Proceedings

The 2nd International Symposium on

HIGH PERFORMANCE DISTRIBUTED COMPUTING

HIGH PERFORMANCE DISTRIBUTED COMPUTING

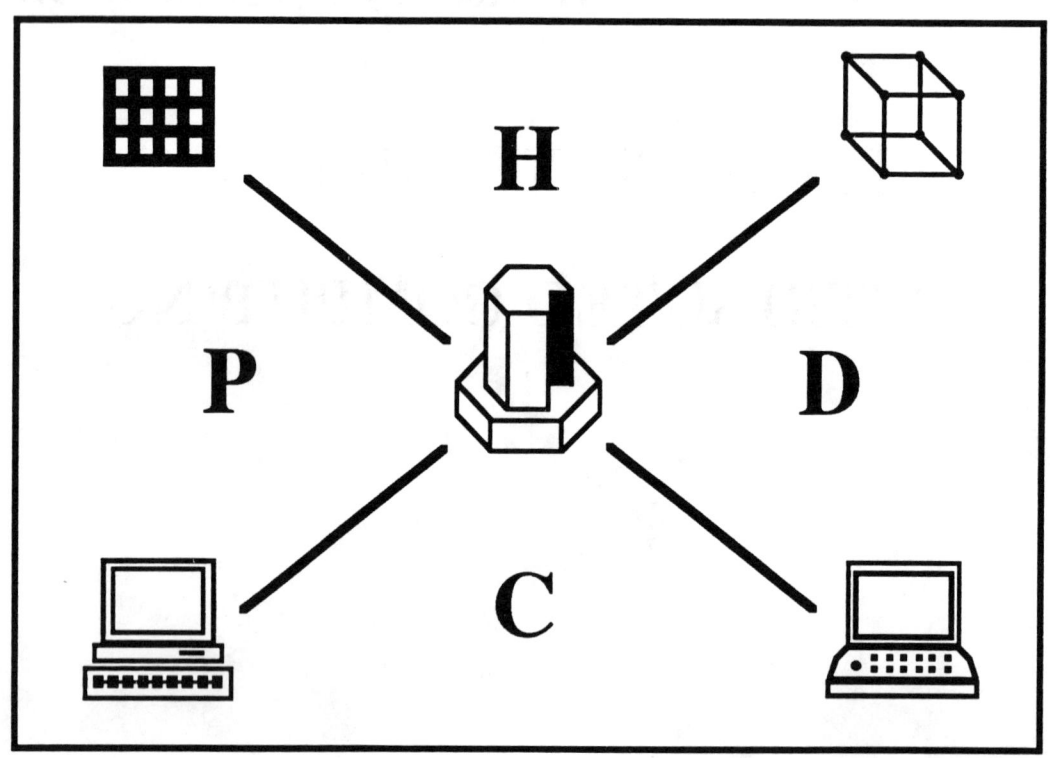

Proceedings

The 2nd International Symposium on

HIGH PERFORMANCE DISTRIBUTED COMPUTING

July 20 – 23, 1993
Spokane, Washington

Cavanaugh's Inn
at the Park

Sponsored by

IEEE Computer Society
Washington State University
Northeast Parallel Architectures Center (NPAC) at Syracuse University

in cooperation with

ACMSIGCOMM
Washington Technology Center, Seattle
IEEE Spokane Section

IEEE Computer Society Press
Los Alamitos, California

Washington • Brussels • Tokyo

The papers in this book comprise the proceedings of the meeting mentioned on the cover and title page. They reflect the authors' opinions and, in the interests of timely dissemination, are published as presented and without change. Their inclusion in this publication does not necessarily constitute endorsement by the editors, the IEEE Computer Society Press, or the Institute of Electrical and Electronics Engineers, Inc.

Published by the
IEEE Computer Society Press
10662 Los Vaqueros Circle
PO Box 3014
Los Alamitos, CA 90720-1264

© 1993 by the Institute of Electrical and Electronics Engineers, Inc. All rights reserved.

Copyright and Reprint Permissions: Abstracting is permitted with credit to the source. Libraries are permitted to photocopy beyond the limit of US copyright law, for private use of patrons, those articles in this volume that carry a code at the bottom of the first page, provided that the per-copy fee indicated in the code is paid through the Copyright Clearance Center, 27 Congress Street, Salem, MA 01970. For other copying, reprint, or republication permission, write to IEEE Copyrights Manager, IEEE Service Center, 445 Hoes Lane, PO Box 1331, Piscataway, NJ 08855-1331.

IEEE Computer Society Press Order Number 3900-02
Library of Congress Catalog Number 93-77714
IEEE Catalog Number 93TH0550-4
ISBN 0-8186-3900-8 (paper)
ISBN 0-8186-3901-6 (microfiche)

Additional copies can be ordered from:

IEEE Computer Society Press	IEEE Service Center	IEEE Computer Society	IEEE Computer Society
Customer Service Center	445 Hoes Lane	13, avenue de l'Aquilon	Ooshima Building
10662 Los Vaqueros Circle	PO Box 1331	B-1200 Brussels	2-19-1 Minami-Aoyama
PO Box 3014	Piscataway, NJ 08855-1331	BELGIUM	Minato-ku, Tokyo 107
Los Alamitos, CA 90720-1264			JAPAN

Production Editors: Mary E. Kavanaugh and Lisa O'Conner
Printed in the United States of America by McNaughton & Gunn Inc.

 THE INSTITUTE OF ELECTRICAL AND ELECTRONICS ENGINEERS, INC.

Chairmen's Message

It has been a pleasure for us to organize the Second International Symposium on High Performance Distributed Computing (HPDC-2), the second in a series of annual symposiums co-sponsored by the IEEE Computer Society. This year, in addition to the IEEE Computer Society, the symposium is being co-sponsored by Washington State University and Syracuse University.

HPDC-2 provides a forum for presenting the latest research findings that unify the parallel and distributed computing fields. In HPDC environments, parallel or distributed computing techniques are applied to the solution of computationally intensive applications across networks of high-performance computers. This symposium facilitates the exchange of ideas in an important and emerging area of technology.

The initial High Performance Computing (HPC) Initiative was correctly enlarged to High Performance Computing and Communications (HPCC) and now supports the Information Infrastructure with a growing emphasis on the communications component. Indeed, we have now moved into the age of High Performance Communications. Thus the presentations in this proceedings not only cover the basic technology but also illustrate the growing convergence of parallel and distributed computing.

The challenging tasks to be addressed by the HPDC community include portability of efficient software over the HPDC environment, low latency that utilizes current advances in gigabit networks and processing technology, and the development of HPDC tools and techniques for parallelizing applications over a network of machines. There is a wide range of topics for conducting research in these areas and we invite researchers to take on the challenge of research in these emerging fields.

We received a total of 69 papers, 52 from North America, 8 from Europe, 8 from Asia, and 1 from Australia. Each submitted paper was reviewed by at least three referees chosen from among the program committee, authors, and other reviewers. Based on the topics and critiques, the program committee selected 36 papers that received favorable reviews and were considered most relevant to the HPDC-2 theme. In addition, we also included four invited papers. These 40 papers are arranged into various sessions, including two panel sessions and two keynote addresses. Additionally, there are five pre-symposium tutorials on relevant topics in high performance distributed computing. We solicited quality research papers that address software, hardware, and network issues of importance to high performance distributed computing and would like to thank the members of the Technical Program Committee and the referees for their timely reviews and good advice.

The success of a symposium such as this depends on the contribution of many individuals. We would like to thank Anujan Varma for organizing the tutorials, Vaidy Sunderam for publicizing this symposium, and the Conference and Institutes staff at Washington State University for their help in processing papers.

Our special thanks go to Kerry Hersh of the School of Electrical Engineering and Computer Science at Washington State University for her help in getting corporate sponsors and to Mike Kibler, also at WSU, for his help in getting the exhibitors for HPDC-2. In addition, our thanks go to Kristin Lingo, Donna McCammon, Deborah Jones and Lee Brink at Syracuse University for their invaluable help in handling the conference organization and symposium registration.

Special thanks also go to Kendall Square Research for their financial support in sponsoring a luncheon and to Dick Russell for his help in coordinating this event. We would like to thank the Washington Technology Center (WTC) and Robert Center, its Director, for their financial contribution to HPDC-2. We would also like to express our appreciation to Olivetti North America for the donation of their equipment for e-mail access and software demonstrations during the Symposium. Our thanks also go to Leonard Byrne, Chair of the IEEE Spokane Section, for his help in coordinating this equipment setup.

Finally, on behalf of the Program Committee, we would like to extend our gratitude to all the authors, panelists, session chairpersons, and reviewers who contributed to the Second International Symposium on High Performance Distributed Computing.

Geoffrey Fox,
General Chair
Director, NPAC
Syracuse University

C. S. Raghavendra,
Program Co-Chair
School of Electrical
 Engineering and Computer
 Science
Washington State University

Salim Hariri,
Program Co-Chair
Electrical and Computer
 Engineering Department
Syracuse University

SYMPOSIUM GENERAL CHAIR

Geoffrey Fox
NPAC, Syracuse University .... hpdc@nova.npac.syr.edu

PROGRAM COMMITTEE CO-CHAIRS

C. S. Raghavendra
Washington State University .... raghu@eecs.wsu.edu

Salim Hariri
Syracuse University .... hariri@cat.syr.edu

PROGRAM COMMITTEE

Tilak Agerwala .... IBM
Dharma Agrawal ..... N. Carolina State University
Pratima Agrawal ...... AT&T Bell Labs
Marco Annaratone ... Digital Equipment Corporation
Gary Craig .... Syracuse University
Dennis Duke .... SCRI/Florida State University
Richard Freund .... NRaD
J.J. Garcia-Luna .... University of California, Santa Cruz/SRI International
Arif Ghafoor .... Purdue University
B. Gopinath .... Rutgers University
Andrew Grimshaw .. University of Virginia
S.H. Hosseini .... University of Wisconsin-Milwaukee
Terry Huntsberger ... University of South Carolina
Malvin H. Kalos ...... Cornell University
Carl Kesselman .... Caltech
H.T. Kung .... Harvard University
T.V. Lakshman .... Bell Communications Research

C.R. Mechoso .... UCLA
Rami Melhem .... University of Pittsburgh
Dick Metzger .... Rome Laboratory
Paul Mockapetris ..... DARPA
Trevor Mudge .... University of Michigan
John Nicholas .... Battelle Pacific Northwest Lab
James C. Patterson ... Boeing Co.
Viktor Prasanna .... University of Southern California
Sanjay Ranka .... Syracuse University
Anthony Reeves .... Cornell University
Karsten Schwan .... Georgia Institute of Technology
Arun Somani .... University of Washington
Vaidy Sunderam .... Emory University
Makoto Takizawa .... Tokyo Denki University, Japan
Anujan Varma .... University of California, Santa Cruz
David Wallace .... University of Edinburgh, UK
Larry Wittie .... SUNY Stony Brook
Pen-Chung Yew .... University of Illinois

PUBLICITY

Vaidy Sunderam
Emory University .... vss@mathcs.emory.edu

TUTORIAL CHAIR

Anujan Varma
University of California, Santa Cruz .... varma@cse.ucsc.edu

LOCAL ARRANGEMENTS

Kristin Lingo
Syracuse University .... KILINGO@fubar.syr.edu

EXHIBITS CHAIR

B. Gopinath
Rutgers University .... gopinath@aramis.rutgers.edu

Exhibitors

AT&T
DEC
Hewlett-Packard
IBM
Kendall Square Research

Mathematrix
Olivetti North America
Parasoft
Sun Microsystems

HPDC '93 Referees

S. Adve
Dharma P. Agrawal
Ian F. Akyildiz
B.R. Badrinath
Prithviraj Banerjee
Laxmi N. Bhuyan
Prabuddha Biswas
P. Bodorik
Ralph M. Butler
Roy Campbell
Russell Carter
Yee-Hsiang Chang
P.D. Coddington
David Cohn
Phyllis Crandall
Chita R. Das
Michel Dubois
Rajendra V. Boppana
Suresh Chalasani
Susan Eggers
Chris Faigle
Mario Gerla
Arif Ghafoor
Joydeep Ghosh
Andrew Grimshaw
Salim Hariri
Mark D. Hill
Robert Hou
S. Hossein Hosseini
Terry Huntsberger
Ashraf Iqbal
Ashish Karkare
Wouter Joosen
Hemanth Kanakia
C.M. Krishna
P. Vijay Kumar
T.V. Lakshman

Tomas Lang
Edward Lazowska
Tong-Yee Lee
Victor O.K. Li
Hwa-Chun Lin
Dan C. Marinescu
Rami Melhem
Lionel Ni
John Nicholas
Zoran Obradovic
Mahamed Osman
Lakshmi N. Pandey
James C. Patterson
Greg Plaxton
Umakishore Ramachandran
K.K. Ramakrishnan
Sanjay Ranka
K. Ravindran
A.L. Narasimha Reddy
Karsten Schwan
Yuan Shi
H.J. Siegel
John A. Silvester
Mukesh Singhal
Harikumar Sivaraman
Arun Somani
M.A. Sridhar
Vaidy S. Sunderam
Alexander Thomasian
Don Towsley
K.S. Trivedi
Anujan Varma
R. Venkateswaran
Michael Wehner
Larry Wittie
Pen-Chung Yew

Table of Contents

Chairmen's Message v
Organizing Committees vii
Referees ix

Keynote Speech: Issues in Gigabit Networks 1
   L. Kleinrock, UCLA

SESSION 1: Invited Papers
   Chair: Walter Johnston, NYNEX Science and Technology

New Flow Control Methods for High-Speed Networks 4
   H.T. Kung

Programming a Distributed System Using Shared Objects 5
   A.S. Tanenbaum, H.E. Bal, and M.F. Kaashoek

Scalable Libraries in a Heterogeneous Environment 13
   A. Skjellum

Parallel Computing for Helicopter Rotor Design 21
   J. Manke, K. Neves, and T. Wicks

SESSION 2: Panel —
The Virtual Heterogeneous Supercomputer: Can It be Built? 30
   Panel Chair: *H.J. Siegel, Purdue University*
   Panelists:
     Henry G. Dietz, Purdue University
     Richard F. Freund, NRaD
     Chani Pangali, Kendall Square Research
     Richard C. Metzger, Rome Laboratory
     Kenneth W. Neves, Boeing Co.
     C.V. Ramamoorthy, University of California at Berkeley
     Andy Tanenbaum, Vrije University

SESSION 3A: Enabling Software Technology
   Chair: Richard C. Metzger, Rome Laboratory

A Parallel Object-Oriented Framework for Stencil Algorithms 34
   J.F. Karpovich, M. Judd, W.T. Strayer, and A.S. Grimshaw

Block Data Decomposition for Data-Parallel Programming on a Heterogeneous Workstation Network 42
   P.E. Crandall and M.J. Quinn

p4-Linda: A Portable Implementation of Linda 50
   R.M. Butler, A.L. Leveton, and E.L. Lusk

Improving Performance by Use of Adaptive Objects: Experimentation with a
Configurable Multiprocessor Thread Package 59
   B. Mukherjee and K. Schwan

SESSION 3B: High Speed Network Protocols
   Chair: Richard Freund, NRaD

DARTS — A Dynamically Adaptable Transport Service Suitable for High Speed Networks 68
   A. Richards, T. Ginige, A. Seneviratne, T. Buczkowska, and M. Fry

Implementation of a Parallel Transport Subsystem on a Multiprocessor Architecture 76
    T. Braun and C. Schmidt

A Message Passing Interface for Parallel and Distributed Computing 84
    S. Hariri, J. Park, F.-K. Yu, M. Parashar, and G.C. Fox

DSMA: A Fair Capacity-1 Protocol for Gigabit Ring Networks 92
    W. Dobosiewicz and P. Gburzynski

Keynote Speech: Distributed Supercomputing — The CASA Gigabit Testbed Experience 100
    Paul Messina, Caltech

SESSION 4A: Applications I
Chair: Dennis Duke, Florida State University

Toward a High Performance Distributed Memory Climate Model 102
    M.F. Wehner, J.J. Ambrosiano, J.C. Brown, W.P. Dannevik, P.G. Eltgroth,
    A.A. Mirin, J.D. Farrara, C.C. Ma, C.R. Mechoso, and J.A. Spahr

Test Pattern Generation for Sequential Circuits on a Network of Workstations 114
    P. Agrawal, V.D. Agrawal, and J. Villoldo

Star Modeling on IBM RS6000 Networks Using PVM 121
    L. Colombet, L. Desbat, and F. Ménard

A Fully Distributed Parallel Ray Tracing Scheme on the Delta Touchstone Machine 129
    T.-Y. Lee, C.S. Raghavendra, and J.B. Nicholas

SESSION 4B: High Speed Networks and Switching
Chair: Daniel McAuliffe, Rome Laboratory

An ATM WAN/LAN Gateway Architecture 136
    G.J. Minden, J.B. Evans, D.W. Petr, and V.S. Frost

Performance Evaluation of a High-Speed Switching System Based on the Fibre Channel Standard 144
    A. Varma, V. Sahai, and R. Bryant

MULTIPAR: An Output Queue ATM Modular Switch with Multiple Phases and Replicated Planes 152
    J. Ma and K. Rahko

A Low-Latency Programming Interface and a Prototype Switch for Scalable High-Performance
Distributed Computing 160
    T. Chen, J. Feeney, G. Fox, G. Frieder, S. Ranka, B. Wilhelm, and F.-K. Yu

SESSION 5: Panel —
Software Tools for High-Performance Distributed Computing 170
    Panel Chair: Vaidy Sunderam, Emory University
    Panelists:
        Geoffrey Fox, NPAC, Syracuse University
        Al Geist, Oak Ridge National Laboratory
        Bill Gropp, Argonne National Laboratory
        Bob Harrison, Battelle PNL
        Adam Kolawa, Parasoft
        Mike Quinn, Oregon State University
        Tony Skjellum, Mississippi State University

SESSION 6A: Applications II
   Chair: Marco Annaratone, Digital Corporation

Parallel and Distributed Systems for Constructive Neural Network Learning 174
   J. Fletcher and Z. Obradovic

An Analysis of Distributed Computing Software and Hardware for Applications in
Computational Physics 179
   P.D. Coddington

Supporting Heterogeneity and Distribution in the Numerical Propulsion System
Simulation Project 187
   P.T. Homer and R.D. Schlichting

Distributed Computing Solutions to the All-Pairs Shortest Path Problem 196
   I. Pramanick

SESSION 6B: Scheduling and Load Balancing
   Chair: Ian Akyildiz, Georgia Institute of Technology

Distributed Control Methods 206
   B. Tung and L. Kleinrock

A Methodology for Evaluating Load Balancing Algoritms 216
   B.S. Joshi, S.H. Hosseini, and K. Vairavan

Distributed Computing Systems and Checkpointing 224
   K. Wong and M. Franklin

Formal Method for Scheduling, Routing and Communication Protocol 234
   L.M.R. Mullin, S.A. Thibault, D.R. Dooling,, and E.A. Sandberg

SESSION 7A: File Systems and I/O
   Chair: Nita Sharma, Ncube Inc.

Accessing Remote Special Files in a Distributed Computing Environment 244
   J. Lilienkamp, B.J. Walker, and R. Silva

Performance Analysis of Distributed File Systems with Non-Volatile Caches 252
   P. Biswas, K.K. Ramakrishnan, D. Towsley, and C.M. Krishna

Trading Disk Capacity for Performance 263
   R.Y. Hou and Y.N. Patt

SESSION 7B: Protocols for Distributed Systems
   Chair: J.J. Garcia-Luna, University of California, Santa Cruz / SRI International

Partial Order Transport Service for Multimedia Applications: Reliable Service 272
   P.D. Amer, T. Connolly, C. Chassot, and M. Diaz

Starvation-Prevented Priority-Based Total Ordering Broadcast Protocol on
High-Speed Single Channel Network 281
   A. Nakamura and M. Takizawa

Design and Analysis of a Hierarchical Scalable Photonic Architecture 289
   P.W. Dowd, K. Bogineni, K.A. Aly, and J.A. Perreault

SESSION 8A: Resource Management
   Chair: Ray Bair, Battelle PNL

Reliable Management of Distributed Computations in Nexus 298
   A. Tripathi, S.P. Koneru, C. Nock, R. Tewari, N.M. Karnik, V. Bandi, K. Day, and T. Noonan

Management of Broadband Networks Using a 3D Virtual World 306
   L.A. Crutcher, A.A. Lazar, S.K. Feiner, and M. Zhou

Resource Management for Distributed Parallel Systems 316
   B.C. Neuman and S. Rao

SESSION 8B: Performance Evaluation
   Chair: Arun Somani, University of Washington

Analytical Performance Evaluation of Data Replication Based Shared Memory Model 326
   S. Srbljic and L. Budin

Hierarchical Distributed System Network Design with Cost-Performance Tradeoffs..336
   N. Sharma and D.P. Agrawal

High-Performance Distributed Shared Memory Substrate for Workstation Clusters 344
   A. Banerji, D. Kulkarni, J. Tracey, P. Greenawalt, and D. Cohn

Author Index 352

KEYNOTE SPEECH

Issues in Gigabit Networks

Leonard Kleinrock

University of California
Los Angeles CA

Abstract of Keynote Speech

Gigabit Networks are coming! A large number of efforts are currently underway to bring about the technology of billion–bit–per–second transmission networks; this is occurring in the research community with the suport of the HPCC initiative.

The move from megabits to gigabits is a far more revolutionary one than that from kilobits to megabits. Indeed, a threshold is about to be crossed whereby the speed of light is now a major issue in wide-area networking. In this presentation, Leonard Kleinrock will discuss the technology of fast packet switching and will address a number of issues in gigabit networking.

SESSION 1:
Invited Papers

Walter Johnston, Chair

New Flow Control Methods for High-Speed Networks

H.T. Kung

Division of Applied Sciences
Harvard University
Cambridge MA 02138

Abstract of Invited Paper

This paper argues that, for high-speed networks such as ATM, it is important to use link-by-link flow control on a per virtual circuit (VC) basis. It can effectively control congestion and maximize network utilization. Three progressively memory-efficient, credit-based flow control schemes, called N123, N123+ and N23, will be described, and simulation results of these schemes will be presented. An ATM switch, which supports credit-based flow control, is under joint development by BNR and Harvard.

Using per VC link-by-link flow control, a VC will receive fast feedback of possible congestion in the network. That is, back-pressure will build up quickly along any congested VC spanning one or more hops. When encountering back-pressure, the traffic source of the VC can be throttled, and as a result, excessive traffic can be blocked at the boundary of the network, instead of being allowed to enter the network. Using per VC link-by-link flow control, one can guarantee that there will be no cell loss inside the network due to congestion.

The "per VC" link-by-link flow control allows multiple VCs over the same physical link to operate at different speeds, depending on their individual congestion status, while fully utilizing the link. In particular, congested VCs cannot block other VCs which are not congested.

The flow control would also allow new services for hosts with high-speed network access links operating, for example, at hundreds of megabits per second. For example, these hosts can be offered a new kind of service, which may be called "greedy" service, where the network will take as much traffic as possible at any instant. There will be no requirements for predefined service parameters. This service will use the network more efficiently as well as provide the host more overall throughput than they could achieve without flow control.

Programming a Distributed System Using Shared Objects

Andrew S. Tanenbaum
Henri E. Bal

Dept. of Mathematics and Computer Science, Vrije Universiteit
Amsterdam, The Netherlands

M. Frans Kaashoek

Laboratory for Computer Science, M.I.T.
Cambridge, MA

Email: ast@cs.vu.nl, bal@cs.vu.nl, kaashoek@lcs.mit.edu

Abstract

Building the hardware for a high-performance distributed computer system is a lot easier than building its software. In this paper we describe a model for programming distributed systems based on abstract data types that can be replicated on all machines that need them. Read operations are done locally, without requiring network traffic. Writes can be done using a reliable broadcast algorithm if the hardware supports broadcasting; otherwise, a point-to-point protocol is used. We have built such a system based on the Amoeba microkernel, and implemented a language, Orca, on top of it. For Orca applications that have a high ratio of reads to writes, we have measured good speedups on a system with 16 processors.

1. Introduction

As CPU prices continue to drop, more and more systems will be constructed from multiple CPUs. The techniques for building the hardware for such systems are beginning to be understood, but the software is in a more primitive state. In this paper we will describe our model for writing software for highly parallel computers, and discuss some example programs and measurements.

Two kinds of multiple CPU systems exist: multiprocessors and multicomputers. A *multiprocessor* is a machine with multiple CPUs that share a single common virtual address space. All CPUs can read and write every location in this address space. Multiprocessors can be programmed using well-established techniques, but they are difficult and expensive to build. For this reason, many multiple CPU systems are simply a collection of independent CPU-memory pairs, connected by a communication network. Machines of this type that do not share primary memory are called *multicomputers*. Because these machines are easier to build and are likely to dominate the highly parallel computer market in the future, our model has been designed for this class of machines, but our software also works on multiprocessors.

The usual approach to programming a multicomputer is message passing. The operating system provides primitives SEND and RECEIVE in one form or another, and programmers can use these for interprocess communication. This makes I/O the central paradigm for multicomputer software, something that is unfamiliar and unnatural for many programmers.

An alternative approach is to simulate shared memory on multicomputers. One of the pioneering efforts in this direction was the work of Li and Hudak [12]. In their system, Ivy, a collection of workstations on a local area network shared a single, paged, virtual address space. The pages are distributed among the workstations. When a CPU references a page that is not present locally, it gets a page fault. The page fault handler then determines which CPU has the needed page and sends it a request. The CPU replies by sending the page. Although various optimizations are possible, the performance of these systems is often inadequate.

Another approach is not to split the shared address space up into fixed-size pages, but into programmer-defined objects. These objects are then sharable among multiple machines. Linda [5], for example, is based on an abstract tuple space. A process can place a tuple in the tuple space, and another process on a different processor can remove it. In this way processes can communicate with one another.

In Emerald [8] location-independent abstract data types can be defined. Processes can perform operations on an abstract data type no matter on which machine it is located. It is up to the system to send the operation to the data or the data to the requesting machine.

Both tuple-based and abstract data type-based schemes eliminate the problem found in Ivy and similar systems of having to move fixed-size units (e.g. 8K pages) around, but they they have other problems. Emerald does not replicate data, which can lead to performance problems; Linda has fixed primitives that are low-level and inflexible.

This work was supported in part by the Netherlands Organization for Scientific Research as part of its *Pionier* program.

2. Shared Data-Objects

Our design is based on the idea of doing parallel programming on distributed systems using shared data-objects. These objects may be replicated on multiple processors, and are kept synchronized by system software, the runtime system, as shown in Fig. 1 Associated with each shared object is a set of operations that are encapsulated with the object to form an abstract data type. Objects are managed by a runtime system, as shown in Fig. 1.

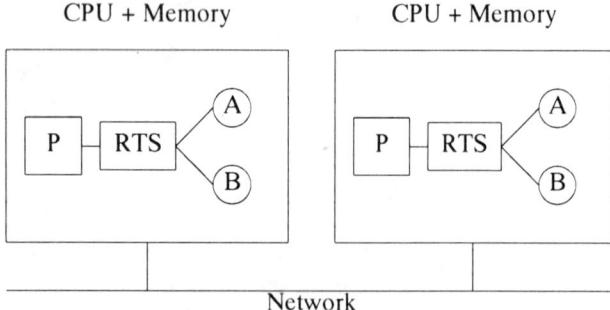

Fig. 1 An object can be replicated on each machine. P = process, RTS = runtime system, A and B are shared data-objects. To the user processes, A and B look like they are in physical shared memory.

Processes on different machines can perform operations on shared objects as though they were in physical shared memory. Shared objects exhibit the property of sequential consistency in that if processes simultaneously perform operations on a shared object, the final result will look like all the operations were performed in some sequential order [11]. The order is chosen nondeterministically, but all processes will see the same order of events and the same final result. It is up to the runtime system to maintain this illusion.

By encapsulating the data inside abstract data types, we insure that processes may not access shared data without the runtime system gaining control. Getting control is essential to make sure objects are consistent when accessed and to guarantee that updates are propagated to other machines in a consistent manner. These properties are not available with a page-based distributed shared memory in which any process can touch any virtual address at will.

Replicating shared objects has two advantages over systems like Ivy. First, reads to any object can be done locally on any machine having a replica. No network traffic is generated. (For our purposes, a read is an operation that does not change the state of its object.) Second, more parallelism is possible on reads, since multiple machines can be reading an object at the same time, even if the object is writable. With page-based schemes, having many copies of writable pages is possible only under restricted circumstances involving weakened consistency.

Whether replication can be done efficiently in software depends on two factors. The first is the ratio of reads to writes. If the vast majority of accesses to shared data are reads, then having a copy of each shared object on each machine that needs it is a good idea. The gain from making reads cheap generally results in a major gain in performance. The other factor is how expensive writes are. If writes are exceedingly expensive (in terms of delay, bandwidth, or computing power required), even a moderately high ratio of reads to writes may not be enough to make replication worthwhile. We have studied this question in detail and reported on it elsewhere [3].

3. Implementation

The idea of sharing objects on a distributed system stands or falls with the efficiency of its implementation. If it can be implemented efficiently, high performance parallel systems can be built as multicomputers and programmed as multiprocessors, combining the hardware simplicity of the former with the software simplicity of the latter. If it cannot be implemented efficiently, the idea is of little practical value. Our results show that shared objects can be implemented efficiently under certain circumstances, and gives good results for a variety of problems.

The system described in this paper consists of three major components: The Amoeba microkernel. The shared object runtime system. The Orca parallel programming language. We will discuss each of these in turn in this section.

3.1. The Amoeba microkernel

Amoeba is a distributed operating system consisting of a microkernel and a collection of server processes [15]. Amoeba was designed for a large number of machines, called the processor pool, called by a (broadcast) network. There are also machines for handling specialized servers, such as the file system, as well as workstations for clients, but the real computing is done on the processor pool machines. A copy of the microkernel runs on all these machines.

The Amoeba microkernel has four primary functions:

1. Manage processes and threads.
2. Provide low-level memory management support.
3. Handle I/O.
4. Support transparent communication.

Let us consider each of these in turn.

Like most operating systems, Amoeba supports the concept of a process. In addition, Amoeba also supports multiple threads of control, or just *threads* for short, within a single address space. A process with one thread is essentially the same as a process in UNIX®. Such a process has a single address space, a set of registers, a program counter, and a stack.

In parallel applications, processes often have multiple threads. Threads can synchronize using semaphores and mutexes to prevent two threads from accessing critical regions or data simultaneously.

The second task of the microkernel is to provide low-level memory management. Threads can allocate and deallocate blocks of memory, called *segments*. These segments can be read and written, and can be mapped into and out of the address space of the process to which the calling thread belongs. To provide maximum communication performance, all segments are memory resident.

The third job of the microkernel is to provide the ability for one thread to communicate transparently with another thread, regardless of the nature or location of the two threads. The model used here is remote procedure call (RPC) between a client and a server [4].

All RPCs are from one thread to another. User-to-user, user-to-kernel, and kernel-to-kernel communication all occur. When a thread blocks awaiting the reply, other threads in the same process that are not logically blocked may be scheduled and run.

The third basic function of the microkernel is to manage I/O devices, handle interrupts, and so on. Device drivers run as threads within the kernel. All other functionality is located in user-space servers and other processes.

Totally-ordered broadcasting

Amoeba also provides totally-ordered, reliable broadcasting on unreliable networks through use of a software protocol [9]. The protocol supports reliable broadcasting, in the sense that in the absence of processor crashes, the protocol guarantees that all broadcast messages will be delivered, and all machines will see all broadcasts in exactly the same order, a property useful for guaranteeing sequential consisting. This feature is heavily used by higher layers of software.

When an application starts up on Amoeba, one of the machines (which normally have identical hardware) is elected as *sequencer* (like a committee electing a chairman). If the sequencer machine subsequently crashes, the remaining members elect a new one. We have devised and implemented two different reliable broadcast algorithms having slightly different properties. In the first algorithm, called *PB* (Point to point - Broadcast), a runtime system needing to reliably broadcast a message (e.g., a new value of an object) traps to the kernel. The kernel adds a protocol header containing a unique identifier, the number of the last broadcast it has received, and a field saying that this is a *RequestForBroadcast* message and sends it as a point-to-point message to the sequencer. When the sequencer gets the message it adds the lowest unassigned sequence number, stores the message in its history buffer, and then broadcasts it.

When such a broadcast arrives at each of the other machines, a check is made to see if this is the next message in sequence. If this is message 25 and the previous message received was 23, for example, the message is temporarily buffered and a request is sent to the sequencer asking it for message 24 (stored in the sequencer's history buffer). When 24 comes in, 24 and 25 are passed to the application program in that order. Under no circumstances are messages passed to application programs out of order. This is the basic mechanism by which it is guaranteed that all broadcasts are seen by all machines, and in the same order.

The other reliable broadcast algorithm is called *BB* (Broadcast - Broadcast). In this method, the user broadcasts the message, including a unique identifier. When the sequencer sees this, it broadcasts a special *Accept* message containing the unique identifier and its newly assigned sequence number. A broadcast is only official when the *Accept* message has been sent.

These protocols are logically equivalent, but they have different performance characteristics. In *PB*, each message appears in full on the network twice: once to the sequencer and once from the sequencer. Thus a message of length m bytes consumes $2m$ bytes worth of network bandwidth. However, only the second of these is broadcast, so each user machine is only interrupted once (for the second message).

In *BB*, the full message only appears once on the network, plus a very short *Accept* message from the sequencer, so only half the bandwidth is consumed. On the other hand, every machine is interrupted twice, once for the message and once for the *Accept*. Thus *PB* wastes bandwidth to reduce interrupts compared to *BB*. The present implementation looks at each message and depending on the amount of data to be sent, dynamically chooses either *PB* or *BB*, using the former for short messages and the latter for long ones (over 1 packet).

3.2. The shared object runtime system

We have developed two runtime systems to use with Amoeba and Orca. The first one is used on networks that have hardware broadcasting or multicasting. The second one is used on systems that have neither of these. Both are described below.

3.2.1. Reliable broadcasting

When the underlying network provides unreliable broadcasting or multicasting, the *PB* and *BB* protocols provided by Amoeba can be used to make broadcasting reliable and totally ordered. The runtime system in this case is straightforward. In the initial implementation, every object is replicated on all machines that need it (an optimizing scheme using partial replication is under development). Reads are then done locally. Writes are done either by doing the operation on the machine doing the write and then broadcasting the result, or by broadcasting the operation code and parameters and letting each machine run the operation itself.

The broadcast RTS has an object manager for each machine. Reads are done directly, bypassing the object manager. Writes are done by asking the local object manager to do the work. Incoming broadcasts are handled by the object managers, which process them in strict FIFO (i.e., sequence number) order, thus guaranteeing that writes are seen by all processes in the system in the same order (necessary for enforcing sequential consistency). When a broadcast packet comes in, the local object is locked to prevent local reads during the update.

3.2.2. The point-to-point runtime system

When the network does not support broadcasting, objects can still be replicated, but they have to be managed using point-to-point messages and completely different protocols. We have implemented and tested two kinds of point-to-point protocols: invalidation and update (the broadcast system always uses update, because it is cheap).

Both protocols allow multiple copies of all objects to exist, so reads can be done locally when a copy is available locally. When an invalidation protocol is being used and an object is written, all copies except one are invalidated (i.e., discarded). When an update protocol is being used and an object is written, all copies are updated to the new value. In general, updating an object is more expensive than invalidating it, since a larger message and more complicated protocol is needed. Also, if you do multiple consecutive writes, invalidation may require one message whereas update may require one per write. On the other hand, if an object is needed on a machine whose copy is no longer valid, a new copy must be fetched, which also has a cost associated with it.

Both our runtime system using invalidation and our runtime system using update are based on the concept of having a primary copy of each object from which all other copies (secondaries) are derived. In the invalidation scheme, when a write is done, a message is sent to the machine holding the primary copy. The runtime system on this machine then locks the object and sends invalidation messages to all the other copies. Each of these sends back an acknowledgement when its copy has been invalidated. When all the acknowledgements have been collected at the primary site, the object is unlocked and made available for reading and copying.

The runtime system using updates also has a primary copy, but the protocol is more complicated due to the need to make multiple simultaneous updates sequentially consistent. A two-phase protocol is used. When a write is done, a message is sent to the primary copy, whose runtime system locks the object and sends an update message to all other copies. This message contains the operation code and parameters to allow the other machines to perform the updates. This approach requires less bandwidth than updating the object at the primary site and sending the result to the other sites.

When each of the secondaries receives the update message, it locks the object, performs the operation, and sends back an acknowledgement, keeping the object still locked. When all the acknowledgements have arrived back at the primary, the second phase of the protocol is entered in which a message is sent to each copy saying that the object can be unlocked and used again for local reads. Reads that are attempted while an object is locked are suspended until it is unlocked.

The decision of where to replicate each object is done dynamically based on runtime statistics. Initially, only one copy of each object is maintained. As accesses to objects are made, statistics are maintained. When the ratio of reads to writes on any machine exceeds a certain threshold, the runtime system concludes that there are so many reads being done and so few writes that having a local copy is worthwhile. A message is sent to the primary to fetch a copy. Similarly, when this ratio falls below another threshold, the runtime system concludes that having a copy is not worth the trouble due to the large percentage of write operations. The local copy is then discarded.

Comparisons of update and invalidation did not show a clear winner. Which one is better depends on the problem being solved. Our experience suggests that updating is better more often than invalidation, but more research is needed.

3.3. Orca

While it is possible to program directly with shared objects, it is much more convenient to have language support for them [1]. For this reason, we have designed the Orca parallel programming language and written a compiler for it. Orca is a procedural language whose sequential statements are roughly similar to languages like C or Modula 2 but which also supports parallel processes and shared objects.

There are four guiding principles behind the Orca design:

- Transparency
- Semantic simplicity
- Sequential consistency
- Efficiency

By *transparency* we mean that programs (and programmers) should not be aware of where objects reside. Location management should be fully automatic. Furthermore, the programmer should not be aware of whether the program is running on a machine with physical shared memory or one with disjoint memories. The same program should run on both, unlike nearly all other languages for parallel programming, which are aimed at either one or the other, but not both. (Of course one can always simulate message passing on a multiprocessor, but this is often less than optimal, especially if there is heavy contention for locks and certain other locations.)

Semantic simplicity means that programmers should be able to form a simple mental model of how the shared memory works. Incoherent memory, in which reads to shared data sometimes return good values and sometimes stale (incorrect) ones, is ruled out by this principle.

Sequential consistency is an issue because in a parallel system, many events happen simultaneously. By making operations sequentially consistent, we guarantee that operations on objects are indivisible (i.e., atomic), and that the observed behavior is the same as some sequential execution would have been. Operations on objects are guaranteed not to be interleaved, which contributes to semantic simplicity, as does the fact that all machines are guaranteed to see exactly the same sequence of serial events. Thus the programmer's model is that the system supports operations. These may be invoked at any moment, but if any invocation would conflict with an operation currently taking place, the second operation will not begin until the first one has completed.

Finally, *efficiency* is also important, since we are proposing a system that can actually be used for solving real problems.

Now let us look at the principal aspects of Orca that relate to parallelism and shared objects. Parallelism is based on two orthogonal concepts: *processes* and *objects*. Processes are active entities that execute programs. They can be created and destroyed dynamically. It is possible to read in an integer, *n*, then execute a loop *n* times, creating a new process on each iteration. Thus the number of processes is not fixed at compile time, but is determined during execution.

The Orca construct for creating a new process is the

fork func(param, ...)

statement, which creates a new process running the procedure *func* with the specified parameters. The user may specify which processor to use, or use the standard default case of running it on the current processor. Objects may be passed as parameters (call by reference). A process may fork many times, passing the same objects to each of the children. This is how objects come to be shared among a collection of processes. There are no global objects in Orca.

Objects are passive. They do not contain processes or other active elements. Each object contains some data structures, along with definitions of one or more operations that use the data structures. The operations are defined by Orca procedures written by the programmer. An object has a specification part and an implementation part, similar in this respect to Ada® packages or Modula-2 modules. Orca is what is technically called *object based* (in contrast with object oriented) in that it supports encapsulated abstract data types, but without inheritance.

A common way of programming in Orca is the Replicated Worker Paradigm [5]. In this model, the main program starts out by creating a large number of identical worker processes, each getting the same objects as parameters, so they are shared among all the workers. Once the initialization phase is completed, the system consists of the main process, along with some number of identical worker processes, all of which share some objects. Processes can perform operations on any of their objects whenever they want to, without having to worry about all the mechanics of how many copies are stored and where, how updates take place, and so on. As far as the programmer is concerned, all the objects are effectively located in one big shared memory somewhere, but are protected by a kind of monitor that prevents multiple updates to an object at the same time.

4. Applications

In this section we will discuss our experiences in implementing various applications in Orca. For each application, we will describe the parallel algorithm and the shared objects used by the Orca program. In this way, we hope to give some insight in the usefulness of shared objects.

In addition, we will briefly consider performance issues of the applications and give some experimental performance results. The performance measurements were carried out on the Amoeba-based Orca system described in the previous section using the broadcast runtime system. The hardware we use is a collection of MC68030s connected by a 10 Mb/sec Ethernet.

The applications we will look at are: the Traveling Salesman Problem, the Arc Consistency Problem, computer chess, and Automatic Test Pattern Generation. Additional Orca applications are described in [2].

4.1. The traveling salesman problem

The Traveling Salesman Problem (TSP) is our favorite example for Orca, since it greatly benefits from object replication. The problem is to find the shortest route for a salesman that visits each of a number of cities exactly once.

We solve the problem using a parallel branch-and-bound algorithm, which is implemented in a replicated worker style program. The problem is split up into a large number of small jobs, each containing a partial (initial) route for the salesman. The jobs are generated by a *manager* process and are stored in a *JobQueue* object. Each available processor runs a *worker* process, which repeatedly takes a job from the queue and executes it. For TSP, executing a job involves searching all possible routes starting with the partial route stored in the job description.

The parallel program keeps track of the best solution found so far by any worker process. This value is used as a bound. A partial route that is already longer than the current best route cannot lead to a better solution, so its search can be abandoned. Significant portions of the search space can therefore be pruned.

The bound must be accessible to all workers, so it is stored in a shared object. This object is read very frequently and is written only when a new better route has been found. In practice, the object may be read millions of times and written only a few times.

In summary, the TSP program uses two important

objects: a global bound and a job queue. The global bound is replicated on all worker processors. Since it has a very high read/write ratio, most operations (i.e., the reads) are done locally, without requiring any communication. Write operations, which occur far less often, are broadcast. If one worker discovers a better value for the bound, all other workers are informed instantly, and can immediately use the new value for pruning parts of their search space. The indivisible operation that updates the object first checks if the new value actually is less than the current value, to prevent race conditions.

The job queue mainly has write operations, since both adding and deleting jobs changes the queue's internal data. The RTS described in this paper (the original one), replicates it on all machines, although keeping a single copy would be better. Despite the global replication of both objects, the speedup is still excellent, as can be seen from the figure.

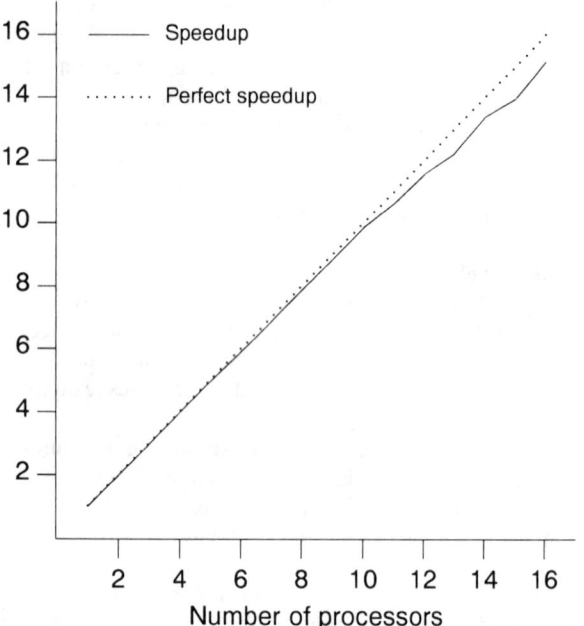

Fig. 2 Speedup for the Traveling Salesman Problem using a 14-city problem.

4.2. The arc consistency problem

The Arc Consistency Problem (ACP) is an important AI problem [14]. The input to the problem is a set of *variables* V_i, each of which can take a value from a domain D_i, and a list of *constraints*. Each constraint involves two variables and puts a restriction on the values these variables can have, for example $A < B$. The goal of ACP is to determine the maximal set of values each variable can take, such that all constraints are satisfied.

A straightforward sequential algorithm for solving ACP is as follows. Assign a set of possible values to each variable V_i; initially, the set for V_i contains all values in its domain D_i. Next, repeatedly restrict the sets using the constraints, until no more changes can be made. An obvious improvement is to keep a list of variables whose sets have been changed, and then only recheck constraints involving such variables.

For example, assume the current set for A is $\{1,10,100\}$ and the set for B is $\{2,3,20\}$. The constraint $A < B$ can be used to delete the value 100 from A's set. Now, all other constraints involving A have to be checked again.

A parallel implementation of the above algorithm is described by Conrad [6], using a message passing program that runs on an iPSC/2 hypercube. The parallel algorithm statically partitions the variables among the available processors. Each processor takes care of determining the value sets for the variables assigned to it.

We have implemented a similar program in Orca, but now using shared objects, and running on the Ethernet-based Amoeba system. The Orca program uses several shared objects. The sets associated with the variables are stored in a shared object, called *domain*. This object thus contains an array of sets, one for each variable. Operations exist for initializing the object, deleting an element from one of the sets, and set membership tests. The object is shared among all processes, since they all need to have this information.

Another object, called *work*, is used to keep track of which variables have to be rechecked. This object contains an array of Booleans, one per variable. If the value set of a variable A has been checked the entry for A is set to *false*. In addition, for all other variables X for which a constraint exists involving both A and X, the corresponding entry is also set to *true* if A was reduced.

The most complicated issue in parallel ACP is how to terminate the algorithm correctly. The algorithm should terminate if none of the variables need to be rechecked. Since the variables are distributed among the processors, however, testing this condition requires careful synchronization.

For this purpose, we use two shared objects. One object contains a Boolean variable that is set to *true* if a process discovers that no solution to the input problem exists, because one of its variables now has an empty set of values. Each process reads the object before doing new work, and quits if the value is *true*.

A second and more complicated object, called *result*, contains an array of Booleans, one per process. A process sets its entry to *true* if it is willing to terminate because it has no more work to do. The program can terminate if two conditions are satisfied: (1) all entries in the *work* object are *false*, and (2) all entries in the *result* object are *true*. In this case, no more work exists and neither will any process generate such work, so the program can safely terminate. The *work* and *result* objects have indivisible operations for testing these two conditions.

The speedups for ACP are shown in Fig. 3. The

program uses at least two processors, since the master process that distributes the work runs on a separate processor.

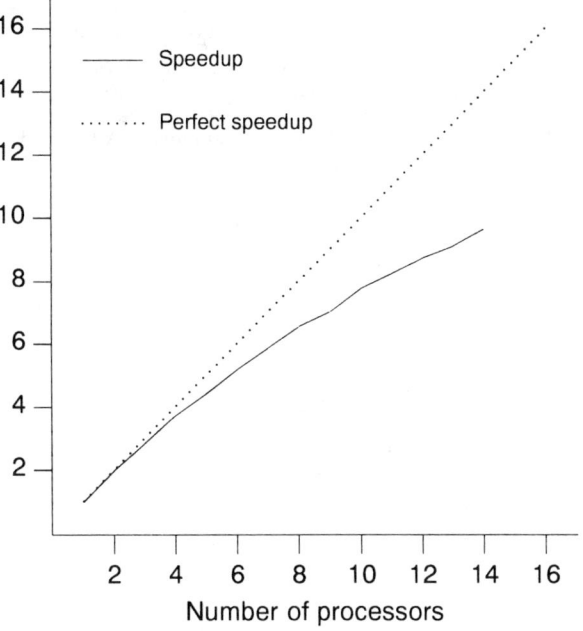

Fig. 3 Speedup for the Arc Consistency Problem using an input problem with 64 variables.

Although the program obtains significant speedups, the speedups are less than those reported for the original hypercube program. The objects used in the program are replicated on all processors, so there is a lot of CPU overhead in handling incoming update messages for these objects. We should also point out, however, that our program uses many operations to handle termination correctly, as explained above. The hypercube program uses a cheaper but far less elegant method to handle termination, based on time-outs.

4.3. Computer chess

Oracol is a chess problem solver written in Orca. It can be asked to look for "mate-in-N-moves" or for tactical combinations that win material. It does not consider positional characteristics.

Oracol's search algorithm is based on alpha-beta with iterative deepening and the quiescence search heuristic. Parallelism is obtained by dynamically partitioning the search tree among the different processors, using simple run-time heuristics. The program uses several shared objects (e.g., a job queue). We will only discuss two objects here, which are of particular interest.

The two objects implement a *killer table* and a *transposition table*. The killer table contains moves that turn out to cause many cutoffs in the alpha-beta algorithm. Killer moves are always considered first. The idea is that if, say, White threatens to capture a rook by playing "Queen to a8", then Black needs to do something against this threat. Any move by Black that does not prevent White from capturing the rook can immediately be refuted by the "Qa8" move, thus saving the trouble of much further analysis.

A transposition table is a table containing positions that have already been analyzed earlier during the search. The same board position can be encountered multiple times during the search, because different sequences of moves can result in the same position. The transposition table thus remembers positions and their evaluation values. Before a position is analyzed, the program first looks in its transposition table (using a hashing function), to determine if it has seen the position before.

Both the killer table and the transposition table can be implemented as local data structures or as shared objects. If used locally, no communication is needed, but processes cannot benefit from each other's tables. For example, a process may evaluate a position that has been evaluated before by another process. If the tables are shared, this will generally not happen, but now communication overhead is introduced for managing the shared tables.

In Orca, it is particularly easy to implement both versions and see which one is best. The tables are implemented using abstract data types (objects types). In the local version, each process declares its own instance of this type. In the shared version, only the main process declares a table object and passes it as a shared parameter to all other processes. The two versions differ in only a few lines of code. For Oracol, we have determined that, especially for the killer table, shared tables are most efficient.

The speedups obtained for the program are not very high, because alpha-beta is hard to parallelize efficiently. On 10 CPUs, we have measured speedups between 4.5 and 5.5. Almost all of the overhead is search overhead, which means that the parallel program searches far more nodes than a sequential program does.

4.4. Automatic test pattern generation

The largest program implemented in Orca so far (nearly 4000 lines) is for Automatic Test Pattern Generation (ATPG). ATPG is an important problem from electrical engineering. It generates test patterns for combinatorial circuits. Such a circuit consists of several input and output lines, and several internal gates (e.g., AND gates, OR gates). The output of a given circuit is completely determined by the input.

To test if a specific gate works correctly, the input lines must be set to certain values, such that the correct functioning of the gate can be determined from the output of the circuit. In other words, at least one of the output lines must be different for a correct and an incorrect gate. The problem is how to determine which inputs to use. In general, all gates of the circuit must be tested, so the problem becomes that of generating a set of input patterns that together test the whole circuit. This problem is called the ATPG problem. The problem is NP complete, so in practice an ATPG program tries to cover as many gates as possible within the time limit imposed on it.

Many ATPG algorithms exist, and several parallel algorithms have been designed and implemented [10]. The Orca ATPG program is based on the PODEM algorithm [7]. The algorithm considers each gate in turn. It assigns values to certain input lines (determined by heuristic rules), and propagates these values through the circuit. If it discovers that the current assignment cannot lead to a test of the gate, it backtracks and tries alternative assignments.

The Orca program parallelizes ATPG by statically partitioning the fault set among the processors. Each processor is given a fixed number of gates, for which it computes the test patterns. Using this basic algorithm, the program achieves good speedups (close to linear) on circuits of reasonably large size.

An important optimization that can be applied to both the sequential and parallel ATPG algorithms is *fault simulation*. If a test pattern has been computed for a certain gate, this pattern will probably test other gates in the circuit as well. Fault simulation determines such gates and removes them from the list of gates for which patterns still have to be computed.

This optimization was easy to add to the Orca program. All processes share an object containing the gates for which test patterns have been generated. If a process adds an element to this set, all other processes also use it to determine which gates they can delete from their set. The Orca program using this optimization is faster in absolute speed (by about a factor of 3), but it obtains inferior speedups. This is partly due to the communication overhead, and partly to the fact that the static partitioning of work may now lead to a load balancing problem. We intend to use a more dynamic work distribution strategy in the future.

5. Summary

Shared objects offer the possibility of programming certain parallel applications on systems lacking physical shared memory. They offer a model comparable to what programmers of multiprocessors get to see. We believe that the shared object model allows systems to be built that have the ease of construction of multicomputers, combined with the ease of use of multiprocessors. For this reason, we see this model as a promising area for future research.

Acknowledgements

The Orca programs for ACP, computer chess, and ATPG, have been written by Irina Athanasiu, Robert-Jan Elias, and Klaas Brink, respectively. Jack Jansen wrote the point-to-point runtime system.

References

[1] Bal, H.E.: *Programming Distributed Systems*, Prentice Hall Int'l, Hemel Hempstead, UK, 1991.

[2] Bal, H.E., Kaashoek, M.F., and Tanenbaum, A.S.: "Orca: A language for Parallel Programming of Distributed Systems," *IEEE Transaction on Software Engineering* vol. 18, pp. 190-205, March 1992.

[3] Bal, H.E., Kaashoek, M.F., Tanenbaum, A.S., and Jansen, J.: "Replication Techniques for Speeding up Parallel Appl. on Distr. Systems," *Concurrency Prac. & Exp.*, vol. 4, pp. 337-355, Aug. 1992.

[4] Birrell, A.D. and Nelson, B.J.: "Implementing Remote Procedure Calls," *ACM Trans. Computer Systems*, vol. 2, pp. 39-59, Feb. 1984.

[5] Carriero, N. and Gelernter, D.: "Linda in Context," *Commun. ACM*, vol 32, pp. 444-458, April 1989.

[6] Conrad, J.M, and Agrawal, D.P.: "A Graph Partitioning-Based Load Balancing Strategy for a Distributed Memory Machine," *Proc. 1992 Int. Conf. Parallel Processing (Vol. II)*, pp. 74-81, 1992.

[7] Goel, P.: "An Implicit Enumeration Algorithm to Generate Tests for Combinational IC Circuits," *IEEE Trans. Computers*, vol. C-30, pp. 215-222, March 1981.

[8] Jul, E., Levy, H., Hutchinson, N., and Black, A.: "Fine-Grained Mobility in the Emerald System," *ACM Trans. Computer Syst.*, vol 6, pp. 109-133, Feb. 1988.

[9] Kaashoek, M.F. "Group Communication in Distributed Computer Systems," Ph.D Thesis, Vrije Universiteit, Amsterdam, 1992.

[10] Klenke, R.H., Williams, R.D., and Aylor, J.H.: "Parallel-Processing Techniques for Automatic Test Pattern Generation," *IEEE Computer*, vol. 25, pp. 71-84, Jan. 1992.

[11] Lamport, L. "How to Make a Multiprocessor that Correctly Executes Multiprocess Programs," *IEEE Trans. on Comp.*, vol. C-28, pp. 690-691, Sept. 1979.

[12] Li, K. and Hudak, P.: "Memory Coherence in Shared Virtual Memory Systems," *ACM Trans. Computer Systems*, vol 7., pp. 321-359, Nov. 1989.

[13] Marsland, T.A., and Campbell, M.: "Parallel Search of Strongly Ordered Game Trees," *Computing Surveys*, vol. 14, pp. 533-551, December 1982.

[14] Mackworth, A.K.: "Consistency in Networks of Relations," *Artificial Intelligence*, vol. 8, pp. 99-118, Feb. 1977.

[15] Tanenbaum, A.S. et al., "Experiences with the Amoeba Distributed Operating System," *Commun. of the ACM* vol. 33, pp. 46-63, Dec. 1990.

Scalable Libraries in a Heterogeneous Environment

Anthony Skjellum
Computer Science Dept. & NSF Engineering Research Center
Mississippi State University
PO Drawer CS
Mississippi State, MS 39762

Abstract

This paper concerns itself with efforts to extend multicomputer libraries to a hierarchical, heterogeneous network environment. Two classes of support for such libraries are discussed: first, the message-passing features needed to establish groups of communicating processes, and communication contexts within which libraries can safely work. Second, we discuss message-passing primitives that encapsulate heterogeneity, hiding it from the user program (and library alike), and eliminating it when it proves unnecessary (within a homogeneous invocation, for instance). The Multicomputer Toolbox first-generation scalable libraries, and Zipcode message-passing systems are the means by which we demonstrate our research, so they are discussed here. We relate Zipcode syntax and semantics to the emerging MPI standard, when appropriate.

1 Introduction

First-generation scalable libraries have been developed within the *Multicomputer Toolbox* schema, described elsewhere [10, 11, 9]. In this system, we have devised distributed data structures for vectors and matrices, defined relative to virtual process topologies (logical grids), as well as an advanced message-passing notation and system, called *Zipcode*, that manages processes, communication scope, and virtual topologies. All of this software has initially been tied to homogeneous assumptions, both in performance, and in data format. We describe steps to relax these assumptions systematically, work that has been underway for the past year.

We describe message-passing operation scope, process groups, and communication contexts, within the framework of parallel libraries. In a heterogeneous environment, the limited message-passing scope attainable by basing message-passing on groups plus a logical partition of receipt selectivity between user-specified and system-registered segments is conceptually pivotal; the data structures that arise are called "mailers" or intra-group-communicators. Libraries can readily be written to work without interference, given communication contexts, because they can acquire (through a registry mechanism) additional communication contexts using a single safe mechanism for communication. Furthermore, the mailer framework is an ideal data structure in which to "cache" information on how operations should be implemented for a particular part of a communication hierarchy. Because of space limitations, we cannot describe in detail here how this is done in *Zipcode* (see [8]), but we do mention that introducing mailer-scope for communication (and data conversion) operations is an important source of runtime optimization for message passing. We mention the issues of library initialization and communication context use. From time to time, we relate *Zipcode* calls to the forthcoming MPI1 standard [3].

We consider the advances in message-passing notation that have been made to help improve the performance potential of codes based on *Zipcode*, particularly those that can incorporate "gather-send" and "receive-scatter" semantics. We describe how these become the building blocks for fully heterogeneous mathematical libraries, and which also offer encapsulation of any heterogeneous conversions. As such, we are able to assure portability between environments with reasonably compatible mathematical precision. We also see these semantics as offering the most optimizable message-passing constructs proposed as yet in any real system (what to do vs. how to do it).

We describe how our invoice notation (aka buffer descriptors) contribute to data-structure-oriented conversions. Reusability of invoices (gather/scatter specifications), and their creation outside inner loops, helps reduce overheads. The use of the ELROS system to implement efficient data conversions is mentioned, as an alternative to XDR, which cannot vectorize/pipeline. We quickly conclude that XDR is a deadend for high-performance data conversion.

We indicate how C++-based systems would further strengthen our efforts, and how abstractions in the current work are seen as a means not only to hide the complexity of heterogeneity, or to manage it, but also as a means to discover runtime optimizations that cannot be discovered with low-level semantics found in other systems. Such work will result in the second-generation scalable mathematical libraries we hope to complete in 1994 and 1995.

2 Language Bindings

Nodal C/C++, Fortran-77, or mixed C, C++, and Fortran-77 programming are the currently most viable approaches to programming on multicomputers / distributed computers (with multicomputer C++ still lagging behind workstation support for it), with a few exceptions. Support for data structures in Fortran-77 is absent, yet scalable libraries need complex data structures to encapsulate communication scope, data layout, methods, and architectural tuning. We do not address the complex issue of supporting Fortran-77 with *Multicomputer Toolbox* libraries here, except to say that macro preprocessing of Fortran-77 will definitely be needed, to provide a reasonable "look and feel" (*e.g.*, m4).

3 Communication System

In this section, we describe how the message passing system *Zipcode*, whose specific design purpose was to support parallel libraries in parallel applications, has been designed and extended to provide basic services useful for library management. We also compare current practice in *Zipcode* to standardization efforts underway in MPI1.

3.1 Programming Model

We assume a multiple-instruction, multiple-data programming model. Multiple program texts are possible within the system. Libraries typically operate in a loosely synchronous fashion. However, multiple independent instances and, overlapping process groups are permitted. Support for asynchronous operations is included (for instance, users could define their own library for an asynchronous collective operation).

3.2 Porting Strategy

Zipcode currently relies on the basic process management (spawn/kill) and messaging services (x-primitives) of the Reactive Kernel / Cosmic Environment, or, more usually, emulations thereof [5, 6, 7]. This strategy has been effective in that we have produced stable, usable ports for the Symult S2010, nCUBE/2, iPSC/2, iPSC/860, Delta, Paragon, BBN TC2000, CM-5 scalar machine, Sun workstation network, and RS/6000 networks during the past five years. A port to the PVM systems is nearly completed [1, 2]; integration of *Zipcode* with ELROS messaging capabilities is also being undertaken [4]; a direct TCP/IP port is also underway, which omits a PVM-like intermediate library,

Zipcode supports the common multicomputer HOST/NODE model of computation, which essentially means that there is an initial process that is responsible for the main part of the "sequential fraction" of computation, including spawning, killing, and initializing the parallel processes of an application. This model is not as general as one would prefer in an hierarchical, heterogeneous environment, but is a reasonable starting point. On a related note, certain multicomputer systems we have addressed in the past do not allow for dynamic process management (*e.g.*, Intel Delta), and many restrict programming to one process per processor. For such systems, operations like "spawn process" and "kill process" are NULL operations, but reasonable portability is still maintained.

3.3 Process Naming

In all *Zipcode* versions to-date, we have utilized the *Reactive Kernel*'s {node, pid}-pairs to describe processes in a pool, whether in a single multicomputer, or attached to a network. For a given implementation, the {node, pid} pair will be mapped to hardware, but this naming remains visible during the initialization process, during which processes are created (spawning). This notation is seen as extremely unattractive for programming by the user, but is rarely used because of automatically generated process groups (addressee lists) and virtual topologies.

Once message-passing has been set up, most *Zipcode* programs work with logical process grids of one-, two-, or three-dimensions. Furthermore, an advanced user can add new virtual topologies to the system. Some libraries might like to have tree topologies, for instance, to make them most natural to program. Virtual topologies provide naming that maps to an addressee list. This level of virtualization hides the implementation of addressee lists from the application, while improving notation.

3.4 Process Groups

A process group is a basic abstraction that has been found to be useful in a number of message-passing systems. A process group might be a way of describing the participants in a communication primitive, such as a synchronization (perhaps with additional information to encapsulate that particular collective operation instance from other operations). In *Zipcode*, a process group is called an "addressee list," and has the following properties:

- It is a logical, ordered collection of {node, pid} pairs.
- It has a rank (number of members).
- It is a purely local object.
- Communication cannot be expressed solely in terms of addressee lists.
- An addressee list can be transmitted in an extant communication context (see below).

In *Zipcode*, we have consistently implemented addressee lists as enumerations of {node, pid} pairs; originally, users assembled addressee lists, but addressee lists are now to be considered opaque; a standard constructor is provided:

```
ZIP_ADDRESSEES *addressees =
zip_new_cohort(int N, int node_bias,
   int cohort_pid, int pm_flag);
```

where

- N is the number of processes involved, or one less than the number of processes involved if pm_flag is true,
- node_bias is the suggested node-number offset to start with when spanning the user's logical allocation of processors,
- cohort_pid is the suggested, constant process ID of the entire collection of processes,
- pm_flag flags whether the process calling zip_new_cohort() is introduced as its zeroth entry, and hence the "postmaster" (group leader) for communication based on this addressee list (see below, under context creation).

This call builds a sensible set of process names over the range of logical nodes available in the user's allocation. The system may choose to override the cohort_pid suggestion never, immediately, or when processes are spawned using the addressee list (see below), The system may choose to override the node_bias naming never, immediately, or when processes are spawned using the addressee list (see below). These relaxations retain the opaque nature of the underlying addressee list, which is important to future generalizations of process naming. Furthermore, the needed transmission of addressee lists during context creation retains this desirable opacity.

Since internal manipulations of addressee lists is denigrated practice, addresee lists can be generalized in future *Zipcode* releases without breaking conforming code. Particularly, there could be additional portable ways to construct, modify, and transmit addressee lists, and particular environments could provide non-portable calls to provide additional addressee lists with appropriate opaque structure. Within the *Zipcode* system itself, there remains the need for non-enumerative representation inside an addressee list, and more general process naming (*e.g.*, PVM task ID's, or, preferably, handles to general opaque name objects). *Zipcode* will be generalized appropriately.

For completeness, *Zipcode* provides the following process management support, for which there is no planned analog in MPI1; the PVM systems also provides this capability, but with different semantics (*e.g.*, after creation, processes join named groups that are cached by dæmons, with possible race conditions):

```
int result = zip_spawn(char *prog_name,
      ZIP_ADDRESSEES *addressees,
      void *state, int not_pm_flag);
```

where

- prog_name is the ASCII name of the program to spawn, local to the spawner's file system,
- addressees addressee list upon which to spawn the program,
- state is unused, future expansion,
- not_pm_flag flags if TRUE, program is spawned on the zeroth addressee, of addressees.

and where result is non-zero on failure. Most implementations require that this spawning function be effected in the HOST process, though this restriction is less likely in a distributed setting. If the caller to zip_spawn is the zeroth entry in the addressee list (role of postmaster), it is erroneous to attempt to set not_pm_flag true. So, a valid HOST/NODE spawning procedure would be

```
#define FALSE 0
#define TRUE ~FALSE
    int N = 256, try_pid = 33;
    addressees = zip_new_cohort(N, 0,
                        try_pid, TRUE);
    result = zip_spawn("./testprog",
                addressees, NULL, FALSE);
```

A compatible zip_kill() is also defined:

```
    result = zip_kill(addressees);
```

With the inclusion of these functions, *Zipcode* specifies an entire programming environment that can be completely divorced from its original relationship with the *Reactive Kernel / Cosmic Environment (CE/RK)*.

3.5 Contexts of Communication

A communication context is an abstraction that was introduced by the author in the original (1988) *Zipcode* system, and which also will appear in the MPI1 standard [12, 3]. In order to write practical, "safe" distributed-memory, and/or distributed-computing libraries, communication contexts are needed to restrict the scope of messages. This is done to prevent messages from being selected improperly by processes when they do message passing. We described contexts in several papers on *Zipcode* [12, 13, 15, 14]. Without this type of scope restriction, it quickly becomes intractable to build up code without globalizing the details of how each portion of a code utilizes the message-passing resource. Communication contexts are therefore central to creating reusable library code, and to maintaining modularity in large-scale distributed application codes, with or without third-party libraries.

A context of communication has the following properties:

- A context of communication is based on an addressee list, the members of which are the assumed participants in the communication,

- A context of communication has one or more system-defined, labelings ("zipcodes," or context_ids in MPI1) of message passing for its addressee list the system,

- It provides a logical partitioning of receipt selectivity into user-defined, and system-registered components.

- If used correctly, allocated zipcodes guarantee that messages will not be misdirected.

- A zipcode is a globally unique quantity, but may be reused in disjoint groups.

To enforce safe programming, the following strictures are placed on message-passing in *Zipcode*:

- Send/receive (point-to-point) and collective communication work only within contexts of communication,

- Wildcarding, where permitted, does not violate context boundaries.

The creation of a context synchronizes the participants in that (future) context, while promulgating the addressee list, and zipcodes (context_id's). Only the "postmaster" (initial member of an addressee list) must know the addressee list initially. All other processes just need to know that they are going to create a communication context. The context server provides the needed zipcodes, and promulgates them with the addressee list information to all participants. A token released by the context server is held to ensure that the process completes without the chance that mailers fail because of race conditions on overlapped collections with distinct postmasters. (A server-free model is also possible, but has not yet been implemented in *Zipcode*.) The following call allocates globally unique zipcodes context_id's, that can subsequently be used to build contexts of communication, when merged with addressee lists:

```
    ZIP_ZIPSET *zips = zip_newzips(int N);
```

The following is the simplest form of the mailer creation call, in the 3D virtual topology (of shape $P \times Q \times R$).

```
ZIP_MAILER *g3_grid_open(int *P, *Q, *R,
    ZIP_ADDRESSEES *addressees)
```

The postmaster for the communication context calls this procedure with a valid addressee list, and valid values for the grid shape. All other participants call with undefined values for the grid shape, and NULL for the addressee list. A variant exists that permits the zipcodes to be specified. In that case, if all participants know their addressee list, then mailer creation is communication-free.

3.6 Zipcode vs. MPI1

A communication context degrades the raw performance of any message-passing system, in return for useful guarantees of program correctness, and manageability; how much degradation results depends on hardware characteristics, number of processes per processor, and whether additional queueing is required to support contexts. This speaks to the need for contexts in vendor primitives, rather than just in a user-level library such as *Zipcode*. With vendor implementations of MPI1, lighter-weight context support will become a reality, and *Toolbox/Zipcode* applications will increase performance either by moving directly to MPI1 primitives, or by our planned light-weight port of *Zipcode* that will run on top of MPI1. We view this evolution as highly satisfactory, as it has provided good portability, performance enhancement to the *Multicomputer Toolbox* libraries. Therefore, no *Zipcode*-based application or library will suffer in face of the standardization, but will instead benefit almost immediately by it, and be even more portable, as multiple vendors will eventually implement MPI1, whereas we were obliged to undertake each *Zipcode* port as new hardware became available.

For reasons of development latency (MPI1 is very large, and vendors have limited resources), and because *Zipcode* provides process management (whereas MPI1 does not), we will continue actively to develop, distribute, and support *Zipcode*, for the next one to two years, and perhaps longer. Particularly, the fully heterogeneous environment has not been addressed or explored fully in practice, and MPI1 does not address dynamic communication contexts. All of these factors suggest that new *Zipcode* features can potentially provide a continued useful role in providing practical input to the 1994 MPI2 effort, while remaining a "full" portability platform. Of course, we hope that MPI2 will include dynamic context support, and process control, and strict guidelines for multi-MPI2-implementation interoperability.

4 Issues from *Toolbox* Libraries

4.1 Initialization

Library initialization is a difficult question for conventional message-passing systems, because it is extremely tricky to predict how the receipt-selectivity-space will be partitioned by multiple invocations of the same library, by distinct libraries, by user programs, and even by collective communications implemented by a vendor (*e.g.*, Intel NX/2 uses the tag space to enforce order in collective combine). Having a library writer publish his/her "range of tags" utilized, which is a common alternative suggested to contexts, simply does not provide enough safety.

Zipcode provides two communication contexts (both encapsulated in the same mailer), by default: one for point-to-point and one for loosely synchronous, collective communication. This is defined to be a basic, safe environment for message passing, from which libraries could acquire additional contexts, as needed. (The second context is needed in the portable *Zipcode* implementation, since point-to-point messages are used to effect collective operations, rather than through alternative network hardware, as a vendor might do.) For each additional type of collective operation that is asynchronous or non-deterministic (*e.g.*, an asynchronous broadcast where the source is not known initially, and where tags must be used with point-to-point operations to preserve correctness), an additional communication context is needed. For each level of stack depth of libraries called, an additional context of communication is needed. For each overlapping pair of addressee lists, separate contexts must be defined for safe communication.

Since users interact mainly with virtual topologies (which are small collections of mailers), it is important to understand virtual-topology requirements and properties. *Zipcode*'s context_id's (zipcodes) are globally unique when issued, yet the built-in functions that implement virtual topologies reuse them safely on non-overlapping children of a virtual topology. As such, a three-dimensional virtual topology of shape $P \times Q \times R$ requires one pair of contexts for transmissions across the three-dimensional collection, and some number $3K$ additional contexts, where K is the number required for any one of the two-dimensional children (any process belongs to three plane subsets). Each of these two-dimensional logical process planes requires a pair of communication contexts for planar communication, and $2L$ additional contexts, where L is the number required by a one-dimensional process grid (a row or column). Evidently, $L = 2$, resulting in a total of two contexts for a one-dimensional grid, six for a two-dimensional grid, and twenty for a three-dimensional grid. If contexts could not be reused as just described, then a total of would grow with P, Q, R, rather than being constant (which is undesirable).

The initialization process for a three-dimensional grid instigates one synchronization of all participant processes, allocates the needed zipcodes (using *Zipcode*'s context server process), and then builds all lower-dimensional children without further communication. This sub-children creation can be done safely without further synchronization because of receipt-selectivity semantics of *Zipcode*: It is legal to post a message to a context before any mailer has been established on the recipient that supports that context of communication. After significant discussion during the definition of MPI1, we have also confirmed the need to support these semantics there, regardless of how system-defined virtual topologies are built in MPI1. For both message-passing systems, libraries can allocate reserve context_id's, and then use them at will, without costly synchronizations. This provides for safe message passing without synchronizations as one nests library calls in an application. So, the natural interpretation of the communication context as partitioning the receipt-selectivity space also leads to the best semantics for libraries, from the point of view of minimizing the number of synchronizations. It does not necessarily lead to the cheapest message-passing system from a low-level implementation perspective.

4.2 Objects & Interactions

Thus far, we have written numerical libraries, such as dense matrix-vector multiplication, to utilize pairs of distributed objects. A dense matrix is defined as distributed on a two-dimensional virtual topology, by specifying a specific mailer that is also identified as a two-dimensional topology. Initially, that mailer has available a safe context of communication for point-to-point and loosely synchronous collective communication. Similarly, we define vectors as replicated objects along one axis of that same topology, again relative to the identical mailer. When objects are created, additional zipcodes (context_id's could have been allocated, to provide safe communication for member functions working on the object. However, when friend functions are applied (*i.e.*, between a matrix and vector, or two matrices), one has to be careful to utilize a valid context of communication for the operations. For instance, validity of operating on two distributed objects is based on the equality of their mailers in the current *Toolbox*, rather than by performing an expensive congruency test on logical process grids. Hence, it is currently necessary for distributed objects to reveal the base virtual topology, and manage extra zipcodes (context_id's) separately (though they imply ephemeral contexts of communication, in general). This is so that the equality test can be satisfied in libraries that do error checking for compatible distributed objects.

We have not fully faced this issue in *Toolbox* libraries as yet, because we have assumed up to now that users do not leave dangling communications before calling a constructor. This is a bad assumption, in general. In fact, one has to question how safe a context of communication is if libraries have no state, but that they only initialize in the sense of creating objects like distributed matrices. One would have to be certain that no spurious communications were pending before creating such objects, or the program would be erroneous. As we don't want to leave this complexity to the user (a decision consistent with our efforts to create contexts), we might not want to rely on the supposedly safe context of communication provided by the mailer, but only rely on a context_id provided to the library (*e.g.*, when it was globally initialized), coupled with the addressee list of the passed-in mailer. So, each unique library in the system needs a pair of zipcodes, so it can bind them when constructing distributed objects. The correct user program is going to have to initialize each library in the system explicitly (or implicitly with static constructors, when we use C++ in the future). This type of library-scope initialization would not be user thread safe, returning the burden to the caller to provide safe context of communication when calling constructors for distributed objects.

5 Implementing Data Conversion

In the fully heterogeneous environment, data conversion will be needed within all heterogeneous communication contexts. We wanted to achieve the following goals (and have done so):

- No explicit conversion calls in user or library code.
- No extra data motion when homogeneous communication contexts are involved.
- Support for collective operations in the heterogeneous model.
- No user intervention with "how" buffers (if any) are formatted, nor how message protocol is handled (who converts, converts to what intermediate form, etc).

In other words, we make the message passing itself opaque. For point-to-point, the user's interface is a gather specification and destination on the sender's side, and a source and scatter specification on the recipient side. For collective communication, a macro procedure is used so that the user specifies the associative-commutative operation; *Zipcode* generates the code needed to handle both the fully heterogeneous and homogeneous cases. For more details, see [14, 8].

5.1 XDR vs. Bandwidth

We note that XDR is a bad system for handling vectors of data conversions because it imposes a function-call overhead for each datum converted, and vendor-supplied basic operations have these semantics as well (no argument for repeat count). So, a system like ELROS [4], which writes pipelineable, or vectorizable conversion code, provides much better bandwidth to the overall communication, than can XDR. Even if ELROS's code does not vectorize or pipeline on a machine, just moving the function call overhead outside the do-loop increases performance dramatically. Though ELROS is an embedded language, it could be used to write the conversion code used by invoices in *Zipcode*. Advanced users could employ ELROS and *Zipcode* together for more complex, hierarchical data structures.

At most, XDR should be used for low-volume negotiations, not for long-haul communications. Otherwise, high bandwidth links will not realize their full potential. A version of XDR that allowed multiple items to be converted per function call, would also be a big step in the right direction. Actually, what one wants is for vendors to implement their conversion operations in assembly language, with such an option. (Then, under *Zipcode*, for instance, something much simpler than XDR can be used to work on messages, because none of this is revealed by *Zipcode* to the user. Everything is done opaquely via invoices. See [8, 14].)

6 Abstraction vs. Performance

One of the clearest lessons of our work thus far, is that abstractions such as the gather/send, receive/scatter semantics of message-passing, because they are expressive, open the way for greater optimization, at the same time they provide the user with greater expressivity, and ease of programming. So, it is not true that higher levels of abstraction always imply less performance, as is commonly held.

The invoice (or buffer-descriptor) semantics allow the total encapsulation of heterogeneity within the calls, removing expensive data motion or conversion when it proves unnecessary (such as when an application is used on a homogeneous subset of machines). Furthermore, the careful binding of a communication context (*Zipcode* mailer) to such calls provides a means to maintain ("cache") appropriate methods, and architectural information about the group of communicating processes. Such information (such as the realization that a context is homogeneous, or in a single memory hierarchy) could be derived at runtime.

The lesson is that moving to a "what-I-want" not "how-I-want-it-done" approach to message passing (which incidently removed buffer structuring from user control), made message passing less error prone, potentially much faster, and simultaneously easier to understand. The limitations of C as the implementation language are relevant in this discussion. In C++ we could discover optimizations at compile-time because of tighter type checking (and overload more appropriate operators), runtime optimizations are no longer our only avenue of improved performance. C++ would open the way for inlining, and would also help instigate much safer message-passing constructs. In fact, the combination of contexts of communication, virtual topologies, and gather/send, receive/scatter semantics could be quite effective (*e.g.*, "a Zipcode++" system), but most of the benefits would be lost if the program were not entirely in C++ (because operator overloading would be lost, and type checking would have to be sacrificed). The invoice-oriented message-passing constructs, plus C++ extensions to allow data-only structs to be transferred would provide a reasonably simple extension to C++ for parallel computing. Such a system is certainly within our immediate reach. The availability of inlining suggests a reduction in the minimum overhead required to effect a message-passing call in C++ compared to C (though C could inline as well), with concomitant potential for better user-level performance. It should be noted that Fortran's minimum granularity is a function call, so using Fortran-77 for message-passing implies a performance hit compared to inlined C++ (or inlined C) calls: message-passing will be more efficient from inlined C/C++ than from Fortran-77, if implemented properly.

7 Summary and Conclusions

In this paper, we have raised issues that emerge when trying to move multicomputer libraries into the fully heterogeneous domain. We have touched on several issues: namely, process control, communication context control, and the semantics for how messages should be transmitted in order to encapsulate heterogeneity. We used our own software, *Toolbox/Zipcode* to motivate this discussion. Future work will include large-scale demonstrations of this software technology on heterogeneous platforms. We drew analogies between *Zipcode*, MPI1, and PVM, to relate these efforts, but this paper was in no way meant as a sincere comparison of these systems.

Acknowledgements

The author acknowledges financial support by the NSF Engineering Research Center for Computational Field Simulation (NSF ERC). Mississippi State University. The author acknowledges the contributions of Steven G. Smith, and Charles H. Still (both of Lawrence Livermore National Laboratory, Livermore, CA) as well as Nathan E. Doss (NSF ERC).

References

[1] A. Beguelin, J. Dongarra, G. A. Geist, R. Manchek, and V. Sunderam. A users' guide to PVM: Parallel Virtual Machine. Technical Report ORNL/TM-11826, Oak Ridge National Laboratory, July 1991.

[2] A. Beguelin, G. A. Geist, W. Jiang, R. Manchek, K. Moore, and V. Sunderam. The PVM project. Technical report, Oak Ridge National Laboratory, February 1993.

[3] Scott Berryman, James Cownie, Jack Dongarra, Al Geist, Bill Gropp, Rolf Hempel, Bob Knighten, Rusty Lusk, Steve Otto, Tony Skjellum, Marc Snir, David Walker, and Steve Zenith. Draft document of the MPI standard. Available on **netlib**, May 1993.

[4] M. L. Branstetter, J. A. Guse, D. M. Nessett, and L. C. Stanberry. An ELROS primer. Technical report, Lawrence Livermore National Laboratory, October 1992.

[5] Charles L. Seitz et al. The C Programmer's Abbreviated Guide to Multicomputer Programming. Technical Report Caltech-CS-TR-88-1, California Institute of Technology, January 1988.

[6] Charles L. Seitz, Sven Mattisson, William C. Athas, Charles M. Flaig, Alain J. Martin, Jakov Seizovic, Craig M. Steele, and Wen-King Su. The architecture and programming of the ametek series 2010 multicomputer. In *Proceedings of the Third Conference on Hypercube Concurrent Computers and Applications (HCCA3)*, pages 33–36. ACM Press, January 1988. (Symult s2010 Machine).

[7] Jakov Seizovic. The Reactive Kernel. Technical Report Caltech-CS-TR-88-10, California Institute of Technology, 1988.

[8] Anthony Skjellum. The Design and Evolution of Zipcode. *Parallel Computing*, 1993. (Invited Paper, to appear).

[9] Anthony Skjellum, Steven F. Ashby, Peter N. Brown, Milo R. Dorr, and Alan C. Hindmarsh. The Multicomputer Toolbox. In G. L. Struble et al., editors, *Laboratory Directed Research and Development FY91 - LLNL*, pages 24–26. Lawrence Livermore National Laboratory, August 1992. UCRL-53689-91 (Rev 1).

[10] Anthony Skjellum and Chuck H. Baldwin. *The Multicomputer Toolbox: Scalable Parallel Libraries for Large-Scale Concurrent Applications*. Technical Report UCRL-JC-109251, Lawrence Livermore National Laboratory, December 1991.

[11] Anthony Skjellum, Chuck H. Baldwin, Charles H. Still, and Steven G. Smith. The Multicomputer Toolbox on the Delta. In Tiny Mihaly and Paul Messina, editors, *Proc. of the First Intel Delta Applications Workshop*, pages 263–272. Caltech Concurrrent Supercomputing Consortium CCSF-14-92, February 1992.

[12] Anthony Skjellum and Alvin P. Leung. Zipcode: A portable multicomputer communication library atop the Reactive Kernel. In *Proc. Fifth Distributed Memory Computing Conf. (DMCC5)*, pages 767–776. IEEE, April 1990.

[13] Anthony Skjellum and Manfred Morari. Zipcode: A portable communication layer for high performance multicomputing. Technical Report UCRL-JC-106725, Lawrence Livermore National Laboratory, March 1991. To appear in Concurrency: Practice & Experience.

[14] Anthony Skjellum, Steven G. Smith, Charles H. Still, Alvin P. Leung, and Manfred Morari. The Zipcode Message-Passing System. In Geoffrey C. Fox, editor, *Parallel Computing Works*. 1992. (Also as LLNL UCRL-JC-112022).

[15] Anthony Skjellum and Charles H. Still. Zipcode: and the Reactive Kernel for the Caltech Intel Delta Prototype and nCUBE/2. In *Proc. Sixth Distributed Memory Computing Conf. (DMCC6)*, pages 26–33. IEEE, April 1991. Also available as LLNL Technical Report UCRL-JC-107636.

Parallel Computing for Helicopter Rotor Design

J. Manke, K. Neves, and T. Wicks
High–Speed Computing Program
Boeing Computer Services
P. O. Box 24346, MS 7L–48
Seattle, WA 98124–0346

Abstract

The High–Speed Computing (HSC) Program was established in 1986 within Boeing Computer Services (BCS) to provide a prototypical environment which could be used to study the problem of integrating new computing technologies into Boeing. The following paper summarizes work within the HSC Program on parallel computing and concentrates on one application area, helicopter rotor design, as an example of how these technologies are being used to prototype critical engineering processes. The discussion will emphasize: (1) The prototypical process; (2) The computing technologies which were employed; (3) Some of the issues which were addressed while investigating these technologies; and (4) The software metrics used to assess the impact of using this technology in the design process.

1. Scientific Computing Trends and Issues

Cost–efficient design of aerospace products at Boeing necessitates that its engineering divisions solve complex problems in computationally intensive areas such as multi–disciplinary optimization. To address these problems, engineers use computing platforms and environments at Boeing that consist of supercomputers, such as the Cray Y/MP, along with mainframes, mini–supercomputers, and high–end workstations, all of which are used separately and sequentially for most tasks. However, traditional mainframes and supercomputers, as they have been designed with proprietary architectures, are nearing the limits of their capability. The amount of research dollars to generate new systems is actually growing while the payoff in performance improvement is dwindling. This suggests that they will meet an economic dead–end before the end of the decade. Accordingly, companies like Cray Research, IBM, Convex, and all the Japanese manufacturers have massively parallel processor (MPP) designs under development. For example, Fujitsu announced that it will be offering an MPP design based on microprocessor technology that can be configured to provide 350 Gflops, with delivery in the third quarter of 1993. The longer term predictions are that the price performance of workstations will overcome minicomputers, mini–supercomputers, and mainframes. Evidence of this already exists even within Boeing. Furthermore, the classical form of supercomputers (large powerful CPU's in relatively small numbers within a single system) will most likely be replaced by MPP's of enormously peak total power as measured in Mflops. We believe that the three following driving forces characterize this form of high performance computing: (1) Computing Power; (2) Hero Problems; and (3) Price Performance.

Computing Power: If one is looking for simply raw power, MPP's will replace traditional supercomputers in this capacity, and will likely be labeled "supercomputers" as well. As an example of the quest for power, one company, Cray Research, is planning a machine with peak performance of a Tflop by mid–decade and sustained performance of a Tflop on meaningful applications before the end of the decade. Even if such machines are more expensive, the new capability will satisfy the needs in the next item.

Hero Problems: The grand challenge problems throughout science abound. Within Boeing we have only scratched the surface of ways in which computing can improve our processes in both design and manufacturing. Technology trends in many fields open up the opportunities for new engineering processes. An example of a Boeing *hero problem* would be the meaningful coupling of structural deformation and aerodynamic loading due to flow over wings, helicopter rotors, and other aerodynamic surfaces. But this is just one example. Most of Boeing's key analysis problems are really the "inner–loops" of a design process that could more greatly benefit from computing. In fact, optimization processes are often more amenable to MPP designs than the original analysis problems from which they derive. As long as Boeing wishes to remain competitive in its products, key *hero problems* will come to the forefront.

Price Performance: This is the most curious change. Traditional supercomputers no longer *own* a price performance advantage. This has caused a considerable confusion for several spurious reasons. There are several ways to achieve superior price performance. As mentioned, microprocessors have the price performance advantage over time. We must remember, however, that price performance is the key measure when the problem being solved is tractable on low-end equipment. If the problem is a critical *hero problem* it could require the high-end of the performance scale. Most of the existing applications at Boeing, if frozen in time, will be tractable on workstations within three years. In fact, most industrial experts predict that workstations with 1 Gflop of power, 1 Gword of memory, and a price tag of $10,000 will be available by the end of the decade. This is approximately three times more powerful than one CPU of our most powerful computer at Boeing today; thus, we must increase performance to solve our biggest problems and we may save money when the problem class is frozen. The key will be knowing when and how fast to move in either direction.

During this period of transition to MPP environments, Boeing faces many interim trends, driven by the above forces, where the near-term future of high performance computing will make use of distributed and parallel computing involving traditional supercomputers, workstations, and advanced visualization systems all linked together by effective high-performance networks. Thus, in meeting requirements for orders of magnitude more computational power, two scenarios (cf. Figure 1) come to mind where one near term trend, the use of many workstations over a network to handle the computing loads once reserved for mainframes or even supercomputers, is used to develop parallel code (using a higher level "portable" communication library) that can make use of the cluster of machines and that will run on MPP platforms once the communication libraries are in place.

2. The HSC Program

The HSC Program provides a prototypical environment to address the changing technology that was discussed in the previous section. The approach taken is three pronged: (1) A prototypical laboratory is provided, The Advanced Systems Laboratory, (ASL); (2) Advances in distributed computing systems, parallel computing tools, languages, and algorithms as well as scientific visualization techniques are actively explored through our Core Technology Program; and (3) Access and meaningful technology transfer of application technology to Boeing's engineering community is provided through the Joint Technology Transfer Program.

The ASL contains both shared and distributed memory parallel machines along with high-end workstations that are connected together by both Ethernet and high-speed networks. The parallel systems inventory includes a 2 processor Cray Y-MP/EL, a 66 processor Intel Paragon, a 32 processor Intel iPSC/860, a 4 processor IRIS 4D/480, and a 4 processor Sun 4/690. The Paragon is (near to) an entry level configuration capable of 5 Gflops peak performance although its design allows it to be scaled to 150 Gflops peak. But even this low-end machine has twice the peak power of the current Y/MP in the Data Center although most current applications would run much slower without modification. In addition, a complement of parallel machines and workstations are connected in the ASL to a FDDI ring and several of these same machines are connected to the Data Center's Y/MP as well as to several high-end workstations in a remote Aerodynamics Research Laboratory via UltraNet. Thus a number of computing "profiles" can be demonstrated and evaluated in this environment.

Technology transfer to and from the HSC Program is provided by the Joint Technology Transfer and Core Technology Transfer Programs. An infrastructure of Parallel Tools such as Forge-90, message-passing software such as PVM and P4, and cluster software such as DQS, UniJes, and LSF is maintained and evaluated by the Core Technology Program for use by projects under the Joint Technology Transfer Program. It is here that intra-organizational teams composed of engineers and HSC Program staff are developing prototypes for the next generation "hero" problem in the areas of Structures, Aerodynamics, Propulsion, and Rotor Wake Modelling. Indeed, we can provide an early look at the promising technology of MPP's that are the likely workhorses of the future as well as workstation clusters that can off-load much of the "routine" work that supercomputers are frequently overloaded with. The HSC Program has a very small fixed staff, which looks at support issues for these future environments, yet the program draws on the broad base of expertise found throughout the more than 500 person Research and Technology Organization of BCS.

3. Helicopter Rotor Design Applications

As an example of how the HSC Program is used to prototype applications from the engineering community on advanced architectures, we consider one of the Joint Technology Transfer Projects which is currently underway with Boeing Helicopters. We will first briefly discuss the problem and the codes that are involved in this work. Afterwards, issues that arose during the parallelization of these codes are discussed and some of the results are presented in the context of a preliminary cost impact analysis.

In 1992, a team of engineers and scientists at Boeing Helicopters and BCS was organized to assess the viability of using parallel computing to reduce costs in the design process of helicopter rotors. As a first step in planning the project, the most computationally intensive procedures currently used for aeromechanics research and rotor design support were reviewed, Figure 2. This review revealed that computational fluid dynamic (CFD) analyses, rotor-wake modelling, blade dynamic and aeroelastic modelling, and optimization offered the greatest potential payoff in the continuous quality improvement of the design process for both the near term, where a cluster of workstations is used for the parallelization, and the long term, where massively parallel systems are integrated into the workstation cluster. HSC Program joint

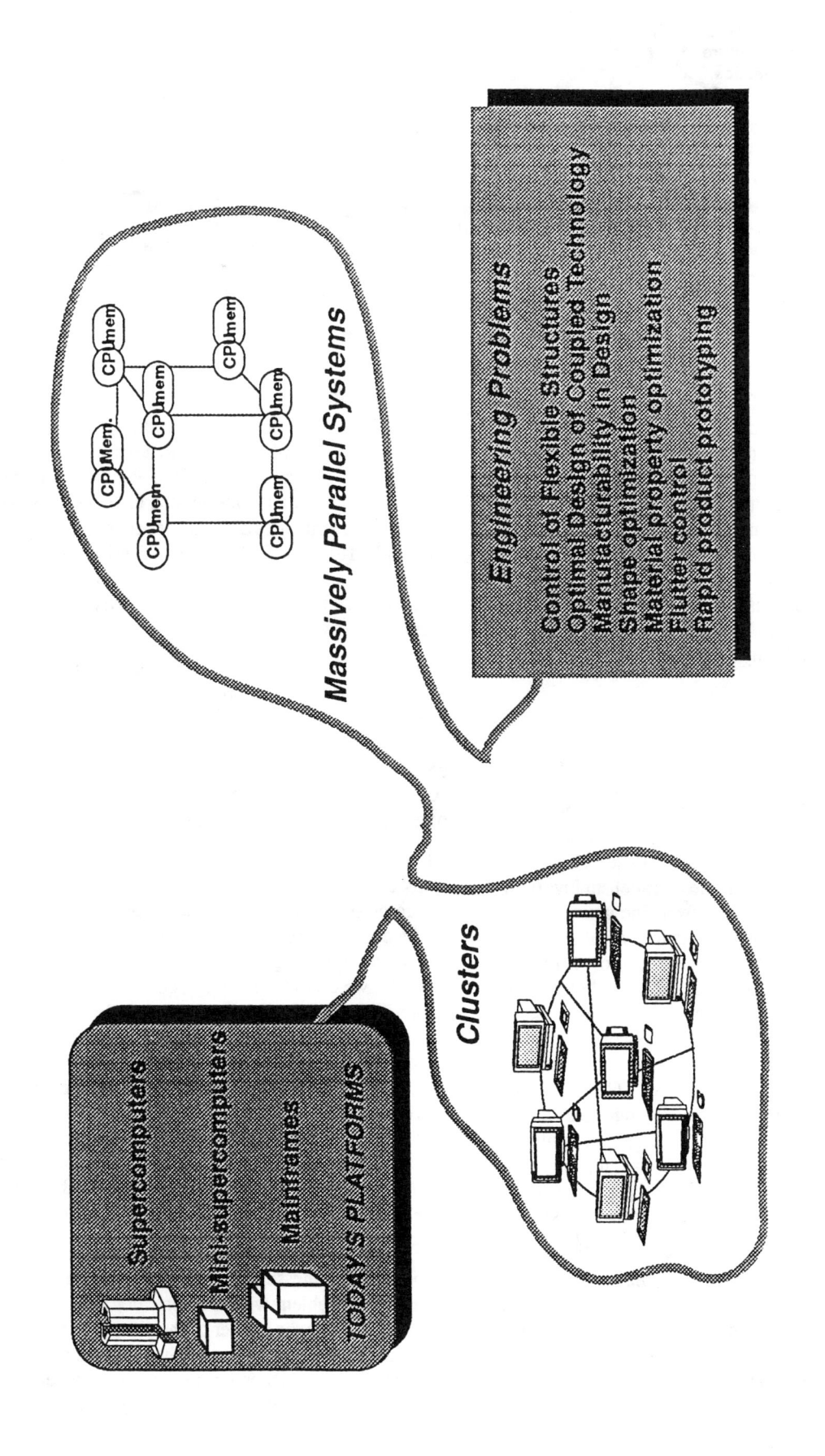

Figure 1. Paths to Meeting Boeing Requirements

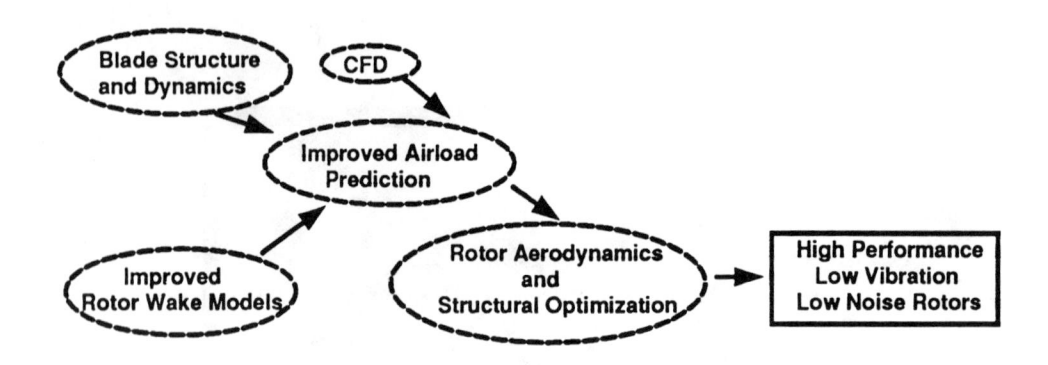

Figure 2. Rotor Design Process

projects between Boeing Commercial Airplane Group (BCAG) and BCS were already addressing areas concerning parallel computing for both internal and external CFD and thus we determined that this project could best be served by targeting three Fortran helicopter analysis and design codes: (1) C–60, a rotor dynamics analysis code with multiple case capability; (2) B–65, a code employing advanced rotor-wake models; and (3) C–06, a structural optimization code that minimizes blade response for a given vibrator airload forcing function. This work, was limited in scope to prototyping and did not include any algorithm research or development activity.

4. The Parallelization

Some of the major requirements imposed on the parallelization were as follows: (1) The computing environment should consist of heterogeneous, distributed memory systems including the Intel iPSC/860 and Paragon along with HP and Sun workstations; (2) Coarse–grained parallelism involving physical tasks should be favoured over fine grained (loop level) parallelization; and (3) Code changes should be minimized. The first constraint was imposed to allow for an investigation that would study both massively parallel systems as well as loosely coupled parallel systems such as workstation clusters that are available at Boeing Helicopters. The P4 message passing library from Argonne National Laboratory was chosen to implement parallelism in C–60, B–65, and C–06 over other process communication languages such as PVM or Linda, or environments such as Express, mainly because at the time this work was started, P4 was the only software which would run on all of the desired platforms. For a more detailed discussion of parallel languages and tools, cf. Gates et al. [1], Chang and Smith [3], and Cheng [4].

One of the more difficult tasks in parallelizing an existing code concerns the determination of potential sections of code which lend themselves to parallelization. This problem is exacerbated by the fact that most of this work is usually done by persons who although familiar with the techniques of parallelism, are unfamiliar with the code or algorithms. In discussing this problem, Gates et al. [1] have looked at tools such as ToolPak from Argonne National Laboratories, and Forge–90 from Applied Pacific Research. During this project much use of Forge was made to obtain timing profiles at both the procedural and loop/block level, as well as to analyze the data structures and data dependencies. When Forge was applied to C–60, B–65, and C–06, codes which are of the order of 70,000 lines and 150 subroutines, a reasonably quick and error free analysis ensued for a process which can normally be overwhelming.

After it is determined what codes should be parallelized, attention can be focused on its implementation using P4. Regarding this, one needs to consider two components, the master and the slave. Implementations involving message passing between master and slaves invokes at least three issues for consideration: memory, performance of the message passing library used, and available bandwidth of a network.

All of the codes in question have been developed over many years and for that reason it was decided that an approach where massive changes were avoided. For this reason, we decided not to separate the master and slave code. In order that issues involving this type of implementation can be discussed, we consider a Fortran code segment of Figure 3 which is similiar to code which needs to be added to an existing application to implement the communication of data between two or more platforms. Here we assume that an array, "data", of floats of length, "len", exists. After initiating P4, this code uses "p4myid" to determine if the code is a "master" running on the machine (or processor) which was used to execute the application or on the "slave" which is automatically executed on a remote machine (or another processor) listed in a file which is read when the "master" executes "p4crpg".

Implementing message passing in an existing code can introduce a problem with memory. For example, whatever memory used by the master or the slave will be required of the other. In situations where either the master or slave has significant different memory requirements, an effort should be made to split the application into master and slave compo-

```
call p4init()

if(p4myid() .eq. 0) then

    call p4crpg()

    call p4send( type, proc, data, len, retc)
    call p4recv( type, proc, data, len, msglen, retc)

else

    call p4recv( type, iprc, data, len, msglen, retc)
    call p4send( type, proc, data, len, retc)

endif
```

Figure 3. Message Passing via Argonne's P4 Communication Library

nents to prevent the case where an excessive amount of memory is requested but not used.

Whilst the problem with requesting too much memory can determine whether the application executes or not, other issues regarding performance can determine how successful the parallelization is in terms of speed–up. For example, consider Figure 4 where the best results of sending a round trip

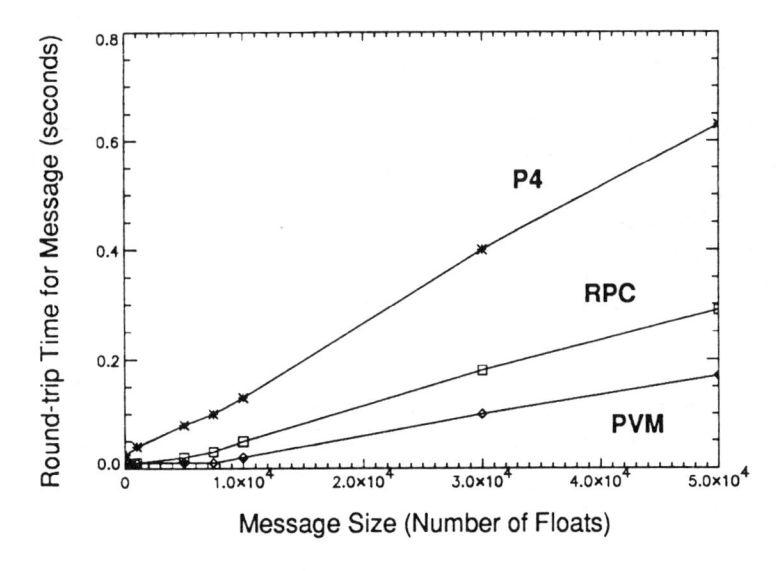

Figure 4. Message Passing Performance between Sun SPARCstation–2's

message between two machines of the same architecture by various techniques are contrasted. When parallelizing various tasks, where data is sent to a slave processor for subsequent computation, it is necessary to consider both the amount of computation which will be carried out on the slave and the time involved in sending the message to the slave. If the message passing time is of the same order as the computation, then the parallelization will suffer a severe inefficiency due to system overhead while the slave is waiting for data with which to compute. Thus, the selection of a particular message passing library (or the use of a message passing library on a different architecture) can hamper ones ability to optimize the parallelization. As an example, we note that in parallelizing C–60, messages of the order of several integers could be used to "feed" separate load cases. For all platforms considered, linear speed–up (with respect to the number of workstations or processors) is guaranteed. However, in the case of B–65, the parallelization was more fragile with the message size for the "best algorithm" entailing arrays of the order of 50,000 floats. As can be seen from Figure 4, if one changed to another message passing library and if the algorithm was not flexible enough to be adjusted for this change, the parallelization might be a failure. In the case of B–65, both the loading and the data were distributed so that difficulties such as this could be minimized.

Before leaving the subject of message passing, the network must be taken into account if a cluster of workstations is to be used. For example, consider Figure 5 where an experi-

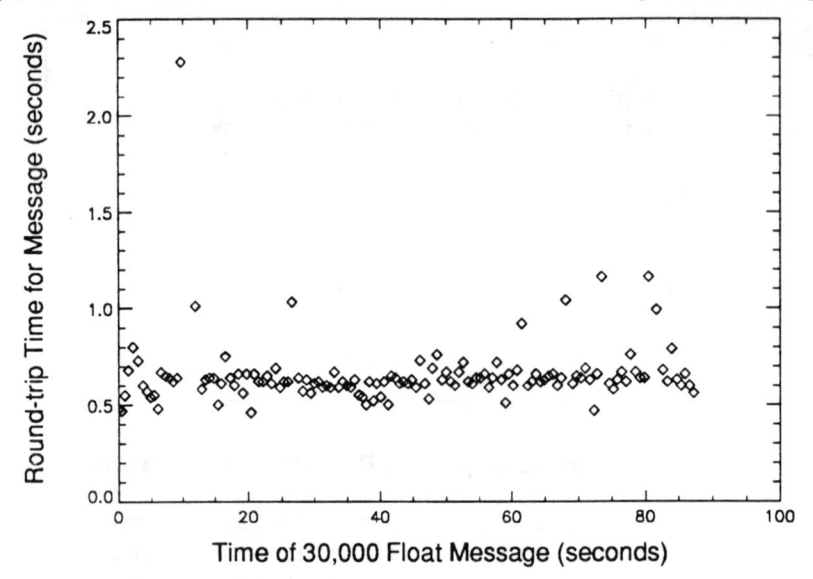

Figure 5. Dependence of Message Passing Performance on the Network

ment was run on a network in which three fileservers and approximately 110 workstations were actively employed for a variety of developmental tasks consuming an average of 15–25 percent of the available bandwidth of that network. During this 1.5 minute experiment, the round trip time for a 30,000 float message varied between 0.48–2.3 seconds, never achieving the best time of 0.4 seconds as computed for Figure 4 on a quiescent network. For codes such as C–60, B–65, and C–06, run–times of 2–360 minutes on the parallelized versions are expected, thus ensuring even more diversity in the time it takes for a message to be passed. At the heart of this problem are administrative issues such as configuration design. Here questions arise such as "how to segment the network to provide for an optimal number of workstations if parallel codes are to be run on that segment" or "how to schedule tasks such as backups and installations to ensure that all tasks complete within an expected and required time frame".

5. Results

Due to the algorithms of C–60 and C–06 being similar, we will only present results for the parallelization of C–60 and B–65.

5.1 C–60 Parallelization

In order to determine the impact that the parallelization has on the design process, we consider an example concerning the use of the parallel version of C–60, C–60P, for a 32 case study and contrast several environments. In Table 1 are projected run times for this assuming available resources such as: (1) A single Apollo DN–10000; (2) A single HP–9000/720; (3) A cluster of HP workstations; and two configurations of an Intel iPSC/860.

System	DN–10000	HP Cluster			Intel IPSC/860	
Processors	1	1	16	32	16	32
Cost	$50,000	$25,000	$400,000	$800,000	$250,000	$500,000
Wait Time	224	122	7.6	3.8	96	48
Cost Index	1	3.67	3.67	3.67	0.47	0.47

Table 1. Software Metrics for C–60P on a 32 Case Study

Here, wait time is measured in the minutes an engineer waits for the results and the cost index is determined by calculating the performance of the configuration (Mflops/cost) with a normalization by the performance of the DN–10000. Because of the linear speed–up of C–60P, the 32 configuration of HP's produces a significantly reduced wait time while the iPSC/860 produces scalable results which are not as robust. (This is due to optimization problems with the iPSC/860 compiler.) On the other hand, if the cost index is used to measure the success of the parallelization then the scalability of the parallelization provides at best, a no cost benefit, due to the necessity of spending the same scalable amount of money to acquire the necessary resource. The primary point of this discussion is the issue of how much benefit an engineer would have generated from spending a reduced amount of wait time, for example 3.8 minutes vs. 122 minutes in the above case for an HP. Data suggests that tradeoffs between cost index and wait time factors need to be considered before determining the potential benefits of using the cluster. For example, if idle workstations can be used, then wait time is the overriding measure; on the other hand, if workstations need to be purchased then the cost index might be more significant.

5.2 B–65 Parallelization

Our next example makes use of the rotor wake model code, B–65, which was parallelized with the help of Forge–90. In particular, a distributed data – distribute load technique was used to obtain a "theoretically" scalable algorithm. That is, "theoretically" if an unlimited amount of bandwidth was available which of course is not. In Table 2, we have tabulated results of this parallelization for a Sun–IPX cluster and the Intel iPSC/860.

System	Sun–IPX	Sun–IPX Cluster			Intel iPSC/860	
Processors	1	2	5	10	16	32
Cost	$10,000	$25,0000	$50,000	$100,000	$250,000	$500,000
Wait Time	1210	671	464	388	439	355
Cost Index	1	0.90	0.52	0.31	0.11	0.07

Table 2. Software Metrics for B–65P

In this case, we see that the best wait time results were obtained for the iPSC/860 with 32 processors. This is because the distributed data algorithm makes use of parallel communication of processors and on an ethernet, wire contention prevents this from occuring. On the other hand, when using a cost index to measure performance, the workstation cluster still out performs the iPSC/860. Of course, the potential for throughput is a factor which is not taken into account here. Indeed, because of bandwidth of the network, two 16–processor jobs on the iPSC/860 will execute faster than two 10–workstation jobs in our environment. When extrapolated to production levels, it is estimated that the cost performance of running on a MPP architecture will exceed that of the workstation cluster if a ethernet is used. Currently under way are experiments to compare throughput studies of running B–65 on FDDI and UltraNet environments in contrast with running on the Intel Paragon.

6. Closure

This article has focused on work regarding portable parallelism. Results for helicopter codes lead us to believe that it is possible to produce portable parallel code which retains the same efficiency (with respect to speed–up and performance) for realistic design applications. Furthermore, the impact of this speed–up can be shown to be significant with respect to rotor designs which were accomplished without the benefit of parallelism.

However, the ability for engineers to make use of parallel computing technology depends on factors (other than those relating directly to proof of principle) concerning its ability to be integrated into the Boeing culture. In particular, engineers use C–60, B–65, and C–06 with a collection of post–processors to visualize the results. By using parallel versions which run on a network, attention to visualizing the distributed data on this network is a must. One of the core projects within the HSC Program has been addressing this problem (see Curtis and Kerlick in this issue). In addition to visualization issues is the fundamental issue regarding the capability to use a cluster of computers. Without some "automatic" mechanism for using the cluster as a transparent resource, it is believed that parallelism will only be used by those willing to struggle with the numerous details concerning its use. Towards the end of providing user friendly parallelism and cluster computing, BCAG Propulsion Research and BCS are conducting a joint project aimed at implementing user friendly parallelism and cluster computing in a production environment. This project employs a heterogeneous cluster of SGI, IBM, and HP workstations that are being used to evaluate network queuing systems such as DQS from Florida State University. Here a utility provided by DQS allows for a user to submit a job to the cluster without needing to be aware of which machines are in the cluster. In the case of a sequential job, the loading of members of the cluster are taken into account so that a target platform can be chosen to run the job. After execution, results are returned automatically. In the case of a parallel job (if one uses P4 or PVM), a list of the most appropriate machines is created and put in files which can in turn be used by the communication libraries to perform the parallelism. Although this work is in its preliminary pilot stage, results demonstrate that a significant cost savings can be realized by using a cluster in this manner. Work in 1993 will focus on expanding this study to Boeing Helicopters and BCS Technology to create a working cluster of several hundred computers. By accomplishing this, significant progress will have been made towards resolving problems associated with the critical issues regarding the use of network queuing software to submit production design codes running in parallel mode.

Acknowledgements

The authors would like to acknowledge the following who have contributed to the projects discussed in this paper: L. Dadone, R. Derham, J. Hirsh and B. Oh of Boeing Helicopters along with M. Gates, D. Kerlick, and J. Patterson of BCS.

References

[1] M. Gates, A. Larrabee, D. Mizell, and J. Patterson, "Using a Network of Workstations for Parallel Computing", *High–Speed Computing Program Technical Report Series*, HSC–91–6, Boeing Computer Services, 1991.

[2] O. Brewer, D. Curtis, D. Kerlick, T. King, and B. Kirby, "Scientific Visualization in a Distributed Environment", *High–Speed Computing Program Technical Report Series*, HSC–92–7, Boeing Computer Services, 1992.

[3] L.–C. Chang and B. Smith, "Classification and Evaluation of Parallel Programming Tools", *Computer Science Technical Report*, CS90–22, The University of New Mexico, 1990.

[4] D.Y. Cheng, "A Survey of Parallel Programming Tools", *NAS Systems Division Report*, RND–91–005, NASA Ames Research Center, Moffett Field, California, 1991.

SESSION 2: Panel —
The Virtual Heterogeneous Supercomputer: Can It be Built?

H.J. Siegel, Chair

PANEL - The Virtual Heterogeneous Supercomputer: Can It Be Built?

Howard Jay Siegel, Panel Moderator
Parallel Processing Laboratory
School of Electrical Engineering
Purdue University
West Lafayette, IN 47907-1285, USA
hj@ecn.purdue.edu

The current advances in processor design, networking technology, and software for parallel/distributed computing lead to the idea of building a virtual supercomputer by dynamically combining an available set of heterogeneous computing resources. However, to achieve this goal there are some challenging problems that need to be solved (design of a programming model, task description and specifications, scheduling machines, task decomposition, matching subtasks to appropriate architectures, portability, etc.). Ineffective solutions to these problems will make the practical implementation of such a virtual system infeasible.

Panelists are expected to argue the feasibility or infeasibility of writing application programs that can run effectively on a set of heterogeneous computing resources with performance in excess of that possible with any single supercomputer. If they think it can be done, then how? What research is needed? Should this heterogeneous approach be pursued, or is enhancing the single parallel machine approach to supercomputing much more realistic?

The following people have agreed to participate as panelists to discuss these issues:

H. J. Siegel (Moderator), Purdue University
Henry G. Dietz, Purdue University
Richard F. Freund, NRaD
Chani Pangali, Kendall Square Research
Richard C. Metzger, Rome Laboratory
Kenneth W. Neves, Boeing Computer Services
C. V. Ramamoorthy, Univ. of California at Berkeley
Andy Tanenbaum, Vrije University

Each member of the panel was asked to prepare a paragraph position statement for these proceedings. Their position statements are reproduced unedited below.

Henry G. Dietz:

The concept of treating a network of computers as a virtual heterogeneous supercomputer is attractive because it seems inexpensive to implement, offers the potential to execute each parallel program on the machine(s) with the most appropriate architecture, and facilitates load balancing. However, the lower cost generally implies that such a network cannot perform as well as a more tightly-coupled parallel machine on fine-grain parallel programs. In addition, matching portions of programs to architectures and accounting for load factors is too complex for most programmers to directly manage; the programming environment must be able to automate these tasks. Thus, we believe that a virtual heterogeneous supercomputer will not replace tightly-coupled parallel machines, but will complement and incorporate them. The primary research tasks involve designing programming models and systems that can automatically and invisibly make good use of these heterogeneous systems. We are currently exploring these issues in a prototype software system called AHS: Automatic Heterogeneous Supercomputing.

Richard F. Freund:

The basic ingredients for a virtual heterogeneous supercomputer (VHS) are already in place. Among these are: a variety of different HPC architecture types, with a growing awareness of both their individual potentials and weaknesses; high-speed interconnectivity amongst the various national hpc labs; development of orchestration tools, e.g., PVM; new programming paradigms; and prototype applications, e.g., Climate Modeling. A basic system implementing all of these has already been developed at NRaD. Development of mature VHS technology offers the possibility of superlinear performance and reduced programming effort. It requires the addition of "smarts," already prototyped at NRaD, to the orchestration tools and a smooth transition path from traditional HPC approaches.

Chani Pangali:

[This abstract not received in time for publication]

Richard C. Metzger:

The feasibility of building a virtual heterogeneous supercomputer can be viewed from two different perspectives. The top down view encompasses programming applications for such a machine. From this view the virtual machine appears to be very feasible. Research into tools such as AHS and PVM have provided prototype capabilities that can analyze an abstract programming model and match the program with the proper execution model. But further research is needed with such tools to provide the proper allocation of segments of code to the proper heterogeneous execution models. The second perspective is from the bottom-up, or the systems perspective. This view supposes that we have the program segments allocated to the proper machines and are ready for execution. From this view the virtual machine is still feasible but when it will be feasible is unknown. This perspective encompasses many of the open issues that still need to be solved. Issues such as a global clock for execution across heterogeneous machines, distributed shared memory across heterogeneous platforms, and global synchronization. The solutions to these problems may be feasible, but the solutions themselves may not be practical to warrant their use. The only means to determine if these solutions exist is with the proper research and resources directed primarily at the systems level.

Kenneth W. Neves:

Axiom: If IT [fill in any technology for IT] is being done somewhere today, IT is not impossible.

Most would argue that the supporting technologies for distributed and parallel computing are understood to some degree. The programming tools, operating system issues, and algorithmic approaches have all been demonstrated in isolated and/or special cases. In fact, there are limited production examples in the aerospace industry. However, we lack emphasis on key issues to make the revolution complete -- ease-of-use and reliability. Efficiency, 100% parallelization, peak performance and host of other academic measures are not important. Rather, time to solution at reasonable cost for competitive problems should be the goal of any new computing paradigm. Ad hoc standards are emerging and the general issues of MPP and distributed computing (through workstations) share some commonality. It is time we attack them as a community, and bring research curiousities into full scale production. We advocate a partnership among academia, computer companies, government labs, and private industry to spur this trend.

C.V. Ramamoorthy:

While the single parallel machine approach is more feasible in the current state of art, virtual machines are likely to become prevalent in the foreseeable future. The needs of the computer user are multiplying, and soon, it will be infeasible to build a single parallel machine that can satisfy all the specific needs of specialized users. The realization of virtual machines on top of heterogenous systems is thus a need driven activity.

Several criteria need to be satisfied for the construction of a virtual machine on top of heterogenous machines - programming abstraction for computation and communication, task description and mapping based on compulsory and optionally satisfiable attributes, scheduling and mapping algorithms, and inter-operatibility and porting considerations.

We have identified some means of achieving at least some of these objectives and believe that future research along these identified directions will yield fruitful realization of our Virtual Machine dream.

Andy Tanenbaum:

I believe that a parallel computer built up of CPU-memory pairs and connected by a fast interconnect is definitely feasible for a wide class of problems. Our experience indicates that good (but not perfect) speedups are possible on problems that exhibit reasonable locality and a high ratio of reads to writes. However, if one looks at a heterogenous system (e.g., 20% SPARC CPUs, 20% DEC Alpha CPUs, 20% HP CPUs, 20% MIPS CPUs, and 20% RS6000 CPUs), I think the difficulties introduced by the different instruction sets and memory models are so great that the project can only succeed for exceedingly loosely coupled applications, like hunting for prime numbers. Thus I believe that a homogenous virtual supercomputer can succeed, but a heterogeneous one will fail.

SESSION 3A:
Enabling Software Technology

Richard C. Metzger, Chair

A Parallel Object-Oriented Framework for Stencil Algorithms

John F. Karpovich, Matthew Judd, W. Timothy Strayer, and Andrew S. Grimshaw

Department of Computer Science, University of Virginia

{jfk3w | mrj2p | wts4x | grimshaw} @virginia.edu

Abstract

We present an object-oriented framework for constructing parallel implementations of stencil algorithms. This framework simplifies the development process by encapsulating the common aspects of stencil algorithms in a base stencil class so that application-specific derived classes can be easily defined via inheritance and overloading. In addition, the stencil base class contains mechanisms for parallel execution. The result is a high-performance, parallel, application-specific stencil class. We present the design rationale for the base class and illustrate the derivation process by defining two subclasses, an image convolution class and a PDE solver. The classes have been implemented in Mentat, an object-oriented parallel programming system that is available on a variety of platforms. Performance results are given for a network of Sun SPARCstation IPCs[1].

1. Introduction

There is a class of applications whose implementation is realized using *stencil algorithms*. In a stencil algorithm, the value of a multi-dimensional array element is a function of the values of other elements within a neighborhood of that element. Exactly which neighboring elements are used is defined by a *stencil*. For example, the four connected neighbors are used to find the next value of an element in an iterative partial differential equation (PDE) solver.

Stencil algorithms are generally computationally expensive and, as a consequence, they are good candidates for parallel execution. Indeed, parallel implementations of stencil algorithms abound. Furthermore, stencil algorithms are structurally very similar.

Stencil algorithms have been ported widely to parallel architectures. Each port represents a considerable investment of time and energy, much of which is spent implementing the same code structures that have already been done by others. This wasted effort is particularly galling when one considers the basic, underlying similarity of these algorithms.

The object-oriented programming paradigm offers an elegant solution to this problem: design a base class that encapsulates the essence of stencil algorithm behavior, implement that class for parallel execution, then derive application-specific stencil classes that implement the details that distinguish the application. This approach allows the programmer to concentrate on the specifics of the problem at hand, and to leverage off the work of others. Ideally, this should result in both reduced implementation time and better performing parallel code (because parallel programming experts can implement the base class). Additionally, if the underlying base class is portable to a wide variety of architectures, then the derived classes should be as well.

This paper reports on our work on a stencil base class with the properties described above. We have implemented a base class, `Stenciler`, and two application-specific derived classes in the Mentat Programming Language (MPL). Mentat [1-3] is an object-oriented parallel programming system that has been implemented on a variety of platforms including networks of workstations. The implementation of the stencil base class has been a success: the stencil class provides the basis for application-specific stencil algorithms, and the parallel implementation of the base class member functions afford the application good performance.

We present the stencil problem in more detail, concentrating on the data decomposition and data communication implications. We then provide a high-level overview of the implementation of the base class. We next present the implementations of two different derived classes, an image convolution class and a PDE solver, followed by the performance of both implementations on a network of Sun IPC workstations. We conclude with a discussion of our future plans.

2. Stencil Algorithms

Stencil algorithms are used in a wide range of scientific applications, such as image convolution, solving partial

---

[1.] This work is partially supported by NSF grants ASC-9201822 and CDA-8922545-01, and DOE grant DE-F605-88ER25063.

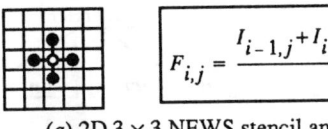

(a) 2D 3 × 3 NEWS stencil and sample function
$$F_{i,j} = \frac{I_{i-1,j} + I_{i+1,j} + I_{i,j-1} + I_{i,j+1}}{4}$$

(b) 2D 3 × 3 eight-connected stencil and sample function 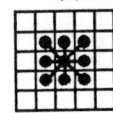
$$F_{i,j} = \sum_{k=0}^{2} \sum_{l=0}^{2} (I_{i+k-1, j+l-1} \times M_{k,l})$$
F - final matrix, I - input matrix, M - convolution mask

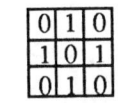

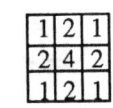

(c) 2D NEWS Stencil

(d) 2D 3 × 3 Gaussian filter

Figure 1 - Typical 2 dimensional stencils.

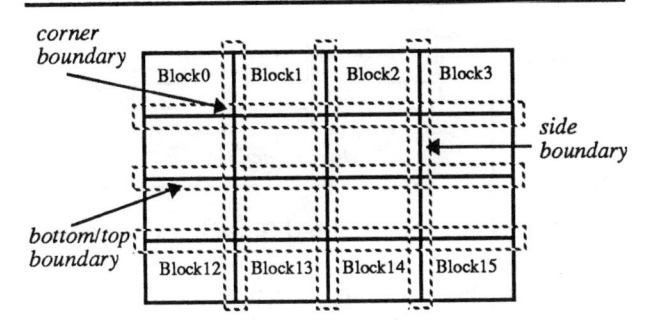

Figure 2 - A 4x4 rectangular decomposition

differential equations (PDE's), and correlation algorithms. Stencil algorithms are a class of algorithms that have several features in common: (1) the input data set is an array of arbitrary dimension and size, (2) there is a *stencil* that defines a local neighborhood around a data point, (3) some function is applied to the neighborhood of points that are "covered" when the stencil is centered on a particular point, and (4) this function is applied to all points in the data set to obtain a new data set.

Figure 1a shows a two dimensional 3 × 3 stencil that indicates that each output value will depend *only* on the "north," "east," "west," and "south" (called NEWS) neighboring points of the corresponding point in the input array. The associated function is an example of a stencil function that uses NEWS neighbors. Figure 1c shows the representation of a NEWS stencil in our implementation.

Figure 1b shows the stencil pattern needed for a 2D image convolution. In two dimensional image convolution, a small matrix, called a *mask*, is applied to the input array of image data. One such mask is shown in Figure 1d. Each point in the result is calculated by multiplying the value of each point in the mask by the appropriate neighbor of the corresponding point in the input image and summing. The equation in Figure 1b shows how to calculate the value of the filtered image at point (i, j) when using a 3 × 3 mask.

2.1. Parallel Solution

The fact that the same function is applied to all points in the input data set in any order and the calculation of each output point uses a regular pattern of neighborhood points around the corresponding input point makes parallelizing stencil algorithms a straight-forward process. Since all calculations logically occur in any order, there is no data-dependence between the output data points, so the problem may be decomposed into several smaller pieces, each computed in parallel. The stencil defines the region of the input data set needed to calculate a piece of the output data set and, as a consequence, also defines the pattern of communication between the decomposed pieces. As shown in Figure 2, if the 2D image convolution problem is decomposed into a 4 × 4 matrix of rectangular "blocks," each of the 16 processors needs its block of input data points as well as data points from the boundary regions of processors above, below, and to the sides of the block. Each piece must therefore exchange data with its eight connected neighbors. In a parallel implementation this implies communication between worker objects.

Different stencils require different communications patterns. Stencil algorithms that don't require data from a neighbor eliminate the need to communicate with that neighbor. The problem decomposition pattern also effects the communication pattern needed. In a 2D problem there are 3 common decompositions: groups of rows, groups of columns, or rectangular blocks. For a given number of pieces, decomposing into rows or columns requires fewer communications, but also requires more overall data volume to be exchanged than a rectangular decomposition. This is a classic trade-off and determining which decomposition is best depends on the specific communications costs of each parallel system.

2.2. Parallel Object-Oriented Solution

The objective of all object-oriented solutions is to provide a framework that exploits the commonality among stencil algorithms and provides an environment for developing efficient parallel code to take advantage of the inherent data parallelism. The object-oriented programming paradigm, through object inheritance, supports exploiting the common attributes of objects while allowing the user to redefine or augment specific details. Our solution is the creation of a 2D parallel stencil class using the object-oriented parallel programming system Mentat.

We have defined a base stencil class that is designed to manage those areas that are common to all stencil

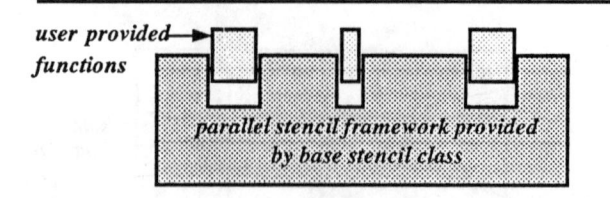

Figure 3 - Object-Oriented Stenciler Framework

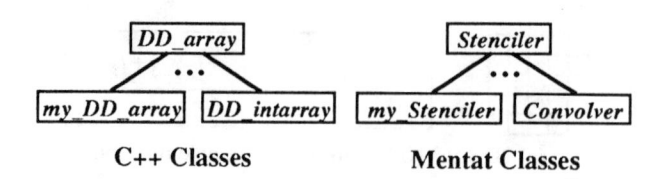

Figure 4 - Class Hierarchies

algorithms while providing a framework for the user to create derived classes that can be tailored to specific applications (Figure 3). The base class contains built-in member functions to perform common tasks, such as managing data communication between pieces. The base class also contains well-commented stubs for member functions that the user must define, such as the stencil function. This approach minimizes the effort needed to create new stencil applications through reuse of common code while supporting flexibility in creating parallel stencil applications.

Our approach is not unique. In fact, there has recently been a movement towards using the object-oriented paradigm in traditionally FORTRAN-dominated scientific computation and numeric analysis applications. An annual conference has been organized for this growing community and the first one was held in April 1993 [4]. This approach has also been used in developing parallel gas combustion code [5].

3. Implementation Sketch

Our implementation consists of two class hierarchies, a C++ *DD_array* class hierarchy and a Mentat *Stenciler* hierarchy (Figure 4). Mentat classes are very similar to C++ classes [6] except that member functions of instances of Mentat classes may be executed in parallel. The Mentat system manages the communication and synchronization of Mentat object member function invocations, exploiting both data and functional parallelism.

DD_array Class Hierarchy

Stencil definitions and input and output data sets of 2D stencil applications are simply 2D arrays. In order to facilitate using arrays in the Mentat environment, a hierarchy of two dimensional array classes has been developed (the 2D array classes should really be a polymorphic class, but we do not currently have a compiler that supports C++ templates). The base class, DD_array, defines commonly used functions including creating arrays, extracting or overlaying sub-arrays, row and point access, etc. This base class has been extended through the creation of derived sub-classes for most of the primitive C data types, including char, int, float, and double. Two features of the DD_array class hierarchy are important:

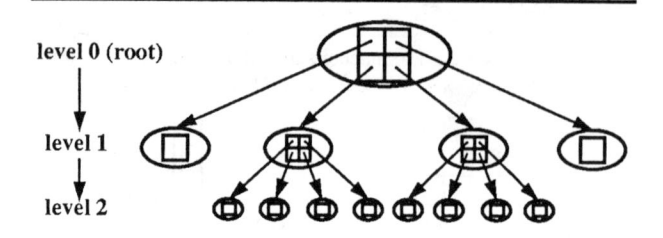

Figure 5 - Sample tree of Stenciler instances

(1) memory space for the matrix is contiguous, and (2) the hierarchy can easily be extended to include a richer set of base data types, including classes and structures, such as a DD_complexarray class. The contiguous allocation of memory allows Mentat to pass DD_array data between process objects easily.

Stenciler Class Hierarchy

The Stenciler class provides the framework for creating 2D stencil applications. The user creates a new class derived from Stenciler. This derived class inherits all of the member functions of the base class, so instances of this new class have all of the built-in common functions provided with the Stenciler class. The user then supplies the application-specific code by overloading certain virtual member functions.

An instance of a Stenciler or derived class is designed to handle one piece of the total array. Each Stenciler instance can create additional workers to split the work-load into smaller pieces. These pieces, in turn, may be further divided, creating a general tree structure of pieces as shown in Figure 5. Each new level of the tree has a "contained-in" relationship to the previous higher level. The pieces at leaves of this tree structure are the workers who perform the stencil function. The interior instances are managers for the workers below them; the managers distribute and synchronize the work of their sub-piece and collect the results. This hierarchical tree structure of processes is a powerful and flexible tool for decomposing a stencil problem, especially when running on different hardware platforms.

3.1. User-Defined Functions

The Stenciler class contains two kinds of member functions: built-in functions to handle common tasks, and

```
persistent mentat class Stenciler {
public:
// ********* BUILT-IN FUNCTIONS *********
    int addStencil(stencil *sten);
    int doStencil();
    int getNumRows();
    int getNumCols();
    MATRIX_TYPE *getRegion(int ulr, int ulc, int lrr, int lrc);
    void init();
    int putRegion(int ulr, int ulc, MATRIX_TYPE *matrix);
    int setDest(string *dNm); // set destination file name
    int setGoal(float convGoal); // set convergence test goal
    int setIterations(int numIterations);// set number of iterations
    int setPieces(int xPieces); // set number of worker pieces
    int setRowsAndCols(int rows, int cols); // set size of data set
    int setRowPieces(int rowPieces); // set number of vertical pieces
    int setSource(string *sNm); // set source file name
    int setWindow(int w_ulrow, int w_ulCol,
                  int w_lrRow, int w_lrCol);
    float checkConvergence();
    int checkConvergence();
// ********* USER DEFINED FUNCTIONS*********
    float checkConvergencePiece();
    int doStencilPiece(stencil *sten);
    int getMatrixPiece();
    stencil *getNextStencil();
    int prepareDest();
    int putMatrixPiece(); };
```

Figure 6 - Stenciler class interface

```
int Convolver::doStencilPiece(stencil* sten) {
// variable declarations (omitted)

// The following functionality is IN THE STUB (omitted here)
// - calc rows and cols in current stencil (stenRows, stenCols)
// - calc coords of this piece's working window (ulr, ulc, lrr, lrc)

// calculate divisor - USER PROVIDED
    stensum = 0;
    for(i=0; i < stenRows; i++)
        for (j=0; stenCols; j++)
            if ((*sten)[i][j] < 0) stenSum -= (*sten)[i][j];
            else stenSum += (*sten)[i][j];
    if (stenSum != 0) divisor = stenSum;
    else divisor = 1;

// outer two loops PROVIDED IN STUB
    for (i=ulr; i <= lrr; i++)
        for (j=ulc; j <= lrc; j++) {
            // begin USER-DEFINED code
            (*destArray)[i][j] = 0;
            for (k=0; k < stenRows; k++)
                for (l=0; l < stenCols; l++)
                    (*destArray)[i][j] += (*sten)[k][l] *
                        (*srcArray)[i + k - stenRows/2][j + l - stenCols/2];
            (*destArray)[i][j] /= divisor;
            // end USER-DEFINED code
        }
}
```

Figure 7 - Convolver stencil function

user-defined functions for application-specific code (Figure 6 shows the `Stenciler` class interface). Stencil applications are tailored by overloading several provided function stubs with user-defined functions. The `doStencilPiece()`, `getNextStencil()` and `checkConvergencePiece()` functions are the heart of the stencil application, defining the work to be done for each data point and controlling which stencil to apply and when processing is complete. In addition to these functions, three user-defined functions, `getMatrixPiece()`, `putMatrixPiece()` and `prepareDest()`, are needed to handle application-specific file I/O operations.

Stencil Function

The `doStencilPiece()` function (Figure 7) defines the stencil function. This is where the actual work of calculating each worker's piece of the result is accomplished. For example, in image convolution this function is a 4-nested loop for performing the multiply and sum necessary to calculate each output value. The stub provided for this function contains information for how a typical stencil function may be coded. Often, the user only needs to copy the stub and provide a small amount of additional code to implement the stencil function.

Control Functions

Stencil applications are often iterative or, in the case of image convolution, several stencils may be applied in succession. To control the application of the stencil function, the user-defined `getNextStencil()` function (Figure 8) is called before each iteration to determine which stencil to apply next. In the case of successive image convolutions, this function simply returns the next stencil in the stencil list. For the PDE problem, `getNextStencil()` determines whether the computation has converged and, if not, continues applying a NEWS stencil.

Iterative stencil algorithms often require a calculation to determine when the convergence criteria has been met. The overloaded `checkConvergencePiece()` function (Figure 9) is defined when necessary to calculate some convergence data for each worker's piece. This data is collected by the built-in `checkConvergence()` function and can be used to determine the next stencil to apply and when the algorithm is completed.

File I/O Functions

Since file formats differ from application to application, the user must define how to read and write the data sets. The `getMatrixPiece()` and `putMatrixPiece()` functions must be defined to read in/write out the data of a worker piece. These functions are called respectively at the beginning and end of the `doStencil()` function (discussed below) for each leaf worker in the `Stenciler` worker tree. The user may also redefine the `prepareDest()` function to set up the destination file by, for example, copying the header of the input file to the output file.

```
stencil *PDE_Solver::getNextStencil() {
// currentStencil points to the next stencil in the stencil list.
// convVal is the value set by the setGoal() function.
// currIter is the current iteration number - declared and set to 0

// local variable declarations - PROVIDED IN STUB
  stencil* next;
// local variable declarations - USER-DEFINED
  float testVal; // convergence value

// begin USER-PROVIDED code
testVal = checkConvergence();
if (currIter == 0) next = currentStencil->st;
else
  if (testVal <= convVal) next = NULL; // we're done
  else next = currentStencil->st; // keep plugging away
currIter++;
// end USER-PROVIDED code
return(next); }
```

Figure 8 - PDE_Solver getNextStencil()

3.2. Built-in Stenciler Member Functions

The built-in functions are designed to perform certain tasks without the user writing any new code. Most of these functions allow the user to tailor a Stenciler object by defining such attributes as the number of sub-pieces, the shape of the decomposition, the names of the source and destination files, if applicable, the stencil(s) to be used, etc. Other built-in functions perform common tasks, for example, retrieving or overlaying a region of the array. These functions can be called from the user-defined code. Once the user-defined code has been provided and the Stenciler object has been initialized, the doStencil() function is called to perform the stencil operation.

Set-up Functions

The functions with the set prefix allow the user to provide information about the current application to a Stenciler object, and the functions with the get prefix allow the user to retrieve current values. The Stenciler implementation contains the notion of a *working window* within the data set where the stencil function is applied. Values outside of this window will not be changed, but will be used as input to the calculation of neighboring values that are within the working window. The window is set up by specifying the upper left and lower right corners in the setWindow() function.

To establish the communication pattern for the application, the stencil(s) must be defined. In our implementation, stencils are represented by small DD_arrays. The non-zero values in the array indicate that a particular neighbor is needed in the calculation. The location of non-zero points and the size of the stencil determine the communication pattern and volume of data communicated. Stencils are kept in a list so that a series of

```
float PDE_Solver::checkConvergencePiece() {
// local variable declarations - USER-DEFINED
  float total; // convergence value to be returned
  float temp;
  int i,j;

// USER-PROVIDED code
total = 0.0;
if (prevArray == NULL) // i.e. if first iteration
  prevArray = new MATRIX_TYPE(myRows+2,myCols+2);
else {
  // calc working window (ulr, ulc, lrr, lrc) - omitted
  // calc convergence test value for my piece
  for (i=ulr; i <= lrr; i++)
    for(j=ulc; j <= lrc; j++) {
      temp = (*srcArray)[i][j] - (*prevArray)[i][j];
      total += temp * temp;
    }
}
// set prevArray to current solution
prevArray->overlay(ulr,ulc,srcArray->extract(ulr,ulc,lrr,lrc));
return(total); }
```

Figure 9 - PDE_Solver checkConvergencePiece()

stencils can be applied in succession. New stencils are added to this list via the addStencil() function.

DoStencil Function

Once a Stenciler object is created and initialized, the doStencil() function is called to execute the stencil. This function does the following:

(1) creates and initializes all additional worker objects needed;
(2) calls each worker to read its portion of the input array (via getMatrixPiece());
(3) while there is more work to be done (via getNextStencil()), loops performing the following tasks:
    (a) exchanges necessary boundary data;
    (b) executes the stencil function (via doStencilPiece());
(4) prepares the destination file and calls each worker to write its piece (via prepareDest() and putMatrixPiece());

It is important to note that the user need only create the root-level Stenciler object and doStencil() does the rest. Also, the user does not need to modify this function, the user need only provide several user-defined functions described above in Section 3.1.

Other Functions

The checkConvergence() function is provided to control calling each leaf worker's user-defined checkConvergencePiece() function and collecting the results. When called, this function determines whether the worker is a leaf node or an interior node. If it is an interior node, it calls checkConvergence() for each of its immediate subordinates, aggregates the partial test values, and sends the result to the next higher level in the worker tree. If the worker is a leaf, then `checkConvergencePiece()` is called to calculate the piece's partial result. The goal of this function is to abstract out the details of the worker hierarchy whenever possible.

The final two built-in functions, `getRegion()` and `putRegion()`, are provided to retrieve or overlay a region of the overall array. These functions are useful, for example, in checking convergence criteria.

4. Sample Stencil Implementations

To illustrate the use of the stencil framework we describe our experience with two sample implementations: an image convolver and a PDE solver using Jacobi iteration.

Image Convolution

Image convolution is a common application in digital image processing and computer vision [7]. In two dimensional image convolution, a small 2D stencil, also called a *filter* or *mask*, defines a region surrounding each picture element (pixel) whose values will be used in calculating the corresponding point in the convolved image. Each element of the filter is multiplied by the corresponding neighbor of the current pixel, and the results are summed and normalized. Figure 1*b* shows the stencil function for a 3 × 3 mask and 1*d* shows a common smoothing filter.

To implement the convolution application, the following steps were necessary:

(1) define the type of the input and output data sets to be `DD_chararray`;
(2) create a `Convolver` class derived from `Stenciler`;
(3) overload `doStencilPiece()` to define the stencil function;
(4) overload the control function `getNextStencil()`;
(5) redefine the file I/O functions to input and output the matrix and prepare the destination file;
(6) create a main program to create, initialize and execute an instance of the `Convolver` class.

Creating the `Convolver` class was straight-forward; in fact, there were no additional variables or functions needed. The stencil function for convolution fits the framework provided in the stub for `doStencilPiece()`. The stub provides code to calculate the bounds of the working window and to loop through each point in the worker's piece. The only new code needed was the inner doubly nested loop to multiply and accumulate the value of a point and the code to normalize the result. An abbreviated version of the overloaded `doStencilPiece()` function is shown in Figure 7. Note that the code shown is used to clearly illustrate the use of the function and that standard C optimization techniques were used in the final code. The

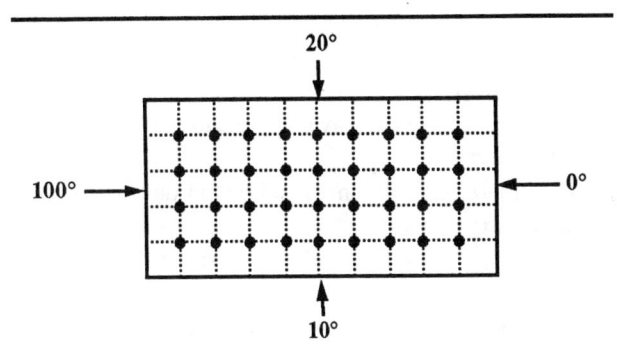

Figure 10 - Grid approximation for heated plate

`getNextStencil()` function simply chains through the list of stencils supplied during initialization, returning each in turn. Therefore, a single `Convolver` instance can apply a series of filters to an image in succession. The `getMatrixPiece()` function was redefined to read from the input file the block of data "owned" by each leaf worker instance. Similarly, the `putMatrixPiece()` function was redefined to write to file the result of each leaf worker instance. Finally, the `prepareDest()` function was overloaded to prepare the header of the output file.

The main program has the following structure: (1) declare, create and initialize an instance of the Mentat class `Convolver`, (2) tailor the instance by setting the source and destination file names, the number of worker pieces, the number of rows and columns in the data set, the number of row pieces (optional), and the list of convolution stencils (filters) to apply, (3) call `doStencil()` to execute the stencil algorithm, and (4) destroy the Mentat object.

PDE Solver Using Jacobi Iteration

Another common and important class of stencil algorithms are iterative methods. Jacobi iteration is a method for solving certain systems of equations of the form $A\vec{x} = \vec{b}$, where A is a matrix of coefficients, $\vec{x}$ is a vector of variables, and $\vec{b}$ is a vector of constants. The general procedure for using Jacobi iteration is to first guess the solution for all variables, and then to iteratively refine the solution until the difference between successive answers is below some pre-determined threshold [8].

The specific application of Jacobi iteration implemented and discussed here is the "heated plate" problem. The heated plate problem consists of a plate or sheet of material that has constant temperatures applied around the boundaries, and the goal is to determine the steady-state temperatures in the interior of the plate (Figure 10). The temperature in the interior region is approximated by dividing the plate into a regular 2D grid pattern and solving for each of the grid points. The values at each point are approximated by the average of the values in the NEWS neighboring points. This transforms the problem into a system of linear equations which can be solved using Jacobi iteration. The form of the stencil function needed for Jacobi iteration is shown in Figure 1a.

To implement the PDE solver application, the following steps were necessary:

(1) define the type of the input and output data sets to be `DD_floatarray`;
(2) create a `PDE_Solver` class derived from `Stenciler`;
(3) overload `doStencilPiece()` to define the stencil function;
(4) overload `checkConvergencePiece()` to calculate the value of the convergence test for each leaf worker's piece;
(5) overload the control function `getNextStencil()`;
(6) redefine the file I/O functions to input and output the matrix and prepare the destination file;
(7) create a main program to create, initialize and execute an instance of the `PDE_Solver` class.

Creating the `PDE_Solver` class was slightly different from the `Convolver` example. The difference is that a new variable, `prevArray`, was added to store the source array of the previous iteration. This value is used in `checkConvergencePiece()` to determine whether the solution has converged. The stencil function for this problem is very simple and uses the framework provided in the `doStencilPiece()` stub with few modifications. The only user-defined code in `doStencilPiece()` is to calculate the average of the 4-connected neighbors for each matrix point.

The control structure of the PDE_Solver requires both an overloaded `getNextStencil()` function and an overloaded `checkConvergencePiece()` function. The `getNextStencil()` function simply calls the provided `checkConvergence()` function using the result to test if the iteration should continue (Figure 8). As discussed in Section 3.1, the `checkConvergence()` function handles calling `checkConvergencePiece()` for each leaf worker and collects and aggregates the results. The `checkConvergencePiece()` function was overloaded to calculate the convergence value of each matrix piece (Figure 9). The test value needed for the PDE solver problem is the sum of the squares of the difference between each point in the current and previous solutions.

The file I/O functions, `getMatrixPiece()`, `putMatrixPiece()`, and `prepareDest()`, were redefined exactly as in the `Convolver` example and the main program follows the same general outline with a few additions. Since the PDE problem defines constant temperature values around the matrix borders, the working window had to be set to include all of the matrix *except* the border region. This prevented the border from being

# Pieces	Convolver Best Execution Time (min:secs)	Speedup	PDE_Solver Best Execution Time (min:secs)	Speedup
1	49:33	N/A	43:39	N/A
2	24:33	2.0	23:01	1.9
4	12:37	4.0	11:37	3.8
6	8:47	5.6	7:53	5.5
8	7:07	7.0	7:08	6.1
10	5:53	8.4	6:47	6.4
12	5:08	9.7	6:23	6.8
14	4:57	10.0	6:10	7.1

Table 1: Performance Results

changed during the stencil calculations. The convergence goal was set to an appropriate value to stop the iteration when the solution was within acceptable limits.

5. Performance

Our goal was to create a framework for stencil algorithms where the user can easily produce parallel code. The reason for wanting parallel code is, of course, speed. In order for our approach to be successful, the framework must provide a user with a program that is fast and exploits the inherent data parallelism of stencil applications. To test our performance we created two versions of each class, a sequential version written strictly in C++, and a parallel version written in C++/MPL. We executed the sequential versions on a Sun SPARCstation IPC and recorded the best of the wall-clock execution times. Similarly, we ran the parallel versions on a network of 16 IPCs connected via ethernet. The parallel versions were executed decomposing the problem into from two to fourteen row pieces. Each decomposition was run several times and the best time for each decomposition was recorded.

For the `Convolver` tests, both the sequential and parallel versions were executed using identical problems: a 2000 × 2000 8-bit grey scale image convolved with three successive 9 × 9 filters. The `PDE_Solver` problem used a 1024 × 1024 grid of floating point numbers to estimate the interior temperatures of the heated plate problem. Table 1 shows the raw best execution times and Figure 11 shows the speedup curve for the problems.

These results show good performance for the parallel implementation. Both speedup curves follow a classic pattern with nearly linear speedup at low numbers of processors and then declining marginal return from the addition of more processors. This phenomenon is caused by two factors. First, computation granularity decreases as the problem is broken into smaller and smaller pieces, causing synchronization and communication to become a larger

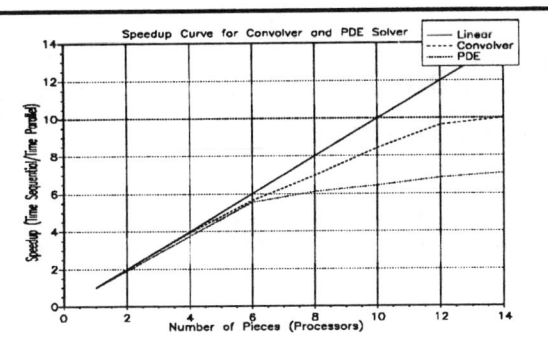

Figure 11 - Stenciler Speedup Curve

percentage of execution time. Second, time spent executing code that is inherently sequential, such as file I/O, increases as a percentage of total run time. We would expect that this decline in performance would be less pronounced with larger problem sizes or a more computationally expensive stencil function. Overall, the convolution example performed better because its computation granularity is significantly greater than for the PDE solver.

6. Summary and Future Work

When we began developing our framework for stencil algorithms, we had several goals in mind: (1) the environment should be easy to use for the application developer, facilitating rapid development of new stencil applications, (2) the framework should provide as much built-in functionality as possible to exploit the similarities among stencil algorithms and to reduce the effort needed by the programmer, (3) the framework should encourage code re-use wherever possible, (4) the programs generated must exploit the parallelism inherent in stencil algorithms and perform adequately, and (5) the code developed should be portable. The Stenciler class hierarchy meets these goals. The object-oriented framework and especially the built-in functions provided in the base class support the goals of ease of use, built-in code for common tasks, and code re-use. The parallel environment of the Mentat system provides the basis for exploiting the data parallelism natural to stencil algorithms. Performance results show that the programs produced using the Stenciler framework are capable of high performance. Finally, the Mentat environment provides an environment for easily porting user code from one environment to another.

The results are encouraging, but there are a number of areas where our approach can be improved and extended. The class interface and hierarchy still needs some clarification and revision. These improvements will become apparent as our experience with using this approach increases. We plan to port the Stenciler class and sample implementation code to a broader range of hardware platforms. We also would like to extend the domain of problems that can be supported using our general approach by creating higher dimensional stencil class hierarchies and applying the same technique to other classes of algorithms. Finally, we would like to extend the model of our base classes to include encapsulation of scheduling and problem decomposition decision information to facilitate better performance while keeping the details away from the user.

Availability

Mentat is available via anonymous FTP for Sun 3, Sun 4, SGI, iPSC/2, and iPSC/860. Paragon, CM-5 and RS6000 versions are expected in Summer 1993. The Stenciler code and related documentation will also be available by the time of the conference (July 1993). For further information, send email to *mentat@Virginia.edu*.

Acknowledgments

We would like to thank Mike DeLong for his help with the mathematics behind the Jacobi iteration PDE solver.

7. References

[1] A. S. Grimshaw, "Easy to Use Object-Oriented Parallel Programming with Mentat," *IEEE Computer*, pp. 39-51, May, 1993.

[2] A. S. Grimshaw, E. Loyot Jr., and J. Weissman, "Mentat Programming Language (MPL) Reference Manual," University of Virginia, Computer Science TR 91-32, 1991.

[3] A. S. Grimshaw, W. Timothy Strayer, and Padmini Narayan, "Dynamic, Object-Oriented Parallel Processing," to appear in *IEEE Parallel and Distributed Technology: Systems and Applications*, May 1993.

[4] *Proceedings of the First Annual Object-Oriented Numerics Conference*, April 1993.

[5] J.F. Macfarlane, et al, "Application of Parallel Object-Oriented Environment and Toolkit (POET) to Combustion Problems," Sandia report, September 1992.

[6] B. Stroustrup, *The C++ Programming Language*, 2nd ed. Addison-Wesley, Reading, Mass., 1991.

[7] Rafael C. Gonzales and Paul Wintz, *Digital Image Processing*, 2nd ed. Addison-Wesley, Reading, Mass., 1987.

[8] M. J. Quinn, *Designing Efficient Algorithms For Parallel Computers*, McGraw-Hill Book Company, New York, 1987.

Block Data Decomposition for Data-Parallel Programming on a Heterogeneous Workstation Network[*]

Phyllis E. Crandall and Michael J. Quinn
Department of Computer Science
Oregon State University
Corvallis, OR 97331-3202

Abstract

We present a block data decomposition algorithm for two-dimensional grid problems. Our method includes load balancing to accommodate heterogeneous processors, and we characterize the conditions that must be met for our partitioning strategy to be of value. While we concentrate on the workstation network model of parallel processing because of its high communication costs and inherent heterogeneity, our method is applicable to other parallel architectures.

1 Introduction

The concept of the *hypercomputer*, a virtual parallel machine formed from a network of workstations [4], has made parallel processing available in a wide range of settings. Workstation networks have become commonplace in scientific, academic, and business environments due mainly to their relatively low cost and general-purpose applicability. The current performance capabilities of workstations make them attractive alternatives to expensive specialized machines for many parallel processing applications.

Parallel processing on a workstation network has much in common with the loosely-coupled multicomputer model of computation, but workstation clusters pose additional challenges that must be met before parallel computing becomes practical. The bandwidth limitation and message preparation latency associated with typical network connections necessitates that careful attention be paid to the placement of tasks to accommodate differing performance characteristics of the various machines and to minimize interprocessor communication. Unlike multicomputers, where all processors normally have the same computing power, workstation networks are often made up of heterogeneous machines with differing computational speeds. Since workstation networks are usually multi-user systems, the workload on any collection of machines may vary over time. This argues for a dynamic load-balancing scheme that can adapt to the changing workload.

Earlier work has shown how to perform dynamic load balancing on two-dimensional problems when contiguous groups of rows or columns are assigned to processors [10]. This paper extends those results by describing a method for block data decomposition. We use a sub-block as the unit of partitioning and load balancing rather than the individual grid point, row, or column. Section 2 describes the parallel workstation network, the problems we wish to solve with this model of computation, and various decomposition methods. In Section 3 we look at related work done in load balancing and block decomposition for parallel processing in the workstation network. The description of our method for block decomposition with load balancing is presented in Section 4 along with a description of the conditions that must be met for our method to be practicable. We conclude in Section 5 with a discussion of the implementation feasibility of our method and future research directions.

2 The problem

For the purposes of our investigation, a workstation network is considered to be a collection of two or more machines connected by a LAN. The network connections typically are Ethernet or Token Ring which have bandwidths varying from 4 to 16 Mbps. However, FDDI (fiber distributed data interface) connections are becoming increasingly available and offer transmission rates of around 100 Mbps. Even faster connections such as HiPPI (high-performance parallel interface) are more rare, but yield bandwidths in the gigabit range. Workstation computing speeds upwards

---

[*] This research was supported by IBM and the Oregon Advanced Computing Institute.

of 10 Mflops are common, and it has been projected that speeds may reach 500 Mflops in the next few years [2].

While the workstation network may be viewed as a loosely-coupled multicomputer suitable for MIMD (multiple instruction, multiple data) processing, the problems we consider in this paper are data parallel in nature. Data parallelism is a model of computation that achieves parallelism through the simultaneous application of the same operation across a collection of data [11]. This model is suitable for many real-world problems in engineering and the sciences. Many of these problem domains are characterized by manipulation of the elements of large matrices. Examples include atmospheric and shallow-water simulations, heat conduction, and imaging problems.

Parallel computers are specifically designed to optimize interprocessor communication. Ethernet or Token Ring connections usually found in workstation networks make interprocessor communication very costly. This indicates a need for careful program design and task placement to reduce interprocessor communication.

Before a program can be executed in parallel mode, it must be divided into tasks. The SIMD model of computation, where every processor performs the same operation on different data, requires that the data be partitioned across the processors. The most effective partitioning of the data depends heavily on the particular problem being solved. Some problems are *embarrassingly parallel* in that the tasks have little or no data dependencies. For these problems there is often little communication until the very end when results are gathered from the processors. Consider, for example, a ray-tracing problem where each pixel may be processed completely in isolation from the others. There are no data dependencies, and no interprocessor communication is required before consolidating the results at the end of execution.

It is more often the case that dependencies exist among the tasks. These may be random or predictable. For example, in Gaussian elimination with partial pivoting, during the ith iteration the row with the largest element in the ith column is chosen as the pivot row. The dependencies are random in the sense that the order of the pivot rows is not known prior to run time.

In other problem domains, such as successive overrelaxation and Jacobi iteration, the problem space may be viewed as a grid with the value of each grid point relying on the data values of each of its adjoining neighbors. In this paper we will refer to problems of

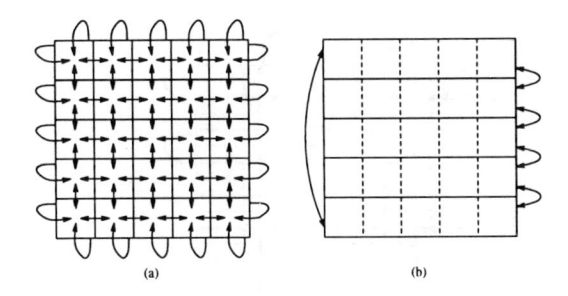

Figure 1: Communication pattern for a grid problem. (a) One grid point per processor. (b) One row of grid points per processor.

this general class as *grid problems*. Figure 1(a) shows an example of communications required for single data points in a grid problem iteration for an $n \times n$ grid (with $n = 5$ in this case). If a single grid point is assigned to each processor, there are $4n^2$ communications at each iteration of the program. This results not only in message preparation overhead and transmission time for all the $4n^2$ data items but also in time spent dealing with contention on the network as all n^2 processors try to communicate at once.

Since each processor usually handles multiple data points in the grid, placing tasks by row, as shown in Figure 1(b), allows $2n^2$ of the communications to be handled internally by each processor at each iteration. Since all northward communications from a given processor are directed to only one other processor, the communications can be optimized by bundling the data. Instead of n communications being transmitted to the north neighbor, all n values can be sent in one packet and unbundled and sorted by the receiver. The same situation applies to the southward communications. Therefore, only $2n$ rather than $2n^2$ external communications are generated at each iteration.

Assigning more than one row of data per processor reduces the number of communications even further. If n rows are divided contiguously among p processors, the number of communications is further reduced to $2p$ without an increase in message length.

Another way to partition the problem space in grid problems is to divide the grid into square blocks of equal size. Each block can then be assigned to a separate processor and communications are required only at the edges. Block decomposition, therefore, requires $4p$ communications during each iteration and each message has length $\sqrt{n^2/p}$ for an $n \times n$ grid. Figure 2 shows a 16×16 grid divided into blocks. If $p = 16$, the grid may be equally divided into squares and apportioned to each of the processors. Interprocessor communication is needed only at the edges, re-

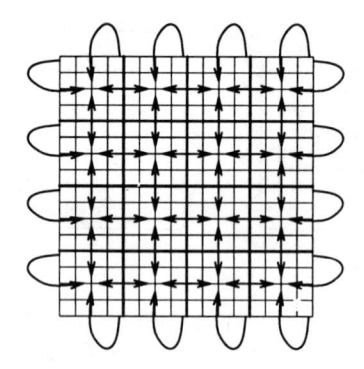

Figure 2: Communication pattern for block decomposition in a grid problem.

sulting in 64 communications at each iteration. Alternatively, if $p = 4$, the number of communications is reduced from 64 to 16, but the length of each message doubles.

While the block decomposition requires twice as many communications as contiguous row (or column) decomposition, there is a point at which the savings in bytes transmitted outweighs the additional message formation overhead. Very large grids are prime candidates for this treatment.

However, the situation is not so tidy when the grid cannot be divided into p squares of equal size or when the processors have different computational speeds. While most multiprocessors and multicomputers consist of collections of homogeneous processing elements (i.e., every processor has the same computing power), workstation networks often consist of machines with different computing speeds.

So there are four cases to consider:

1. all processors have the same computing power and p evenly divides the grid into squares,

2. all processors have the same computing power but p does not evenly divide the grid into squares,

3. p evenly divides the grid into squares but the processors have different computational power, and

4. p does not evenly divide the grid into squares and the processors have unequal computing power.

Figure 3 shows possible partitionings for each case.

Performance varies inversely with the number and size of external communications, so there is a delicate balance between using a large number of machines to achieve high computational performance and small communication size, and using a small number of machines to limit the number of interprocessor communications. In the case of block decomposition, the

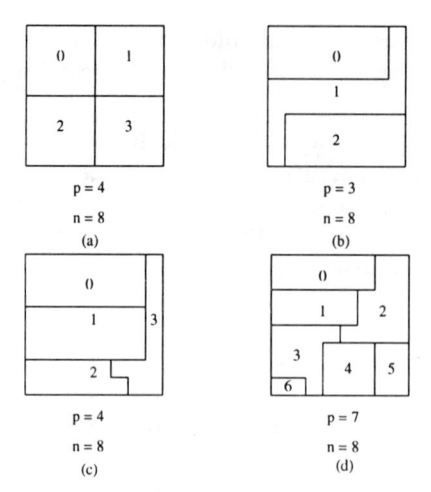

Figure 3: Possible grid layouts. (a) All processors have the same computing power and evenly divide the grid. (b) All the processors have the same computing power but do not equally divide the grid. (c) The number of processors equally divides the grid but they have different computing power. (d) The number of processors does not evenly divide the grid and they have differing computing power.

number of line segments occurring in the grid layout is indicative of the number of necessary external communications [3]. Therefore, it is desirable for the layout to be as regular as possible. Squares of equal size are the ideal target.

In addition to the heterogeneous nature of the workstation network, these machines are multi-user systems whose workloads may vary widely. This indicates a need for load balancing at both the static and dynamic level. We use the term *static* load balancing to mean the initial partitioning of the grid among the machines in the workstation network. If the performance characteristics of the various machines are known beforehand, the work may be divided so that the more powerful processors receive the larger share. If information about the current machine loads is also available, this may be incorporated when making the initial placement decision. Without considering the computational power of the machines, the attainable performance is limited by the slowest or most heavily loaded machine regardless of the decomposition method

3 Related work

Load balancing in a distributed computing environment has received a great deal of attention over the last few years. Only some of this research is specific to parallel processing, and even less is applicable to the heterogeneous environment of the workstation network.

Cheung and Reeves [5] pay careful attention to static load balancing (data partitioning) based on the heterogeneous nature of the machines and their networks. The data distribution scheme and load balancing strategy assume large arrays or matrices like the grid problems we consider here. The grid is partitioned across either one or two dimensions, with the two-dimensional case creating contiguous rectangles. The communication patterns of the application are not considered and the workload distribution is immutable and cannot respond to changing conditions in the network load.

The PARFORM [4] is specifically targeted for the high-performance workstation environment with Ethernet connections. Message passing is handled using TCP and Berkeley sockets. It provides static placement according to actual current load of the workstations. Provisions for dynamic load balancing are included in the PARFORM, and UNIX kernel variables are scanned periodically to check the load situation on the various machines. A heuristic is used to optimize the size and number of subtasks to be performed given the current network load, but the possible variance in the computational speeds of the machines is not considered.

PVM (Parallel Virtual Machine) is not specifically targeted for the workstation environment, but lends itself to a number of different architectures and networks [1]. PVM 2.4.1 has no load balancing facilities. Machines are assigned in round-robin fashion, and PVM is completely ignorant of their relative speeds and current workloads. The user, however, may request specific machines or architectures [6]. Communication is by explicit message-passing in the code.

The issue of block data decomposition is addressed in Berger and Bokhari [3]. Their work targets problems where certain subregions of the domain are given extra grid points. The problem space is decomposed into rectangles by recursively dividing the partitions into sub-partitions of equal computational effort until all processors have been allotted their share of the domain. Snyder and Socha [13] have devised a method for mapping an $I \times J$ array of grid points to a $K \times K$ array of processors. Placement is static and the processors are considered to be homogeneous. Other data decomposition strategies include static mapping of data to processors based on programmer-supplied information as incorporated in the DINO language [12], and automatic data partitioning techniques based on constraints [7].

Our investigation is carried out in the Dataparallel C programming environment. Dataparallel C is a superset of the Kernighan and Ritchie C language [9]. It is a high-level parallel language that permits a SIMD model of programming in a distributed environment. The model of computation presented to the programmer is characterized by a global name space, synchronous execution, and virtual processors as the unit of parallelism [8]. The programmer is allowed to specify the dominant communication pattern so that data may be partitioned in the most effective way.

The load balancing feature in the current Dataparallel C compiler relies on two sources of information. Initial placement of virtual processors is based on *a priori* information regarding the relative speeds of the machines. Dynamic load balancing is accomplished through periodic exchange of load information during calls to the routing library at runtime. Entire processes are not moved in this load-balancing scheme, merely some number of the virtual processors assigned to a given machine are shifted. Since a virtual processor is characterized by its data, migrating the data alone is sufficient.

The Dataparallel C environment has been successfully ported to a number of multiprocessor and multicomputer systems and has recently been enhanced for use on a heterogeneous network of workstations [10]. The workstation compiler is currently installed on IBM RS/6000's, Sun SPARCstations, and HP Snakes. Programs execute across any combination of these machines.

Two dimensional grid problems where the communication patterns involve all four nearest neighbors may benefit from `block` decomposition. The current Dataparallel C compiler, however, provides only limited facilities for block partitioning the problem space. Block decomposition is permitted only when the number of processors p is a power of 2 and this number divides the grid into p equal rectangles. The number of processors must be declared at compile time for block partitioning. For a more complete description of load balancing in Dataparallel C, see Nedeljković and Quinn [10].

4 The method

Our goal is not to reach optimal partitioning for either the static or dynamic task allocation case, but to achieve an acceptable performance level given the conflicting goals of maximizing computation speed and

p	number of processors
n^2	number of grid points
α	software overhead to initiate a message
β	network bandwidth (seconds per byte)
t	computation time per grid point
c	number of communications per iteration
D	number of bytes transmitted by each processor per communication
W	wait time due to load imbalance and network contention
d	length of the each data item to be transmitted (i.e., 4 bytes for floating point)

Figure 4: Notation used to analyze execution time of grid algorithms.

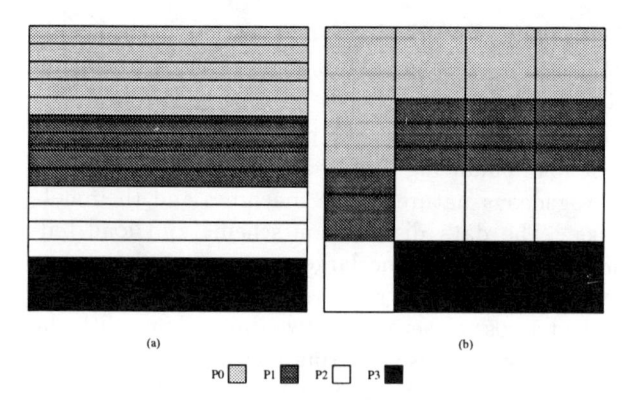

Figure 5: Partitioning with 4 processors with relative speeds of (5, 4, 4, 3) by (a) Contiguous row and (b) naïve contiguous placement of sub-blocks.

minimizing communications. Block decomposition requires a greater number of communications than row decomposition, so the size of the communications must be small enough to offset the additional message-passing overhead.

Referring to the notation in Figure 4, if we are given a grid problem where the values of the four nearest neighbors are used by each grid point to calculate its new value at each iteration, a sequential program will take tn^2 seconds per iteration. Executing the same program on p homogeneous processors ideally should take

$$(\frac{tn^2}{p}) + c(\alpha + p\beta D) + W \qquad (1)$$

We see from (1) that the computation time is evenly divided among the processors so that, in the absence of message-passing overhead, execution would complete in $1/p$ th the time of the sequential program. The message-formation overhead represented by α is incurred within each processor concurrently and therefore is not multiplied by a factor of p. We make the simplifying assumption that α does not depend on D, which we feel is justifiable since the number of data packets per communication is typically small. The β overhead involves time actually spent in transmission. Assuming that only one workstation can be sending a message at any one time over the physical medium of the network, β overhead must be multiplied by a factor of p as well as D. We will ignore wait time in the calculations that follow.

We assume in this investigation that the grid for our problem space is square and divides evenly into n sub-squares of size $\sqrt{n} \times \sqrt{n}$. Additionally, we assume that $\sqrt{n}$ is an integer. We use these sub-blocks as our unit of partitioning and dynamic load balancing so that the granularity is the the same as contiguous-row or contiguous-column decomposition.

At run time in the Dataparallel C environment, the user specifies p, the number of machines to use in the computation. The run-time system consults a data file containing host machine information, and the first p machines are engaged. The user can dictate the identity and order of machines by changing the data file prior to execution.

Once the relative speeds of the processors are known, the number of sub-blocks that should be given to each processor may be calculated. Often this number is not an integer. To address this case, we round the result of this calculation.

One naïve approach is to allocate the sub-blocks contiguously in row (or column) fashion. This has the advantage of simplicity, but may result in greater communication overhead than the contiguous row or column approaches. Figure 5 shows an example of this. The contiguous row case generates 8 communications with a total of $8n$ data items during each iteration. The block decomposition, on the other hand, generates 22 communications and $10.5n$ total data items including wraparound. Using equation (1), we see that performance for the block partitioning is not as good as that for row allocation.

Obviously, the ideal block partitioning scenario occurs when the grid portion assigned to each processor is a square. This is the configuration we strive to approximate by assuring that the rectangularity of the partitions is maintained, even at the cost of some load imbalance.

When the processors are homogeneous, each block has no more than 4 communications per iteration. Recall that the number of line segments indicate the

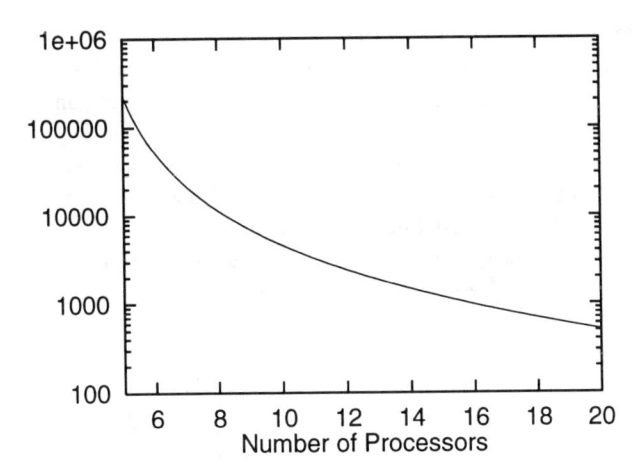

Figure 6: Minimum number of grid points required for block allocation to be superior to contiguous row or column allocation, as a function of number of processors. Block allocation is never superior to contiguous row or column allocation when there are fewer than 5 processors.

number of necessary communications. Regular partitioning keeps these at a minimum.

We can see by equation (1) that the communication time for block decomposition with homogeneous processors is more favorable than contiguous row when the problem size is larger and/or there are more processors. Block partitioning makes sense when

$$2(\alpha + pdn\beta) > 4(\alpha + pd\frac{n}{\sqrt{p}}\beta) \qquad (2)$$

or when

$$\alpha < pdn\beta - pd\frac{2n}{\sqrt{p}}\beta \qquad (3)$$

Figure 6 shows the conditions on problem size and number of processors that must be met before block decomposition in the homogeneous case is advantageous. For our calculations we have assumed that $\alpha = 1$ msec, $\beta = 1$ μsec per byte, and data length $d = 4$ bytes. Equation (3) tells us that block decomposition with any number of processors less than 5 will not give better performance than contiguous row or column partitioning.

Our method of block partitioning is inspired by the binary decomposition scheme of Berger and Bokhari [3]. However, instead of dividing the domain into regions of equal computational effort at each iteration, we divide the domain according to the relative speeds of the processors. Our algorithm appears in Figure 7.

Initial conditions:
- The current grid is the entire problem space.
- dimension = vertical.
- P = the list of processors being used in the computation in descending order of relative speed.
- p = the total number of processors to be used (the cardinality of P).

Partition(current grid, dimension, P, p)

1. If $p = 1$, end.
2. Sum the relative speeds of the processors in P and consider the $p/2$ fastest processors.
3. Divide the current grid into two partitions along the indicated dimension according to the ratio that the relative speed total of the fastest $p/2$ processors bears to the sum of all the relative speeds of the processors in P.
4. If $p/2 > 1$
   (a) Set $t = p$.
   (b) Set $T = P$.
   (c) If dimension = vertical, set dimension = horizontal else set dimension = vertical.
   (d) set $p = t/2$.
   (e) Set P to the first p processors.
   (f) Partition(first partition, dimension, P, p).
   (g) Set $p = t - p$.
   (h) Set $P = T - P$.
   (i) Partition(second partition, dimension, P, p).
5. End.

Figure 7: Block Decomposition Algorithm

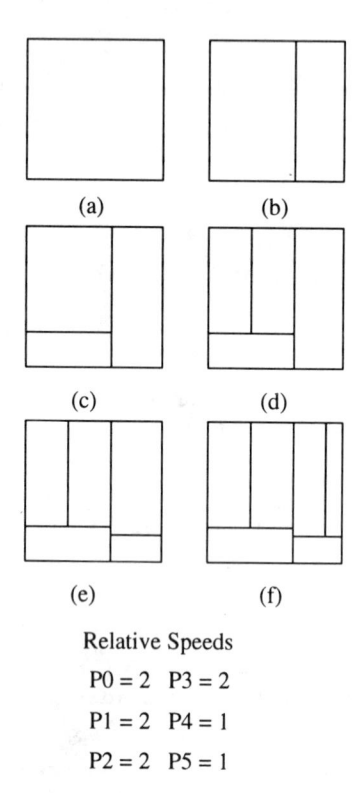

Figure 8: The steps necessary to partition a grid with 64 sub-blocks for 5 heterogeneous processors. The relative speed table is given at bottom right.

Relative Speeds
P0 = 2   P3 = 2
P1 = 2   P4 = 1
P2 = 2   P5 = 1

Figure 8 shows the steps necessary to partition a grid with 64 sub-blocks for 6 heterogeneous processors. The table of relative speeds for each processor is also given.

The decomposition calculation is done independently by all processors, and all reach the same conclusion on partitioning so no communication is required other than the initial table identifying the participating processors and their relative speeds.

Notice that our line segment count has increased over what we would expect in the homogeneous case. Including wraparound communications, there is a need for 8 additional messages over those that would be required in the homogeneous case.

Clearly, performance under block decomposition will be better than contiguous row or column only when the overhead of these additional communications does not outweigh the gains realized from increasing the number of neighbor communications.

Dynamic load balancing for block decomposition takes the same form as the initial partitioning. Dataparallel C periodically monitors the performance of the processors and new relative speeds are determined. All processors have the performance data and all can calculate the partitioning changes independently. Since moving the data associated with the virtual processors is costly, load balancing should only be done when the benefit clearly outweighs the cost. The Dataparallel C workstation run-time system suppresses load balancing unless the necessary adjustment is 5% or more on at least one workstation [10].

In Dataparallel C, the location of virtual processors is calculated using two arrays: one which indicates the number of the beginning virtual processor on each machine, and one showing the total number of virtual processors on each machine. Our requirement of rectangularity necessitates very few changes to the data structures. Using a *top-left, bottom right* procedure, the calculation of the location of any virtual processor is easily accomplished. Substituting a single array with these values allows each processor to find the location of any other processor. Also, a border structure must be maintained for each processor that indicated the identities of the neighboring processors along each border.

In our block decomposition scheme there is no longer a need for the number of physical processors to be some power of 2. Also, the number of processors no longer needs to be declared at compile time. These minor changes add considerable flexibility to Dataparallel C.

5 Conclusions and Future Directions

In this paper we have proposed a method for block data decomposition for parallel processing in the heterogeneous workstation network. We have seen that there are certain conditions that must be met before block partitioning is advantageous in a system such as this where communication costs dominate performance characteristics. Initial results confirm the performance predicted by the graph in Figure 6. Using 8 processors on a wrapping grid problem, homogeneous block decomposition began outperforming contiguous-row partitioning when the grid size exceeded 65000 elements. However, heterogeneous block partitioning yields no benefit at this grid size. When the wrapping grid problem was executed across 8 machines with relative speeds of 2,2,2,1,1,1,1,1, performance still lagged behind contiguous-row, even when the grid exceeded 250000 elements. The decomposition generated by the algorithm is shown in Figure 9. Further investigation, both theoretical and empirical, is needed to determine the suitability of heterogeneous block partitioning to real-world sized problems.

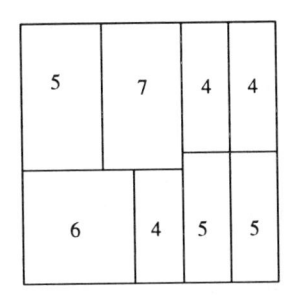

Figure 9: Heterogeneous block decomposition of an $n \times n$ grid for 8 processors with relative speeds 2,2,2,1,1,1,1,1.

More sophisticated analysis tools must be available to the compiler and the runtime environment to allow the system to make decisions regarding the efficacy of using the workstations specified by the user. There may be times when careful analysis shows that better performance may be realized by using fewer machines and taking advantage of the greater number of local neighbor communications. The Dataparallel C runtime system could be enhanced to analyze the problem size and relative speeds of the designated processors during the initial partitioning of the problem space. This information could be given to the user as a suggestion, or the user could optionally relinquish this decision to the system. This would allow the system to ignore machine ordering in the host information file, to use fewer machines if communication costs would be reduced, or to use more machines if indicated by the problem size. If analysis showed that block decomposition was not cost effective, the system could change the partitioning to contiguous row or contiguous column as the default. These improvements go beyond what we have proposed in this paper, and they warrant future investigation.

References

[1] Adam Beguelin, Jack Dongarra, Al Geist, Robert Manchek, and Vaidy Sunderam. A users' guide to PVM. Technical Report ORNL/TM-11826, Oak Ridge National Laboratory, 1991.

[2] Gordon Bell. Ultracomputers: A teraflop before its time. *Communications of the ACM*, 35(8):26–47, August 1992.

[3] Marsha J. Berger and Shahid H. Bokhari. A partitioning strategy for nonuniform problems on multiprocessors. *IEEE Transactions on Computers*, C-36(5):570–580, May 1987.

[4] Clemens H. Cap and Volker Strumpen. The PARFORM–A high performance platform for parallel computing in a distributed workstation environment. Technical report, University of Zurich, 1992.

[5] Alex L. Cheung and Anthony P. Reeves. High performance computing on a cluster of workstations. In *Proceedings of the First International Symposium on High-Performance Distributed Computing*, pages 152–160, 1992.

[6] Brian K. Grant and Anthony Skjellum. The PVM systems: An in-depth analysis and documenting study–concise edition. Technical Report Lawrence Livermore National Laboratory Massively Parallel Computing Initiative Annual Report 1992, Lawrence Livermore National Laboratory, 1992.

[7] Bidyut Gupta and Sandip Roy-Chowdhury. A probabilistic dynamic load balancing algorithm for homogeneous distributed systems (with extension to hypercubes). Technical Report 91-06, Southern Illinois University at Carbondale, 1991.

[8] Philip J. Hatcher and Michael J. Quinn. *Data-Parallel Programming on MIMD Computers*. MIT Press, Cambridge, MA, 1991.

[9] Brian W. Kernighan and Dennis M. Ritchie. *The C Programming Language*. Prentice-Hall, Inc., Englewood Cliffs, NJ, 1978.

[10] Nenad Nedeljković and Michael J. Quinn. Data-parallel programming on a network of heterogeneous workstations. In *Proceedings of the First International Symposium on High-Performance Distributed Computing*, pages 28–36, 1992.

[11] Michael J. Quinn. *Parallel Computing: Theory and Practice*. McGraw-Hill Book Company, New York, (in press).

[12] Matthew Rosing and Robert P. Weaver. Mapping data to processors in distributed memory computations. In *Proceedings Fifth Distributed Memory Computing Conference*, April 1990.

[13] Lawrence Snyder and David G. Socha. An algorithm producing balanced partitionings of data arrays. In *Proceedings of the Fifth Distributed Memory Computing Conference*, April 1990.

p4-Linda: A Portable Implementation of Linda

Ralph M. Butler [*]
Alan L. Leveton

College of Comp. and Inf. Sci.
University of North Florida
Jacksonville, FL 32224
rbutler@sinkhole.unf.edu

Ewing L. Lusk [†]

Math. and Comp. Sci. Division
Argonne National Laboratory
Argonne, IL 60439
lusk@mcs.anl.gov

Abstract

Facilities such as interprocess communication and protection of shared resources have been added to operating systems to support multiprogramming and have since been adapted to exploit explicit multiprocessing within the scope of two models: the shared-memory model and the distributed (message-passing) model. When multiprocessors (or networks of heterogeneous processors) are used for explicit parallelism, the difference between these models is exposed to the programmer. The p4 tool set was originally developed to buffer the programmer from synchronization issues while offering an added advantage in portability, however two models are often still needed to develop parallel algorithms. We provide two implementations of Linda in an attempt to support a single high-level programming model on top of the existing paradigms in order to provide a consistent semantics regardless of the underlying model. Linda's fundamental properties associated with generative communication eliminate the distinction between shared and distributed memory.

1 Introduction

We have implemented two compatible versions of Linda on top of the p4 portable parallel programming system, one to take advantage of shared-memory architectures, the other to utilize a network of heterogeneous processors, offering an advantage in portability. Each implementation is based on a different programming model: an abstract data structure called a monitor synchronizes access to shared data in shared-memory architectures, whereas processes in distributed-memory space communicate through message-passing operations. Both programming paradigms are high-level abstractions in themselves and provide an intelligent means to construct parallel programs in diverse environments. The challenge was to bootstrap the approaches to a higher level of abstraction - that of the Linda model.

Although shared-memory seems natural for Linda's tuple space, some means is required to make the operations on tuple space atomic. During the brief moment in which a process either places a tuple into tuple space or consumes a tuple, the process must be assured of being the sole process operating on the data. Monitors provide a coherent means to protect tuples from simultaneous access by processes executing in parallel.

The message-passing programming model provides a means for distributed, loosely-coupled processes to communicate solely through messages. It supports an implementation of Linda that works on both shared-memory machines and distributed machines that communicate over a network. This model may run on a large multicomputer, or on a collection of heterogeneous machines, including a network of workstations. It provides a more portable system at the possible risk of suffering some loss in performance.

2 Linda Background

Linda is described in [8]. Gelernter introduces generative communication, which he argues is sufficiently different from the three basic kinds of concurrent programming mechanisms of the time (monitors, message-passing, and remote operations) as to make it a fourth model. It differs from the other models in requiring that messages be added in tuple form to an

---

[*] This work was partially supported by National Science Foundation grant CCR-9121875.

[†] This work was supported by the Applied Mathematical Sciences subprogram of the Office of Energy Research, U.S. Department of Energy, under contract W-31-109-Eng-38.

environment called tuple space where they exist independently until a process chooses to receive them.

The abstract environment called tuple space forms the basis of Linda's model of communication. A process generates an object called a tuple and places it in a globally shared collection of tuples called tuple space. Theoretically, the object remains in tuple space forever, unless removed by another process [6].

Tuple space holds two varieties of tuples. Process or "live" tuples are under active evaluation, incorporate executable code, and execute concurrently. Data tuples are passive, ordered collections of data items. For example, the tuple ("mother","age",56) contains three data items: two strings and an integer. A process tuple that is finished executing resolves into a data tuple, which may in turn be read or consumed by other processes [6].

Four operations are central to Linda: *out, in, rd* and *eval*. Out(t) adds tuple t to tuple space. The elements of t are evaluated before the tuple is added to tuple space [1]. For example, if array[4] contains the value 10, out("sum",2,array[4]) adds the tuple ("sum",2,10) to tuple space and the process continues immediately.

In(m) attempts to match some tuple t in tuple space to the template m and, if a match is found, removes t from tuple space. Normally, m consists of a combination of actual and formal parameters, where the actuals in m must match the actuals in t by type and position and the formals in m are assigned values in t [1]. Thus, given the tuple noted above, in("sum",?i,?j) matches "sum", assigns 2 to i, 10 to j, and the tuple is removed from tuple space. Rd is similar to in except that the matched tuple remains in tuple space. Unlike the other operators, the executing process suspends if an in or rd fails to match a tuple.

Eval(t) is similar to out(t) with the exception that the tuple argument to eval is evaluated after t is added to tuple space. A process executing eval creates a live tuple and continues. In creating the active tuple, eval implicitly spawns a new process that begins to work evaluating the tuple [6]. For example, if the function abs(x) computes the absolute value of x, then eval("ab",-6,abs(-6)) creates or allocates another process to compute the absolute value of -6. Once evaluated, the active tuple resolves into the passive tuple ("ab",-6,6) which can now be consumed or read by an in or rd. Eval is not primitive in Linda and is actually constructed on top of out and provides Linda with a mechanism to dynamically create multiple processes to assist in a task. Implementations of Linda exist that do not recognize the eval operation [1], including a network model based on worker replication - n nodes are given n copies of a program, thereby obviating the need for dynamic process creation.

Tuple members are usually simple data types: characters, one-dimensional strings, integers, or floats. In some Linda implementations tuples can include more complex data types (e.g., integer arrays) [6]. These data structures are removed from or added to tuple space just like the more fundamental types.

Operations which insert or withdraw from tuple space do so atomically. In theory, nondeterminism is inherent; it is assumed that the tuples are unordered in tuple space so that, given a template m and matching tuples t1, t2 and t3, it can not be determined which tuple will be removed by in(m) [8]. In practice, implementations of tuple space fall short of pure nondeterminism. Some ordering is inescapable but remains implementation dependent. It is in the spirit of Linda programming not to presuppose any ordering of tuples in the underlying mechanism. Sequencing transactions upon tuple space is facilitated using a sequencing key as an additional tuple element [10], a method employed to program distributed arrays in Linda. Thus the ith element of vector "A" is accessed via

```
in("A",i,<some_number>)
```

while the ith + 1 element is added to tuple space with

```
out("A",i+1,<some_number>)
```

Several properties distinguish Linda. Generative communication simply means that a tuple generated by process p1 has independent existence in tuple space until removed by some process p2. This property facilitates communication orthogonality because a receiver has no prior knowledge about a sender and a sender has none about the receiver - all communication is mediated through tuple space. Spatial and temporal uncoupling also mark Linda. Any number of processes may retrieve tuples, and tuples added to tuple space by out remain in tuple space until removed by in [8].

A property called structured naming deserves special consideration. Given the operations out(t1) and in(m1), all actuals in t1 must match the corresponding actuals in m1 for matching to succeed. The actuals in t1 constitute a structured name or key and, loosely speaking, make tuple space content addressable. For example, if ("sum",10,9) is a tuple in tuple space, then the success of the operation in("sum",?x,10) is predicated upon the structured name ["sum",10]. We are reminded both of the restriction operation in relational databases and instantiation in logic languages [8]. The structured name should not be confused with the logical name, which is simply the initial

3 p4 Background

p4 [4] [2] [9] is a set of parallel programming tools designed to support portability across a wide range of multiprocessor/multicomputer architectures (hence the name "Portable Programs for Parallel Processors"). Three parallel processing paradigms are supported:

- shared-memory multiprocessors;

- a set of processors that communicate solely through messages (typically, a distributed-memory multiprocessor, or a group of machines that communciate over a network);

- communicating clusters (sets of large multiprocessors that communicate via shared-memory locally and via message-passing remotely).

The tools that support these paradigms achieve portability by hiding machine dependent details inside C procedures.

Programming multiprocessors in which processes can communicate via globally shared-memory requires that shared objects must be protected against unsafe concurrent access. One approach to programming such systems involves the use of an abstract data type called a *monitor* to synchronize access to shared objects. Monitors coordinate efficient use of locking mechanisms to guarantee exclusive access to shared resources and protect critical sections of code at any one time. They are responsible for suspending processes that wish to enter the monitor prematurely, and releasing processes blocked on the condition queue when the resource is free and use of the monitor relinquished.

p4 includes high-level monitor operations built on top of low-level, machine-dependent primitives. One special-purpose mechanism is called the *askfor* monitor. A common pattern in multiprocessing, sometimes called agenda parallelism [6], focuses on a list of tasks to be performed and is epitomized in the master/worker paradigm. A master process initializes a computation and creates worker processes capable of performing, in parallel, a step in the computation. Workers repeatedly seek a task to be performed, perform the task, and continue to seek tasks until an exhaustion state is reached. The askfor monitor manages just such a pool of tasks and is invoked with:

```
askfor(<monitor_name>,<num_processes>,
       <get_problem>,<task>,<reset>)
```

where monitor_name is a unique name of the monitor, num_processes is the number of processes that share the task pool, get_problem is a user-defined function that provides the logic required to remove a task from the pool, task is the actual piece of work removed from the pool, and reset is the logic required to reinitialize the pool. Askfor includes the logic required to delay and continue processes if tasks cannot be taken from the pool.

Message-passing is the most widespread method for coordination of cooperating processes. In message-passing, we create parallel processes and all data structures are maintained locally. Processes do not share physical memory, but communicate by exchanging messages. Processes must send data objects from one process to another through explicit send and receive operations. For algorithms that can be formulated as such, the p4 package includes the following primitives:

```
p4_send(<type>,<id>,<msg>,<size>)
p4_recv(<type>,<id>,<msg>,<size>)
```

where id is the process identification of the intended recipient of the message (for send) or the process id of the sender (for receive), type is the message type, and size is the length of the message. The message type actually points to a structure in which the message is 'packetized' and must be of a consistent specified format across all nodes that use the particular message type. *p4_sendr* (send with rendezvous), an alternative to send, forces the sending process to suspend until it receives acknowledgement from the recipient.

Processes are created in p4 via *p4_create_procgroup*(). It reads a file, called the *procgroup* file, to determine on which machines processes are to be started, and the number on each machine.

4 Interface to p4-Linda

Linda operations must adhere to a strict format in our implementations. In particular, a format string or mask, must be present as the first argument to some of the Linda operations; it should not be confused with the tuple elements themselves. This mask is unusual in our implementation, but is typical for many C libraries that contain functions which accept variable length argument lists (e.g., printf). The range of valid data types for tuples include integers, one-dimensional strings, floats (doubles), and aggregates (arrays of any of the other types). The value of each element is formatted according to the codes embedded in the mask. For simple actuals (actuals that are not aggregates), the mask format specification is $<\%Type>$, where Type is d (integer), f (double), or s (string). For aggregates the format specification is $<:Type>$. The Linda operations must distinguish between actuals and formals; thus a different type separator is used for simple formals: $<?Type>$, where type is again d, f, or s. Another restriction is that the first tuple element (the logical name) must be a string or integer actual. Out is exemplified in the following code:

```
func()
{
  int i, num, big[10];
  int size = 10;
  char buf[20],mask[20];

  num = 100;
  strcpy(buf,"anything");
  for (i=0; i < 20;i++)
    big[i] = i;
  ...
  out("%s%s%d:d","key",buf,num,big,size);
}
```

A necessary limitation of our model is that tuple arguments to out must be actuals. Furthermore, a tuple may contain one more element than type identifiers because aggregates require an integer dimension following the array name. When the parser recognizes the aggregate type separator, it automatically pops the dimension (size) off the argument stack. Given the same declarations and assignments, when executing

```
in("%s?s?d:d","key",buf,&num,big,&size)
```

the parser interprets all arguments as formals, except the key. Since all formals are addresses of C variables, ampersands are required for the integers (names for strings and arrays are the addresses for these types). Note that the first tuple argument is the only one used for matching criteria. If we execute

```
in("%s?s%d:d","key",buf,2,big,&size)
```

then the matching criteria consists of "key" and "2". One may wonder why the type separator for an aggregate formal (:) is the same as its actual counterpart. In our implementation, aggregate arguments to rd and in are restricted to formals and no distinguishing specifier is necessary.

p4-Linda requires that the user program include a header file and invoke initialization and termination procedures. Processes are created as part of the initialization procedure, by reading a procgroup file that includes the following information:

- the name of each (remote) machine on which processes are to be created
- the number of processes that are to be created and share memory on each remote machine
- the full path name of the remote program on each machine

We wanted to design a Linda model, not a complete Linda kernel; hence, the fundamental decision to code the Linda operations as functions. Further, we observed that much of what is standard in C (i.e. the library of I/O functions) are procedures built on top of a minimal set of instructions and we simply viewed the p4-Linda primitives as an extension of this standard. This decision resulted in certain limitations on eval and out. A Linda kernel cited in [7] allows eval tuples to have more than two elements. For example, a typical eval may appear as:

```
eval("key",i,primes(i))
```

which spawns a process to compute whether or not i is prime. After the tuple is evaluated, the tuple ("key",i,$<result>$) is added to tuple space. In our implementation it is impossible to defer the evaluation of primes(i) - the function will return a value prior to process creation. Instead we use:

```
out("prime_args",i)
eval("key","primes")
```

where "primes" is the name of a function which is found in a table supplied by the user at initialization. The primes procedure would then obtain its arguments by doing:

```
in("prime_args",&i)
```

Also, our implementation of eval does not place a tuple in tuple space, rather the invoked procedure (primes in this case) is responsible for doing an out operation when it completes.

In p4-Linda, the arguments to out are restricted to actuals. Some Linda kernels allow for inverse structured naming, in which formals are permitted as elements in tuple space. Although the monitors model can be enhanced to include a restricted form of inverse naming (the formals would have to be shared variables), without special locators or distributed pointers this is would be quite difficult to implement in a loosely-coupled environment.

5 Design of the Shared-Memory Implementation

Tuples are stored in shared-memory as self-contained data structures. The representation of tuples includes not only data, but also typing information required for matching and retrieving the tuple. The first element of the tuple structure, called the hanger, contains the data, i.e. formals or actuals that constitute the tuple. The tuple mask is the second element and contains the typing information required to process the tuple. Note that all elements are actuals, a necessary restriction placed on out in our implementation. Actuals that are integers, floats, or simple strings are copied into the hanger. For actuals that are aggregates, a global copy is made and a pointer to the copy is stored in the tuple hanger. The tuple structure is hashed into any one of 256 linked lists. These hash lists, in their entirety, are at any time the physical embodiment of tuple space.

We considered two possible implementations for eval in the shared-memory model. One method dynamically creates processes as needed, i.e. eval("key",func) would cause a new process to be created. The other method would cause a set of processes to be created at initialization. These processes would then share the task of handling any new work that is generated, remaining active until termination of the user's program. The latter approach was selected because it follows the established p4 model which assumes that process create/destroy may be an expensive operation on many machines.

The four basic Linda operations are implemented as functions in the shared-memory model. A single monitor protects two resources: a queue of unevaluated functions and the linked list representation of tuple space. Two askfors control respective access to tuple space and process-to-task initiated by eval.

Out is relatively easy to process. A statement of the form

out(mask,arg1,arg2,...,argN)

invokes a function which examines each argument for its type based on the relative position in mask. The mask informs the function how to build the hanger. All that remains is to claim access to the monitor, link the tuple structure to the appropriate hash list, and relinquish the monitor.

In and rd are more complicated because a process must suspend if no tuple matching occurs. A statement of the form

in(mask, arg1, arg2,...,argN)

where the arguments are a collection of actuals and formals, invokes a function that constructs a local template based on typing information in mask. The process must then gain exclusive access to the tuple space monitor to search for a matching tuple. The askfor monitor provides the answer. Recall that one of the parameters to askfor is $< get_p roblem >$, a pointer to a routine whose purpose is to return a task from a pool of work. In our case that routine includes the following logic:

- search the appropriate hash list for a matching tuple
- if a match is found, delete the tuple structure from the hash list and return success to askfor
- if no match is found, return failure to askfor

Two characteristics of askfor are crucial to the p4-Linda operations. If a match is found, the matched tuple is returned in $< task >$, another of the parameters to askfor. If no match is found, the askfor monitor automatically delays the process on a monitor queue. Rd initiates a similar process, except that the tuple structure is not deleted from the hash list.

Eval's basic design is best explained by example. Suppose we have defined a function to compute the number of primes within the range 2 to N. If primes is a pointer to a function, eval("some_tag","primes") spawns a process that calls the function. Arguments to the function are passed via tuple space - the process executing the eval adds the arguments to tuple space; the process allocated by eval removes the arguments from tuple space. The example is coded in our system as:

```
main()
{
  /* masks omitted for convenience */
  out("prime_arg",3);
  eval("prime_test","primes");
  /* collect primes with */
  /* "is_prime" tag      */
}
```

```
primes()
{
  int i,result;

  in("prime_arg",i)
  /* compute result and */
  /* put in tuple space */
  out("is_prime",result);
}
```

With these restrictions in mind, the design of eval only has to assign unevaluated live tuples to waiting processes. A separate askfor is used to this end. Eval is basically a three step operation: enter the evaluation monitor, add the function name to the pool of tasks (a linked list of pointers to functions), and exit the monitor. Note that we have slightly altered the traditional semantics of eval. Heeding the caveat, process creation may be expensive on many machines, we decided to create N processes up front where N is the number of processes specified by the user in the procgroup file. This permits us to "reuse" processes rather than repeatedly create them. The p4 procedure *p4_create_procgroup*() spawns processes which begin execution at a procedure that invoke an askfor that manages the assignment of unevaluated tuples to available processes, and then invoke the function in the tuple retrieved from the pool.

6 Design of the Message-Passing Implementation

A p4-Linda program based on message-passing requires a minimum of two processes: a master process to initialize the environment and a process to act as tuple space manager. Of course, if there are not other processes, then the master process will be the only process to alter tuple space. All communication between the master process and slaves is mediated through p4-Linda operations and tuple storage handled by the manager.

A fundamental decision in the message-passing model was whether tuple space should be centralized, distributed, or even replicated. We opted for a centralized tuple space because the alternative methods require building fast deletion and broadcast protocols, an effort beyond the scope of the project. For an interesting discussion of these schemes see [5].

Tuples are stored as structures in the local memory of the tuple space manager. A tuple structure includes the following elements: a mask contains the typing information; the hanger contains the data corresponding to simple data types; a type identifier indicates whether a request is in, rd, or out; size identifiers store the tuple and aggregate lengths; and a separate area stores aggregate data. Note that all data, including aggregates, are copied into the tuple structure's data areas; pointer storage is meaningless in distributed-memory space. Once again, a tuple structure is hashed into any one of 256 linked lists. A similar structure, which we call the tuple channel, serves as the primary message type through which processes communicate tuple information to the tuple manager.

The initial steps of in and rd require argument examination and template construction. The tuple channel is used to send the template to the tuple space manager and to receive the actual tuple from tuple space. The two statements:

```
p4_send(type,manager_id,channel,size)
p4_recv(type,from_id,channel,size)
```

not only communicate a matched tuple to the process executing the in or rd, but suspend the process until a match is found. A process retains a copy of the template, and defers the assignment of actuals to formals until receiving a matched tuple. Send was preferred to sendr because the dialogue between a Linda process and the manager uses self-synchronizing pairs - a send is immediately followed by a receive in any process executing rd or in. Out examines the argument list, populates the tuple channel and uses send to communicate the information to the tuple manager.

The tuple manager takes the place of the monitor in the message-passing implementation. It's sole job is to receive a request on tuple space, process the request dependent on the tuple type, and iterate. If the tuple type is rd or in, the manager searches the appropriate hash list. If a match is found, data is packed into the tuple channel and returned to the suspended process. When no match is found the identity of the requester, the tuple type and the template are linked to a wait queue. Upon receipt of a tuple of type out, the manager first searches the wait queue, satisfying all pending requests (there may be several rd's waiting on the same tuple) until the first matched in is encountered or the search is exhausted. If no in is encountered, the information in the tuple channel is copied into a tuple space structure and linked to the appropriate hash list. The manager serves requests until it receives a special tuple of type END which signals termination.

7 An Example Program

As an example, we present a simple program whose mainline procedure puts MAXVAL items into tuple space. For each item inserted, it evals the procedure named consumer to process the item, and then extracts an acknowledgement from tuple space indicating that the item was processed. To process an item, consumer simply removes it from tuple space and outs the acknowledgement.

```
#include "sr_linda.h"

#define MAXVAL 1000

main(argc,argv)
int argc;
char **argv;
{
  int primes();
  int last,i,ok;
  struct linda_eval_tbl linda_eval_funcs[2];

  linda_eval_funcs[0].ptr = consumer;
  strcpy(linda_eval_funcs[0].name,"consumer");
  linda_eval_funcs[1].ptr = NULL;

  linda_init(&argc,argv,linda_eval_funcs);

  for (i=0; i <= MAXVAL; i++)
  {
     out("%s%d","msg",i);
     eval("%s","consumer");
     in("%s%d","ack",i);
  }

  printf("mainline exiting\n");

  linda_end();
}


int consumer()
{
  int i,val;

  in("%s?d","msg",&val);
  out("%s%d","ack",val);
  return(1);
}
```

This program works with both versions of the code if we merely replace the include for *sr_linda.h* with *mon_linda.h*. When the program executes *linda_init*, p4 will spawn some number of processes to participate in the execution. The number of processes spawned will be determined by the contents of the p4 procgroup file. The sr_linda version will use one of those processes to manage the tuple space. The mon_linda version will use all processes to evaluate live tuples and coordinate their access to tuple space via monitors; each process will be in a loop looking for live tuples to evaluate. Thus, note that the mainline program does one eval for each number to be examined. Each eval causes the procedure primes to be invoked as part of the evaluation.

To reiterate an important point however, note that if the program is run in a message-passing environment, it can run on a shared-memory machine, and p4 will handle message-passing through the shared-memory. The program could even run on a network of shared-memory machines, and p4 would use shared-memory when possible, passing messages over the network only when necessary.

Table 1 contains the run times for three executions of the program, one in which all communications are handled via monitors, one in which communications are handled via message-passing through shared-memory, and one in which all communications are handled via message-passing over a network. Note that the message-passing versions are slower because all ins and outs must be handled by an extra process, the tuple space manager.

Synchronization Method	Communication Medium	Time in Seconds
Monitors	Shared-memory	3
Message-passing	Shared-memory	25
Message-passing	Ethernet	70

Table 1: Times for Example Program Executions

8 A Semigroups Problem

There exists a class of programs in which communication costs decrease as execution time increases. The *semigroups problem* [11] falls into this category, and thus is a very good candidate for p4-Linda's message passing implementation. A short discussion of an algorithm suggested by [3] follows the problem description.

As input, the program is given a set of words and an operation table that defines how to build new words from existing ones. The object is to build a unique set of words by applying the operation table to the original set and any newly derived words. The set of all possible words is usually very large when compared with the solution set. For example, if there are six unique values for a character in a word, and a 6x6 operation table defining the product of a character pair, for a 36 element word one can derive 6 to the 36th words. Eliminating duplicates yields a solution set of only 223 words.

A p4-Linda parallel solution to the problem requires a master and any number of slaves. For efficiency, all slaves are required to build local copies of the word list and no two slaves can receive the same piece of work, represented by an index into the local word list; thus, it is incumbent upon the master to communicate new words to slaves via tuple space. To meet this requirement, new-word tuples are indexed by slave. Initially the master must communicate unique id's to each slave by placing into tuple space n tuples of the form ("id",i) where n is the number of slaves and i is some arbitrary integer. After the master places the operation table and initial word list into tuple space, it in's tuples of the form:

("master",&type,&id,word);

where type takes the value Candidate (a slave found a word it thinks is new) or Work_request (a slave needs an operand from which to generate new words). If the master in's a Candidate that is indeed a new word, it adds the word to the master list and outs the tuple:

(id,type,word,idx)

where type is New_word, id is the unique id of the target slave, and idx is an indication of where word is to be placed in the local list.

Slave processes in tuples of the form:

(id,&type,word,&idx)

where type contains one of two flags: New_word, which informs the slave to add word to its local list; or Work, which prompts the slave to generate new words from the word pointed to by idx. If a derived word exists locally, it is discarded. If a derived word is not in the local list, the slave outs the tuple:

("master",type,id,word)

where type is Candidate. The master now searches the primary list for the word. If the master discovers the word is truly new, he adds it to the primary list and outs n copies into tuple space, where n is the number of slaves.

Communication costs are substantially curtailed by maintaining a master list and several local lists. If each slave's list is a subset of the master list, a slave can eliminate as many duplicates a possible on a local level, rather than communicate all generated tuples to the master.

Some results for problems of two different word sizes are recorded in Table 2. All processes were running on a shared-memory Sequent Symmetry. The results are promising for loosely-coupled processors also because, as execution time increases, generated words are more likely found in local lists, and communication through tuple space only occurs infrequently.

Number of Processes	Word Size 25	Word Size 36
1	3.5	31.5
2	2.3	19.6
4	2.3	11.3

Table 2: Time (seconds) for Semigroup Problem

9 Future Directions

The p4-Linda implementations provide a minimal set of Linda operations: eval, out, in, and rd. Boolean versions of the primitives might prove useful to perform existence tests on tuples in tuple space. *Inp* and *rdp* would attempt to locate a matching tuple and return 0 if they fail; otherwise they would return a 1 and perform the usual matching of actuals to formals that are found in a normal in or rd. Constructing these predicate versions on top of in and rd would require minimal modification to the existing code.

Our hashing scheme works best when tuples are restricted to a single unique key. Once such a key is identified in tuple space, the tuple will match any template with the same key. If the hash distribution is good, this translates into a match with the first tuple in the hash list. Unfortunately, not all tuples fall into this category. In problems where the matching criteria include two tuple elements (the logical name and one or more additional actuals) hashing on a combination of these elements should result in a faster search for a matching tuple. Our hashing method is less than optimum for tuple patterns like these, and we therefore recommend experimentation with concatenated index schemes to alleviate potential search bottlenecks.

Finally, there is the issue of a distributed tuple space. Suppose we wished to add two matrices "A" and "B". To inform matrix "A" of its row index and data we write:

out("A",index,data).

The logical "A" identifies a specific vector, while index points to a specific element of the vector. An element is retrieved by matching on the first two tuple members:

rd("A",index,&data).

The amount of searching can be reduced if we placed vector "A" in one segment of tuple space, thus eliminating the need for combined keys. In the message-passing model, this translates into multiple tuple managers. A distributed askfor, or use of several monitors, may provide the answer to distributed tuple spaces in the monitors model. A Linda kernel described in [10] implements multiple tuple spaces.

10 Conclusions

We have implemented two compatible versions of Linda on top of the p4 portable parallel programming system, one to take advantage of shared-memory architectures, the other to utilize resources of networked machines, offering an advantage in portability. We have described the advantages and disadvantages of each implementation and methods in which the performance of each might be enhanced. We view these implementations as being prototypes and suggest that if there is sufficient interest, we would like to further develop them. The code for these systems is available in the pub/p4 directory at info.mcs.anl.gov.

11 Bibliography

References

[1] S. Ahuja, N. Carriero, and D Gelernter. Linda and friends. *IEEE Computer*, 19(8):26-34, August 1986.

[2] James Boyle, Ralph Butler, Terrence Disz, Barnett Glickfeld, Ewing Lusk, Ross Overbeek, James Patterson, and Rick Stevens. *Portable Programs for Parallel Processors*. Holt, Rinehart, and Winston, 1987.

[3] R. Butler and N. Karonis. Exploitation of parallelism in prototypical deduction problems. In *Ninth International Conference on Automated Deduction*, pages 333-343, 1988.

[4] Ralph Butler and Ewing Lusk. User's guide to the p4 parallel programming system. Technical Report ANL-92/17, Argonne National Laboratory, Mathematics and Computer Science Division, October 1992.

[5] N. Carriero and D. Gelernter. The s/net's linda kernel. *ACM Transactions on Computer Systems*, 4(2):110-129, May 1986.

[6] N. Carriero and D. Gelernter. How to write parallel programs. *ACM Computing Surveys*, 21(3):323-356, September 1989.

[7] N. Carriero and D. Gelernter. Linda in context. *Communications of the ACM*, 32(4):444-458, April 1989.

[8] D. Gelernter. Generative communication in linda. *ACM Transactions on Programming Language Systems*, 7(1):80-112, January 1985.

[9] Virginia Herrarte and Ewing Lusk. Studying parallel program behavior with Upshot. Technical Report ANL-91/15, Argonne National Laboratory, Mathematics and Computer Science Division, August 1991.

[10] W. Leler. Linda meets unix. *IEEE Computer*, 23(2):43-54, February 1990.

[11] E. Lusk and R. McFadden. Using automated reasoning tools: A study of the semigroup f2b2. *Semigroup Forum*, 36(1):75-88, 1987.

Improving Performance by Use of Adaptive Objects: Experimentation with a Configurable Multiprocessor Thread Package

Bodhisattwa Mukherjee

College of Computing
Georgia Institute of Technology
Atlanta, GA 30332

Karsten Schwan

College of Computing
Georgia Institute of Technology
Atlanta, GA 30332

Abstract

Since the mechanisms of an operating system can significantly affect the performance of parallel programs, it is important to customize operating system functionality for specific application programs. In this paper, we first present a model for adaptive objects and the associated mechanisms, then we use this model to implement adaptive locks for multiprocessors which adapt themselves according to user-provided adaptation policies to suit changing application locking patterns. Using a parallel branch and bound program, we demonstrate the performance advantage of adaptive locks over existing locks.

1 Introduction

Earlier research with parallel and distributed machines has demonstrated that the attainment of high performance requires the customization of operating system mechanisms and policies to suit each class of application programs. For example, for real-time applications executing on shared memory multiprocessors, the object-based operating system kernels described in [9] offers several representations of objects and object invocations to support the different degrees of coupling, task granularities, and invocation semantics existing in real-time applications[5]. Such experiences in the real-time domain are mirrored by work in multiprocessor scheduling[2] that demonstrates the importance of using application-dependent information or algorithms while making scheduling decisions.

This paper explores the support of application programs by kernel-level assembly of program-specific mechanisms and policies[10]. Specifically, we address the following questions: (1) How can an operating system kernel's abstractions be represented so that they can detect changes in application requirements and adjust to suit such changes? (2) Are the runtime costs incurred due to dynamic adaptation justified by the possible performance gains? (3) What basic mechanisms are required for dynamic kernel adaptation?

In this paper, we first present a model and associated mechanisms for adaptive objects. We then use this model to implement a class of multiprocessor locks, adaptive locks. Adaptive lock objects detect changes in application defined lock attributes at runtime, and adjust to such changes by using application specific adaptation policies. In this paper, we demonstrate that the added runtime cost of dynamic adaptation is outweighed by the ensuing performance gains, using measurements on a 32 node BBN Butterfly GP1000 multiprocessor.

The next section mentions a few results from our previous research to motivate the use of adaptive objects. Section 3 introduces the notions of adaptive objects. Section 4 demonstrates the utility of such objects for multiprocessor synchronization using three implementations of a well-known multiprocessor application, Travelling Sales Person(TSP) program. The implementation of adaptive locks and some basic measurements are presented in section 5. Section 6 compares our work with related research and finally, section 7 concludes the paper and presents some future directions.

2 Previous work

Experiments with artificial work-loads demonstrate [7] that any locking mechanism offered by an operating system kernel should permit the mixed use of spinning, back-off spinning, and blocking as waiting strategies. The implementation of a reconfigurable lock object that offers such multiple waiting strategies is presented in [7]. Such a lock object permits the explicit alteration (statically and/or dynamically) of its waiting and scheduling behaviors. Experiments with reconfigurable locks with a workload generator on a 32 node BBN Butterfly multiprocessor (using a multiprocessor version of Cthreads[6] as the basis) demonstrate that the application performance gains due to dynamic reconfiguration outweigh any performance penalties caused by the added runtime costs. First, for improved performance, an application requires lock schedulers that are most appropriate for the locking patterns exhibited by its threads. One experiment compares the performance of three lock schedulers – FCFS, Priority, and Handoff using a common class of multiprocessor applications: applications structured as client-server programs. For such applications, priority locks exhibit the best performance whereas FCFS locks exhibit the worst, thus demonstrating the importance of application-specific lock schedulers[7]. Second, the optimal waiting policy for a lock depends on the application's locking pattern and can be improved by dynamic configuration. This is demonstrated by experiments that dynamically alter selected attributes of reconfigurable locks to effect different waiting policies. Furthermore, these experiments suggest that a speculative or advisory lock[7] performs well for variable length critical sections.

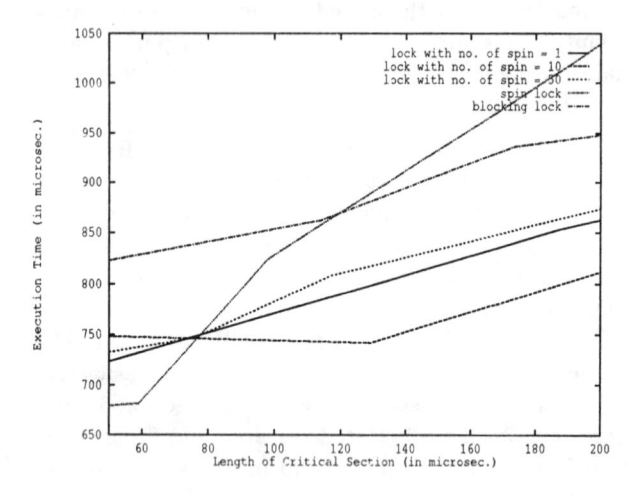

Figure 1: Critical section length vs. Execution time

We show one result of our previous research in Figure 1 which suggests that a waiting policy based on dynamic feedback is essential for improved application performance. The figure compares the performance of an application using combined locks[1] vs. pure spin and blocking locks. It shows the performance of three combined locks – one that spins 10 times initially before blocking, one that spins 50 times before blocking, and one that spins only once before blocking. The results demonstrate that the lock spinning 10 times performs better than that spinning once for certain lengths of critical sections. However, the lock spinning 50 times performs worse than the lock spinning 10 times for critical sections of the same length. This shows that the optimal number of initial spins of combined locks depends on various application characteristics such as its locking pattern, length of critical sections *etc*. Furthermore, the optimal waiting policy for a lock might differ during different phases of a computation. These results give credence to the main contribution of this paper. Namely, a waiting policy based on dynamic feedback should lead to improved performance for a large number of shared memory multiprocessor applications (especially important for applications with unknown locking patterns, applications with frequently changing locking patterns *etc.*). The contribution of our work is twofold: (1) presenting a structure for adaptive objects which can be used to build different operating system abstractions for parallel and distributed systems, and (2) applying the structure to implement multiprocessor locks to investigate the usefulness of adaptability. Specifically, although the mechanisms required for gathering information and for dynamic lock reconfiguration introduce additional overheads, we show that these overheads are outweighed by performance gains due to adaptability using a Travelling Sales Person program.

3 Adaptive objects

The object model is important to our research because the encapsulation property of objects hide their implementation from other program components, thereby permitting the alteration of an object implementation without changing its interface. With respect to configurability of objects, we classify objects into three types: non-configurable, reconfigurable and adaptive.

Non-configurable objects: Such objects are mainly used to encapsulate code and data. An instance of such an object is uniquely described by its names and methods, the latter implementing the object's functionality. They are used by invocation of their methods, where both the semantics of invocation and the representation of objects may be class-specific[5].

Reconfigurable objects: Reconfigurable objects provide mechanisms to alter the implementation of one or more of their methods dynamically (at exe-

---

[1] A thread waiting for a combined lock spins as well as sleeps while waiting according to a user-defined policy[7]

cution time) without changing their interface. Figure 2 (see the dotted line) illustrates the structure of reconfigurable objects presented in [7]. In the figure, "Configurable Methods" represent the set of object methods including its configurable methods, and the methods implemented by the reconfiguration mechanism.

Reconfiguration is possible only if the components being changed offer an immutable interface to the remainder of the application program. However, for reconfiguration and for attainment of high performance, application programs must be aware of additional object properties. These properties may be represented as object *attributes* that may be specified and changed orthogonally to the object's class determined by its methods. We use an attribute-based specification to investigate a class of dynamically changeable attributes. Specifically, we are concerned with object attributes that characterize an object's internal implementation. Changes in object attributes may be performed both synchronously or asynchronously with method invocations[5]. This requires the introduction of two additional time-dependent properties of object attributes: (1) mutability and (2) ownership. An attribute is *mutable* whenever its current value may be changed. Since attribute mutability is subject to change over time, the implementation of a reconfigurable lock object possesses an internal *mechanism* to enact the object's reconfiguration. This policy makes use of object state describing its *ownership* by invokers. Such ownership of an object attribute is acquired in one of the two ways – implicitly, when an object method belonging to a specific predefined set of methods is invoked, explicitly when the "acquisition" method is invoked by an external agent[7].

Adaptive objects: In addition to the components of a reconfigurable object, an adaptive object (Figure 2) contains a built-in monitoring mechanism that provides information about its attributes and a "user-provided adaptation policy" that guides the reconfiguration of the object.

The monitor module senses changes in those object characteristics that are required for reconfiguration of the mutable attributes and of the method implementations. The implementation of this module needs to be efficient to avoid extra overhead associated with the adaptation. Section 5 presents an implementation of such a monitoring mechanism. The monitor information may be fed to an external agent (possibly a thread belonging to the same application or to an adaptation module) for interpretation. The external agent thus senses the current state of the object, and may choose to dynamically configure it to suit the changing application requirements. Additionally, an adaptive object permits users to define adaptation policies thus implementing a feedback loop consisting of the monitor mechanism, the adaptation policy, and the reconfiguration mechanism. Issues and tradeoffs regarding adaptive objects are reviewed in the remainder of this section.

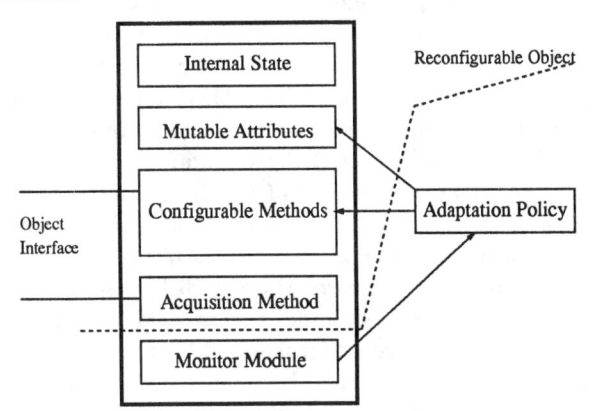

Figure 2: Structure of Adaptive Objects

Monitoring cost vs. Amount of information: The quality of monitored data depends on: (1) the range of data monitored and (2) the sampling Rate. As the range and the sampling rate increase, the quality of adaptation decision improves but monitoring overhead increases as well. Furthermore, as the complexity of the adaptation algorithm increases, adaptation cost increases.

Coupling of the feedback loop: The coupling between the monitor module and the adaptation module, and between the adaptation module and the reconfiguration mechanism affect the performance of adaptive objects. If the adaptation module lags the monitor module by a large amount, overflow of information may cause the adaptation module to make a reconfiguration decision based on a past object state rather than the current state. The adaptation lag becomes even more pronounced if the reconfiguration mechanism also lags the adaptation module. To avoid such lags, our current adaptive objects implement "closely-coupled" feedback loops.

4 Experimentation with the TSP application

An adaptive lock object, used for task or thread synchronization in multiprocessor operating system kernels and/or user-level thread libraries, detects changes in application request (locking) patterns and adapts itself for improved performance. Adaptation concerns altering the waiting and scheduling policies of locks to suit application requirements. Section 5 presents the implementation of such locks in detail. In this section, we discuss the performance advantage of using such locks in a branch-and-bound application.

Branch-and-bound algorithms are commonly used in optimization problems. We studied a specific application belonging to the class of branch-and-bound algorithms, called the travelling sales person problem. This specific algorithm is the LMSK algorithm for finding the shortest tour of a fully connected graph. The algorithm [8] proceeds by dynamic construction of a search tree, at the root of which is a description of the initial problem. Independent subproblems are generated by selection of some edges from the graph and creation of children of the root. The algorithm continues to choose leaf nodes and expand them until a tour is found. Once a tour is found for any subproblem, the search space may be pruned by deletion of some unnecessary branches and leaf nodes. When all leaf nodes have been expanded and pruned, the lowest tour is the minimum tour of the graph.

The TSP algorithm is implemented as a collection of asynchronous cooperating threads[6]. Threads cooperate via two shared abstractions: (1) a shared work queue of subproblems which stores the search-space tree, and (2) a shared value representing the current best tour found so far. To start a computation, the main thread of the program first enqueues the node of the initial problem (the root node) in the work queue, it then forks a number of searcher threads and finally waits until all of them terminate.

The above algorithm's implementation is varied in three different ways using alternative implementations of the shared abstraction ranging from centralized to distributed queue and tour representation, with and without a load balancing strategy. All implementations use four synchronization locks – qlock for mutual exclusion of the shared queue, glob-act-lock for mutual exclusion of the variable containing the number of active slaves, glob-low-lock for mutual exclusion of the lowest tour value (for the distributed representation, each processor keeps its own local copy of the value), and globlock which is a multi-purpose lock to keep the global data structure consistent. Studies of the locking patterns show that glob-low-lock and globlock do not suffer from any contention. The lock adaptation policy identifies such no-contention locks and configures them to low-latency spin-locks. qlock and glob-low-lock, on the other hand, exhibit considerable lock contention. As expected, the distributed implementation (Figure 5) exhibits a much lower lock contention for qlock than the centralized implementation (Figure 3).

The customized lock monitor for the adaptive locks, used in the following experiments, senses the number of waiting threads (sampled once during every other unlock operation) to be used by the adaptation module. The adaptation policy used by the adaptation module is simple and straightforward as given below:

```
FUNCTION simple-adapt()
        <input:  no-of-waiting-threads> IS
  IF no-of-waiting-threads = 0
     Configure the lock to be pure spin;
  ELSIF no-of-waiting-threads ≤ Waiting-Threshold
     Increase no-of-spins by n;
  ELSIF no-of-waiting-threads > Waiting-Threshold
     Decrease no-of-spins by 2*n;
     IF no-of-spins ≤ 0
        Configure the lock to be pure blocking;
END
```

In the above algorithm, *Waiting-Threshold* specifies the threshold of the number of waiting threads for a lock which determines when the number of spins should be raised and n is a lock-specific constant. The threshold and n are different for different locks and depend on the locking pattern and the length of the critical section. The constants *Waiting-Threshold* and n need to be varied in order to attain the optimal adaptation policy for each specific lock.

The remaining part of this section briefly discusses each implementation focussing on the application locking patterns, and the effect of adaptive locks on the performance of these implementations. The measurements shown in this section are taken using 10 processors with one thread per processor (each searcher thread executes on a dedicated processor) on a BBN Butterfly NUMA multiprocessor for a problem of size 32 (*i.e.*, the number of cities of the initial TSP problem is 32).

Blocking Lock milliseconds	Adaptive Lock milliseconds	Percentage Improvement
3207	2636	17.8%

Table 1: Performance of the Centralized Implementation using blocking lock vs. adaptive lock

Centralized implementation: This implementation uses a global centralized tour value and a global centralized work queue. As a result, the best tour value and the work sharing queue are consistent (global ordering is strictly maintained in the work sharing queue) and pruning of the search-space tree is optimal. However, as shown in Figure 3 and Figure 4, both locks (especially for qlock) exhibit a high lock contention.

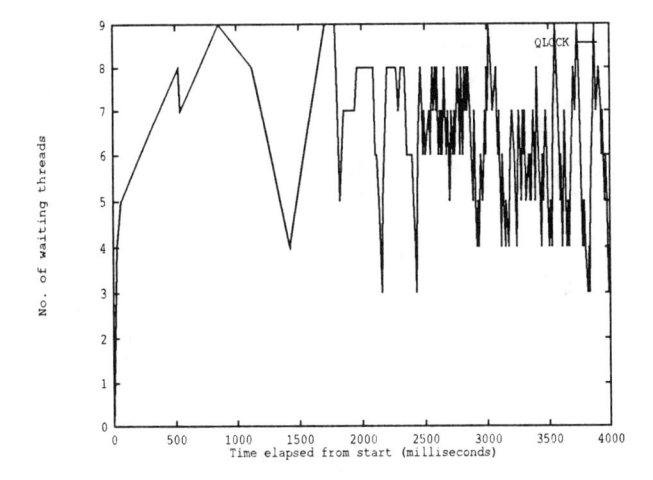

Figure 3: Locking Pattern for "QLOCK" in the Centralized Implementation

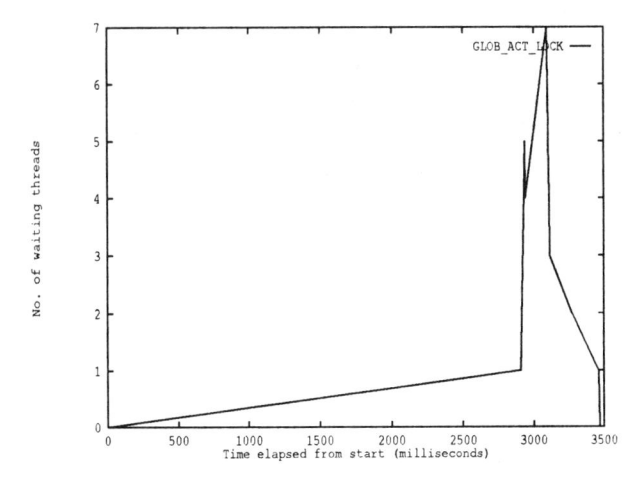

Figure 4: Locking Pattern for "GLOB-ACT-LOCK" in the Centralized Implementation

The execution time of the sequential implementation of TSP is 20666 milliseconds. Table 1 compares the execution time of the centralized parallel implementation using blocking vs. adaptive locks. The implementation using blocking lock exhibits speedup of 6.5 over the sequential implementation. However, when the blocking locks are replaced by adaptive locks, the same application's speedup improves by 17.8%. This performance gain can be attributed to two factors: (1) the adaptation policy identifies the no-contention locks and alters them to lowest-latency locks, and (2) the adaptation policy varies the waiting policy by varying the spin time and blocking time depending on the monitor input to decrease the average waiting time of each thread.

Blocking Lock (milliseconds)	Adaptive Lock (milliseconds)	Percentage Improvement
2973	2596	12.7%

Table 2: Performance of the Distributed Implementation using blocking lock vs. adaptive lock

Distributed implementation without load balancing: The second implementation of TSP uses a distributed work sharing queue and a distributed best tour value. Each processor maintains a local work queue; the local queues are connected by a ring. When the local queue is empty, a searcher thread gets work from the next non-empty remote queue along the ring. Similarly, each processor maintains a local copy of the tour value and once a new best tour is found, propagates it to the rest of the processors. As a consequence, the distributed implementation may suffer from useless node expansions due to an inconsistent tour value and partially ordered work sharing queues. However, as shown by Figure 5 and 6, lock contention is lower compared to that of the centralized implementation.

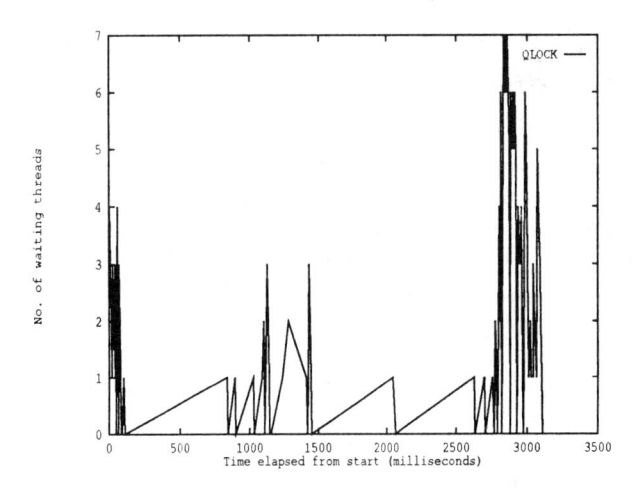

Figure 5: Locking Pattern for "QLOCK" in the Distributed Implementation

Table 2 compares the performance of this implementation using blocking vs. adaptive locks, and demonstrates a 12.7% of performance improvement in favor of the latter. The distributed implementation performs better than the centralized implementation because most of the work is performed locally reducing the number of remote memory accesses.

Distributed implementation with load balancing of work queues: The third implementation uses a distributed work sharing queue and best tour value with a specific load balancing strategy among the local work queues to improve the global ordering of queue elements. Each time a searcher gets a node, it gets a sub-problem from the queue of the next processor, puts this sub-problem into the local queue, and then gets the best sub-problem from the local queue. As expected, lock contention of `qlock` (Figure 7) and `glob-act-lock` (similar to figure 6) for this implementation is lower than for the centralized implementation.

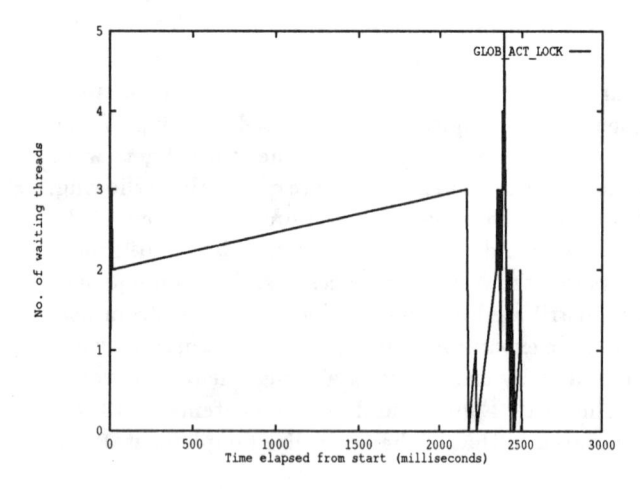

Figure 6: Locking Pattern for "GLOB-ACT-LOCK" in the Distributed Implementation

Table 3 compares the performance of this implementation using blocking lock vs. adaptive locks showing a 6.5% performance advantage in favor of adaptive locks. The performance advantage is low compared to the centralized version because of reduced synchronization activities.

Blocking Lock (milliseconds)	Adaptive Lock (milliseconds)	Percentage Improvement
2054	1921	6.5%

Table 3: Performance of the Distributed Implementation (with load balancing) using blocking lock vs. adaptive lock

In summary, the results in this section demonstrate that it is important to consider dynamic locking patterns to determine the appropriate waiting policy for a lock. Performance enhancements demonstrated in this section are attributed mainly to finding the most suitable waiting policy for a lock (causing a minimum locking cycle *i.e.*, an unlock operation followed by a lock operation). For massively parallel applications we expect the gain to be even higher because the effect of blocking vs. spinning (useful processing vs. wasted processor cycles) is more pronounced. This topic will be addressed in our future research, where we will study a massively parallel application to see the effect of adaptive locks.

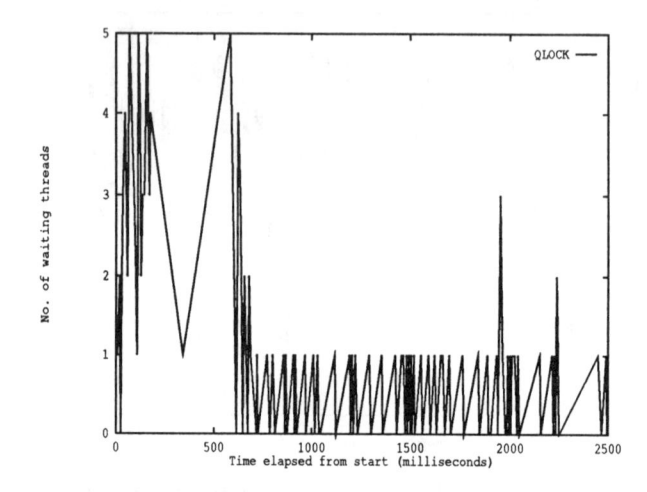

Figure 7: Locking Pattern for "QLOCK" in the Distributed Implementation (with Load Balancing)

5 Adaptive locks

This section describes the model and the implementation of adaptive multiprocessor locks, then lists some basic measurements demonstrating the performance penalties due to lock monitoring and adaptation.

5.1 Implementation

Adaptive locks consist of the following components:

Internal state: current lock state, current lock owner, registration information, *etc.*

Mutable attributes: specify the waiting policy of the lock (the policy that governs the manner in which a thread is delayed while attempting to acquire the lock). Sample attributes are `spin-time`, `sleep-time`, `timeout` *etc.* [7].

Configurable methods: Lock and Unlock operations are reconfigured by alteration of the lock scheduling policy. Each configurable lock *scheduling* component may be divided into three sub-components: *registration, acquisition* and *release*[7].

Monitor module: The lock monitor module is a customized monitor system obtained from a general purpose thread monitor which provides users with a mechanism to insert data collecting sensors and probes into the target application program. The thread monitor implements a local monitor using a monitor thread on a dedicated processor which receives trace data from application threads, performs some low-level processing if necessary and sends them to a central monitor (possibly running in a remote machine) or to the adaptation module. We found such an implementation to be too loosely coupled to be used in adaptive lock objects. Therefore, the customized lock monitor uses the application threads (executing the object methods) to perform information collection, thus making the monitor module closely coupled with the adaptation module.

Adaptation policy: A user-provided adaptation policy that takes input from the monitor module, and alters the mutable attributes and the scheduling subcomponents for improved performance.

Given the lock implementation outlined above, each lock access request involves the following steps[7]:

Lock operation: (1)*registration:* A requesting thread registers itself with the lock object. At this time, attribute information like thread-id, priorities, ownership, *etc.* is processed by the lock's policy. The overhead of policy execution depends on the number of attributes processed and the complexity of the processing being performed (the "registration" component of the lock scheduler). (2)*acquisition:* If lock status indicates that the thread must wait for the lock, then the waiting method is determined by the acquisition module of the lock object. A simple implementation of adaptive lock maps requests to methods for spinning, blocking, back-off spinning, conditional locking, and advisory locking depending on the current state of the object and the application locking pattern.

Unlock operation: (1)*release:* The last part of the lock object's policy is the release module, which selects the next thread that is granted access to the lock. The release module's selection (scheduling) policy may consist of a simple access to a thread-id noting the next thread to be executed (as in handoff scheduling[3]) or it may execute more complex scheduling strategies depending on the current configuration.

5.2 Performance evaluation

This section describes the basic costs of non-adaptive lock implementations and compares them with the costs of the operations provided by the adaptive lock object. A formal characterization of reconfiguration operations and their costs is presented in [7].

The following measurements are taken on a 32-node BBN Butterfly GP1000 NUMA multiprocessor using a multiprocessor version of Cthreads as the basis[6]. Table 4 lists the latencies of the lock and unlock operations for different lock implementations available on the BBN multiprocessor (provided by the hardware, operating system and the Cthreads library). A "local lock" refers to a lock which is located in the local physical memory whereas a "remote lock" is located in a non-local memory module. The atomior function (provided by the BBN Butterfly hardware), which implements a low level atomic "or" operation (similar to test-and-set), is used to implement various locks. The *spin-with-backoff* lock is a variation of the backoff spin lock suggested by Anderson et al.[1]. A thread requesting ownership of such a lock spins once, and if the lock is busy, waits (back offs) for an amount of time proportional to the number of active threads waiting for the processor. As expected, the primitive spin-lock has minimum latency, whereas maximum latency is obtained for the blocking-lock. The latency of the adaptive lock is comparable to that of a primitive spin lock because a lock operation for adaptive locks initially spins for the lock before deciding to block the requesting thread.

Type of	Lock		Unlock	
Lock	local	remote	local	remote
atomior	30.73	33.86	-	-
spin	40.79	41.10	4.99	7.23
spin-backoff	40.79	41.15	5.01	7.25
block	88.59	91.73	62.32	73.45
adaptive	40.79	41.17	50.07	61.69

Table 4: Basic lock operations (μsecs.)

The costs of the locking cycle for adaptive locks as well as other existing locks and costs of the basic mechanisms associated with adaptation are reviewed in detail in [7]. Scheduler reconfiguration is more expensive than waiting policy reconfiguration because a simple dynamic configuration of the waiting policy requires only one memory read and one memory write whereas an alteration of the scheduler requires three memory writes for three submodules, one memory write to set a flag (to implement the configuration delay), and another memory write to reset the flag (when all the pre-registered threads are served, the old scheduler is discarded). The cost of monitoring one state variable is 66.03 μsec.

6 Related research

Some of the notions introduced in CHAOS[5], PRESTO[2] and CHOICES[4] are related to this work.

CHAOS[2] is a family of object-based real-time operating system kernels. The family is *customizable* in that existing kernel abstractions and functions can be modified easily. As opposed to CHAOS objects, the adaptive objects used in this research contain their own mutable attributes, internal user-provided adaptation policies, and monitoring mechanisms to aid adaptation decisions. PRESTO uses the encapsulation property of objects to build a configurable parallel programming environment. Structurally, PRESTO's synchronization object is somewhat similar to adaptive locks. However, a synchronization object does not support dynamic attribute reconfiguration, adaptation, and object state monitoring. CHOICES is an example of an object based reconfigurable operating system which can be tailored to a particular hardware configuration or to a particular application. The focus of CHOICES is to structure the operating system kernel in an object oriented way whereas, the focus of our research is to build a configurable operating system kernel at the thread level. Even though we use the object model at the application level, we do not use objects to build the run-time system.

7 Conclusion and future work

In this paper, we demonstrate that application performance can be improved with dynamic adaptation which does not require any alteration of the applications's code. The contribution of our work is twofold: First, we propose a model for adaptive objects. Then, we apply the model to implement adaptive multiprocessor locks, and demonstrate their utility using various implementations of a branch-and-bound application. We show that "closely-coupled" adaptations can be used in operating system kernels for improved performance.

This paper also demonstrates that locking patterns vary significantly across different applications, program execution phases, and locks used in the program. For high performance applications and operating system kernels, it is essential to take these patterns into consideration when building efficient waiting policies for particular locks.

In future research, we will apply the concept of "closely-coupled" adaptation to other operating system components, and finally we will construct an adaptive operating system kernel for large scale parallel systems.

---

[2]A **C**oncurrent, **H**ierarchical, **A**daptable **O**perating **S**ystem supporting **a**tomic, real-time computations.

Acknowledgements

We would like to thank Christian Clemencon for implementing the TSP application using the Thread library on a BBN Butterfly multiprocessor. We would also like to thank Kaushik Ghosh for his valuable comments and suggestions on our results.

References

[1] Thomas E. Anderson, Edward D. Lazowska, and Henry M. Levy. The performance implications of thread management alternatives for shared-memory multiprocessors. *IEEE Transactions on Computers*, 38(12):1631–1644, December 1989.

[2] B. Bershad, E. Lazowska, and H. Levy. Presto: A system for object-oriented parallel programming. *Software: Practice and Experience*, 18(8):713–732, August 1988.

[3] D. Black. Scheduling support for concurrency and parallelism in the mach operating systems. *IEEE Computer Magazine*, 23(5):35–43, May 1990.

[4] R. Campbell, G. Johnston, and V. Russo. Choices (class hierarchical open interface for custom embedded systems). *Operating Systems Review*, 21(3):9–17, July 1987.

[5] A. Gheith and K. Schwan. Chaos-arc – kernel support for multi-weight objects, invocations, and atomicity in real-time applications. *ACM Trans. on Comp. Sys.*, pages 33–72, April 1993.

[6] Bodhisattwa Mukherjee. A portable and reconfigurable threads package. In *Proceedings of Sun User Group Technical Conference*, pages 101–112, June 1991. Techreport no: GIT-ICS-91/02.

[7] Bodhisattwa Mukherjee and Karsten Schwan. Experiments with a configurable lock for multiprocessors. In *Proc. of International Conference on Parallel Processing*, August 1993. Also TR# GIT-CC-93/05.

[8] Karsten Schwan, Ben Blake, Win Bo, and John Gawkowski. Global data and control in multicomputers: Operating system primitives and experimentation with a parallel branch-and-bound algorithm. *Concurrency: Practice and Experience, Wiley and Sons*, pages 191–218, Dec. 1989.

[9] Karsten Schwan, Prabha Gopinath, and Win Bo. Chaos – kernel support for objects in the real-time domain. *IEEE Transactions on Computers*, C-36(8):904–916, July 1987.

[10] William A. Wulf, Roy Levin, and Samuel R. Harbison. *Hydra/C.mmp: An Experimental Computer System*. McGraw-Hill Advanced Computer Science Series, 1981.

SESSION 3B:
High Speed Network Protocols

Richard Freund, Chair

DARTS – A Dynamically Adaptable Transport Service Suitable for High Speed Networks

Antony Richards, Tamara Ginige,
Aruna Seneviratne and Teresa Buczkowska

School of Electrical Engineering,
University of Technology, Sydney.
Sydney, N.S.W., Australia.

Michael Fry

School of Computer Science,
University of Technology, Sydney.
Sydney, N.S.W., Australia.

Abstract

It has been shown that protocol processing represents a severe bottle-neck for high speed computer networks. The disadvantage of proposed solutions are their incompatibility with existing standardised protocol implementations and/or their complexity. One method of alleviating this limitation is to have an adaptable protocol stack, as proposed in this paper. Preliminary results are presented which show that significant gains in throughput can be achieved while still maintaining compatibility with existing standard protocol stacks.

1 Introduction

The development of distributed computing applications are being influenced by two major factors: the increasing capabilities of the high performance end systems and communication networks, and the diversity and dynamism of new applications. In terms of the OSI Reference model, the above two factors have moved the performance "bottle-neck" to the higher layers (above layer 3). In particular there is a concern that the existing transport and presentation protocols are the most processing intensive protocols.

Many studies [1, 3, 5, 6, 7, 8, 9, 15, 19, 25] support the argument that the overheads associated with the processing and operating system support for network protocols will prevent the full network bandwidth from being made available to the application. The severity of this bottleneck is so great that only 20% of the speed of the underlying network filters its way back to the application [2]. However, Clark et al. [6] has demonstrated that a protocol properly implemented in software is capable of alleviating some of the bottlenecks. The current protocol mechanisms used (ie flow control, error control, etc) may still be suitable with minor modifications to their configurations and realisations.

This article will analyse current protocol designs and their evolution. A solution to the problems outlined will then be given, namely a dynamically adaptable protocol. Finally, a comparison with similar proposals will be presented.

1.1 Problems with Existing Network Protocols

Currently a range of views are being proposed for dealing with the cause of the bottlenecks in protocols. Literature indicates that the problem is caused by the operating system support, protocol mechanisms and/or its implementation.

Clark [8] argues that the inefficiencies in the current protocol stacks, are due to the implementation methodologies as well as the protocol mechanisms being used. Both Clark [8], and Crowcroft [9] argue that it is the layering concept itself that can lead to inefficient protocol implementation. This is because a layered protocol model tends to produce optimal solutions for each layer, rather than producing an overall optimal system. Other implementation issues; such as the number of context switches, the number of data copying operations and the excessive use of timers will also cause inefficiencies.

Considering the above, current protocol designs and implementations, and operating system designs must be revised so that high speed data communications can be supported.

1.2 Proposed Solutions

The proposed solutions range from restructuring the computer's operating system to suit the requirements of protocols, investigations into protocol implementation methodologies, to the implementation of totally new protocol mechanisms and architectures. Other proposals include using parallel processing, either by creating custom silicon protocol implementations, or by using multiple processors.

Optimise Existing Protocols

Clark [6] have analysed TCP/IP and concluded that when properly implemented, the control part of protocol processing is capable of handling the throughput requirements of high speed networks. Clark has also proposed a new method of structuring and scheduling a protocol, using a system called *Upcalls* [5]. This strategy reduces the number of context switches required by making the sequence of protocol execution more logical. Clark's aim with this work was to show that the layering concept is not inefficient, but that it is the current implementation strategies used that introduce the inefficiencies.

The x-kernel is a good example of an operating system platform based on Upcalls. Protocol efficiency is also improved within x-kernel by the use of buffer management strategies which dramatically reduce the amount of data copying required [13]. This results in a significant reduction in the CPU overhead.

Another approach [23], has improved the efficiency of layered protocols by using a protocol layer bypassing technique. This technique removes unnecessary layers of the protocol when it is initialised. The size of the protocol stack is reduced to only the required components, with an associated reduction in the processing overhead.

Implement the Protocols in Hardware

Chesson (XTP) [3], Siegel et al. [18] and Zitterbart [25] are working on VLSI versions of the transport layer. The advantage of this method is that it results in a general purpose protocol. However, complex (and thus expensive) silicon implementation designs are required, because the designers of the existing transport layer protocols assumed it would be realised in software.

A silicon implementation of the protocols would also tend to halt the evolution of future protocols, at a time when the underlying network is evolving rapidly [20]. Further, special purpose hardware will still need to interact with the host operating system, and the general computing environment [6].

Invent New Protocols and Protocol Architectures

New generation general purpose transport protocols such as VMTP [1] and NETBLT [7] have been designed specifically for high speed networks. A close examination of these specialised protocols show that their main differences with the standard protocols mechanisms, are in the buffering techniques, flow and error control, and timer and connection management areas [12].

1.3 New Protocol Mechanisms

Table 1 summarises the major differences between the new generation and standard protocols. This section will describe some of the optimisations used by VMTP and NETBLT.

Error Control

Errors in end-to-end protocols are caused by damaged, lost, duplicated and mis-sequenced packets. Timers and checksums are used in conjunction with a retransmission scheme to detect and correct errors. In earlier networks, a common cause of error was due to the bit error rate of the underlying network. Correction was achieved by retransmitting the corrupted packet.

The mechanisms need to be different for high speed networks because of its low bit error rates and its high bandwidth-delay product. In these networks, if a packet is lost, it is most likely due to a buffer overflow, which would be caused by congestion. If retransmission of the packet is required (for non real-time applications), it must be done within the bandwidth allocated to the communication channel, otherwise the congestion will be increased. This scheme requires an agreed data rate to be negotiated during connection establishment, which can be re-negotiated at a later stage.

A common error control scheme (used by TCP and OSI/TP4) is to use a sliding window in conjunction with an acknowledgement scheme. At the transmitter, a retransmission timer is set when ever a packet is sent. The value of the retransmission timer is normally greater than the time taken to transfer a packet and receiver its corresponding acknowledgement. If the transmitter has not received an acknowledgement on expiry of the retransmission timer, it will retransmit the packet. This is very process intensive, as timers

Protocol	Connection Management	Error Control	Flow Control	Comments
TCP	Hand-shake based.	Checksum on TPDU. 1 by 1 ACK. SR or GBN window. Timer at Tx.	1 by 1 ACK. Coupled with error control.	Tx must timeout for lost packets. Has a heavy reliance on timers.
OSI/TP4	Hand-shake based.	Length Field of packet. Checksum over TPDU Optional. 1 by 1 ACK. GBN (SR Optional) window. Timer at Tx.	1 by 1 ACK.	
NETBLT	Modified hand-shaking arrangement.	State info sent when a block is received. Receiver based timeouts, using inter-arrival times. SR window. Allows CTS Xmission with errors. Inter-arrival timer at Rx.	Uses Window & rate modulation. Tx and Rx buffers are allocated & negotiated for each frame. RTD dependent.	If the Window is larger than the buffers then rate modulated required to reduce prob. of buffer overflow. Runs on top of IP.
VMTP	Timer Based	Response to requests acts as an implicit ACK. One Tx timer per request. SR window.	Based on message groups. Stop & wait at buffer level. Assumes lost packets from queue overflows, not bit errors.	Assumes best effort datagram subnetwork (eg IP). Geared for REQUEST / RESPONSE type applications. Designed as a simple base for higher level connection control.

This table is primarily based on information from [1, 10, 12].

Table 1: A Comparison of Different Transport Protocols.
Note: CTS – Continuous; RTD – Round Trip Delay.

frequently need to be set and reset. Furthermore, it is difficult to determine an appropriate time out value. It depends on the application, system load, system resource scheduling characteristics and round trip delay. Long time out periods will drastically affect the throughput of erroneous connections. A short time out period will lead to unnecessary retransmissions.

Both NETBLT and VMTP have reduced the number of timers required by grouping the packets, and acknowledging the reception of the blocks. NETBLT measures the inter-packet arrival time because this is less variant than the round trip delay time measured by TCP and OSI. It also allows the timers to be placed at the receiver, which knows exactly which packets have arrived.

Flow Control

Flow control bounds the rate of data transfer. This is so that there is a bound on the maximum amount of resources used by the connection. Good resource usage dictates that the rate of packet transmission needs to be as smooth as possible.

Flow control in the standardised protocol is coupled with error control. However, from their definitions, it can be seen that they represent very different functions. Further, as shown by Clark et al. [7], when these two functions are coupled it may result in very poor network performance. For example, when packet retransmissions takes place, it takes place outside the flow control's window, and thus increases congestion.

Most transport protocols do not explicitly address network congestion. However, general purpose transport protocol implementations can attempt to avoid it. In one proposal [14], the protocol implementation observes a principle of *conservation of packets* by adjustment of its behaviour in response to timeouts. In another case [16] the transport layer uses explicit feedback from the network layer in order to regulate network congestion. In both of the above, the action taken to alleviate congestion is to modify the window size, which effectively controls the rate of transmission.

NETBLT uses a rate based flow control mechanism, rather than the usual window based one. At the beginning of each buffer transmission, the rate of transmission between the transmitter and receiver is agreed. This allows either end to control the rate of data transfer. VMTP has flow control implemented at the packet group level. A packet group cannot be transmitted until the previous group has been acknowledged. This scheme provides efficient flow control if (and only if) the sender is slightly faster than the receiver.

Timers

Ultimately, timers are essential for a protocol's operation over an unreliable network. However, the number of timers used must be limited for several reasons. Firstly, timers represent a high processing overhead for a protocol. This is because timers are used to monitor many events. Thus a large number of timers are required. This problem is compounded because most operating systems did not consider the needs of data communications when the timer operations were optimised. VMTP has reduced the need for timers by only monitoring groups of packets.

Secondly, as argued by Zhang [24], a timeout only indicates to the protocol that something is wrong. A guess, based on incomplete information, is required to determine the cause of the timeout. The decision, which is based on a guess, cannot be optimal, and thus the response is non optimal. For congested networks, the current use of timers (to cause a packet to be retransmitted) will typically exacerbate the situation.

The variance of the interval to be timed also reflects on the protocol's overhead. If the interval is highly variable, then it must be over-estimated. This leads to a slow response to errors. However, if the timed interval is reduced, then false time-outs will occur. NETBLT measures the packet inter-arrival time instead of the normal measurement of the round trip delay time for this reason. This requires only a single timer at the receiver.

1.4 A Diagnosis of the Protocol Bottlenecks

Ginige [12] has analysed the cost of providing a transport service. The overwhelming result is that data copying must be eliminated. A buffer management scheme known as buffer cut through [23] was used to significantly reduce the CPU overhead in the protocol. Protocol mechanisms such as delayed acknowledgements also improved the throughput, as shown in Table 2.

Support	Th'put (Kbps)
Maximum throughput that can be obtained from the system (without any transport layer)	1300
BCT at both ends and delayed ACKs	1163
BCT at both ends	938
BCT at transmitter only	443
Original ISO-TP4	435

Table 2: The throughput of an OSI TP4 implementation on a 286 PC with a message size of 21Kbytes. *This implementation assumes a perfect network, so issues such as error handling and recovery were not addressed. Buffer Cut Through (BCT) [23] is a memory management technique that minimises memory copying.*

It can be seen from these results, and as asserted by Watson & Mamrak [20], that properly designed general purpose protocol mechanisms can be utilised in high speed networks environments.

2 General Purpose Protocols

Each network type has its own useful, and inhibiting properties. A general purpose protocol must be designed to handle the inhibiting properties of all common networks. Some inhibitions of networks include the bit error rate and the overall delay of the connections. These problems result in packets being lost, and duplicate packets. Thus, over-sized, *able to handle everything*, protocols tend to be developed. Unfortunately, for most networks this extra robustness is not required.

Further, some of the design optimisations for different network types causes conflicts. For example, the packet size should be large for high speed, low bit error rate networks; but a small packet is more suitable for a slow speed, high bit error rate network. It is for these reasons that Clark [4] has stated that there will never be successful general purpose protocol.

Light-weight protocols have been developed for particular networks and applications. These protocols work efficiently under the conditions that they have been designed for. By using specialised protocols, the usability, inter-operability, and flexibility of the equipment becomes limited.

A method is required to allow a general purpose protocol to match an application's requirements to the services provided by the network. This can be achieved by having a self configuring adaptable protocol stack.

A sample multimedia application is presented with the aim of showing some of the inadequacies of the current protocols used. These inadequacies will be addressed by an adaptive protocol. Consider the multimedia document in Figure 1, which is being edited at two different workstations simultaneously. The attention of the two parties editing this documents will keep switching between the five windows shown. An adaptive protocol can take advantage of the change in attention of the user by dynamically changing the quality of service provided to each of the windows.

A typical change in attention will occur when the pause button is pressed. Now, the user is focussing into a specific area. If the defect is in this region, then the user will be unable to get any useful information from the picture.

While the image is paused, the (real time) network connection is not being used. Even if an ATM (or any other underlying network that allocates resources on demand) network is used, bandwidth will still be wasted because real time connections require a certain amount of resources to be reserved. To optimise the use of the reserved resources, and thus improve the

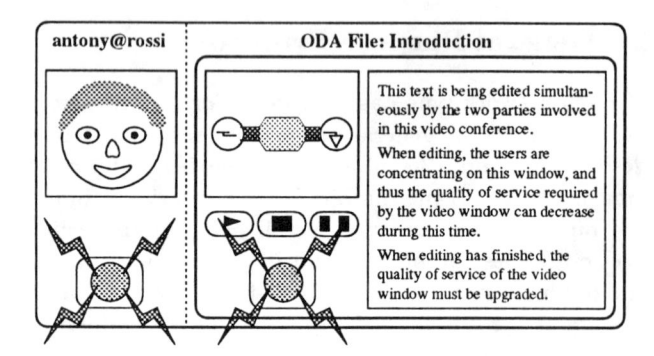

Figure 1: A sample Multi-media Workstation Desktop.

picture quality, the application and protocol should adapt to the current requirements of the user. In this case, the displayed image should have the defects removed by the appropriate retransmission of data.

3 The Proposed Solution

It has been shown that the current protocol mechanisms and implementation methodologies are not capable of fully utilising the services, and the raw bandwidth offered by the new generation of high speed networks. In parallel, real time networked multimedia applications, such as video conferencing have emerged. These applications will place different constraints on acceptable packet delivery time and residual error rates.

An efficient general purpose protocol is much more usable, and will be more widely applicable than a specialised protocol. Further, a protocol that is backward compatible with OSI will be more acceptable. This can be achieved by a dynamically adaptable protocol implementation.

There are two ways that the protocol can be adaptive. Firstly, the various protocol mechanisms can be optionally incorporated into the overall protocol during connection establishment, by using dynamic linking [22]. Configuration involves decisions based on the required quality of service, and the statistics of the data that will be communicated.

The time spent initially configuring the system must be small compared to the total time of transmission. Thus, for file transfers and other quick data transfers, a fast hand-shaking algorithm must be used to select the protocol components used.

An extended real time video connection, on the other hand, can take longer to initialise. This may be implemented by using a fast hand-shaking algorithm, and then use the protocol's ability to adapt mid-stream to improve the connection (see below). Alternatively, an extended hand-shaking algorithm may be used.

The following examples are suitable to apply dynamic linking during connection establishment.

- For networks with short delays and low delay variances, delayed and grouped acknowledgements reduces the number of returning packets, and thus the amount of processing associated with them. Networks with other delay characteristics should send acknowledgements immediately.

- Virtually all the encoding aspects of the presentation layer are either on or off for the whole connection. Thus, all the presentation layer functions can be dynamically linked in when required.

A the protocol can also change its operation mid stream. Mid stream adaptation does not only mean fine tuning the variables, but it also means that any algorithm or aspect of the overall protocol is changeable. This will allow the protocol to trade off throughput, jitter, delay and residual error; so that these parameters are best matched to the requirements of the application. Again, dynamic linking will be used to allow adaptation.

The following are examples of mid stream adaptation.

- Change the packet size depending on the loss probability and bit error rate.

- Introduce a selective repeat error correction scheme for a network with large delays, and a large uniform packet loss probability; or when the end system resources need to be shared amongst many applications.

- Switch between delayed ACK and immediate ACK depending on the prevailing network conditions.

- When used with header prediction, certain aspects of the protocol can be dynamically turned on and off.

By doing this is it is possible for the protocol to optimise its operation for the instantaneous network conditions, illustrated by Figure 2. This aspect of adaptation will require an advanced (but with a low processing cost) decision algorithm. The algorithm must be conservative enough so that the overhead of adapting does not exceed the benefits of instantaneous optimisation.

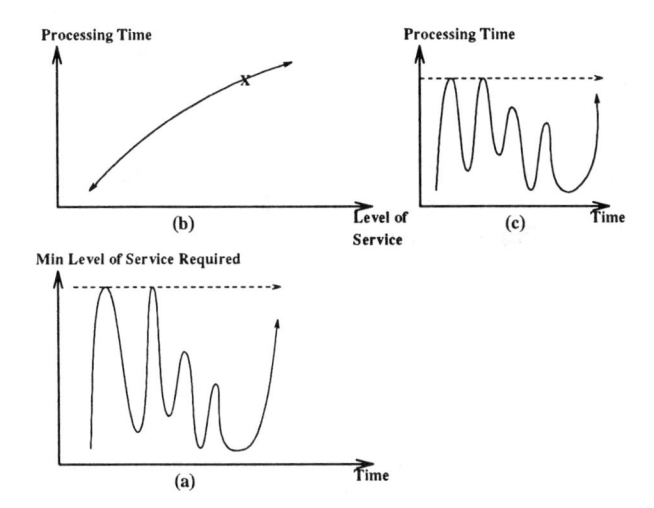

Figure 2: An illustration showing how adaptivity will reduce the average cost of a protocol.
Graph (a) shows the instantaneous minimum grade of service required from the protocol under the prevailing network conditions. Graph (b) equates the processing cost of a protocol that is required to give a specified level of service. X represents the minimum processing time of a non-adaptive protocol. Finally, graph (c) shows the instantaneous processing time of an adaptive algorithm. This on average is less than that of a non-adaptive protocol.

3.1 Proof of Concept Implementation

The viability of an adaptive protocol can only be demonstrated through an experimental implementation. This section will describe issues associated with such an implementation.

3.1.1 Backward Compatibility with OSI

The transport service that has been chosen is based on an enhanced OSI TP0, TP4 and LLC. As shown in Figure 3, the protocol will be able to switch on and off mechanisms defined within these protocols.

If an OSI protocol stack is required, when the protocol is initiated then all that is required is to link in the desired OSI protocol stack modules. This will allow the protocol to be backward compatible with OSI.

3.1.2 Dynamic Linking

The primary aim of this research is to prove that the performance of adaptive protocols are superior to existing protocols. Dynamic linking[22] will be used to allow the software to change the modules used within it, and thus its operation.

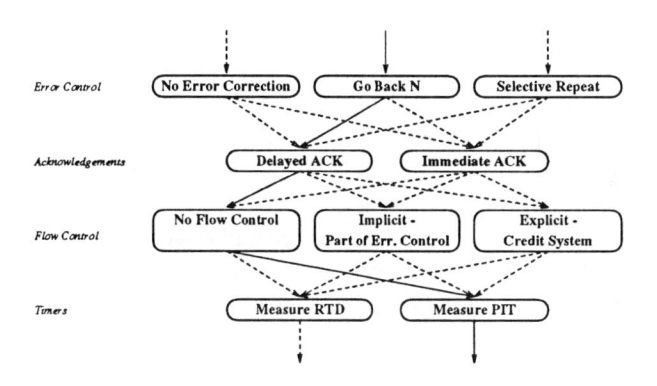

Figure 3: An illustration of selectable modules.
The solid lines represents the current configuration of the protocol. Key: PIT – Packet Inter-Arrival Time.

Dynamic linking is different to the traditional approach to software development in that the various software modules are linked into the executable program (by itself) during run time, as shown by Figure 4. Traditionally, all the modules required in the executable are linked during compilation. The major advantage of dynamic linking is that a program can offer a very large range of options, but the executable remains small.

Figure 4: The compilation process using dynamic linking.
Not all of the <SomeFiles>.o need to be read into the executing process.

An object oriented extension of the Dynamic Link/unlink eDitor (DLD) package [21] was chosen because; it not only allows dynamic linking, but modules can also be unlinked when they are no longer required, furthermore DLD is platform independent.

A similar concept has also been implemented in Lipto [11], an extension of the x-kernel.

3.1.3 The Cost of Dynamic Linking

There are two costs involved with dynamic linking. Firstly, when a module is required, the object file must be read from disc, and then linked into the executing program. Secondly, every function call to the dynamically linked part of the program involves an extra table look up. This overhead is required for any adaptive software, whether dynamic linking is used or not, because either all the functions will require case statements (with its associated overhead), or function pointers are required to provide adaptation. These are the same function pointers used to call a dynamically linked function.

If the first cost is unacceptable, a second process can be created to load the modules, allowing the first process to continually operate the protocol. Alternatively, if a certain function is continually being selected and then unselected, it can be kept in the computer's memory, and only the linking operation needs to be performed.

3.2 A Comparison with similar Solutions

Other researchers are working in the area of adaptive protocols. ADAPTIVE [17] is an example. This project aims to provide a complete communication environment, based on the x-kernel. Discussions with the designers of this protocol reveals that their decision to create a whole communication environment was because literature indicated that only 20% of the processing bottleneck was due to the protocol (the rest being due to the operating system and the implementation environment).

Given the current work on operating system support for data communications, and the general reluctance of users to change operating system platforms; it has been decided to concentrate on protocol mechanism efficiency. This allows the protocol to operate over any of the current operating systems. It is in this respect, that ADAPTIVE differs from the protocol proposed in this paper.

Lipto [11] is an extension of the x-kernel, that allows amongst other things, object implementations to be dynamically loaded while the system is running. This is similar to the functionality of the DLD package. The aim of the x-kernel project (and Lipto) is to provide an environment suitable for protocol development; not to prove that adaptivity will improve network throughput.

The functional based communication model being developed by Zitterbart [25] represents a finer grain and more flexible communication model compared to the OSI reference model. The use of this model allows flexibility to be introduced into protocol mechanisms used. However, the protocol mechanisms cannot be changed mid-stream. Further, the emphasis is on parallel implementation of protocols.

4 Conclusions

Preliminary experiments on an Apollo workstation, shows that an OSI TP4 protocol has a maximum throughput of about 20% less than an OSI TP0 protocol. This does not take the cost of adapting into account. However, from the discussion in Section 3.1.3, it has been estimated that the maximum throughput will need to be reduced by no more than 4% to allow for the cost of adaptation. This results in a 16% reduction in processing overheads.

A LLC implementation that is being carried out also indicates that similar results could be achieved. Therefore, if dynamic adaptation gives improvements in most of the layers, significant gains are possible.

It has thus been shown that dynamically adaptable protocol implementations will enable the OSI protocol stack to be utilised in high speed network applications. Furthermore, the implementation methodologies will provide means of supporting specialised application requirements, without jeopardising OSI compatibility.

The work is being carried out on a high speed network of multimedia workstations supplied under Digital Equipment Corporation's External Research Program. Companion projects are investigating and implementing operating system resource allocation mechanisms for high bandwidth streams, and investigating synchronisation techniques for multimedia transport connections.

5 Acknowledgement

The work of Antony Richards is partially funded through a Telecom Australia postgraduate fellowship.

References

[1] D. R. Cheriton and C. L. Williamson. VMTP as the transport layer for high-performance distributed systems. *IEEE Communications Magazine*, pages 37–44, June 1989.

[2] G. Chesson. Protocol engine design. In *Usenix Conference*, pages 209–215, June 1987.

[3] G. Chesson. XTP/PE design considerations. pages 27–33. IFIP WG 6.1/WG 6.4, Elsevier Science Publishers B.V. (North-Holland), May 1989.

[4] D. Clark. Modularity and efficiency in protocol implementation. RFC-817, July 1982.

[5] D. Clark. The structuring of systems using upcalls. In *Proceedings of the 10th ACM Symposium on Operating Systems Principles*. ACM, Dec. 1-4 1985.

[6] D. Clark, V. Jacobson, J. Romkey, and H. Salwen. An analysis of TCP processing overhead. *IEEE Communications Magazine*, 27(6):23–29, June 1989.

[7] D. Clark, M. Lambert, and L. Zhang. NETBLT: A high throughput transport protocol. In *Proceedings of the SIGCOMM'87 Workshop on Frontiers in Computer Communications Technology*, pages 353–359, Aug. 11-13 1987.

[8] D. Clark and D. Tennenhouse. Architectural considerations for a new generation of protocols. In *Proceedings of SIGCOMM'90, Communications Architectures and Protocols*, pages 200–208, Sept. 1990.

[9] J. Crowcroft, I. Wakeman, Z. Wang, and D. Sirovica. Is layering harmful? *IEEE Network Magazine*, Jan. 1992.

[10] B. T. Doshi and P. K. Johri. Communication protocols for high speed packet networks. *Computer Networks and ISDN Systems*, 24:243–273, 1992.

[11] P. Druschel, L. L. Peterson, and N. C. Hutchinson. Lipto: A dynamically configurable object-oriented kernel. *IEEE Technical Committee on Operating Systems and Application Environments*. Available by FTPing /pub/tcos/v#n# at ftp.cse.ucsc.edu.

[12] T. Ginige. Performance evaluation of standardised transport protocols for high speed data communications. Master's thesis, University of Technology; Sydney, Sept. 1992.

[13] N. C. Hutchinson, S. Mishra, L. L. Peterson, and V. T. Thomas. Tools for implementing network protocols. *Software-Practice and Experience*, 19(9):895–916, Sept. 1989.

[14] V. Jacobson. Congestion avoidance and control. *SIGCOMM'88*, pages 314–329, 1988.

[15] A. N. Netravali, W. D. Roome, and K. Sabnani. Design and implementation of a high-speed transport protocol. *IEEE Journal on Selected Areas in Communications*, 38(11):2010–2024, Nov. 1990.

[16] K. K. Ramakrishnan and R. Jain. A binary feedback scheme for congestion avoidance in computer networks. *ACM Transactions on Computer Systems*, 8(2):158–181, 1990.

[17] D. C. Schmidt, D. F. Box, and T. Suda. ADAPTIVE: A flexible and adaptive transport system architecture to support lightweight protocols for multimedia applications on high-speed networks. In *Proceedings of the Symposium on High Performance Distributed Computing*, Sept. 1992.

[18] M. Siegel, M. Williams, and G. Rößler. Overcoming bottlenecks in high-speed transport systems. 16th *IEEE Conference on Local Computer Networks*, Oct. 1991.

[19] C. Tschudin. Flexible protocol stacks. In *SIGCOMM Symposium on Communications Architectures and Protocols*, pages 197–205. ACM, Sept. 1991.

[20] R. W. Watson and S. A. Mamrak. Gaining efficiency in transport services by appropriate design and implementation choices. *ACM Transactions on Computer Systems*, 5(2):97–120, May 1987.

[21] W. Wilson Ho. Dld. A Dynamic link/Unlink Editor. Version 3.2.3., 1991. Available by FTPing /pub/gnu/dld-3.2.3.tar.Z at metro.ucc.su.oz.au.

[22] W. Wilson Ho and R. A. Olsson. An approach to genuine dynamic linking. *Software – Practice and Experience*, 21(4):375–390, Apr. 1991. Also available by FTPing /pub/gnu/dld-3.2.3.tar.Z at metro.ucc.su.oz.au.

[23] C. M. Woodside, K. Ravindran, and R. G. Franks. The protocol bypass concept for high speed OSI data transfer. pages 107–122. IFIP WG 6.1/WG 6.4, North-Holland Publ., Amsterdam, The Netherlands, Nov. 1990.

[24] L. Zhang. Why TCP timers don't work well. In *SIGCOMM'86*, pages 397–405, 1986.

[25] M. Zitterbart, B. Stiller, and A. Tantawy. A model for flexible high-performance communication subsystems. Technical Report RC17801, IBM Thomas J. Watson Research Center, Feb. 1992.

Implementation of a Parallel Transport Subsystem on a Multiprocessor Architecture

Torsten Braun, Claudia Schmidt

Institute of Telematics, University of Karlsruhe, W-7500 Karlsruhe, Germany

Requirements of emerging applications together with rapid changes in networking technology towards gigabit speeds require new adequate transport systems. Integrated designs of transport services, protocol architecture, and implementation platforms are needed for the requirements of forthcoming applications in high-speed network environments. The transport subsystem PATROCLOS (parallel transport subsystem for cell based high speed networks) is designed with special emphasis on a high degree of inherent parallelism to allow efficient implementations on multiprocessor architectures combined with specialised hardware for very time critical functions. The paper presents transport system design guidelines based on experiences gained with parallel implementations of transport and network layer protocols on transputer networks, an implementation architecture for PATROCLOS based on transputer networks and results of a performance evaluation, which indicate promising throughput values.

1. Introduction

During the last years, the characteristics of communication networks changed dramatically. The bandwidths of the networks are growing into the gigabit range and are providing an increasing variety of services. However, there is still a lack of adequate *transport systems*, which combine the functions of the four lower layers according to the OSI Reference Model and deliver the performance of the networks to the applications. The concept of parallelism may significantly increase the performance of *transport subsystems*, which cover only a subset of a complete transport system. Transport subsystem entities use *protocols* for communication. Parallelism should be based on a relatively fine granularity together with low overhead (e.g., communication overhead among parallel building blocks) to support efficient mappings of transport subsystem protocols on multiprocessor architectures. Several parallel protocol implementations have already shown possible performance advantages [1, 2, 3, 4, etc.].

Because parallelising standard protocols (e.g., OSI or TCP/IP) suffers from their inherent sequential structure, PATROCLOS realises a parallel protocol architecture with fine granularity adequate for parallel implementations on hybrid multiprocessor platforms. In addition, several characteristics of emerging cell based networks such as ATM and DQDB influence the protocol design for the transport system [5]. A number of protocol mechanisms (e.g., connection management, error control, flow control) need to be changed in order to take advantage of the provided network bandwidth [6]. Moreover, since a large amount of data may be travelling between communicating end systems, it is impractical to maintain a consistent view of the state in both systems. The exchange of connection state information piggy-backed in user data can not be recommended for high performance communications. Mechanisms based on exchanges after dedicated requests (e.g., XTP [7]) or periodic exchanges (e.g., SNR [2]) seem to be more suitable.

The parallel transport subsystem PATROCLOS presented in this paper attempts to overcome the performance limitations by the integration of protocol and implementation issues and by providing the required functionalities between the media access layer interface of cell-based networks and the transport layer interface in a single, modular designed protocol component.

2. Design Guidelines for Parallel Transport Subsystems

Considering processing speeds and memory bandwidth as major bottlenecks for high performance communication subsystems, the use of multiprocessor platforms is an adequate approach to increase their performance. Different levels of granularity have been chosen for several approaches in parallelising standard protocols. Most of them remain at a level that is based on protocol entities or even complete protocol stacks. The approach followed in the PATROCLOS design uses a finer granularity with a protocol function-oriented decomposition into basic building blocks.

A sophisticated protocol example supporting parallelism is XTP [7]. Parallelism has been considered in the design process and has resulted in the specification of multiple concurrent extended finite state machines (FSMs) [8]. Several XTP features, such as the integration of transport and network layer, the fixed header format etc., are extremely helpful in designing a parallel high performance implementation on multiprocessor architectures such as transputer networks [3]. This XTP implementation is able to process send and receive part in parallel without significant interactions. Processing of information and control packets can be performed partly in parallel. Communication overhead caused by event signalling among the FSMs and by context information updates is the major limiting factor. Based on the analysis of the XTP FSMs and the performance results of the corresponding parallel implementation, we derived several guidelines for protocol architectures appropriate for parallel processing [5]:

- *Reducing data dependences*
- *Decoupled control and user data processing*
- *Modular function-oriented decomposition*
- *Reducing event signalling among parallel units*
- *Minimising common resources*

3. PATROCLOS

The presented design issues have influenced the architecture of PATROCLOS, which combines a modular design and the avoidance of layering to achieve a high degree of parallelism. The transport subsystem has the functionality of the OSI layers 2b-4 and is based on a specification as parallel finite state machines. This section describes the decomposition of the protocol functions into autonomous units to support the implementation on a parallel architecture and introduces the specifications of the FSMs.

PATROCLOS is mainly designed around a set of independent protocol functions [5]. There is a high degree of independence among functions involved in send and receive processing. Furthermore, the protocol functions are classified as transfer control, data access and data control functions. **Data access functions** process user data units and can be divided into the subclasses *data manipulation functions* and *data analysis functions*. **Data control functions** decide the actions to be performed on data units. Data control functions can also be divided into two subclasses called *send control functions* and *receive control functions*. Data control and data access functions are called **data transfer functions**. **Transfer control functions** (e.g., connection management, flow control) control the connection and its user data flow and exchange control information for control and management purposes.

3.1. Parallel FSM Specification

The components of the PATROCLOS architecture are realised by parallel FSMs. FSMs belonging to the same PATROCLOS entity exchange messages for synchronisation and communication purposes. They form a system of extended finite state machines (FSM system) with the functionality of the transport subsystem.

3.2.1. FSM System Definition

A FSM is defined by the quintuple [9]:
$$\langle A_e, A_a, S, s_0, \Delta \rangle, \text{ with}$$
A_e: a finite set of input characters
A_a: a finite set of output characters
S: a finite set of states with main states and variables
s_0: a special element of S (initial state)
Δ: set of transitions, i.e., a relation of $(S \times A_e \cup \{\varepsilon\}) \times (A_a \cup \{\varepsilon\}) \times S$, with the null element ε

Several FSMs, which interact by message exchange over channels, can be combined to a FSM system. The input and output characters encode the message types and the channels, on which the interactions take place. A channel addressing function performs the mapping of the messages to channels. The FSM system has two interfaces, an input interface allows an external influence on the system, the output interface indicates the reactions of the system. A FSM system is defined by [9]:
$$\langle D, C, f_k, N_e, N_a, A_e', A_a' \rangle, \text{ with}$$
D: a finite set of FSMs
C: a finite set of channels with unlimited capacity. The channels are based on a FIFO service discipline.
N_e: union of the sets of input characters of the FSMs in D
N_a: union of the sets of output characters of the FSMs in D
f_k: channel addressing function, i.e., a partial mapping from $N_e \cap N_a$ to C
N_e': input interface message types
N_a': output interface message types
A_e: input mapping function, i.e., a partial mapping from N_e' to N_e
A_a: output mapping function, i.e., a partial mapping from N_a to N_a'

PATROCLOS can be characterised as a FSM system according to this definition. The FSMs belonging to the same entity exchange messages, which are classified as internal messages and external messages. Internal messages are exchanged between FSMs inside a FSM system. A special case of internal messages are timer messages. Timers are regarded as small FSMs, which receive commands to start or stop a timer and send timeout messages to other FSMs. External messages, which represent the interface messages of the FSM system definition, are used for the communication with other FSM systems, i.e., the external messages in PATROCLOS are messages from/to the transport system user or the underlying network. The functions A_e and A_a perform together the mapping between the internal message types of a FSM system and the message types used at the interface. For formal FSM description we used charts and PROMELA [10]. The specification has been simulated and validated with SPIN (simple PROMELA interpreter) [10].

3.2.2. The PATROCLOS FSM System

PATROCLOS consists of two types of FSMs:
- *Interface FSMs* for interactions with neighboured layers, which are located at the interfaces of the transport subsystem.
- *Protocol FSMs* communicating by separate protocols with peer FSMs at the peer entity.

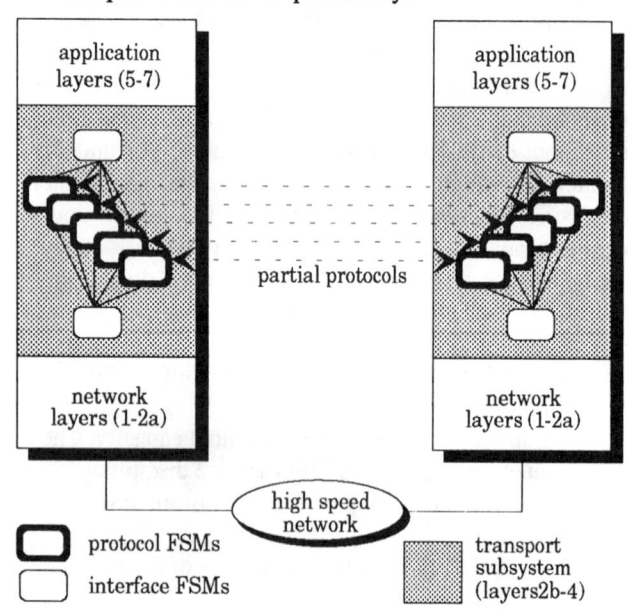

Figure 1 : Architecture of PATROCLOS

The system interface of PATROCLOS is subdivided in two interface FSMs. These interface FSMs support interactions of PATROCLOS with the transport service user or with the underlying network unit. They are only involved in local communications inside one entity, and they do not have to communicate with FSMs at the peer entity. The transport interface FSM exchanges TSDUs with the transport service user, triggers actions of the protocol FSMs dependent on the received TSDUs, delivers TSDUs to the transport service user, and is involved in performing secure connection termination. The network interface FSM controls and schedules transmission of P-frames to the underlying network unit.

The protocol FSMs are designed to decouple the connection state information exchange from user data exchange effectively. Acknowledgements and connection state information exchange are triggered by expired timers, explicit requests, or error situations. Protocol FSMs communicate directly with the corresponding peer FSMs. Each communication relation has its own protocol and separate packets (P-frames). Multiplexing of P-frames by different FSMs is avoided to support parallelism. The FSM protocols have their individual error recovery mechanisms and timers. The decomposition into independent FSMs permits parallel execution and it has the benefit of a highly modular system, which can be configured easily depending on the requirements of the applications and the characteristics of the networks. Configuration issues of transport systems are covered in [11].

3.2.3. Communication among Protocol FSMs

The independent protocol functions identified in the previous section are realised by autonomous protocols, which build together the PATROCLOS protocol. Each partial protocol is performed by communicating peer FSMs, which use data units containing only the necessary information for their functions. This results in a parallel execution of different protocol functions. Moreover, most of the functions allow parallelism between send and receive part. Several FSMs are discussed in the following:

- *Connection management*

  A single connection management FSM manages the complete duplex connection. It supports establishment, monitoring, maintenance, and correct termination of connections. Therefore, this FSM has to activate and initialise the other FSMs of the same entity for each new connection and has also to deactivate these FSMs after connection termination. To provide a correct connection release, the connection management FSM has to ensure by co-operation with several other FSMs that all data, which are delivered to the transport system before initiating connection termination are sent and acknowledged. Handshake-based or implicit establishment mechanisms are provided according to the requested service.

- *User data transfer*

  User data transfer FSMs send and receive user data. The main tasks of the two FSMs are formatting and analysing P-data-frames. Therefore, the user data send FSM uses the header fields of the P-data-frames to describe the user data, while the user data receive FSM operates on these informations to detect duplicates and errors or it checks the lifetime of the packet.

- *Acknowledgement and retransmissions*

  The acknowledgement/retransmission functions can be divided into two FSMs. The FSM on the send side (retransmission FSM) receives acknowledgements from the peer's FSM on the receive side (acknowledgement FSM). The retransmission FSM may also request acknowledgements, or send the state of acknowledged data to the peer's acknowledgement FSM. Retransmission strategy and management of unacknowledged data are implemented in this FSM.

- *Flow and rate control*

  For flow and rate control, there exist two FSMs for each connection, i.e., one FSM for each transfer direction. The flow control send FSM controls data flow by the interpretation of the peer entity's feedback signals, e.g., window and buffer sizes, and rate values.

For rate control, both peer FSMs negotiate appropriate rate parameters.

- *Congestion control*
The congestion control FSMs control data flow by the interpretation of feedback signals from the network or the peer entity, e.g., congestion indications, round trip times, and inter-arrival times of test packets. The FSMs exchange test P-frames to identify congestions or to estimate round trip times. Based on test packet delays and inter-arrival times, congestion situations are detected and the rate can be decreased [12, 13]. The FSM may also react to the feedback signals of the network nodes.

- *Routing and relaying*
The FSM performs functions required in intermediate systems such as relaying, routing, route management, and monitoring.

- *Delay jitter control*
The jitter control FSMs support the timing relationships between sent and received data. Several applications require well defined data packet inter-arrival times. These FSMs send and receive time stamps for transferred user data. The receive FSM controls the orderly delivery of user data to the transport system user considering the received time stamps.

3.2.4. Co-operation among FSMs of one Entity

The system is designed to minimise interactions among FSMs of the same entity, i.e., all FSMs are designed as autonomous as possible [14]. Because bi-directional communications reduce the achievable parallelism considerably, the communication among FSMs is uni-directional to allow a higher degree of parallelism. If possible, the necessary information exchange is performed periodically to reduce the communication overhead. The co-operation among the PATROCLOS FSMs in the cases of flow control and data transfer with retransmission and acknowledgement is described in the following.

Data transfer, retransmission, and acknowledgement

Data transfer can be divided into a sending path and a receiving path. The sending path includes most of the data manipulation functions, the receiving path consists of most of the data analysis functions. Because data transfer often performs the critical path in communication protocols, retransmission and acknowledgement are handled by special control functions, i.e., the user data send FSM gives control over previously sent data packets to the retransmission FSM, which is responsible for further retransmissions to the peer's user data receive FSM. Retransmissions depend on incoming acknowledgements from the peer's acknowledgement FSM.

Because processing the user data transfer functions usually performs the critical path in communication protocols, communication between the participating FSMs is reduced to a minimum. In the case of error-free communication, the FSMs in one entity communicate periodically instead of exchanging messages after each packet. E.g., the user data send FSM gives the control over the sent packets to the retransmission FSM periodically. To avoid delays in error cases, the information is sent as quick as possible.

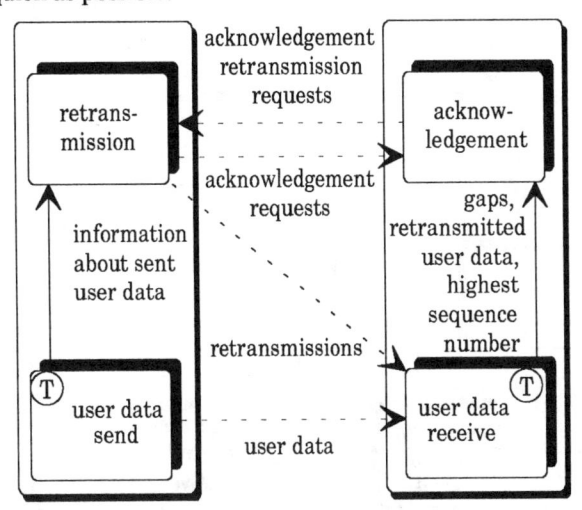

Figure 2: Co-operation among FSMs for data transfer and retransmission

Flow control

Flow control in PATROCLOS is a combination of window-based and rate-based mechanisms. Two flow control FSMs exist in each entity, one FSM for each data flow direction (cf. Figure 3). These FSMs negotiate flow control parameters with the remote peer and use these parameters to control the data flow. On the receiving side, the user data receive FSM has to signal buffer state information to the flow control FSM. The flow control receive FSM calculates from these informations new flow control parameters and sends them periodically to the remote peer's flow control send FSM. This one controls the FSMs of the user data sending functions by the negotiated flow control parameters. The user data send FSM is responsible for the window-based part of the flow control and, therefore, receives the new window bounds from the flow control send FSM. If required, the user data send FSM can request new credit values. The rate-based part of the flow control is performed by the flow control send FSM and the send control FSM. The flow control send FSM is interrupted periodically by the rate control timer to send a new credit value to the send control FSM, which decrements the credit value, whenever a new data packet has been sent. Simultaneously, the congestion control send FSM informs it about the actual traffic patterns. To minimise the communications among FSMs, messages are sent periodically if possible, e.g., buffer state information from the user data receive FSM to the flow control receive FSM. Other messages are exchanged only in exception cases, e.g., the user data send FSM requests a new credit, if it is blocked on the sliding window.

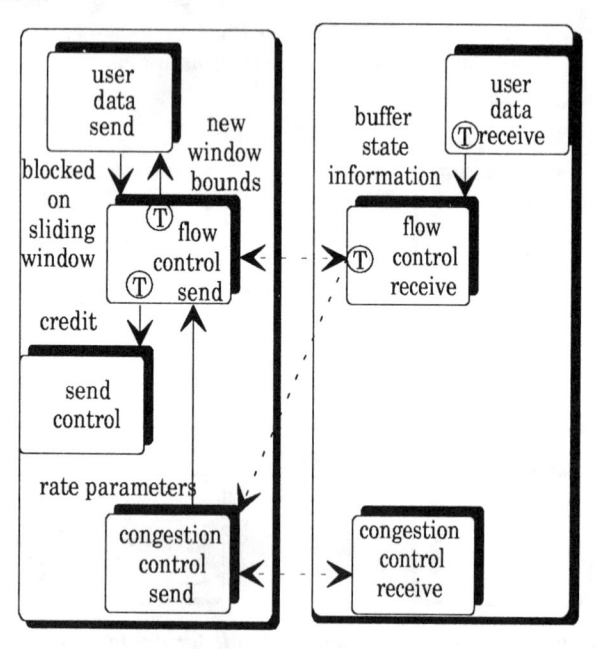

Figure 3: Co-operation of FSMs involved in flow control

4. Prototype Implementation

PATROCLOS is appropriate but not limited to be implemented on a hybrid multiprocessor architecture. Parallel architectures for communication subsystems are successfully built with transputer networks [1, 3, 4]. This section describes the mapping of the protocol specification based on a set of parallel FSMs to appropriate implementation building blocks. Based on these implementation concepts, a hybrid multiprocessor architecture has been developed. Finally, the achievable performance of the parallel implementation is analysed.

4.1. Implementation of FSMs by Processes

The FSMs have been implemented as processes (main processes). Each process may be mapped to a single processor of a suitable multiprocessor configuration. Processes of the same entity communicate with each other via asynchronous message passing across interconnecting inter-process channels. Timer processing is supported by special timer processes, which do not need to run on the same processor as the protocol process, and, therefore, may be performed in parallel. A protocol process has to send command messages to the appropriate timer process to start, modify or stop timers. The timer process notifies the protocol process for each time-out by sending a time-out message. Processes on the same processor are interconnected by software channels, processes on different processors are interconnected by hardware channels.

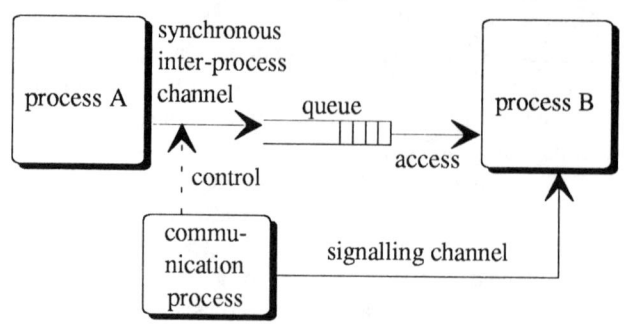

Figure 4: Asynchronous communication between processes

Each main process starts a subprocess, the so-called communication process, which supports asynchronous inter-process communication across synchronous channels (cf. Figure 4) and avoids deadlocks. A communication process receives incoming messages from another main process over a synchronous inter-process channel and stores the received messages in a queue. The communication process co-operates with the according main process by this queue and wakes up the main process whenever a message arrives by sending a signal over the signalling channel. Then, the main process performs computations dependent on the contents of the received message. Transputers provide special capabilities to perform inter-processor communication concurrently with computations of any process. A parallel C language [15] with additional elements for message passing and process management has been used for implementation.

```
process data_send () {
  while (TRUE) {
    read_message_from_queue();
    switch (message_type) {
      case FRAME_FROM_SEGMENTATION:
        format_frame ();
        deliver_frame_to_send_control ();
        break;
      ...
      case OPEN_MSG_FROM_CONN_MANAGER:
        initialise_new_context ();
        break;
}}}
```

Figure 5: Process implementation

The program in Figure 5 shows the structure of the data send process as example for the implementation of protocol processes. Different processing steps have to be performed dependent on the incoming message from another process or a timer process. After each processing step, the process waits for the arrival of new messages.

4.2. Multiprocessor Based Implementation Architecture

The multiprocessor-based implementation architecture uses transputers as universal processors. Each process derived from the PATROCLOS protocol architecture can be mapped to a separate processor. A demultiplexing unit to demultiplex incoming P-frames to the appropriate processor, access control units to control the access of several processors to the shared memory buses, and protocol functions on cell level (SAR processing according to AAL4) have been implemented by dedicated hardware units to support the high network bandwidth. The combination of universal processors and specialised processors results in a hybrid multiprocessor architecture. The implementation architecture will be connected via a DMA unit to a host system. On the send side, TSDUs are segmented by the segmentation processor and delivered to the data send processor. The use of shared memories avoids copying of data between different processors. The send control processor receives P-frames from the data send processor and from the transfer control processors, determines the next P-frame to be sent, and delivers corresponding P-frame informations to the segmentation hardware, which performs cell segmentation for a cell-based network.

On the receive side, the demultiplexing hardware distributes incoming cells to the reassembly hardware units of the data manipulation processor and the transfer control processor modules. The reassembly hardware units reassemble incoming cells to P-frames and signal completely received P-data-frames and errors (e.g., bit errors, cell loss, and missequenced cells). The received P-data-frames are delivered via the receive control processor to the reassembly processor, which generates TSDUs. The TSDUs are delivered via the transport service interface to the transport service user.

Memory management tasks are distributed among the processors of the send and receive pipeline. Special data structures are required, which have been designed in order to reduce copying of data to a minimum. They permit efficient memory management and access by several processors without any inconsistencies and conflicts.

4.3. Performance Evaluation

Figure 6 shows the communication among the protocol processes in the case of regular, and error-free data flow. The processes exchange window and credit values, and information about P-data-frames received or to be sent. Most of the processing steps of a process are triggered by received information from another protocol process. These messages are depicted in Figure 5 by an arrow. Time-out messages from timer processes, are indicated by a circle near the beginning of an arrow.

The time periods needed for the processing steps are presented close to the arrowheads of the processing steps triggered by received messages and close to the time-out symbol of the processing steps triggered by timeouts. E.g., the data send process sends messages to the retransmission process periodically. The processing time for the data send process to react on the time-out by sending a message to the retransmission process, and to restart the timer is 101 µs, the retransmission process needs 86 µs for processing the incoming message.

Because P-control-frames are sent and received periodically and, therefore, usually less frequently than P-data-frames, processing of user data to be sent and received will be the critical path. The send path consists of the processes transport interface → segmentation → data send → send control, the receive path consists of the processes data receive → reassembly → transport interface. The processing times of the send and receive pipeline are highlighted in Figure 6. Because both paths may be processed by pipelines, the throughput values depend on the processes with the largest processing time of the pipeline. These so-called *bottleneck processes* are the data send process on the send pipeline with more than 159 µs, and the data receive process on the receive pipeline with more than 179 µs.

To compute the average processing time per frame of the data send process, we have to take into account that the data send process is being triggered by three events during the regular data flow periods:

- The data send process gets P-data-frame information from the segmentation process, formats the P-data-frame header, and delivers the P-data-frame to the send control process, if the credit is large enough. This time needed for this procedure is called t_{seg}.
- The flow control send process controls the available credit of the data send process and sends new credit values to the data send process periodically. Processing an incoming credit value from the flow control send process needs t_{fcs}. Assuming that this message arrives every w P-data-frames, the data send process requires the time $\frac{t_{fcs}}{w}$ per P-data-frame to process the incoming new credit values.
- The data send process has to send informations about sent P-data-frames (t_{ret}) to the retransmission process, which monitors missing acknowledgements. The time period between two messages must be lower than the minimum round trip time (*rtt*), i.e., the minimum time between sending a P-data-frame and receiving its acknowledgement. With p as the packet rate [packets/s], the processing time per P-data-frame for sending information about sent P-frames is $\frac{t_{ret}}{p*rtt}$.

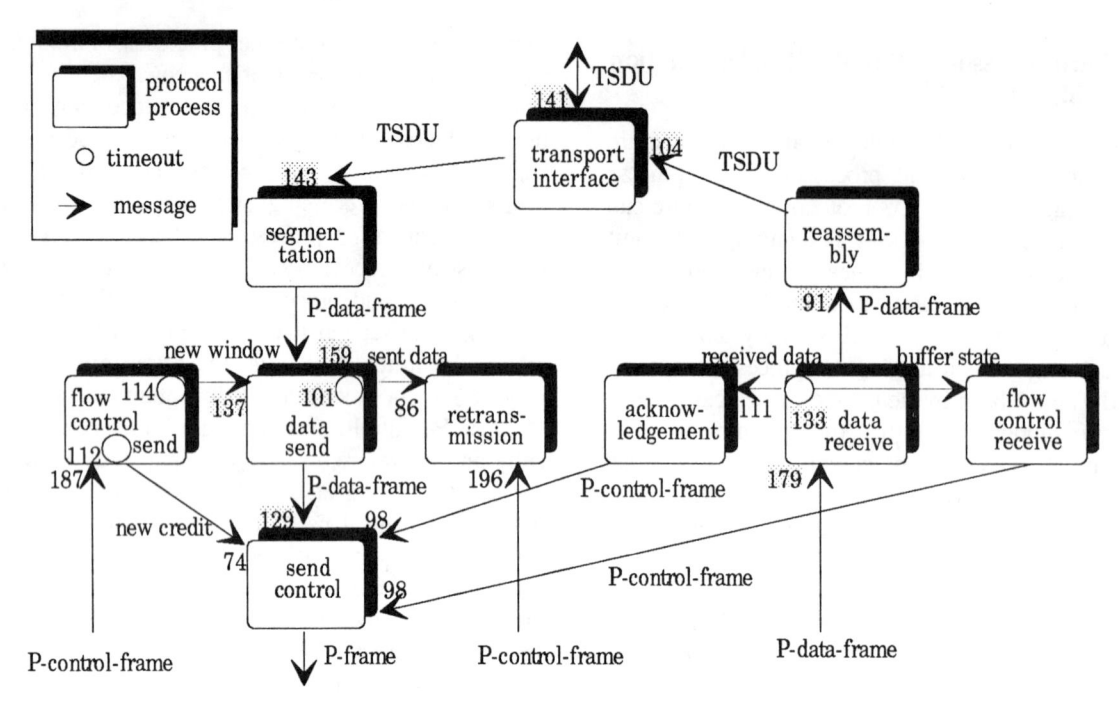

Figure 6: Performance evaluation of the PATROCLOS processes on transputers

The maximum achievable packet rate can now be calculated by the following formula:

$$p = \frac{1}{t + \frac{t_{fcs}}{w} + \frac{t_{ret}}{p*rtt}} \Rightarrow p = \frac{1 - \frac{t_{ret}}{rtt}}{t + \frac{t_{fcs}}{w}}$$

Figure 7 shows the throughput in packets (P-data-frames) per second dependent on the parameters w and rtt (t_{seg} = 159 µs, t_{fcs} = 137 µs, t_{ret} = 101 µs). Increasing the values of rtt and w results in a higher performance. The achievable throughput is higher than 5000 packets/s for rtt > 5 ms and w > 5, but is limited to 6300 packets/s by the time of 159 µs of the data send process to format a packet.

Assuming a regular data flow, two actions of the data receive process have to be considered to get the average processing time per frame of the data receive process:

- The data receive process gets P-data-frames from the network, analyses the lifetime, checks on duplicates etc., and delivers the P-data-frames to the reassembly process. This procedure takes the time t_{net}.
- The data receive process has to inform the acknowledgement process periodically about P-data-frames correctly received (t_{ack}). Also, the flow control receive process, expects buffer state information within certain periods of time. These messages should be exchanged at least once per rtt. If the generation and distribution of these messages is performed n times per rtt, it costs $\frac{n*t_{ack}}{p*rtt}$ per P-data-frame.

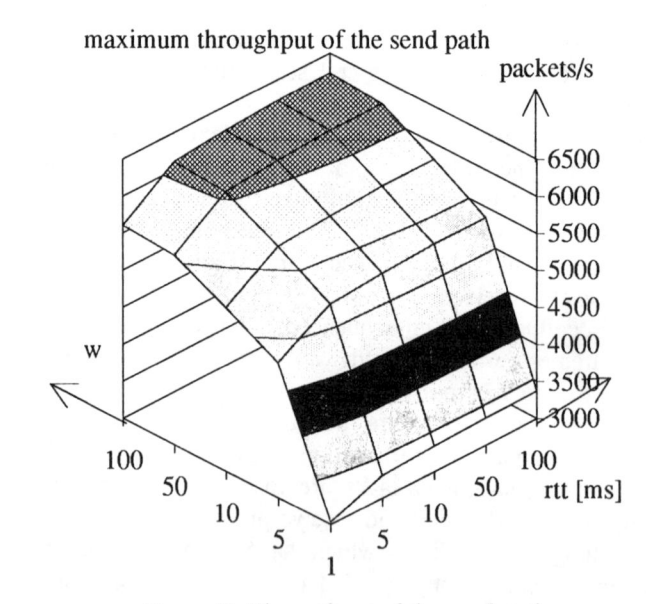

Figure 7: Throughput of the send path

The maximum throughput of the receive pipeline is calculated by the following formula:

$$p = \frac{1}{t_{net} + \frac{n*t_{ack}}{p*rtt}} \Rightarrow p = \frac{1 - \frac{n*t_{ack}}{rtt}}{t_{net}}$$

Figure 8 shows the throughput dependent on the parameters n and rtt (t_{net} = 179 µs, t_{ack} = 133 µs). The throughput grows with an increasing value of the ratio $\frac{rtt}{n}$, but is limited by t_{net} to 5600 packet/s and is higher than 5000 packets/s for rtt > 5 ms.

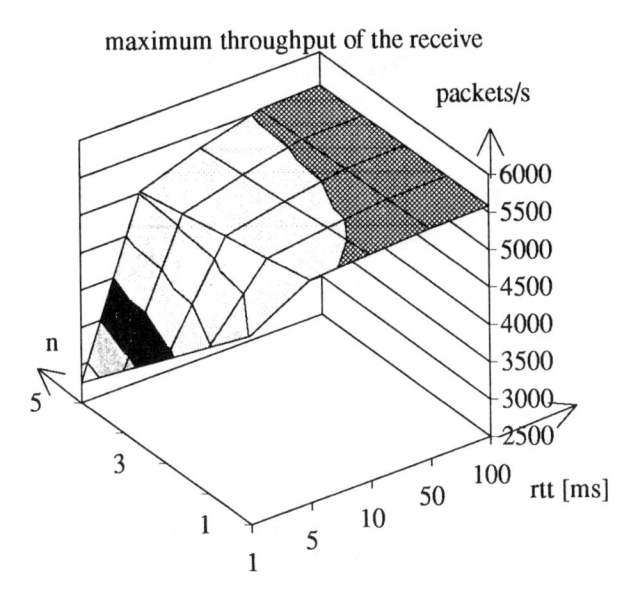

Figure 8: Throughput of the receive path

Compared with other implementations, the PATROCLOS implementation achieves very high performance. The XTP implementation [3], which, however, uses an other memory management scheme, accomplishes a maximum throughput of less than 1330 packets/s. A TCP/IP implementation [4] running on a faster transputer architecture (parallel protocol engine, PPE) than the one used for PATROCLOS and XTP achieves up to 2800 packets/s. The throughput values of PATROCLOS will at least be 15 % higher on the PPE.

5. Conclusions

In this paper, PATROCLOS, a parallel transport subsystem appropriate for high performance communication subsystems, has been presented. The general goal was an integrated design of protocol and implementation architecture issues. Multiprocessor systems may be applicable candidates for future gigabit rate networks and, thus, a protocol design appropriate for efficient implementation architectures is required.

The presented design is highly influenced by guidelines for parallel protocol design. The key issue is the decomposition of a protocol entity into concurrently executable FSMs. Therefore, the protocol consists of multiple modular FSMs operating almost independently from each other. The design comprises separate FSMs for each control function and for user data processing. With respect to concurrent processing, synchronisation among FSMs of a single protocol entity is reduced by associating each FSM with an individual protocol for message exchange between FSMs residing in different entities.

A prototype version of PATROCLOS has been implemented on a multiprocessor architecture using transputers as general purpose processors and dedicated hardware for time-critical protocol functions. Performance evaluations show significant improvements compared to similar implementations of other protocols.

References

[1] Zitterbart, M.
High Speed Transport Components
IEEE Network Magazine, Vol. 5, No. 1, January 1991, pp. 54-63

[2] Sabnani, K.; Netravali, A.; Roome, W.
Design and Implementation of a High Speed Transport Protocol
IEEE Transactions on Communications, Vol. 38, No. 11, November 1990, pp. 2010-2024

[3] Braun, T.; Zitterbart, M.
A Parallel Implementation of XTP on Transputers
16th Annual IEEE Conference on Local Computer Networks, October 14-17, 1991, Minneapolis, pp. 172-179

[4] Rütsche, E.; Kaiserswerth, M.
TCP/IP on the Parallel Protocol Engine
4th IFIP Conference on High Performance Networking, HPN92, December 14-18, 1992, Liège, Belgium

[5] Braun, T.; Zitterbart, M.
Parallel Transport System Design
4th IFIP Conference on High Performance Networking, HPN92, December 14-18, 1992, Liège, Belgium

[6] La Porta, T.F.; Schwartz, M.
Architectures, Features, and Implementation of High-Speed Protocols
IEEE Network, Vol. 5, No. 3, May 1991, pp. 14-22

[7] Strayer, W.T.; Dempsey, B.J.; Weaver, A.C.
XTP: The Xpress Transfer Protocol
Addison-Wesley Publishing Company, 1992

[8] Protocol Engines Inc.
XTP Protocol Definition
Revision 3.4, July 17, 1989

[9] Krumm, H.
Functional Analysis of Communication Protocols
Informatik-Fachberichte 247 (in German), Springer, 1990

[10] Holzmann, G.J.
Design and Validation of Protocols: A Tutorial
Computer Networks and ISDN Systems, Vol. 25, 1993, pp. 981-1017

[11] Zitterbart, M.; Stiller, B.; Tantawy, A.
A Model for Flexible High-Performance Communication Subsystems
Journal of Selected Areas in Communication, May 1993

[12] Keshav, S.; Agrawala, A.; Singh, S.
Design and Analysis of a Flow Algorithm for a Network of Rate Allocating Servers
in: Johnson, M.J. (ed.): Protocols for High-Speed Networks, II, North-Holland, 1991, pp. 55-72

[13] Haas, Z.
Adaptive Admission Congestion Control
Computer Communication Review, Vol. 21, No. 5, October 1991, pp. 58-76

[14] Schmidt, C.
Design of a Transport System Based on Parallel Finite State Machines
Diploma thesis (in German), University of Karlsruhe, July 1992

[15] INMOS Ltd.
ANSI C Toolset Language Refernce
INMOS Ltd., Bristol, U.K., 1990

A Message Passing Interface for Parallel and Distributed Computing

Salim Hariri, JongBaek Park, Fang-Kuo Yu, Manish Parashar and Geoffrey C. Fox
Northeast Parallel Architectures Center
Syracuse University
Syracuse, NY 13244

Abstract

The proliferation of high performance workstations and the emergence of high speed networks have attracted a lot of interest in parallel and distributed computing (PDC). We envision that PDC environments with supercomputing capabilities will be available in the near future. However, a number of hardware and software issues have to be resolved before the full potential of these PDC environments can be exploited. The presented research has the following objectives: (1) to characterize the message-passing primitives used in parallel and distributed computing; (2) to develop a communication protocol that supports PDC; and (3) to develop an architectural support for PDC over gigabit networks.

1 Introduction

The proliferation of high performance workstations and the emergence of high speed networks have attracted a lot of interest in parallel and distributed computing (PDC). We envision that PDC environment with supercomputing capability will be available in the near future. Current workstations are capable of delivering tens and hundreds of Megaflops of computing power. A recent report from the IBM European Center for Scientific and Engineering Computing [2] stated that a cluster of 8 RX/6000 Model 560 workstations connected with IBM serial optical channel converter achieved a performance of 0.52 Gigaflops for the Dongarra benchmarks for massively parallel systems. The obtained result outperforms a number of existing parallel computers like a 24 node Intel iPSC/860, 16 node Intel Delta, 256 node nCube2 or a 24 node Alliant CAMPUS/800. Further, workstations are general-purpose, flexible and much more cost-effective, and it has been shown that the average utilization of a cluster of workstations is only around 10% [11]; this unutilized or wasted fraction of the computing power is sizable and, if harnessed, can provide a cost-effective alternative to expensive supercomputing platforms.

Current trend in local area networks is toward higher communication bandwidth as we progress from Ethernet networks that operate at 10 Mbit/sec to higher speed networks such as Fiber Distributed Data Interface (FDDI) networks. Furthermore, it is expected that soon these networks will operate in Gigabit/sec range. However, the application-level transfer rates on existing local area networks remain much lower and it is doubtful that they can keep pace with medium speed. For example, out of the 10 Mbit/sec available at the medium of an Ethernet network, only around 1.2 Mbit/sec bandwidth is available for applications [10].

Consequently, it has been established that current clusters of workstations have the aggregate computing power to provide an environment for high performance distributed computing, while high speed networks, capable of supporting these computing rates, are becoming a standard (e.g., ATM, SONET, HUB-based LAN) [9]. It has also been established that it is not cost-effective to introduce new parallel architectures to deliver the increased computing power. Consequently, we envision that future computing environments need to capitalize on and effectively utilize the existing computing resources. The objective of the presented research is to develop an environment that can harness the computing potential of existing, cost-effective heterogeneous computers and high speed networks.

The organization of the paper is as follows: Section 2 describes an environment for parallel and distributed computing based on hardware and software support that utilizes efficiently the existing heterogeneous computers and the emerging high speed networks. Section 3 analyzes the performance of the communication protocol described in section 2. Section 4 summarizes the paper and provides some concluding remarks.

2 An Environment for Parallel and Distributed Computing

The main objective of the PDC environment is to provide parallel and distributed applications with message passing primitives as well as the host-network interface required to achieve efficient environment over the emerging Gigabit networks. The hardware portion of this environment consists of a host interface processor (HIP), a high speed network (HSNet) and a normal speed network (NSNet) as shown in Figure 1. The software portion of this environment consists of a high speed communication protocol (HCP) and a HCP runtime system. The HCP runtime system is an interface between a parallel and distributed programming tool and the HCP services running on an interface processor. In a distributed programming environment, software tools such as EXPRESS [5] or PVM [6] provide a communication library for message passing. The current implementations of these tools utilize low-level communication programming interfaces (e.g., BSD socket library) that are supported by a standard transport protocol (e.g., TCP/IP). Because these interfaces involve a large number of system calls, data copying and memory management, they can not provide the high-bandwidth and the low-latency communication needed for PDC. To solve the problems above, HCP provides all the services (data transfer, synchronization and control) needed for efficient parallel and distributed computing. Furthermore, these services run on the HIP processor and therefore offload the host. In what follows, we present hardware and software support to build such PDC environment.

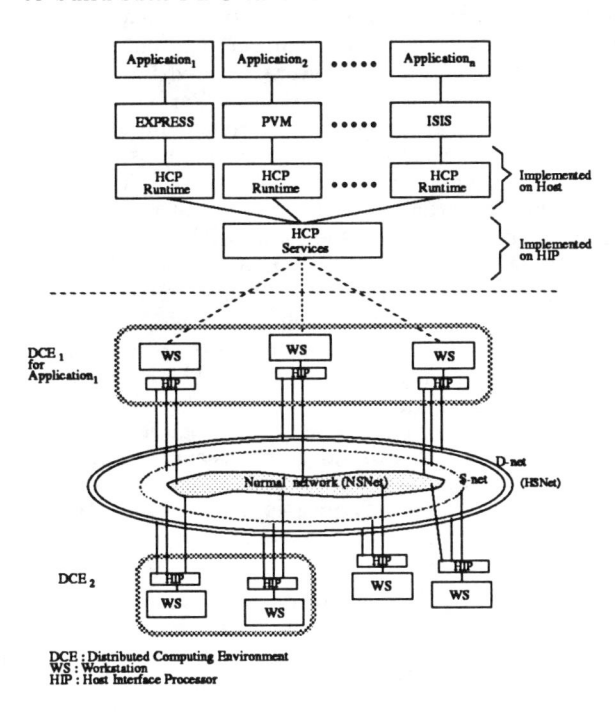

Figure 1: An environment for PDC

2.1 Architectural Support for PDC

A high speed local area network (HLAN) for PDC environment consists of two types of networks: High-Speed Network (HSNet) and the Normal Speed Network (NSNet). These two networks could be two physically separated networks or could be logical networks (e.g., in an ATM-based network, a large portion of the communication bandwidth is allocated to HSNet traffic). The network supports two modes of operation: Normal-Speed Mode (NSM) where a standard transport protocol is used to transmit and/or receive data over NSNet and High-Speed Mode (HSM) where processes communicate with each other through the HSNet to achieve low application transfer latency with effective transfer rates close to the medium transmision rate. The HSNet consists of two sub-networks: the Data network (D-net) and the Status network (S-net). The D-net could be a ring network with n bidirectional rings; each consists of two counter-rotating channels. While one ring is used for data transmission, the other ring is used for acknowledgments. The S-net is a token-ring based network. The purpose of the S-net is to distribute control and status information about the activities of computers connected to the D-net. The S-net can also be used to support some control and broadcasting capability that might be required to achieve parallel and distributed computing. The HLAN utilizes two types

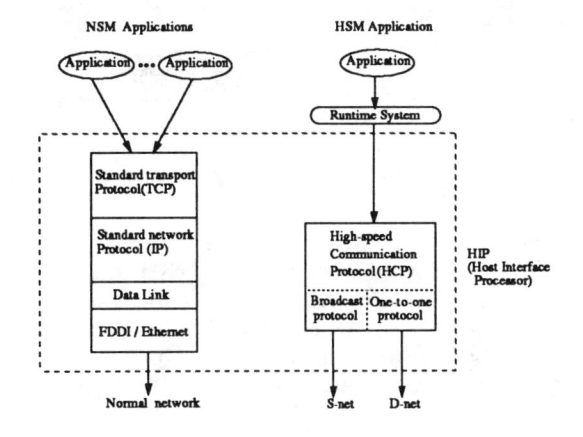

Figure 2: A configuration of protocol stack with HCP

of protocol stacks as shown in Figure 2. In this subsection, we present briefly an architecture of a host interface that provides the hardware support needed for efficient PDC.

HIP is a communication processor capable of operating in two modes of operation such that either or both of these modes can be active at a given time. In HSM, HIP provides applications with data rate close to that offered by the communication medium. This high speed transfer rate is achieved by (1) using simple communication protocol, HCP, to be discussed in the next subsection (2) decomposing the transmit/receive tasks into several subtasks that can run concurrently on a separate engine and (3) using point-to-point channels that allow all nodes to transmit and receive data concurrently when conflicts are not exist. In NSM, the standard transport protocols can run efficiently on HIP and thus off-load the host from running these protocols. Figure 3 shows a block diagram of the main functional units of the proposed HIP. The HIP design consists

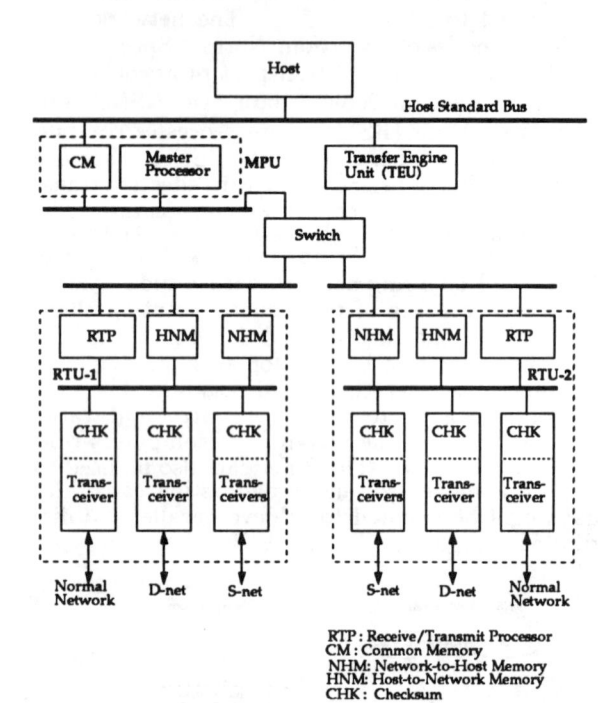

Figure 3: Blockdiagram of HIP

of five major subsystems: a Master Processing Unit (MPU), a Transfer Engine Unit (TEU), a crossbar switch, and two Receive/ Transmit units (RTU-1, RTU-2). The architecture of HIP is highly parallel and uses hardware multiplicity and pipeline techniques to achieve high-performance transfer rates. For example, the two RTUs can be configured to transmit and/or receive data over high-speed channels while the TEU is transferring data to/from the host. More details of HIP architecture can be found in [11].

2.2 Software Support for Parallel and Distributed Computing

In this subsection we develop a communication protocol that exploits the support of HIP and provides services needed in PDC. Most existing protocols were designed in the 1970's, when the available communication bandwidths were in the Kb/s range and the existing computing nodes had limited computing power. Since these protocols regarded the communication bandwidth as a scarce resource and the communication medium as inherently unreliable, they were designed to be very general to handle complex failure scenarios, which resulted in complicated protocols implemented as a stack of software layers. The last decade, however, has seen tremendous advances in computing and networking technology. Current networks are highly reliable and can supports high transmission speeds. Further, the computing power of processors has increased while their cost decreased significantly. Consequently, special purpose communication processors like HIP proposed in the previous section can be built to offload hosts from running communication protocols. Furthermore, many services required in parallel and distributed computing can be handled more efficiently by this special interface processor.

We present the design and the implementation of a high speed communication protocol (HCP) that could run on a communication processor such as the HIP. The approach followed in developing HCP is carried out in two steps: 1) analyze the message-passing primitives provided by existing software tools on current parallel and distributed systems; and 2) identify a maximal subset of message passing primitives that can be efficiently implemented by a communication protocol for parallel/distributed computing.

2.2.1 Characterization of Message Passing Primitives for PDC

In oder to identify the HCP services for PDC, we first study the primitives provided by some current parallel/distributed programming tools. The software tools studied include EXPRESS [5], PICL [3], PVM [6], ISIS [1], the iPSC communication library [4] and the CM5 communication library (CMMD) [7]. These tools were selected because of their availability at the Northeast Parallel Architecture Center at Syracuse University and also the following two reasons: (1) they support most potential computing environments, i.e., parallel, homogeneous and heterogeneous distributed systems; and (2) they are either portable tools (EXPRESS, PICL and PVM) or hardware dependent tools (CMMD and the iPSC communication library). There is an increased interest in the standardization of message-passing primitives supported by software tools for parallel/distributed computing [8]. The characterization provided in this section can be viewed as step in this direction. The communication primitives supported by existing libraries can be characterized into five classes, viz., point-to-point communication, group communication, synchronization, configuration/control/management, and exception handling.

Point-to-Point Communication The point-to-point communication is the basic message passing primitive for any parallel/distributed programming tools. To provide efficient point-to-point communication, most systems provide a set of function calls rather than the simplest *send* and *receive* primitives.

• **Synchronous and Asynchronous Send / Receive:** The choice between synchronous and asynchronous primitives depends on the nature and requirements of the application. As a result, most tools support both, asynchronous and synchronous send/receive primitives. To provide asynchronous message processing, additional supporting functionality must be provided in the tools.

For example, 1) poll/probe the arrival and/or information of incoming messages e.g., *extest*, *probe*, or *CMMD_msg_pending* used in EXPRESS, PVM, or CMMD, respectively; 2) install a user-specified handler for incoming messages e.g., *exhandle* or *hrecv* used in EXPRESS or iPSC, respectively; and 3) install a user-specified handler for outgoing messages e.g., *hsend* used in iPSC.

- **Synchronous/Asynchronous Data Exchange:** There are at least two advantages for providing such primitives. First, user is freed from having to decide which node should read first and which node should write first. Second, it allows optimizations to be made for both speed and reliability.

- **Non-contiguous or Vector Data:** One example of transferring a non-contiguous message is sending a row (or column) of a matrix that is stored in column-major (or row-major) order. For example, *exvsend/exvreceive* and *CMMD_send_v/CMMD_receive_v* used in EXPRESS and CMMD, respectively.

Group Communication Group communication for parallel or distributed computing can be further classified into three categories, *1-to-many*, *many-to-1*, and *many-to-many*, based on the number of senders and receivers.

- **1-to-Many Communication:** Broadcasting and multicasting are the most important examples of this category. Some systems do not explicitly use a separate *broadcast* or *multicast* function call. Instead, a wild card character used in the destination address field of point-to-point communication primitives, provides multicasting functions. It is important to note that in ISIS broadcast primitives with different types and order are available to users. Users can choose the proper broadcast primitives according to the applications.

- **Many-to-1 Communication:** In many-to-1 communication, one process collects the data distributed across several processes. Usually, such function is referred to as *reduction operation* and must be an associative, commutative function, such as, addition, multiplication, maximum, minimum, logical AND, logical OR, or logical XOR. For example, *g[op]0* and *g[type][op]* in PICL and iPSC, where *op* denotes a function and *type* denotes its data type.

- **Many-to-Many Communication:** There are several different types of many-to-many communications. The simplest example is the case where every process needs to receive the result produced by a reduction operation. The communication patterns of many-to-many operations could be regular or irregular. The regular cases are *scan* (e.g., CMMD's *CMMD_scan*), *concatenation* (e.g., EXPRESS's *exconcat*), *circular shift*, and *all-to-all broadcasting*, while the irregular cases are *gather* and *scatter* (e.g., CMMD's *CMMD_gather_from_nodes*) operation.

Synchronization A parallel / distributed program can be divided into several different computational phases. To prevent asynchronous message from different phases interfering with one another, it is important to synchronize all processes or a group of processes. Usually, a simple command without any parameters, such as, *exsync*, *sync0*, *gsync* in EXPRESS, PICL, and iPSC, can provide a transparent mechanism to synchronize all the processes. But, there are several options that can be adopted to synchronize a group of processes. In PVM, *barrier*, which requires two parameters *barrier_name* and *num*, blocks caller until a certain number of calls with the same barrier name made. In PICL, *barrier0* synchronizes the node processors currently in use. In iPSC, *waitall* and *waitone* allow the caller to wait for specified processes to complete.

Another type of synchronization is that one process is blocked until a specified event occurred. In PVM, *ready* and *waituntil* provide event synchronization by passing the signal. In ISIS, the order of events is used to define *virtual synchrony* and a set of token tools (e.g., *t_sig*, *t_wait*, *t_holder*, *t_pass*, *t_request*, etc.) are available to handle it. Actually, event detection is a very powerful mechanism for exception handling, debugging, as well as performance measurement.

Configuration, Control, and Management The tasks of configuration, control, and management is quite different from system to system. A subset of the configuration, control and management primitives supported by the studied software tools are such as to allocate and deallocate one processor or a group of processors, to load, start, terminate, or abort programs, and for dynamic reconfiguration, process concurrent or asynchronous file I/O, nad query the status of environment.

Exception Handling In a parallel or distributed environments, it is important that the network, hardware and software failures must be reported to the user's application or system kernel in order to start a special procedure to handle the failures. In traditional operating systems such as UNIX, exception handling is processed by event-based approach, where a signal is used to notify a process that an event has occurred and after that a signal handler is invoked to take care of the event. Basically, an event could be a hardware condition (e.g., bus error) or software condition (e.g., arithmetic exception). For example, in the iPSC library, a user can attach a user-specified routine to respond to a hardware exception by the *handler* primitive. In ISIS, a set of *monitor* and *watch* tools are available to users. EXPRESS supports tools for debugging and performance evaluation. PICL supports tools for event tracing.

2.2.2 HCP Message-Passing Primitives

Based on the characterization of message-passing techniques used in parallel/distributed computing

	EXPRESS	PICL	PVM	ISIS	iPSC Library	CM5 Library CMMD
Point-to-point Communication	exread/exwrite exsend/exreceive extest exhandle exchange exvsend/exvreceive	send0/recv0 message0 recvinfo0 probe0	snd/rcv vsnd/vrcv rcvinfo rcvmulti probe probemulti	[x]bcast[2] [x]bcast_1[2] reply reply_1	csend/crecv isend/irecv hsend/hrecv csendrecv isendrecv	CMMD_send/CMMD_receive CMMD_msg_pending CMMD_swap CMMD_send_and_receive CMMD_send_v CMMD_receive_v
Group Communication	exbroadcast excombine exconcat	bcast0 g[op]0 [1]			g[type][op] [3] gopf gcol	CMMD_distrib_to_nodes CMMD_receive_bc_from_host CMMD_reduce_<type> CMMD_scan_<type> CMMD_concat_with_nodes CMMD_gather_from_nodes
Synchronization	exsync exsem	sync0 barrier0	barrier ready waituntil	token tool	waitall waitone gsync	CMMD_barrier_sync CMMD_sync_with_nodes CMMD_sync_host_with_nodes CMMD_sync_with_host
Configuration Control Management	exopen/exclose fmulti/fsingle/fasync exgrid exparam exload exstart abort	open0 close0 load0 setarc0/getarc0	initiate leave pstatus terminate	isis_init isis_remote isis_entry isis_rexec msg_read/msg_write	getcube relcube load cread/cwrite iread/iwrite	CMMD_enable CMMD_disable CMMD_suspend CMMD_resume
Exception Handling	(not address)	(not address)	pvm_perror	monitor tool watch tool	handler	(not address)

[1] For PICL, op={max, min, sum, prod, comb, and, or, xor}.
[2] For ISIS, x = {a, c, f, g, m} is the type of broadcast.
[3] For iPSC, type = {d(double), i(integer), s(real)}, op = { high, low, sum, prod, and, or, xor}.

Table 1: A Characterization of message-passing primitives for parallel / distributed computing

primitive	Description
Data transfer	
1-1 communication • hcp_Send • hcp_Recv • hcp_Exch Group Communication • hcp_MCast/BCast	point-to-point send primitive point-to-point receive primitive primitive for exchanging data between nodes multicasting (broadcasting) for one-to-many(all) data transfer
Synchronization	
• hcp_Lock • hcp_Barrier	primitive to logically lock a resourec so that mutual exclusion is ensured within a single DCE barrier synchronization routine to allow a specified number of hosts to synchronize on a specified barrier name
System Management	
• hcp_Probe • hcp_MsgStat • hcp_NetStat • hcp_HostStat • hcp_Config • hcp_AddHost • hcp_DeleteHost	primitive to query the arrival of messages for a particular host message arrivals can be queried by message type, message source or by wildcards return the status of a transmitted message to the source node return the current status of the network return the current configuration and status of the hosts allocate the requested number of nodes and configure them as a logical group add a host to a logical group delete a host from a logical group
Error Handling	
• hcp_Signal • hcp_Log/ChkPt	sends a high priority message to the hosts to communicate error status sends a signal to all hosts of a logical group to allow them to save predefined check-pointing data

Table 2: Primitives Supported by HCP

presented in Table 1, we identify the set of primitives (shown in Table 2) which can efficiently implement the primitives supported by most software tools for parallel and distributed computing. The services can be broadly classified as data transfer services, synchronization services, system management/ configuration services and error handling services. Data transfer services include point-to-point services for sending, receiving and exchanging messages and group communication services for broadcasting and multicasting data(*hcp_Send, hcp_Recv, hcp_Exch, hcp_Mcast/Bcast*). Synchronization services allow a processor to lock resources so that no other processor can access them(*hcp_lock, hcp_Barrier*). This service enables mutually exclude access of resources shared between processors. The *hcp_Barrier* primitive enables a specified number of processor to synchronize at a logical barrier before proceeding. System management/ configuration services(*hcp_ Probe, hcp_MsgStat, ...*) include calls to monitor sent and arriving messages, the current status of the network and hosts and to configure the hosts into logical groups and for adding/ deleting hosts from/to these logical groups. Special error handling services include the *hcp_Signal* primitive which sends a high priority message to all hosts to propagate any error status and the *hcp_Log/ChkPt* primitive to enable checkpointing and logging of previously specified data for debugging purposes. When the *hcp_Log/ChkPt* signal is sent, all processors dump this data into a log file and proceed with their computation. In what follows, we describe how some of the services shown in Table 2 are implemented in HCP.

2.3 HCP Implementation Issues

• **Operation Modes:** Each node participating in a computation over the D-net is in one of the following modes during its operation: Idle (ID), Receive-only (RO), Transmit-only (TO), Receive and transmit (RT), Receive-and-Receive (RR), Transmit-and-Transmit (TT) or Bypass (BP) mode. Initial mode is ID. In BP mode, a node is just isolated from the network and all the incoming data is forwarded to the next node with minimum delay.

• **Routing Policy:** If a node has data to transmit, it has to determine first which path of the D-net to use; for example, in ring-based HSNet, there are two paths to reach any destination node. The routing policy selects the available path that minimizes the number of hops between the source and destination nodes. The other channel segments from the destination to the source with opposite direction is automatically assigned for sending acknowledgment frames.

• **Long Message Transfer:** We distinguish between two transfer schemes depending on the message size: long message transfer and short message transfer. A message with length of less than a data frame size is designated as a short message and otherwise it is regarded as a long one. Each long message is transferred as a sequence of data frames.

The size of a data frame is determined as large as possible because larger frames perform better as will be shown later. However, the maximum frame size should be within the limit where clock skewing does not lead to a synchronization problem at the receiver. For long messages, data transmission is performed in two phases: connection establishment and data transfer. A connection request (CR) frame is sent first to the destination node. Once the connection is established successfully, all intermediate nodes are set to BP mode. After receiving a connection confirm (CC) signal from the destination node, the source node sends data, and finally the acknowledgment of the last frame releases the circuit connection. Figure 4 shows all the steps involved in long message transfer; establishing a connection, receiving a confirmation of a successful connection, transferring the data frames, and then disconnect the connection, respectively. In this figure, node 0 is set to mode TO and communicates with node 3 that is set to mode RO. The intermediate nodes are set to BP modes while all other nodes are in the idle mode.

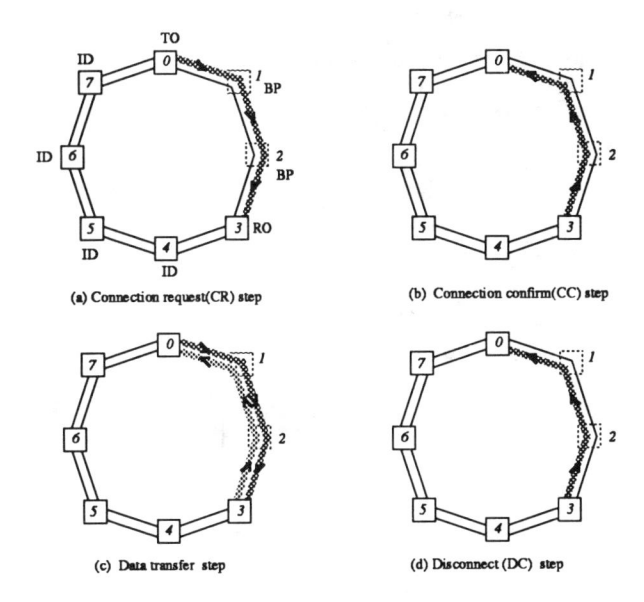

Figure 4: Steps of long message transfer

• **Error and Flow Control:** Sender transmits a frame and then waits for ACK signal from the receiver. When the sender receives a positive ACK (PACK), it sends the next frame; otherwise it retransmits the same frame. Retransmission is repeated a predefined number of times and after that an error signal is raised to the higher layers. The acknowledgment frame serves as a mechanism to achieve flow control between the transmitter and receiver nodes. When the receiver does not have enough buffer space for next frame, it responds with a not-ready indication by setting a flag in ACK frame. If the source receives the not-ready indication from the destination, it stops transmitting frame until it receives ready indication. This simple scheme is attractive because it does not impose any limit on the transmission rates that could be in Gigabit or even Terabit range. However, it is doubtful that the current error and flow control methods used in existing standard protocols can cope with such high transmission rates.

• **Frame Formats:** In Figure 5, we show four types of frames which are used in the D-net during HSM: CR frame with short data, CR frame with long data, Data frame, and ACK frame. The preamble field (PA) is used to achieve synchronization between the receiver and the sender. The delimiter fields (SD and ED) denote the start and the end of a frame, respectively. The type field is used to distinguish between the different kinds of frames. The Source (SRC) and Destination (DST) fields in CR frame indicate the network address of source and destination nodes. The length and frame size fields denote the number of bytes to be transmitted, and the frame size in bytes, respectively. The number of frames to be received is $n_f = \lceil$ length/ frame size$\rceil$. The status field in ACK frame distinguishes acknowledgments of connection confirm (CC) and disconnect (DC) as well as positive (PACK) and negative (NACK) acknowledgment of data frames. The RDY field in ACK frame denotes the readiness of the receiver to receive data frames. The checksum field (CHK) uses a cyclic redundancy code to detect errors in received frames.

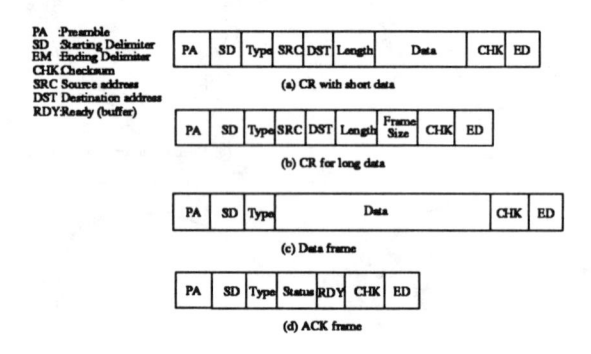

Figure 5: Frame formats for D-net

3 Performance Analysis

In this section, we analyze the application-to-application latency in HLAN and estimate its effective transfer rates for different message sizes. We illustrate in Figure 6 the sequence of events from the moment an application process initiates a request to send a message to the time when the data sent is received in the host buffer of the receiving application.

The application program at the sender side calls the runtime library to send a message. Once the parameter checking is done by a library routine (C), another routine writes a send request in the Common Memory of HIP (N_1) and then interrupts the Master Processor. The send request includes the address of the destination node and a pointer to the message and its size. The Master Processing Unit

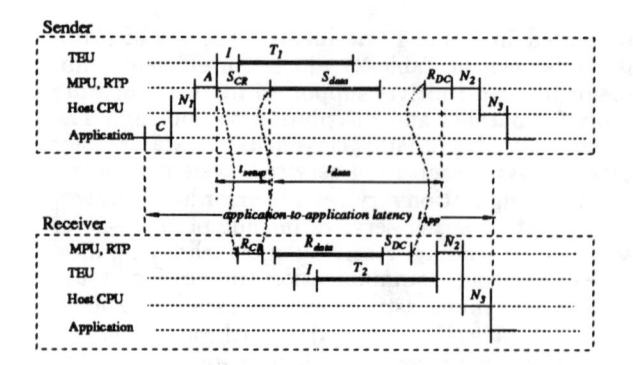

Figure 6: Application-to-application latency

(MPU) selects one of the Receive-Transmit Processor (RTP) to handle the transfer (A). After the Transfer Engine Unit (TEU) is initialized (I) and has started transferring data from the host memory to the buffer (T_1), the RTP sends the Connection Request to the destination node (S_{CR}). On receiving the Connection Confirm, the RTP sends the message data (S_{data}) stored in HNM. The host is notified when the data transfer is complete (N_2). The host then notifies the application (N_3).

At the receiver side, while frames are being received and stored in the (NHM) buffer (R_{data}), the TEU transfers data NHM buffer to the host memory (T_2). When the last frame is received, the RTP sends the disconnect (CC) frame to the sender (S_{DC}). The process R_0 then notifies the host of the message arrival by writing in Common Memory and interrupting the host processor (N_2), which in turns notifies the application (N_3).

The application-to-application latency is indicated in Figure 6 as the time elapsed between the events C and N_3 at the sender and the receiver, respectively. Due to the concurrent operations of the TEU and RTP in the sender such that data transfer from host memory to HIP buffer (T_1) is overlapped with that from the HIP buffer to the network (S_{data}), the latency is minimized. Similarly, the receiving time is also minimized due to the parallel operations of R_{data} and T_2 at the receiver side.

Having analyzed the latency, we consider the transfer rates of long messages. We assume the D-net is lightly-loaded so that no waiting time is consumed at the intermediate nodes when the connection is being established between the source and the destination nodes. The connection establishment will be successful most of the time and the CR frame will not be blocked at intermediate nodes because the CR frame will not be issued unless the required path is available.

We define the application-level data transfer rate $\mathcal{R}$ as the ratio of the data length to be transmitted (l_M) to the total application-to-application transmission time (t_{App}).

$$\mathcal{R} = \frac{l_M}{t_{App}} \quad (1)$$

Based on the discussion in [11], $\mathcal{R}$ can be computed as follows.

$$\mathcal{R} = \frac{l_M}{t_C + t_{N_1} + t_A + t_{setup} + t_{data} + t_{N_2} + t_{N_3}} \quad (2)$$

where t_{setup} denotes the connection setup time, t_{data} represents the time for data transmission and other terms are for the events described earlier.

In Figure 7 and 8, we plot the effective application transmission rate with respect to different message and frame sizes. We consider two channel speeds: 100 Mbit/sec and 1 Gbit/sec. In this analysis we assume the following values for frame fields: 25 byte CR frame, 15 byte length of overhead fields in a data frame, and 15 byte of the ACK frame. Also, we assume that the number of intermediate nodes is 5, the probability of a bit error is 2.5×10^{-10}, the propagation delay between source and destination is $= 0.5$ μsec for average distance of 100 m. Furthermore, we assume each of the following events: $t_C, t_{N_1}, t_{N_2}, t_{N_3}, t_A$ needs around 10 instructions to be processed; i.e. each event can be processed in 1μsec when the performance of HIP processor is 10 MIPS.

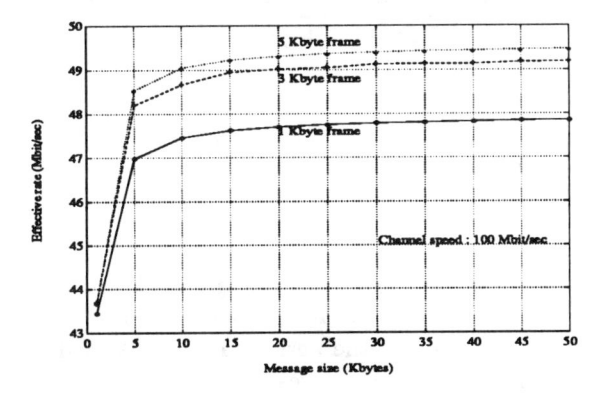

Figure 7: Application-level transfer rate with 100 Mbit/sec channel

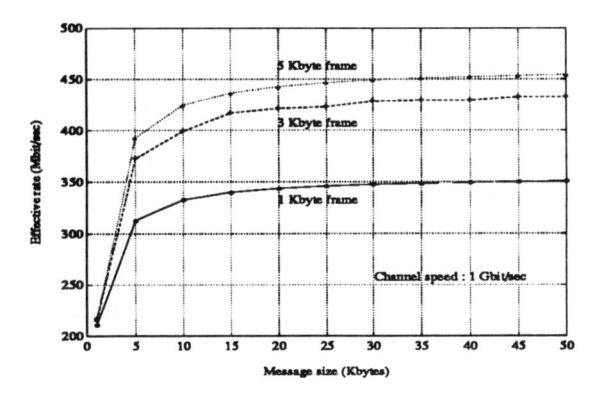

Figure 8: Application-level transfer rate with 1 Gbit/sec channel

4 Conclusion

In this paper, we analyzed the current advances in computing technology, network technology, and software tools for developing parallel and distributed computing applications. We analyzed the primitives, supported by existing parallel and distributed software tools and characterize them into five categories; viz., *point-to-point communication, group communication, synchronization, configuration / control / management*, and *exception handling*. We proposed an environment that capitalizes on the current advances in processing and networking technology and software tools to provide cost-effective parallel and distributed computing. We also presented the design of a communication processor (HIP) that alleviates the host-interface bottleneck and a high speed communication protocol (HCP) that provides the needed bandwidth and services for PDC applications.

References

[1] K. Birman, R. Cooper, T. Joseph, K. Kane, and F. Schmuck. *The ISIS System Manual*.

[2] IBM European Center for Scientific and Engineering Computing. Usenet news item, 1992.

[3] G. A. Geist, M. T. Heath, B. W. Peyton, and P. H. Worley. A user's guide to picl, a portable intrumented communication library. Technical Report Tech. Rep. ORNL/TM-11616, Oak Ridge National Laboratory, Oak Ridge, Tennessee 37831, Oct 1991.

[4] Oregon Intel Supercomputer System Devision, Beaverton. ipsc/2 and ipsc/860 user's guide. 1991.

[5] Parasoft Corporation. *Express Reference Manual*, 1988.

[6] V. S. Sunderam. Pvm: A framework for parallel distributed computing. Technical report, Oak Ridge National Laboratory, Oak Ridge, Tennessee 37831, 1991.

[7] Massachusetts Thinking Machines Corporation, Cambridge. Cmmd reference manual, version 1.1. 1992.

[8] David W. Walker. Standards for message-passing in a distributed memory environment. *ORNL/TM-12147*, Aug 1992.

[9] H. T. Kung, " Gigabit Local Area Networks: A Systems Perspective," *IEEE Communications Magazine*, pp. 79-89, April 1992.

[10] G. Chesson, " The Protocol Engine Project," *Proceedings of the Summer 1987 USENIX Conference*, pp. 209-215, June 1987.

[11] J.B. Park and S. Hariri, "Architectural Support for a High-Performance Distributed System," *Proceedings of the 12th Annual IEEE International Phoenix Conference on Computers and Communications'93 (IPCCC-93)*, pp. 319 –325, March 1993.

DSMA: A Fair Capacity–1 Protocol for Gigabit Ring Networks

W. Dobosiewicz and P. Gburzynski
Department of Computing Science
University of Alberta
Edmonton, Alberta, Canada, T6G 2H1

Abstract

We present a simple MAC-level protocol for high-speed ring networks. The protocol is fair and its maximum achievable throughput does not deteriorate with the increasing propagation length of the ring. The proposed protocol operates on the so-called "spiral ring" topology, including the single-segment regular ring as a special case. It accommodates synchronous traffic automatically, without any bandwidth preallocation or similar special efforts, yet with an arbitrarily low jitter and without packet loss.

1 Introduction: The Spiral Ring

The **spiral ring** is a fibre-optic cable looping in the form of a spiral. The ends of the spiral are connected and the fibre constitutes a closed, multiple, unidirectional loop which visits each station a number of times. The number of segments in the spiral is a configuration parameter. The protocol discussed in this paper can operate on a single-loop spiral retaining most of its advantageous properties. A two-loop spiral with a different MAC protocol was presented in [2]. Figure 1 shows the layout of a 5–loop spiral. Only one station is shown for clarity: all the other stations have identical connections.

Every station has a transmitter port and a receiver port connected to each loop of the spiral. A station should expect packets addressed to it on every receiver port; therefore, the number of receivers per stations must be equal to the number of loops. The number of transmitters is flexible. We found it best to have only one transmitter per station. This transmitter is switched among the multiple transmitter ports. With this approach, a single station can transmit only one packet at a time (although it can receive multiple packets simultaneously).

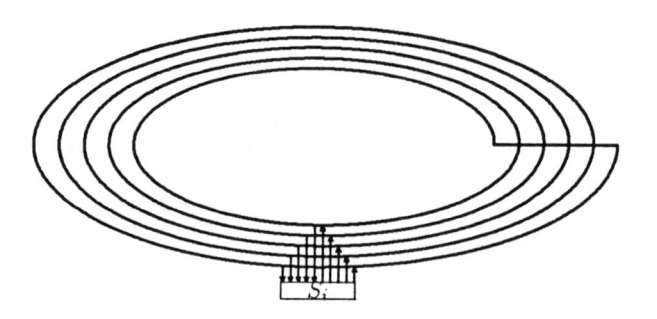

Figure 1: The spiral ring.

Our proposed protocol (dubbed DSMA—for *Distributed Spiral Multiple Access*) can be viewed as a refinement of FDDI [4] towards very high transmission rates. Unlike in FDDI, the performance of DSMA does not deteriorate with the increasing ratio of the channel length (expressed in bits) to the packet length.[1] Moreover, in contrast to FDDI, DSMA incurs zero access delay when traffic is low.

The stations' ports are constructed in such a way that they introduce a constant[2] delay, whether they operate in bypass mode or in regular mode. Consequently, the latency between two adjacent ports of a station is fixed: let it be denoted by L. Each port of every station is capable of operating independently, possibly in parallel with other ports of the same station.

DSMA can occur in three versions: slotted, semi-slotted, and unslotted. The semi-slotted version is an interesting compromise between the other two extreme versions: no explicit slot markers are inserted into the ring, but the packet length is fixed. In this paper we

---
[1] Protocols with this property are called *capacity-1* protocols.
[2] Constant in principle, but allowed to vary with some small and known tolerance.

discuss the semi-slotted and slotted versions of DSMA. In the semi-slotted version, we assume the same packet format as in FDDI, except, of course, that its length is fixed. The slot format in the slotted version has been borrowed from DQDB [3].

2 DSMA

We start from presenting the semi-slotted version of DSMA.

At any given time, one port of each station is logically differentiated from all the others: we will call it the "yellow" port while all the other ports are "green." The "colour" of each location changes dynamically.

A token-passing mechanism is used to single out the station that disconnects the spiral and the port in which the ring is disconnected. A token packet travels along the spiral. When it reaches a port, the station that owns that port grabs the token and holds it for a prescribed amount of time. While holding the token, the station disconnects the spiral at the port where the token was captured. When a station releases the token, it labels the port that held it as "yellow"; all the other ports are labelled "green."

A station i must hold the token for an amount of time equal to the value of THT_i, a constant associated with the station.[3]

2.1 Timing

Unlike in FDDI, stations do not release the token early if they have no packets to transmit; they must hold it for the whole amount of time assigned to them. Thus, the time that elapses between two consecutive token captures by the same station is constant and the same for all stations.[4] Paraphrasing the terminology of FDDI, we will denote this time by TTRT which, in our case, stands for *Total Token Rotation Time*. The value of TTRT is given by the formula:

$$TTRT = L + \sum_{i=1}^{n} THT_i + \varepsilon$$

L is the propagation length of one loop of the ring. The role of ε is to compensate for the variability of repeater delays. Thus, TTRT represents a slightly inflated upper bound on the actual value of the token rotation time.

---

[3] Priorities may be implemented by assigning different values of THT to different stations.

[4] Note that this property of DSMA greatly simplifies the procedure for lost token recovery.

Each station is equipped with a timer called the *Token Rotation Timer* (TRT) which counts the time elapsed since the moment the station last acquired the token. Whenever a station acquires the token, it resets this timer to 0. As TTRT is slightly pessimistic, the token arrives at a station a moment before its TRT timer equals TTRT; however, this difference is small and no phenomenon similar to the *early token* in FDDI can occur.

2.2 Transmission rules

1. Stations willing to transmit constantly check for silence in their ports. Possession of the token is not relevant.

2. Whenever a station willing to transmit a packet senses a period of silence in a "green" port, it starts transmitting, first the preamble, then the packet itself.

3. Whenever a station willing to transmit senses some activity in all its "green" ports, but senses silence in its "yellow" port, it checks whether the condition TRT>TTRT − L holds; if it does, the station starts transmitting from its "yellow" port; otherwise, it resumes checking at step 1.

4. When a transmitting station senses the arrival of another packet frame, sent by an upstream station (a collision), it immediately stops transmitting and resumes the checking loop in step 1.

5. Having completed a successful packet transmission, the station immediately resumes the checking loop 1.

Each packet is preceded by a preamble which absorbs a collision. The preamble should be long enough to fulfill its purpose (synchronising the receiver's clock to the incoming packet) despite the fact that some initial part of it may be destroyed.[5] The preamble can be disturbed at most once: it never triggers more than one collision.

The rules for packet removal are similar to FDDI:

- The station holding the token removes from the network all the traffic reaching the port where the token was captured.

- Every station is responsible for removing the packets that it created.

---

[5] The preamble in FDDI includes superfluous bits.

- The token is removed by the first station that sees it. This station is responsible for inserting the token back into the network.

Packets are removed entirely, including the preamble. To do so, each station records the time τ when it started a successful transmission of a packet and starts expecting the arrival of this packet at its next port at time $\tau + L - f/2$, where f is the length of a packet frame, preamble included. Starting at this moment, when the port senses a period of silence followed by the beginning of some activity, it removes that activity. Removal is also triggered by sensing an unfinished packet frame (i.e., the result of a collision). A removed packet leaves a period of silence of length at least f, which can be reused to send another packet, as stated by the rules for transmission. The token is absorbed by the station in the same way, i.e., it is removed entirely. Timing is based on the value of the TRT clock.

The protocol permits stations to transmit from their "yellow" ports, if a specific condition holds. This condition guarantees that the packet will make at least one full circle through the ring before being absorbed by a token-holding station.

2.3 Synchronous and isochronous traffic

DSMA does not explicitly differentiate between synchronous and asynchronous traffic. With each turn of the token, every station gets a guaranteed share of the bandwidth at fixed time intervals, which it can use as it pleases. Likewise, when a station absorbs its own packet, it can reuse the packet's frame with a guaranteed success.

Essentially, there exist three possible transmission strategies as far as synchronous traffic is concerned:

Transmit only during token possession. This strategy offers the lowest possible jitter (bounded by ε) and should be used if low jitter is the primary concern. Each station S_i has a guaranteed synchronous (isochronous) bandwidth equal to THT_i/TTRT. Bandwidth guaranteed for synchronous traffic, but unused, may be used freely for transmitting other packets. Because no packet reuse takes place for synchronous traffic, the maximum synchronous throughput is limited to:

$$\left(1 - \frac{\text{L}}{\text{TTRT}}\right) \times \frac{p}{p+h+\delta}$$

where h and δ represent the length of the packet header and preamble, and p is the length of the packet payload.

Transmit at all opportunities. A higher *maximum* bandwidth for synchronous traffic may be obtained by allowing the transmission of synchronous packets from every port—at the expense of a non-zero jitter. There still will be no packet loss if the synchronous load in station S_i does not exceed the value of $\mathcal{K} \times \text{THT}_i/(\text{TTRT}-\text{L})$. With this strategy, synchronous traffic is given priority over asynchronous traffic, but treated in the same way in all other respects.

Token possession and frame reuse. This strategy is a compromise between the other two. Synchronous transmissions are allowed during token possession and at predictable transmission windows by stations reusing their own frames. Note that if a station transmits m frames at time t from a green port, it is guaranteed to get a transmission window of m frames at time $t + L$. It can be shown, that if the sum of the token holding times at stations is a divisor of $\mathcal{K} \times L$, these transmission windows are not only predictable, but they also occur at highly regular intervals.

The last approach seems to be particularly well suited for synchronous traffic organised into sessions of more or less constant intensity. A station willing to sustain the regularity of its transmission windows should make sure that it reuses all its frames.

2.4 Optimal packet frame length

The idea of fixing the frame length in DSMA stems from the fact that a substantial portion of the achieved network bandwidth comes from frame reuse. With fixed frames, a station reusing a stripped frame will always succeed in placing a new packet frame.

The fixed-length frames should not be too long, as, the longer the packet, the greater the chance that a "spontaneous" transmission will collide with an upstream transmission and be wasted. Moreover, shorter packets decrease the average amount of padding needed for each message. On the other hand, shorter packets imply more preambles and headers needed for each message, thus taking away part of the total bandwidth.

The optimal packet length is impossible to determine, as the impact of collisions varies with traffic pattern and intensity. Assuming saturated traffic, the following formula gives the part of the bandwidth wasted due to fixed-length packet frames:

$$\sum_{m=1}^{\infty} \Phi(m) \times \left(1 - \frac{m}{\lceil \frac{m}{p} \rceil \times (p+h+\delta)}\right)$$

μ	Packet length	Wasted bandwidth due to headers	stuffing
512	429	0.52214	0.09817
1024	589	0.38030	0.14999
2048	797	0.28105	0.16188
4096	1070	0.20934	0.15294
8192	1429	0.15675	0.13395
16384	1905	0.11785	0.11153

Table 1: Optimal packet frame length.

where Φ is the density function of message length distribution, p, h, and δ are the lengths of the payload part, the header, and the preamble of the packet frame, respectively. In the FDDI packet format we have $h = 160$ bits and $\delta = 64$ bits. If message lengths are assumed to be exponentially distributed with a mean of μ, Table 1 gives the optimal packet frame length for selected values of μ.

2.5 The slotted version

The fixed-length frames in DSMA can be replaced with explicit slots. With this approach, the station holding the token is responsible for inserting slots into the network—on the output port of the disconnected loop segment. No packet preambles are necessary and collisions do not occur. The full/empty status of a slot is indicated by a special (*full*) bit in the slot header. A station willing to transmit a packet (assuming the terminology of DQDB, we would call it a segment) awaits the first slot with the *full* bit cleared. Then the station sets the *full* bit *on the fly* (similarly as in DQDB) and inserts the segment into the payload part of the slot. Note that the station holding the token is also the first station to "see" the new slots inserted into the network. Thus is has a temporary priority in using the slots over all the other stations.

All the time intervals used by the protocol, i.e., TTRT, TRT, and THT are expressed in slots. This way the task of measuring time is greatly simplified. One can even argue that the explicit token becomes now unnecessary. Indeed, following the network initialisation phase, each station can learn when it gets the token by simply counting slots that are passing by. A natural way to implement the token is to use a reserved bit in the slot header. Thus, the total number of special bits in the segment header required by the protocol is two.

3 Simulated environment

The performance of DSMA was investigated by simulation and compared to the performance of FDDI and METARING. The networks and their protocols were modeled in SMURPH [5, 6]. Typically, each point in a performance curve was produced as an average of four independent experiments. The number of messages transmitted in one experiment depended on several criteria aimed at ensuring the stability of the results. The network would start from an idle state, and the observed message delay was monitored after every reception of 40,000 messages. When this delay ceased to grow (meaning that the network has reached an equilibrium state), the experiment was continued for a further 300,000–1,000,000 messages, depending on the propagation length of the spiral. During this phase the proper measurements were taken.

3.1 Network geometry

The results presented here have been obtained for spirals with 1, 3, and 5 loops. A one-loop spiral, the simplest possible spiral network, is an important special case for DSMA. The protocol offers zero access delay under light load with any number of loops greater than one, but not in the single-loop network (all ports are always "yellow").

The results for the other two cases (3 and 5 spirals), and also for other configurations not discussed here, demonstrate that when the number of loops is bigger than one, the protocol behaviour is practically independent of this number, if the observed throughput is scaled properly, i.e., multiplied by the number of loop segments.

Three lengths of a ring (one loop segment) were considered: 10^5 bits, 10^6 bits, and 10^7 bits. In all networks, the number of stations was 32. Therefore, the increasing propagation length of the ring corresponds to the increasing transmission rate rather than the geographical area covered by the network. Assuming a 200 km ring, the three propagation lengths represent transmission rates of 100Mb/s, 1Gb/s, and 10Gb/s. The 32 stations were equally spaced along the spiral.

3.2 Packet format

In the semi-slotted version of DSMA, the packet format of FDDI was assumed. With this format, each packet frame is preceded by a 64-bit preamble followed by a 112-bit header.[6] Two (fixed) payload lengths

---

[6] We are not concerned here with the details of turning bits into optical signals. Transmission rates, timing, and distances

were used in the experiments, namely 8192 and 1056 bits. In the FDDI networks used for comparison, the packet length was variable with the maximum of 36000 bits. In the unslotted version of METARING, we also assumed the packet format of FDDI—to make the comparison meaningful.

In the slotted protocols, the slot format of DQDB was assumed. The slot in DQDB consists of an 8-bit header (containing the control bits), 32-bit address field, and the 384-bit payload part. Similarly as in the simplest version of DQDB, two bits from the 8-bit header are used by DSMA: one to indicate the full/empty status of the slot, the other to pass the token.

3.3 Traffic patterns

Except for one experiment (figure 11), the traffic pattern was uniform with the likelihood of every pair *sender, receiver* being the same. For the semi-slotted version (compared with FDDI and unslotted METARING), the message length was either fixed at 8192 bits or exponentially distributed with the mean of 4096 bits. In the first case, the packet payload length for DSMA matched exactly the fixed message length. The goal of these experiments was to determine the maximum throughput achieved by the network under advantageous, although perhaps somewhat unrealistic, conditions. In the second case, the packet payload length in DSMA was set to 1056 bits which is close to the optimal fixed packet length from Table 1.

For the slotted protocols, the message length was fixed and assumed to match exactly the payload length of the segment (384 bits). Thus, the results obtained for these protocols do not account for fragmentation from splitting a message into multiple slots.

A simple model of packetised voice traffic was used to investigate the network behaviour under synchronous load. These experiments were carried out for the slotted version of DSMA. In the synchronous traffic model, we assumed two-segment voice messages, produced every 10 ms. The traffic was organised into multiple streams (each stream involving one sender and one receiver) randomly assigned to stations. The traffic intensity was adjusted by changing the number of streams.

3.4 Token holding time

The protocol is parametrised by THT—the token holding time definable individually for each station. In our experiments, THT was the same for all stations.

---
are all expressed in bits.

The smallest value of THT (the *unit* of THT allocation) allowed each station to transmit one complete maximum length packet together with the preamble. For the slotted variant of DSMA, the smallest (and also recommended) token holding time is clearly one slot. For the semi-slotted version, the minimum value of THT was arrived at by considering the frame size. For example, with the fixed packet length of 8192 bits, the unit of THT was set to 8424 bits. This value is the sum of the following components: the packet payload length (8192 bits), the length of the packet preamble (64 bits), the length of the packet frame information (160 bits), and 8 bits of safety margin. Similarly, with the packet length of 1056 bits, the unit of THT was $1056 + 64 + 160 + 8 = 1288$ bits.

When comparing FDDI with DSMA, the value of TTRT for FDDI was obtained as $L + \text{THT} \times N$, where N was the number of stations (32), L was the propagation length of the ring, and THT was the holding time per station for DSMA.

In METARING, there is an analogue of THT, called k [1]. This parameter is used to prevent starvation. We assume that one *unit* of THT in FDDI or DSMA corresponds to one increment in the value of k.

3.5 Performance measures

The performance of the protocols discussed here is compared by relating their throughput-versus-delay graphs. Throughput tells the number of useful bits received by all stations within a time unit. Time is measured in bits; thus, throughput is normalised w.r.t. time. It is also normalised w.r.t. the number of loop segments, i.e., divided by this number.

Throughput presented in the figures is actually the *effective throughput*, i.e., preambles, packet headers and trailers do not count to the bits passed through the network. If we account for this difference, the maximum throughput achieved by a $\mathcal{K}$-segment network is $\mathcal{K}$, irrespective of the order of magnitude of the propagation length of the ring. The maximum throughput depends on the sum of the token holding times at all stations and the value of L: when the latter is a multiple of the former, the network can operate at full capacity; otherwise, a portion of the bandwidth is lost (limited from above by 0.5). To achieve its maximum throughput, the spiral ring must be tuned, i.e., its length adjusted, possibly by inserting a short fibre loop into the ring. In the figures below, non-optimal values of L were used, so the maximum throughput shown there for DSMA is less than 1.

The delay measure is the so-called *message access delay* understood as the amount of time (expressed in bits) elapsing since a message is queued for transmission, until the message has been completely transmitted by the sender. It includes all the waiting time at the sender, but excludes the propagation time. This approach seems reasonable for comparing networks with different propagation lengths.

4 Comparison

In all the figures below, the throughput of multi-loop (spirals) and multiring networks (METARING[7]) was normalised, i.e., divided by the number of loops.

Figures 2 and 3 illustrate the performance of unslotted DSMA for a 100Kb ring and compare it to the performance of FDDI. The 3 and 5 segment versions of DSMA incur no access delay under light traffic (as transmission time is included in the access delay).

For a short ring, DSMA performs slightly better than FDDI. The difference becomes visible for longer rings. Figures 4 and 5 show the performance of DSMA for a 1Mb ring. These figures also include curves for METARING. Although in principle METARING is a capacity-1 protocol, it trades this property for fairness or, for longer rings, exhibits a behaviour similar to FDDI.[8]

For a very long ring, both FDDI and METARING are outclassed by DSMA (figure 6). The maximum throughput achieved by FDDI and METARING can be pushed by increasing the value of THT (TTRT, k), but this approach has obvious negative implications. In FDDI, it increases the token rotation time and further worsens the network response time. Moreover, stations must have sufficiently many backlogged messages to take advantage of the increased holding time. In METARING, increasing k introduces a potential for starvation and increases jitter for synchronous traffic.

Figure 7 illustrates the behaviour of the same 10Mb networks with the same protocols and traffic pattern as in figure 6, but with THT (k) increased to 4 units. Although the other protocols exhibit much better behaviour than before, they still perform quite poorly in comparison with DSMA.

Figures 8, 9, and 10 compare the performance of the slotted version of DPMA with the performance of DQDB and a slotted clone of METARING. DSMA performs worst for the single-loop 100Kb ring: its message access time for light load is higher and its maximum throughput is lower than for the other protocols. Note however, that the value of k for METARING is 10.

With very short transmission units (as a DQDB slot) it is reasonable to use bigger values of k in METARING. The situation changes as we move to multiple-loop and/or longer networks. Even with a very big value of k (100), the maximum throughput achieved by METARING puts it far behind the other two networks. Under uniform load, slotted DSMA exhibits a performance characteristics similar to DQDB; however, in contrast to DQDB, DSMA is absolutely fair and it is better suited for synchronous traffic.

Figure 11 shows the message access delay in slotted DSMA for synchronous traffic. The measurements were performed against the background of uniform asynchronous traffic of varying intensity (l_a). The transmission strategy for synchronous traffic was the "compromise" strategy in which synchronous segments are transmitted during token possession and at the "predictable" moments when previously transmitted synchronous segments are reused. The observed indifference of the network's behaviour for synchronous traffic with respect to the uniform load is quite spectacular. One would expect such behaviour if synchronous segments were only transmitted during token possession, but the high stability of the message access time for the "compromise" strategy is not so obvious.

5 Summary

We presented a network topology (the **spiral ring**) and a MAC-level protocol for this topology. The proposed solution can be viewed as a family of networks parametrised by the number of loop segments. The maximum throughput achieved by our protocol does not degrade with the increasing propagation length of the ring. Even in the special case of only one segment, the network is able to use a fixed fraction (close to 1) of the channel bandwidth irrespective of its length. Moreover, in contrast to other *capacity-1* solutions (e.g., DQDB), our network is absolutely fair. If there is more than one segment, the network incurs no access delay when the traffic is light.

The protocol implicitly supports isochronous traffic up to any predetermined level not exceeding 1; additionally, it supports synchronous traffic up to the 100% of the available bandwidth with marginal jitter but without packet loss if stations obey their individual limits.

References

[1] I. Cidon and Y. Ofek. A full-duplex ring with fair-

---

[7] In the unidirectional world, METARING is made of 2 rings.
[8] It still offers zero access delays for light load.

ness and spatial reuse. In *IEEE INFOCOM'90*, pages 969–981, 1990.

[2] W. Dobosiewicz and P. Gburzyński. An alternative to FDDI: DPMA and the pretzel ring. *IEEE Transactions on Communications*, 1993. (To appear.).

[3] IEEE Project 802.6, Proposed Standard, Distributed Queue Dual Bus Metropolitan Area Network. Doc. No. P802.6/D15, Oct. 1990.

[4] Fiber Distributed Data Interface (FDDI) – Token Ring Media Access Control (MAC). American National Standard for Information Systems, Doc. No. X3, 139–1987, Nov. 1987.

[5] P. Gburzyński and P. Rudnicki. Object-oriented simulation is SMURPH: A case study of DQDB protocol. In *Proceedings of 1991 Western Multi Conference on Object-Oriented Simulation*, pages 12–21, Anaheim, California, Feb. 1991.

[6] P. Gburzyński and P. Rudnicki. *The SMURPH Protocol Modelling Environment*. University of Alberta, Department of Computing Science, Edmonton, Alberta, Canada T6G 2H1, 1991.

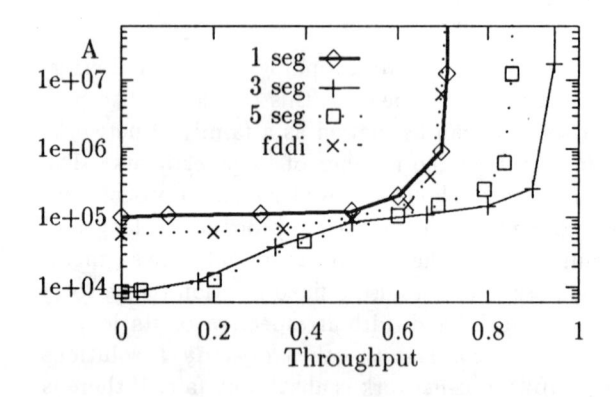

Figure 2: Loop length 100Kb, (fixed) packet length 8192 bits, fixed message length 8192 bits, THT = 1 unit.

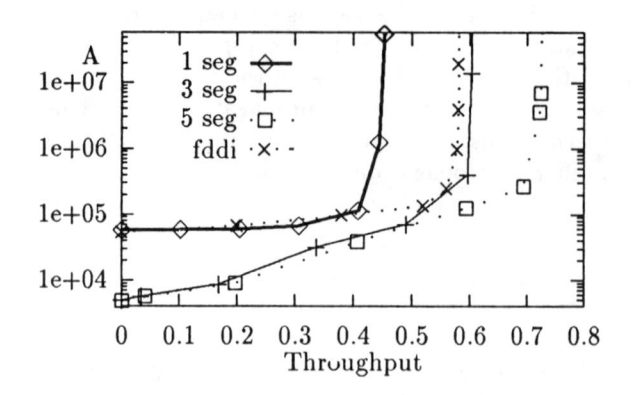

Figure 3: Loop length 100Kb, (fixed) packet length 1056 bits, variable message length 4096 bits, THT = 4 units.

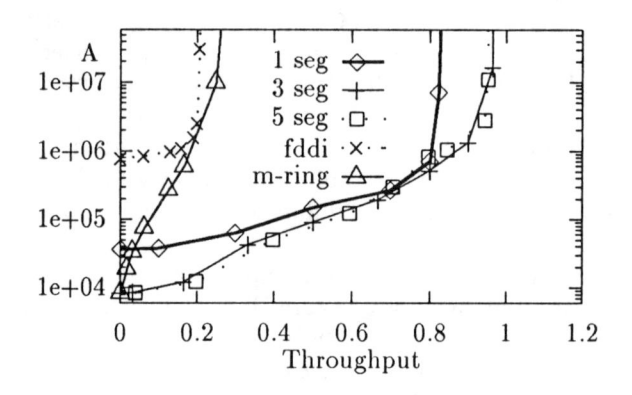

Figure 4: Loop length 1Mb, (fixed) packet length 8192 bits, fixed message length 8192 bits, THT (k) = 1 unit.

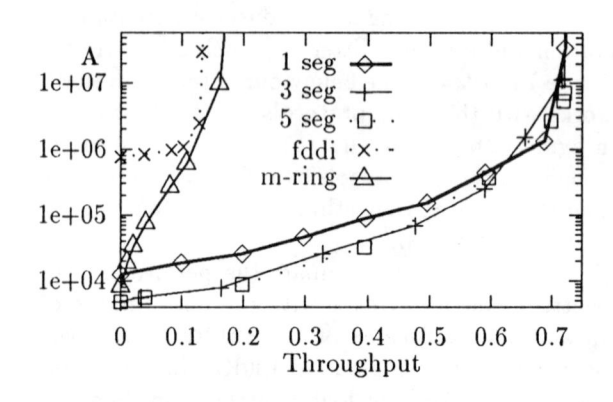

Figure 5: Loop length 1Mb, (fixed) packet length 1056 bits, variable message length 4096 bits, THT (k) = 4 units.

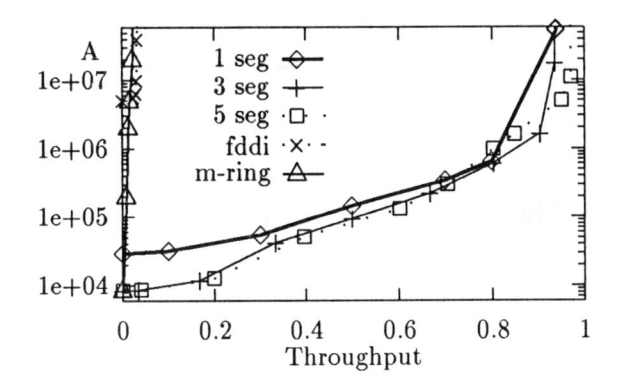

Figure 6: Loop length 10Mb, (fixed) packet length 8192 bits, fixed message length 8192 bits, THT (k) = 1 unit.

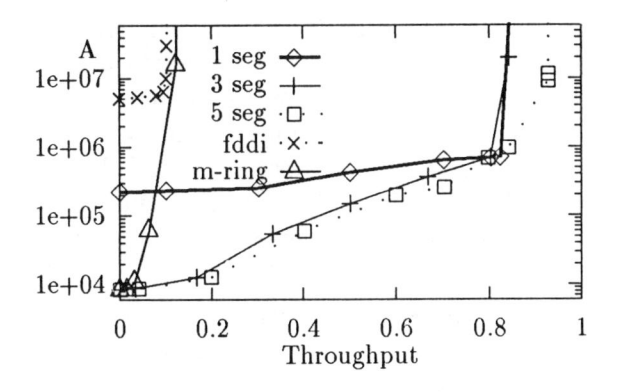

Figure 7: Loop length 10Mb, (fixed) packet length 8192 bits, fixed message length 8192 bits, THT (k) = 4 units.

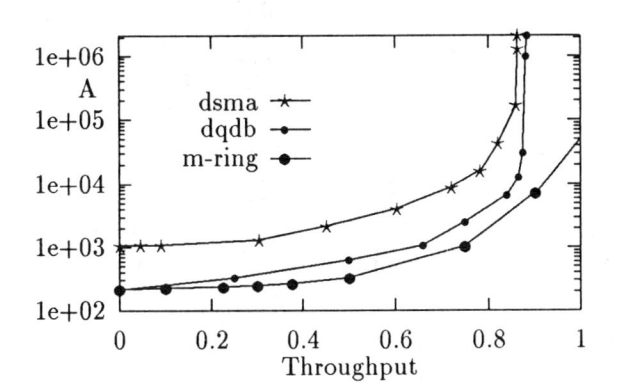

Figure 8: Single segment 100Kb, slotted protocols, THT = 1 slot, k = 10 slots.

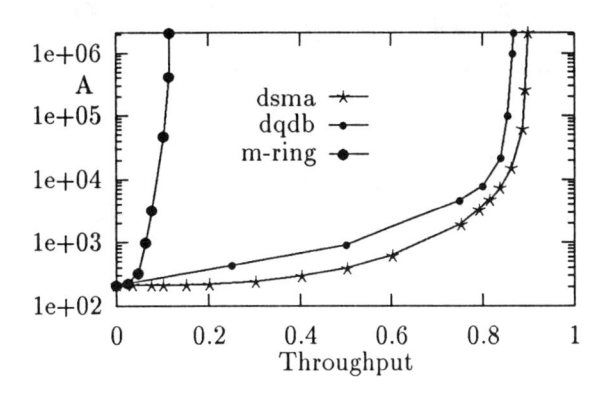

Figure 9: Three segments 1Mb, slotted protocols, THT = 1 slot, k = 10 slots.

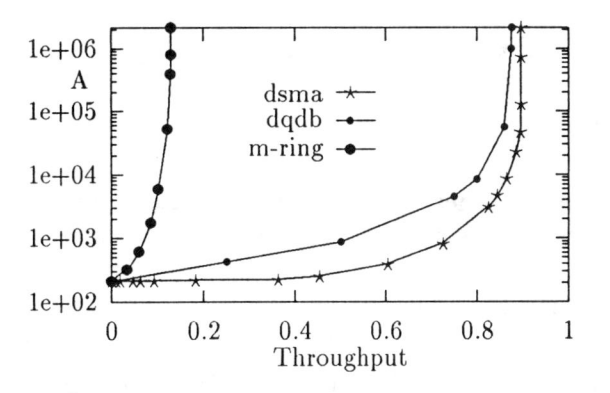

Figure 10: Five segments 10Mb, slotted protocols, THT = 1 slot, k = 100 slots.

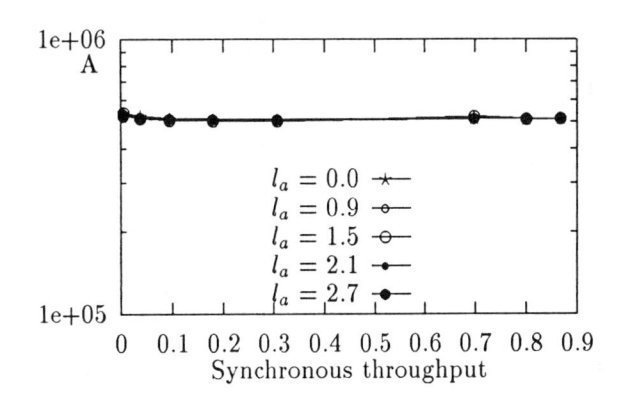

Figure 11: Three segments 1Mb, slotted DSMA, THT = 22 slots, synchronous traffic against uniform background.

KEYNOTE SPEECH

Distributed Supercomputing – The CASA Gigabit Testbed Experience

Paul Messina

Caltech
Pasadena CA

Abstract of Keynote Speech

The key goal of the CASA testbed research project is to characterize the role that high-speed wide area networks can play in providing better resources for solving large-scale scientific applications.

The CASA testbed is exploring the use of high-speed networks to provide the necessary computational resources for leading-edge scientific problems, regardless of the geographical location of these resources.

The vehicles for carrying out this research are three important scientific problems from the areas of chemistry, geophysics, and climate modeling. Each has computational profiles and data movement patterns that differ from the others and that are characteristic of broad classes of scientific and engineering computations. Through the application of supercomputer networking to these three problems, we are gaining insights into what aspects of computational problems present problems in the use of networks and into algorithm and implementation strategies that will overcome the difficulties.

The research issues addressed in the project to date include how to design application communications to hide latency and how to write or modify applications software to run in a distributed fashion. These algorithms in turn are being analyzed to identify new programming models and the network services and functionality needed to support distributed applications. We have also derived hardware design parameters for high bandwidth networks. A significant activity has been the design and implementation of a programming environment that is common to all the supercomputers that are being used in CASA experiments and that provides facilities for executing programs in both distributed and parallel computer environments.

The software infrastructure needed to support the applications, including network protocols and user interface libraries has been ported to each of the supercomputer platforms. Part of this effort has been the identification of appropriate performance metrics for analyzing the performance of the testbed.

Key elements of the applications have been implemented as parallel programs on one or more computers and in most cases have been run distributed across network-connected computers.

High speed (HIPPI) interfaces have been installed and tested on almost all of the major hosts that will be put on the CASA network and that will be used by the three applications.

In summary, the CASA network hardware and software environment has been designed to provide a testbed for demonstrating the feasibility of distributing large-scale applications across a gigabit/second Wide Area Network. Results of early experiments with this environment will be given.

SESSION 4A:
Applications I

Dennis Duke, Chair

Toward a High Performance Distributed Memory Climate Model

M.F. Wehner, J.J. Ambrosiano, J.C. Brown, W.P. Dannevik, P.G. Eltgroth, A.A. Mirin
Lawrence Livermore National Laboratory
Livermore, California 94550
and
J.D. Farrara, C.C. Ma, C.R. Mechoso, J.A. Spahr
Department of Atmospheric Sciences
University of California, Los Angeles 90024-1565

As part of a long range plan to develop a comprehensive climate systems modeling capability, we have taken the Atmospheric General Circulation Model originally developed by Arakawa and collaborators at UCLA and have recast it in a portable, parallel form. The code uses an explicit time-advance procedure on a staggered three-dimensional Eulerian mesh. We have implemented a two-dimensional latitude/longitude domain decomposition message passing strategy. Both dynamic memory management and interprocessor communication are handled with macro constructs that are preprocessed prior to compilation. The code can be moved about a variety of platforms, including massively parallel processors, workstation clusters, and vector processors, with a mere change of three parameters. Performance on the various platforms as well as issues associated with coupling different models for major components of the climate system are discussed.

1 Introduction

1.1 The Need to Understand and Predict Climate Change

Since the Industrial Revolution, humankind has inadvertantly mounted a grand-scale and largely uncontrolled experiment on the earth's global environmental systems. The growing consumption of fossil fuels, deforestation, and other human activities are increasing the atmospheric concentration of gases such as carbon dioxide, methane, nitrous oxide, and chlorofluorocarbons. Along with water vapor, these "greenhouse" gases are major factors in the radiation budget of the atmosphere, which in turn plays a critical role in controlling the earth's climate. Under a variety of reasonable growth scenarios for population and industrial activity, the increasing concentration of greenhouse gases over the next few decades could result in a radiative forcing equivalent to that produced by a doubling of preindustrial levels of carbon dioxide.

While it is likely that this process will eventually affect global climate, we are far from being able to predict accurately the timing, magnitude, and regional pattern of such changes. Attempts to alter the present global system of energy production to effectively counter a possible world-wide temperature rise could incur enormous social and economic costs. However, the effects of global climate change resulting from an unchecked temperature increase could prove equally costly. For these reasons it is vitally important to improve the scientific basis for understanding and predicting the response of the earth's environmental systems to substantial perturbations, both natural and human-induced.

1.2 The Need for Models and High-Performance Computing

The inadvertant experiment described above is difficult to interpret for at least two reasons. First, there is no "control" experiment. The record of the unperturbed climate system is too sparse and unreliable to provide a comparison or reference dataset, especially as other factors also affect climate. Second, our knowledge of the magnitude and spatial pattern of perturbing influences is inadequate. For example, the time histories of the concentrations of greenhouse gases, the amount of volcanic aerosols aloft, and the record of solar radiation are all poorly known. In addition, only about half of the anthropogenic emissions of carbon dioxide increase its concentration in the atmosphere.

We know little about what happens to the remaining half, particularly with respect to how the global carbon dioxide sink is partitioned between the ocean and terrestrial biosphere.

All these uncertainties, combined with the practical impossibility of comprehensive laboratory-based climate experiments, have created a unique and vital role for computer-based climate simulation experiments. By enabling climate scientists to quantify their models and to test them in detail against a wide array of observational datasets, such experiments can provide an objective basis for understanding the climate system and for estimating future changes.

The bewildering diversity of physical processes that together determine a given climate regime occurs over a wide range of space and time scales that are activated by nonlinear couplings. Models that attempt to encapsulate these processes are necessarily complex and overtax the capabilities even of current supercomputers.

This disparity between computer requirements and capabilities will become more acute with the next generation of models. Current estimates of climatic change are often based on atmospheric models run with limited chemical reactions, simplified oceans, and essentially no representations of terrestrial and marine biosystems. Such limitations, together with the delayed response currently evident in the global temperature record, point clearly to the need for more comprehensive and better-tested models. Future models of the climate system will need increased spatial resolution, enhanced representation of processes, and full coupling of additional major components of the earth system, including dynamic representation of the oceans, ecosystems, and interactive biogeochemistry.

It is clear that substantially faster algorithms and increased throughput are imperative if we are to move forward to advanced simulations of the climate system during this decade. Parallel processing offers significant potential for attaining increased performance if the basic algorithms can be recast in a suitable parallel form.

2 The UCLA Atmospheric General Circulation Model

The general circulation of the atmosphere is one of the major component subsystems of the earth's climate system. Atmospheric General Circulation Models (AGCMs) solve a set of primitive equations to simulate the long-term (climatic) behavior of the atmosphere. They generally fall into two categories defined according to the algorithms used to solve the hydrodynamical equations of motion. The more conventional of the two is characterized by a grid point discretization. An alternative method of solution is provided by a spectral transform method using a spherical harmonic approximation to calculate certain horizontal derivatives. At currently attainable horizontal grid resolutions, spectral methods have an edge over grid point methods on traditional vector supercomputers. It is felt by many that at the desired higher resolutions this situation will reverse. Additionally, spectral methods require numerous Fourier transforms per time step. Hence on distributed memory computer systems, large amounts of data must be communicated between processors. As is well known, parallel algorithms generally are limited by the time spent communicating data relative to that spent actually calculating data. For these and additional reasons, we have chosen to implement a grid-point-based AGCM.

The AGCM developed by Arakawa and coworkers at UCLA beginning in the mid-1960's [1] is such a grid point model. The current version of the UCLA AGCM incorporates advanced finite differencing techniques [1, 3], state of the art parameterizations of physical processes, and has been extensively tested and used to study a variety of climate problems [12, 13]. In a separate study, the UCLA AGCM has been coupled to the NOAA Geophysical Fluid Dynamics Laboratory / Princeton Universtity Modular Ocean Model (MOM) for investigations on the seasonal cycle and interannual variability of the atmosphere-ocean system [15]. Also underway at UCLA is addtional study of the distribution of the coupled AGCM/MOM across high speed networks [14]. We have recast an existing vectorized version in a portable, parallel form. We have also extended the model to include a number of additional atmospheric processes and have imbedded the AGCM into a framework intended to allow coupling to the other major sub-models (ocean, biosphere, atmospheric chemistry, etc.) defining an earth system model (ESM).

Atmospheric general circulation models typically consist of two parts. The first part is the solution of the equations of hydrodynamics suitably approximated to the regimes encountered by the atmosphere. This typically involves a straightforward derivation beginning with the Navier-Stokes equations. The second part is a collection of physically based parameterizations of the other processes important to the simulation of the atmosphere. These process parameterizations are generally considerably less connected to physical "first principles" than the hydrodynamics due to the complexity of the processes involved. In some cases, a lack of understanding of the details of the relevant physical mechanisms forces these parameterizations to be oversimplified.

The hydrodynamics portion of the UCLA AGCM is a grid point based explicit finite difference model. The horizontal differencing scheme is designed to conserve the potential enstrophy, the global integral of the potential vorticity, as well as the total energy [2, 4]. The solution of the inertial terms of the momentum conservation equation is fourth order. Other terms of this equation and the continuity equation are solved to second order in the spatial dimensions. The horizontal advection of the scalar quantities is also fourth order accurate in the spatial dimensions.

The vertical differencing scheme under the hydrostatic approximation reduces the problem from fully three-dimensional equations to a set of coupled two-dimensional equations closely related to the shallow water equations. From these, the velocity components and the pressures are determined. All differencing schemes in the vertical dimension are second order accurate.

The thermodynamic energy equation, formulated in terms of the potential temperature, describes the variation of the internal energy in both the vertical and horizontal directions. Advection of moisture (formulated in terms of specific humidity) and ozone concentration are performed. The ideal gas law provides a closure to solve for the density, which also varies in each of the directions. This then allows the pressure gradient force to vary in the vertical dimension even within a finite difference cell.

The finite difference mesh is staggered in both the vertical and horizontal directions. In the horizontal direction, the Arakawa C-mesh in latitude/longitude coordinates is used because of its superior properties for large scale atmospheric motion [1]. In the vertical direction, the thermodynamic variables and the (derived) vertical velocity are staggered. The net result in three dimensions is a cell shaped as a cube in spherical geometry with the velocity components centered on each of the faces and the thermodynamic variables (potential temperature, pressure, specific humidity, ozone, etc.) at the cell center.

The vertical domain is divided into three distinct regions. These are the stratosphere, the troposphere and the planetary boundary layer (PBL). The vertical coordinate is a modified σ coordinate system with $\sigma = -1$ at the top of the atmosphere, $\sigma = 0$ at the tropopause, $\sigma = 1$ at the troposphere-PBL boundary, and $\sigma = 2$ at the earth's surface [5]. The PBL is represented by the lowest model layer, and the free atmosphere-PBL boundary is considered as a material boundary surface with no mass or momentum advected through it via the hydrodynamic equations. The only exchange between these layers occurs via parameterized source terms depending on model specific physics. The top and bottom of the model are also considered as material surfaces, with no exchanges across them except for parameterized fluxes of momentum, heat and moisture. The horizontal boundary condition is that of periodicity in the longitudinal coordinate. In the latitudinal coordinate, a regularity condition is imposed at each of the poles.

The second portion of the UCLA AGCM, the parameterized physical processes, consists of several subprocesses that are operator split. These are a layer cloud instability calculation at the troposphere-PBL boundary[5], cumulus convective transport of energy, momentum and moisture [6], moist convective instability adjustment [5], long wave (infrared) radiation transport [7], short wave (visible and UV) radiation transport, surface fluxes of momentum, moisture and energy to the PBL [5], the evolution of the ground temperature and snow cover [8], and simplified ozone photochemistry[9]. All of these subprocesses involve quantities only from a single horizontal mesh cell. However, because of the staggered mesh, these quantities are not all at the same physical location. Instead, quantities relating to the thermodynamic state are cell-centered and those relating to the hydrodynamic state are face-centered. Typically, no further information for these parameterized processes is needed in the horizontal dimensions other than the horizontal velocity components located on each of the four faces of the cell. In the vertical direction, however, some of these processes require an implicit solution. Hence, these subprocesses are collectively described as the "column physics" modules to denote their dependence on a vertical column of air.

The time differencing of the AGCM equations is mostly explicit. Because of the substantial computational burden of the column physics, the hydrodynamics is subcycled with respect to it. The time step governing the hydrodynamics is considerably more restrictive than that required by the more slowly varying column physics processes. In explicit hydrodynamics schemes, the time step is usually governed by the Courant-Friedrich-Levy (CFL) condition in order to ensure stability. In a spherical coordinate system, the longitudinal spacing between cell centers converges as points approach the polar singularity. Hence, in a grid point model with a fixed time step scheme, the time step is usually determined by the cells nearest the poles. For a simulation of the atmospheric dynamics, this extra resolution near the poles is physically unnecessary since the accuracy of the calculation is typically determined by the cells near the equator. Various attempts have been made to overcome this restrictive time step. In the UCLA AGCM, Arakawa and Lamb [1] developed a set of discrete Fourier filters specifically designed to damp unstable modes which may arise when violating the CFL condition in the vicinity of the poles. These filters contain a latitudinal dependence but are applied over the complete longitudinal domain. This allows a choice of hydrodynamic time step in violation of the CFL condition in the higher latitudes but consistent with it near the equator. A typical operational time step in a 4° by 5° calculation is one hour for the column physics and 7.5 minutes for the hydrodynamics. It is desirable to reduce the column physics time step somewhat since some of these processes vary on a faster time scale. However, as the horizontal resolution is increased, this time step may not need to be decreased further since the scaling of these processes is essentially determined by the vertical structure of the model. This is not the case for the hydrodynamics, as the CFL condition still determines the time step.

3 Parallelization Strategy

3.1 Domain Decomposition Methodology

The parallel AGCM is designed for a distributed memory multiple-instruction-multiple-data (MIMD) computing environment. A two-dimensional latitude/longitude domain decomposition method is used, so that each subdomain actually consists of a number of contiguous vertical columns extending from the earth's surface into the upper atmosphere (see Fig. 1). The choice to decompose in only two dimensions is based on the fact that column processes strongly couple the elements within the column and do not naturally parallelize along the column. Additionally, the number of meshpoints in the vertical direction is usually small. We choose the two dimensional decomposition over a one dimensional decomposition because the latter does not provide the necessary concurrency for mesh sizes of interest and has an asymptotically larger communications cost[10].

Subdomains are assigned to processors in a deterministic manner and data are transmitted between subdomains in the form of messages. In order to calculate the fourth order solution of the horizontal part of the hydrodynamics [4], two points on each of the four sides of a cell are required. For cells in the interior of a subdomain, this data is readily available in local memory. For cells bordering on the edge of a subdomain, some of this data is contained in a neighboring subdomain and hence, on a different processor's local memory. This is the data that must be communicated.

The structure of a subdomain is rectangular (in logical space) with an inner rectangle consisting of the cells to be calculated by the assigned processor and a border or frame of cells into which data will be transmitted from the neighboring subdomains. These "phony" cells do not have their solutions advanced in the hydrodynamics portion of the calculation. Rather, they may be thought of as the implements of interface conditions between subdomains. At the physical boundaries, these phony cells provide the imposed physical boundary conditions instead. For the fourth order scheme, this border is two cells wide in order that the last "real" cell may be calculated. We have made a conscious effort to maintain a uniformity of the subdomains. Since the subdomain interface and imposed boundary conditions are used at the same point in the calculation, we have written a subroutine that determines which of these two cases must be invoked. In the subroutines that difference the equations, no knowledge of the physical location of the subdomain is necessary. In this manner, we have been able to use the same code on multiple and single subdomain decompositions, allowing us access to traditional single processors computers for purposes of debugging and comparison.

Communication of any particular quantity is required only once per time step due to the explicit time differencing of the algorithm. Communication is accomplished in two steps. Data is first exchanged between subdomains bordering each other at a given latitude. This is followed by an exchange between subdomains bordering each other at a given longitude. Diagonal communication of data at the extreme corners of the subdomain frame is thus implicitly accomplished without further messages.

The communications described thus far are necessary to implement calculation of difference approximations to horizontal derivatives for the hydrodynamics. These communications require that messages be sent only to each of a subdomain's four nearest neighbors. There are two other parts of Arakawa's algorithm that require interprocessor data communication. Both of these are global in the longitudinal direction. The simpler of the two is a calculation of the vorticity on the grid points nearest to the polar singularity. Because of the staggered mesh, this is accomplished via a circulation theorem that requires a knowledge of the latitudinal velocity component at each of the points encircling the pole. Since this is needed at only a single latitude line for each hemisphere, the amount of data communicated is not large. A larger and more complex communication procedure is required to implement the discrete Fourier filters used to increase the time step. Calculation of these filter functions involves the convolution of two vectors about the entire longitudinal domain. The filtering of a given variable takes the form

$$\phi'(i) = \sum_{i'=1}^{M} S(i-i')\phi(i') \; . \qquad (1)$$

Here, S is a fixed set of coefficients, M is the number of longitudinal cells and ϕ is the vector to be smoothed. For each grid point, a sum involving some combination of each of the elements of both of these vectors is required. For the fixed coefficient vector, we copy every longitudinal element for the range of latitude lines contained in the subdomain into the local memory of that subdomain's processor at problem generation. To calculate the actual summations, partial sums of the inner product of S and the portion of ϕ contained in the subdomain are first calculated. These partial sums are then communicated via messages to the appropriate subdomain and the summation is completed. The resulting equation is

$$\phi'(i) = \sum_{n=1}^{n_p} \Big(\sum_{i'=L_n}^{U_n} S(i-i')\phi(i') \Big) \; . \qquad (2)$$

Here, L_n and U_n are the lower and upper longitudinal elements of the subdomain n. For each subdomain, the inner sum is calculated for all values of $i = 1, ..., M$ and hence uses all the elements of the fixed coefficient vector, S. The partial sums are communicated by messages from each subdomain to all the other subdomains (at that latitude), requiring of order N messages where N is the number of longitudinal subdomains. Alternatively, a tree-based communications pattern would allow a reduction to of order $\log N$ messages. We are also investigating equivalent filter functions having a limited rather than global extent to further reduce communication cost.

The filtering procedure can seriously affect overall performance on distributed memory computers. There are several issues. The filters are constructed to be latitude dependent. This means that there is a load imbalance between subdomains containing high latitudes and those near the equator. This load imbalance is caused by both the communication and the extra computation required to perform the summations. This is further accentuated by the use of two types of filters, "strong" and "weak". Under the operational conditions described above, the weak filter operates on only about 10% of the cells in the vicinity of the poles, while the strong filter operates on about half. It may be possible to alleviate some of this load imbalance by tailoring the size of the subdomains. This would involve making the latitudinal size smaller in the near-polar subdomains than in the near-equatorial subdomains. Unfortunately, this strategy runs opposite to that dictated by the column physics, where increased tropical cumulus convective activity leads to another load imbalance. An implicit barrier communication between these two sections of the model further complicates matters.

Another performance issue regarding filters is specific to the UCLA AGCM. The functions that are altered by the filters are not the prognostic variables themselves but rather the terms that comprise the hydrodynamical operator functions. This procedure is demanded by conservation requirements. The impact on performance is that communication must be interspersed throughout a portion of the algorithm rather than being performed at one specific point. We have designed the code to perform the border communication of all of the prognostic variables at the end of a time step. However, the calculation of the filtered quantities involves three stages that cannot be performed at this point. The first stage is the calculation of the unfiltered quantities at the interior cells of the subdomain using the previously communicated prognostic variables. This is followed by the filtering procedure and its requisite global communication. Finally, a border communication of the same type as required by the prognostic variables must be performed. In fact, all of these communications cannot be performed simultaneously either, since the strongly filtered quantities depend on the weakly filtered quantities as well. Our chosen method is to calculate the filtered quantities as close to the beginning of the current time step as possible so that the filtering occurs reasonably near the prognostic variable border communication of the previous time step.

3.2 Data Structures

Data structures in the parallel AGCM are designed to be uniform across the subdomains. A single processor is assigned the role of initializing global data. It also calculates the subdomain decomposition and divides the global data appropriately among the subdomains. This processor may optionally be responsible for i/o and aggregation facilties. The processors assigned to specific subdomains are directed to receive in a message from the global domain processor certain scalar information prior to any subsequent operations. Once the subdomain array bounds have been determined, dynamic allocation of arrays and other initialization procedures may be completed.

We have designed the array structures used by both the global domain and the local subdomain processors to have an identical structure. That is, these arrays are contained in FORTRAN header files with the same array names and same variable dimension names. However, the values of these dimensions are different between subdomains and the global domain. In this manner, data may be communicated easily between the global and subdomain processors. We do this by copying the relevant portions of a global array in the global processsor's local memory into a scratch array to be sent to a subdomain via a message. The subdomain processor then receives this data directly into an array with the original (and proper) name. In addition to providing concise coding, this technique has the added advantage of allowing us to skip this communication procedure entirely in a single processor configuration. In this case, the global domain and the single subdomain are identical.

4 Portability

The rapid evolution in computing technology has produced a multiplicity of platforms from a variety of vendors. Because we wish to carry out scientific studies in a reliable production environment while developing advanced computational versions for high performance systems, it is of paramount importance to maintain a portable source code. We have addressed two issues that affect portability: dynamic memory management and interprocess communication.

4.1 Dynamic Memory Management

Allocating memory at run time, rather than at compile time, allows memory to be used more efficiently and makes it much easier to resize domains dynamically (for example, when attempting to balance the load between processors). Because the language constructs for dynamic memory management are nonstandard, we are using the M4 preprocessor to handle

Table 1: Variation of array allocation syntax with architecture. The symbol pntr_a stands for the pointer to the array a (when relevant).

Architecture	Syntax
Sun-4	pntr_a = malloc(nbytes)
Cray-C90	call hpalloc(pntr_a,nwords,err_flg,0)
BBN-TC2000	allocate a

macro constructs that are processed prior to compilation. This practice confines nonportable constructs to the bodies of the macros, allowing the code to be easily modified to accommodate new architectures.

For example, the variation of array allocation syntax with architecture is shown in Table 1. On the Sun-4 the storage in bytes must be specified, on the Cray-C90 the unit of storage is words, and the BBN-TC2000 computes the memory to be allocated from the array bounds information specified in the array declaration statement. The memory allocation macro has the syntax:

`ALLOCAT(A(I1:J1,I2:J2,...,IN:JN), NBYTES),`

where on the Cray-C90 the second argument is divided by 8, and on the BBN-TC2000 it is not used. In all of the above cases the array bounds information is not explicitly needed in the allocation command. However because the Fortran-90 standard requires that information to be present in the allocation syntax, it is included in the macro call for flexibility and future portability.

We have designed macros to handle storage allocation and deallocation, equivalencing, and real and integer declarations (both local and common). An optional error handling procedure is provided.

4.2 Interprocess Communication

Message passing constructs also vary from platform to platform. Each parallel architecture has its own message passing library, and message passing software designed to accommodate a variety of platforms is available. Here too, we have chosen to construct macro commands for sending and receiving messages. These macros take the form:

`MSEND(DESTINATION PROCESS I.D., MESSAGE I.D.,`

DATA TYPE, DATA, LENGTH, BLOCKING FLAG)

MRECV(SENDING PROCESS I.D., MESSAGE I.D., DATA TYPE, DATA, LENGTH, BLOCKING FLAG)

Support is provided for packages in which the receiving process specifies either both message identifier and sending process or message identifier only. In the latter case one can invoke an optional message identifier conversion in which unique message identifiers are generated to handle the case where multiple processes spawn messages having the same identifier. Another feature of these macros is a data type flag to facilitate data conversion for heterogeneous systems. As with the memory management macros, an optional error handling procedure is provided.

Macros have been constructed to handle Parallel Virtual Machine (PVM) 2.4.1, the Argonne P4 package, the Livermore Message Passing System (LMPS), Thinking Machines' CMMD 2.0, and Parasoft's EXPRESS.

These macro constructs, along with CPP precompile directives, allow movement between the Cray-C90, the BBN-TC2000, the TMC CM-5, and a Sun or IBM workstation cluster with a simple change of only three parameters.

5 Performance

5.1 Performance Scaling Model

The parallel performance of any code depends on a number of factors. First, it is important to balance the computational load so that some processors do not idle while others are doing most of the work. It is also important to minimize interprocessor communications costs, again to avoid significant processor idle time. While some systems will allow message traffic simultaneously with computation, it is nevertheless informative to estimate communications costs by assuming that the two do not overlap.

One can define the speedup obtained from parallelization as the wall clock time for a serial calculation divided by the wall clock time for the same calculation in parallel. A perfectly efficient calculation will have a parallel speedup equal to the number of processors applied to the problem. Assuming the arithmetic time to be inversely proportional to the number of active processors, the speedup becomes a function of the communications time relative to the time to carry out arithmetic computations.

For the two-dimensional domain decomposition strategy used in the atmospheric model, the speedup S takes the form

$$S(n_p, n_g) = n_p \left[1 + c\left(\frac{n_p}{n_g}\right)^{\frac{1}{2}}\right]^{-1} \quad (3)$$

where n_p is the processor count, n_g is the number of horizontal zones, and c is a machine and algorithm dependent constant. This formula assumes a load balanced computation having subdomains of nontrivial size and reflects well known scaling of communications overhead with subdomain surface to volume ratio for domain decomposition of algorithms explicit in time. This is approximately correct for the explicit time advance scheme used for the hydrodynamic fields of the UCLA AGCM.

The longitudinal global filtering operation that is applied to certain terms in the momentum equation modifies the speedup scaling. The filtering operation is designed to eliminate unstable computational modes that originate from the convergence of meridians in polar regions. This introduces the need for non-nearest neighbor subdomain communications. As a result, the parameter c is modified to the form[11]

$$c' = c \frac{1 + \alpha \sqrt{n_g}}{1 + \beta \sqrt{n_g}}, \quad (4)$$

where α and β are constants that depend on the form of filter arithmetic and the number of processors n_p. It should also be noted that c is inversely proportional to the amount of arithmetic operations required to implement the column physics parameterizations, which require no interprocessor communications.

5.2 Performance on BBN-TC2000

We have carried out a series of timing runs with the parallel code in order to validate the preceeding scalings and determine absolute performance levels. All of these runs were performed with the 9 layer 4° by 5° version of the AGCM with square (N by N) subdomain decompositions. In the standard operational mode of this configuration of the model, the total AGCM time step is taken as one hour. The hydrodynamics is subcycled over this time step eight times resulting in a hydrodynamic time step of 7.5 minutes. Since the initialization and termination phases of the calculation involve serial operation of the code, we have measured the performance of only the time advance segments of the model. Furthermore, because of a large penalty due to the page faulting process on the BBN TC-200 which occurred as code and data were loaded into appropriate locations upon these phases, we computed speedups only over the middle three time steps of a five hour simulation. The amount of calculation required per time step is variable in the AGCM, being dependent on the state of the atmosphere at the given moment. This is mainly due to branching in the convective parts of the model. However, from a set of longer serial runs, we have inferred that these runs are representative of the typical calculation.

Measured and predicted parallel speedups are shown in Fig. 2 for the hydrodynamics module of the code, with filtering and column physics turned off. The predicted scaling is from Eq.(3) with $c = 4.5$. Note that the time step must be artifically lowered in this case in order to ensure stability of the calculation.

The addition of filtering should decrease the parallel performance, since α in Eq.(3) is usually larger than β. This trend is confirmed in Fig. 2. The agreement is better than expected, especially since the surface-to-volume ratio is not small at the larger processor count, whereas the scaling estimates assume that this ratio is small.

From Eq.(3), we would expect that the addition of column physics would increase parallel speedup, because column physics increases the gridpoint computational intensity while requiring minimal additional communication. This trend is also confirmed in Fig. 2. In the largest decomposition (10 by 10), we see that the parallel speedup for the complete model is about 45. Examination of the timing statistics for the individual portions of the model reveals a load imbalance caused by unequally sized subdomains. This is a result of a mismatch between the subdomain decomposition and the number of zones in each direction. A more suitably matched decomposition to the 4° by 5° horizontal resolution is a 9 by 11 subdomain configuration. In this case, the overall calculation time is about 9% less than in the 10 by 10 subdomain configuration with most of the savings occurring in the hydrodynamics part of the calculation. In the column physics, the overall load is more evenly distributed in this case but the cost for the slowest subdomain remains about the same.

From the scaling estimates, it can be seen that increasing the horizontal resolution should increase parallel efficiency. In the near future, horizontal resolutions on the order of 1° by 1° will be performed, increasing the number of horizontal zones by a factor of 20. Also, it is hoped that improvements to the filtering algorithm should substantially reduce the communications penalty without adversely affecting the model predictions.

5.3 Performance on Workstation Clusters

The AGCM has been run on a cluster of small computers, using IBM RS/6000-550 workstations and ethernet communications under the PVM 2.4.1 system. Timings were performed for up to 16 processors and were taken on a dedicated system, with a minimum set of other processes and communicators. The times reported by the operating system inferred initial efficiencies near 100 percent for small numbers of processors, dropping to 50 percent at approximately 16 processors. However, a disparity was noted between the times reported by the system and the actual wall clock times for configurations which needed increased communication at the poles. This discrepancy correlated well with a large and increasing number of voluntary context switches reported by the individual CPUs. A voluntary context switch typically occurs when an unavailable service has been requested by the user. When additional communication measurements were taken, it was observed that the average communicating workstation bandwidth never exceeded 3.7 Megabits/s. on the cluster. The data transfer rate for the high communication configurations was typically in the range 2.0 - 3.0 Megabits/s. Peak ethernet bandwidth is specified to be 10 Megabits/s. Further experimentation using both public and private ethernet capability and using both UDP-IP and TCP-IP protocols did not materially change the observations. Similar testing on the BBN system revealed that, although the communication needs increased for these configurations, the BBN communication system yielded minimal performance degradation, reaching a peak observed throughput of 14.2 Megabits/s.

The message passage performance monitoring revealed that message lengths were distributed in a bimodal fashion for all domain decompositions. Messages clustered at lengths of 1 kilobyte for one group and near 100 kilobytes for the second group. The first group of messages was more numerous and contained most of the traffic. The second group of messages appeared to deal with data transfers at problem initiation and termination. The median message length ranged between 1.2 and 2.4 kilobytes. When varying domain decompositions with a fixed number of processors, the number and length of messages increased dramatically as the number of longitude segments increased. As the number of longitude segments increased from 1 to 16, the number of messages went up by a factor of five, and the total data transferred went up by a factor of seven.

Although at first glance the performance degradation of the IBM cluster under heavy communication load would seem to be the fault of the message passing implementation, it is likely that the operating system attributes, combined with the basic structure of PVM 2.4.1 are the major contributors to inefficiency. While it is very useful at our present stage of code development to have explicit accounting and control of data transfer, there is inadequate operating system support on the cluster to permit separate monitoring of such factors as operator system switching times and PVM daemon overhead. It is likely that future enhancements in PVM structure and implementation will lead to efficiency improvements.

A second set of performance tests have been made using a cluster of SUN workstations using local ethernet communications. In this series of tests, the system was not made available to other users. Two message passing systems were tested, P4 and PVM v.2.4.1 in configurations up to 16 subdomain processors. In Fig. 3, it is seen that PVM v.2.4.1 is slightly more efficient than P4 on the SUN workstation. Also in Fig. 3, we show the results for the IBM cluster using the reported system times. Note that since the individual IBM nodes are faster than the SUN nodes, the parallel speedup obtained is somewhat lower.

6 Coupling of Climate System Components

In the near future, the AGCM model will be coupled with a variety of other applications models, such as an ocean GCM (OGCM), a land surface and terrestial ecosystem model, an atmospheric chemistry model and a ocean biogeochemistry model. These packages must be coupled in a flexible framework that will allow efficient concurrent execution under a variety of control and synchronization strategies, and that supports intermodular exchange of a wide variety of data structures.

6.1 Inter-Module Data Communication

A well established practice that contributes to the modularity of complex computer codes is the art of data hiding, attaining its highest form in the methods of object-oriented programming. The principle of data hiding states that the internal representation of data in an object should be of no concern to the ultimate user of that data and so should be hidden. In principle, well-crafted objects simply provide data on request. In practice, the line between major science packages may not be so clean.

Rather than being written in an object-oriented language, the major portions of our physics models are written in FORTRAN, the *lingua franca* of scientific programming. Therefore, we need some additional tools to accomplish data hiding.

We have constructed a set of services in a small library called the Run-Time Data Base (RTDB). The RTDB maintains a set of global arrays that have been created by the various packages in the model and links a global name or alias with each such array. The data base stores the dimensionality, data type, and memory location of the array in structures that are accessible by hash table lookup of the alias. One can copy the entire array or subarray into a user-provided buffer, or dispense a pointer. Both FORTRAN and C application interfaces are provided.

Using the Run-Time Data Base, we can make data available for interchange between packages directly whenever the physical representations match. That is, whenever the data type, units, and data point locations of one model match those of another we can allow the models to share the same data structure through the RTDB. For instance two packages that each need temperature in degrees Kelvin on the same grid can share the same array, referring to it as say "temperature" when accessing the RTDB and using any other convenient variable names internally.

For a more general and robust interface, we must provide a higher degree of data hiding by building interface routines. We must assume that in general the data type, units, and locations (time or space) do not match in going from one package to the next. In addition, the quantities needed by one package may not be the same as those of another, but rather are derived from them. For convenience, the raw data going into the package interface routine as well as the transformed data destined for the next package can be posted to the Run-Time Data Base.

The interface routines A/B, A/C, that make data from package A available to packages B and C respectively, are considered part of the communications wrapper of A. Writing these routines is like providing a set of labeled output jacks on an electronic component module. To facilitate this process, we may in some cases write export functions for a particular package. These are functions that provide data values at specified temporal and spatial points on request, interpolating from the values stored in the internal representation of the package. Thus, instead of working with an internal array that stores temperature at the grid points of package A, the interface routine calls an export function, say Temp_A(x,y,z,t), to obtain the data. This allows the internal representation of temperature in A to be changed easily (e.g., converting from a structured to an unstructured grid) without a major rewrite of the interface routines. The symmetric analog to an export routine is an import routine that provides further insulation for the receiving package. We plan to place a variety of interpolation functions in a portable library to enable these export and import functions to be written easily, perhaps by a contributing author.

At the moment, the data exchanged between packages via the RTDB is assumed to reside in local processor memory, or if not, to be made available on that processor by the programmer, for example by explicit message passing. We plan to remove this restriction by designing a distributed data base for communication. The distributed data base would have a global representation for the data to be shared between packages, together with information on how the data is distributed. A package requesting a subset of that data would not have to know the details of how the data is distributed among the processors. Data not in the local memory of the requesting processor would be gathered via messages from wherever it resides.

6.2 Time Integration and Synchronization Issues

The AGCM program comprises a rather large and complex parallel code. However, it forms only a portion of a much more complex modeling system that includes different modules for calculating various physical aspects of the earth system. Each module can be an independent parallel program, typically using domain decomposition to implement parallelism within a module. It is desirable to run the entire suite of programs in parallel, thus exploiting high level functional decomposition as well as data decomposition.

We have chosen to build a general work distribution code section above the existing AGCM code in order to accommodate other physics modules such as ocean circulation, chemistry, biological processes, and more. The code section, written in standard Fortran, is executed by each processor taking part in the overall model. In the following discussion, we use the term package to denote a collection of procedures that model a related set of physical processes. The AGCM code is one such package. We have identified at least six packages that will be needed for the entire earth system model. At the work distribution level for packages, it is assumed that each package can be characterized by a single time. This implies that any parallelism within a package has been controlled at least to the extent that all data subdomains in the package are synchronized in time before any subdomain processor returns control to the scheduling phase. All communication between or among packages is carried out explicitly, typically using messages or file entries.

Earth system model packages are assumed to be written in Fortran or C and to use messages with blocking receives in order to transfer data. In this scheme, there is no facility to interpret the content of a message before accepting it. Therefore, a known scheduling must be used to direct each package. In order to make the task of the package builder easy, we have assumed that each package has some schedule of times at which it must prepare (and possibly send or receive) data. This allows a package to serve as a stand alone code, provided needed information can be gotten from files or internal means. Issues of consistency and differing resolutions are dealt with at the level of intermodule communication, not within the packages themselves. Clearly, the scheduling algorithm must be known within both the package and the work delivery code sections.

The actual scheduling of a package is accomplished by determining the next time at which a message must be received by that package from each other package. If all other packages that must transmit information to the original package (to allow it to advance beyond its present state) have done so, then the earliest next message reception time is used and the package is advanced from its present time to the earliest next message reception time. Although the package has been scheduled to be advanced using knowledge of event times of senders, the scheduling process does not guarantee that messages are received. Thus the package may encounter a wait while attempting to receive information from others. Two options are available for dealing with this synchronization issue. For direct package to package communication, the wait can be absorbed within the receiving package. If the communication is to take place via some intermediate process, such as a run time data base entry, then the scheduling process itself calls a check-in procedure that receives tokens from other processes as their data placement is completed. When all needed information is in place, then the actual advance can occur.

It is assumed that the actual preparation of data for communication to other packages takes place within the sending package. When a package exits from its own advance, the scheduling process assumes that all needed data has been placed into messages or made available to an intermediate process. In the latter case, the scheduler sends tokens to appropriate receivers to maintain synchronization. An error message will be generated if the scheduling process finds no package available for scheduling. It is allowable to have non-symmetric information transfers, such as, for example, one package sending data to another at a different rate than it receives data from that same package. At present, the "coupling times" for information transfers are specified by the user at run time. A system of priorities has been placed into the scheduling so that, if two or more packages could be advanced at the same time, the higher priority package is scheduled first. A simple priority reversal scheme has been instituted to allow fairness, if desired. Leapfrog time advance schemes are also supported, in order to allow the types of time centering between packages that are customary in many physics codes.

The work scheduling module is an attempt to allow data flow style parallel processing within the restrictions of an imperative language. It allows the exploration of a variety of coupling schemes for earth system modeling without restriction to specific non-portable approaches. It is undergoing continuing development as the number and complexity of physics modules in the earth system model increase.

7 Outlook

Our work with parallelization of the AGCM, as well as similar work with an oceanic general circulation model, suggest that the domain decomposition/message passing (DDMP) method represents a flexible, robust paradigm with favorable scaling properties for a wide range of anticipated climate modeling applications. Many of the additional physics process modules which will be added in the future (e.g., atmospheric chemistry and terrestrial ecosystem models) have large gridpoint computational intensity with only modest horizontal connectivity. In addition, future applications will often feature increased horizontal resolution in many of the modules. Both of these trends will lead to increased parallel efficiency in a predictable fashion. In addition, the increased options for concurrent execution of multiple modules, each parallelized via the DDMP approach, will lead to a rich environment for implementation of load balancing strategies. We believe that one of the next major issues to be addressed will relate to the question of how to understand exactly what is being produced by the next-generation climate model, i.e., the challenge of high-performance scientific visualization and efficient manipulation of truly enormous data volumes on distributed-memory platforms.

Acknowledgement

Particular thanks are expressed to Professor Akio Arakawa at UCLA. His research on atmospheric dynamics has provided us a most suitable algorithm for the beginnings of a high performance distributed memory climate model. Work performed under the auspices of the U. S. Department of Energy by the Lawrence Livermore National Laboratory under contract No. W-7405-ENG-48. Partial support has been provided by the Department of Energy CHAMMP program.

References

[1] A. Arakawa and V. Lamb, *Methods in Comp. Phys.* **17**(1977) 173-265.

[2] A. Arakawa and V. Lamb, *Mon. Weath. Rev.* **109**(1981) 18-36.

[3] A. Arakawa and M. Suarez, *Mon. Weath. Rev.* **111**(1983) 34-45.

[4] K. Takano and M. Wurtele, *Air Force Geophysics Laboratory Report AFGL-TR-82-0205*(1982)

[5] M. Suarez, A. Arakawa and D. Randall, *Mon. Weath. Rev.* **111**(1983) 2224-2243.

[6] A. Arakawa and W.H. Schubert, *J. Atmos. Sci.* **31**(1974) 674-701.

[7] Harshvarden, *et. al.*, *J. Geophys. Res.* **92**(1987) 1009-1016.

[8] A. Arakawa, "Design of the UCLA general cirulation model", (1972) Technical Report No. 7, Dept. of Meteorology, University of California, Los Angeles.

[9] M.E. Schlesinger and Y. Mintz, *J. Atmos. Sci.* **36**(1979) 1325-1361.

[10] R. Procassini, S. Whitman, and W. Dannevik, "Porting a Global Ocean Circulation Model Onto a Shared-Memory Multiprocessor", to appear in *J. Supercomputing*.

[11] W. Dannevik, "Geophysical Fluid Dynamics, Large Eddy Simulations and Massively Parallel Computing", in B. Galperin and S.Orszag, eds., *Large Eddy Simulations of Complex Engineering and Geophysical Flows*, Springer Verlag, New York (in press).

[12] C.R. Mechoso, M.J. Suarez, K. Yamazaki, A. Kitoh, A. Arakawa, *Adv. Geophys.* 29(1986) 375-413.

[13] C.R. Mechoso, S.W. Lyons and J.A. Spahr, *J. Climate* 3(1990) 812-826.

[14] C.R. Mechoso, C.-C. Ma, J.D. Farrara, J.A. Spahr, R.W. Moore, "Parallelization and distribution of a coupled atmosphere-ocean general circulation mode.", *Mon. Weath. Rev.*, in press.

[15] C.-C. Ma, Y. Chao, C.R. Mechoso, W.M. Weibel and D. Halpern, "Comparison of vertical mixing schemes for ocean general circulation models.", Preprints of the Fifth Conference on Climate Variations, Denver, CO, Amer. Meteor. Soc. (1991) 388-391.

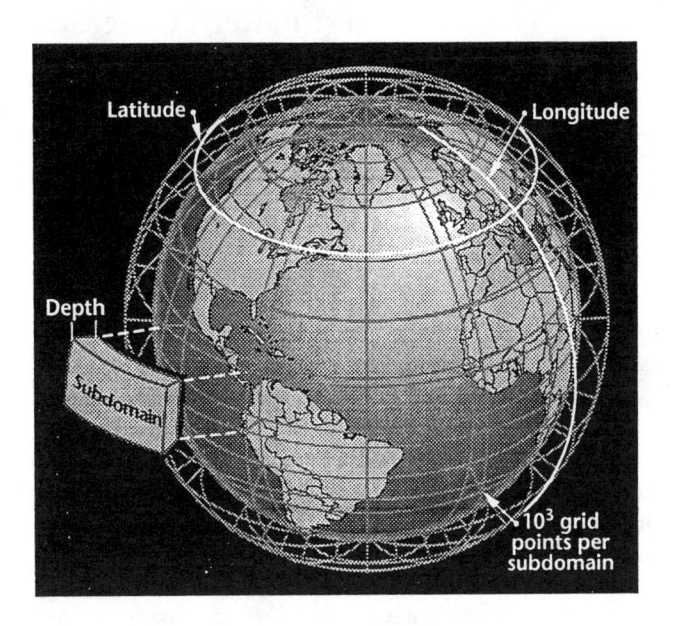

Figure 1. Two-dimensional domain decomposition used for parallelizing the atmospheric general circulation model.

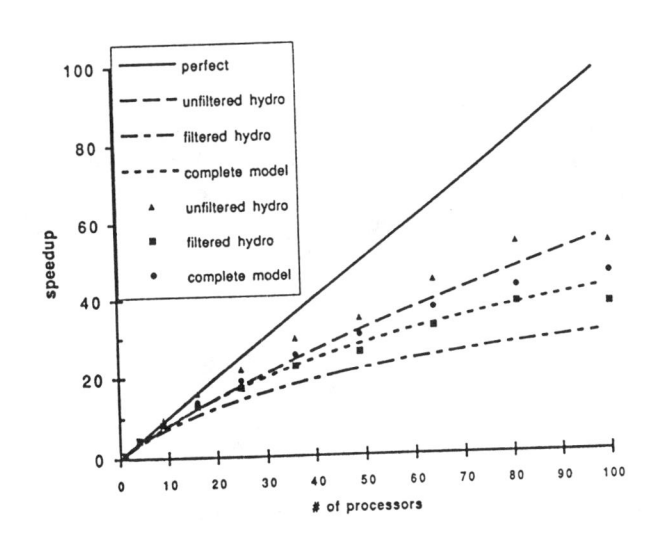

Figure 2. Parallel performance of the AGCM on the BBN-TC2000. Speedup as defined in eq.(3). vs. number of processors.

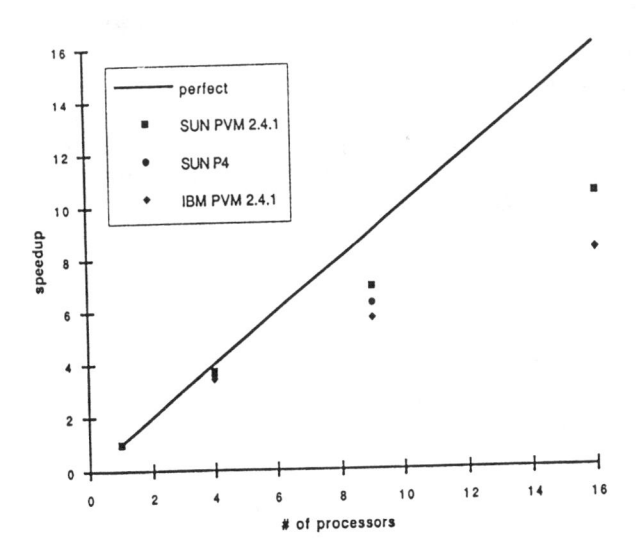

Figure 3. Parallel speedup of the AGCM on clusters of workstations.

Test Pattern Generation for Sequential Circuits on a Network of Workstations

Prathima Agrawal, Vishwani D. Agrawal, and Joan Villoldo

AT&T Bell Laboratories
Murray Hill, NJ 07974

Abstract—A sequential circuit test generation program is parallelized to run on a network of Sparc 2 workstations connected through ethernet. The program attempts to compute tests to detect all faults in a given list. The fault list is equally divided among the processors. The entire process consists of a series of parallel computing passes with synchronization occurring between passes. During a pass, each processor independently generates test sequences for the assigned faults through vector generation and fault simulation. A fixed per-fault CPU time limit is used within a pass. Faults requiring more time are abandoned for later passes. Each processor simulates the entire fault list with its vectors and communicates the list of undetected faults to all other processors. Processors then combine these fault lists to create a list of faults that were not detected by all processors. This list is again equally divided and the next pass begins with a larger per-fault time limit for test generation. The process stops after either the required fault coverage is achieved or the pass with given maximum per-fault time limit is completed. Some benchmark results are given to show the advantage of distributed system for large circuits. Finally, we study a speedup model that considers duplicated computation and interprocessor communication.

I. INTRODUCTION

Test generation for sequential circuits is computationally expensive. For example, a fast test generation program may take a few minutes on a Sparc 2 computer to generate test for a 5,000 gate combinational circuit. The CPU time for a sequential circuit of comparable size can be several hours. Test generation time increases nonlinearly with the size of the circuit. Multiprocessing, therefore, offers a potential solution to speeding up of test generation.

Most of the work reported on parallelization of test generation deals with combinational circuits. Several approaches are possible, namely, partitioning of (1) circuit netlist, (2) fault list, (3) vector space, or (4) test generation algorithm. Parallelization for sequential circuits differs from that for combinational circuits due to the presence of the memory elements. In addition, the architecture of the multiprocessor system also influences parallelization.

Patil *et al* [1] have reported a parallel test generator for sequential circuits using an eight processor Encore system. Encore is a shared memory system and the processors communicate through a shared bus. All processors cooperate in generating a test sequence for a fault by a combination of reverse-time and forward-time processing. For fault simulation, gates are distributed over processors. Their method, which is rather specific to a system of strongly connected processors, shows a definite speed improvement over single processor execution. In a more recent paper [2], the Illinois group has presented results for a network of Sun workstations. The parallelization strategy is still based on the division of search space.

In this paper, we study parallel test generation on a distributed system of computers. We distribute faults among processors. To reduce interprocessor communication and to avoid circuit initialization problem, the vectors generated by separate processors are not shared. Fault list is, however, synchronized using a multipass procedure. The parallelization strategy is outlined in Section 3. Our system consists of sixteen Sparc 2 processors communicating through ethernet. A file-server manages the disc storage for all processors. The processors belong to separate users and the network is similar to a real VLSI design environment.

II. BASIC TEST GENERATOR

We parallelize an existing test generator program, Gentest [3]. Using the time-frame expansion method, Gentest conducts a branch and bound search for a test sequence for the given *target* fault in the reverse time mode. Heuristics based on testability measures guide the search. Once a test sequence is found, all faults detectable by it are removed from the fault list through fault simulation.

The fault simulator in Gentest is a parallel pattern version of the differential simulator [4]. Experience with Gentest has shown that its fault simulation is one to two orders faster than test generation. We, therefore, emphasize the parallelization of test generation.

A. Multi-Pass Operation

Gentest works with a multipass strategy. In the first pass, it begins with a small per-fault CPU time limit. A target fault is picked from the given fault list. If a test is found within the time limit, fault simulation is performed before moving to the next fault. If the time limit exceeds and no test is found, the target fault is abandoned. The abandoned fault is retained in the list of undetected faults and the test generator moves on to the next fault. A pass is completed when each fault is either detected by test generator, or detected by fault simulator, or abandoned. In the next pass, the undetected faults are processed with a higher per-fault CPU time limit. Depending upon the user specified upper limit on the per-fault CPU time, the test generator may make several passes. Results of Gentest on the sequential benchmark circuits may be found in a recent paper [5].

B. Initialization

Gentest supports several options for initialization. The user can supply a sequence of vectors which is simulated to remove the detected faults from the list. The test generator then picks a target fault. Both the true state and the faulty state are known at the end of the simulated vectors. The test for the target fault starts from these states. If, however, there are no user-supplied vectors given, a completely *unknown* state is assumed. The test sequence for the first target fault thus includes an initialization sequence. The state at the end of the first test sequence then becomes the initial state for the second fault.

III. PARALLELIZATION

The main considerations in executing Gentest on a distributed system are as follows:

A. Inter-Processor Communication

Since the ethernet communication between processors is expensive in time, we must minimize it by letting the processors work independently. The fault list is, therefore, equally divided among processors each of which processes its own faults.

B. Duplicated Work

Every fault is targeted in only one processor. Still it is possible that the fault is detected by vectors in other processors. Theoretically, such duplication of work can be avoided by proper partitioning of faults into independent sets. This means that the faults in one set are not detectable by the tests for faults in another set. Methods for such partitioning for sequential circuits are not known and we must rely on arbitrary partitioning. Duplication of work is reduced by *synchronization*, of course, at the cost of interprocessor communication.

C. Synchronization

Since each processor independently initializes the circuit, the vectors are not shared. As explained in the previous section, the test generator makes multiple passes. A pass is characterized by a per-fault CPU time limit. We let all processors work independently within a pass. At the end of a pass, each processor locally updates the *complete* fault list by simulating *all* faults against its vectors. The *locally* updated fault list is broadcast to all other processors. After a processor has received the locally updated fault lists from all other processors, it generates a *globally* updated fault list by taking only those faults that are included in all local lists. The processor then divides the updated fault list and continues with the next pass. In this way, even though the vectors are not shared, the fault lists are globally synchronized after each pass.

D. Initialization

No global reset capability in the circuit is assumed. If the user supplies initial set of vectors, each processor begins with these vectors. If no vectors are supplied by the user, each processor separately initializes the circuit during the generation of its first test sequence. The accumulated vectors in a processor at the end of a pass become the initial vectors for the next pass in that processor. At the end of the first pass, if a processor is found to have generated no vectors, the vectors generated in another processor are supplied to it as starting vectors for the next pass.

E. Assembling the Test Sequence

The program terminates on reaching a user selected limit which can be either maximum per-fault time or the required fault coverage. All subsequences generated in separate processors are concatenated to form the final vector sequence. Since each subsequence begins with its own initialization vectors, the coverage of the concatenated sequence cannot be lower than the coverage determined during multiprocessing. The final sequence, however, contains several sets of initialization vectors which is one reason for its longer length compared to the test sequence generated entirely by a single processor. Actual details of vector by vector fault coverage can be determined by fault simulation with the concatenated sequence. Except the first subsequence, since all others now begin with known flip-flop states, the coverage can be higher than what was found during the multiprocessor operation.

IV. SYSTEM ARCHITECTURE

The architecture of the computer system is shown in Fig. 1. The user initiates the program from any processor which then acts as the host. All communication to and from the user is through the host. The user input consists of (a) circuit netlist, (b) per-fault maximum CPU time limit, (c) number of processors to be used, and (d) required fault coverage. The host compiles the circuit netlist to produce fan-in, fan-out and other tables used by Gentest, checks the workload on the other processors and schedules jobs. For each job, a new copy of the circuit data structure is created in the file server for the assigned processor. On completion of the job, all such copies except the original belonging to the host are deleted. On completion of the program, vector sets from all processors are concatenated to form the test sequence.

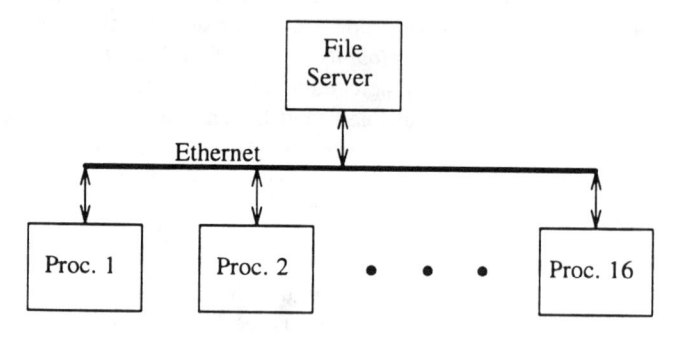

Fig. 1. The system of sixteen Sparc 2 workstations.

Our system is completely automatic. Apart from Gentest, which is a C program, all other procedures are implemented as Unix programs using *cat, grep, sort, uniq, awk,* and *sed* [6] and other utilities.

V. Experimental Performance Measures

Figure 2 shows the multipass operation of a three-processor system. The horizontal scale is elapsed time that may include CPU time, communication time and other overheads due to paging, I/O and the file server queue. The passes are separated by vertical solid lines. Within a pass, there is a computing phase and a communication phase separated by a dashed vertical line. The duration of the computing phase is determined by the processor that take the longest CPU time. For example, processor 3 determines the duration of computing phase in pass 1 and processor 2 determines this duration in pass 2. During the communication phase, the fault lists are communicated among processors which then update their own fault lists and start the next pass synchronously. Similar model has been used to analyze the synchronized parallel logic simulation [7].

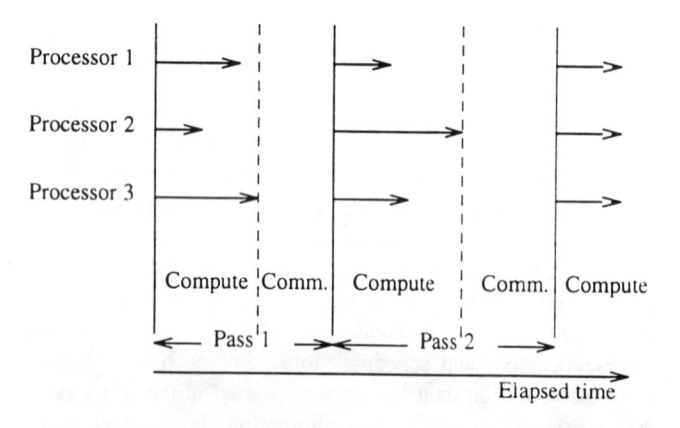

Fig. 2. Parallel computing phases and synchronization.

We use several performance measures. As explained, test generator synchronizes the fault list at the end of each pass. Since the next pass cannot begin until all processors have completed the present pass, the lower bound of time for a pass is the time of processor taking the longest. A lower bound (t_{min}) for the entire task can be found as:

$$t_{min} = \sum_{passes} \max_p (CPU\ time)$$

where p is the number of processors. The actual amount of CPU time used by the task is given by:

$$t_{CPU} = \sum_{passes} \sum_p (CPU\ time)$$

The total system time used by the task is:

$$t_{sys} = t_{min} + \sum_{passes} (Communication\ time)$$

As an example, consider test generation for the circuit s349. The results are given in Table I. The last column gives the *elapsed time* seen by the user. This is higher than the system time (t_{sys}) due to several reasons. First, the user communicates with the host through a remote terminal requiring communication external to the ethernet. Second, the user time includes delays involved in paging, I/O, etc. Although the user time can vary depending upon the state of the communication network, it follows the behavior of t_{sys}. Notice that t_{sys} has two components. The first component, t_{min}, reduces as more processors are used. For an ideal load balance, $t_{min} = t_{CPU}/p$. With sixteen processors, $t_{CPU}/p = 173/16 = 10.8s$. Due to the unbalanced load on these processors, the actual t_{min} was 20s. The second component in t_{sys}, which is due to interprocessor communication, increases with the number of processors used. For larger number of processors, communication time dominates.

TABLE I
TEST GENERATION FOR S349 ON A DISTRIBUTED SYSTEM

No. of CPUs p	No. of Vectors	Fault Coverage %	t_{min} s	t_{CPU} s	t_{sys} s	User Time s
1	81	95	112	112	247	300
2	90	90	58	85	143	245
4	113	96	44	118	139	209
8	153	94	36	165	232	320
16	219	95	20	173	266	382

Table I shows that for s349, the best performance was obtained with four processors. Notice that even with single processor, the communication overhead is not zero. This is due to the communication between the host processor and the file server.

The computing cost to the user can be obtained as a weighted sum of the total CPU time (t_{CPU}) and the communication time ($t_{sys} - t_{min}$).

VI. RESULTS

We generated tests for several benchmark circuits using the distributed version of Gentest. The results are summarized in Table II.

Several observations are made from these results. For a very small circuit like s27, there is no benefit of multiprocessing. This is because the communication time dominates the computing time. For circuits, where computing time is large, multiprocessing is beneficial. The fault coverage can vary with number of processors. There are two reasons for this. First, the faults are targeted in different order. Whether or not Gentest finds a test for a target fault can be influenced by the state produced by the previous vectors. Second, the stopping heuristics in Gentest sometimes terminate a pass if many successive target faults are abandoned.

Multiprocessor runs always produced more vectors. This is not different from the results reported by Patil *et al* [1]. Fault coverages in Table II were computed by including the faults reported as *untestable* among tested faults. Gentest identifies a fault as untestable if no test is possible. Some of these faults are, in fact, redundant. Thus, the fault coverage corresponds to the faults that are either detected by the generated vectors or not detectable at all by Gentest's algorithm. Any lower than 100% coverage is due to the per-fault CPU time limit specified by the user. Depending upon the circuit size, this limit was varied from 1s to 128s. The comparative speed advantage of multiprocessing is significant. Consider, for example, the s5378 circuit. The system time for a single Sparc 2 is 202275s or over two days. With four processors, this time is reduced to less than two hours. Such superlinear speedup is observed for several circuits for which the single processor CPU time was large.

One possible reason for superlinear speedup is the different order in which the test space is explored in the cases of single and multiple processors. In the latter case, multiple searches are simultaneously conducted. In case of easy to test circuits, the run time is dominated by the communication time and distributed system gives no advantage. The circuit s1196 is an example of this type.

Figure 3 shows the four-processor speedup as a function of the single-processor time. For smaller jobs, the speedup is lower than the ideal value of *four*. Load unbalance is the main cause for this result. Lowering of speedup due to interprocessor communication is also evident. For some larger jobs, as explained earlier, there is superlinear speedup. Surprisingly, for s526, s832 and s5378, the speedup with communication is higher than the speedup when the communication is neglected. A possible reason is that computing and communication are overlapped; while a processor communicates with the fileserver, others may compute. In the single processor case, no computing is done while communication with fileserver is carried out.

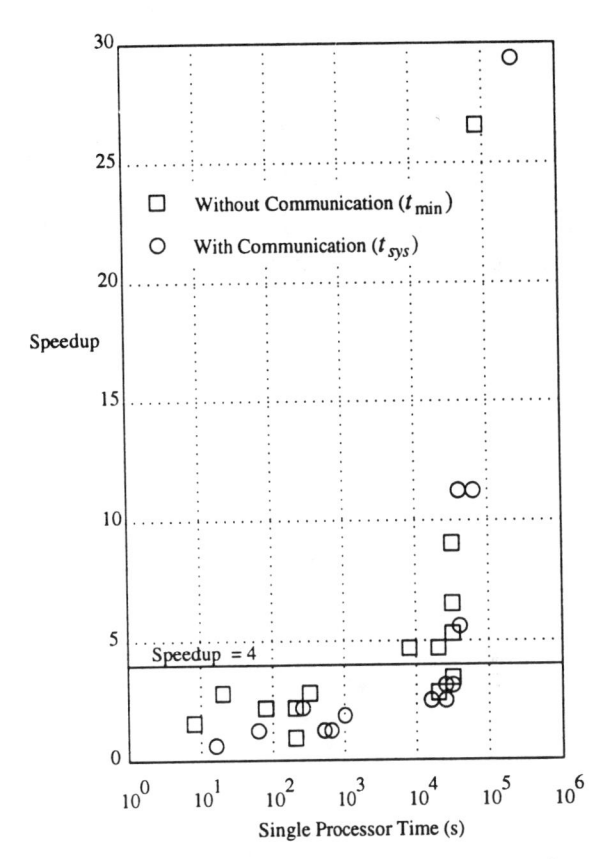

Fig. 3. Four-processor speedup versus single processor time.

Possible Improvements

In our system, all processors are served by a common file server. Although the processors can compute in parallel, memory management (paging, etc.) is essentially serial. Improved performance is possible with distributed file system where the processors may communicate through Unix *socket*. The system can also accommodate dissimilar processors. The fault list can then be divided unequally in proportion to the computing capability of processors.

Partitioning of faults in our system is arbitrary. Intelligent partitioning where faults are divided into independent sets can reduce duplication of computation. An optimal partitioning will be such that the faults in one partition are not detectable by tests for faults in another partition. Finding optimal or even near optimal partitioning of faults in a sequential circuit is an open problem.

Although the present strategy of synchronized multi-pass execution gives significant speedup, improvements are possible. A simple strategy is to start with small number of processors. With small CPU time limit, easy to detect faults are covered. In later passes, as the time limit is increased to cover hard to detect faults, more processors can be added. In general, hard to detect faults require separate tests while any test might detect many easy to detect faults.

TABLE II
Test Generation on a Distributed System

Circuit Name	No. of CPUs p	No. of Vectors	Fault Coverage %	t_{min} s	t_{CPU} s	t_{sys} s
s27	1	18	100.0	0.2	0.2	5.6
	2	21	100.0	0.13	0.23	13.2
	4	27	100.0	0.13	0.44	11.4
	8	37	100.0	0.18	0.80	17.1
	16	57	100.0	0.15	1.08	24.9
s208	1	132	100.0	8.2	8.2	20.0
	4	223	100.0	3.7	9.0	64.0
	12	347	100.0	2.1	12.0	31.0
	16	416	100.0	1.8	12.0	64.0
s298	1	190	87.3	240.2	240.2	387.0
	4	426	93.3	193.1	589.0	444.0
	12	792	90.4	19.6	118.0	104.0
	16	822	90.4	24.0	191.0	121.0
s344	1	144	93.9	208.6	208.6	995.0
	4	242	95.0	105.9	343.0	583.0
	12	326	94.2	57.1	402.0	590.0
s349	1	81	94.8	112.0	112.0	247.0
	4	113	95.7	44.0	118.0	139.0
	8	153	94.0	36.0	165.0	232.0
	16	219	94.8	20.0	173.0	266.0
s382	1	3488	94.0	6129.8	6129.8	14724.0
	12	997	100.0	47.4	392.0	797.0
s400	1	2079	93.4	7290.0	7290.0	13351.0
	12	3548	93.6	648.0	5648.0	6765.0
s420	1	131	100.0	290.0	290.0	571.0
	4	300	99.5	125.1	404.0	713.0
	12	389	99.5	63.6	510.0	636.0
s444	1	507	97.0	8206.8	8206.8	18996.0
	4	541	96.2	1714.8	5245.0	6185.0
	12	1743	97.5	1320.3	13098.0	8655.0
s526	1	2582	76.4	27085.7	27085.7	65487.0
	4	2158	73.9	4381.1	8663.0	5930.0
	12	5925	81.2	3641.3	24972.0	8855.0
s526n	1	2592	81.5	20176.5	20176.5	28644.0
	4	1377	72.9	4966.9	9855.0	9061.0
	12	4414	78.1	3576.6	22952.0	9044.0
s820	1	465	89.2	22166.3	22166.3	26279.0
	4	424	81.5	4275.9	7671.0	5914.0
	12	558	85.9	1763.9	11763.0	2836.0
s832	1	362	84.1	30457.3	30457.3	46656.0
	4	376	78.0	3281.8	6923.0	4170.0
	12	567	79.9	2309.4	13939.0	3175.0
s953	1	26	99.9	150.5	150.5	178.0
	4	50	99.9	3.8	12.0	24.0
	12	74	99.9	2.9	15.0	32.0
s1196	1	328	100.0	20.0	20.0	54.0
	4	528	100.0	7.8	27.0	63.0
	12	668	100.0	4.8	44.0	101.0
s1488	1	373	88.4	19691.7	19691.7	31432.0
	4	413	82.5	6554.4	15506.0	8415.0
	12	724	88.8	5400.9	28728.0	6473.0
s1494	1	143	83.6	23160.1	23160.1	41039.0
	4	529	90.1	6745.8	10941.0	6622.0
	12	870	90.3	6962.2	34466.0	6468.0
s5378	1	436	76.2	89247.0	89247.0	202275.0
	4	874	77.2	3388.4	10250.0	7014.0
	12	1157	73.4	2268.9	15293.0	11201.0

VII. A Theoretical Performance Model

Test generation is a search problem. We search for tests for the given set of faults. Let us first consider test generation on a single processor. Once a test is found for some chosen target fault, fault simulation is performed to remove all other faults from the list that are also detected by the generated test. Such elimination of faults results in considerable efficiency in test generation.

Two problems arise when we parallelize a test search problem. First, the tests cannot be communicated between processors. This is because of the sequential nature of the circuits and the tests generated in two processors may require different initial states. Information on detected faults can be communicated. However, the communication in a distributed system may be more expensive and will reduce the overall speedup. Still, the communication of the detected fault data can reduce duplication of work. Since the faults are distributed among processors, a fault is targeted by only one processor for test generation. The same fault can be detected by the tests generated by another processor for some other target fault. That processor should then communicate this information to the processor to which the fault was assigned. Reducing duplication of work, therefore, requires interprocessor communication.

Consider the single processor case again. Assume that the test generation for a target fault and simulation of the test to update the fault list is *one unit* of computing effort. Also, assume that d is the probability of detecting a fault by the test generated for some other target fault. For simplicity, we assume d to be the same for all faults, though that is not the case in reality. Having detected the first fault in the list, we find that the generated test also detects the second fault with probability d. The average computing effort for detecting the second fault is $1-d$. Similarly, the effort of detecting the third fault is $(1-d)^2$. If the list contains N faults, the total effort of test generation by a single processor is

$$E_{comp}(N) = 1 + (1-d) + (1-d)^2 + \cdots + (1-d)^{N-1}$$
$$= \frac{1-(1-d)^N}{d} \qquad (1)$$

For $d = 0.0$, $E_{comp}(N) = N$. However, for any nonzero d, $E_{comp}(N)$ is always less than N.

Next, consider a system of p processors. N faults are equally divided. Thus each processor works on its own list of N/p faults. Suppose, we allow no interprocessor communication. We also assume that either there is no statistical variation between the efforts of generating tests for various target faults or these variations can be averaged out. Then, the time taken by the multiprocessor system is given by $E_{comp}(N/p)$, which is obtained by substituting N/p for N in Equation (1). The speedup without communication is

$$S_{no\_comm}(p) = \frac{E_{comp}(N)}{E_{comp}(N/p)} = \frac{1-(1-d)^N}{1-(1-d)^{N/p}} \qquad (2)$$

This is shown in Figure 4 for $N = 1,000$. For $d = 0.0$, the speedup is ideal. As d increases, the probability of processors duplicating the work increases and the speedup reduces significantly. It is interesting to note the massively parallel case, $p = N$, where just one fault is assigned to each processor. The parallel system takes only one unit of computing effort.

However, the effort of single processor is $E_{comp}(N) \approx \frac{1}{d}$. Thus, the speedup is $\frac{1}{d}$.

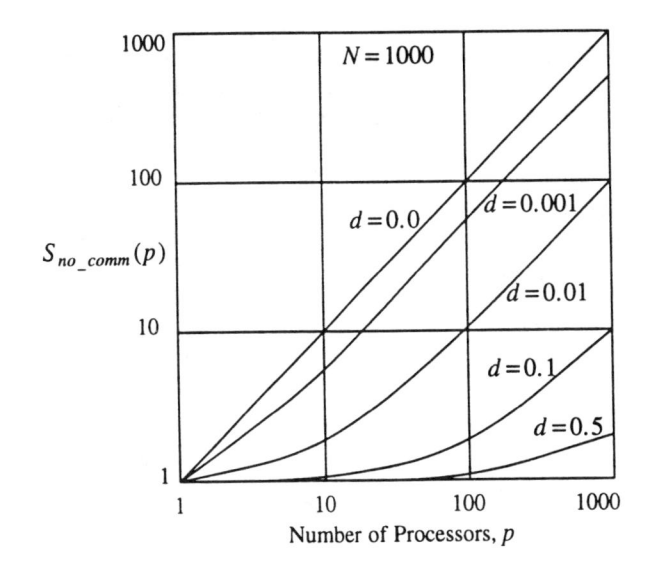

Fig. 4. Speedup without communication.

Next, let us consider the effect of interprocessor communication. Assume that the data generated for communication is proportional to the amount of computation. Also, the data generated by a processor is communicated to $p-1$ processors. Thus the total amount of communication effort is

$$\alpha \, p(p-1) \cdot E_{comp}(N/p)$$

where α is a constant of proportionality that accounts for the relative cost of computing and communication. It is related to the bandwidth of the communication network; $\alpha = 0.0$ corresponds to infinite bandwidth. The total speedup is

$$S_{with\_comm}(p) = \frac{E_{comp}(N)}{E_{comp}(N/p)} \cdot \frac{1}{1+\alpha p(p-1)} \qquad (3)$$

Suppose, now if we assume that $d = 0.0$, that is, there is no duplication of effort in computing, then $E_{comp}(N) = N$ and $E_{comp}(N/p) = N/p$. Equation (3) shows that the total speedup contains two factors. The first factor, as given by Equation (2), is the speedup when communication overhead is neglected. The second factor accounts for communication. For considering the effect of interprocessor communication, we take the ideal value of the first factor obtained by substituting $d = 0.0$ in Equation (2) which corresponds to *no duplicated effort*. Thus

$$S_{no\_dupl}(p) = \frac{p}{1+\alpha p(p-1)} \qquad (4)$$

For very small α, the communication cost is negligible and the speedup rises linearly with p. However, as the number of processors increases, for any α, eventually $\alpha p(p-1) \gg 1$, and the speedup drops as $\frac{1}{p\alpha}$. For small but nonzero α, Equation (4) provides the maximum speedup when $p = \alpha^{-\frac{1}{2}}$. This speedup is $\frac{p^2}{2p-1}$. For example, with $\alpha = 0.01$, the maximum speedup of 5.26 will occur at $p = 10$. With $\alpha = 0.1$, the maximum speedup is only 1.8 which occurs at $p = 3$. An interesting case is $\alpha = 1.0$. Now the maximum speedup is 1. This indicates that when communication is as expensive as computation, it is better to compute in the same processor than communicating data to other processors. Obviously, we need not consider the cases with $\alpha > 1.0$. A plot of Equation (4) is shown in Figure 5.

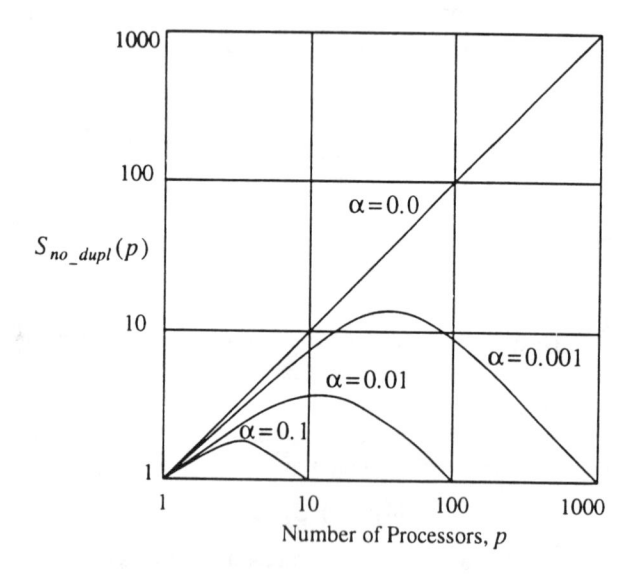

Fig. 5. Speedup with communication ($d = 0.0$).

VIII. Conclusion

Computer networks are a common feature of today's computing environment. Conventional methodology requires execution of a program on a single CPU. This results in under utilization of the combined computing capacity of the system. Expensive solutions requiring supercomputers have been considered in the past. The present work shows that distributed computing can speed up programs at practically no additional cost.

The key idea is to use a synchronized independent multiprocessing model of computation [7]. We were able to complete test generation for a complex sequential circuit in two hours which would have required two days on a single processor. Distributed processing may have similar advantages in other computing tasks.

Our parallel processing models identify the influence of duplicated computing and interprocessor communication on speedup. The influence of these two factors cannot be simultaneously minimized. In order to minimize one, the other must increase. Thus, a proper distribution of a task should take into account the characteristics of the computing network as well as that of the problem being solved. In parallelization, some duplication may be essential when we search a solution space.

Acknowledgment

Authors thank T.J. Chakraborty for assistance with the Gentest program.

References

[1] S. Patil, P. Banerjee, and J.H. Patel, "Parallel Test Generation for Sequential Circuits on General-Purpose Multiprocessors," *Proc. 28th Design Automation Conf.*, pp. 155-159, June 1991.

[2] B. Ramkumar and P. Banerjee, "Portable Parallel Test Generation for Sequential Circuits," *Proc. Int'l Conf. CAD*, pp. 220-223, November 1992.

[3] W.-T. Cheng and T.J. Chakraborty, "Gentest - An Automatic Test-Generation System for Sequential Circuits," *Computer*, Vol. 22, pp. 43-49, April 1989.

[4] T.M. Niermann, W.-T. Cheng, and J.H. Patel, "PROOFS: A Fast, Memory-Efficient Sequential Circuit Fault Simulator," *IEEE Trans. CAD*, Vol. 11, pp. 198-207, February 1992.

[5] B. Bencivenga, T.J. Chakraborty, and S. Davidson, "The Architecture of the GenTest Sequential Circuit Test Generator," *Proc. Custom Integrated Circuits Conference*, pp. 17.1.1-17.1.4, May 1991.

[6] A.V. Aho, B.W. Kernighan, and P.J. Weinberger, *The AWK Programming Language*, Addison-Wesley, Reading, MA, 1988.

[7] V.D. Agrawal and S.T. Chakradhar, "Performance Analysis of Synchronized Iterative Algorithms on Multiprocessor Systems," *IEEE Trans. Parallel Distr. Syst.*, Vol. 3, pp. 739-746, November 1992.

Star Modeling on IBM RS6000 Networks using PVM

Laurent Colombet
LMC-IMAG
46, avenue Félix Viallet
38031 Grenoble France
colombet@imag.fr

Laurent Desbat
TIMC - IMAG
Faculté de Médecine
38706 La Tronche - France
desbat@chrug.imag.fr

François Ménard
Observatoire de Grenoble
B.P.53X D.U.
38041 Grenoble France
menard@gag.observ-gr.fr

Abstract

We present the parallelization of a Monte Carlo radiative transfer code on a workstation network using PVM. In order to measure parallel performances on heterogenous networks, we propose a generalization to heterogenous parallel architectures of the classical speedup and efficiency definitions. We apply these formulae to the study of our parallel code. We then show some scientific results obtained using this program on a Gflops peak performance network.

1 Introduction

Today's scientific problems need more and more computing power. The present trend in supercomputer architecture development is to design parallel machines with powerful processors of more than 100Mflops. A good way to get ready for this future generation of supercomputers is to use workstation networks. Indeed, everybody has access to workstation networks. Furthermore, their total power apparently has no limits and some may even surpass actual supercomputers.

New software like PVM [10] allow us to program such computer networks easily. We did it in Astronomy to illustrate the full potential of this approach, study the performances on a useful application and increase our knowledge of the star formation process.

We parallelized a Monte Carlo type code to study multiple scattering of photons propagating through a dense envelope of dust grains surrounding a central star. The decision to use the Monte Carlo method is justified by the fact that it is the only one versatile enough to allow arbitrary densities and geometries of the scattering medium. This is of fundamental importance since the stars are thought to originate in the gravitational collapse of large molecular clouds. Depending on the amount of initial rotation of these clouds, the geometry of the final stages of formation (before a star like our sun appears for example) can deviate greatly from spherical symmetry. Indeed, following extensive observation campaigns, we now know that most of the low-mass forming stars (stars that will one day become similar to our sun) go through a violent phase of mass loss. This is detected via the presence of high-velocity jets for example, i.e., narrowly collimated streams of material escaping from the "poles" of the forming stars. The collimation mechanism of these jets is still uncertain but a good possibility is the presence of an equatorial disk that would somehow force material to flow preferentially towards the poles.

But these disks are also interesting for another reason: they are a material reservoir out of which planets may very well form. And it is interesting to note that in our own solar system all the planets are located in the same plane, the equator of the sun! We therefore feel that the study and if possible the evaluation of the geometrical parameters of the disks surrounding the forming stars can yield decisive clues about the uniqueness and the origin of our own planetary system.

It was shown [2, 16] that polarization observations of forming stars contain, if the viewing angle is appropriate, direct information about these disks. Indeed, the pattern of the linear polarization vectors thoughgout the surrounding dust envelope is modified by the presence of the disk. The code we used here was written to produce synthetic polarization maps of this phenomenon for comparison. The first simulations we made gave us, for the first time, the size, mass and inclination of ~ 30 star-disk systems [16, 3]. These calculations suffered however from a lack of CPU power. The synthetic maps produced were low-signal ($\sim 5 \times 10^6$ photons) low-resolution (11×11 grid) replicas of the observations. They confirmed that the basic idea of a disk surrounding a star in formation is right, but did not allow very precise comparison with the observations. As we will see, the use of PVM on a network of only 20 workstations allowed us to produce better maps of the intensity and more precise linear polarisation at the same resolution and signal-to-noise ratio than the observations now available.

These calculations allowed us to ascertain that the size of the disks surrounding young stars are of similar sizes and masses as those in our own solar system. This is a very important result as it proves that our planetary system is not the exception anymore, at least in our Galaxy. We cannot directly detect the planets yet, but we see and measure their precursor: the equatorial disk. And this is only one aspect of the results.

In §2 we describe the workstation network we used and the parallelization, with PVM, of the radiative transfer code on an IBM RS6000 network. In §3 we propose a generalization of the classical speedup and efficiency definitions to heterogeneous processor networks that we then use to study the performance of our parallel application. A presentation of the principal astrophysical results follows.

2 Parallelization of the Monte Carlo code on an IBM RS6000 network

A present-day challenge in supercomputer design is to reach *Teraflops* performances. Manufacturers like CRAY, DEC, HP, IBM, TMC, all have Tflops projects based on powerful processors like those used in modern workstations. Meanwhile, that high-speed processor technology is also used to build workstation networks [1, 21, 19, 20] widespread in companies and universities, that can mimic parallel virtual machines, thanks to softwares like CHARM [14], Parform [8], P4 [7], PVM [10, 11]. This is the approach we chose for our scientific calculations.

2.1 Description of the network

The computational ressources of the Observatoire de Grenoble are principally based on a workstation network (see figure 1). Different machines are used for two different purposes: some (at the top of the figure) are dedicated to interactive work, with restricted access for each of the three constitutive groups of the Observatoire. They are mostly load-free at night. The others (at the bottom) are machines dedicated to number-crunching and belong to the common observatory pool. They are heavily used through DNQS (Dis-

tributed Network Queueing System). For final calculations, the network was used at night and further extended by including the workstations of the Magistère de Physique de Grenoble, located several kilometers away. These machines are not represented in the figure.

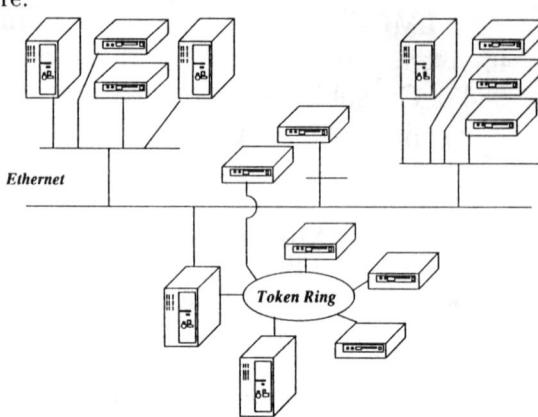

Figure 1: IBM RS6000 network used at the Observatoire de Grenoble.

2.2 The PVM system

PVM (Parallel Virtual Machine) is a software developed at the Oak Ridge National Laboratory; it allows to use a set of heterogeneous computers as a single computational resource like a MIMD parallel computer. The computing elements of the network (e.g., workstations, vector machines, and multiprocessors) may be interconnected by one or more networks, which may themselves be different (e.g., Ethernet, Token Ring, FDDI,...). In fact, PVM consists of two parts, the first one is a daemon process and the second one is a library that contains routines for the initiation of processes on other machines, communication between processes, and synchronization of processes. Users' programs, in C or Fortran, can access PVM features through calls to the PVM library. The PVM environment also offers debugging and administrative facilities, a graphical interface tool that permits the specification of applications using a variant of DAGs[1] and the post-mortem analysis HeNCE [4, 5].

On distributed memory machines, the cost of accessing data that do not reside on the local memories severely affects the performance of an algorithm. For an IBM RS6000 workstation network interconnected by Ethernet and Tokeng Ring, the communication cost is a critical issue. In our case, the use of a Monte Carlo method to follow the evolution of trajectories

---
[1]Directed acyclic graphs

of photons scattered by dust grains assures the independence of each photon calculation and renders the parallelization trivial. Furthermore, since the volume of communications between processors is small (sending the start-up input parameters and retrieving the final results only) the ratio of data communication to the amount of computation is almost negligible. But the Monte Carlo method is a statistical one and a large number of events has to be simulated to obtain accurate results, implying a lot of CPU time. Thus, we decided to implement an algorithm based on dynamic load balancing to fully use the resources of the available network. The parallel programming model that we chose is of the master-slave type. The master task is in charge of broadcasting the work by equal packets of nb photons to the stations (slaves) dedicated to calculation. It also redistributes new work loads when needed. Adapting nb to every machine would slightly improve the efficiency but is not critical and therefore not done. Another critical issue is the possible fault of some computer(s) in the network during calculation. To avoid losing all the results, if the crash of a slave-machine were to cause an interruption of the whole network, we devised a fault tolerant algorithm. If a slave processor crashes during calculation, the master task will not communicate with it anymore and equivalent work will be done by another processor, therefore tolerating faults.

Algorithm 1

Master Task algorithm

> Enroll this program in PVM
> Send to each processor the initial parameters
> of the modeling and nb
> dowhile ($N > 0$)
>   receive results from processor $inum$
> $N \leftarrow N - nb$
>   if ($N > 0$) then
>   send work of amount nb to proc. $inum$
>   endif
>   Treat results
> enddo
> kill all slaves
> Treat and save all results
> Stop

Algorithm 2

Slave Task algorithm

> Enroll this program in PVM
> Receive parameters of the modelling and
> nb the number of photons
> dowhile (I have work)
>   Compute
>   Send results
>   Wait for new work
> enddo
> Stop

3 Efficiency and speedup on an heterogeneous computer network

Speedup and efficiency are well defined for homogeneous parallel architectures, i.e., parallel machines built with P identical processors [12, 15, 17, 22] (for more extensive studies [18, 13] and references therein). In this case the definition of speedup for an algorithm is:

$$S(P) \stackrel{def}{=} \frac{T(1)}{T(P)}$$

where $T(j)$ is the algorithm execution time with j processors. If a basic operation has the same execution time on a processor both during the parallel execution and during the sequential one (for example, we suppose that the memory is large enough to hold the problem for a sequential execution), then it is clear that the speedup is less or equal to the number P of processors. So, the notion of efficiency for parallel algorithms on homogeneous architecture is given by:

$$E(P) \stackrel{def}{=} \frac{S(P)}{P} = \frac{T(1)}{PT(P)}.$$

When using a heterogeneous processor network, the concept of speedup and efficiency has to be generalized. In fact, what does "the sequential time" $T_{\text{seq}} = T(1)$ mean in this case? The power p of a processor on a sequential algorithm is defined by:

$$p \stackrel{def}{=} \frac{W}{T},$$

where W is the work to be done and $T = T_{\text{seq}}(p)$ is the corresponding execution time. In numerical computation, we generally evaluate the power of a processor in Mflops (the work W being the number of floating point operations). In the classical homogeneous case, the speedup is implicitly related to the sequential execution time on *one* of the processors, because they are identical. In the heterogeneous case, this relativity with respect to the power p of a processor (defined as the reference processor or RP) used for the sequential time measurement has to be explicitly expressed, because the processors are different. We propose a new general definition of the speedup:

$$S_P(p) \stackrel{def}{=} \frac{T_{\text{seq}}(p)}{T(P)} \text{ where } T_{\text{seq}}(p) = \frac{W}{p}.$$

During the parallel execution of the algorithm involving the work W, the processor i executes a work W_i such that $W = \sum_{i=1}^{P} W_i$. The power of the processor i on this work is defined by:

$$p_i \stackrel{def}{=} \frac{W_i}{T_i},$$

where T_i is the sequential execution time of the work W_i on the processor i. The total power available on the P processors network for our algorithm is $\sum_{i=1}^{P} p_i$. We can define the relative power of processor i by $\frac{p_i}{p}$. If the power of the processor i is independent of the exact nature of the work executed (i.e., p_i constant $\forall W_i$) we say that the behaviour of the processor is homogeneous. A homogeneous processor i is equivalent to $\frac{p_i}{p}$ reference processor (RP) for our sequential algorithm. Let's note

$$\#(p_1, \ldots, p_P, p) = \frac{\sum_{i=1}^{P} p_i}{p}$$

the relative power of the processor network. When the processors are homogeneous the following proposition gives us a constant upper bound for the speedup.

Proposition 1

$$S_P(p) \leq \#(p_1, \ldots, p_P, p)$$

The previous bound is reached when the times T_i are all the same and when the communications are completely overlapped. If the processors are not homogeneous, this bound depends on the work mapping. If we want to define the efficiency and speedup of an algorithm on a heterogeneous network of heterogeneous processors, we must introduce a model of the execution time taking into account the processor differences, i.e., their different ability to compute different types of operations. We suppose that the total work W is composed by J different types of operations: $W = \sum_{j=1}^{J} W^j$. We define $c_{i,j}$ and $w_{i,j}$ as the cost and work respectively of one operation of type j on processor i, thus $T_i = \sum_{j=1}^{J} c_{i,j} w_{i,j}$. We can prove that the solution $T_{//}$ of the following linear program is a lower bound of the parallel execution time of the application:

$$T_{//} \stackrel{def}{=} \min_{w_{i,j}} \sum_{j=1}^{J} c_{P,j} w_{P,j}.$$

$$\begin{cases} w_{i,j} \geq 0 \\ \sum_{j=1}^{J} c_{i,j} w_{i,j} = \sum_{j=1}^{J} c_{P,j} w_{P,j} \; \forall i = 1, \ldots, P-1 \\ \sum_{i=1}^{P} w_{i,j} = W^j \; \forall j = 1, \ldots, J \end{cases}$$

(1)

Remark that $T_i = T_{//}, \forall i$ is a constraint of the previous linear program. As for the lower bound given in the case of a homogeneous network, we solve the problem with real numbers and thus obtain a underestimation of the optimal parallel time obtained with integers: $T_{//} \leq T(P)$. We note that the simplex (1) is always feasible with:

$$w_{i,j} = \frac{\prod_{k=1, k \neq i}^{P} c_{k,j}}{\sum_{l=1}^{P} \prod_{k=1, k \neq l}^{P} c_{k,j}} W^j.$$

We can prove (see [9]) that:

- If the cost vectors $c_{i,\cdot}$ are two by two dependent, each feasible solution of (1) yields the optimality, i.e., gives the same bound $T_{//}$. To simplify we suppose that $\forall i = 1, \ldots, P, \exists \lambda_i \in \mathbb{R}$ like $\forall j = 1, \ldots, J, c_{i,j} = \lambda_i c_j$ where $(c_1, c_2, \ldots, c_J)$ is the cost vector of the processor RP, then the solution for the problem (1) is:

$$T_{//} = \frac{T_{\text{seq}}(p)}{\sum_{i=1}^{P} \frac{1}{\lambda_i}}.$$

A majoration of the speedup is given by $\#(p) = \#(p_1, \ldots, p_P, p) = \sum_{i=1}^{P} \frac{1}{\lambda_i}$ and we can use the following definition:

$$E(P) = \frac{S(P)}{\sum_{i=1}^{P} \frac{1}{\lambda_i}}$$

This definition is a generalization of the well-known classical definition with $\lambda_i = 1$ (identical processors).

- If there exists a cost vector linearly independent from the others, all feasible solution to problem (1) is not necessarily optimal. Let $w_{i,j}^*$ be a solution, then $W_i^* = \sum_{j=1}^{J} w_{i,j}^*$, $p_i^* = W_i^*/T_{//}$ and $\#(p) = \sum_{i=1}^{P} p_i^*/p$. In this case the following definition of the efficiency is consistent (i.e., $0 \leq E(P) \leq 1$):

$$E(P) = \frac{S(P)}{\#(p)}$$

where $\#(p) = \#(p_1^*, \ldots, p_P^*, p)$ is a constant (for more details see [9]).

4 Results

In this section we present performance measurements of our Monte Carlo code on an heterogeneous network of IBM-RS6000 workstations. The first test experimentations presented were done on a dedicated small and local network (one to five RS6000-320, one RS6000-550, one RS6000-560), with the same astrophysical parameters as in the final runs, to study the behavior of the programs (sequential and parallel) and later to allow performance analysis. Then we present some measurements on actual experiments with 20 IBM RS6000 (fifteen 320, one 520, one 530, two 550 and one 560) on a wider network (machines several km apart).

4.1 Test experiments

4.1.1 Sequential execution time

We present, in figure 2, the sequential execution time for the various types of workstations we used as a function of the number N of photon trajectories to be computed. For the usual value of N ($N \in [10^5, 10^8]$), we see that the statistical time variations are negligible and the behavior linear. Thus we can predict the sequential execution time on each workstation for any large N ($\sim 10^9$) from the execution time for a small N ($\sim 10^5$).

We can also measure that a 520 model has the same power as a 320 on our code, the 530, 550, 560 models are respectively 1.25, 2 and 2.5 times more powerful. We will accept the following approximation to perform an efficiency analysis: we suppose that the various model cost vectors are two by two linearly dependent. Indeed, the workstations have no major differences in their architecture (all are super-scalar processors). Under this hypothesis and taking a 320 as RP, we have $\#(p) = \sum_{i=1}^{P} \frac{1}{\lambda_i}$ with $\lambda_i \in \{1, 1.25, 2, 2.5\}$ depending on the type of machine.

4.1.2 Parrallel execution time

Influence of nb: We present, in figure 3, the execution time on a network of five workstations as a

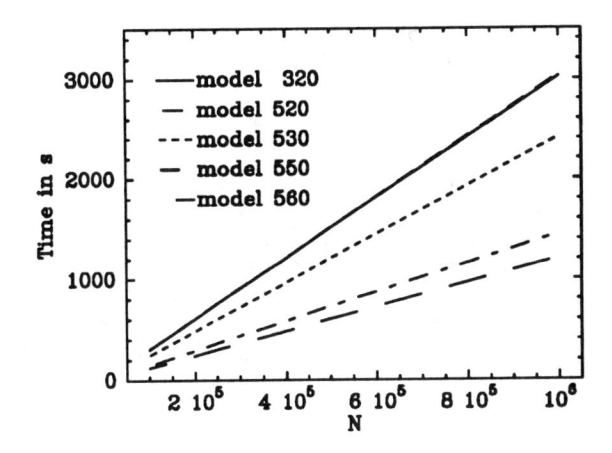

Figure 2: Sequential execution time (in seconds) as a function of photon number N.

function of N for different nb. According to the small amount of data exchange at each communication, the parameter nb is not very critical (unless it is chosen very small (~ 1) or very large ($\sim N$)).

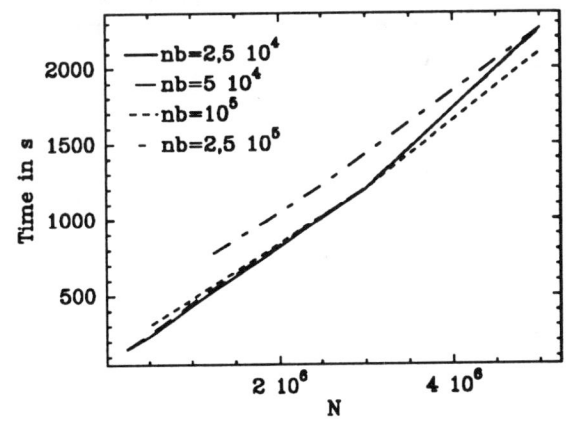

Figure 3: Parallel execution time as a function of photon number N for different parameters nb.

Influence of P: In figure 4 we show that the parallelization yields excellent results on a small number of workstations. When using only IBM-RS6000 320, the Speedup goes almost as P. When using a small heterogeneous network (three 320, one 560 and one 550, see figure 5) the speedup is almost $\#(p)$ where the RP is a 320 ($\#(p)$ has the successive values : 1,2,3,5.5,7.5 when we increase the number of stations).

4.2 Astrophysical experiments

Finally, we present results (run time, speedup, efficiencies...) for actual experiments in astrophysics cal-

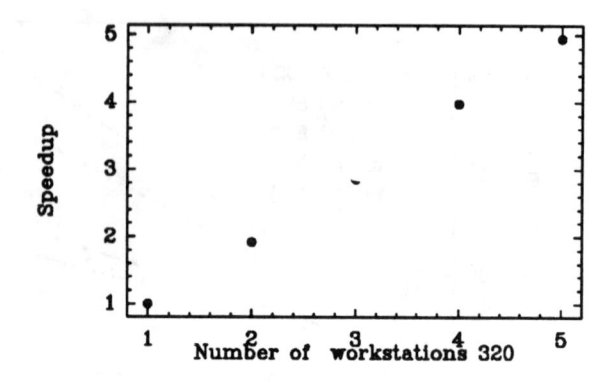

Figure 4: Speedup as a function of the number P of RS6000 320 used.

culated with up to 20 IBM RS6000 (320, 520, 530, 550 and 560) workstations, which represent a peak power of 1 Gflops.

We first measured, for a small number $N = 10^5$ of photons, the sequential execution time on each kind of workstation and for each experiment. The latter differ only by physical parameters, e.g., the grain size.

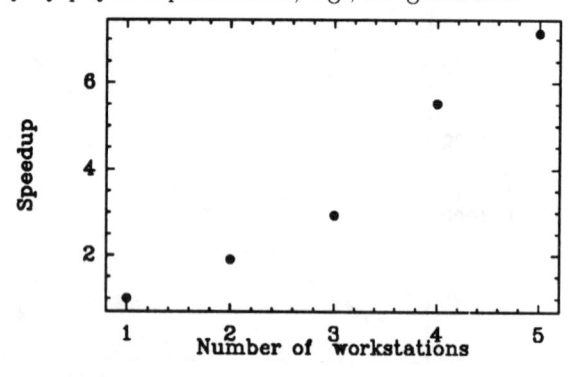

Figure 5: Speedup for a network of three 320's, one 560 and one 550 in the aforementioned order.

Exp.	320	520	530	550	560
1	288 s	286 s	228 s	136 s	114 s
2	294 s	294 s	232 s	138 s	116 s
3	285 s	283 s	227 s	134 s	113 s
4	285 s	284 s	226 s	134 s	113 s

According to paragraph 4.1.1, we can predict the sequential time of each calculation on each workstation. Thus, we are able to measure the speedup relative to each kind of processor in our network.

In the following tabular T_{seq} represents the sequential execution time (in 10^3 seconds) on the RP, a RS6000-320, $S_P(p)$ the speedup and E the efficiency. As in the preceding paragraph, we suppose that the vector costs of the processors for the work to be done are two by two dependent. Thus we can use the results from section 3 and the information from the previous tabular to compute very simply the value of $\#(p)$. We note that the efficiency is of order 80% in this case. This is because we cannot forbid the access to all the machines during the calculations: other jobs were running on some of them. 80% is therefore an underestimation of the actual efficiency. We can verify in section 4.1.2 that the efficiency is close to 100% when the network is totally allocated to our application.

Exp.	N	$\#(p)$	T_{par}	T_{seq}	$S_P(p)$	E
1	$5\ 10^7$	23.75	8.5	144	16.9	.71
2	$8\ 10^7$	23.75	12.7	235	18.5	.78
3	$8\ 10^7$	23.75	11.9	228	19.2	.81
4	$8\ 10^7$	23.75	12.3	228	18.5	.78

5 Astronomical results

Presented on the next page are the actual observations (left panel) of a Young Star known as R Monocerotis together with a synthetic image (right panel) whose upper part closely resembles the image obtained at the telescope. On the observed image, the intensity contours are indicated by the full lines. Note their conical shape, opening towards the top of the page, with the brightest spot (the star) located at the base of the cone. The synthetic image nicely simulates the opening angle of the cone and the relative brightness of the contours throughout the nebula.

From the parameters used in the calculations to produce this result, it is possible to understand the nature of the underlying system: a star surrounded by an asymmetric dust shell and an equatorial disk, probably the precursor of a planetary system.

In the observed image, the southern "cone" remains undetected because it is buried deeper in a molecular cloud detected by other techniques. The short lines covering the image indicate the polarization across the nebulosity, a feature not discussed here, but also precisely and nicely reproduced by our program.

6 Conclusion

We presented the parallelization of a Monte Carlo code on a network of workstations to study an astrophysical problem. In such a favorable context (independent calculations and almost no communications) the use of PVM enabled us to achieve very high efficiency and speed, leading to unprecedented astronomical image simulation. Geometrical parameters for the environment, and more specifically the disks, surrounding stars in formation are now available, giving us invaluable new insight into the physics of star formation.

The construction of a dynamic load-balancing algorithm made our calculations more efficient and tolerant to machine faults. When calculations are performed in multi-user mode, this algorithm balances the work to make the best use of all available resources, the efficiency becomes close to optimal when a large fraction of the machines is fully dedicated to the problem.

We also proposed a generalization of the speedup and efficiency notions to heterogeneous networks. Simple formulae were obtained for the case of weak heterogeneity, i.e., when the processors differ only by their clock rates. Our formulae are valid only when one application is running on the computer network. In the multi-user case, our formulae underestimate of the speedup and efficiency, but are nevertheless good indicators.

Since, in our problem, the communication fraction is negligible compared to the volume of calculations, other applications may not be as efficient on similar workstation networks. Nevertheless, many applications exist (e.g., in geophysics, fluid mechanics, matrix computation [6]) for which the use of a network of workstations greatly increases the performance. Furthermore, because they are easily available in large numbers and quite simple to use in an everyday environment, these workstations potentially totalize a large calculation power when forming a network and therefore offer a very appealing way to simulate and get ready to use large Teraflop parallel supercomputers. This is a key issue as those computers are expected to be available by 1995-96. Acquiring sufficient expertise in the art of parallel programming and developing the proper tools today is therefore "a must" to optimize the throughput of the next generation of computers and to address the myriad of new problems we will then be able to solve.

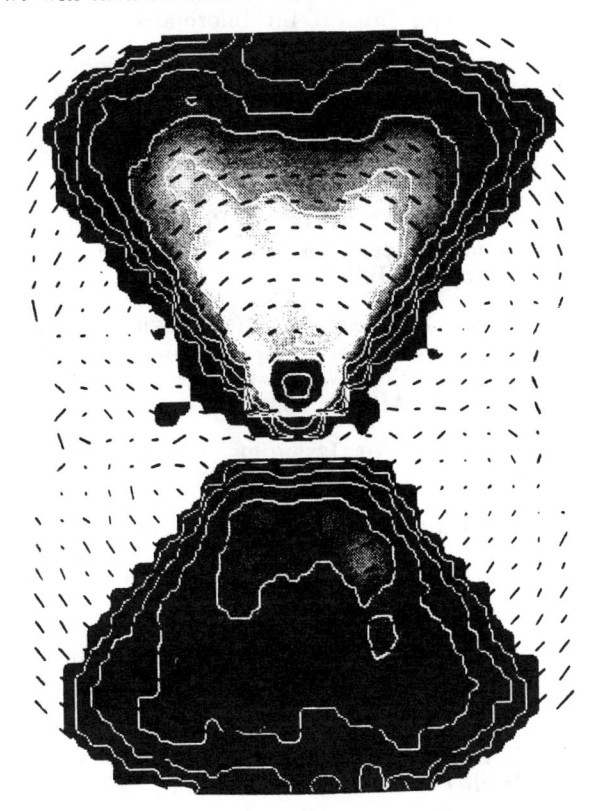

References

[1] A. ANANDA, B. TAY, AND E. KOH, *A Survey of Asynchronous Remote Procedure Calls*, ACM Operating Systems Review, 26 (1992).

[2] P. BASTIEN AND F. MÉNARD, *On the Interpretation of Polarization Maps of Young Stellar Objects.*, Ap. J., 326 (1988), pp. 334–338.

[3] ——, *Parameters of Disks Around Young Stellar Objects from Polarization Observations.*, Ap. J., 364 (1990), pp. 232–241.

[4] A. BEGUELIN, J. DONGARRA, ET AL., *Graphical Development Tools for Network-Based Concurrent Supercomputing.* HeNCE document, 1992.

[5] ——, *HeNCE: A Users' Guide Version 1.2*, Oak Ridge National Laboratory, Feb. 1992.

[6] A. BENZONI, G. RICHELLI, AND V. S. SUNDERNAM, *Concurrent LU Factorization on Workstation networks*, in Parallel Computing 91, G. J. D.J. Evans and H. Liddell, eds., Elsevier Science Publishers, 91.

[7] R. BULTER AND E. LUSK, *User's Guide to the p4 Programming System*, Tech. Rep. ANL-92/17, Argonne National Laboratory, 1992.

[8] C. CAP AND V. STRUMPEN, *The Parform : A High Performance Platform for Parallel Computing in Distributed Workstation Environment*, tech. rep., Institut für Informatik, Universität Zürich, 1992.

[9] L. DESBAT AND L. COLOMBET, *Speedup and Efficiency on Heterogeneous Networks.*, Preprint, Informatique Médicale, Faculté de Médecine, 38706 Grenoble (France), (1993).

[10] J. DONGARRA ET AL., *A Users' Guide to PVM Parallel Virtual Machine*, Oak Ridge National Laboratory, July 1991.

[11] G. A. GEIST AND V. S. SUNDERAM, *Network Based Concurrent Computing on the PVM System.* Oak Ridge National Laboratory and Emory University Atlanta, 1992.

[12] HOCKNEY AND JESSHOPE, *Parallel Computers*, Adam Higler, Bristol and Philadelphia, 1988.

[13] R. HOCKNEY, *Performance parameters and benchmarking of supercomputers.*, Parallel Computing, 17 (1991), pp. 1111–1130.

[14] L. KALE, *The CHARM (3.2) Programming Language Manual*, tech. rep., University of Illinois at Urbana Champaign, (e-mail : kale@cs.uiuc.edu), Dec. 1992.

[15] T. LEWIS AND H. EL-REWINI, *Introduction to Parallel Computing*, Prentice-Hall, 1992.

[16] F. MÉNARD, *Etude de la polarisation causée par des grains dans les enveloppes circumstellaires denses.*, PhD thesis, Univ. of Montréal, 1989.

[17] H. STONE, *High-Performance Computer Architecture*, Addison&Wesley, 1987.

[18] X. SUN AND J. GUSTAFSON, *Toward a better parallel performance metric.*, Parallel Computing, 17 (1991), pp. 1093–1109.

[19] A. TANENBAUM, *Computer Networks*, Prentice-Hall, second ed., 1989.

[20] ——, *Modern Operating Systems*, Prentice-Hall, 1992.

[21] A. TANENBAUM AND R. VAN RENESSE, *Distributed Operating Systems*, ACM Computing Surveys, 17 (1985).

[22] J. WORLTON, *Toward a taxonomy of performance metrics.*, Parallel Computing, 17 (1991), pp. 1073–1092.

A Fully Distributed Parallel Ray Tracing Scheme on the Delta Touchstone Machine*

Tong-Yee Lee, C.S. Raghavendra

School of EECS
Washington State University
Pullman, WA 99164

John B. Nicholas

Battelle Pacific Northwest Laboratory

Richland, WA 99352

Abstract

We describe a fully distributed, parallel algorithm for ray-tracing problem. Load balancing is achieved through the use of comb distribution to roughly assign the same amount of pixels to each processor first, and then dynamically redistribute excessive loads among processors to keep each processor busy. In this model, there is no need for a master node to be responsible for dynamic scheduling. When each node finishes its job, it just requests an extra job from one of its neighbors.

We implement our algorithm on Intel Delta Touchstone machine with 2-D mesh network topology and provide simulation results. With our scheme, we can get good speedup and high efficiency without much communication overhead.

1 Introduction

Realistic 3-D image synthesis is computationally very expensive. Among all rendering techniques, the ray-tracing[1] is the most popular algorithm to create high quality image. With ray-tracing, the main rays are sent from the eye through pixels on an imaginary viewplane and traced as they are reflected and transmitted by objects, shown in Figure 1. The reflected and transmitted rays are in turn traced until a maximum tracing depth is reached or the rays no longer hit any object. However, ray-tracing is also very noted for its high computational complexity, taking considerable CPU time to produce each image. There have been many efforts to accelerate computation.

Arvo[2] and Kirk describe three general classes of techniques for speeding up raytracing. The faster intersection technique consists of algorithms for intersecting rays with specific primitive objects[3, 4, 5, 6] and exploits the use of spatial coherence[7, 8, 9, 10]. The fewer rays technique reduces the number of rays needed to be traced, as proposed by [11, 12, 13, 14], and the generalized rays technique, based on the idea of ray's coherence[15, 16]. Despite these improvements, they are still too slow to make raytracing a common rendering method, especially when very realistic images, including stochastic sampling and sophisticated illumination models, are to be rendered.

Recently, with the advent of many commercially available massively parallel machines such as Intel Delta Touchstone, Connection Machine, and Intel IPSC-860 with parallel algorithms for raytracing provide an excellent way to decrease the computation time. While ray tracing appears to be easily parallelized, load imbalances and communication overhead still can be problems, particularly with increasing numbers of processors. The goal of this paper is to get efficient use of large numbers of processing nodes and yield a good speedup and high efficiency for raytracing.

The rest of this paper is organized as follows. In section 2, the previous work in parallel ray-tracing will be reviewed. Our parallel algorithm is introduced and implemented on Intel Delta Touchstone machine in section 3. Finally, the results and conclusions are given in section 4.

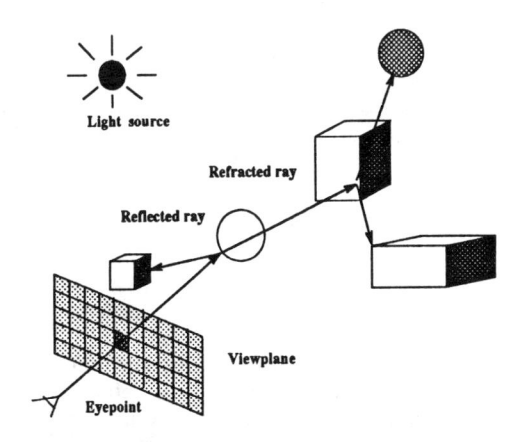

Figure 1: The process of raytracing

2 Overview of Previous Works

There have been different hardware configurations[17, 18, 19], such as linear arrays and hypercubes

---
*This research is supported in part by the NSF Grant No. MIP-9296043.

used to implement parallel raytracers. Among these, most previous implementations prefer hypercube systems with high connectivity, such as Intel IPSC-860 and Connection Machine. The main design issues are the schemes used for load balancing and the model of computation, such as data-driven and demand-driven models.

Carter[20] and Teague use comb assignment, a static load balancing scheme, to distribute the same amount of pixels among processors. Each processor node performs only its allotted job. The drawback of comb assignment is that it can not guarantee the same loading for each node. To improve load balancing, they[21] also use a blocking scheme to distribute pixels across processors and require a master processor to dynamically allocate pixel blocks to idle processors. Dippe[22] describes an adaptive subdivision algorithm which divides the screen into different hexahedral regions on a 3D array of processors. He includes a very complex technique to measure the relative load of neighboring nodes and dynamically reshapes the hexahedral regions to allocate more loading to other processors with light loading. This dynamic load balancing scheme suffers a significant computation and communication overhead. Delany[23] uses the numbering of a preorder traversal of tree to map the bounding volume hierarchy tree structure on CM2 and assigns each ray to a processor. At each iterations, use general communication to fetch the next bounding volume as the rays traverse the tree. With this algorithm, the root of the tree will be the bottleneck of both communication and computation. This scheme causes high congestion in communication and slows down the execution.

Badouel[24] and T.Priol consider both load balancing strategy and database distribution problems on a hypercube iPSC/2. They use a control oriented parallelization for load balancing and dynamically exploit the data access locality using data paging and cache memory for decreasing the remote data access latency. With this scheme, the static load redistribution can not completely reflect the need of nodes with lighter loads and must take extra computation to avoid incorrect synchronization and deadlock.

In this paper, we implement ray tracing on Intel Delta Touchstone machine, containing 512 computational nodes with 20MByte main memory in each node. Generally, this memory size is large enough for complex scenes. Therefore, we are primarily concerned with how to design an efficient parallel raytracer with a good speedup and high efficiency. The data distribution problem is out of our scope in this paper. As described previously, most algorithms are based on central control master/slave models. Their obvious drawback is the burden on the master processor and possible congestion. To alleviate this problem, we have developed a fully distributed parallel algorithm for ray-tracing which is explained in the following section.

3 Parallel Raytracing on the Delta Touchstone Machine

This section will deal with the description of our fully distributed parallel ray-tracing algorithm and the implementation issues on the Intel Delta Touchstone machine.

3.1 The Delta Touchstone machine

The Delta[25] Touchstone machine is a high-speed concurrent multicomputer, consisting of an ensemble of nodes connected as a 2-D mesh. The nodes are independent processors, each with its own independent memory space. Groups of nodes can work on the same problem and communicate with each other by message passing. The interconnection network is a 2-D mesh, illustrated in Figure 2.

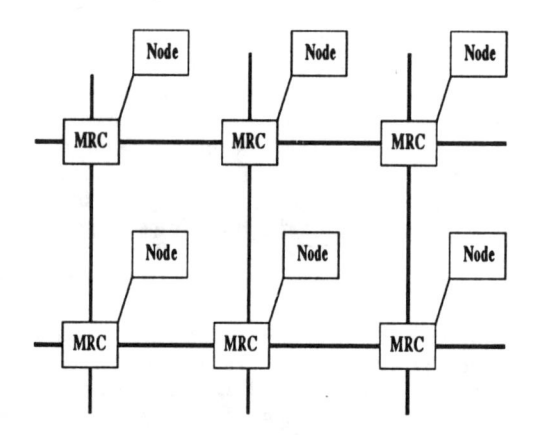

Figure 2: The Delta Touchstone system scalable interconnection network

Each node is connected to the mesh through a mesh routing chip(MRC). After the sending node transmits a message to its MRC, the message moves from MRC to MRC until it reaches the destination node. No intermediate processors are interrupted. Only the sending and receiving nodes participate in the message transfer. Each message is divided into packets which undergo wormhole or cut-through routing. Currently, it contains 512 computational nodes, arranged as a 16 by 32 mesh in nine cabinets. Each numeric node is an Intel i860 microprocessor operating at 40 MHz and rated at 33 MIPS. It is believed to be the fastest computer in the world.

3.2 Fully distributed parallel raytracing algorithm

Our parallel algorithm consists of two parts at each node, where the computation part is responsible for raytracing computation and requesting more regions from its neighbors, and the service part for dynamically allocating extra regions to idle neighboring nodes. Figure 3 shows our fully distributed parallel ray-tracing algorithm.

3.3 Implementation issues

In the Delta Touchstone machine, nodes internal to the mesh have four nearest neighbors, nodes on the boundaries have three, and nodes on the corners

```
Computation part
{
    Initially, use "Comb assignment" to equally divide image
    screen for each processors;
    over = false;
    Direction = inward direction, relative to the center node;
    /** Each node has four neighbors: E,N,W,S directions **/
    While (!over)
    {
        if there are more regions
        {
            raytrace(one region); /** 2x2 pixels **/
            decrease one region;
        }
        else {for all neighbors
        {
            gets a half of the neighbor's regions located on Direction;
            if succeeds then break;
            else Direction = next direction;
        }
        if no more region from all neighbors then Over = True;
        }
    }
}
```

```
Service part
{
    Receive region request from neighbors;
    if has extra regions(over a threshold)
    {
        allocate a half of my regions to this request;
        updatae my own region size;
    }
    else acknowledge request "No more region";
}
```

Figure 3: Parallel raytracer algorithm

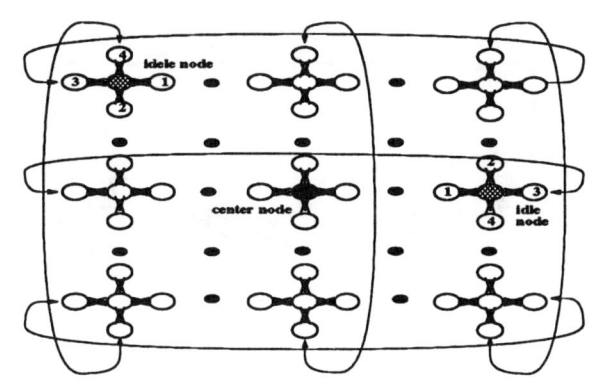

Request order is by 1 > 2 > 3 > 4, relative to the center node

Figure 4: Request order in torus configuration

```
Request Packet: char ask; /** only one byte **/
Service Packet: {
    int base_address;
    int start_page;
    int end_page;
};
```

Figure 5: Packet format

have two. So, if we do not take these boundary or corner cases into account, these nodes always have a higher probability of completing their computation early, which result in less load balancing. To improve this, we logically extend 2-D mesh network topology into a Torus configuration, illustrated in Figure 4. Thus, each node has four neighbors to share work to improve load balancing.

Owing to the characteristics of images, the internal nodes would initially like to get heavier loads. So, we require that when each node requests additional work, it preferentially requests from inner nodes to accelerate the load distribution from high to low density. With our parallel algorithm, each node has two parts - the computation part and the service part. At any point, its neighboring nodes can request job from it. So, providing an ideal and efficient way to schedule both parts and handle incoming requests is crucial to the whole system performance. In this paper, we exploit the use of interrupt handler scheme to schedule both parts. With this scheme, we treat incoming requests as interrupts and attach service part as an interrupt handler routine to the requests' response. Before calling this handler routine, the computation part will perform its computation without blocking. After a request comes, the computation will be suspended until the end of handler routine. For requests arriving at the same time, we use the FCFS strategy to honor all requests. Thus, there is no need for any synchronization between a node and its neighbors; each node can spend most of its time in the computation part to achieve better performance.

The communication overhead is another important factor which affects the performance of the parallel raytracer. When each node responds to requesting node, it should provide more computation than overhead in communication activity. Experimental results show that about half the workload of service node should be moved to requesting node to obtain a good performance. Our two message data structures are described in Figure 5. These two message formats are very compact and efficient without involving large amount of data transmission. To verify the feasibility of our communication model, we compare our results with the master/slave communication model regarding communication overhead.

We consider the worst case for both models. For master/slave model, we calculate the total response time of master node when all slave nodes request jobs from it at the same time. For our scheme, we con-

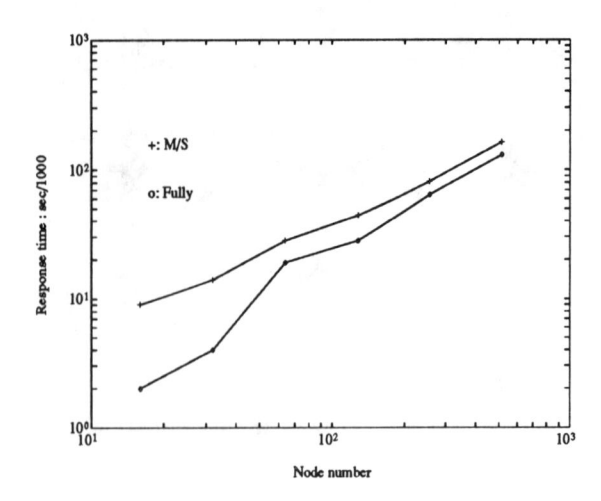

Figure 6: Response time of both models

sider the response time when each node issues a request from one of its neighbors at the same time. Both response times will include the message transmission time and waiting time of all nodes. Figure 6 shows the response time for both models with various number of nodes. We can see that ours is consistently better than the master/salve model. Within the master/slave model, all slaves would like to request jobs from master simultaneously at any point, so the average waiting time experienced by a slave increases with the number of slaves. This will globally effect the performance of the system. In our scheme, each node just needs to issue request from one of the four neighboring nodes. Since each node finishes its job at a different time, the worst case scenario does not occur very often. Our model will be more suitable for massively parallel computations than the master/slave model.

To speed up the processing of ray-tracing at each node, we follow Kay's[26] algorithm to create a best-fit bounding volume hierarchy, which is very efficient for both ray intersection tests and hierarchy traversal. In our implementation, we also include shadow hit caches to accelerate the shadow computation for objects.

Most highly-parallel computers have remarkably inadequate I/O capabilities. Especially, for the I/O intensive tasks such as raytracing which needs massive data read/write operations on disk space, I/O problem can be a bottleneck. Particularly, when multiple nodes output their data on the same output file. Based on this observation, we scatter the image output data of each node among different files to alleviate this I/O problem. After this output phase, a global gather function can be invoked to collect and re-arrange all image files on a single output file.

Without the above scatter/gather process, it is hard to get a better throughput on our remote parallel raytracer. There are two more reasons for this. First, it is hard to perform any compression/decompression manipulation over many scattered files. Second, with these unorganized subimage files from all nodes of the Delta, it is not very efficient to transfer these data by different packets across long haul networks. At any time, it is very difficult for the local, received site to predict and allocate buffers for receiving data during raytracing computations. Therefore, the received site easily gets I/O explosion on its incoming/outgoing system buffers(the I/O exceeds the size of the incoming/outcoming system buffers).

Our parallel raytracer will create about 3Mbytes image data for each image frame with 1024 x 1024 resolution. Without exploiting any compression technique, it is impossible to achieve high-speed data transfer over a single, bandwidth-shared 56kbytes/sec line between WSU and Caltech. Within our environment, we include JPEG library [27] to reduce the size of image data transfer. The JPEG compression/decompression technique [28], a ISO standard for still,high-quality image, is based on the 8*8(two dimensional) Discrete Cosine Transform(DCT), followed by psychovisual quantization and statistical coding. We adjust the compression ratio to about 1/10 to 1/20 without too much loss of original image data.

3.4 Remote visualization application

Recently, scientific visualization is rapidly becoming an important part of scientific discovery, enabling researchers to explore more of their data with greater efficiency and increased comprehension. In our experimental environment, it is easy for us to extend it into a remote visualization system. At local WSU site, we can use some distributed system software such as PVM(Parallel Virtual Machine) to cluster many workstations to do simulation works. After they finish their job, they can submit their render jobs to our remote parallel raytracer. Finally, the rendered image will be sent back to display at local SGI workstations. Figure 7. shows our remote visualization system.

4 Results and conclusion

We used a set of standard scene databases from Eric Haines[29] to perform our experiments. Table 1. shows the geometry characteristics of different scenes. All test images are traced by 1024 x 1024 resolution with antialiasing. Antialiasing is very important to increase visual realism since it can smooth out jagged edges and create razor sharp lines. With antialiasing, we use 8 more rays to trace each pixel. Efficiency is defined as the speedup over the number of nodes used for a given scene. Table 2,3 and 4 demonstrate the simulation results. We find our parallel algorithm can provide expected speedup and efficiency, for up to 512 nodes. In the future, we will consider databases which are too large to be replicated at each node. This will be a task assignment problem dealing with how to minimize the access time of data stored at different nodes. We also plan to include more space and ray coherence to accelerate the ray-tracing algorithm.

	Mountain	Balls	Teapot	Rings	Tree
Primitives	8196	7382	4805	23101	8191
Lights	1	3	2	3	7

Table 1: Database characteristics

Unit: second

Database set Node number	Mountain	Balls	Teapot	Rings	Tree
16	2920	1536	1202	2313	1034
32	1466	769	603	1156	518
64	733	391	305	581	259
128	370	199	156	307	132
256	187	102	84	164	68
512	101	56	47	81	36

Table 2: Rendering time for different database with 1024 x 1024 resolution

Assume the speedup is 1 unit for 16 nodes in use

Node number Database set	16	32	64	128	256	512
Mountain	1.0	2.02	3.96	7.89	15.61	28.91
Balls	1.0	2.00	3.93	7.72	15.06	27.43
Teapot	1.0	1.99	3.94	7.71	14.31	25.57
Rings	1.0	2.0	3.99	7.83	15.21	28.76
Trees	1.0	2.0	3.99	7.83	15.21	28.76

Table 3: Speedup for different database

Assume the efficiency is 100% for 16 nodes in use

Node number Database set	16	32	64	128	256	512
Mountain	100	101.00	99.00	98.63	97.56	90.34
Balls	100	100.00	98.25	96.50	96.38	85.72
Teapot	100	99.50	98.50	96.38	89.44	79.91
Rings	100	100	99.50	94.13	88.13	89.25
Trees	100	100	99.75	97.88	95.06	89.88

Table 4: Efficiency for different database

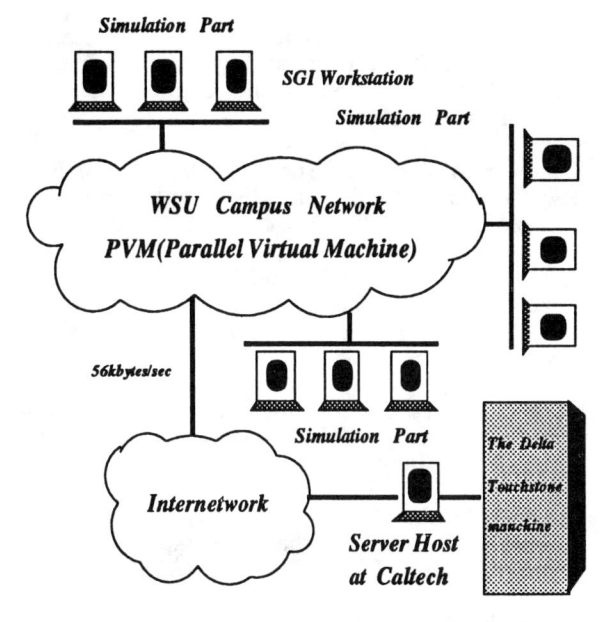

Figure 7: Remote Visualization System

Acknowledgment

This research was performed in part using the Intel Touchstone Delta System operated by Caltech on behalf of the Concurrent Supercomputing Consortium. Access to this facility was provided by Pacific Northwest Laboratory.

References

[1] Whited, Turner, "An Improved Illumination Model for Shaded Display", Comm. of ACM, Vol. 23, No. 6, June 1980.

[2] Arvo, James, and David Kirk, "A Survey of Ray Tracing Acceleration Techniques", SIGGRAPH '88 Tutorial on Introduction to Ray Tracing, 1988.

[3] Kajiya, James T., "New Techniques for Ray Tracing Procedurally Defined Objects", Computer Graphics, Vol. 17, No. 3, July 1983.

[4] Sederberg, Thomas W., and David C. Anderson, "Ray Tracing of Steiner Patches", Computer Graphics, Vol. 18, No. 3, July 1984.

[5] Sweeney, Michael A. J., and Richard H. Bartels, "Ray Tracing Free-Form B-Spline Surfaces", IEEE Computer Graphics and Applications, Vol. 6, No.2, February 1986.

[6] Toth, Daniel L., "On Ray Tracing Parametric Surfaces", Computer Graphics, Vol. 19, No. 3, July 1985.

[7] Arvo, James, and David Kirk, "Fast Ray Tracing by Ray Classification", Computer Graphics, Vol. 21, No. 4, July 1987.

[8] Fujimoto, Akira, Takayuki Tanaka and Kansei Iwata, "ARTS: Accelerated Raytracing System", IEEE Computer Graphics and Applications, Vol. 6, No.4, April 1986.

[9] Glassner, Andrew S., "Space Subdivision for Fast Ray Tracing", IEEE Computer Graphics and Applications, Vol. 4, No.10, October 1984.

[10] Haines, Eric A. and Donald P. Greenberg, "The light Buffer: A Shadow Testing Accelerator", IEEE Computer Graphics and Applications, Vol.6, No.9, September 1986.

[11] Cook, Robert L., "Stochastic Sampling in Computer Graphics", ACM Transaction on Graphics, Vol.5, No. 1, January 1986.

[12] Dippe, Mark, and Erling Henry World, "Antialiasing Through Stochastic Sampling", Computer Graphics, Vol. 19, No.3, July 1985.

[13] Hall, R. A., and D.P. Greenberg, "A Testbed for Realistic Image Synthesis", IEEE Computer Graphics and Application, Vol. 3, No. 10, November 1983.

[14] Lee, Mark, Richard A.Redner, Samuel P. Uselton, "Statistically Optimized Sampling for Distributed ray tracing", Computer Graphics, Vol. 19, No.3, July 1985.

[15] Amanatides, J., "Ray Tracing with Cones", Computer Graphics, Vol. 18, No. 3, July 1984.

[16] Shinya, Mikio, Tokiichiro Takahashi, and Seiichiro Naito, "Principles and Applications of Pencil Tracing", Computer Graphics, Vol. 21, No. 4, July 1987.

[17] Kobayashi H, Nishimura S, Kubota H, Nakamura T, Shiegi Y,"Load Balancing Strategies for a Parallel Ray Tracing System based on constant subdivision", The Visual Computer, 1988, 4(4).

[18] Nishimura H, Ohno H, Kawata T, Shirakawa I, Omura K, "LINKS-1: a Parallel Piplined Multimicrocomputer System for Image Creation", In Proc 10th Ann. Int. Symp. Computer Architecture, 1983.

[19] Salmon J, Goldsmith J, "A hypercube Raytracer", Proc 3rd Conf. Hypercube Computers and Applications, 1988.

[20] Carter, M. B. and Teague, K. A., "The Hypercube Ray Tracer", In Proc. of the 5th Distributed Memory Computing Conference, 1990.

[21] Carter, M. B. and Teague, K. A., "Distributed Object Database Ray Tracing on the Intel iPSC/2 Hypercube", In Proc. of the 5th Distributed Memory Computing Conference, 1990.

[22] Dippe, M., and Swensen, J., "An Adaptive Subdivision Algorithm and Parallel Architecture for Realistic Image Synthesis", Computer Graphics, July, 1984.

[23] Delany, H. C. "A Simple Hierarchical Ray Tracing Program for the Connection Machine System", Tech. Rep. VZ 88-4, Thinking Machine Corporation, Cambridge, MA, December 1988.

[24] D. Badouel and T. Priol, "An efficient Parallel Tracing Scheme for High Parallel Architectures", Fifth Eurographics Workshop on Graphics Hardwares, Septmber, 1990.

[25] "Touchstone Delta User's Guide", Intel Corporation, October, 1991.

[26] Kay, Timothy L.,and James T. Kajiya, "Ray Tracing Complex Scenes", ACM SIGGRAPH 1986, 20(4), August.

[27] The Independent JPEG Group's JPEG software, release 4 ,1992.

[28] Gregory K. Wallace, "The JPEG Still Picture Compression Standard" , IEEE Transactions on Consumer Electronics, December, 1991.

[29] E. Haines, "A Proposal for Standard Graphics Environments", IEEE Computer Graphics and Applications, July, 1987.

SESSION 4B:
High Speed Networks and Switching

Daniel McAuliffe, Chair

An ATM WAN/LAN Gateway Architecture

Gary J. Minden, Joseph B. Evans, David W. Petr, Victor S. Frost

Telecommunications & Information Sciences Laboratory
Department of Electrical & Computer Engineering
University of Kansas
Lawrence, KS 66045-2228

Abstract

This paper describes a gigabit LAN/WAN gateway being developed for the MAGIC gigabit testbed. The gateway interfaces a gigabit LAN developed by Digital's Systems Research Center and the MAGIC SONET/ATM wide area network. The gateway provides 622 Mb/s throughput between the LAN and WAN environments, and supports either a single STS-12c or four STS-3c tributaries. Traffic measurement capability and support for multiple bandwidth management schemes are provided by this architecture.

1: Introduction

Computer communications networks are reaching transmission capacities exceeding one gigabit per second. Networks are traditionally partitioned into Local Area Networks (LANs) and Wide Area Networks (WANs) for a variety of economic and regulatory reasons. While LANs have been primarily oriented toward data traffic, they are increasingly viewed as the medium for the real-time traffic associated with multimedia applications. On the other hand, WANs have traditionally carried real-time circuit oriented traffic, primarily voice, but data traffic is gaining growing importance. Evolving standards and systems under the label "Broadband ISDN" (B-ISDN) will integrate data and real-time traffic to provide a variety of services to users. The convergence of integrated traffic and the possibility of new services has led both exchange carriers and computer network providers to embrace technologies such as SONET (Synchronous Optical NETwork) and particularly ATM (Asynchronous Transfer Mode) for both local and wide area networks.

The use of similar technology in the LAN and WAN environments provides the opportunity for geographically distributed high performance networks. A key element in realizing this goal is the development of efficient user-network interfaces (UNIs) between the LAN and WAN environments; although the basic technology used on both sides of the interface may be similar, the operational aspects of LANs and WANs are significantly different. The gateway architecture described in this paper supports communication between LANs and WANs operating at gigabit per second rates.

The authors can be contacted via e-mail at evans@tisl.ukans.edu. This research is partially supported by ARPA under contract F19628-92-C-0080, Digital Equipment Corporation, the Kansas Technology Enterprise Corporation, and Sprint.

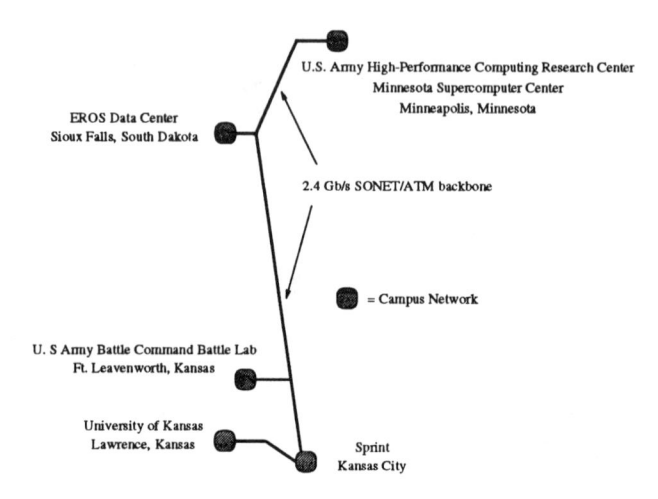

Figure 1. MAGIC Network

1.1: Gigabit LAN/WAN Overview

The Multidimensional Applications and Gigabit Internetwork Consortium (MAGIC) is a group of industrial, academic, and government organizations participating in gigabit network research. The MAGIC backbone network operates at 2.4 Gb/s and each site on the network includes LANs or hosts communicating at gigabit per second rates. The MAGIC network is depicted in Figure 1.

The University of Kansas (KU) will deploy an experimental gigabit LAN called the AN2, provided by Digital Equipment Corporation and developed by Digital's Systems Research Center [1]. The AN2 is a local area network based on ATM technology [7]. The KU network is shown in Figure 2. The network will consist of several switches (initially two), connected by interswitch links operating at 0.8 Gb/s. DECStation 5000 hosts equipped with AN2 host adapter boards will be attached to the switches. These hosts will communicate locally via the AN2 switches, and with remote MAGIC sites via a LAN/WAN gateway developed at KU.

1.2: The LAN/WAN Interface

The gateway supports B-ISDN ATM traffic between the KU local area network and the MAGIC wide area network at SONET STS-12 or STS-12c rates (622.08 Mb/s) [2, 14]. The architecture of the gateway is based on the existing AN2 gigabit interswitch line card design. The gateway and associated hosts support signaling and connection management procedures for the LAN/WAN interface.

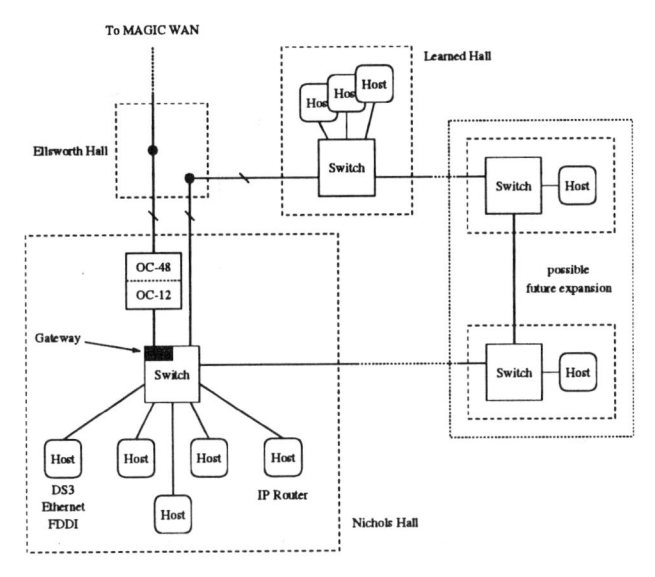

Figure 2. University of Kansas AN2 Configuration

A variety of research issues are being addressed through implementation and application of the LAN/WAN interface. A significant issue to be addressed in the testbed is the internetworking of the connection-oriented WAN environment and connectionless LAN environments. Connection setup procedures are being developed to provide virtual circuits for IP datagram traffic traveling from LAN to LAN via the B-ISDN WAN. These procedures will initially focus on permanent virtual circuits (PVCs), but this will later be extended to switched virtual circuits (SVCs).

In addition to the issues of simple connection management, more complex network control issues that arise in an ATM network need to be addressed. In particular, dynamic bandwidth allocation mechanisms promise to provide LAN/WAN services more economically. The gateway architecture is designed to allow the testing and evaluation of dynamic bandwidth allocation algorithms.

The architecture proposed for B-ISDN is a connection-oriented (CO) transmission service [9]. Most data communications based LANs and common protocols (e.g. IP), however, implement a connectionless (CL) service. A well recognized [5, 8, 10] challenge in B-ISDN is the integration of connectionless services over a connection-oriented B-ISDN. Agents are needed between connectionless and connection-oriented services to manage and control the flow of information. It is further expected that the data rates of future LANs (i.e., integrated access points) and B-ISDN will be of comparable orders of magnitude, so that assigning the peak access rate to each connection would result in a significant waste of resources. The challenge in this new environment is to match the unknown dynamics of the internet connectionless traffic to the characteristics of the virtual circuit (VC) carrying this traffic in the connection-oriented system.

2: The AN2 Gigabit Local Area Network

The AN2 LAN is a switch based local area network. Hosts are connected to switches by one or more 155 Mb/s full duplex links, and switches are interconnected by 0.8 Gb/s links.

Switches are 16 by 16 port crossbars and can switch at a maximum aggregate rate of 12.8 Gb/s and greater than 95% throughput. The AN2 is a virtual-circuit based system. Packets, received from the host, are segmented by host adapters into streams of ATM cells that are transmitted on a virtual circuit using AAL 5 [13]. The host adapter transmits cells to its attached switch. Switches then move the cells through the network and deliver them, in order, to the destination host adapter via a virtual circuit. The receiving host adapter re-assembles packets from the cell stream and, once a packet is completely re-assembled, sends the packet to the host's main memory. Host adapters plug into the Turbochannel I/O bus of the DECStation 5000.

Traffic is divided into two classes, sporadic and periodic or guaranteed bandwidth traffic. Hosts can request at call setup time a guaranteed bandwidth in units of 1 Mb/s. If the bandwidth is available, switches along the route cooperate to establish individual crossbar schedules to provide the guaranteed bandwidth.

2.1: AN2 Switches

Switches implement the following features:

- ordered delivery of cells within a virtual circuit
- no head-of-line blocking
- guaranteed bandwidth
- hop-by-hop based flow control
- shortest path routing

The following three types of line cards plug into the switch crossbar: (1) link line cards have a single full duplex link operating at 0.8 Gb/s, (2) host line cards have four full duplex links operating at 155 Mb/s, and (3) the AN2/SONET Gateway operating at 622 Mb/s using the SONET transmission protocol. Line cards consist of an input side and an output side. The input side receives cells over the link, routes those cells, queues them, and sends them through the crossbar. The output side receives cells from the crossbar, buffers them, transmits the cells on the link, and manages the flow control mechanism. Queues will not overflow because the flow control mechanism (described below) will not allow it.

Cells are synchronously switched through the crossbar with a slot period of 520 ns. During arbitration, lasting one slot period, each line card requests access to each output line card for which it has traffic. The arbitration mechanism will result in either no connection or a single connection to an output line card. By posting requests to each output for which there is traffic and implementing a distributed arbitration mechanism [1], the AN2 avoids the usual head-of-line blocking in the input queues. Cells from the crossbar are immediately transmitted on the output link.

Switching slots are grouped into frames of 1024 slots. Slots within a frame can be dedicated to a specific connection between an input line card and output line card. This mechanism supports the guaranteed bandwidth feature.

The AN2 implements a strict, window flow control mechanism on a link by link and virtual circuit by virtual circuit basis. During call setup, buffers are allocated on the input side of each line card along the route for the virtual circuit. The number of cell buffers necessary in each line card depends on the maximum bandwidth on the virtual circuit and the distance between output and input cards. The necessary number of buffers N_b is:

$$N_b = \frac{C \text{ bits/second} * 2D \text{ km} * 4.95 \mu s/\text{km}}{53 \text{ bytes/buffer} * 8 \text{ bits/byte}},$$

where C is capacity in bits per second, D is distance in kilometers, 4.95 μs/km is the propagation velocity of light in fiber, and the denominator is the number of bits per cell buffer. For a one kilometer link operating at 155 Mb/s, four cell buffers per virtual circuit are needed on each line card input along the route. The buffer sizes are thus relatively small for LATM systems.

A line card will not transmit a cell on a link unless it is sure there is a buffer at the receiving end to store that cell. Line card outputs maintain an account balance of the number of buffers available at the receiver for each virtual circuit. As each cell is transmitted, the account balance for that virtual circuit is decremented. When the account balance reaches zero, the output notifies the input line card, through the crossbar, to stop the virtual circuit. The input line card marks that virtual circuit stopped and will not attempt to transmit further cells on that virtual circuit until it is started again.

When an line card sends a cell through the crossbar the virtual circuit identifier is sent to that line card's output side. The output side piggybacks the virtual circuit identifier of the forwarded cell on the cell stream going back to the far end (an empty cell will be used if there is no return traffic). This is an acknowledgment that a cell buffer on the forwarded virtual circuit has been freed. Note that other mechanisms are possible, such as batching acknowledgments into a return cell. The input side of the line card at the far end strips off the piggybacked acknowledgment and sends it to the output side. The output side increments the buffer account balance for the virtual circuit. If cells are flowing smoothly, an acknowledgment for a virtual circuit will arrive at the account just before the next cell on that virtual circuit is transmitted. Acknowledgment loss and account resynchronization between output and input are beyond the scope of this paper.

Each line card has a microprocessor, called the LCP, to control, monitor, and manage the line card. The LCP is involved in call setup, call tear down, route finding, resource allocation, periodic bandwidth allocation, monitoring the line card, and performance measurement.

3: The Gateway Architecture

The AN2/SONET Gateway is a hardware device that connects the Digital Equipment Corporation AN2 Local ATM network to the SONET based B-ISDN ATM network. The purpose of the gateway is to provide a means for data to move between the AN2 and the SONET based wide area network.

The AN2/SONET Gateway supports the following features:

- operation at the SONET STS-12/STS-12c (622.08 Mb/s) capacity on the wide area side via fiber optic connection
- operation within the DEC AN2 Local ATM switch by connecting to the AN2 switch backplane

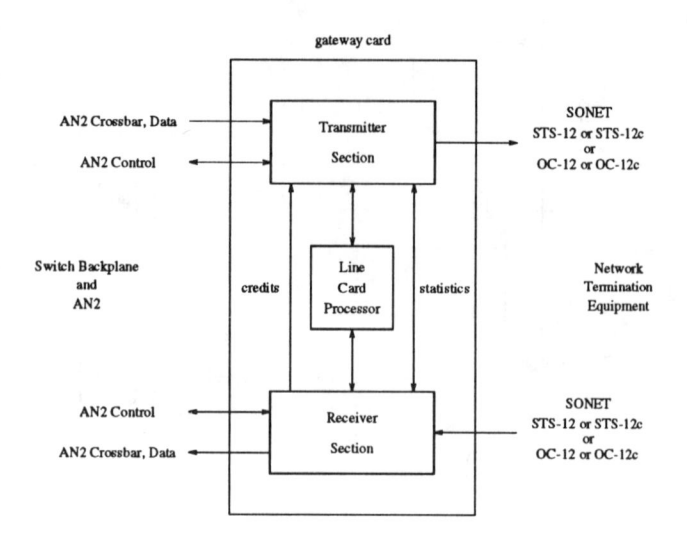

Figure 3. AN2/SONET Gateway

- experimental techniques for dynamic bandwidth allocation
- experimental techniques for interoperability between connection-oriented and connectionless protocols; in particular, the gateway supports TCP/IP traffic, but it is not restricted to that protocol suite
- experimental signaling protocols for call setup and call parameter negotiations
- measurement of network performance

The AN2/SONET Gateway is a single card that plugs into an AN2 switch port. The gateway, shown in Figure 3, contains three primary sub-systems: the receive section, the transmit section, and the line card processor (LCP) section.

3.1: Transmit Section

The transmit section, shown in Figure 4, connects the AN2 switch crossbar to the transmit SONET Network Termination Equipment (NTE) of the WAN provider. The transmit section interface to the NTE is via single mode optical fiber at OC-12 rates (622.08 Mb/s). The transmit section may optionally connect to the NTE at OC-3 rates (155.52 Mb/s). The transmit section will normally use clocks derived from the receive section, but will also have a crystal controlled local clock oscillator. The transmitter receives ATM cells from the AN2 crossbar. The cells are buffered and merged with the SONET overhead information stream. The combined stream forms a SONET frame. The LCP will be able to receive cells from the AN2 crossbar. The transmit section will maintain status for each possible virtual circuit (VC). The status information will include the number of buffers available at the remote end. This will allow the transmitter to participate in the AN2 flow control strategy, within the limits imposed by memory, latency, and the WAN. The transmit section will forward cell acknowledgements issued by the receive section when appropriate. The transmit section supports a single STS-12c stream or four STS-3c streams multiplexed into a single STS-12.

The AN2 Crossbar Interface connects the gateway card to the AN2 switch backplane. Cells are received at the AN2 Crossbar Interface in thirteen clock cycles, 32 bits per cycle. The transmit section only accepts cells destined for the

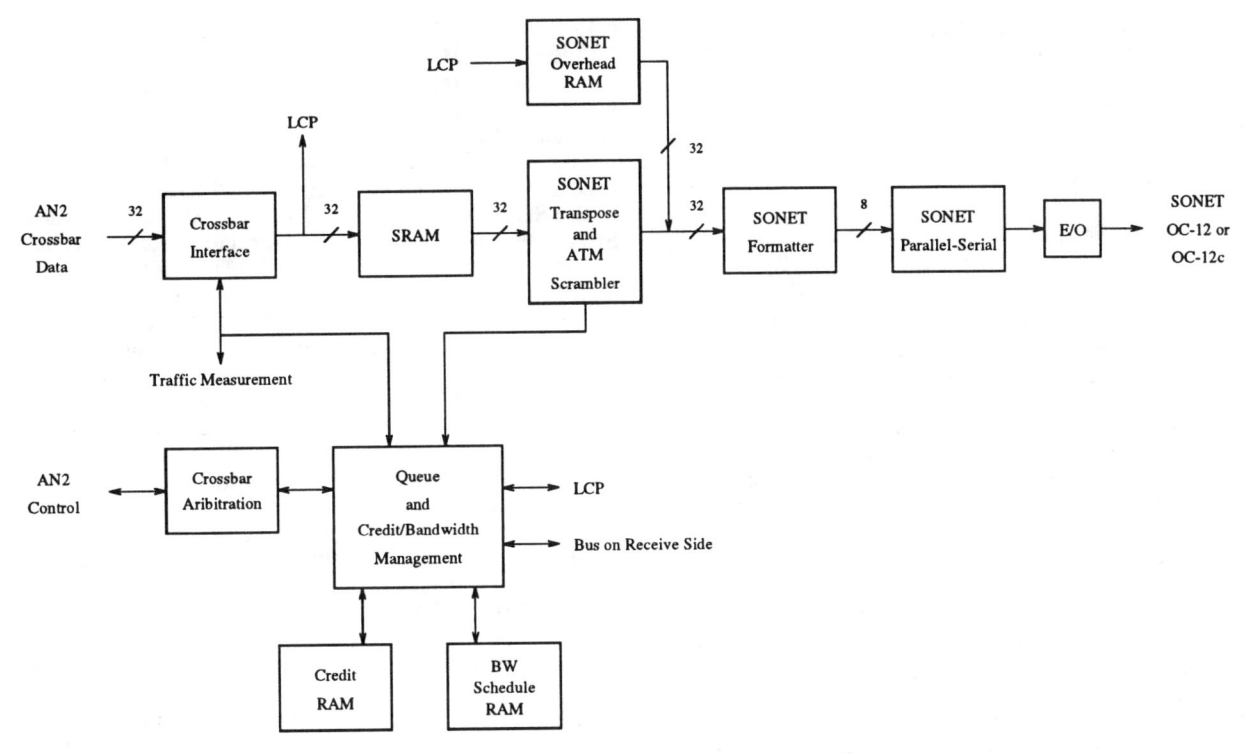

Figure 4. Gateway Transmitter Architecture

gateway. The Crossbar Interface temporarily buffers partially received cells arriving from the AN2 crossbar. Upon completion of a cell arrival, and given successful arbitration, the Crossbar Interface writes the cell to the SRAM unit. The transmit section only participates in arbitration if there are sufficient buffer resources in the SRAM. Traffic measurements of cell and packet arrivals are extracted at the Crossbar Interface, packaged into cells, and forwarded to hosts for off-line analysis.

The SRAM unit is used to temporarily buffer cells arriving from the crossbar. The SRAM unit also serves as a rate adaptation unit. The AN2 operates at a clock rate of 40 ns (25 MHz) per 32 bit word and a cell rate of 520 ns, since 13 words per cell are forwarded across the AN2 crossbar (the HEC byte is not passed through the crossbar). In contrast, the SONET transmission clock is 12.86 ns per byte or 681.6 ns per cell (peak rate). Cells are loaded into the SRAM unit at the AN2 rate and read from the SRAM unit at the SONET rate.

The SRAM unit is controlled by the Queue and Credit/Bandwidth Management unit. The Queue Management module schedules memory accesses to the SRAM unit and maintains pointers to the cell stream locations in SRAM. The Credit/Bandwidth Management module subtracts credits from the credit bank for end-to-end flow control, and generates batches of acknowledgements (credits) for forwarding to the transmitting entity. This unit also maintains the scheduling tables for the i slots out of m slots bandwidth control [6]. The LCP can access the various tables through the Queue and Credit/Bandwidth Management unit.

The SONET Transpose and ATM Scramble unit operates in one of two modes: a single STS-12c ATM stream, or four STS-3c ATM streams multiplexed into an STS-12.

The mode is selected at system configuration time. When operating in STS-12c mode, the Transpose unit acts as a two cell ping-pong buffer, so that one cell can be byte transposed and injected into the SONET frame while a second is read from the SRAM. In four by STS-3c mode, four streams are multiplexed into a single byte stream for encapsulation in a SONET frame. When operating in the four by STS-3c mode, the Transpose unit buffers two sets of four ATM cells. In this case, byte interleaving can be performed by simply extracting a byte from each stream in a round-robin fashion. In either mode, byte multiplexing is performed on the ATM streams using multiplexers under the control of a finite state machine. The payload section of each ATM cell stream is scrambled according to the prescribed self-synchronous scrambler polynomial [6].

The SONET Overhead RAM is a fast, dual-ported SRAM containing the SONET overhead bytes. The LCP loads the SONET Overhead RAM with the proper section, line, and path overhead bytes. Sixteen overhead buffers are provided so that the contents can be altered while the system is in operation. The SONET overhead is multiplexed with the byte interleaved ATM cell streams via a tristate bus to generate the input stream to the SONET Formatter. Because the path frame is aligned with the section and line overhead at transmission, the control for the multiplexing is straightforward.

The SONET Formatter takes payload and overhead data from the preceding stages and performs the remaining functions required to complete a SONET frame. In particular, the SONET Formatter performs the combinational operations necessary to fill the parity bytes of the path, section, and line overhead, and scrambles the SONET signal according to the standard polynomial [12, 14].

The SONET Parallel-Serial unit performs the conversion

from the byte-wide parallel stream to a serial stream. The serial data is then fed into the Electrical-to-Optical interface.

The transmit section is implemented using a combination of Xilinx FPGAs, a commercially available SONET parallel to serial conversion integrated circuit, and commercially available memory chips.

3.2: Receive Section

The receive section, shown in Figure 5, connects to the received signal from the wide area SONET NTE. The interface to the NTE is via single mode optical fiber at OC-12 or OC-3 rates. Timing information (bit, byte, and frame) is extracted from the received SONET signal, and is used in both the receive and transmit sections. The receive section extracts the SONET overhead and the SONET payload from the incoming stream. The SONET payload is processed as ATM cells in accordance with evolving SONET/ATM standards. The ATM header is checked for errors prior to further processing. ATM cells are buffered on a virtual circuit basis. The destination of the received ATM cells is determined by a routing table. ATM cells forwarded through the switch or sent to the LCP are acknowledged to the remote end via a return path through the transmit section, specifically through the credit management mechanism. The receive section supports a single STS-12c stream or four STS-3c streams multiplexed into a single STS-12.

The Optical-to-Electrical converter receives and detects the optical serial bit stream and outputs an electrical serial bit stream. A bit clock is recovered from the received signal. The SONET Synchronization and Serial-Parallel unit searches for and synchronizes itself with the SONET frame synchronization pattern. At the beginning of each frame, the start of frame is detected and an indication signal is asserted. A frame lock signal is also asserted as long as synchronization is maintained. This unit also generates a byte clock that is used throughout the gateway system. The SONET Synchronization and Serial-Parallel unit converts the serial bit stream to a 32-bit wide parallel stream for further processing.

The SONET Descramble and BIP Check unit applies the standard descrambling function to the received signal [12, 14]. This unit also checks the SONET section and line bit interleaved parity (BIP) bytes.

The ATM Cell Delineation and Descramble unit searches for valid ATM cell headers in the received payload byte stream, using the standard cell synchronization method. In particular, the Cell Delineation unit performs the header error check CRC, and performs comparisons until a match is found in the byte stream. When a prescribed number of consecutive matches occur, synchronization is indicated. If a prescribed number of consecutive matches then fail, loss of synchronization is indicated. The system supports both a single STS-12c and four STS-3c streams. ATM cell stream alignment across the four STS-3c payload streams is not assumed. Idle cells are dropped by the cell delineation unit and are not forwarded for further processing. ATM cells with incorrect headers are dropped; no error correction is currently attempted. The Descrambler unit applies the cell descrambler polynomial to the cell payload.

Once they are delineated and descrambled, partial cells are written to the SRAM unit for buffering and routing. The SRAM unit also provides the rate adaptation between the SONET clock rates and the AN2 crossbar clock rates. The cells containing batches of credits which were collected by the Credit Management unit on the transmit side are inserted on the input bus to the SRAM unit, as are the cells generated by the Traffic Measurement unit, and cells that are transmitted by the LCP.

The SONET Termination unit extracts the SONET overhead bytes of the received frame, and writes those bytes to the SONET Overhead SRAM. The SONET Overhead SRAM buffers the overhead information for subsequent reading and processing by the LCP. The SONET Termination unit uses the path frame pointer in the SONET line overhead to determine the location of the path overhead. In the case of an STS-12c stream, this is a single pointer, but in the case of four STS-3c streams, pointers to four offset frames must be tracked. This unit also checks the SONET path parity bytes, and informs the cell delineation unit about path slippage in the SONET frame.

The SRAM unit performs buffering of the ATM cell streams prior to buffering on a per VCI basis in the VRAM unit. The SRAM unit is managed by the Cell Stream Management unit, which schedules memory accesses for the cell streams and provides indication when cells are ready to be buffered in the VRAM. The Cell Stream Management unit also controls VC extraction from the received cells.

The VRAM Buffer is used to provide sufficient buffering for ATM cells, so that congestion in the AN2 network will not cause cell loss due to buffer overflow. As in the standard AN2 line card, cells are buffered on a per VCI basis, so that flow control on one VC will not effect other VCs.

The Queue Management and Crossbar Arbitration unit controls the VRAM Buffer and maintains the queue tables. This unit also manages the crossbar arbitration cycle and controls the write operation from the VRAM to the AN2 crossbar. The Queue RAM holds pointers to the cells in the VRAM; this structure allows buffer resources to be dynamically allocated.

The receive section is implemented using a combination of Xilinx FPGAs, a commercially available SONET synchronizer integrated circuit, a three port video dynamic access memories for the VRAM Buffer, and commercially available memory chips.

3.3: Line Card Processor

The Line Card Processor (LCP) manages the resources of the receive section, transmit section, and communications paths. It is responsible for setting up circuits, releasing circuits, monitoring circuits, allocating bandwidth to circuits, and other network management operations both within the AN2 and with the WAN. The LCP communicates with other switch processors via ATM cells. The LCP can receive cells from the AN2 crossbar, and transmit signals into the AN2 crossbar. The LCP communicates with the WAN via cells which pass through the AN2 crossbar, and hence are subject to the standard resource management logic. The LCP can also communicate with SONET equipment via the path, section, and line overhead bytes. The LCP is composed of a general purpose RISC processor and support chips.

4: LAN/WAN Interface Issues

The hosts on the various networks that comprise the MAGIC gigabit testbed will initially communicate using the TCP/IP suite [4]. The IP datagrams generated by hosts will be carried on the connection-oriented ATM LAN and

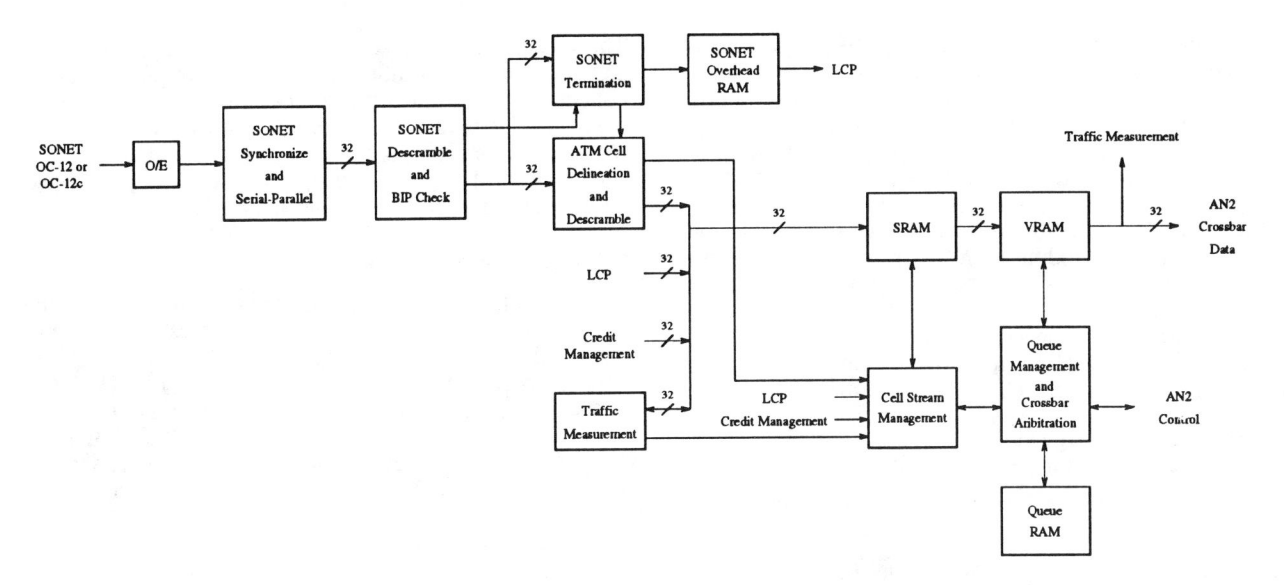

Figure 5. Gateway Receiver Architecture

WAN networks. The gateway and associated hosts support the assignment and mapping of IP traffic to virtual circuits, the provisioning of virtual circuits, and the dynamic management of virtual circuits. This section describes how connectionless IP services will utilize the connection-oriented ATM service provided by the AN2 and B-ISDN WAN.

4.1: Internetworking

The hosts on the MAGIC network will use AAL 5, the Simple and Efficient Adaptation Layer (SEAL) [13] for carrying IP datagrams on ATM cell streams. An intermediate IEEE 802.2 LLC layer may also be supported, for interoperability with the IEEE 802 protocols. The protocol stack is shown in Figure 6.

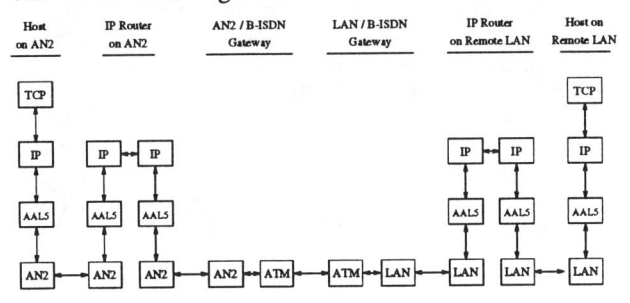

Figure 6. Gateway Protocol Stack

In order to direct IP packets to local AN2 hosts or to remote hosts via the WAN, IP routing functionality will be provided in the network. Initially, IP routing will be accomplished using a selected host (or hosts) on the local subnet, as shown in Figure 7. This corresponds to the current practice for networks connected to the Internet. Future research will explore other options which will alleviate the potential performance bottlenecks imposed by the use of a single router. An number of possibilities exist, for example, multiple routers, each managing a set of virtual circuits.

The initial MAGIC testbed configuration will use permanent virtual circuits (PVCs) across the wide area network. It is envisioned that the provisioning of PVCs will be done using SNMP [3] according to the MIB published by the ATM Forum [6]. The gateway will support signaling according to this standard.

Later MAGIC testbed configurations will include ATM switches, and hence use switched virtual circuits (SVCs). The gateway LCP will support the signaling required, most likely the proposed Q.93B extensions to Q.931 [11].

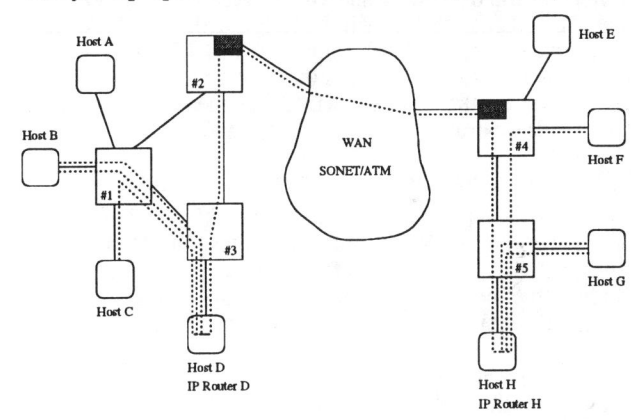

Figure 7. Initial Routing Configuration for MAGIC

4.2: Bandwidth Allocation

Many data protocols and services are connectionless; connection-oriented applications are frequently built on top of these connectionless protocols. Connectionless applications tend to generate short bursts of packets followed by idle periods. Even connection-oriented applications, such as file transfer applications, may require high data rates at some times and lower data rates at others. The evolving local ATM networks and wide area networks are connection-oriented, so services must be provided to interface connectionless protocols to connection based communication networks. This section outlines the issues involved in providing such a service and the implications on the gateway architecture.

In the B-ISDN environment, it will be necessary to match the dynamics of the connectionless traffic to the characteristics of the virtual circuit carrying this traffic in the connection-oriented system. The common solution [5, 8] to this problem is to initially request a modest amount of connection-oriented network bandwidth and dynamically adjust the requested capacity as the interface service detects the need for additional capacity. Renegotiation of call parameters during a session is a facility expected in B-ISDN [7]. We plan to implement a service on the local area network, called the CL/CO service, to monitor the bandwidth requirements of connections through the system and adjust bandwidth allocations among those connections.

Connectionless to connection-oriented services and the dynamic bandwidth allocation process should posses attributes listed below. The CL/CO service should:

- use infrequent signaling between the CL/CO service and the connection-oriented service,
- not be sensitive to the specific nature of the traffic statistics,
- be able to operate at gigabit/sec speeds,
- be insensitive to the relative latencies of gigabit networks,
- induce minimum latency,
- not require extensive special switch interaction.

The gateway is designed to provide the data necessary to implement the dynamic bandwidth allocation CL/CO service. The CL/CO service will be tested within the MAGIC network by fixing the WAN capacity available to the gateway and executing several remote applications simultaneously. During the tests we will experiment with several dynamic allocation algorithms and signaling protocols.

4.3: Performance Measurements Collection

In order to develop fundamental base of knowledge about the nature of LAN/WAN traffic statistics, and to provide a method to evaluate the effectiveness of the dynamic bandwidth allocation and management algorithms just discussed, the gateway supports traffic measurement functions.

Measurements are made on traffic flowing through the gateway, from which a number of statistics can be calculated. The statistics that are targeted for calculation are:

- packet interarrival time series
- packet length distribution over time
- packet delay statistics, including evolution of statistics over time
- cell interarrival time series
- cell delay statistics, including evolution of statistics over time
- credit queue statistics (length, idle time, time evolution)
- loss statistics across WAN
  - those due to bit error
  - those due to WAN congestion
  - evolution of statistics over time (loss bursts)

These statistics can be calculated for both specified VCs and the aggregate traffic stream. Measurements can be collected on both a per packet and a per cell basis, using the payload type identifier specified in the AAL 5 definition [6]. The measurements are buffered at the gateway for a short period of time, and then forwarded using dedicated VCs to hosts for bulk collection and analysis.

5: Conclusions

This paper has described the gateway architecture for the interconnection of a Digital AN2 gigabit local area network and the 2.4 Gb/s MAGIC gigabit wide area network. The gateway is designed to support the transport of ATM LAN traffic over a B-ISDN wide area network at SONET STS-12 rates. While the MAGIC testbed will use the TCP/IP suite and AAL 5, the gateway architecture is designed to support a variety of higher level protocols and adaptation layers. The gateway can be configured to support a single SONET STS-12c tributary, or four STS-3c tributaries multiplexed into an STS-12 frame. The extensive use of programmable logic devices in this system has provided this configurability, as well as facilitated the rapid development of the design as standards have evolved, which would have been more difficult using traditional approaches such as custom application-specific integrated circuits.

References

[1] T. Anderson, C. Owicki, J. Sax, and C. Thacker. High speed switch scheduling for local area networks. In *Proc. Int. Conf. Arch. Supp. Prog. Lang. and Op. Sys.*, Boston, Oct 1992.

[2] R. Ballart and Y. Ching. SONET: Now it's the standard optical network. *IEEE Commun. Mag.*, 27(3):8–15, Mar 1989.

[3] J. D. Case, M. S. Fedor, M. L. Schoffstall, and J. R. Davin. Simple Network Management Protocol. Internet Working Group Request for Comments 1157, Network Information Center, SRI International, Menlo Park, California, May 1990.

[4] D. E. Comer. *Internetworking with TCP/IP, Volume I*. Prentice-Hall, Englewood Cliffs, New Jersey, 1991.

[5] P. Crocetti, G. Gallassi, and M. Gerla. Bandwidth advertising for MAN/WAN connectionless internetting. In *Proc. IEEE INFOCOM*, Bal Harbor, Florida, Apr 1991.

[6] ATM Forum. Network Compatible ATM for Local Network Applications. Apple Computer, Bellcore, Sun Microsystems, Xerox, Apr 1992.

[7] 1990 CCITT Study Group XVIII Recommendation I.150. B-ISDN Asynchronous Transfer Mode Functional Characteristics. CCITT, Geneva, 1990.

[8] L. Mongivoni, M. Farrell, and V. Trecorido. A proposal for the interconnection of FDDI networks through B-ISDN. In *Proc. IEEE INFOCOM*, Bal Harbor, Florida, Apr 1991.

[9] M. T. Mullen and V. S. Frost. Dynamic bandwidth allocation for B-ISDN based end-to-end delay estimates. In *Proc. IEEE ICC*, Chicago, Jun 1992.

[10] G. M. Parulkar and J. Turner. Towards a framework for high speed connection in heterogeneous networking environments. In *Proc. IEEE INFOCOM*, Ottawa, Canada, Apr 1989.

[11] 1989 CCITT Study Group XI Recommendation Q.931. Specifications of Signaling System No. 7. CCITT, Geneva, 1989.

[12] S. W. Seetharam, G. J. Minden, and J. B. Evans. A parallel SONET scrambler/descrambler architecture. In *IEEE Int. Symp. Circuits and Syst.*, pages 2011–2014, May 1993.

[13] ANSI Committee T1 Contribution T1S1.5/91-449. AAL 5 – A New High Speed Data Transfer AAL. Bellcore Technical Reference Issue 2, IBM et al, Dallas, Texas, Nov 1991.

[14] Bellcore Technical Reference TR-NWT-000253. Synchronous Optical Network (SONET) Transport Systems: Common Generic Criteria. Bellcore Technical Reference Issue 2, Bellcore, Dec 1991.

Performance Evaluation of a High-Speed Switching System Based on the Fibre Channel Standard

Anujan Varma[*]
Vikram Sahai
Computer Engineering Department
University of California
Santa Cruz, CA 95064

Robert Bryant
Lawrence Livermore National Laboratory
P.O. Box 808
Livermore, CA 94551

Abstract

We present a performance study of a switching system being designed for use in the High-Performance Switching System (HPSS) project at the Lawrence Livermore National Laboratory. The HPSS is a distributed switching system designed to operate with the protocols of the proposed ANSI Fibre Channel Standard (FCS). The system is based on a folded version of the Clos three-stage network and its largest configuration has 4096 ports, each operating at 1.0625 Gbits/s. A detailed simulation model is used to evaluate the throughput, setup time, and blocking at various stages in an HPSS configuration with 512 ports. Our results indicate that the system can sustain a throughput that is within 70 to 80 percent of the maximum theoretical limit for our choice of operational parameters.

1 Introduction

In this paper, we present a performance study of a switching system being designed for use in the High-Performance Switching System (HPSS) project at the Lawrence Livermore National Laboratory. The aim of this project is to provide a high-speed network testbed based on the Fibre Channel Standard being developed by ANSI. The testbed will use fiber-optic links, operating at a speed of 1.0625 Gbits/s, and a distributed switching fabric to interconnect the laboratory's Cray supercomputers and high-performance workstations.

The switching system is based on the CXT-1000 switch from Ancor Communications, the details of which can be found in [1]. The operational parameters and algorithms we use in this analysis, however, are our own and do not correspond to Ancor's design. The results in this paper, therefore, should not be interpreted as applicable to the Ancor product.

In this paper, we evaluate the performance of HPSS in the circuit-switched mode. We first derive some simple upper bounds on the throughput of the switch as a function of its operational parameters and the traffic distribution. These are then compared with results from a detailed simulation of the system. The results indicate that a throughput in the range of 70 to 80 percent of the maximum theoretical limit can be obtained from the system.

The paper is organized as follows: Section 2 provides an overview of the Fibre Channel Standard, and a brief discussion of the structure and operation of the HPSS. In section 3, we derive some simple upper bounds on the throughput of an example configuration with 512 ports. In section 4, we present the results from a detailed simulation of the system. Concluding remarks are given in section 5.

2 Fibre Channel and HPSS

2.1 Fibre Channel Overview

Fibre Channel is a standardization effort undertaken by ANSI to define a serial I/O channel for connecting peripheral devices to computer systems. The standard defines a layered architecture starting from the physical layer (FC-0) and ending with the device layer (FC-4). A number of technologies and implementations are supported at the physical layer including multimode and single-mode fiber and coaxial cable. Four different link-bandwidths are specified, ranging from approximately 125 Mbits/s to 1 Gbits/s. By providing choices for physical-layer implementation and bandwidth capability, it is hoped that that the Fibre Channel will find application in systems over a wide range of cost and performance, from low-end workstations to mainframes and supercomputers. A summary of the Fibre Channel is given in [3] and details can be found in [4]. The analysis in this paper is based on Version 1.6 of the Fibre Channel.

An important feature of the ANSI Fibre Channel is the support for multiple classes of traffic. Both circuit-switched traffic and datagrams are supported. This allows the Fibre Channel to be used as a high-speed communication network. Fibre Channel supports three classes of service: *Dedicated connection* (Class 1), *multiplex* (Class 2), and *datagram* (Class 3). A dedicated connection requires a dedicated path to be set up between the communicating nodes before data can be transferred. This corresponds to the operation of a circuit-switch. Multiplex and datagram are packet-oriented services. The HPSS currently sup-

---

[*]Supported by NSF Young Investigator Award MIP-9257103, NSF Grant No. MIP-9111241, and a grant from the Institute for Scientific Computing Research at Lawrence Livermore National Laboratory.

ports only class-1 service. Hence, we have studied its performance under class-1 traffic only.

Instead of defining a specific interconnection topology, the Fibre Channel defines a functional model for the interconnection network, called *fabric*. The fabric is defined in terms of the functions it must support, rather than its specific topology and implementation. The standard defines two types of ports, N-ports (node-ports) and F-ports (fabric ports). An N-port is a point of attachment of the network to any of the nodes in the system, analogous to the network interface of a node in a communication network. The F-port is the point of attachment of a link on the fabric side. Thus, a communication link connects either an N-port to an F-port, or two N-ports together.

The interaction between two nodes in the Fibre Channel consists of a hierarchy of data units, the lowest of which is called a *frame*. The frame is the smallest indivisible unit of information transfer across the Fibre Channel. In the Version 1.6, each frame consist of a 4-byte start-of-frame sequence, a 16-byte frame header, a variable-size data field with a maximum length of 2112 bytes, 4 bytes of a cyclic redundancy check (CRC) code, and finally, a 4-byte end-of-frame sequence. Thus, the length of the largest frame is currently 2140 bytes. The individual bytes are encoded by the IBM 8-bit/10-bit transmission code.

The highest data-unit in the Fibre Channel hierarchy that is of interest to us is the *connection*. Connection is the level at which two nodes establish communication and negotiate various parameters in a class-1 interaction.

2.2 HPSS Design

The HPSS is a distributed switching system designed to operate with the Fibre Channel protocols. The largest configuration of the switch has 4096 full-duplex ports. The system is constructed from interconnected crossbars, based on a folded version of the Clos three-stage network. The system uses distributed control, unlike most of the previous designs based on Clos networks. Each fabric port supports a data rate of 1.0625 Gbits/s, corresponding to the highest speed of Fibre Channel.

The design of HPSS is based on three-stage Clos networks [2]. A Clos network, in its basic form, consists of three cascaded switching stages. The middle stage consists of m crossbar switches, each of size $r \times r$, and the first and last stages each consists of r crossbars, each of size $n \times m$. Thus, the total number of ports is nr. The number of middle-stage switches m determines the blocking characteristics of the network. Clos showed that the network is *nonblocking in the strict sense*, if $m \geq 2n - 1$; that is, a path from any idle input terminal to any idle output terminal can be found at any time if this condition is satisfied, independent of the way other terminals are connected through the switch.

The Clos construction can be used to design a network with $N = nr$ full-duplex ports by pairing each input terminal of the switch with the corresponding output terminal. One way of doing this is to fold the Clos network to obtain the topology shown in Figure 1. The figure shows the largest configuration of an HPSS switch; this configuration has 4096 ports, designed from individual crossbars of size 64×64.

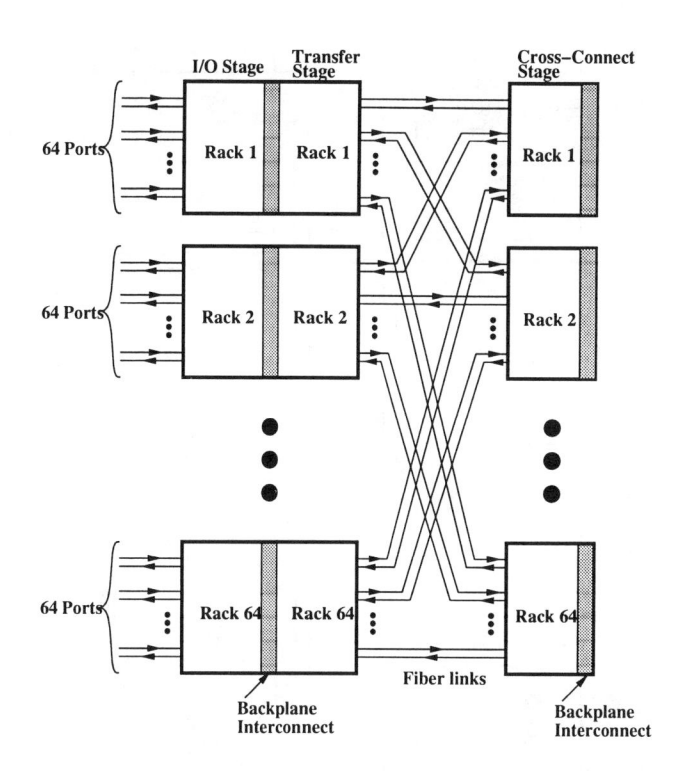

Figure 1: An HPSS configuration with 4096 ports.

The HPSS switch in Figure 1 still has three stages, although they do not correspond to the stages in the three-stage Clos network. The switching stages in the HPSS, starting from the F-ports of the switch, are referred to as *I/O*, *transfer*, and *cross-connect* stages, respectively. The building blocks of the switch are called *racks*, which have somewhat different functionality than single crossbars. A crossbar in the first stage of the Clos network extends from an I/O-stage rack to the corresponding transfer-stage rack; a crossbar in the second stage of the Clos network is completely contained within a cross-connect stage rack; and a crossbar in the third stage of the Clos network extends from a transfer-stage rack to the corresponding I/O-stage rack.

An I/O-stage rack is packaged together with the corresponding transfer-stage rack, and the combination is referred to as an *IOT rack*. Figure 2 shows the internal structure of an IOT rack. Each IOT rack consists of up to four boards (called I/O modules) implementing the I/O stage, up to four boards (called transfer modules) implementing the transfer stage, and a pair of backplane buses interconnecting the two stages. Every module has sixteen duplex fiber-link interfaces on it. We shall refer to this fiber inlet/outlet pair of a rack as a *channel*. Thus, a fully populated IOT rack has 64 channels on either side. Note that the degree of blocking can be controlled by varying the number of I/O modules in each rack, keeping the number of

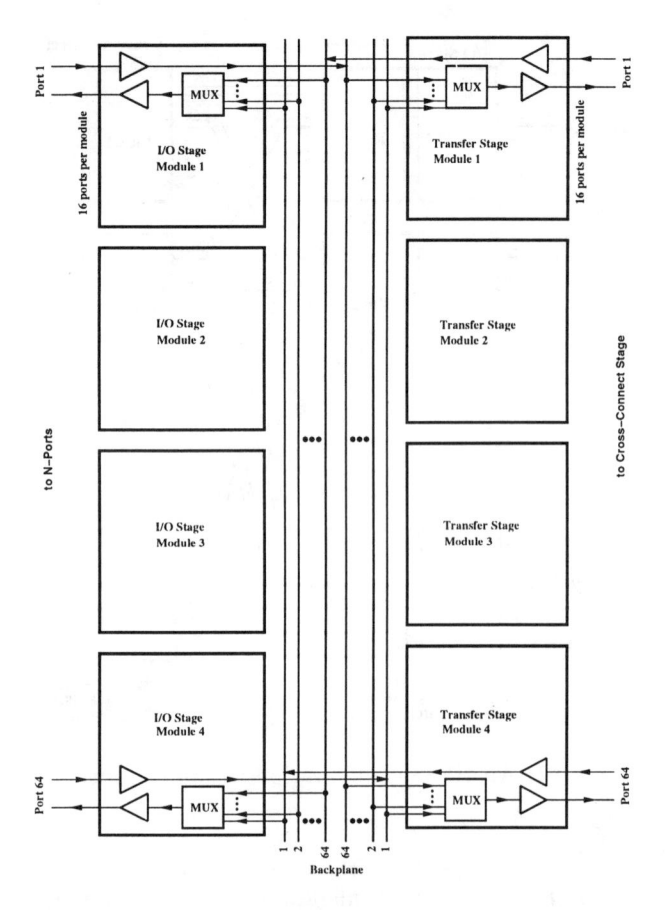

Figure 2: Internal structure of an IOT rack in the HPSS.

transfer modules constant, or vice-versa. The configuration in Figure 1 is the largest configuration of the HPSS switch, where each of the 64 IOT racks is fully populated. It is easy to see that, if half of the I/O modules (that is, 32 ports), are removed from each IOT rack, the resulting configuration is a strictly nonblocking network with 2048 ports.

The crossbar function within the IOT rack is implemented by a combination of drivers and multiplexers. Drivers drive the backplane bus lines and multiplexers select one input from 64 lines of the backplane bus. There are two such sets of drivers, buses, and multiplexers in each IOT rack. Each module has an autonomous microcontroller on it for control. The individual microcontrollers within a rack exchange control messages via a time-shared control bus local to each rack. The control bus in an IOT rack may be serving up to eight microcontrollers.

A CC (cross-connect) rack has about half the hardware of an IOT rack as it implements a single crossbar. Each CC rack has a backplane bus and up to four modules (called CC modules) with 16 channels each. Each module drives the 64 lines of the bus and takes multiplexer inputs from the same backplane bus. This rack exactly corresponds to a crossbar in the middle stage of the Clos network. As in the IOT racks, each CC module has an autonomous microcontroller for control functions, and a separate time-shared control bus for communication between microcontrollers within the same rack.

A three-stage network with any number of ports $N \leq 4096$ can be constructed using these racks as building blocks. For example, a switching system with 512 channels can be constructed using 8 IOT racks with 64 bidirectional channels per rack, and the same number of CC racks with 64 bidirectional channels per rack. Such a system allows a maximum of $64 \times 8 = 512$ I/O ports; in a nonblocking configuration, however, only 256 ports can be used. It should be noted that any three-stage network constructed using the fixed-size racks provides multiple routing paths from an IOT rack to a CC rack whenever the total number of channels is less than the maximum size (4096). Thus, in a smaller configuration, there are more routing choices available at the transfer stage.

The specific HPSS configuration we study in this paper has 512 channels, with 8 fully-populated CC racks and the same number of IOT racks. Each IOT rack is assumed to have all four transfer modules, but the number of I/O modules is varied from 2 to 4 to control the degree of blocking. When the number of I/O modules per IOT rack is 2, the resulting system has 256 ports, and is a strictly nonblocking configuration. When all the IOT racks are fully populated, a blocking configuration with 512 ports results. Each interconnecting fiber link between IOT and CC racks is assumed to be 1 km long, as the racks are distributed across the campus.

Clos networks were initially proposed for telephone switching, and consequently used circuit-switching with a central controller. Such a centralized control scheme would be impractical if the crossbars in the individual stages are distributed over large distances, as is the case with the HPSS. The HPSS system, therefore, uses a distributed control scheme where different sections of the switch are controlled independently. Thus, each microcontroller makes routing decisions on its own based on the information about the status of the paths available to it at that time. The microcontrollers need to exchange control messages to set up and remove connections, and to communicate the most recent status of their connections among themselves. This signaling can be either *in-band* or *out-of-band*. The HPSS switch uses both mechanisms:

1. Microcontrollers within the same rack exchange messages through the local control bus using out-of-band signaling. Access to the bus is serialized, but once a microcontroller gains access to it, it may *broadcast* a message to any number of microcontrollers within its rack.

2. Microcontrollers located in the CC and transfer stages exchange messages using an inband signaling scheme defined by the Fibre Channel. The Fibre Channel mandates a minimum of 24 idle characters to be inserted between consecutive data frames at the time of transmission. Up to 16 of these characters may be removed and replaced by

signaling information; thus, these characters represent excess bandwidth the switch may use for internal signaling. When signaling information needs to be transmitted between two microcontrollers in the transfer and CC stages, a control frame is constructed and queued at one of the channels connecting the two modules. The control frame is transmitted immediately if the channel is idle; otherwise it waits until an excess idle character is found, and is then transmitted. If a subsequent data frame arrives before the transmission of the control frame is complete, it is delayed in an elastic buffer. This delay in the data stream is eventually absorbed by removing excess idles in subsequent frames.

While simulating the HPSS, we need to distinguish between *data frames* and *control frames*. Control frames are the signaling messages between the microcontrollers within the HPSS; examples of control frames include status-update frames, frames to indicate path-busy and port-busy conditions, etc. Any frame generated by an N-port for delivery to another N-port is referred to as a data frame. We shall use the term *port* to encapsulate an N-port with its corresponding F-port on the switch, since in most of our discussions we do not need to distinguish between them.

2.3 HPSS Operation

A connection is set up in the HPSS switch starting at the source part and proceeding through the I/O and transfer stages into a CC-stage module, subsequently to a transfer-stage module, and finally to the I/O-stage module corresponding to the destination port. This path setup is performed in a distributed fashion, with each microcontroller choosing an available path to the next stage. If no path is found, the request backs off to the previous stage. This is similar to a *depth-first search*. The choice of paths among the available ones can be made randomly at each step. The path can be chosen more intelligently, however, if each microcontroller knows the entire state of the system at that time. The HPSS uses a *status update scheme* to broadcast state changes from each microcontroller to others.

In the HPSS, status updates are conveyed by control frames originating at the CC stage. These updates are received by the transfer-stage microcontrollers, which then combine their status to the frames, and broadcast the combined status to the I/O-stage microcontrollers. The update messages are assumed to be timer-driven, and the interval between updates can be varied in the simulations. The interval can also be selected as infinite, corresponding to a completely random selection of paths at every stage. Note that the update scheme is useful only if the update interval is small compared to the average lifetime of a connection. Because long block transfers (typically 3 Mbytes of data) are expected to be a significant fraction of the HPSS traffic, such an update scheme is worthy of investigation. Note that, even if path selection is performed in a totally random manner, such a status-update scheme is still useful for communicating the temporary unavailability of certain links or switch modules because of faults or error conditions.

Each microcontroller maintains an availability table which stores a list of available paths to the next stage of the switch to reach a given destination. For example, a microcontroller in the transfer stage stores the available CC-stage choices to reach each IOT rack. These tables are updated by the status-update messages. Note that the availability tables store possible choices to route a connection to the next stage of the switch, but do not store the status of the I/O ports. The availability tables are meant to increase the probability of the selected path reaching the destination port without being blocked in a subsequent stage, but the path-selection is still random. That is, a random choice is made from the set of available paths when more than one path is shown by the availability table. If no available paths are found, a *path-busy* control frame is returned to the previous stage, which then tries a different path.

2.4 Connection Setup Algorithm

An important distinction of HPSS from earlier implementations of Clos-type networks is its distributed control structure. State information is maintained by every microcontroller for each inlet/outlet pair (or channel) on the microcontroller's module. Since all data traffic is bidirectional, separate status information need not be maintained for each inlet and outlet.

Channels and ports in the HPSS can be in one of three states: *idle*, *reserved*, and *connected*. The connected and reserved states are busy states, and idle is the state in which the port or channel is readily available for a connection. The reserved state is a resource-reservation state, where channels are reserved and will be used if the connection is successfully set up, else will eventually be released and made available to other connection requests.

Connection establishment between two I/O ports can involve up to six microcontrollers. Currently, each I/O port is allowed to have only one outstanding connection request at any time. For each connection request, the switch must set up a route from the source I/O port to the destination I/O port, and a return path from the destination I/O port to the source I/O port. We shall refer to the control frame used to set up the forward path as the *request*, and the frame use to set up the return path as the *acknowledgment*. Since no port-status information is maintained in the modules, a request must reach the destination I/O port's microcontroller to determine if the port is available to engage in a data exchange. Note that blocking (or path busy condition) can occur even in a strictly non-blocking HPSS configuration because of distributed control. For example, two IOT racks may simultaneously request the same outgoing path from the CC stage, and one of them will have to be rejected.

There are two methods of connection establishment in the HPSS, depending on whether the destination I/O port is in the same rack as the source I/O port. When the ports involved in a connection request belong to distinct I/O racks, the connection can be set up through a single CC-rack; such a connection is referred to as a *type-1* connection. When the pair of ports to be connected are located within the same IOT rack, however, connection setup is more complex because an IOT rack does not allow local connections between its I/O ports. In general, such a communication path between two I/O ports located on the same IOT rack may use two distinct CC racks, one for the forward path and the second for the reverse path.[†] Such a connection — between two I/O ports located within the same I/O rack — is called a *type-2* connection.

Setting up a connection in the HPSS involves propagating a connection-request control frame from the source I/O port to the destination I/O port and receiving a response. At each stage, the servicing microcontroller selects one of the available paths to the next stage from its availability tables to forward the message. On reaching the destination IOT rack, if the destination I/O port is found idle, the corresponding microcontroller returns an acknowledgement frame to the requesting port. For a type-1 connection, setup is complete when the acknowledgement frame reaches the source that originated the request. The connection setup for a type-2 connection is more complex as it requires the paths in each direction to be set up separately. Details of the connection setup algorithm are described in [5].

If a requesting I/O port receives another incoming request from a port while its request is in transit, the incoming request is given priority. The generated request is then aborted by sending an abort frame to follow the partial path set up by the request frame.

When a microcontroller selects a channel (or another microcontroller) to route the request to the next stage, the request may get blocked at a switch module because no outgoing paths are available. In such cases, a path-busy control frame is returned to the previous stage. The receiving microcontroller then frees the channel on which the path-busy frame was received and tries to set up the path through an alternate outgoing channel (or microcontroller). Thus, path setup proceeds in a depth-first tree, backing off to the previous stage whenever no paths are found in a certain stage. If the search backs off all the way to the root of the tree, that is to the requesting F-port. The F-port must then retry the request at a later time.

3 Upper Bounds on Switch Throughput

Before we present results from a detailed simulation of the HPSS switch, we first derive some simple upper bounds on its throughput as a function of certain design and operational parameters of the system. These bounds are useful for comparison with the actual results obtained from simulations.

[†]One CC rack may implement the paths in both directions if there are multiple paths between the transfer and CC stages, as is the case when the number of channels is less than 4096. Two distinct CC racks are always needed in a full configuration as there is a unique channel between every pair of IOT and CC racks.

3.1 Effect of Traffic Model

It is important to realize that the data traffic distribution has a significant impact on the true offered load. The traffic in the HPSS network is expected to have a bimodal distribution, with "long" connections for transmission of image data and "short" frames for other network traffic. In our simulations, we used two sizes of connections, long connections that transfer 3 Mbytes of data (roughly corresponding to one screenful of graphics data at 1024×1024 resolution with 24 bits per pixel), and short connections that transfer a single Fibre-Channel frame of 2140 bytes. Thus, a long connection takes about 30 milliseconds as against approximately $20\mu s$ for a short connection.

I/O ports go through a cycle of setup, data exchange, and idle periods. Although not all attempted connections are established successfully, we can obtain an upper bound on the throughput of the switch by counting the number of connections attempted per second by each active port. Assuming a uniform spatial distribution of connections, each port must serve as many incoming connection requests, on the average, as the number of requests it generates. In the ideal case, each port would go through a cycle of connection setup, data exchange, response to an incoming connection request, data exchange, and response to a disconnection. The minimum amount of time required for each such cycle is

$$t_{\text{setup}} + t_{\text{data}} + \frac{1}{2} t_{\text{setup}} + t_{\text{data}} + \frac{1}{2} t_{\text{setup}},$$

where t_{setup} is the minimum connection setup time and t_{data} is the average time to transfer the data in the connection. The $\frac{1}{2} t_{\text{setup}}$ terms represent the time for disconnection.

Thus, an upper bound on the number of connections *attempted* per second per port is given by

$$C_{\text{attempt}} = \frac{1}{2(t_{\text{setup}} + t_{\text{data}})}. \quad (1)$$

Let α denote the fraction of connections that are short. Then,

$$t_{\text{data}} = \alpha t_{\text{short}} + (1-\alpha) t_{\text{long}}, \quad (2)$$

where t_{short} and t_{long} denote the durations of a short and long connection, respectively. With our choice of transfer sizes (2140 bytes/3 Mbytes), $t_{\text{short}} \approx 21$ μs and $t_{\text{long}} \approx 3$ ms. We have considered three values of α in our simulations — 90, 95, and 100 percent.

The minimum setup time t_{setup} can be estimated easily. A type-1 connection involves at least 11 microcontroller processing delays, 6 control bus transmissions, and 4 fiber-link delays. A type-2 connection involves at least 9 microcontroller processing delays, 4 control bus transmissions, and 4 fiber-link delays. We assumed a processing time of 4 μs per request at each microcontroller (approximately 100 instruction-cycles in a 25 MHz Intel-960 microprocessor). Transmission time for a control frame was taken as 3.2 μs

(32 bytes per control frame and a control-bus bandwidth of 10 Mbytes/s). The propagation delay in 1 km of fiber is approximately 4.76 μs. Furthermore, for a switch with 512 channels per stage (8 racks per stage), type-1 connections are 7 times as likely to occur as type-2 connections when the spatial distribution of requests in uniform. Therefore,

$$\begin{aligned}t_{\text{setup}} &= 0.875\,(11\times 4 + 6\times 3.2 + 4\times 4.76)\\ &\quad + 0.125\,(9\times 4 + 4\times 3.2 + 4\times 4.76)\\ &\approx 80\ \mu s.\end{aligned}$$

It is now easy to see that when $\alpha = 1$, t_{setup} is the dominant factor in determining C_{attempt}, whereas for $\alpha = 0.95$ and 0.9, $(1-\alpha)t_{\text{long}}$ is the dominant factor. From equations (1) and (2), the the maximum number of connections per port attempted by the traffic model for $\alpha = 0.90, 0.95$, and 1, is obtained as 161, 312, and 4950, respectively. These will serve as upper bounds for comparison of the results from simulation.

3.2 Effect of Rack Control Buses

The bandwidth of the rack control buses imposes an upper limit on the HPSS throughput. The control bus in an IOT rack serves as the signaling means for a maximum of 8 switch modules, whereas the control bus in a CC rack serves a maximum of 4 CC-stage modules. Therefore, the control bus in an IOT rack is likely to saturate earlier than the control bus in a CC rack.

Each connection established results in 4 IOT control-bus transmissions during setup; the number of control-bus transmissions for a disconnect operation is 2 for a type-1 disconnect and 3 for a type-2 disconnect. Hence, the average number of IOT bus transmissions in a 512-port switch is 6.25 per connection. We assumed a uniform size of 32 bytes for control frames, and a control-bus bandwidth of 10 Mbytes/s. Therefore, in an HPSS configuration with 8 racks in each stage, the aggregate IOT control-bus bandwidth available over the 8 racks is 80 Mbytes/s. When the system is fully populated, that is with 512 ports, the maximum number of connections per second per port that can be supported is:

$$\frac{8\times 10\times 10^6}{32\times 6.25\times 512}\approx 781.$$

Similarly, the upper bounds for the cases of 2 and 3 I/O modules per IOT rack are obtained as 1042 and 1562, respectively. By comparing with the maximum attempt rates obtained in section 3.1, it is easy to see that these upper bounds are much higher than the attempt rates for 90/10 and 95/5 traffic-mixes. With 100% short frames, however, the signaling bandwidth imposes a limit on throughput that is well below the attempt rate. Note that these upper bounds do not take into account control traffic not directly related to connection setup, such as status updates, instrumentation, etc.

3.3 Effect of Microcontroller Processing Time

The delays involved in the processing of control frames by the microcontrollers in the HPSS also imposes limits on its throughput. An upper bound on the throughput can be obtained by accounting for the total time needed to process the control frames for a connection setup, assuming that no path-busy or port-busy conditions are encountered. In an HPSS configuration with fully-populated IOT racks, the setup protocol causes a microcontroller in the transfer-stage to process slightly more control frames than the other microcontrollers. Each connection established results in 4 control frames processed by transfer-stage microcontrollers during set-up, and 2 frames during disconnect. Hence, the average number of control messages processed by the transfer-stage microcontrollers for each connection is 6. Note that each transfer-stage microcontroller services 16 ports. Assuming $4\mu s$ of processing time for each message, the maximum number of connections that can be supported is

$$\frac{1}{6\times 4\times 10^{-6}\times 16}\approx 2{,}600\ \text{connections/sec./port.}$$

Again, this number is much higher than the rate of connection attempts by the 90/10 or 95/5 traffic mixes, but almost half of the attempt rate with a 100/0 mix.

4 Experimental Evaluation

Here we present and interpret the results obtained from simulations of the HPSS switch. About 400 simulation runs were done with varying parameters, and selected results are presented here. The simulation source, written in the C-based language CSIM, consists of over 6000 lines of code. In the figures that follow, the parameter that is varied to obtain each plot is the average idle interval between connection requests generated by active I/O ports. This affects the *offered load* (number of connections attempted per second), and consequently, the number of connections actually set up per second. The x-axes in the figures show the number of successful connections set up per active I/O port per second. The per-port value is used to normalize the effect of switch-size.

We used a traffic distribution where a fraction α of the attempted connections are short (one Fibre-Channel frame with 2140 bytes) and $(1-\alpha)$ are long connections (a total of 3 Mbytes per connection). The results reported here are for $\alpha = 0.95$, unless stated otherwise. Connections of each type were generated from an Erlang-2 distribution and the destinations of connections were chosen from a uniform distribution. The HPSS configuration studied has 512 channels, with 8 fully-populated CC racks and the same number of IOT racks. Each IOT rack has all four transfer modules, while the number of I/O modules is varied from 2 to 4 (that is, the total number of F-ports were varied from 256 to 512.).

The setup times are plotted in Figures 3 and 4, respectively, for the cases of two and four I/O modules per IOT rack. The setup times are shown for various values of the status-update interval. The update period of infinity should be interpreted as making a random selection of channels and microcontrollers in the routing phase, since all channels and microcontrollers are initialized to the 'available' state in all status tables. This corresponds to completely random selection of paths. The minimum time to set up a connection in the HPSS switch is approximately 80 μs with our choice of parameters, assuming no queueing of requests anywhere in the system. As observed in section 3.1, this places an upper bound on the throughput of the switch of approximately 312 connections per second per port for the 95/5 traffic distribution. The saturation throughput in Figure 3 is approximately 80% of the upper bound in section 3.1, demonstrating excellent performance.

It is easy to observe from Figure 3 that frequent status-updates actually degrade performance, and a completely random selection of paths performs extremely well. This is because the probability of blocking in the system with random path-selection is not high enough to justify the overhead of transmitting and processing status-update messages. On increasing the number of I/O modules per rack, the update scheme becomes increasingly effective, as is evident from Figure 4. Due to the increased blocking in the racks in this case, random guesses do not fare as well. The traffic mix also has a significant influence on the effectiveness of status updates. We observed that a 90/10 traffic mix improves the effectiveness due to the lower rate of state changes in the system. On the contrary, the update scheme almost always degraded the performance with 100/0 traffic.

Figure 5 shows the average sum of queueing and processing delays experienced by control frames at a microcontroller in the I/O stage. Only the fully-populated I/O-rack cases are shown (4 modules per I/O rack). The queueing and processing times are a function of availability of IOT control buses (since microcontrollers block on a bus-transmit until they get access to the bus), of the rate of arrival of control frames, and of the processing speed (service rate) of the microcontrollers.

Another useful and interesting performance metric is the probability of blocking at each of the three stages. By blocking, we refer to a situation where a particular microcontroller is unable to find a path to the destination, and returns a path-busy control frame to its requesting microcontroller in a preceding stage. In almost all simulations, probability of blocking at the I/O stage was found to be negligible. Figure 6 shows the probability of blocking at the transfer stage. Here the effect of increasing the number of I/O modules per rack is clearly visible. With four I/O modules per rack, the probabilities increased rapidly at approximately 200 connections per second per port, but with two I/O modules per rack the probabilities were insignificant.

Figure 7 shows the utilization of the control buses in the IOT racks. The load on the control bus in the IOT rack was observed to be slightly higher as compared to the load in the CC stage, but the bandwidth of 10 Mbytes/s was seen to be adequate for both for the case of 95/5 traffic distribution.

Figure 8 shows the bandwidth used by control messages between the transfer and CC stages as a function of the aggregate link-bandwidth between the two stages. The signaling bandwidth is almost linear at low loads but increased faster at high loads because of the increase in path-busy and port-busy conditions. Even at high loads, however, the signaling bandwidth used was very low, less than 0.05 percent.

5 Concluding Remarks

We found that the performance of the switch from our simulations is close to the theoretical upper bounds with our choice of operational parameters. With a 95/5 mix of short and long connections, an aggregate capacity of approximately 63,000 connections per second was obtained from a 256-port nonblocking configuration. A 512-port blocking configuration provided a maximum throughput of over 100,000 connections per second.

We observed that the traffic model has a significant influence on the performance; our choice of operational parameters (control-bus bandwidth, microcontroller processing time, etc.) provided adequate performance for the 95/5 and 90/10 traffic distributions. For the 100/0 traffic mix, however, the control-bus bandwidth clearly was a bottleneck.

The 100/0 traffic mix corresponds to the worst-case traffic, consisting of short frames only. Clearly, if the traffic consists of predominantly short frames, the setup time dominates the overall throughput of the switch and significant performance gains can be obtained only by eliminating or simplifying the connection setup operation (for example, by the use of class 2 or 3 of the Fibre Channel Standard).

Acknowledgements

This work benefited from discussions with Paul Rupert, Bill Lennon, and Jed Donnelly at Lawrence Livermore National Laboratory.

References

[1] T. Anderson and R. Cornelius, "High-Performance Switch with Fibre Channel," *Proceedings of IEEE COMPCON*, February 1992.

[2] V. E. Beneš. *Mathematical Theory of Connecting Networks and Telephone Traffic*, Academic Press, 1965.

[3] D. Getchell and P. Rupert, "Fiber Channel in the Local Area Network," *IEEE LTS*, Vol. 3, No. 2, May 1992, pp.38–42.

[4] *Fibre Channel Physical and Signaling Interface (FC-PH)*, Working Draft Rev. 2.2, ANSI X3T9.3, January 1992.

[5] V. Sahai, *Performance Evaluation of a High-Speed Switching System*, Masters Dissertation, Computer Engineering Department, University of California at Santa Cruz, September 1992.

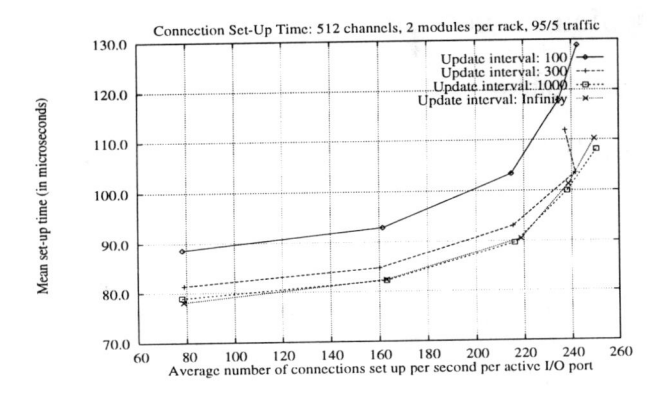

Figure 3: Setup time for an HPSS configuration with 2 I/O modules per rack (256 ports).

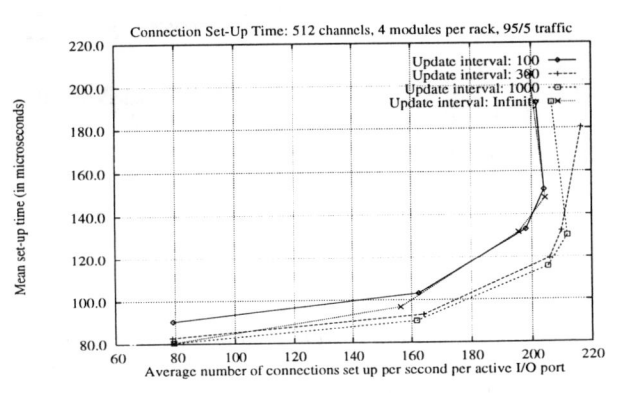

Figure 4: Setup time for an HPSS configuration with 4 I/O modules per rack (512 ports).

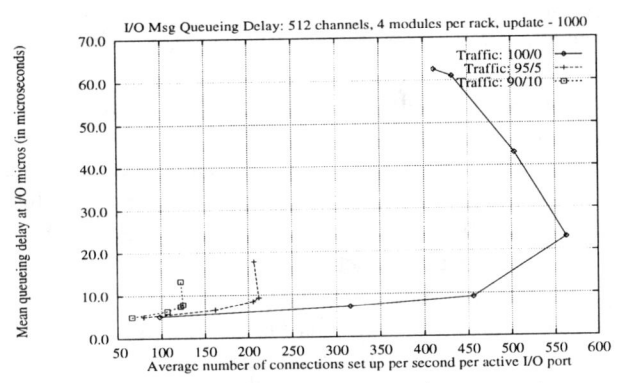

Figure 5: Mean processing delay at an I/O-stage microcontroller.

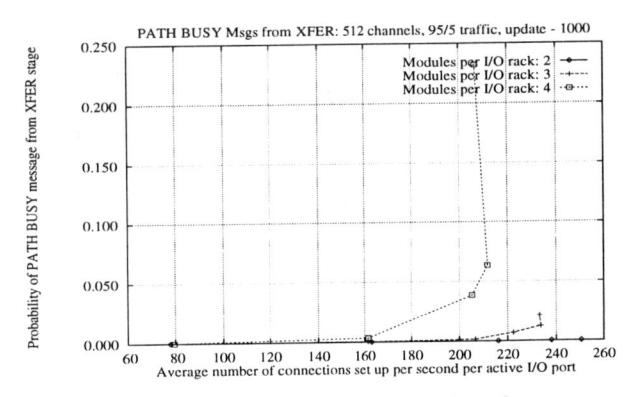

Figure 6: Transfer-stage blocking.

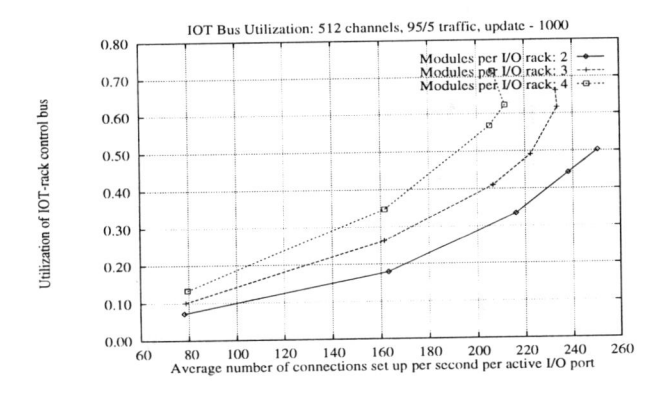

Figure 7: Utilization of the control bus in an IOT rack.

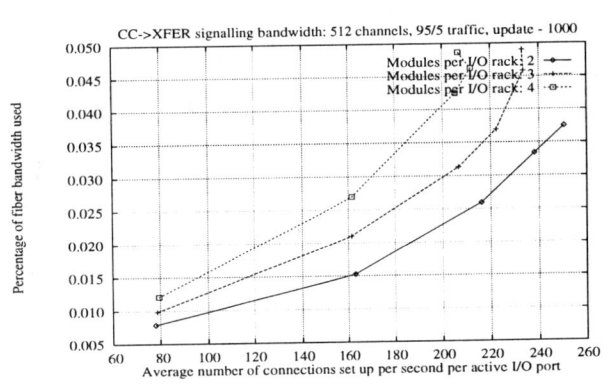

Figure 8: Bandwidth used by CC – transfer stage signaling.

MULTIPAR: An Output Queue ATM Modular Switch with Multiple Phases and Replicated Planes

Jian Ma and Kauko Rahko

Laboratory of Telecommunications Technology, Helsinki University of Technology

Abstract

In this paper, we propose a novel output queuing ATM modular switch which has memoryless two-stage interconnection with disjoint-path topology. The goal of achieving the modular switch is to relax the limitation of VLSI implementation, to simplify interstage wiring and synchronization, furthermore to reduce complexity of the overall switch. A pure output queue is constructed by providing multipath in each output port and replicated switching module planes. The switch with certain cell loss requirement can be ensured by choosing a suitable path set of L_1 and L_2. For instance, cell loss probability in the switch can be kept less than 10^{-6} for various N, under 90% load, if a set of $L_1=9$ and $L_2=4$ (or $L_1=8$ and $L_2=5$) is chosen.

1: Introduction

A high performance ATM switch should have very high throughput, low cell delay, and low cell loss probability; it must be able to handle many cells destined for a same output port in same time slot. A number of such switch architectures has already been proposed. The Knockout switch [1] achieves a pure output queue with N ($N \times L$)-concentrators to construct modular switch. Lee's switch [2] has a modular structure, and output contention is overcome by output space extension. However, both switches have to bear high overall complexity. The Sunshine switch [3] uses a cascade of an $N \times N$ Batcher network and multiple parallel banyan networks to achieve a certain degree of output buffer, and to achieve small complexity. But, achieving this switch becomes increasingly more difficult for larger networks, because the Batcher/banyan network is a synchronous network and requires that all cells are aligned on a common boundary at each column of switching elements. The other designers [4,5,6] focus on minimizing the cost of switch. However, the path conflict requires extra control[6] and a larger buffer [4,5] especially in the case of burst traffic, thus the switches are inevitably expensive. Currently, especially for packet switching, the cost of switch element has become less significant; greater proportion of the cost is for buffer size, input synchronization and switch control. In this paper, we focus on relaxing the limitation of VLSI implementation, reducing buffer size, simplifying interstage wiring and synchronization, to propose a novel switch fabric, called <u>mult</u>iple <u>p</u>hases' <u>a</u>nd <u>r</u>eplicated planes'(MULTIPAR) modular packet switch. This switch has memoryless two-stage modular fabric with disjoint-path topology, it is self-routing in which the cell routing is based on a certain phase address, it has pure output queue which achieves the best delay/throughput performance [7].

We arrange this paper as the following. In section 2, we describe the switch architecture. In section 3 we give analysis and simulation results of the cell loss due to the limited number of paths and due to buffer overflow. In section 4, we discuss on implementation of the module, complexity, reliability, and growability of the switch.

2: MULTIPAR modular switch architecture

Fig. 1. illustrates the basic fabric of the MULTIPAR modular switch. An $N \times N$ switch fabric (where $N = n \times m$) is partitioned into two stages(or phases). The first stage consists of m <u>m</u>ultipath <u>s</u>witching <u>m</u>odules(MSMs); each MSM has n distinct input and output ports; each output port has L_1 paths. The second stage consists of L_1 identical parallel planes, each one having n MSMs; each MSM has m distinct input and output ports; each output port has L_2 paths. The same number MSMs in the L_1 planes compose a <u>g</u>roup <u>m</u>odule (GM). All particular number outputs of a GM are connected to an <u>o</u>utput <u>p</u>ort <u>c</u>ontroller(OPC). To ensure that up to L_1 cells destined for a same GM can pass through the first stage MSM, and arrive then to the different plane of the GM, respectively, the L_1 paths of an output port in the first stage MSM are connected to the different planes of a GM respectively. and If more than such L_1 cells are present, then the excess cells within the first stage MSM must be discarded. As same as above in the first stage case, the second stage MSM offers L_2 paths to pass arriving cells destined for same OPC. The OPC statistically multiplexes and buffers the cells to access to the transmission links. Thus, a pure output queue switch is constructed. The switches with the output queue have been proven to give the best delay/throughput performance [7].

Each cell has equal probability $\frac{1}{N}$ of being addressed to any given output. Thus, in the first stage MSM, the probability of an input cell destined for a second stage GM is simply $\frac{m\rho}{N}$. $P1(k)$, the probabilities of k cell arrivals all destined for the GM in a time slot has the binomial probabilities:

$$P1(k) = \binom{n}{k}\left(\frac{m\rho}{N}\right)^k\left(1-\frac{m\rho}{N}\right)^{n-k}. \quad (1)$$

If we only allow up to L_1 such cells to pass through the MSM, the probability for a cell to be dropped in the first stage is

$$P1_{loss} = \frac{1}{\rho}\sum_{k=L_1+1}^{n}(k-L_1)\binom{n}{k}\left(\frac{\rho}{n}\right)^k\left(1-\frac{\rho}{n}\right)^{n-k}. \quad (2)$$

If $n \to \infty$,

$$P1_{loss} = \left[1-\frac{L_1}{\rho}\right]\left[1-\sum_{k=0}^{L_1}\frac{\rho^k e^{-\rho}}{k!}\right] + \frac{\rho^{L_1} e^{-\rho}}{L_1!} \quad (3)$$

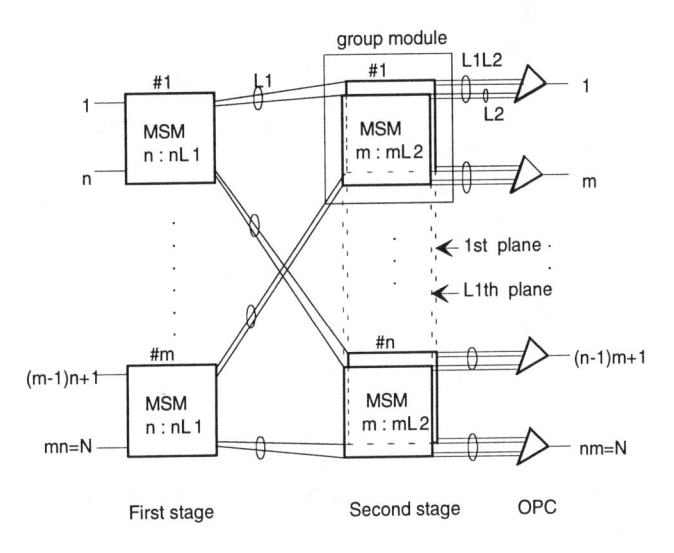

Fig. 1. The two-stage MULTIPAR switch

The switch is self-routing that the cell routing in each MSM depends only on a phase address. The destination address contains $\log_2 N$ bits which are divided into two phases. The first phase of the address consists of $\log_2 n$ bits, and it is used in first stage MSM to direct a cell to a particular second stage GM. The second phase consists of $\log_2 m$ bits, and it is used in the second stage MSM to direct a cell to a particular OPC.

3: Switch performance

3.1: Cell loss due to limited number of paths

We consider a random traffic model. Under the random traffic model, arrivals on the N inputs are independent Bernoulli processes in which the probability that a cell arrives on an input in any given time slot is ρ.

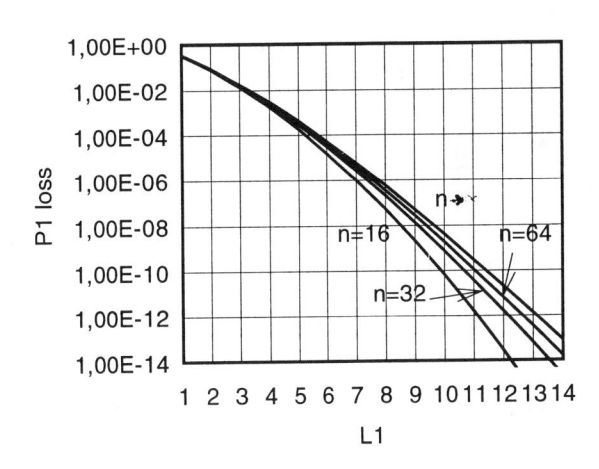

Fig. 2. The cell loss probability in first stage versus L_1, under 90% input load, for n=16, 32, 64 and infinite.

Fig. 2. shows the cell loss probability versus L_1 under 90% load (i.e., ρ=0.9), for n=16, 32, 64, and infinity. We note that eight paths per output port achieves the cell loss probability less than 10^{-6} for arbitrarily large n. Furthermore, in Fig. 3., we see that number of paths required to achieve a particular cell loss probability is not sensitive to the switch loading when the load is high.

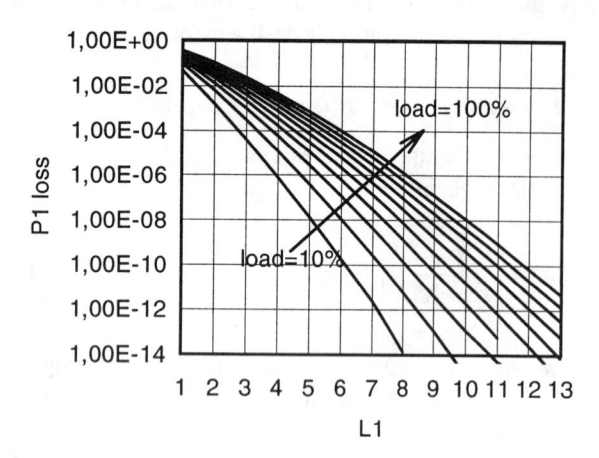

Fig. 3. The cell loss probability in first stage versus various loads, for $m \to \infty$.

In the second stage MSM, the probability of cell arriving at an input port is assumed to be $\frac{\rho}{L_1}$, because we are interested in low cell loss rate. Thus the probability of an arriving cell destined for an OPC is $\frac{\rho}{mL_1}$. $P2(k)$, the probability of k cells arriving in a time slot all destined for the OPC is

$$P2(k) = \binom{m}{k}\left(\frac{\rho}{mL_1}\right)^k \left(1-\frac{\rho}{mL_1}\right)^{m-k}. \quad (4)$$

If we only allow up to L_2 such cells to pass through the MSM, the probability for a cell to be dropped in the second stage can be obtained from (2) and (3) by replacing ρ and L_1 with $\frac{\rho}{L_1}$ and L_2 respectively,

$$P2_{loss} = \frac{L_1}{\rho} \sum_{k=L_2+1}^{m} (k-L_2)\binom{m}{k}\left(\frac{\rho}{mL_1}\right)^k \left(1-\frac{\rho}{mL_1}\right)^{m-k} \quad (5)$$

If $m \to \infty$,

$$P2_{loss} = \left[1-\frac{1}{\rho}\right]\left[1-\sum_{k=0}^{L_2} \frac{(\rho/L_1)^k e^{-\rho/L_1}}{k!}\right] + \frac{(\rho/L_1)^{L_2} e^{-\rho/L_1}}{L_2!}. \quad (6)$$

Fig. 4. shows the cell loss probability versus L_2, for n=16, 32, 64 and infinity, in the case of L_1=8. Fig. 5 gives the cell loss probability in the second stage versus L_1 and L_2, for $m \to \infty$. Comparing Fig. 3. and Fig. 5., we see that the L_2 requires less size than the L_1 for same cell loss probability, thanks to input load reduction in the second stage MSMs. For example, we note that five paths per output port in the second stage module can archive the cell loss probability less than 10^{-6}, for arbitrarily large m, in the case of L_1=8.

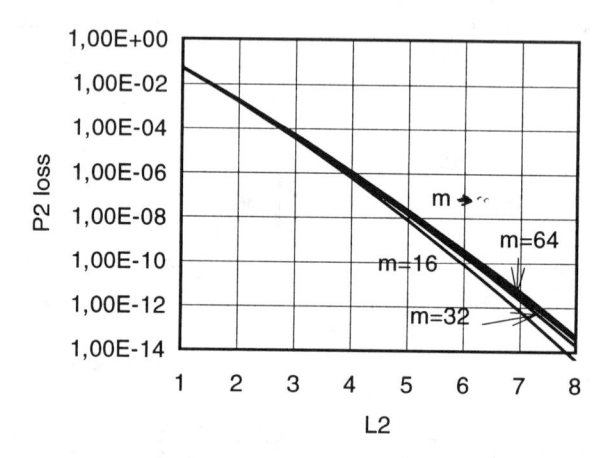

Fig. 4. In the case L_1=8, the cell loss probability in second stage versus L_2, under 90% input load, for m=16, 32, 64 and infinite.

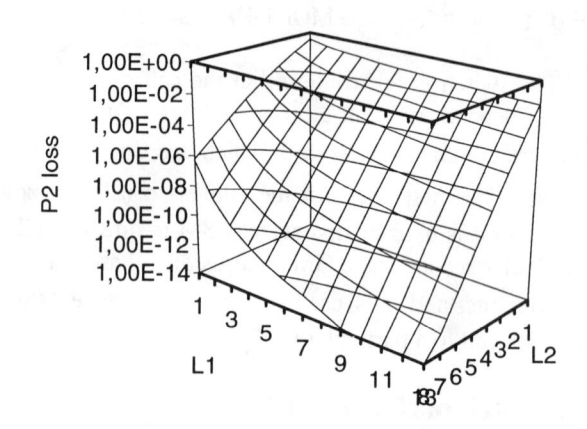

Fig. 5. The cell loss probability in second stage versus L_1 and L_2, under 90% input load, for $m \to \infty$.

Assuming that lost cells in the first stage and in the second stage are independent reciprocal, the total cell loss probability of the overall switch can be written as

$$P_{loss} = P1_{loss} + P2_{loss} - P1_{loss} \times P2_{loss} \quad (7)$$

In Fig. 6., we see that cell loss probability of the overall switch can be decreased to about 10^{-3} time, as L_1 increases by three and L_2 increases by one, and a few of increasing of the L_1 and L_2 leads to a big reduction of cell loss probability. If the reasonable set of $L_1=9$ and $L_2=4$ (or $L1=8$ and $L_2=5$) are chosen, the probability can be kept below 10^{-6} for arbitrarily N under 90% load(See Fig. 6.)

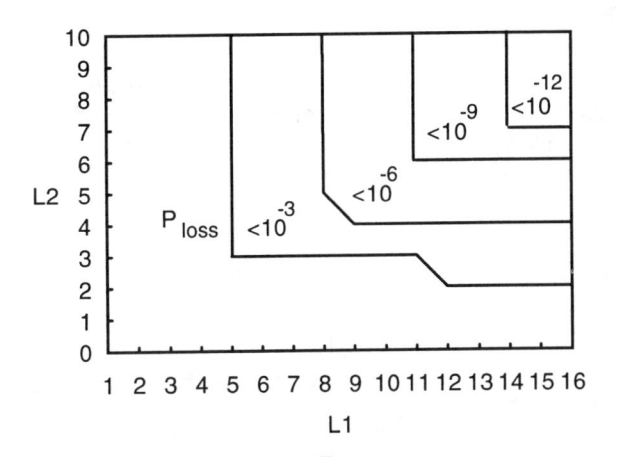

Fig. 6. Required L_1 and L_2 size versus the cell loss probability of overall switch, under 90% input load, for $N=n^2 \to \infty$

Table 1. gives the comparison of the packet loss probabilities in the random traffic and in the bursty traffic with the mean burst length A of 8 (see section 3.2) for some sets of L_1 and L_2. As can be seen, the cell loss probabilities for the random traffic and the bursty traffic are almost same, i.e., the effect of the bursty traffic on the number of paths can be ignored.

Table 1. Comparison of cell loss probabilities for the random traffic and the bursty traffic(Load=80%).

		Random Traffic (analysis)		Bursty Traffic (simulation)	
L1	L2	$P1_{loss}$	$P2_{loss}$	$P1_{loss}$	$P2_{loss}$
2	2	6,36E-02	1,65E-02	6,45E-02	1,49E-02
4	2	1,18E-03	5,03E-03	1,28E-03	5,35E-03
5	3	1,09E-04	1,06E-04	1,10E-04	1,06E-04
6	3	7,94E-06	6,20E-05	9,34E-06	6,68E-05
6	4	7,94E-06	1,24E-06	9,34E-06	1,56E-06
8	4	2,10E-08	3,98E-07	2,25E-08	4,50E-07

Since cells in ATM network have different cell loss rate requirements, (for instance telephone service requires cell loss rate below 10^{-3} and data transmission service requires cell loss rate below 10^{-6},) the number of concentrator outputs(i.e. L_i) can be reduced by applying priority bit in cell header to satisfy the different cell loss requirements. This further reduction of the number of paths is our ongoing work.

3.2: Cell loss due to buffer overflow

In this section, we present cell loss performance for the output buffers. The results are obtained via simulation for $N=256$, $n=m=16$ ATM switch design. We consider two different traffic models: a random traffic model like above and a bursty model. The bursty model that we consider is uniform geometrically bursty traffic in which an input alternates between active and idle periods of geometrically distributed duration. Cells destined for the same output arrive continuously in consecutive time slots during an active period. The duration of the active period is characterized by a parameter p. The mean bursty length is given by $A = \frac{1}{p}$. (Note: we assume that there is at least one cell in the burst.) The idle period is geometrically distributed with parameter q. Unlike the duration of an active period, the duration of an idle period can be 0. The mean idle period is given by $I = \frac{1-q}{q}$. Given p and q, the offered load ρ can be found by $\rho = \frac{A}{A+I}$. We assume the destination of each burst is uniformly distributed among the outputs.

For the random traffic model, Fig. 7 shows the cell loss probability in an output buffer versus the buffer size for various offered loads ranging from the 80% to 100%, and $L_1=8$, $L_2=4$. For 80% load, a buffer size of 30 cells is needed to keep cell loss probability below 10^{-6}. This conclusion of buffer size is similar to Knockout switch. For the bursty traffic model, Fig. 8. shows cell loss probability vs. mean burst length for 80% load. For mean burst length $A=4$ and $A=8$, buffer sizes 250 and 450 are estimated to keep cell loss probability below 10^{-6}. For the bursty traffic, the larger buffer size associates with the increasing burst length.

N=256 (m=n=16), L1=8, L2=4

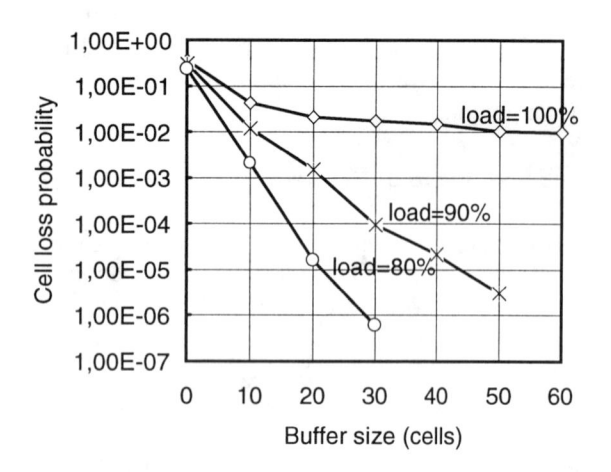

Fig. 7 Cell loss probability in an output buffer for the random traffic.

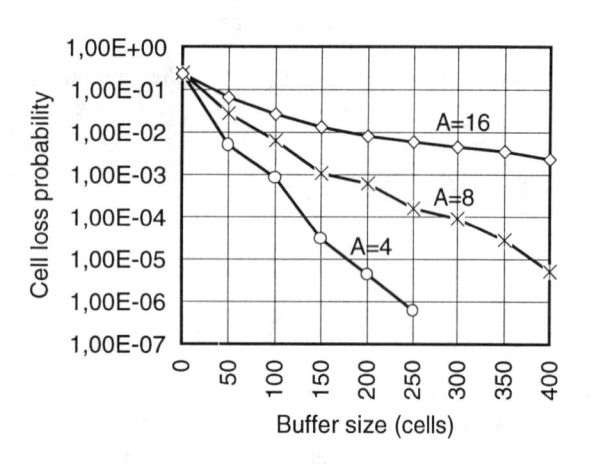

N=256 (m=n=16), load=80%, L1=8, L2=4

Fig. 8. Cell loss probability in an output buffer for the burst traffic.

4: Implementation of the MULTIPAR switch

4.1: Implementation of the MSM

Each MSM in either first stage or second stage is a cascade of an $n \times n$ (or $m \times m$) Batcher sort network and a group of parallel routing networks (See Fig. 9), each routing network consisting of a trap network and an $\left\lceil \frac{n}{L_1} \right\rceil \times n$ (or $\left\lceil \frac{m}{L_2} \right\rceil \times m$) expansion Banyan network. The Batcher network sorts incoming cells in a non-increasing order according to a phase address. The interconnection pattern between the Batcher network and L_i (i=1 or 2) parallel routing networks is a perfect shuffle which ensures that up to L_i cells with same phase address can be directed to the different routing networks. In the trap network, if more than one cell with same phase address appear at the input port of the trap network, only the cell with highest priority is accepted and the rest are dropped. Thus, all the cells at the input of the Banyan network have different phase addresses and are in a decreasing order. Therefore, the banyan network becomes non-blocking. They ensure that up to L_i cells with the same phase address can pass through the module. We should mention that this Banyan network is an expanded Banyan network as an example shown as Fig. 10., which has less switching nodes than Banyan network, and the dimensions of the nodes are 2×2 and 1×2.

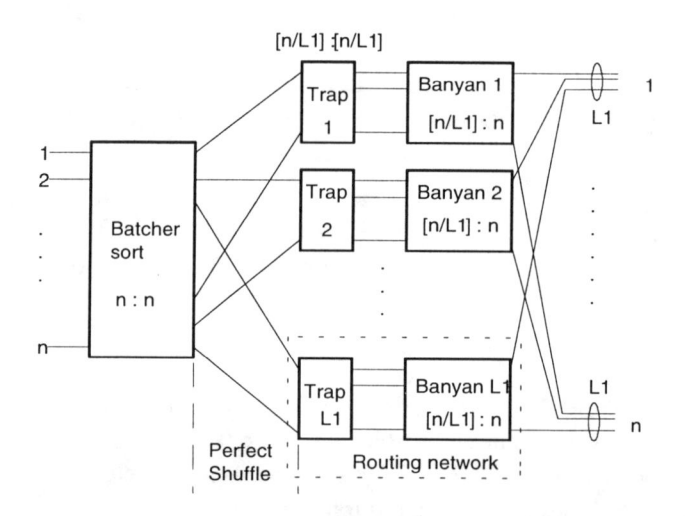

Fig. 9. The configuration of an MSM (e.g., first stage module).

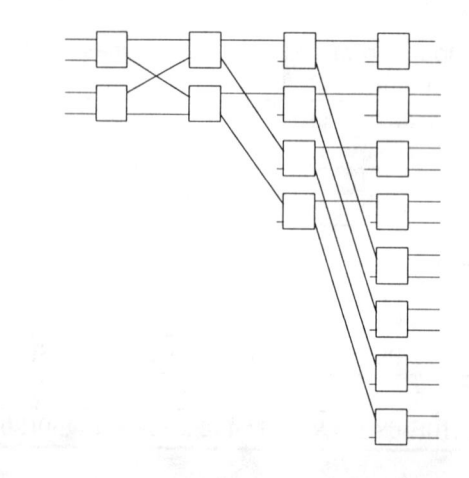

Fig. 10. An example of 4×16 expanded Banyan network.

The modular architecture can be realized as an array of 3-dimensional parallel processors(see Fig. 11.). The 3-D configuration reduces interconnection wire length, and the perfect shuffle interconnections between modules ensure the minimal interconnection wire length.

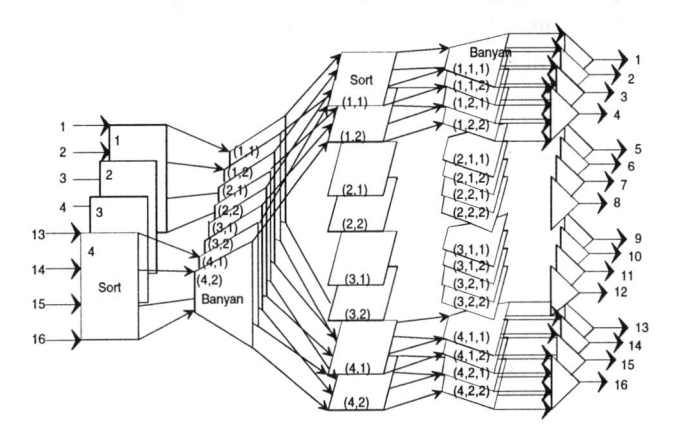

Fog. 11. MULTIPAR switch in 3-D space. (e.g., N=16, n=m=4, $L_1=L_2=2$)

4.2: Complexity Comparassion

Table 2. The complexity and modularity of the MULTIPAR modular switch.

		Number of modules	Dimension of module	Number of nodes
1st stage	Batcher	m	$n \times n$	$\frac{n}{4}\log_2 n(\log_2 n+1)$
	Banyan	mL_1	$\left[\frac{n}{L_1}\right] \times n$	$\frac{n}{2k_1}\log_2 n$
2nd stage	Batcher	nL_1	$m \times m$	$\frac{m}{4}\log_2 m(\log_2 m+1)$
	Banyan	nL_1L_2	$\left[\frac{m}{L_2}\right] \times m$	$\frac{m}{2k_2}\log_2 m$
OPC		N	$L_1L_2 \times 1$	$L_1L_2 \times 1$

Note: [x] is the nearest integer to x and [x]≥x; k_1, $k_2 > 1$.

Table 2. gives a statistics of the complexity and module. The maximal module of the MULTIPAR switch dimension does not exceed $n \times n$ or $m \times m$. If balance factor $n = m = \sqrt{N}$ is chosen, the maximal module dimension is only $\sqrt{N} \times \sqrt{N}$. The OPC size is $L_1L_2 \times 1$ which is not relative to the switch size, is depends on the switch performance. The number of the nodes of the switch increases as n, m, L_1 and L_2 increase, and the number of the nodes in second stage seems to increase more sensitively as L_1 and L_2 increase. Fortunately, the L_1 and L_2 are small constants which depend on the required performance of the switch, in addition, the L_2 has less size than the L_1.

Table 3. The comparison of complexity and modularity(N=1024, balance factor $n=m=\sqrt{N}$, load=90%, cell loss probability<10^{-6})

	Proposed switch	Lee's switch	Knockout switch	Sunsine switch
Batcher element	76,800	7,680	no	28,160
Banyan element	50,688	327,680	no	40,960
Binary tree element	no	130,048	no	no
Packet filter	no	no	1,048,576	no
Content element	no	no	8,912,896	no
1-bit delayer	no	no	4,456,448	no
Dimension of OPC	36×1	128×1	8×1	8×1
Dimension of maximum module	32×32	32×32	128×8	1024×1024

Table 3. compares the complexity of the proposed switch, the Knockout switch, the Lee's switch and the Sunshine switch. The comparison is carried out under the same conditions where all the four switches have the same cell loss probability and output queue. For example of an N=1024 switch, the output queued Lee's switch has an extended output space with L=4 parallel paths; each 1024×8 concentrator of the Knockout switch comprises one 64×8 and eight 128×8 concentrators [8]; and the Sunshine switch employs eight parallel banyan networks. The proposed switch has 32 MSMs in first stage and 32×9 (here the set of L_1=9 and L_2=4 is selected) MSMs in the second stage; each $\left[\frac{32}{9}\right] \times 32$ and $\left[\frac{32}{4}\right] \times 32$ banyan network has 32 and 36 switching nodes respectively. From the comparison, it is clear that the MULTIPAR modular switch has much smaller number of switching nodes than the Knockout switch and the

Lee' modular switch, and has small module size and very few different kinds of modules. As we know, the Sunshine switch has less complexity among some high-performance output queue switch, but it is not a modular switch. It is very difficult to implement a large switch like the one mentioned before. The proposed switch has only about the double number nodes of the Sunshine switch.

4.3: Growability and Reliability

In practice, it is estimated that a central exchange of a broadband network is expected to require switch fabric with very large number of high-speed ports, say 10,000. The most important feature of this switch architecture is its simple modular growth capability. In the following, we present three approaches to realize a large size switch from small size modules, and we show how large switch size can be realized by using the different growing approaches.

1. The switch capacity can be expanded incrementally by increasing dimension of the Batcher module and banyan module, without increasing planes and paths as well as OPC size. For instance, $N=4096$ switch size can be realized by using 64×64 dimension Batcher modules and $\left[\frac{64}{L_i}\right] \times 64$ dimension banyan modules which are within recent VLSI technology. If a 128×128 dimension module can be realized, up to $N=16,384$ size switch can be achieved by using this growing approach.

2. If switch building block is limited by a small size chip, for instance $32 \times 32 \cdot L_i$ chips, a $N \times N$ switch could be constructed by multistage structure if above two-stage structure can not archive a large switch size. For instance, a three-stage structure can construct a switch with 32,768 ($N=32^3$) input/output ports. In general, if building blocks are $a \times aL_i$ (i=1,2,3) dimensions, the three-stage structure needs $N\frac{1+L_1+L_1L_2}{a}$ such building blocks, where $N=a^3$. However, in the case of $N \neq a^3$, the switch needs more sorts of modules and every large number of modules. It could be very expensive.

3. The other way to expand the switch size is found below. A $kn \times knL_1$ switch can be build from the basic $n \times nL$ building modules by using a single-stage growing approach. Fig. 12. shows an example of a $2n \times 2nL_1$ switch (here $k=2$) configured from four $n \times nL$ switch modules and some extra concentrators. The left two basis $n \times nL$ building modules accept only cells destined for destinations from 1 to n; while the right two basic modules accept only cells destined for output destinations from $n+1$ to $2n$. In general, to build a single-stage $kn \times knL_1$ fabric from a basic $n \times nL$ module, k^2 building modules and kn concentrators are required. In fact, several concentrators can be integrated in a single chip. Here the L can be obtained from the following equations for a cell loss probability.

$$P = \frac{k}{\rho} \sum_{i=L+1}^{n} (i-L) \binom{n}{i} \left(\frac{\rho}{kn}\right)^i \left(1-\frac{\rho}{kn}\right)^{n-i}. \qquad (8)$$

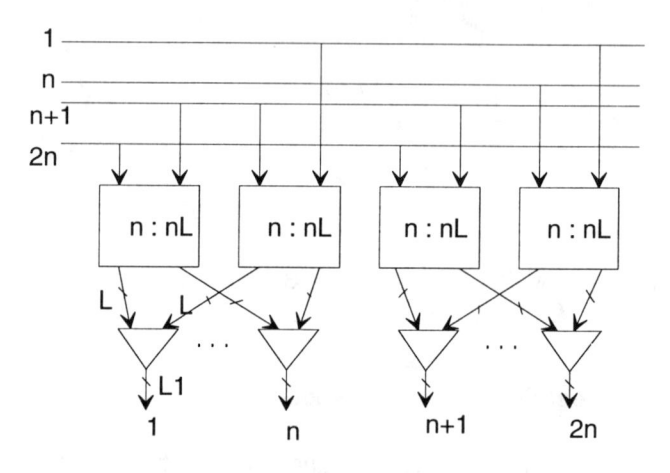

Fig. 12. Single-stage expansion from n:nL building blocks to 2n×2nL₁ module.

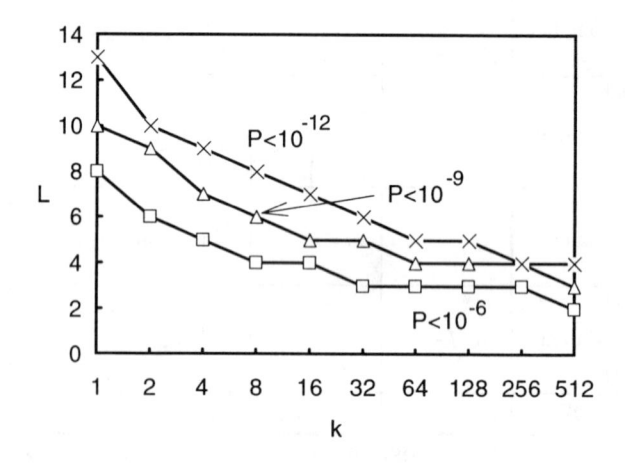

Fig. 13. Cell loss probability versus L and k, for n=32, in single-stage expansion scheme.

Note that the L is less than L_1 and it decreases as k increases (see Fig. 13.). This is just our expectation. For a moderate size switch, the single-stage approach seems to be feasible. According to this idea, we find a way to compose an arbitrarily size switch. To construct $N=kn^2$ (the balance factor $n=m$ is chosen) size switch, we still use the two-stage architecture. In the first stage, the MSM is $kn \times knL_1$ dimension, if k is moderate size(i.e., 2, 4, 8, 16); in the second stage, the MSM dimension is $n \times nL2$. Using the single-stage growing approach within each first stage MSM, the $(kn \times knL_1)$ MSM can be composed of k^2 $(n \times nL)$ modules. Therefore, total number of the $n:nL$ and $n:nL_2$ building blocks in both stages can be obtained from $N\frac{k+L_1}{n}$. Comparing with the three-stage growing approach, the approach has less number of the building blocks, if k is not very large. In practice, we can implement very large switch by using this approach.

Reliability is also an important issue for large switch. A single device failure within a module can cause the entire module to fail. The MULTIPAR modular architecture limits the failure group size to a single module. The failure of single module only disturbs a local traffic. In the case of an failure of a single module, the worst case is a failure in the first stage Batcher module which disrupts the traffic of n input ports. Other failures, such as banyan module in the first stage or the second stage MSM, only increase the cell loss probability and reduce the quality of communications. Sparing strategies need to be explored to improve reliable operation. In the first stage, a fault tolerant design could be achieved by providing a spare Batcher which can take over the operation of any one of the m Batcher modules if a failure occurs, while the design of replacing L_1 with L_1+1 increases the quality of the switch and makes it possible to achieve a fault tolerant design.

5: Conclusion

The proposed MULTIPAR modular switch is a self-routing and pure output queue network with the best delay/throughput performance. An $N \times N$ switch fabric is partitioned into two-stage modules, each of which is about $\sqrt{N} \times \sqrt{N} L_i$ dimension disjoint-path switch which is realized from a cascade of a $\sqrt{N} \times \sqrt{N}$ Batcher network and L_i parallel $\left[\frac{\sqrt{N}}{L_i}\right] \times \sqrt{N}$ expansion banyan networks. For various N, under 90% load, a small number set of $L_1=9$ and $L_2=4$ (or $L_1=8$ and $L_2=5$) is needed to keep cell loss probability below 10^{-6}. The buffers are only located at the output stage and buffer size has similar requirement as one stage output buffer switch. The switch fabric can be expanded to a very large size by using small building modules. A comparison has shown that the MULTIPAR modular switch has smaller module size and less complexity than some typical module switches.

References:

[1] Yeh, M. G. Hluchyj and A. S. Acampora, " The Knockout Switch: A Simple, Modular Architecture of High-performance Packet Switching," IEEE J. on Selected Areas in Comm., Vol.SAC-5, No.9, December 1987.

[2] T. T. Lee :"A Modular Architecture for Very Large Packet Switches", IEEE Trans. on Commun. 1990, VOL. 38(7), pp. 1097-1106.

[3] N. Giacopelli and W. D. Sinocoskie "Sunshine: a high performance self-routing broadband packet switch architecture," in proc. ISS'90, Stockholm, May, 1990, pp.112-129.

[4] C. M. Weng, and C. T. Hwang :"Distributed double-phase switch", IEE Proceedings-I, 1991, Vol. 138, pp.417-425

[5] J. Ma and K. Rahko:" A Growable Architecture for Broadband Packet (ATM) Switch," in proc. International Conference on Communication Technology, Beijing, Sept. 1992.

[6] K. Y. Eng, M. J. Karol, and Y. S. Yeh :"A growable packet(ATM) switch architecture: design principles and applications", Proc. GLOBECOM, 1990, pp. 1159-1165

[7] G. Hluchyj and M. J. Karol "Queuing in space-division packet switching," in INFOCOM '88, pp.334-343.

[8] K. Y. Eng, M. G. Hluchyj, and Y. S. Yeh " A Knockout Switch for Variable-Length Packets," IEEE J. on Selected Areas in Communications, Vol. SAC-5, No.9, Dec. 1987, pp.1426-1435.

A Low-Latency Programming Interface and a Prototype Switch for Scalable High-Performance Distributed Computing

Taitin Chen   Jim Feeney*   Geoffrey Fox   Gideon Frieder[†]   Sanjay Ranka[‡]
Bill Wilhelm*   Fang-kuo Yu

Northeast Parallel Architectures Center
Syracuse University

Abstract

This paper discusses the architecture and performance of a prototype switch for interconnecting IBM RISC System/6000 workstations. The paper describes the interconnection architecture and performance on a cluster of four IBM RISC System 6000 model 340 workstations. It also describes the driver level software interface to the switch and the features incorporated to minimize communication overhead.

The performance measurements cover communication latency and bandwidth. In addition, performance measurements of Express, a popular parallel-programming interface, are provided.

1 Introduction

Although a large variety of parallel computers are available on the market today, the impact of parallel computing on the industry is relatively insignificant. The use of high-performance parallel machines has been primarily limited to research laboratories and academics. This can be largely attributed to two factors: The cost of these machines is prohibitive, and software environment available to application scientists is relatively primitive [1].

Most industries own a large variety of high-performance workstations that are typically clustered by a local area network such as Ethernet [2]. Due to the wide availability and relatively small cost of such networks, there is a large resource of "Idle" cycles available for doing high-performance computing at a relatively small cost. However, since the Ethernet is a bus structure and not a dedicate device, the contention would be very heavy if all nodes tried to communicate at the same time. The problem gets worse as the node number increases. In addition, the AIX kernel controls every file operation that causes a big overhead for communication. All these factors make sure local area networks have poor latency and small bandwidth. The classes of applications that can be solved using these workstation clusters are relatively limited, which is why we proposed a dedicated prototype switch device instead of Ethernet, a low latency programming interface instead of a socket library, and a streaming and exchange protocol instead of TCP/IP to explore the benefits of these configurations, thus achieving a high-performance distributed system.

This paper discusses the architecture and performance of a scalable switch that can achieve low latency and high bandwidth, thus making it possible to use a cluster of high-performance workstations for solving a large variety of computationally intensive scientific and engineering applications. In section 2 we describe related work with some background information; in section 3 we describe the architecture of the prototype switch; in section 4 we describe LLPI (Low Latency Programming Interface); in section 5 we describe the performance of LLPI, Express, and some applications (matrix multiplication, Nbody, and Gaussian elimination.)

2 Preliminaries

2.1 Related work

There has recently been much research in the use of high-speed networks for high-performance computing, including the development of the Protocol Engine Design by G. Chesson [3], and the VMP Network Adapter Board by H. Kanakia and D. Cheriton [4].

---

*IBM, Endicott, New York.

[†]Present address: School of Engineering and Applied Science, George Washington University, 725 23-rd street NW, Washington DC 20052.

[‡]Author to whom all correspondence should be sent.

These projects tried to off-load the processing task of specific transport protocols to the network interface. In addition, the Nectar (Network Computer Architecture) project at Carnegie Mellon University is a high speed network with low latency, high bandwidth, and scalability properties [5]. The optical switching network by A. Guha and M. Agrawal of Honeywell, Inc., uses fiber optics to achieve high bandwidth and low loss and to reduce the need for signal regeneration and power consumption [6]. The closest project to ours is the Bit 3 VME project of Motorola Semiconductor, Inc. It also stresses the low-latency communication issue, but is a bus architecture rather than a distributed system. These projects are representative of a great deal of work in this area.

2.2 An overview of AIX

AIX (Advanced Interactive Exchange) is a UNIX compatible operating system that is available to IBM workstations. It provides more features by adding a set of software services to extend the UNIX kernel rather than modify it.

VRM (Virtual Resource Manager), a part of AIX, controls the real hardware and provides a stable, high-level machine interface to advanced hardware features and devices. It provides services to implement a multi-tasking operating system while insulating the kernel from most of the details of the hardware implementation. The kernel has to be aware only of the problem state instructions. All other services, such as I/O device and memory management, are provided by VRM [7].

For I/O subsystems, VRM provides an extensive queued interface to all I/O devices. The devices that the kernel typically sees are generic, such as generalized fixed-disk drives or serial ports. These generic devices are not efficient enough for applications that need real-time capabilities. This problem can be solved by writing C or assembly programs to implement necessary functions and dynamically add those features to VRM. This feature of VRM can make adding the hardware specific requirements relatively easy. Thus, VRM can make the operating system very flexible.

2.3 Express

Express provides an architecture-independent interface to a variety of parallel machines, and it provides basic tools to access the parallel processing system. For example, it provides low-level communication primitives for sending messages between processors, peripherals, and other system components. It also provides high-level message-passing routines that perform broadcasting, global averaging, global maximum/minimum, data redistribution, etc. Moreover, a transparent I/O system is provided to allow any node in the machine access to operating system facilities that would normally be available to the host node. There is an automatic domain-decomposition library that allows programs to be completely independent of the hardware on which they run, and that also allows scalable processors through run-time parameters. Parallel programs written in Express can run on machines of any size with no software changes, and they are independent of the topology of the underlying hardware system. The prototype system configuration is shown in Figure 1.

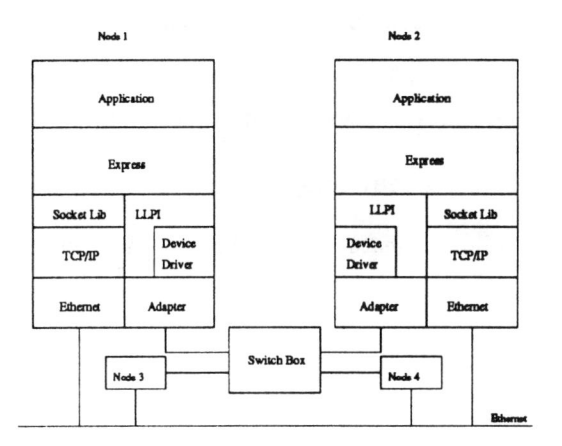

Figure 1: Express interface of the switch

2.4 Micro Channel architecture

The IBM RISC System/6000 series workstation uses Micro Channel architecture that provides a standard hardware interface for adding I/O devices to a computer. Implementation of this architecture provides a number of slots that electrically connect to I/O device adapters. Each Micro Channel adapter provides addressable resources that reside in either an I/O address space, bus-memory address space, or the IOCC (I/O Channel Controller) address space. An adapter also provides a set of POS (Programmable Option Select) registers that can be programmed by the software to configure the adapter. No DIP switches or jumpers are required on the adapter.

The Micro Channel is the interface between the computer and the prototype switch. A prototype adapter and twisted pair cable have been implemented to connect the computer to the switch.

3 Prototype switch architecture

3.1 Design features

The following features were chosen to help with the goal of low-latency communication.

1. Asynchronous circuit connection allows all nodes to connect independently as opposed to a central switch controller.

2. Positive acknowledge by hardware eliminates necessity for software

3. Acknowledge processing and extra acknowledge messages.

4. Hardware-generated routing relieves software of this step.

5. Hardware retries and selection of alternate paths reduces burden on software to manage fault tolerance.

6. Hardware guaranteed ordered delivery removes this burden from software.

We also chose to assign the prototype adapter to a single application rather than to being shared by two or more applications on a single node at the same time. The lowest latencies are attained by assigning the adapter to a single application. This mode of operation is aimed at parallel applications that require dedicated nodes to achieve minimum elapsed times. On the other hand, throughput may be more important, and using the prototype switch and adapter in shared mode may be more efficient in a distributed-batch environment. In shared mode the latencies are 5 to 10 times longer, depending on the node processor performance. The low-latency code supports operating in either mode, and a resource management system is required to support the allocation of adapter resources to applications.

3.2 Implementations

The prototype switch connected to 16 computers using a multi-stage circuit switch is shown in Figure 2. When one computer wants to send data to another computer, a connection (circuit) is established in the switch between the two computers. The data is then transmitted as a message from the sending computer to the receiving computer. The establishment of the circuit and transfer of the message are not synchronized with operations between other pairs of computers. Therefore, these operations are very fast and can be done in parallel. In addition to transmitting a message, the circuit also provides positive acknowledgement of a successful or unsuccessful transfer. This allows the sending adapter to re-send unsuccessful messages and, in the case of hard failures, to return a message to the software for analysis. This removes the burden of message acknowledgement and management from the software, thereby improving performance.

The prototype switch also provides fault tolerance in the form of power detection and alternate paths. Power detection consists of a signal between the prototype adapter in the computer and the prototype switch. As long as the prototype adapter has power, this signal is active; if it becomes inactive, the prototype switch disables the interface to that computer, insuring that noise created by turning the computer on or off will not interfere with the operations of the prototype switch. Alternate paths provide four circuits between each pair of prototype switch connections. If one path fails, the message can be retried over an alternate path. This feature, along with the positive hardware acknowledgement, allows the prototype adapter to bypass both intermittent and hard switch faults without software involvement.

The interface between the prototype switch and adapter consists of 25 signals: 8 data and 4 control in each direction (to and from the switch) and the power detect signal (see Figure 3). The control signals include valid message, message accepted, message rejected, and broadcast mode. The prototype adapter has timeout logic and multiple signal checks to detect failures of the acknowledge and reject signals. The receiving prototype adapter also checks destination node, message length, and a CRC code to be sure the received message is not corrupted. It issues a reject signal if any of these checks fails. The broadcast mode signal supports a hardware-level broadcast and multicast. Messages may be transmitted across this interface in both directions simultaneously.

The prototype adapter provides format conversion and speed matching between the 4-byte-wide Micro Channel and the byte-wide prototype switch. It contains a transmit FIFO buffer and a receive FIFO buffer for message buffering and speed matching. The transmit and receive functions are performed in parallel from the prototype switch interface to the Micro Channel interface. At the Micro Channel these operations become 4-byte serial because the Micro Channel

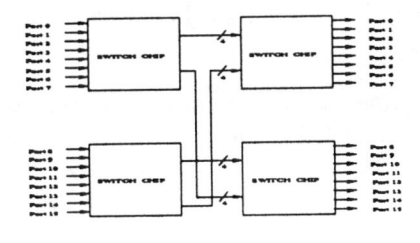

Figure 2: 16-port prototype switch 1412

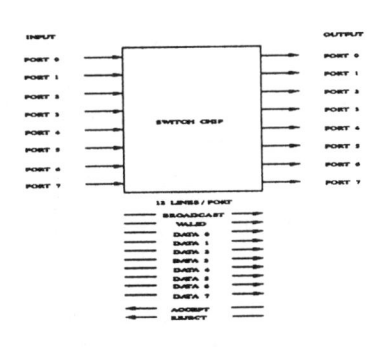

Figure 3: 8-port switch chip

cannot transfer in both directions simultaneously.

A significant result of this prototype switch/adapter architecture is the achievement of low-latency and high-bandwidth data transfers. In the clustering of Micro Channel-based workstations, the transfer of data into and out of the processor is the bottleneck, not the transfer through the switch. By designing a switch that minimizes the burden on the processor software and Micro Channel interface, low latency and high bandwidth can be attained.

4 Low-latency programming interface

In this section, we present a special device driver interface for the prototype adapter. The special device driver interface LLPI (Low-Latency Programming Interface) has been developed for Express. However, this could potentially be used for other high-level programming interfaces.

A device driver is a low-level software for a hardware device. It hides all the device-dependent information from its users and supports a uniform, easy-to-use interface for them. In AIX, a device is regarded as a special file and can be accessed by the standard file operations such as "open," "close," "read," "write," and "ioctl." This approach has two advantages. First, users can use the standard "open" and "close" operations to initialize and release the device. The standard "read" operations receive data from the device, the standard "write" operations send data to the device, and the standard "ioctl" operations perform the special control. All the file operations can be easily used without having detailed knowledge about the hardware device. Second, since the device driver is the only part in the entire system that handles device-dependent codes, it is relatively easy to maintain the system when the hardware environment is upgraded or modified.

One disadvantage of the standard AIX kernel (without any extension) approach is that each file operation must go through the AIX kernel, which is a time-consuming task that may cause heavy system overhead and access delay, especially when the hardware device is a time-critical, high-speed communication adapter such as the prototype adapter. Since this approach based on kernel system service of AIX has high latency, it is not a suitable communication interface for a cluster of high-performance workstations.

The major goal of LLPI is to address the above problem. The basic idea is to map the prototype adapter control registers directly into user address space. Based on this approach, the sending FIFO and receiving FIFO on the prototype adapters are directly accessible to the user. No system calls or user-to-kernel memory-copy-operations are required to send or receive messages, thus the system overhead and access delay can to a great extent be avoided. The design issues and the design characteristics of the LLPI will be discussed in the following subsections.

4.1 Design issues

In order to achieve the goals of LLPI, two design philosophies are addressed. First, LLPI must be as simple as possible since LLPI is only an interface between Express and the prototype adapter. LLPI does not try to cover the data link layer or the network layer in the seven-layered approach of the OSI reference model [2]. The major purpose of LLPI is to speed up the transmission rate when sending messages to or receiving messages from the prototype adapter. As a result, LLPI leaves several important services to the upper layer (the Express kernel) or to the lower layer (the prototype adapter). For example, the major task of the data link layer is left to the prototype adapter. In other words, the prototype adapter and the prototype switch box deal with reliable data communication between the source node and the destination node.

Second, system overhead of LLPI must be kept as small as possible: LLPI adopts memory mapping mechanism for sending and receiving messages. There are no kernel calls involved in sending or receiving messages. However, the LLPI must use standard "open" and "close" kernel function calls to initialize and release the prototype adapter. In addition, the standard "ioctl" function call is used to control the prototype adapter for getting device-dependent information. These standard function calls are used to keep LLPI as simple as possible. Actually, "open" and "ioctl" are used by entry point init_init, and "close" is used by entry point int_release entry point. The system overhead is tolerated in these phases of initialization. We will discuss all entry points of the LLPI in section 4.3.

4.2 Design characteristics

The design characteristics of the current user-level programming interface list are as follows:

1. Single application: LLPI is dedicated to a single application under Express. When the LLPI is active, the prototype adapter cannot be opened by another application on that node. This is handled by address protection in the device driver. LLPI respects the partition protection and will only communicate with nodes that are a part of that partition or serve the partition. The prototype switch AIX device driver protects against erroneous message delivery through the use of the AIX file descriptor, logical channels and node partitioning.

2. Address binding: The goal of address binding is to map the logical address of Express to the physical address of the prototype adapter. The physical address of the prototype adapter is dependent upon the port of the switch box to which it is attached. When device driver attached the prototype adapter, the LLPI got the local physical address and returned it to the Express daemon. After all the Express daemons got the physical address, these daemons exchanged the information and built the mapping table on every workstation. When the Express calls LLPI for sending messages, the Express must use the mapping table to specify the physical address of the destination node.

3. Data fragmentation: In current implementation of the sending FIFO, the maximum message size allowed by the prototype adapter is 2040 bytes. The Express kernel must fragment the user's message into smaller messages (each message less than 2040 bytes) and send them to LLPI.

4. No data buffering: Memory copying is another degradation factor in interprocessor communication. In order to decrease the overhead of memory copying, LLPI does not support internal buffers for sending or receiving of messages. When called, LLPI just pulls the messages in the prototype adapter to the user space if the messages are required by the user. If the messages are not wanted (source node or the data type in the header of the messages is not right), put them in the buffers of the Express kernel and keep pulling messages until the needed messages come.

5. Multiplexing: LLPI always returns the first received message from the receiving FIFO to the Express kernel. However, the source node identification or the data type of the receiving message may not satisfy the current user's requirement. Therefore, the Express kernel supports internal buffers to store the incoming messages and multiplex the incoming messages.

6. Destination check: The sending prototype adapter doesn't check the user identification before delivering a message via LLPI, but the receiving prototype adapter does check the destination node number to see if it is for this specific node, providing the high bit of the destination node identification field is set to 1.

7. Flow control: The Express kernel is responsible for only part of the flow control and leaves other parts to the LLPI and the prototype adapter. Basically, there are two parts to flow control—sending and receiving. In order to let the prototype adapter receive new messages from the other nodes, the Express kernel must continue reading messages to make certain that the receiving FIFO on the prototype adapter has enough room for incoming messages. On the other hand, LLPI and the prototype adapter on the sending node must

make sure that messages are successfully sent to the destination nodes through the acknowledgement signal.

8. Retry count: If the receiving FIFO is full, the sending node cannot successfully send messages to the receiving node. In this case, a specific message may get "stuck" in the sending FIFO. The prototype adapter sending node will keep trying to send this message until the hardware's retry count is expired. Then, a software retry count will be active to send the message again. If the receiving FIFO is still full, the specific message still can't be sent. If the software's retry count is also expired, LLPI will return an error code to the Express. At that time the application can retrieve the stuck message and any messages that may be queued behind it. The application can then decide what it wants to do.

9. First-in-first-out: The basic policy for sending and receiving messages from LLPI is "First-in-first-out." Thus, LLPI cannot choose to read incoming messages out of order in the receiving FIFO (for example, messages from a specific source node or with some specific data type). The prototype switch guarantees ordered delivery of all messages from one node to another node on a given channel.

10. Byte vs. word: The prototype adapter can only transfer word-sized data elements (4 bytes) while Express allows any arbitrary byte-sized message. Thus, for sending messages, LLPI must transform byte-sized messages to word-sized messages by byte stuffing. Since the software header of the Express message contains the information of the actual length of the message, LLPI returns received messages directly to the Express kernel without eliminating stuffing bytes.

The major tasks of the data link layer and the network layer are covered by the prototype switch and adapter. The prototype switch system provides a reliable datagram service between the source node and the destination node. Error control, flow control, and routing are handled by the prototype switch system.

4.3 Programming interface

LLPI supports five entry points for the Express kernel:

1. int int_init(max, min, node_id);
   int *max, min, *node_id;

   - The int_init entry point initializes the prototype adapter.

2. int int_write(buf, length, dest, type);
   char *buf;
   int length, dest, type;

   - The int_write entry point sends the message to another prototype adapter without blocking.
   - There is an error if "length" is equal to zero, because LLPI will not accept a message with zero length. Another error occurs when "length" is greater than "max," because LLPI will not accept it and Express has to fragment it into smaller messages.

3. int int_read(buf, length, src, type);
   char *buf;
   int length, *src, *type;

   - The int_read entry point returns the first received message without blocking.

4. int int_test(src);
   int *src;

   - The int_test entry point returns the information for the first received message without blocking.
   - Two consecutive int_test commands without int_read command will give the same information for the first received message.

5. int int_release()

   - The int_release entry point releases the prototype adapter.

5 Performance measurement

An experimental environment is installed at Syracuse University. There are four IBM RISC System/6000 model 340 workstations connected by two transmission media—an Ethernet and a prototype switch box. They all run AIX 3.2.1 and have 16 MBytes memory each. In the current version of our software, the configuration of Express and the loading of node programs are done via Ethernet.

5.1 Performance of the LLPI

The goal of performance evaluation for the LLPI-LLPI level is to measure the transmission rate up to the LLPI interface through the prototype adapter between two workstations. Two performance measures, latency and bandwidth, are considered at this level. The software for testing is based on two different high-level protocols—the exchange protocol and the streaming protocol. For the exchange protocol both nodes send a message, then both receive a message. This results in a synchronized message exchange between two nodes. For the streaming protocol, the

LLPI — LLPI	Latency
1 to 2 streaming send side	7.7 usecs
1 to 1 streaming receive side	15.3 usecs
1 to 1 exchange	30.0 usecs
1 to 1 exchange with 48 data bytes	58.2 usecs
LLPI — LLPI	Bandwidth
1 to 2 streaming send side	5.3 MBytes/sec
1 to 1 streaming receive side	4.0 MBytes/sec
1 to 1 exchange	3.6 MBytes/sec

Table 1: Performance of LLPI

Fixed send software	6.300 usecs
Processor to adapter	1.500 usecs
Fixed message preparation	1.250 usecs
Adapter to adapter via switch	1.500 usecs
Fixed message store	0.875 usecs
Adapter to processor	1.920 usecs
Fixed receive software	13.280 usecs
Total message latency	26.625 usecs

Table 2: Latency breakdown

Interface — Interface	Latency
File System Interface Echo	250.0 usecs
Express Interface Exchange	153.0 usecs
Interface — Interface	Bandwidth
File System Interface Streaming	2.3 MBytes/sec
Express Interface Streaming	3.5 MBytes/sec

Table 3: Performance of Express and file system

sender sends one message to the receiver without waiting for the return message from the receiver. The message sizes used for testing are 12 and 2000 bytes. For latency, the message size is 12 bytes (The hardware header of the message is 8 bytes, and the data size of the message is 4 bytes.) For bandwidth, the message size is 2000 bytes (the current maximum message size the prototype adapter can handle is 2K bytes). The raw performance figures in Table 1 are averaged over 1,000,000 messages.

Since the write function on the sending node is quicker than the read function on the receiving node, the receiving node has a hard time keeping its receiving FIFO available to receive more messages in 1-node-to-1-node streaming mode. But, for the 1-node-to-2-nodes streaming case, the sending node does not have to wait for enough space in the receiving FIFOs, so the sending nodes perform better than the receiving nodes.

Table 2 is a latency breakdown of the prototype switch and adapter. Note that the processor-to-adapter (via Micro Channel) cycle time is 500ns per word (4 bytes). The prototype adapter-to-processor (via Micro Channel) cycle time is 640ns per word. Both of these times are limited by the prototype adapter, not the processor or the Micro Channel. The prototype switch cycle time is 125 ns per byte. This is also limited by the prototype adapter.

Included in the timings are both fixed overhead times and the times that are dependent on message size. All measurements were performed on a one-data-word message that included an additional 2 words of message header. This resulted in an overall message size of 3 words or 12 bytes.

The fixed send time (#1) came from a 7.8 usecs time measured by streaming messages from one node to three nodes minus the Micro Channel transfer time (7.8 - 1.5 = 6.3). The fixed receive time (#7) came from a 15.2 usecs time measured by streaming messages from three nodes to one minus the Micro Channel transfer time (15.20 - 1.92 = 13.28). The other times (#2-6) are calculated based on the hardware cycle time, the operations performed, and the message size.

The total time is less that the measured 30 usec exchange latency time in the paper because the exchange gives an upper bound on message latency due to its synchronized behavior. An echo measurement between two nodes should give a lower bound less than or equal to the calculated total message latency of 26.625 usecs.

5.2 Performance of Express and file system

In this subsection, we'll describe the performance of latency and bandwidth under a prototype adapter on the standard file system interface through device driver and on Express interface through LLPI. In standard file system interface, latency was calculated by sending one million messages, with each message 4 bytes long. Bandwidth was measured by sending one million messages, with each message 2,000 bytes long. In the Express interface, latency was measured by sending 4 data bytes messages plus an Express software header, but the method for measuring bandwidth was the same as for the standard file system interface.

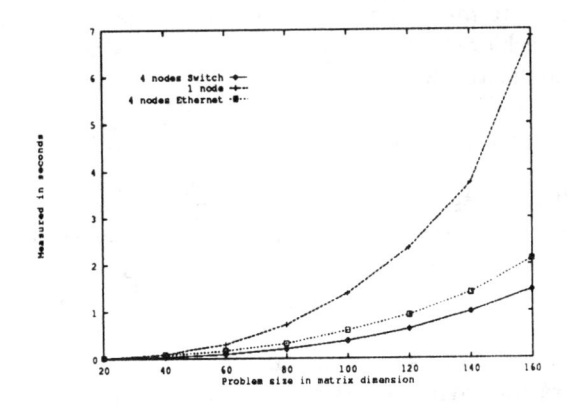

Figure 4: Performance of matrix multiplication

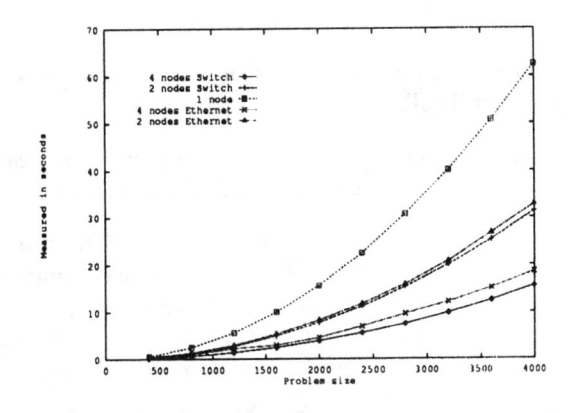

Figure 5: Performance of Nbody problem

Both exchange and streaming protocols are measured in Table 3. The Express Interface latency exchange mode has 44 more header bytes than the Standard File System Interface.

The lower-than-expected bandwidth is due to the prototype adapter interaction with the Micro Channel. This will improve slightly in a production implementation. A direct memory access (DMA) adapter is required to attain maximum bandwidth for large messages. Our goal was to minimize latency and, therefore, because of time and cost constraints, the initial implementation does not contain the DMA feature. The design, however, does not prevent this from being added at a later date.

5.3 Performance of some applications

We implemented matrix multiplication, Nbody, and Gaussian elimination algorithms to measure the performance of applications on the prototype switch box and Ethernet. The experimental results for different problem sizes are measured on 1, 2, and 4 nodes (in 4, 5, and 6. The switch communication time of Gaussian elimination is shown on Figure 7. For our workstation cluster, the host is also one of the node. Thus, the time measured in this node may not be accurate (the execution time of this node should actually be lower). We measured the execution time by averaging every node's execution time.

Matrix multiplication and Nbody algorithms were derived from [1], and are based on a cubix programming model (allows parallel input/output in every node). The matrix multiplication problem is to multiply two $N \times N$ matrices to another $N \times N$ matrix. The algorithm can accept any order of the matrices as long as the size is within the system limit. The elements can be randomly generated or entered from disk file. Each node is assigned a square subblock of the input elements, so the nodes are arranged as a two dimensions grid structure. We can't measure two nodes of configuration because the node number must be an exponent of 2 to form a grid.

The Nbody problem algorithm is also based on the cubix model. We measured the execution time by as few as 400 particles to as many as 6000 particles. Each node gets approximately an equal number of particles, and the nodes are arranged in a ring structure. At each step, the interaction between the particles is calculated, the force on each particle is updated, and the potential energy is summed. After the rotation, the total potential energy is found by summing all nodes.

Gaussian elimination is used to solve an $N \times (N+1)$ linear equation system. It is implemented in the Express host node model, and only the host can execute input/output functions in this model. This is a transitional parallel programming model, and it would be hard to debug programs. The elements of the input matrix are distributed from the host to nodes by block, and the nodes are arranged as a one-dimensional structure. The program used extensive broadcast functions to broadcast various length elements among the nodes.

The experimental results clearly suggest that by using the prototype switch we can achieve near linear speedup for all of these applications. On the other hand, by using the Ethernet the performance is worse than when using the prototype switch. For applications like Gaussian elimination which require a large amount of communication, the improvement in per-

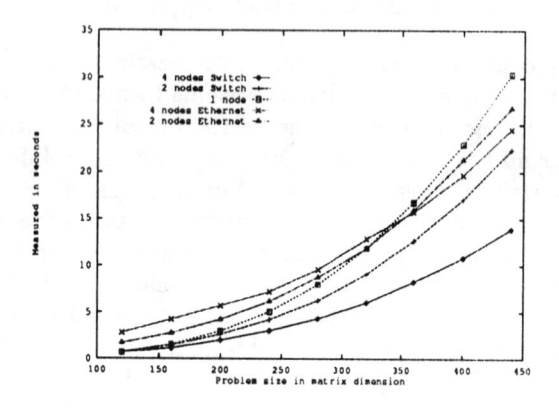

Figure 6: Performance of Gaussian elimination

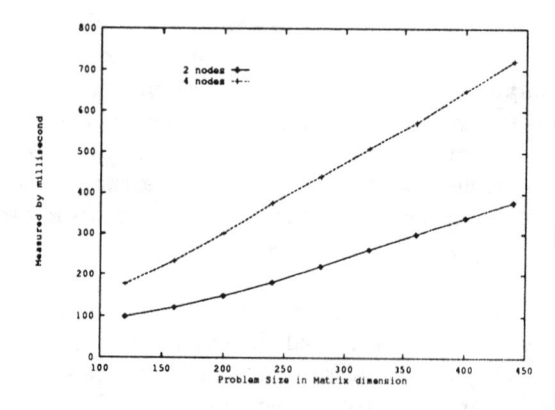

Figure 7: Switch communication of Gaussian elimination

formance by adding additional nodes is negligible on Ethernet.(In fact, by adding more nodes the performance deteriorates for problem sizes as large as 300.)

6 Conclusion

This paper presents the design and implementation of a low-latency programming interface for a high-performance prototype switch. Our experimental results of applications using Express, the message latency, and the bandwidth of LLPI suggest that we can achieve scalable performance using LLPI on a cluster of RISC System/6000 connected by the prototype switch. However, our experimental results are limited to only four nodes, and making any generalizations about higher nodes may be imprecise. At this point, the communication performance achieved is close to many contemporary parallel machines that have achieved scalable performance for a wide variety of applications.

Acknowledgements

This paper discusses a prototype which has not been announced as a product and which may never be announced or made generally available as a product. Any performance data contained in this document was determined in a specific controlled environment, and therefore, the results which may be obtained in other operating environments may vary significantly.

References

[1] Geoffrey Fox, "Solving Problems on Concurrent Processors," V. I, II, Prentice Hall.

[2] Andrew Tanenbaum, "Computer Networks," Prentice Hall.

[3] Greg Chesson, "Protocol engine design," *Proceedings of the Summer 1987 USENIX Conference.*

[4] Hemant Kanakia and David Cheriton, "The VMP network adapter board (NAB): High performance network communication for multiprocessors," *Proceedings of the SIGCOMM 1988 Symposium on Communications and Architectures and Protocols.*

[5] H. T. Kung et al, "The Design of Nectar: A Network Backplane for Heterogeneous Multicomputers," *Proceedings of Third International Conference on Architectural Support for Programming Languages and Operating Systems,* April 1989.

[6] Aloke Guha and Mukul Agrawal, "A Scalable Packet Switch for Distributed Computing," *First International Symposium on High Performance Distributed Computing,* Sept. 1992.

[7] IBM International Technical Support Center, "Writing a Device Driver for AIX Version 3," May 1991.

[8] IBM International Technical Support Center, "Performance Monitoring and Tuning Guide," Nov. 1990.

SESSION 5: Panel –
Software Tools for High-Performance Distributed Computing

Vaidy Sunderam, Chair

Software Tools for High-Performance Distributed Computing

Vaidy Sunderam

Emory University
Atlanta GA

Abstract of Topics

Parallel processing on distributed memory architectures is rapidly becoming the methodology of choice for high-performance computing — but, as usual, lagging software techniques preclude exploitation of the full power of such platforms. Active research is in progress, however, in areas such as parallel languages, graphical tool kits, and abstract methodologies for application development, debugging, monitoring, profiling, and various other aspects of the software life-cycle.

Panelists will summarize and discuss their opinions on the state-of-the-art software for high-performance distributed computing, and discuss the future, "best" approaches, promising ideas for investigation, and short-term as well as long-term strategies, both form the pragmatic and scientific perspectives.

Panelists:

Geoffrey Fox is Professor of Physics and Professor of Computer Science at Syracuse University, Syracuse, and is director of the Northeast Parallel Architectures Center. Professor Fox is regarded as a pioneer and leading researcher in the field of computational science to which he has made numerous contributions.

Al Geist is group leader of Computer Science in the Math Sciences Section of Oak Ridge National Laboratory. His interests are in high performance parallel computing, numerical linear algebra, and Grand Challenge applications, and he is a co-PI in the PVM and HeNCE projects.

Bill Gropp is a research scientist at Argonne National Labs, and his research interests include methodologies and tools for concurrent and distributed computing. His is one of the principal investigators in the P4 project, a system for portable distributed memory parallel computing on a variety of hardware environments.

Bob Harrison is a research scientist at Pacific Northwest Laboratories, and has worked on systems for distributed and parallel computing. He is the author of the TCGMSG package for parallel distributed computing.

Adam Kolawa is co-founder of ParaSoft Corporation, whose charter is the development of software tools for parallel and distributed computers. The Express tool kit from ParaSoft is a coordinated set of tools for the development, execution, debugging, and profiling of parallel programs on various multiprocessors and cluster systems.

Mike Quinn is an associate professor of computer science at Oregon State University. He has made numerous contributions to the field of parallel processing, notably in the form of data parallel languages and high level abstractions for distributed memory parallel computing.

Tony Skjellum is a faculty member at Mississippi state University, and his research interests are in tools and standards for message passing parallel processing. He is the developer of the Zipcode system, and is active in the MPI standards effort.

Moderator:

Vaidy Sunderam is Associate Professor of Computer Science at Emory University. His interests are in heterogeneous distributed computing, high-speed networks and protocols, and tool kits and methodologies fro parallel processing. He is co-PI in the PVM and Eclipse projects, systems for high-performance heterogeneous concurrent computing.

SESSION 6A:
Applications II

Marco Annaratone, Chair

Parallel and Distributed Systems for Constructive Neural Network Learning*

J. Fletcher   Z. Obradović[†]

School of Electrical Engineering and Computer Science
Washington State University
Pullman WA 99164-2752

Abstract

A constructive learning algorithm dynamically creates a problem-specific neural network architecture rather than learning on a pre-specified architecture. We propose a parallel version of our recently presented constructive neural network learning algorithm. Parallelization provides a computational speedup by a factor of $O(t)$ where t is the number of training examples. Distributed and parallel implementations under p4 using a network of workstations and a Touchstone DELTA are examined. Experimental results indicate that algorithm parallelization may result not only in improved computational time, but also in better prediction quality.

1 Introduction

A *neural network* is a weighted graph of simple processing units (or *neurons*). The interconnection graph of a *feed-forward* network is acyclic with processing units arranged in multiple layers consisting of input, zero or more hidden, and output layers. All units in any layer are fully connected to the succeeding layer. Units compute an *activation function* of their weighted input sum. Here we consider *binary neural networks* where the activation function of each unit is of the form $g(x) : \mathrm{R} \to \{0, 1\}$,

$$g(x) = \begin{cases} 0 & \text{if } x < t \\ 1 & \text{if } x \geq t. \end{cases}$$

Traditional neural networks learning (e.g. back-propagation [12]) involves modification of the interconnection weights between neurons on a pre-specified network. Determining the network architecture is a challenging problem which currently requires an expensive trial-and-error process. In selecting an appropriate neural network topology for a classification problem, there are two opposing objectives. The network must be large enough to be able to adequately define the separating surface and should be small enough to generalize well [7]. Rather than learning on a pre-specified network topology, a *constructive algorithm* also learns the topology in a manner specific to the problem. The advantage of such constructive learning is that it automatically fits network size to the data without overspecializing which often yields better generalization. Examples include the tiling algorithm of Mézard and Nadal [9] and the cascade-correlation algorithm of Fahlman and Lebiere [4]. Our goal is to explore the use of distributed and parallel systems in constructively learning a single hidden layer binary neural network architecture. We argue that a parallel approach improves computational efficiency and generalization quality.

In a single hidden layer feed-forward binary neural network, each hidden unit with fan-in k is a representation of a k-1 dimensional hyperplane. The hyperplane corresponding to the hidden unit may be determined through solution of the equation system defined by k points on the hyperplane. Our work is inspired by a constructive algorithm proposed by Baum [1] where a sequence of oracle queries are used in conjunction with training examples to find these k points. Here the learner is allowed to ask an oracle for the correct class associated with arbitrary points in the problem domain in addition to using the training examples provided. The hyperplanes are sequentially determined by partitioning the problem domain space using training examples and queries. The hidden units of a single hidden layer feed-forward binary neural network and corresponding connections are then created from the hyperplanes. The connection weights from the hidden layer to the output layer are determined by an algorithm which separates the hidden layer represen-

---

*Research sponsored in part by the NSF Industry / University Cooperative Center for the Design of Analog-Digital ASICs (CDADIC) under grant NSF-CDADIC-90-1 and by Washington State University Research Grant 10C-3970-9966.

[†]Also affiliated with the Mathematical Institute, Belgrade, Yugoslavia.

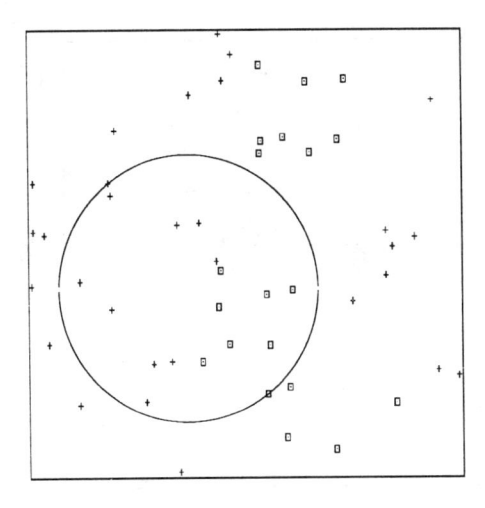

Figure 1: First unknown region

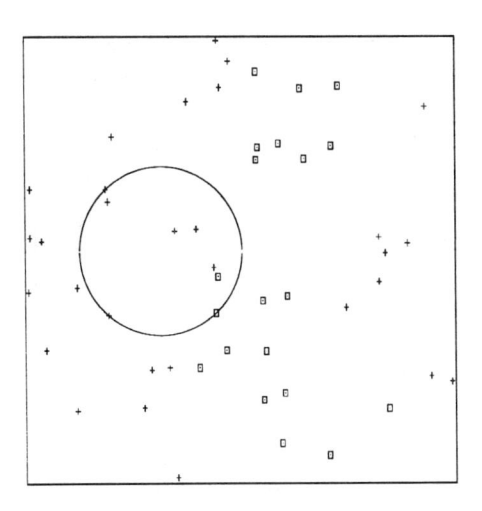

Figure 2: Next unknown region

tation of the problem by a single hyperplane (e.g. the perceptron algorithm [11]).

In Section 2 we describe our constructive learning algorithm which does not require oracle queries. In Section 3 a new parallel approach to this algorithm is explored with analysis and experimental results following in Section 4.

2 Sequential hidden layer construction

While Baum's algorithm is applicable where an oracle for the classification of any given point exists, in many cases such an oracle is not available or may be too expensive for practical use. In [5] we proposed a modification of Baum's algorithm which does not assume the availability of such an oracle and incrementally constructs the neural network from examples alone. In this modification, approximations of the points on the hyperplane are found by repeatedly interpolating between example points of the various classes T_1 and T_2 in the training set T. The interpolation begins by selecting positive and negative examples $m \in T_1$, $n \in T_2$. The unknown region between m and n is then searched for the nearest point $q \in T$ to the midpoint of m and n. The unknown region is defined as the the circle centered at the midpoint of m and n with a diameter of the distance between m and n, as shown in Figure 1. If q is found, the search is then repeated in the smaller unknown region between q and m or q and n respectively depending on whether q is positive or negative (Figure 2).

If no point from T is found in the current unknown region, its midpoint p^1 is the closest approximation to a point on the separating hyperplane. If p^1 is determined to be within a specified tolerance of an existing hyperplane, a new pair of points is selected and the search is repeated. The remaining points p^2 through p^k that define the hyperplane are found by taking a random vector from p^1 to a point $v \in T$ (Figure 3) and interpolating between either m and v or n and v to p^i based on the class of v. The interpolated points from T and the generated hyperplane are shown in Figure 4.

As in Baum's algorithm, the connection weights from the hidden layer to the output layer units must be computed once the hidden unit layer has been generated. In the modified algorithm, the hidden layer units are generated from examples alone, and so may not correspond to the optimal separating hyperplanes. As such, the hidden layer problem representation of the generated network with the same number of hidden units as in the minimal network may not be linearly separable. In order to account for this possibility, hidden units continue to be generated beyond the minimal architecture; for example, until the data is exhausted, a number of data points have been examined without generating a new hidden unit or a predetermined number of units have been created.

The pocket algorithm [6] is a single-layer neural network learning algorithm that finds the optimal separation under a given topology for problems that are not linearly separable. The algorithm keeps the best set of weights in the "pocket" while the perceptron is trained incrementally. A practical modification of the pocket learning algorithm is proposed in [10] which is faster and still has the same guarantee for convergence to the optimal separating hyperplane. This parallel dynamic algorithm is used to determine the output layer weights in the constructed network.

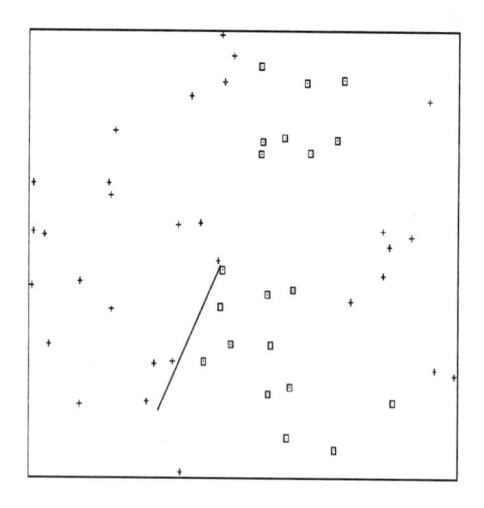

Figure 3: Random vector

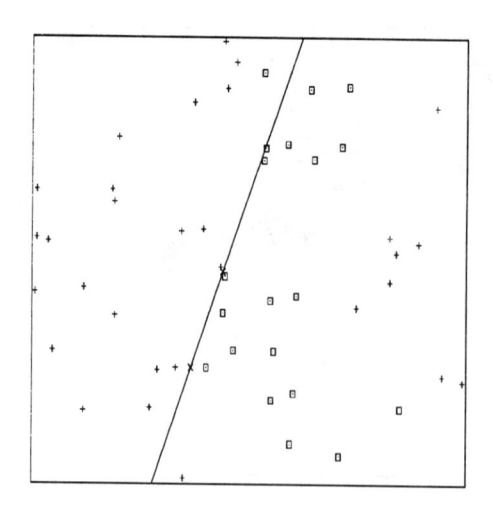

Figure 4: Separating hyperplane

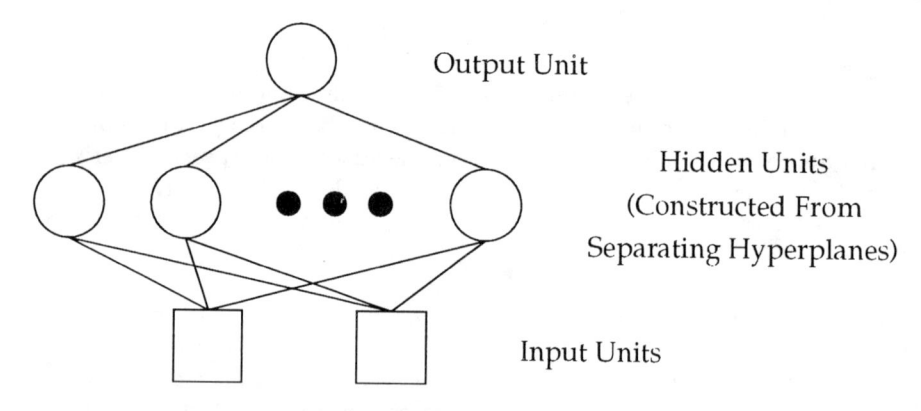

Figure 5: Hidden layer construction

3 Parallel hidden layer construction

While the sequential algorithm provides good generalization, significant computational resources are required. Here we propose a speedup by a parallelization that distributes the computational load across a number of processors. In order for parallelization to be efficient, an appropriate partitioning of the input space is required. This is accomplished by assigning the example points of one class evenly across the available processors. Given training set T of t examples belonging to classes T_1 and T_2 let t_1 and t_2 ($t_1 \geq t_2$) be the number of examples in each class respectively. In a system with $P + 1$ processors each of P slave processors ($1 \leq P \leq t_1$) is assigned $\lceil t_1/P \rceil$ examples of class T_1. Each slave processor examines the input subspace formed by pairing its assigned examples of T_1 with all examples in T_2. A system with a balanced computational load is obtained by this partitioning of the initial pairs.

Figure 6 shows the proposed parallel architecture. Each processor may be either a workstation in a distributed environment or a processor on a parallel machine. One processor is responsible for the master process. This master process distributes the training data at initialization and creates neural network hidden layer units from the determined separating hyperplanes. All slave processors search for separating hyperplanes as described in Section 2 starting from the initial pairs in their assigned data partitions. When such a separating hyperplane is found, it is communicated to the master process. The master process then compares the hyperplane to those that currently exist. If it is not sufficiently similar to an existing hyperplane, a new hidden unit corresponding to the hyperplane is generated (Figure 5).

Hidden layer construction is completed when a predetermined number of hidden units have been generated, the input space has been exhaustively searched, or a number of initial pairs have been examined with-

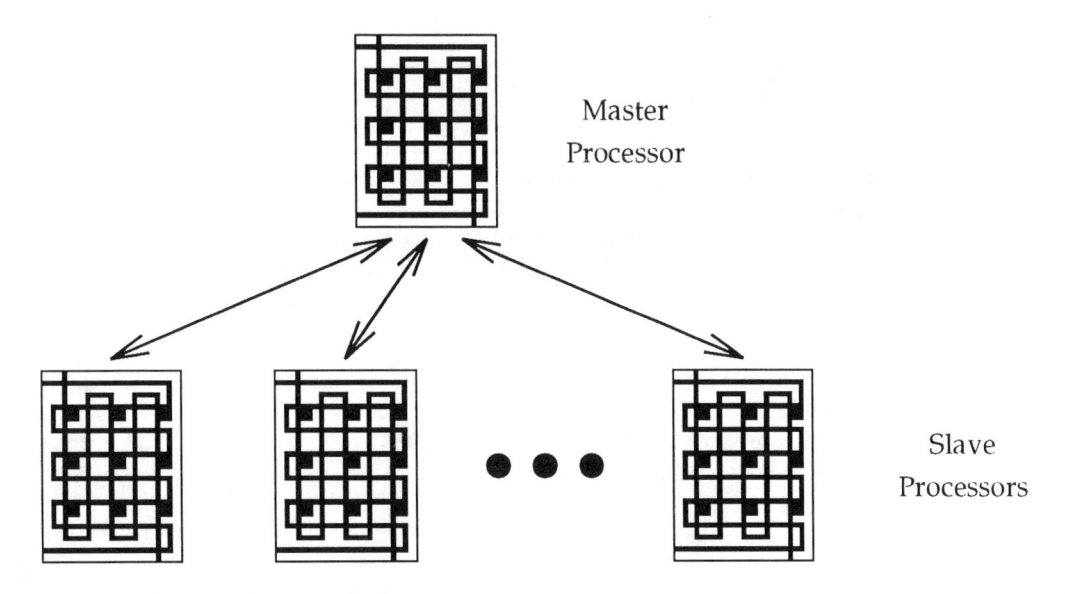

Figure 6: Parallel architecture

out determining a new separating hyperplane. Finally, the master process performs the relatively simple task of training the output layer weights as in the algorithm of Section 2.

4 Analysis and Experimental Results

The total running time of our algorithm depends primarily upon the time required to determine if a separating hyperplane can be constructed starting from a given pair of training examples. Search for a point on the hyperplane takes $O(\log t)$ interpolation steps since each interpolation removes at least half of the t training examples. In each interpolation step, finding the nearest training example to the center of an unknown region can be determined in time $O(\log t)$ through use of the k-d tree of Bentley [2]. Thus, the worst case time required to search for one point on the hyperplane is $O(\log^2 t)$. A hyperplane is defined by k points, and so the total time to determine if a hyperplane can be found starting from a given pair of training examples is $O(k \log^2 t)$.

In the sequential algorithm an exhaustive data partitioning starting from all $t_1 t_2$ training pairs of examples can be performed in worst case time of $O(k t_1 t_2 \log^2 t)$. In the parallel algorithm an initial overhead of $O(t)$ is required for data distribution. A minimal overhead of $O(k)$ is incurred for transfer of generated hyperplane data from the slave to the master processor. Since $t_1 + t_2 = t$ the worst case parallel time for an exhaustive data partitioning is thus $O((k t_1 t_2 \log^2 t)/P)$ where P is the number of slave processors.

In learning problems w.l.o.g. we can assume that both t_1 and t_2 are of order $\Theta(t)$ as both classes have to be well represented in the training set. With that assumption the worst case parallel computing time of the maximal distributed system ($P = \max(t_1, t_2)$) is $O(k t \log^2 t)$ compared to a sequential time of $(k t^2 \log^2 t)$. Algorithm parallelization thus provides a computational speedup by a factor of $O(t)$.

The algorithm was implemented using $p4$ [3]. Developed at Argonne National Laboratory, $p4$ supports parallel programming for both distributed environments and highly parallel computers. Two implementation platforms were used: a distributed system of 19 DECStations and a Touchstone DELTA. The Touchstone [8] is an Intel high-speed concurrent multicomputer, consisting of 576 nodes in a 19 × 36 mesh. Of these, 64 nodes were allocated for our experiments. Implementation under $p4$ allowed the same code to be used for the Touchstone as for the DECStation network.

Experiments were performed using the MONK's problems [13] to compare the quality of generalization between the sequential and parallel implementations. The MONK's problems consist of three six-feature binary classification problems which represent specific challenges for standard machine-learning algorithms, such as the ability to learn data in disjunctive normal form, parity problems and performance in the presence of noise. To allow the random vector to search equally in each dimension, the input data is normalized to points on a hypersphere.

	Sequential		Distributed		Parallel	
Processors	1		19		64	
Accuracy	Train	Test	Train	Test	Train	Test
Problem 1	100.00	85.42	100.00	81.02	100.00	81.71
Problem 2	81.07	70.37	85.80	72.45	91.72	75.23
Problem 3	96.72	72.92	99.18	77.08	100.00	78.94

Table 1: Percentage Accuracy on the MONK's Problems

The generalization ability of the sequential and parallel implementations is compared in Table 1. It is interesting to note that in the more complex problems 2 and 3 the generalization of the parallel algorithm exceeds that of the sequential algorithm. This improvement may be due to the fact that as the number of processors increases, a greater diversity in the input space will be searched.

While these results are promising, the principles described here are being further evaluated on the large-scale problem of predicting protein structure.

5 Conclusions

Neural networks efficiency and prediction quality depends significantly on how we select network architecture, learning algorithm and initial set of weights. The constructive learning algorithm of Section 2 efficiently learns not just connection weights but also creates the required architecture. A parallel version proposed in Section 3 provides a significant speed-up in the construction of the hidden layer and a greater diversity in the input space searched, also resulting in improved generalization quality.

References

[1] E. B. Baum. Neural net algorithms that learn in polynomial time from examples and queries. *IEEE Transactions on Neural Networks*, 2(1):5–19, January 1991.

[2] J. L. Bentley. Multidimensional binary search tree used for associative searching. *Communications of the ACM*, 18(9):509–517, September 1975.

[3] R. Butler and E. Lusk. *User's Guide to the p4 Parallel Programming System*, November 1992.

[4] S. Fahlman and C. Lebiere. The cascade-correlation learning architecture. In D. Touretzky, editor, *Advances in Neural Information Processing Systems*, volume 2, pages 524–532, Denver 1989, 1990. Morgan Kaufmann, San Mateo.

[5] J. Fletcher and Z. Obradović. Creation of neural networks by hyperplane generation from examples alone. In *Neural Networks for Learning, Recognition and Control*, page 23, Boston, 1992.

[6] S. I. Gallant. Perceptron-based learning algorithms. *IEEE Transactions on Neural Networks*, 1(2):179–191, June 1990.

[7] S. Geman, E. Bienstock, and R. Doursat. Neural networks and the bias / variance dilemma. *Neural Computation*, 4(1):1–58, 1992.

[8] Intel Supercomputer Systems Division, Beaverton, OR. *Touchstone Delta System User's Guide*, October 1991.

[9] M. Mézard and J.-P. Nadal. Learning in feedforward layered networks: The tiling algorithm. *Journal of Physics A*, 22:2191–2204, 1989.

[10] Z. Obradović and R. Srikumar. Dynamic evaluation of a backup hypothesis. In *Neural Networks for Learning, Recognition and Control*, page 71, Boston, 1992.

[11] F. Rosenblatt. *Principles of Neurodynamics*. Spartan, New York, 1962.

[12] D. Rumelhart, G. Hinton, and R. Williams. Learning internal representations by error propagation. In D. Rumelhart and J. McClelland, editors, *Parallel Distributed Processing*, volume 1, chapter 8, pages 318–362. MIT Press, Cambridge, 1986.

[13] S. B. Thrun et al. The MONK's problems: A performance comparison of different learning algorithms. Technical Report CMU–CS–91–197, Department of Computer Science, Carnegie Mellon University, Pittsburgh, PA, 1991.

An Analysis of Distributed Computing Software and Hardware for Applications in Computational Physics

P. D. Coddington
Northeast Parallel Architectures Center
Syracuse University
Syracuse NY 13244, U.S.A.

Abstract

We have implemented a set of computational physics codes on a network of IBM RS/6000 workstations used as a distributed parallel computer. We compare the performance of the codes on this network, using both standard Ethernet connections and a fast prototype switch, and also on the nCUBE/2, a MIMD parallel computer. The algorithms used range from simple, local, and regular, to complex, non-local, and irregular. We describe our experiences with the hardware, software and parallel languages used, and discuss ideas for making distributed parallel computing on workstation networks more easily usable for computational physicists.

1 Introduction

Many academic institutions and research laboratories own large numbers of high performance workstations. These workstations are typically connected by a local area network (LAN) such as Ethernet. Surveys have shown that in most instances the average CPU usage of these workstations is less than 10%. Due to the wide availability of such networks, there is a huge resource of unused cycles available for doing high performance computing. For example, a network of 50 IBM RS/6000-550 machines represents a 1.1 Gflop computing resource.

The problems hindering the effective use of these workstation networks as powerful distributed computers are threefold – hardware, systems software and programming languages. Due to the relatively high latency and small bandwidth of Ethernet LANs, the type of applications which can be run effectively on these networks is limited. Sophisticated systems software is also needed to allow a heterogeneous network of workstations to be used in this way, without degrading the performance of workstations which are being used interactively (users can be very possessive of their own CPUs), and with some kind of load balancing. Finally there is the difficult problem of coding efficient parallel programs so that these loosely coupled networks of workstations can be used as parallel computers.

Here we describe our experiences in distributed computing using some applications from the field of computational physics; in particular Monte Carlo simulation of spin models of magnetic crystals. The same kind of techniques and algorithms are also used for the simulation of quantum field theories such as QCD (the theory of the strong nuclear force), and in simulations of theories of quantum gravity using dynamically triangulated random surfaces. Similar techniques are also used to tackle general optimization problems using simulated annealing. We will consider two types of Monte Carlo methods: the standard Metropolis algorithm, which is regular and local and therefore easy to parallelize; and the cluster-style algorithms, which are irregular and non-local and thus much more difficult to parallelize.

We have developed and studied a range of parallel algorithms for these problems on different parallel architectures. Here we describe the use of a network of workstations for distributed computing, and examine the performance of these parallel algorithms on such a network. We are particularly interested in the suitability of distributed computing for our physics codes, and whether new algorithms are required for efficient use of a distributed workstation network as a parallel computer.

The computing facilities used for this work consisted of 4 IBM RS/6000 model 340 workstations connected with both Ethernet and a high performance prototype switch [1]. This is a copper wired switch based on 8 × 8 prototype crossbars, with an adapter which connects directly to the Micro Channel of the RS/6000. The same programs have also been run on an nCUBE/2, a MIMD parallel computer with a hypercube topology.

The software we have used to make the network behave as a parallel computer is Express, from ParaSoft Inc. [2] Express is the result of research by the Caltech Concurrent Computation Group, and is a powerful and portable message passing environment which has tools for inter-processor communication, domain decomposition, parallel I/O, graphics, debugging and profiling. It can be used on most Commercial MIMD parallel computers, including those from nCUBE, Meiko and Intel, as well as on workstation networks. Express can be used with C or Fortran, which simplifies the modification of sequential code. The programs described below were written in Express Fortran.

2 Monte Carlo Simulation of Spin Models

Magnetic materials usually undergo a transition from a magnetic to a non-magnetic phase as the temperature is increased. These phase transitions can generally be described very well by simple models of interacting spins on a lattice, such as the Ising model [3, 4]. Numerical simulations of these spin models are mainly done using Monte Carlo methods such as the Metropolis algorithm [3, 4, 5]. This algorithm works by making small, local changes to the configuration of spins. This leads to the problem of "critical slowing down", meaning that many iterations are required to generate a new uncorrelated configuration, especially near a phase transition or critical point of the system. Non-local Monte Carlo algorithms have been introduced for some spin models [6, 7]. These so-called "cluster algorithms" can dramatically reduce critical slowing down, and thus give a huge improvement in computational efficiency over standard Monte Carlo algorithms. Here we look at two different types of cluster algorithm – the Wolff algorithm [7] which finds a single cluster to update, and the Swendsen-Wang (SW) algorithm [6] which partitions the entire lattice into clusters which are all updated.

Parallel algorithms for spin models offer an interesting challenge for parallel machines, languages, and compilers, since they have widely varying levels of difficulty. The local Metropolis algorithm can be easily and efficiently parallelized using standard domain decomposition, since it is regular and needs only local edge communication. This is a simple case which is easy to express in a language such as Fortran 90, and should be well handled by any parallelizing compiler. The cluster algorithms, on the other hand, are difficult to parallelize, since they are non-local and irregular, and lack the structure of regular multi-scale algorithms such as multi-grid. Consequently they provide a challenging problem for any parallelizing compiler, or even a high level parallel language.

3. The Metropolis Algorithm

The Metropolis algorithm for simulating a spin model is very similar to the standard algorithm for solving simple differential equations such as Laplace's equation on a discretized grid of points [8]. The update of the spin depends only on the values of neighboring spins, which means that a parallel implementation of this algorithm is very simple and efficient, since only local communication is required. Since the algorithm is regular we do not have to worry about load balancing.

The dependence of the update on the values of neighboring spins means that not all spins can be updated simultaneously in parallel. We need to set up a checkerboard or red/black partitioning of the lattice, in which all the red sites can be updated in parallel, and then all the black sites [8]. In this way the sites updated simultaneously are completely independent of one another, and the parallel algorithm therefore obeys the technical constraint known as "detailed balance" which ensures that the Monte Carlo procedure is valid [3, 4].

As long as this constraint is taken into account, writing a parallel Metropolis algorithm is very simple. In fact if we insist that there be more than 2^d sites per processor for a d-dimensional lattice and that we update one site at a time on each processor, then we automatically satisfy detailed balance. The resulting code on each node looks almost exactly like the sequential code, the only difference being that the function which is called to find the neighboring spin value handles periodic boundary conditions for the sequential code, while in the parallel code it performs message passing if the neighboring site is on another processor. This regular local communication is particularly simple in Fortran 90, with just a call to a periodic SHIFT operation.

This is the type of algorithm we would use for a fine grained parallel computer such as the CM-2, which has relatively low latency and high bandwidth nearest-neighbor communication. In Fig. 1 we show the results for the efficiency (the speed-up compared to the sequential program running on one node divided by

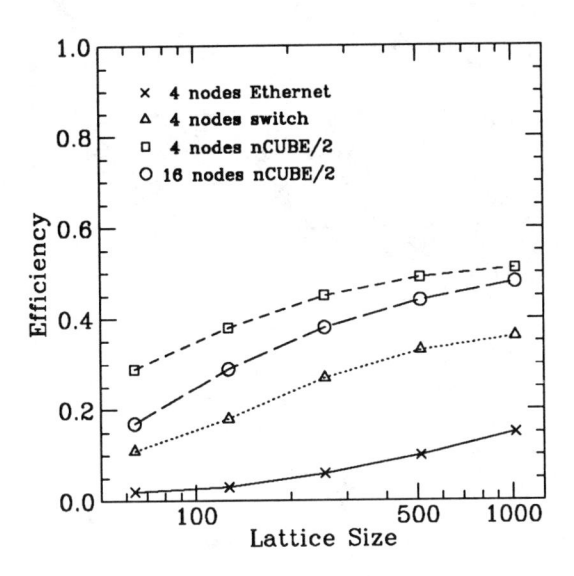

Figure 1: Efficiency of fine-grained Metropolis algorithm for different parallel architectures.

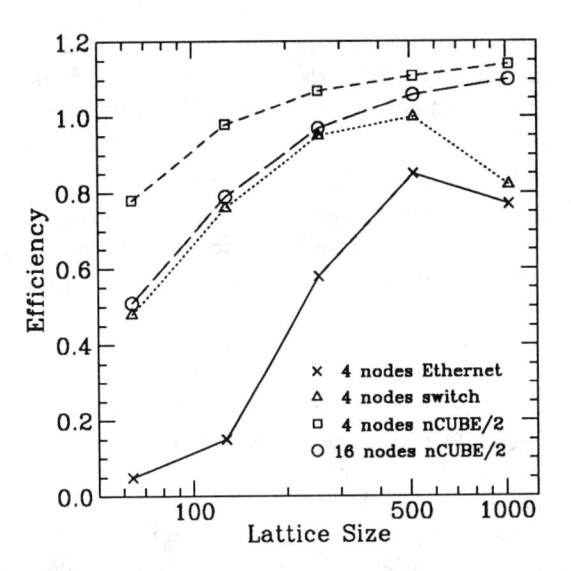

Figure 2: Efficiency of coarse-grained Metropolis algorithm for different parallel architectures.

the number of nodes) of the algorithm on different parallel architectures. Here the lattice size L refers to an L^2 lattice of sites. We can see that the fine grained algorithm also works reasonably well for coarser grained parallel machines such as the nCUBE/2. However this is clearly not an efficient algorithm for coarse grain parallel machines with high latencies, such as networks of workstations, since it involves passing a lot of very small packets of data (the spin value at a single site). In fact, using the 4 processor network is much slower than using a single processor. The calculation time for this problem scales linearly with the lattice volume, whereas the communication time scales as the length of the lattice. The time taken by this fine-grained parallel algorithm using the Ethernet LAN scaled roughly as the length of the lattice, and thus was was totally dominated by communication. Note that the low latency of the prototype switch gives dramatically improved performance over the standard Ethernet connections. The efficiencies are comparable with those for the nCUBE/2, even though the calculation time on the IBM workstations is very much smaller (for this problem the IBM RS/6000-340 processor is about 8 times faster than the custom nCUBE/2 processor).

For coarse grain machines this algorithm can be optimized by passing a smaller number of messages, each containing a larger amount of data. This can be done by using the red/black algorithm for the sub-lattice on each processor. In this case we can pack all the spin values along a processor boundary into a single message, which we only need to pass before every red or black update. This greatly reduces the latency, and since for a local coarse grain algorithm we have a large calculation-to-communication ratio (basically the ratio of the volume of the sub-lattice to its perimeter), we obtain very good efficiencies (see Fig. 2). Notice that the prototype switch still outperforms the Ethernet, and gives efficiencies close to that of the nCUBE/2. In some cases the efficiency is greater than 1, presumably due to more use of cache memory when the data is distributed over multiple processors. We believe that the decrease in efficiency at the largest lattice size for the workstation network is also an artifact of this kind. For the nCUBE/2, the performance of this algorithm is scalable to larger numbers of processors as long as the amount of data per processor remains constant, and this should also be true for a workstation network.

4. Cluster Algorithms

The main computational task in cluster algorithms is the identification and labeling of the clusters. This is an instance of the well-known problem of connected component labeling [9]. Connected component labeling is used in a number of other applications, most notably percolation theory and image processing. The problem is very simple: there are connections between sites of the lattice, and we want to give the same label to all sites which are part of a connected cluster, with each of these clusters having a different label. This means that local information (connectivity) must be processed and converted into global information (the cluster labels).

There are very efficient sequential algorithms for this problem which execute in a time of $O(V)$, where V is the number of sites [10]. However this is a very difficult problem to implement efficiently on a parallel machine, since sites in the same cluster may be on distant processors, and the path connecting two sites may be quite labyrinthine. Parallel component labeling algorithms are generally rather complicated, and can be very different to the sequential algorithms. There are many algorithms in the computer science literature for tackling this problem. We have studied a number of these methods, and have also developed and implemented our own algorithms for use in a parallel SW cluster update algorithm, for both MIMD and SIMD machines [10, 11, 12].

The extreme irregularity (in both size and shape) of the clusters in spin models means that this problem is not well suited to SIMD machines [12]. However MIMD parallel machines (which includes distributed workstation networks) can handle the irregular clusters, since they allow processors to follow branch points in the program completely independently. For our problem, this means that each processor can run the very efficient sequential labeling algorithms in parallel on their own section of the lattice. If we do a standard domain decomposition of the data so that each processor has the same number of lattice sites, the sequential algorithm will take approximately the same time for each processor, and we will also have good load balancing. A small amount of edge information then needs to be passed between processors in order to give the same labels to sub-clusters connected across processors. As long as the ratio of the number of sites per processor to the number of processors is relatively large, this method is fairly efficient on MIMD parallel computers [10].

This algorithm has been considerably optimized for coarse grain parallel computers, by minimizing both the amount of communication and the number of communication calls required. This optimization is vital for workstation networks where the latency is high. We can see from Fig. 3 that it allows us to obtain good performance, comparable to the much simpler and more regular parallel Metropolis algorithm. However we expect the parallel Metropolis algorithm to scale much better to larger networks, as is the case for larger numbers of nodes on parallel computers such as the nCUBE/2 [10].

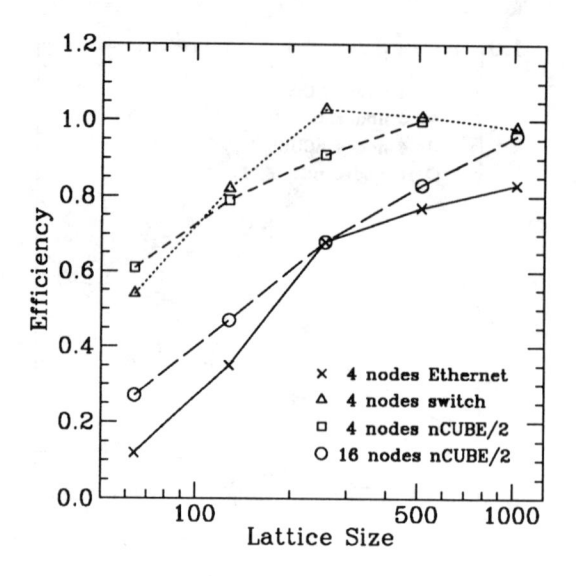

Figure 3: Efficiency of parallel cluster algorithm for different architectures.

Note that the parallel labeling algorithm outlined above will only work efficiently for the SW algorithm, which identifies clusters on all the lattice sites. It is difficult to see how the Wolff algorithm, which only grows a single cluster, can be parallelized without having serious load imbalance.

3 Independent Parallelism

Quantitative studies of cluster Monte Carlo algorithms require extremely accurate data on large systems in order to make reliable calculations of quantities of interest, such as dynamic critical exponents. For the SW cluster algorithm we can use parallel or distributed computers to study larger systems, using the parallel algorithms discussed above. However the Wolff algorithm, which grows a single cluster, cannot be efficiently parallelized or vectorized. A network of high performance workstations is the most suitable architecture for simulations using this algorithm. Workstations have enough memory and power to handle large systems, and the IBM RS/6000 runs the Wolff code almost as fast as a CRAY X-MP.

Although the Wolff algorithm is not parallelizable over a single simulation, we can utilize the network by parallelizing over multiple simulations. The individual workstations in the network can be running simulations with different parameter values, such as the system size or the temperature. Independent parallelism is especially applicable to Monte Carlo simulation, which can be parallelized in this way even without varying the parameter values. This is because the Monte Carlo procedure is basically a sum over a large number of sample configurations of the system. This is a statistical process, with a corresponding statistical error which is proportional to the square root of the number of independent configurations sampled. Monte Carlo simulations are therefore "embarrassingly parallel", in that different processors can be generating different configurations completely independently, by using different starting configurations and different random number streams. These independent results can then be combined to reduce the statistical error in the simulation.

This kind of independent or "job level" parallelism is common to many kinds of simulations in science and engineering. Usually simulation involves studying changes in the system as parameters are varied. Sometimes the choice of new parameters will depend on the results of the simulation with the current parameters, so this is a sequential process. However in many cases one would like to know results for a large number of parameter values which can all be run independently.

As long as the system size is small enough so that each processor can hold all the data for a simulation, this procedure will give perfect speedup, since the sequential program is run independently on each processor. The data obtained using a network of workstations in this way allowed us to make accurate measurements of dynamic critical exponents for the Wolff algorithm for spin models [13, 14]. This method has also been used for Monte Carlo simulations of dynamically triangulated random surfaces, which are highly irregular and very difficult to parallelize [15, 16].

This approach is ideally suited to very coarse-grained parallel machines, and especially for distributed computing over networks of workstations. There are at least three methods of invoking job level parallelism on distributed networks, which we discuss below. We have done our physics production runs using the first two methods, neither of which we found to be satisfactory. This has led us to think of programming paradigms and systems software which would be ideal for these types of physics applications, and this is what we propose as the third method.

(1) The Brute Force Approach

The simplest but most tedious method is just to log on to any available machines in the network and submit a different job to each of these machines. This method is too time consuming to use on any more than a handful of workstations. It would be possible to set up a shell program to remotely run these jobs on different processors, however deciding which machines to use generally requires first checking that the machine is not already in use. Physicists and other scientists who might wish to use networked workstations in this way usually do not have (and should not need to have) the systems programming knowledge to implement such an approach automatically. Some systems software to deal with these problems would make the utilization of networked workstations very much easier.

(2) Portable Parallel Software

Job level parallelism can be used on distributed computing networks and MIMD parallel computers using parallel software. It is easy to set up parallel code to do this, since only data input and output need to be managed, as all computation is sequential and requires no communication. The problem with this method is that although the programs are run independently, they generally require synchronization every time data is input or output. This will lead to performance problems if one or more of the processors in the network is slower than the others, perhaps because it is also running other processes. This can be avoided by writing the data from each processor into separate files which can be accessed asynchronously. This can be done in Express, for example. This approach allows all the processors to run completely independently. However we are still left with the "load balancing" problem, of arranging for processes to be run on workstations which are idle or lightly loaded.

(3) A Transparent Network

It would be preferable to be able to run multiple jobs over the network without having to deal with parallel software (such as Express) at all. Ideally, one would like to be able to just set up a standard Unix runfile which submits multiple jobs, with different input and output files, to the *network*, rather than to a particular workstation. Some clever systems software would then distribute these jobs to whichever machines on the network had the smallest load and were not being used interactively. Again, some load balancing software would be required, so that if an interactive session was started on a workstation, the job would be suspended or migrated to another workstation. This would all be transparent to the user, who would just submit jobs to the network and not care where they were run.

Some shared memory parallel machines, such as the Sequent Symmetry and BBN Butterfly allow this kind of programming paradigm. No knowledge of parallel computing or parallel languages is required to run on these machines using job level parallelism. A number of independent Unix processes are submitted to the parallel computer, and each one runs on a separate node. Of course these machines can also be programmed as parallel computers. Ideally a distributed network of workstations could be programmed in the same fashion, using these two paradigms. The new IBM SP-1 machine has this functionality.

4 Parallel Languages

The main problem hindering the use of distributed and parallel computing for scientific applications has been the difficulty of parallelizing sequential codes, and the lack of simple, portable and efficient high level parallel languages. High level languages such as Fortran 90 are now becoming available, and a lot of effort is going into the development of future parallel languages such as High Performance Fortran (HPF) [17] and parallelizing compilers such as Fortran D [18]. The Northeast Parallel Architectures Center (NPAC) at Syracuse University is playing a major role in these efforts, including the development of the Fortran 90D compiler.

We used the Express parallel programming tools for all the work described here. The most appealing features of Express are that it can be used with standard C or Fortran, so sequential codes can be easily utilized, and it is portable. We have also coded our algorithms in CMFortran, a variant of Fortran 90 used on the Connection Machine. We found that programming in CMFortran (or Fortran 90) was much simpler than programming in Express Fortran (or Fortran with message passing). Explicit message passing allows the user the extra control over communications that one would expect from a lower level language, which can help in optimization of parallel algorithms. A simpler higher level language would be preferable, however we must be careful that the implementation of such a language is efficient enough to make using it worthwhile.

Methods for parallelizing simple, regular programs such as the Metropolis algorithm for spin models are straightforward, but tedious and error-prone, in Express Fortran. A parallelizing compiler such as Fortran D should therefore have no problem with algorithms of this kind, even when starting with sequential Fortran 77 code. The implementation of the Metropolis algorithm in Fortran 90 was very simple.

Implementing the irregular, non-local parallel algorithm for the cluster Monte Carlo program was quite difficult in Express Fortran, but surprisingly easy to code in Fortran 90. However this would be a tough problem for a parallelizing compiler starting from sequential Fortran 77 code. One of the difficulties in developing parallelizing compilers such as Fortran D lies in the fact that for many problems, including this one, very different algorithms are required for parallel and sequential machines, and even for different parallel architectures, such as SIMD and MIMD, or coarse and fine grain machines. Also, many modern computational physics applications, such as cluster algorithms, hierarchical N-body simulations, dynamically triangulated random surfaces, and adaptive grid finite element and computational fluid dynamics simulations, use complex, irregular, and dynamic data structures which may be difficult for parallelizing compilers (and even parallel languages) to handle. We expect that substantial user input will be required for efficient parallelization of these problems, especially over distributed computers with high latency and low communications bandwidth.

Portability of parallel software is crucial for the advancement of parallel and distributed computing. Software portability is one of the driving forces behind the High Performance Fortran initiative. Currently there are a number of different proprietary parallel languages, such as CMFortran and C* for the Connection Machine, MP Fortran and MPL for the Maspar, Fortran Plus for the AMT DAP, and different message passing software libraries for the nCUBE, Intel, and Meiko. These cannot be migrated between similar architectures, let alone between SIMD, MIMD, vector, distributed, and sequential machines. We were able to run our Express programs *unchanged* on different MIMD parallel computers and on distributed workstation networks. Such portability is a great asset to computational physicists who would rather spend their time doing physics than porting codes between different computers. Many portable parallel software packages now exist, such as Express, PVM, PICL, Linda, and Strand. The Fortran 90 standard and the development of Fortran D and HPF should further improve the situation and entice more computational scientists to move to parallel and distributed computing.

Setting up the network of workstations to act as a distributed parallel computer was very simple under Express. The user need only run an initialization program and specify the names of the machines to be used. One of the problems with running on the network was that if one of the workstations in the network is loaded with another process, then the efficiency of the distributed computer drops to under 50%, and other processors are under utilized. A solution to this problem would require some kind dynamic load checking and load balancing by the systems software, perhaps by migrating processes to other machines which are idle (or at least less loaded).

The main problem with Express is that it uses a fairly low-level implementation of parallelism, using explicit message passing. Writing distributed memory MIMD parallel programs can be extremely difficult, and debugging such programs can be even harder. We have seen that producing code which works efficiently, especially on a loosely coupled distributed network, requires an additional level of effort. Optimization usually requires carefully adjusting the communications strategy, and sometimes changing the algorithm. This tends to be very time consuming and error-prone. Clearly a higher level parallel language such as HPF is required, but it is also clear that developing and implementing such a language to work efficiently for a wide class of problems is a very difficult task.

5 Discussion and Conclusions

The performances we obtained on the workstation network using standard Ethernet were, as expected, not nearly as good as for distributed memory parallel computers such as the nCUBE. However we were able to use the large memory and processing power of each node to get reasonable performance for very large physical systems distributed over small numbers of nodes, where the amount of data per node is large.

To exploit parallel computing systems based on networks of workstations, it is necessary to construct algorithms that take advantage of very coarse grain parallelism and the large processor memory, minimize latency, and maximize the ratio of calculation to communication. This is much more crucial than for parallel computers. For instance the simplest parallel implementation of the Metropolis algorithm, which works very well on fine grained machines like the CM-2, and passably well on the nCUBE/2, performs so poorly on the Ethernet LAN that it runs slower using more than one workstation. However an improved coarse grained algorithm gives good speed-ups for this network. The cluster applications performed well on small numbers of processors, since a lot of effort had already gone into optimizing the code for large numbers of processors on massively parallel MIMD computers such as the nCUBE/2. Other applications, such as the simple independent parallelism of the Wolff code, required no extra effort to gain maximum benefit from using multiple workstations across a network.

Since we only have a very small number of workstations in our network, it is difficult to assess the scalability of the hardware. From results we have obtained for scaling to larger numbers of nodes on the nCUBE/2, it is unlikely that our applications will be scalable to large numbers of workstations using standard Ethernet connections, mainly due to high latency. However the prototype switch which we have used gave efficiencies comparable to the nCUBE/2, even though the nCUBE/2 has much slower processors. This implies that communications bandwidth, and more importantly the latency, of the switch is comparable to or better than a parallel MIMD computer. Such as switch should thus provide scalability on a par with MIMD computers, and thus allow the use of a large number of connected workstations to be used as a parallel computer on a single problem.

Developing parallel programs for many regular scientific applications is rather tedious, but straightforward, with current parallel software tools. The introduction of Fortran 90, Fortran D, and HPF compilers will greatly simplify this task. We have seen that useful parallel algorithms can be developed even for complex, irregular problems requiring non-local data access, such as the cluster Monte Carlo programs. These problems are much more difficult to implement with current languages and compilers, however higher level parallel languages should improve this situation.

Our results suggest that a cluster of workstations used as a parallel computer can be an economical way of providing a high performance computing resource. However improvements in hardware (fast switches and high bandwidth communications), systems software (making the network transparent and easily accessible without unduly impacting interactive users), and parallel software (portable high level languages such as HPF) are necessary for easy and efficient use of such a system. All of these improvements should be readily implementable in the near future.

Acknowledgements

I would like to thank John Apostolakis, Clive Baillie, Taitin Chen, Geoffrey Fox, Leping Han, Enzo Marinari and the NPAC systems staff for discussions and programming support.

This work was supported in part by the Center for Research on Parallel Computation with NSF cooperative agreement No. CCR-9120008, and a grant from the IBM Corporation.

This paper discusses a prototype which has not been announced as a product, and which may never be announced or made generally available as a product. Any performance data contained in this document was determined in a specific controlled environment, and therefore, the results which may be obtained in other operating environments may vary significantly.

References

[1] T. Chen et al., "A Prototype Switch for Scalable High-Performance Distributed Computing", NPAC Technical Report SCCS-392 (1992).

[2] "Express Reference Manual", ParaSoft Corporation, 2500 E. Foothill Blvd., Pasadena, CA 91107 (1988).

[3] K. Binder ed., *Monte Carlo Methods in Statistical Physics*, (Springer-Verlag, Berlin, 1986).

[4] H. Gould and J. Tobochnik, *An Introduction to Computer Simulation Methods*, (Addison-Wesley, Reading, Mass., 1988).

[5] N. Metropolis et al., *J. Chem. Phys.* **21**, 1087 (1953).

[6] R.H. Swendsen and J.-S. Wang, *Phys. Rev. Lett.* **58**, 86 (1987).

[7] U. Wolff, *Phys. Rev. Lett.* **62**, 361 (1989).

[8] G. Fox et al., *Solving Problems on Concurrent Processors, Vol. 1*, (Prentice-Hall, Englewood Cliffs, 1988).

[9] E. M. Reingold, J. Nievergelt and N. Deo, *Combinatorial Algorithms: Theory and Practice* (Prentice-Hall, Englewood Cliffs, N.J., 1977); E. Horowitz and S. Sahni, *Fundamentals of Computer Algorithms*, (Computer Science Press, Rockville, Maryland, 1978).

[10] C.F. Baillie and P.D. Coddington, *Concurrency: Practice and Experience* **3**, 129 (1991).

[11] J. Apostolakis, P. Coddington and E. Marinari, *Europhys. Lett.* **17**, 189 (1992).

[12] J. Apostolakis, P. Coddington and E. Marinari, "New SIMD Algorithms for Cluster Labeling on Parallel Computers", NPAC Technical Report SCCS-279 (1992).

[13] P.D. Coddington and C.F. Baillie, *Phys. Rev.* **B 43**, 10617 (1991).

[14] P.D. Coddington and C.F. Baillie, *Phys. Rev. Lett.* **68**, 962 (1992).

[15] C.F. Baillie and R.D. Williams, "Numerical Simulations of Dynamically Triangulated Random Surfaces on Parallel Computers with 100% Speedup", Proc. of the 5th Distributed Memory Computing Conference, Charleston (April 1990), eds. D.W. Walker and Q.F. Stout (IEEE Computer Society Press, Los Alamitos, California, 1990).

[16] M. Bowick, P. Coddington, L. Han, G. Harris and E. Marinari, "The Phase Diagram of Fluid Random Surfaces with Extrinsic Curvature", NPAC Technical Report SCCS-357 (1992), to be published in *Nucl. Phys.* **B**.

[17] The High Performance Fortran Forum, "High Performance Fortran Language Specification", Center for Research in Parallel Computing Technical Report CRPC-TR92225.

[18] G.C. Fox et al., "Fortran D Language Specifications", NPAC Technical Report SCCS-42C (1990); A. Choudhary et al., "Compiling Fortran 77D and 90D for MIMD Distributed Memory Machines", NPAC Technical Report SCCS-251 (1992).

Supporting Heterogeneity and Distribution in the Numerical Propulsion System Simulation Project

Patrick T. Homer
Richard D. Schlichting

Department of Computer Science
The University of Arizona
Tucson, AZ 85721

ABSTRACT

The Numerical Propulsion System Simulation (NPSS) project has been initiated by NASA to expand the use of computer simulation in the development of new aircraft engines. A major goal is to study interactions between engine components using multiple computational codes, each modeling a separate component and potentially executing on a different machine in a network. Thus, a simulation run is a heterogeneous distributed program controlled by a simulation executive. This paper describes a prototype executive composed of the AVS visualization system and the Schooner heterogeneous remote procedure call (RPC) facility. In addition, the match between Schooner's capabilities and the needs of NPSS is evaluated based on our experience with a collection of test codes. This discussion not only documents the evolution of Schooner, but also serves to highlight the practical problems that can be encountered when dealing with heterogeneity and distribution in such applications.

1. Introduction

The Numerical Propulsion System Simulation (NPSS) project, sponsored by NASA Lewis Research Center, aims to reduce the high cost of designing and implementing new propulsion technologies by using computer simulation [7]. Specifically, the project, which is part of the High Performance Computing and Communications (HPCC) initiative, involves developing both computational codes to model various engine components, and a simulation executive to control the simulation and model component interactions. Codes have already been written for a number of engine components, with others currently under development. The hardware used by these codes ranges from vector processors to parallel machines to clusters of workstations. Work on the simulation executive is also underway. The focus in this effort is on providing sophisticated capabilities to interact with codes, as well as the ability to substitute different codes at varying degrees of fidelity. A scientific visualization system such as AVS [2] or Khoros [20, 18] will likely form a major component of the finished product.

The nature of the NPSS project makes it imperative that the simulation executive support *heterogeneous distributed processing*, in which diverse software and hardware elements on local- or wide-area networks are incorporated into a single simulation. Providing such support poses many non-trivial problems. For example, a given code may be suitable for execution only on a specific machine architecture, thereby requiring the ability to pass data and control transparently to and from codes executing elsewhere. The role of the executive, then, is to act as the "glue" that connects new and existing codes to produce a program that encompasses all aspects of a given simulation. The user of such a program should not see individual codes that execute in isolation, but rather a single integrated program. In addition to being simpler and more intuitive, such a model allows interaction capabilities not possible when codes are run separately. For example, intermediate results can be viewed and parameters modified to affect subsequent parts of the computation; long running computations can easily be monitored and controlled.

This paper describes how heterogeneous distributed processing is supported in a prototype version of the NPSS simulation executive. The key to this capability is the Schooner interconnection system [14, 15], an application-level remote procedure call (RPC) facility that includes a simple specification language, an intermediate data representation, a collection of stub compilers, and a run-time system implementing cross-machine control transfer. These pieces, together with an execution framework provided by AVS, form a simple simulation executive that supports heterogeneous distributed processing with capabilities approaching those required by NPSS.

In addition to describing the way in which this executive works, we also analyze how well Schooner's capabilities matched the needs of NPSS. Where deficiencies in Schooner were discovered, remedies are outlined; some have already been incorporated, while others are in the implementation stage. Discussing how Schooner has evolved in this way not only documents the evolution of the system, but also serves to highlight the

---

This work supported in part by the National Science Foundation under grant ASC-9204021. Homer is supported by the National Aeronautics and Space Administration under GSRP grant NGT-50966.

practical problems that can be encountered when dealing with heterogeneity and distribution in such applications.

This paper is organized as follows. In Section 2, we describe the NPSS project in more detail, including its hardware and software aspects. The way in which heterogeneity is supported in NPSS using Schooner is the topic of Section 3, while Section 4 outlines how Schooner has and will change based on this experience. Finally, Section 5 offers some conclusions.

2. The NPSS Project

2.1. Overview

The NASA Numerical Propulsion System Simulation (NPSS) is designed to reduce the cost of designing and implementing aircraft propulsion systems through the use of numerical computation and simulation. Typically, one major difficulty in the design process lies in understanding the interaction among engine components. In the past, these interactions could not be studied until the engine components were built and tested, too often resulting in major re-design at a fairly late stage in the development cycle. The goal of NPSS is to provide improved component codes and a numerical testbed where these engine components can be tested together and interactions between components identified at a much earlier stage.

The project has two aspects. One is the improvement of existing codes and the development of new codes to model engine components. Existing codes are being improved to take advantage of improvements in current hardware. New codes are being developed to make use of new advances in massively parallel machines and clustered workstations. However, even with these improved machines and algorithms, it will still prove too costly to simulate all the components of an engine in complete detail. Thus, five levels of fidelity are being used; these range from level 1, a steady-state thermodynamic model, to level 5, a three-dimensional time accurate model.

The second aspect is development of a simulation executive that enables a user to select from the available codes to construct a complete engine model. This is the computational equivalent of an engine test cell, with a primary motivation being to simulate the interactions between engine components by exchanging data values and boundary conditions between the codes modeling different parts of the engine. The user will be able to model the entire engine or a subset of the engine through the specific component codes selected. The model will typically have most of the engine components at the same level of fidelity, although one or two components of interest will often be modeled at a higher level. This strategy allows a reasonable compromise between the need to model the entire engine to capture properly the interactions among the components, and the need to keep the computational costs and time factors at affordable levels.

2.2. Hardware

NPSS will use a variety of hardware architectures. Historically, vector machines have been used in simulating engine components. NPSS intends to use these existing codes and the machines they run on. Improvements in vector machines, particularly those improvements that result in faster execution, will allow these codes to execute in less time and/or include additional physics in the simulation.

A major goal of NPSS, however, is to bring parallel algorithms into more common use in engine simulation. This effort seeks to achieve higher performance at lower cost than can be achieved with sequential algorithms and platforms. Again, the performance improvements gained can be used to speed the simulation, or traded to allow more detail. The effort includes current machines such as the Intel i860 and the CM-5, as well as planning for future generations of massively-parallel machines and clusters of workstations. In some cases, parallel machines can also provide a more natural solution to a problem, i.e., being able to assign one processor to each blade row when modeling an engine fan.

It is quite likely that all the component codes for an engine will not run optimally on the same type of hardware. Thus, mechanisms must be incorporated into NPSS that will allow codes to communicate across machine boundaries. In many cases, this will result in communication across long distances, since not every site will have local access to all the types of machines needed to run a complete engine simulation. Part of NPSS, then, is to explore methods for efficiently running simulations in such a widely-dispersed, heterogeneous environment. The intent here is to take advantage of advances in network hardware to improve the bandwidth between nodes, and improvements in network software to reduce latency.

2.3. Software

The NPSS software effort is concentrating in three areas:

- Connecting codes that execute on different architectures and/or use different programming models,
- Integrating various software packages, such as graphics tools and existing simulation codes, into the system, and
- Improving user interaction with the simulation.

In the first area, the key problem is dealing with data exchanges between a variety of different machines. This facet involves not only solving the problems associated with differing data formats, but also potentially the need to communicate between different computational models. A parallel algorithm, for example, needs to be able to collect scattered values to pass on to a sequential algorithm executing on a vector machine or workstation. As another example, differences in the ability of machines to handle communications will need to be accommodated in the design of the application and algorithms. Bottlenecks, such as occur when fast machines are talking to slow machines, need to be addressed. In some cases, simple buffering to allow the slow machine to catch up will be sufficient. In others, the slower machine may need to filter the data selectively rather than attempt to use all of it.

In the second area, the goal of NPSS is to take advantage of existing software when available. This includes the incorporation of existing codes to model engine components and the use of such tools as graphics packages for displaying results. Having the ability to handle multiple graphics packages will allow a particular code to be incorporated without the need to convert its output.

In the third area, the rationale is that the user is ultimately responsible for deciding the right tradeoffs in applications such as NPSS. For example, it is the user who must decide on such issues as whether a non-optimum local machine is better than an optimum remote machine, or on what the best level of fidelity for each engine component should be. Thus, the system has to provide reasonable default actions, while still allowing a high-degree of user interaction. This interaction extends not only to the selection of which engine components to model, but also to the setting of parameters, both for the individual codes and for the simulation as a whole. The user will also need the ability to monitor the simulation through selectively viewing graphical results or monitoring particular values from selected component codes.

2.4. Simulation Executive

The NPSS simulation executive brings together all the individual codes and coordinates them to simulate the entire engine. The overall goal is a system where the user is able to sit at a workstation and build an engine from various component codes. In general, the user will bring up one of several complete engine models, and then make code substitutions for one or more of the components. The simulation executive must also allow interaction with the engine model and its various codes, as noted above. For example, the user will be able to set starting parameters, change values during a run, resume execution from a particular point, etc. Such capabilities allow the user to model the engine at steady state, to "start" the engine and bring it up to speed, to simulate various atmospheric conditions, or to test operation of the engine in the presence of failures.

A prototype of such a simulation executive is being built using a combination of the AVS scientific visualization system and Schooner. Along one dimension, AVS provides a state-of-the art environment for viewing scientific data. In particular, it provides a large number of tools for processing and displaying data. Another important feature of AVS—and the one that is actually most important for the purposes of NPSS—is the ability to create, modify, and save programs using its Network Editor. This editor allows the user to create programs by visually dragging modules into a workspace and connecting them into a dataflow graph. In addition to the modules supplied with AVS, the user is free to write additional AVS modules that can be integrated into a network in the same way. In the context of NPSS, the Network Editor allows the user to incorporate the specific codes needed for a simulation. The dataflow in this case models the flow of air through the engine.

Interaction with the modules is possible through the setting of parameters associated with each component. In AVS, this is realized using "widgets" that appear in control panels as dials, sliders, type-in boxes, etc. Using the widgets, the user is able both to set initial values for each module and also to modify values during execution, giving a great degree of control over each engine component during a simulation run.

3. Supporting Heterogeneity using Schooner

As alluded to in the Introduction, the need to incorporate heterogeneous hardware and software components follows naturally from the goals of NPSS. Heterogeneity is reflected in the nature of jet engines and the different algorithms needed to simulate their various components. It is also reflected in the variety of machine architectures and programming models being used in and developed for the NPSS project. The need to deal with the distribution of these resources is also inherent in NPSS, since different parts of the simulation may execute on different machines. Indeed, given the special-purpose nature of these machines, it is not unreasonable to expect that they may be separated by significant geographic distances.

These issues of heterogeneity and distribution are dealt with in the prototype NPSS simulation executive by using Schooner, a heterogeneous RPC facility. This section presents an overview of Schooner and describes the prototype executive formed by the combination of AVS and Schooner.

3.1. Schooner Overview

Schooner is designed to be an application-level RPC facility that can be used by programmers to invoke procedures on other machines in a straightforward manner despite the complications of heterogeneity and distribution. As such, a Schooner program is designed in the same manner as a normal procedural program, but with the significant advantage that the programmer is not constrained to a single machine, architecture, programming model, or programming language. Instead, procedures can be written that are tailored to the hardware and software combination most suited to a given application. At runtime, the procedures are instantiated as processes, with calls implemented using a message passing library. The Schooner system handles all data conversions and message passing between processes, thereby preserving a familiar and easy method for constructing programs from a collection of procedures.

Being procedure-oriented, the execution of a Schooner program is essentially sequential, with control proceeding from one procedure to the next as shown in Figure 1. Note, however, that this does not preclude the use of parallel algorithms where appropriate; to use such an algorithm, it is only necessary to encapsulate it within a procedure as illustrated in the figure. This allows the use of, for example, a particular hardware platform's native parallel library, or the incorporation of a computation in which a system such as PVM [22] is used to achieve parallel execution on a cluster of workstations.

To carry out its task of connecting components and masking heterogeneity, Schooner provides three largely orthogonal services: the Universal Type System (UTS) [12], which includes a type specification language and intermediate data format, a collection of stub compilers, and a runtime system. The UTS type specification language uses a Pascal-like syntax to describe the parameters that are expected for each procedure. It provides for the common simple types such as float, integer, byte, and string, as well as structured types such as arrays and records. An *export specification* is written for each procedure that is to be publically available, while a nearly identical *import specification* is written and associated with the invoking code. UTS also provides a common data interchange format. This is implemented by library functions that handle conversions between a machine's native format and the common interchange format.

A stub compiler is provided for each supported language to read the specification files and produce a stub for each imported and exported procedure. This stub acts as the interface between the user's code and the Schooner runtime. Specifically, it handles the marshaling and unmarshaling of arguments through calls to the UTS library, and utilizes the Schooner library to locate and communicate with the remote procedures. Schooner currently supports C and Fortran, while the predecessor MLP system [10, 11] also incorporated languages as diverse as Pascal, Icon [9], and Emerald [5].

The Schooner runtime system consists of a communication library and two types of system processes. The communication library is linked with every procedure to handle the sending and receiving of messages implicit in RPC. The system processes are the Schooner Manager and Schooner Servers, respectively. The Manager is responsible for startup and shutdown of processes, maintaining a table of exported procedures and their locations, and performing runtime type-checking of procedure calls based on the UTS specifications. There is one such process per executing program. The Servers are used by Manager processes to start processes on remote machines. There is one Server per machine involved in a given computation.

Systems such as PVM, p4 [6], and APPL [19] also support heterogeneous distributed processing. However, these systems are oriented primarily towards exploiting clusters of workstations and/or parallel machines to achieve affordable parallel speedup, and as such, support a general message passing paradigm. Schooner, on the other hand, is oriented primarily towards connecting heterogeneous resources to increase the functionality available to the programmer, a task for which RPC is sufficient. Given that RPC is closer to the standard procedural paradigm familiar to most users and simpler to implement, it is a logical choice for the type of problems addressed by Schooner. Also, as compared with these other systems, the availability of UTS simplifies the task of generating the library calls needed to convert and transmit data between machines.

Schooner's use of an external data representation, a specification language, and stub compilers is similar to other RPC systems [1, 4, 21, 23]. Several of these systems also emphasize heterogeneity, including Matchmaker [16],

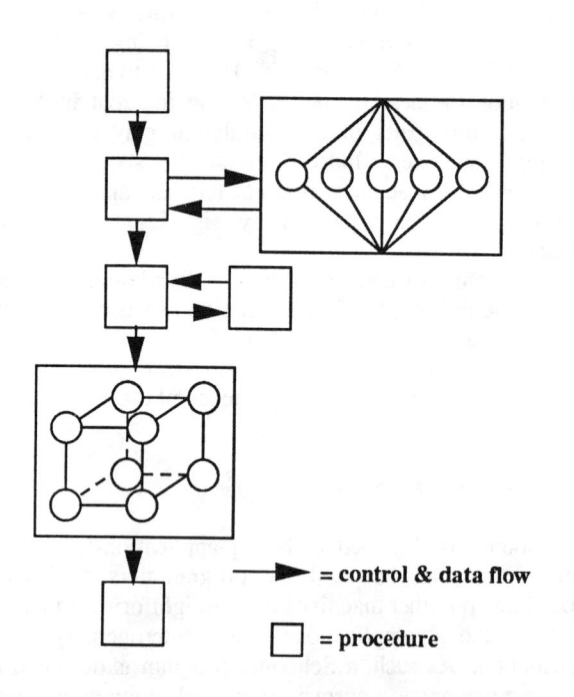

Figure 1 — A Schooner program

Horus [8], and HRPC (Heterogeneous RPC) [3]. Schooner differs from these systems mainly in its orientation toward designing applications in a distributed environment, rather than as a client-server operating system mechanism.

3.2. The Prototype Executive

A prototype NPSS executive has been constructed by combining the capabilities of the AVS scientific visualization system and Schooner. AVS, executing on a workstation, provides visualization capabilities and an execution framework through its dataflow graph of modules. Schooner, in turn, provides the ability to perform the actual computation associated with a module—that is, the simulation code itself—on a remote, potentially heterogeneous, machine. The executive is being tested using an NPSS test simulation based on Digtem, a complete component-level set of engine codes developed by NASA. Figure 2 shows the AVS network that implements this model, with the AVS widgets for the combustor module on the left. While not an especially complex model, it is sufficiently realistic to test most aspects of the problem being addressed.

At this time, three of the engine modules have been modified so that their computations are executed remotely using Schooner: the fan, compressor, and combustor modules. The changes made in adapting the combustor module are described below; the changes needed in the other two cases were similar.

In adapting an existing code to use Schooner, four tasks must be performed. The first is to decide which procedure or procedures should be executed remotely. This requires evaluating available architectures and programming languages to decide which would be most appropriate for the given computation. In some cases, the decision may also take into account factors such as the most convenient place to locate data files containing, for example, the computational grid. Once a decision has been reached, the procedure, along with any supporting code, is separated and moved to the remote machine. In the case of the combustor code, for example, the central procedure `combustorn` was placed into its own file `combustor.f`, and then moved together with a supporting file `npss-procom.f` to the destination machine.

In the next step, two UTS specification files are written. The two are nearly identical, differing only as to whether they are designated an import or an export. (UTS actually allows the import to be, in essence, a subset of the export, but this facility is not currently exploited in NPSS.) For `combustorn`, the export specification is co-located with the `combustor.f` file on the remote machine, while the

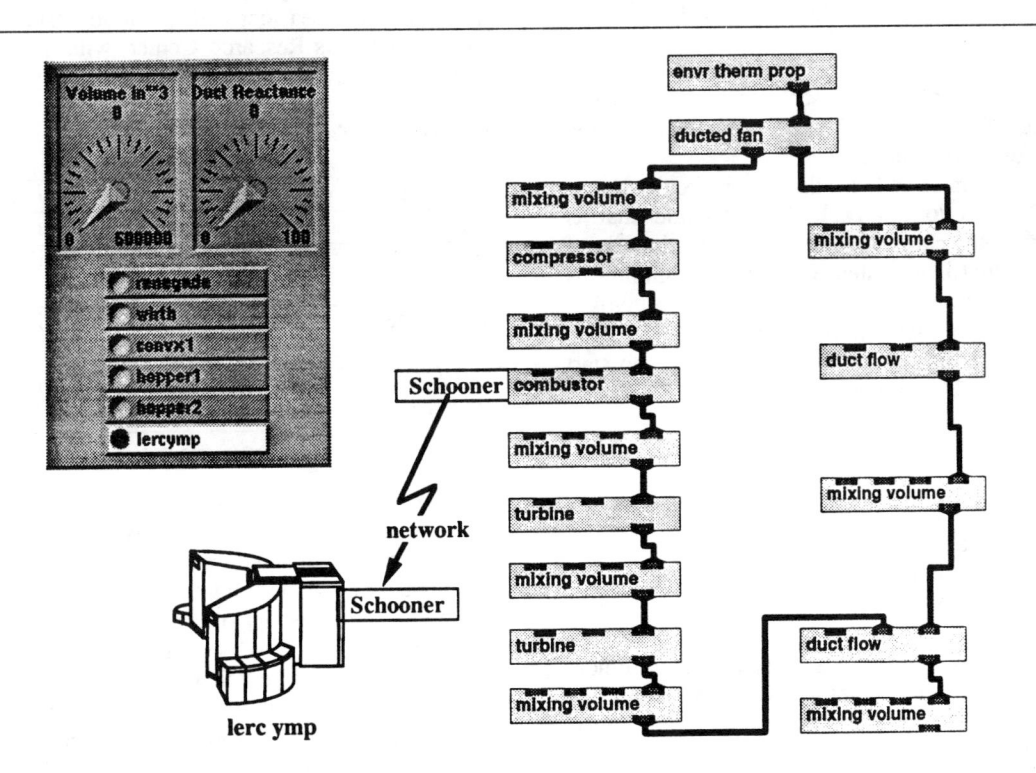

Figure 2 — Prototype simulation executive

matching import specification is co-located with the code for the invoking AVS module. The export specification is as follows:

```
export combustorn prog(
    "wchempt" val float, "etab"   val float,
    "pin"     val float, "pind"   val float,
    "pout"    val float, "poutd"  val float,
    "tin"     val float, "tind"   val float,
    "tout"    val float, "wdotid" val float,
    "betacmb" val float, "farin"  val float,
    "wdotin"  res float, "hout"   res float,
    "eout"    res float)
```

Note that, in this example, all parameters are specified as either value or result parameters; UTS supports `var` parameters as well.

The final step involves modifying the AVS module slightly to add whatever interaction facilities are desired and to coordinate startup with the Schooner Manager. In general, three short pieces of code are needed to accomplish these tasks. The first is placed in the `spec` function of the module, which specifies the AVS input and output data streams, and the widgets the module will use. For `combustorn`, a widget was added to allow the user to specify the machine on which to execute the remote procedure, as follows:

```
iparm3=AVSADD_PARAMETER('Remote Machine',
        'choice', 'renegade', 'renegade:wirth:
        convx1:hopper1:hopper2:lercymp', ':')
CALL AVSCONNECT_WIDGET(iparm3,
                        'radio_buttons')
```

The strings between colons represent machines at Lewis Research Center that can be chosen interactively as the location to run the computation.

The second section of code is added at the beginning of the `compute` function in each AVS module that is invoking a remote computation. This function is a standard routine that is executed each time the module is scheduled for execution by AVS. The added code invokes a Schooner library function that registers the AVS module with the Schooner Manager and asks the Manager to start the remote process. This is done as follows:

```
character*(*) machine
save          first_time_combustor
logical       first_time_combustor/.true./
if (first_time_combustor) then
    CALL sch_contact_schx(machine,
          'path/combustor')
    first_time_combustor = .false.
endif
```

The value of `machine`, which is passed as an argument to `sch_contact_schx`, is set when the user makes the selection of a remote machine using the radio button widget described above.

The final piece of additional code is placed in the AVS `destroy` function, which is invoked when the module is removed from a network or the entire network is cleared.

This code is simply a call to the Schooner library function `sch_i_quit`, which notifies the Manager that the AVS module is being destroyed. When this occurs, the Manager sends shutdown messages to each remote procedure to terminate the Schooner program.

As already mentioned, the steps followed for the other two adapted modules were essentially the same. One deviation is that, in the case of the compressor module, the code was structured as two remote procedures, one to initialize the simulation parameters and the other to do the computation itself. This was done mostly to allow the prototype executive to be tested in the case where multiple remote procedures were invoked from within a single AVS module. The steps used to create this pair of remote procedures were the same as described above for the combustor computation. For interaction capabilities, two widgets appear in the control panel that allow the user to specify which machine to use for each of the two remote procedures. This allows the user to, for example, place the initialization code on the local workstation and the compressor code on a Cray, or any other combination desired.

3.3. Experiments

All three of the adapted AVS modules were tested separately on a variety of machine combinations over both local and wide-area networks. These tests took place primarily at Lewis Research Center, with one set of tests also involving a machine at The University of Arizona. Some of the more interesting combinations are summarized in Table 1.

AVS	Remote	Connecting Network
Sun Sparc 2	SGI 4D/480	local Ethernet
Sun Sparc 2	Convex C220	same building multiple gateways
SGI 4D/480	Cray YMP	same building multiple gateways
SGI 4D/480 NASA Lewis	Sun Sparc 2 U. of Arizona	via Internet

Table 1 – NPSS and Schooner Tests

In one experiment, two of the computations were performed remotely. Specifically, the ducted fan computation was executed on a Cray YMP at Lewis, while the combustor computation was executed on a Sun Sparc 2 located at The University of Arizona. AVS with its NPSS network ran on an SGI 4D/480 at Lewis.

Finally, it should be reiterated that the engine model being used is designed to test the executive and not to represent all the complexities of an engine simulation. Thus, while the interfaces to the modules contain all the correct parameters and the control widgets can be used to pass values to the modules, the computations themselves are minimal and no attempt is made to generate "correct" results. As such, this test case has been used primarily to ascertain the feasibility of performing remote computations and controlling them from within AVS, rather than to do production simulations.

4. The Evolution of Schooner

A primary reason for constructing and testing the prototype executive was to determine how well Schooner's capabilities matched the needs of scientific applications like NPSS. Although Schooner fared well in general, deficiencies were found that led to the evolution of the system. In this section, we first document the incremental changes that were made to Schooner as minor deficiencies were inevitably uncovered during our experimentation. These modifications were designed to overcome specific and relatively small problems, or to extend the functionality of the system. We then turn to describing the one more significant extension that we now feel is desirable based on our experience with NPSS. This extension involves modifying Schooner's programming model to support more dynamic configuration of remote procedures into the overall computation. The incremental changes were made as work with the prototype executive progressed and have already been implemented, while the modifications needed to realize the programming model extension are still in progress.

4.1. Incremental Changes

Incremental changes to Schooner included the addition of the Cray YMP to the list of supported machines, the addition of a new floating point type to UTS, and a change in the Schooner startup protocol. Adding the Cray was straightforward and involved work in two areas. The first was writing UTS conversion routines for the Cray data types, especially the ones for integer and floating point values, which are used heavily in NPSS. Such routines are easily written since they simply involve converting the Cray's internal data representations to and from the UTS intermediate representation. The only problem was that the Cray's integer and float representations support larger magnitudes than the IEEE standard used by UTS. Two remedies were considered: treating such out-of-range Cray values as an error, or converting them to the IEEE "infinity" value. After consultation with researchers involved in developing NPSS code, the first option was chosen.

The other area where work was needed to incorporate the Cray was modifying the Schooner runtime system to support communications with the machine. In general, this was no more difficult than for other machines, requiring only a few changes to include files and type declarations. The one area where an unexpected problem did arise was in the naming of Fortran procedures. On most machines, procedure names are converted to lower case by their respective Fortran compilers, while the compiler on the Cray uses upper case. This inconsistency caused a surprising number of naming problems, both for the writer of Schooner programs and for the Schooner implementation itself. For example, if this inconsistency had been retained, a user writing a program that calls a remote Fortran procedure would need to know beforehand whether it would be run on a Cray or some other machine. Moreover, having Schooner standardize all procedure names to, for example, lower case is not satisfactory because that would interfere with common naming conventions in other languages such as C. In the end, the choice was made to accept both upper and lower case names for Fortran procedures, and then treat them as synonyms within Schooner. This was done primarily by changing the Manager so that it stored both the upper and lower case alternatives in its mapping tables.

The second incremental change was expanding the UTS type system to include both single- and double-precision floating point types instead of just double-precision. The original decision to include only double-precision was in keeping with the Kernighan and Ritchie C specification [17], which requires that values of both float and double types passed as arguments be coerced to double for the call. With the addition of Fortran to Schooner and the development of the ANSI C specification, this practice is no longer adequate. Additionally, having both types is an advantage since it allows the user to specify more precisely the size of the argument value to be passed.

To support both sizes of float values, two changes were required. The first was to add both *float* and *double* to the UTS specification language, with the corresponding changes to the parsers for the stub compilers. The second change involved adding the appropriate encode and decode functions to the UTS library for each of the supported architectures.

The third area where changes to Schooner were needed involved the startup protocol. Previously, Schooner programs were started by executing the Manager as a command and specifying the various files containing Schooner procedures and the appropriate machines as its arguments. Once started, the Manager would fork processes to execute all the remote procedures on the appropriate machines, and then invoke the program's main routine. Since the Manager controlled everything, it could easily collect the mapping information needed to resolve subsequent remote invocations. When AVS is involved, however, the Manager is no longer in control. Specifically, it now has no way of inferring when or where a process should be instantiated for a remote procedure, since this now occurs when a module is configured into an AVS network rather than when the Manager is started. To solve this problem, a new protocol was devised that allows a newly-configured module to contact the Manager and request that a given remote procedure be started on a specific machine.

4.2. Extended Schooner Model

As mentioned above, the original Schooner model of how a program would be executed was oriented around the traditional command line paradigm where everything is specified *a priori*. Unfortunately, this model has proved too restrictive for NPSS, where the pieces of the overall application are configured dynamically at runtime using the Network Editor. In fact, this would be the case for any application written using AVS or similar systems.

One easy change that extended this model to a degree was the new startup protocol described above. This allows remote procedures to be initiated only when needed, thereby facilitating such features as interactive user placement of a remote computation using a widget. However, this change did not solve all the problems, largely because certain simplifying assumptions had been made in the implementation; while these assumptions were valid given the original orientation, they became less so as the orientation changed. For example, it was assumed that there would be only one procedure of a given name in a Schooner program. While reasonable for traditional programs, such an assumption is too restrictive for NPSS. In this environment, there may well be multiple instances of the same module in the network, and therefore, multiple remote procedures with the same name. This scenario, in fact, appears in Figure 2 where the network contains two instances each of the turbine and duct flow modules. A (non-exhaustive) list of similar problems includes:

- The Schooner runtime is written assuming no concurrent execution of remote procedures; with the dataflow model of AVS, this may not be true.

- The original Schooner shutdown procedure terminates the entire program when any part executes sch_i_quit or an error occurs; deleting an individual module in AVS should, in fact, result only in the termination of those remote computations associated with the module.

- Remote procedures cannot be moved once instantiated as processes; given the potentially long-running nature of codes in NPSS, moving the computation should be an option so that, for example, scheduled downtimes can be avoided.

All these problems forced a rethinking of the Schooner model and corresponding changes to the implementation. Our goals in doing so were first, to retain an intuitive, easy to use, and general programming model for the user, and second, to minimize implementation effort.

One option for an extended model that was considered and quickly discarded was to treat each module in an AVS network and its associated remote computations as a separate Schooner program. In this model, each module would have its own Manager process to handle remote startup, name mapping, etc. While workable, this strategy would put an undue burden on the user, who becomes responsible for managing which AVS module is associated with which Manager. It would also preclude sharing remote procedures between modules, something that is desirable in certain situations.

The option that was, in the end, chosen involves extending the model of a Schooner program to include multiple threads of control, which we call *lines*. (Line is the nautical term for rope.) Each line is equivalent to the previous notion of a Schooner program; that is, it is a sequential execution of procedures, some of which may be located on remote machines and/or written in various programming languages. Any procedure in a line can request the initiation of other remote procedures by using the appropriate Schooner library function; such newly started procedures are considered part of the requesting procedure's line and are callable only from other procedures in that line. As before, there is a single Manager, but it now handles the initiation and name mapping chores for multiple control threads. Given the more dynamic nature of the computation, the Manager also becomes a persistent process that must be explicitly initiated and terminated by the user.

The extension of the model to include multiple lines solves many of the problems associated with the original model without unduly complicating either the user's task or the implementation. For example, concurrency is possible, but controlled; each line is sequential and executes independently of the others with no synchronization. Similarly, no duplicate procedure names are permitted within a line, but multiple lines can contain remote procedures with the same name; in this case, each line will have its own instance. Sharing can also be easily realized. To do so, a procedure is designated as shared at startup time, indicating that it is not part of the line from which the startup request originated, but is available for use by any line. Future mapping requests to the Manager are then checked first against procedures in the local line, and then against a list of shared procedures. When a shared procedure is terminated or moved, the mapping database is updated for all lines.

Reasonable shutdown semantics and the ability to move computations are also supported easily in this extended model. The shutdown protocol now involves only the procedures in a single line. Thus, when an AVS module is removed from the network or an error occurs, the Manager terminates only the remote procedures within the affected line. To move a computation, a Schooner library function is invoked in which the process to be moved and the target machine are specified as arguments. This results in the Manager first sending a shutdown message to the original process, and then forking a new copy on the specified machine. The Manager also updates the procedure name mapping information so that future calls go to the new location. Note, however, that this kind of migration is feasible only if the procedure is stateless. This condition is satisfied by many of the Digtem codes being used as our test case and by many other scientific codes.

This extension to the Schooner model represents, we believe, a good compromise between the overly restrictive model used previously and the complexity that results from a complete generalization. With this scheme, the user can manipulate an NPSS network from within AVS in such a way that the remote computations behave reasonably, while still retaining simplicity of use. As mentioned, implementation of this extended model is currently underway.

5. Conclusions

Developing a suitable simulation executive is undoubtedly one of the most important and challenging aspects of the NPSS project due to the myriad of responsibilities assigned to the software. Not only must it provide features that can be used to control and interact with the computation, but it must also mask from the user the effects of heterogeneity and distribution. Here, we have described a prototype executive that takes a step towards meeting these needs by combining the strengths of AVS and Schooner. Specifically, AVS provides the ability to compose and control a simulation using a high-level network editor and associated widgets, while Schooner provides transparent access to heterogeneous and distributed resources. In evaluating the capabilities of Schooner in this regard, we concluded that, although the system was a reasonable match when the project started, some modifications were needed to provide stronger support for the requirements of NPSS and similar scientific projects. Work is continuing on making these changes and evaluating the results in the context of NPSS.

Acknowledgements

Thanks to A. Afjeh, C. Putt, B. Perry, and B. Armstead, who provided assistance with understanding the software and hardware requirements of NPSS. Special thanks also to G. Follen for his support and advice. This work was performed in part on computing resources at the Advanced Computing Concepts Laboratory and the Computer Services Division at NASA Lewis Research Center.

References

[1] Almes, G.T., Black, A.P., Lazowska, E.D., and Noe, J.D. The Eden system: A technical review. *IEEE Trans. on Softw. Eng. SE-11*, 1 (Jan. 1985), 43-59.

[2] Advanced Visual Systems Inc. *AVS Developer's Guide* (Release 4.0), Part number: 320-0013-02, Rev B, Advanced Visual Systems Inc., Waltham, Mass., May 1992.

[3] Bershad, B.N., Ching, D.T., Lazowska, E.D., Sanislo, J., and Schwartz, M. A remote procedure call facility for interconnecting heterogeneous computer systems. *IEEE Trans. on Softw. Eng. SE-13*, 8 (Aug. 1987), 880-894.

[4] Birrell, A. D. and Nelson, B. J. Implementing remote procedure calls. *ACM Trans. on Computer Systems 2*, 1 (Feb. 1984), 39-59.

[5] Black, A., Hutchinson, N., Jul, E., Levy, H. and Carter, L. Distribution and abstract types in Emerald. *IEEE Trans. on Softw. Eng. SE-13*, 1 (Jan. 87), 65-76.

[6] Butler, R. and Lusk, E. User's guide to the p4 parallel programming system, Argonne National Laboratory, Argonne, IL, August 1992.

[7] Claus, R.W., Evans, A.L., Lylte, J.K., and Nichols, L.D. Numerical Propulsion System Simulation. *Computing Systems in Engineering 2*, 4 (Apr. 1991), 357-364.

[8] Gibbons, P.B. A stub generator for multi-language RPC in heterogeneous environments. *IEEE Trans. on Softw. Eng. SE-13*, 1 (Jan. 1987), 77-87.

[9] Griswold, R. and Griswold, M. *The Icon Programming Language*, Prentice Hall, Englewood Cliffs, New Jersey, 1990.

[10] Hayes, R. and Schlichting, R.D. Facilitating mixed language programming in distributed systems. *IEEE Trans. on Softw. Eng. SE-13*, 12 (December 1987), 1254-1264.

[11] Hayes, R., Manweiler, S., and Schlichting, R.D. A simple system for constructing distributed, mixed-language programs. *Software—Practice and Experience 18*, 7 (July 1988), 641-660.

[12] Hayes, R. *UTS: A Type System for Facilitating Data Communication*, Ph.D. Dissertation, Dept. of Computer Science, Univ. of Arizona, August 1989.

[13] Hayes, R., Hutchinson, N.C., and Schlichting, R.D. Integrating Emerald into a system for mixed-language programming. *Computer Languages 15*, 2 (1990), 95-108.

[14] Homer, P.T., and Schlichting, R.D. Adapting AVS to support scientific applications as heterogeneous, distributed programs (extended abstract). *Proc. Workshop on Heterogeneous Processing*, Beverly Hills, CA (Mar. 1992), 50-53.

[15] Homer, P.T., and Schlichting, R.D. A software platform for constructing scientific applications from heterogeneous resources. Tech. Report 92-30, Dept. of Computer Science, Univ. of Arizona, Nov. 1992.

[16] Jones, M.B., Rashid, R.F., Thompson, M.R. Matchmaker: An interface specification language for distributed processing. *Proc. 12th Symp. on Prin. of Prog. Lang*, New Orleans, LA (Jan. 1985), 225-235.

[17] Kernighan, B.W., and Ritchie, D.M. *The C Programming Language*, second edition, Prentice Hall, Englewood Cliffs, NJ, 1988.

[18] Mercurio, P.J. Khoros. *Pixel 3*, 2 (Mar./Apr. 1992), 28-33.

[19] Quealy, A., Cole, J., and Blech, R. Portable programming on parallel/networked computers using the Application Portable Parallel Library (APPL), NASA Technical Manual, 1992.

[20] Rasure, J. and Williams, C. An integrated visual language and software development environment. *Jour. of Visual Languages and Computing 2* (1991), 217-246.

[21] Sun Microsystems, Inc. *Network Programming Guide* (Revision A), Part number 800-3850-10, Sun Microsystems, Inc., Mountain View, CA, March 1990.

[22] Sunderam, V. S. PVM: A framework for parallel distributed computing. *Concurrency—Practice and Experience 2* (Dec. 1990), 315-339.

[23] Xerox Corp. *Courier: The Remote Procedure Call Protocol.* Xerox System Integration Standard XSIS 038112, Xerox Corp., Stamford, Conn., Dec. 1981.

Distributed Computing Solutions to the All-Pairs Shortest Path Problem

Ira Pramanick

IBM Corporation
Kingston, NY 12401

Abstract

This paper proposes two distributed solutions to the all-pairs shortest path problem, and reports the results of experiments conducted on a network of IBM RISC System/6000s, containing up to seven such workstations. It discusses the issues that become critical in a distributed environment as opposed to a parallel environment, and the results obtained underline the importance of reducing communication between the loosely coupled subtasks in a distributed environment. The results demonstrate that properly designed distributed algorithms, which take into account the limitations (in terms of a slower communication medium and/or the non-dedicated mode of machines) of a distributed computing environment, can yield significant performance benefits.

1. Introduction

Shortest path problems constitute an important class of graph theoretic problems, finding extensive use in the study of transportation and communication networks. The all-pairs shortest path problem can be stated as follows:

Given:

A directed graph $G = (V, E)$, where V = {vertices of G}, E = {edges of G}, $|V| = n$, and W = weight matrix such that w_{ij} is the weight of the edge (cost of the edge) from vertex v_i to vertex v_j. In particular $w_{ii} = 0$, and $w_{ij} = \infty$ ($i \neq j$) if there is no edge between v_i and v_j. It is assumed that there are no cycles of negative length.

Objective:

For every pair of vertices v_i and v_j, determine the shortest path along the edges of the graph. That is, find a matrix A such that a_{ij} (the ith row, jth column element of A) is the shortest path from v_i to v_j.

Several well known sequential algorithms exist for the all-pairs shortest path problem [Dijk, Floy, PaKr], and many theoretical [ArCo, FrRu, Lakh, PaKr, Sava] and experimental [DePL, JeSa, QuYo] studies of parallel algorithms for this problem have been conducted. However, no work has been reported on algorithms for this problem on a Distributed Computing System (*DCS*) such as a network of workstations.

The objective of high performance distributed computing is to utilize the resources available in a DCS and maximize the resulting performance. Given that most current DCSs have a relatively slow communication medium, high performance distributed computing requires minimization of inter processor communication for reasonable performance benefits. Additionally, often the processors in a DCS may be available only in a non-dedicated mode. The challenge lies in examining parallel (as well as serial) algorithms for these problems and determining which ones will be most amenable to distributed computing. As we will see in this paper, a good parallel algorithm may not translate into a good distributed algorithm. The characteristics of a given DCS will typically be different from those of a parallel environment and redesigning/reassessing the serial and/or parallel algorithms may be necessary.

This paper proposes two distributed algorithms for the solution to the all-pairs shortest path problem — distributed Dijkstra's algorithm and distributed Floyd's algorithm. Results on a network of IBM RISC System/6000 workstations demonstrate that reasonable performance benefits can be derived from a DCS, provided a suitable distributed algorithm is used to solve a given problem. For the distributed algorithms investigated in this paper, it was observed that as the number of processors was increased, the execution time of the algorithms decreased significantly. Even for medium-sized graphs, the speedups obtained with both the proposed algorithms were in the range 2 — 4 with 6 processors.

The two distributed algorithms differ in their communication and computation patterns. The distributed Dijkstra's algorithm has three phases (which may overlap): an initial communication phase, a computation phase, and a final communication phase. During its computation phase, a processor in the DCS does not communicate with other processors. As opposed to that, the distributed Floyd's algorithm has no computation phase as such, and a processor needs to communicate with other processors in between the steps of its computation. Thus we get two different perspectives for distributed algorithm design for the same problem, with respect to issues such as the ratio of computation time to communication time, work allocation among the processors, and load balancing.

2. Proposed Distributed Solutions

The two distributed algorithms proposed in this paper to solve the all-pairs shortest path problem are based on the sequential Dijkstra's single source and Floyd's all-pairs algorithms respectively. Dijkstra's algorithm was chosen because its distributed implementation has no inter processor communication while a processor is executing its sub-task and hence it is a good candidate for a distributed environment. Floyd's algorithm was chosen because it is considered the best sequential algorithm, and it was considered worthwhile to try to distribute it in a manner consistent with the goals and limitations of distributed computing.

Both the proposed distributed algorithms are based on a master-server paradigm where the *master* process runs on the host processor, and *server* or *worker* processes run on all the processors in the DCS. At the beginning of the computation, the master sends input data to all the servers, who then execute their tasks and send results back to the master. The software package used for synchronization and communication among the processors/processes was *Parallel Virtual Machines (PVM)* [BDGM].

2.1. Distributed Dijkstra's Algorithm

Dijkstra's sequential algorithm [Dijk] is a very popular algorithm for the single-source shortest path problem. It can be used to calculate the solution to the all-pairs problem by running it once for each vertex as the source vertex. In a parallel/distributed environment, each processor can execute Dijkstra's algorithm for a disjoint subset of the vertices. This scheme has been used in [JeSa] for comparison purposes with two parallel versions of Floyd's algorithm. It was observed there that the parallel version of Dijkstra's method outperforms parallel versions of Floyd's method only when the number of processors in the hypercube is large (32 or 64), and provided enough memory is available on each hypercube processor to accommodate W. As discussed in Sections 3 and 4, we shall see that regarding distributed Dijkstra, our conclusions are different.

The proposed distributed implementation of Dijkstra's algorithm uses concurrent applications of the sequential algorithm for different vertices. Each processor in the DCS calculates the shortest paths from a disjoint subset of vertices to all the vertices in the graph, and the collection of results from these processors constitutes the all-pairs solution. Each processor needs the entire W matrix for its calculation. The master process, which has the input graph W, broadcasts the entire graph to all the server processes in the system, and waits for results back from the servers. Each server executes the algorithm in Figure 1.

```
begin
    wait for matrix W from master;
    p = number of servers in the DCS;
    myinum = my instance id;
    for (i=myinum; i<n; i+=p) {
        dijkstra (i);
    }
    send results to master;
end
```

Fig. 1: Server algorithm for distributed Dijkstra

Assuming that all the processors in the DCS are more or less equally powerful, this static scheme of work distribution at run time provides automatic load balancing. Section 3 describes the hardware used for our experiments, which satisfies this assumption. Additionally, this scheme allows each server process to determine its own work load, and the master does not have to perform any task scheduling. At the end of its computation, a server process sends its result back to the master process. The master process collects all the results and puts them together into A which constitutes the final result.

2.2. Distributed Floyd's Algorithm

Floyd's sequential algorithm [Floy] initializes A to W, and conditionally updates this matrix in n^3 iterations. In the parallel version proposed in [JeSa], the A matrix is partitioned and each partition assigned to one of the multicomputer (hypercube) processors. It considers two partitioning schemes: by stripes and by rectangles. Their analysis and experiments indicate that partitioning by rectangles is slightly better than that by stripes for large graph sizes. The rectangular partitioning approach assumes that there are 2^d processors (which is always true for a hypercube). However, such an assumption can not be made for a general DCS. In a general DCS, partitioning by squares could lead to load imbalance situations, thus offsetting the advantage (if any) of lower communication costs for the rectangles partitioning scheme. Furthermore, the analysis of communication costs of the two partitioning approaches is based upon the architectural features of a hypercube, which will not hold for a general DCS.

The proposed distributed Floyd's algorithm therefore employs a partitioning by stripes scheme. That is, the master partitions the original A matrix (initialized to W) into p disjoint stripes, where p is the number of server processes. Each stripe consists of contiguous columns of

A. The master process then sends to each server process its corresponding stripe. Each server computes the values for its partition of A according to Floyd's sequential algorithm [Floy], communicating with the other servers as necessary, and sends its final updated partition of A back to the master.

Figure 2 gives the sub-algorithm executed by each server process of the proposed distributed Floyd's algorithm. Each server waits for its stripe to be sent by the master. Let A^q be the version of A at the start of iteration q. Each server updates its stripe values for $k = 0,...,(n-1)$ iterations. For this, it needs the corresponding segments of $A^{k-1}[i,k]$ and $A^{k-1}[k,j]$, where i and j are the row and column indices of its partition. As a result of the stripes partitioning approach, for each process, i varies between $0, \cdots, n-1$, and j has disjoint range values across the processes. Hence each process always has the segment $A^{k-1}[k,j]$ that it needs for its kth computation. Thus, it need only wait for the segment $A^{k-1}[i,k], i=0, \cdots, n-1$. Correspondingly, if a server process has a segment $A^{k-1}[i,k], i=0, \cdots, n-1$ (i.e., the kth column), it must broadcast this to all other server processes.

```
begin
   wait for striped partition of A;
   m = no. of columns in my stripe;
   beg_col = stripe's beginning col. no.;
   end_col = stripe's ending col. no.;
   for (k=0; k<n ; k++) {
      if ((k >= beg_col) && (k <=end_col)){
         broadcast kth col. to all other
         servers;
      }
      else {
         wait for the kth col. from another
         server;
      }
      update my stripe elements;
   }
   send results to master;
end
```

Fig. 2: Server algorithm for distributed Floyd

That is, for each iteration of k, every server needs the kth column of the A matrix. This column resides on exactly one server process, which will broadcast it to the other server processes. Thus each server enters a "broadcasting" phase for some contiguous values of k. During this phase, it broadcasts its columns, one column per iteration, interleaving that with the required computation to update its striped partition. For the remainder of its working time, it is in a "receiving" phase, when it does not have the required column and waits for that to be broadcast from the process that has it, and then updates its stripe. The widths (m in Figure 2) of stripes assigned to different servers may not be the same, since we are not making any assumptions about the number of processors in our DCS. This is discussed in more detail with respect to load balancing below.

Thus for the distributed Floyd's algorithm proposed here, unlike the case of distributed Dijkstra's algorithm discussed above, the server processes do not determine their respective work but are assigned work by the master; additionally, the server processes do not require the entire initial A matrix to perform their computations.

The work allocation scheme that is determined at run time (when the number of processes available is determined) is again aimed toward proper load balancing. If n is divisible by p, then each stripe has equal width. Otherwise, the server process that is located on the same processor as the master process is assigned the remaining columns. The underlying assumption here is that communication between processes on the same physical processor takes much less time than between those on physically different processors; thus the server process located on the same processor as the master process has more time to devote to computation. This ensures load balancing to a greater extent.

3. Experiment Design & Results

The distributed computing environment used was a network of IBM RISC System/6000 workstations connected via a 16 mbs token ring. Six of these workstations were used for our experiments. These six machines have comparable hardware and speed, thus no significant load imbalance is expected in program execution due to differences in the computing power of the machines, other factors aside. Of course, since these workstations were not used in dedicated mode (i.e., they could be running other jobs), deviations from expected performance could result. Although an attempt was made to use them at times when most of these were idle, one or more workstations could still be executing some other job(s). However, this situation is representative of a normal distributed computing system, and the results will reflect that.

A seventh workstation which was slower than the above six was used to investigate the gain in performance that could be achieved (with additional computing power) for larger problem sizes in spite of the resulting potential load imbalance. This would also highlight the importance of issues such as static versus dynamic scheduling, and load balancing.

This study was performed on ten graphs, with vertices ranging from 50 to 1000. These graphs were randomly generated, with a user-defined maximum on the weight of an edge. The probability of an edge between any two vertices was set at 0.5, with no self loops or negative edges allowed. An infinite edge weight between two vertices indicated no connection between them. Three different experiments were conducted: experiment with distributed Dijkstra, experiment with distributed Floyd, and experiment with the strictly sequential version of both the algorithms (to obtain speedup figures and derive further conclusions). The sequential implementations were run on one of the faster of the six processors used in our DCS.

PVM was used to establish a DCS with the number of processors ranging from 1 — 7. For all the experiments, a master process was started on one of the processors (the host processor), and it initiated server processes on all the processors (including itself), one server per processor. We will use p to refer to both the number of processors and the number of server processes.

As described in Section 2, the master sent the input data to all the server processes, and collected the results back from the servers. The time used to complete a distributed job included the time for sending the data to the servers, and receiving and putting together the partial results obtained from the servers. It should be noted here that for some studies in the literature, the time to send input information to the processors in a parallel/distributed environment is not included in the execution time; for example, for parallel Dijkstra's algorithms discussed in [KuSi], it is assumed that the input data is already available on all the processors. Thus, the distributed execution times (or parallel time, as we will sometimes refer to it as) reported in our experiments represent an upper bound; often the data may be available at the server processes as a result of another computation and need not be distributed by a master process.

Table 1 shows the results obtained from our experiments. The first three columns give the example number, the number of vertices in the graph, n, and the number of processors used, p. The next two columns state the times taken (in msecs.) by distributed Dijkstra, T_{Dp}, and distributed Floyd, T_{Fp}. The time taken for the value of $p=1$ is that for using one worker process under the PVM paradigm, and not the time for the sequential algorithm. Since Floyd's sequential algorithm is considered to be the best sequential algorithm [JeSa] for the all-pairs shortest path problem, it is used in our speedup calculations. The sixth column gives the time taken (in msecs.) by the sequential Floyd's algorithm, T_{F1}. The last two columns state the speedups obtained by distributed Dijkstra, S_{Dp} and distributed Floyd, S_{Fp}. The speedups are calculated as follows:

$$\text{Speedup of distributed Dijkstra} = S_{Dp} = \frac{T_{F1}}{T_{Dp}}$$

$$\text{Speedup of distributed Floyd} = S_{Fp} = \frac{T_{F1}}{T_{Fp}}$$

For distributed Dijkstra, the results demonstrate the advantage of distributed computing for all the examples, the results differing in the best choice for the number of processors (giving least execution time) to use. For the smallest graph (Ex. 1), using three processors results in a smaller execution time than using either one or two. Thus the communication costs in distributing the input to the three processors and getting the results back is not large enough to offset the gain obtained from dividing the computational load per processor by three. As the number of processors is further increased, communication costs predominate and the execution time increases. For Ex. 2, using four processors seems to be the optimal choice.

For the remainder of the graphs (Ex. 3 — Ex. 10), the advantage of a DCS becomes significantly evident. As the number of processors is increased from one to six, the execution time decreases rapidly and is the best for the case of six processors. For instance, for Ex. 7, the time taken on four processors (61228 msecs) is about half that on two processors (119503 msecs.), and the time taken on six processors (44379 msecs) is a little greater than one-third of that on two processors. Hence, for these graphs, the amount of computation per processor is large enough to partially offset the communication cost.

For the medium and large graphs, the seventh (slower) processor was also included in the experiments to examine any performance vs. load imbalance tradeoffs. The table includes parallel times with seven processors for all the examples for the sake of completeness. Adding a slower seventh processor still yields performance benefits and the execution time decreases further for most of the larger graphs. However, this decrease in execution time is not as large as when p was increased from 3 to 4 (say). This is to be expected, since the seventh processor is slower, and load imbalance occurs. Consistent with this conjecture, it was observed during this experiment that the worker process on the seventh processor was typically the last one to send results back to the master.

For distributed Floyd, for Ex. 1 and Ex. 2, the execution time typically increases as the number of processors is increased — this indicates that the communication costs incurred far exceed any advantage obtained from dividing the computation among two or more processors for these graph sizes. As the graph size is increased, for Ex. 3 — Ex. 6, when the number of processors is increased from 1 to 6, the execution time first decreases, and then starts increasing. As the number of processors is initially increased, the advantage of dividing the computation among multiple processors offsets part of the communication cost, thus decreasing the parallel time. However, as the number of processors is further increased, the amount of computation per processor decreases, and communication costs predominate, increasing execution time. Thus for instance, using four processors seems to be the best choice for Ex. 4. For Ex. 7 — Ex. 10, the parallel time decreases with increasing number of processors. For these graphs, the benefit from decreasing the amount of computation per processor significantly dominates the communication costs, and as in the case of distributed Dijkstra, the need for (and advantage of) a DCS becomes evident. For instance for Ex. 8, using four processors (67930 msecs.) instead of two (120265 msecs.) reduces the execution time by almost half.

Table 1: Experimental Results

Ex.	n	p	T_{Dp} (msec.)	T_{Fp} (msec.)	T_{F1} (msec.)	S_{Dp}	S_{Fp}
1	50	1	293.7	476.0	62.6	0.21	0.13
		2	282.6	726.0		0.22	0.09
		3	229.6	878.7		0.27	0.07
		4	315.7	823.3		0.20	0.08
		5	300.0	1072.4		0.21	0.06
		6	319.9	1416.7		0.20	0.04
		7	298.9	1611.9		0.21	0.04
2	100	1	991.8	1186.4	513.6	0.52	0.43
		2	832.9	1377.8		0.62	0.37
		3	790.4	1698.4		0.65	0.30
		4	655.2	2030.4		0.78	0.25
		5	928.5	2381.4		0.55	0.22
		6	1012.9	2788.4		0.51	0.18
		7	1198.7	3247.6		0.43	0.16
3	200	1	7107.2	5718.4	4098.5	0.58	0.72
		2	4875.3	4631.9		0.84	0.89
		3	3446.9	4464.5		1.19	0.92
		4	3012.1	4529.7		1.36	0.90
		5	2627.6	5245.3		1.56	0.78
		6	2558.8	5649.3		1.60	0.73
		7	2581.0	6468.1		1.59	0.63
4	300	1	22742.7	16713.5	13833.3	0.61	0.83
		2	15323.9	11636.6		0.90	1.19
		3	10684.7	10065.7		1.30	1.37
		4	8628.4	8956.5		1.60	1.55
		5	7451.3	9740.2		1.86	1.42
		6	6584.4	10272.4		2.10	1.35
		7	7000.6	11282.8		1.98	1.23
5	400	1	53103.6	37100.3	34507.2	0.65	0.93
		2	42339.4	25043.1		0.82	1.38
		3	28073.5	19605.8		1.23	1.76
		4	21318.2	17337.2		1.62	1.99
		5	17646.2	17439.0		1.96	1.98
		6	14741.1	17526.4		2.34	1.97
		7	14353.1	18902.8		2.40	1.83
6	500	1	103257.1	69023.1	66877.0	0.65	0.97
		2	68537.1	45692.6		0.98	1.46
		3	47121.3	34602.2		1.42	1.93
		4	36888.5	28715.6		1.81	2.33
		5	30855.3	28929.6		2.17	2.31
		6	26280.6	28207.9		2.55	2.37
		7	26038.2	28753.2		2.57	2.34
7	600	1	177455.3	118022.8	111065.7	0.63	0.94
		2	119503.0	78162.9		0.93	1.42
		3	80661.2	56718.2		1.38	1.96
		4	61228.1	45890.6		1.81	2.42
		5	52386.2	42136.1		2.12	2.64
		6	44379.3	40274.2		2.50	2.76
		7	42976.8	40640.5		2.58	2.73

Table 1: Experimental Results (cont'd)

Ex.	n	p	T_{Dp} (msec.)	T_{Fp} (msec.)	T_{F1} (msec.)	S_{Dp}	S_{Fp}
8	700	1	281016.6	183534.6	176362.3	0.63	0.96
		2	189095.7	120265.7		0.93	1.47
		3	127050.7	87375.4		1.39	2.02
		4	95937.2	67930.0		1.84	2.60
		5	81166.1	62400.1		2.17	2.83
		6	69074.9	58134.1		2.55	3.03
		7	66299.8	56763.3		2.66	3.11
9	800	1	417392.9	270617.0	264727.0	0.63	0.98
		2	276712.8	178299.7		0.96	1.49
		3	188146.8	128889.8		1.41	2.05
		4	144489.6	99992.2		1.83	2.65
		5	119613.9	89996.8		2.21	2.94
		6	101008.1	82564.0		2.62	3.21
		7	96760.2	81501.4		2.74	3.25
10	1000	1	816443.0	518292.3	512738.9	0.63	0.99
		2	547191.5	344128.2		0.94	1.49
		3	364147.0	244169.2		1.41	2.10
		4	275319.3	188471.9		1.86	2.72
		5	225246.7	168332.0		2.28	3.05
		6	193538.9	151311.3		2.65	3.39
		7	181228.4	145933.7		2.83	3.51

Comparing the execution times for the two proposed solutions, we see that distributed Floyd stabilizes (in terms of reducing execution time with increasing number of processors) at a larger graph size than distributed Dijkstra does. That is, the benefits of distributing Floyd's algorithm start materializing at a larger graph size than for distributing Dijkstra's algorithm. However, once this occurs, the execution time of distributed Floyd becomes typically less than the corresponding execution time of distributed Dijkstra. For distributed Dijkstra, execution time starts decreasing monotonically with increasing number of processors from Ex. 3 onwards, whereas for distributed Floyd, this happens from Ex. 6 onwards. For Ex. 7 onwards, the execution time for distributed Floyd is always less than that for distributed Dijkstra for $p=1,\cdots,6$.

Floyd's distributed algorithm is characterized by an overlap of computation and communication between the processors. Thus adding a slower processor to the system would be expected to cause greater load imbalance than in the case of distributed Dijkstra. The results in column 5 of the table demonstrate this point. In this case, adding a seventh (slower) processor to the DCS becomes advantageous only for the three largest graphs considered in this study.

In the case of distributed Dijkstra, adding a slower processor has the effect that the slower processor takes a longer time to perform its share of computation, leading to this processor sending the results back later than the other processors. For distributed Floyd, since part of the computation on each of the processor depends on the results from the slower processor, a worker on a faster processor may end up waiting for the results from the slower one. Using load balancing techniques could make the performance better with a slower processor in the system for both the distributed algorithms. However, it is not clear whether the overhead of dynamic load balancing would not overshadow any advantages obtained from it for examples in the graph size range considered in this study. Clearly, for larger problem sizes, load balancing would improve the performance of both the distributed algorithms in a DCS containing processors with significantly different processing power.

We thus see the advantages of using a DCS to solve even small to medium sized instances for the all-pairs shortest path problem. We will now assess each algorithm in terms of the traditional parallel processing performance metric, speedup. The calculation of speedup (as explained above) for the two algorithms, given in the last two columns of Table 1, demonstrate that reasonably good performance benefits are achieved by the proposed algorithms. Distributed Dijkstra yields speedups in the range 2 — 3 with 6 processors for most of the examples. This is a desirable figure in light of the relatively slow communication hardware, and the non-dedicated mode of workstations used in our DCS. Also, it must be kept in mind that its execution time is being compared to the sequential time of Floyd's algorithm. Distributed Floyd yields speedups in the range of 2 — 3.5 with 6 processors once it stabilizes, thus giving better speedup values than distributed

(a) $n = 200$

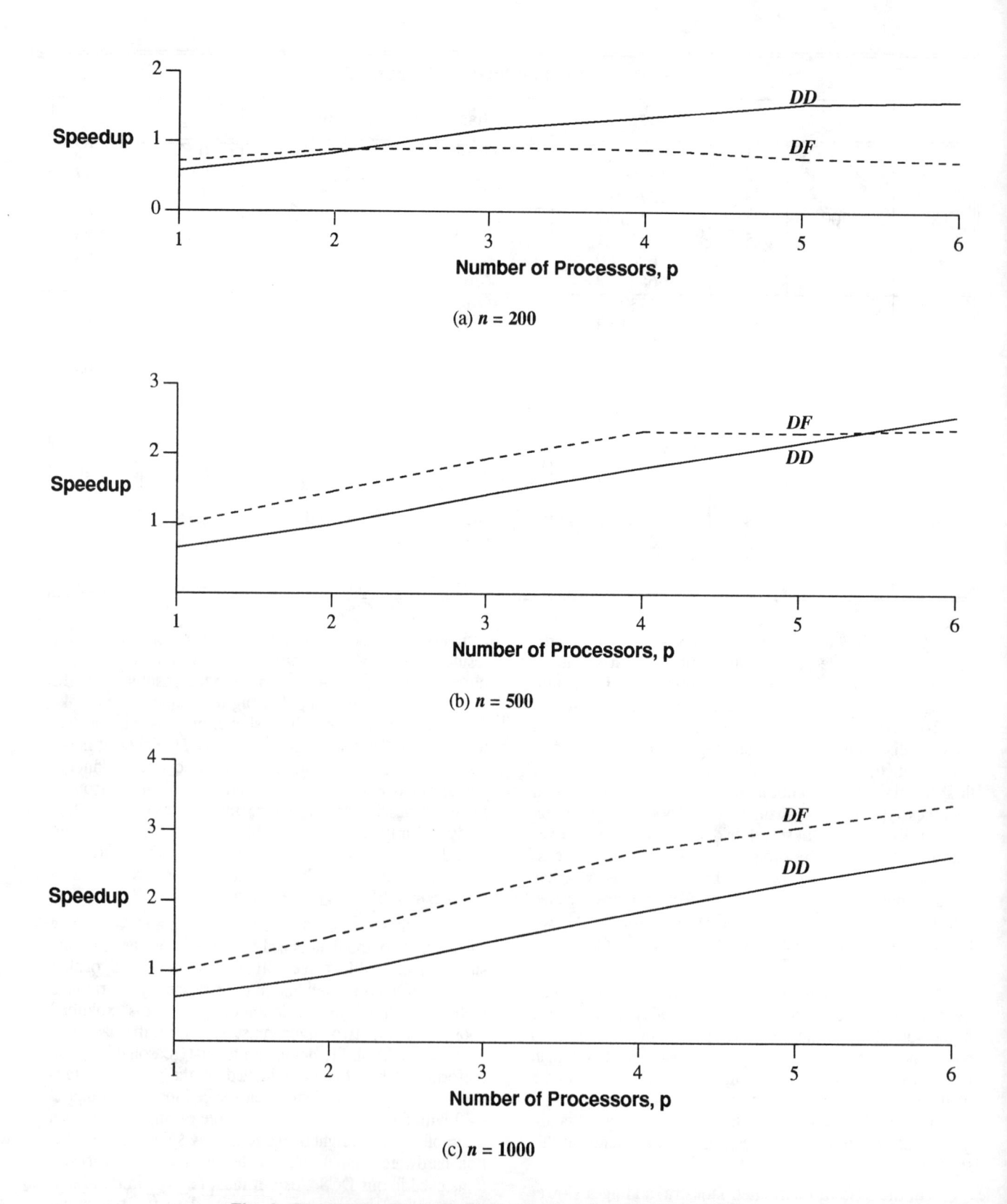

(b) $n = 500$

(c) $n = 1000$

Fig. 3: Distributed Dijkstra (DD) VS. Distributed Floyd (DF).

Dijkstra. It must be noted that these sequential times are for a workstation in a dedicated mode (i.e. not running any other jobs) as opposed to our DCS where the workstations were used in a non-dedicated mode.

Additionally, the workstation chosen for the sequential algorithms was a faster one among the six used in our study. These times degraded, sometimes significantly, when run on one of the slower of the six. For instance for Ex. 6, sequential Floyd took 97,803 msecs. on the slower machine as opposed to 66,877 msecs. given in the table.

These speedup figures can be used to further compare the two distributed algorithms. For the smaller graphs (Ex. 1 — Ex. 4), distributed Dijkstra typically yields better speedup values (lower execution times) than distributed Floyd. As the graph size increases, distributed Floyd catches up with distributed Dijkstra and soon starts giving better speedup values (lower execution time) than distributed Dijkstra. This comparison is illustrated in Figure 3(a) where the speedups for the two algorithms are plotted for Ex. 3, in Figure 3(b) where Ex. 6 is considered, and in Figure 3(c) which plots these values for Ex. 10.

Thus, we see that properly designed distributed algorithms can yield good performance benefits in a DCS in spite of its various constraints. We see that the benefits obtained from a reduction in computation per processor in a suitably designed algorithm quickly dominates the communication costs of a distributed computing environment. A speedup of about 3.0 with 6 processors is a very desirable figure, given the DCS on which the experiments were performed. And adding additional (albeit slower) hardware to get better execution times (although not as good a speedup figure) is desirable too. One of the objectives of DCSs is to reduce execution time by stealing idle cycles. In most industrial situations, problem sizes are significantly larger than the ones considered in this study and thus require execution times in the order of hours and days. In such a scenario, while good speedup is definitely a desirable objective, reducing the execution time as much as possible with the use of inexpensive hardware is probably a more desirable one.

4. Conclusions

In this paper, we considered distributed solutions to the all-pairs shortest path problem. The results demonstrated that designing a distributed algorithm which minimizes communication costs can yield significant performance benefits. For medium sized graphs considered in this study, speedups in the range 2 — 3 were observed for distributed Dijkstra's algorithm, and in the range 2 — 4 were observed for distributed Floyd's algorithm with six processors in the DCS. These are desirable speedup figures, even for a parallel environment.

The two distributed algorithms proposed here differ in their communication and computation patterns. Thus we get two different perspectives for distributed algorithm design for the same problem, with respect to issues such as the ratio of computation time to communication time, work allocation among the processors, and load balancing.

References

[ArCo] E. Arjomandi and D. Corneil, "Parallel Computations in Graph Theory," *SIAM Journal of Computing*, 7(2), 1978, pp. 230 — 236.

[BDGM] A. Beguelin et al, "A User's Guide to PVM Parallel Virtual Machines," *ORNL/TM-11826*, July 1991.

[DePL] N. Deo, C. Pang and R. Lord, "Two Parallel Algorithms for Shortest Path Problems," *Proc., Int'l Conf. on Parallel Processing*, 1980, pp. 244 — 253.

[Dijk] E. Dijkstra, "A Note on Two Problems in Connexion with Graphs," *Numerische Mithematik*, 1, 1959, pp. 269 — 271.

[Floy] R. W. Floyd, "Algorithm 97: Shortest Path," *Communications of the ACM*, 5, 1962, pp. 345.

[FrRu] A. Frieze and L. Rudolph, "A Parallel Algorithm for All Pairs Shortest Paths in a Random Graph," *Proc., 22nd Allerton Conf.*, 1984, pp. 663 — 670.

[JeSa] J. Jenq and S. Sahni, "All Pairs Shortest Paths on a Hypercube Multiprocessor," *Proc., Int'l. Conf. on Parallel Processing*, 1987, pp. 713 — 716.

[KuSi] V. Kumar and V. Singh, "Scalability of Parallel Algorithms for the All-Pairs Shortest Path Problem: A Summary of Results," *Proc., Int'l Conf. on Parallel Processing*, 1990, pp. III-136 — III-140.

[Lakh] G. Lakhani, "An Improved Distribution Algorithm for Shortest Path Problem," *IEEE Transactions on Computers*, C-33, 1984, pp. 855 — 857.

[PaKr] R. Paige and C. Kruskal, "Parallel Algorithms for Shortest Path Problems," *Int'l. Conf. on Parallel Processing*, 1985, pp. 14 — 20.

[QuYo] M. Quinn and Y. Yoo, "The Efficient Solution of Graph Theoretic Problems on Tightly-coupled MIMD Computers," *Proc., Int'l Conf. on Parallel Processing*, 1984, pp. 431 — 438.

[Sava] C. Savage, "Parallel Algorithms for Graph Theoretic Problems," *Ph.D. Thesis*, Univ. of Illinois, Urbana, August, 1977.

SESSION 6B:
Scheduling and Load Balancing

Ian Akyildiz, Chair

Distributed Control Methods

Brian Tung*

Computer Science Department
University of California, Los Angeles
Los Angeles, CA 90024

Leonard Kleinrock

Computer Science Deparment
University of California, Los Angeles
Los Angeles, CA 90024

Abstract

The distributed system is becoming increasingly popular, and this produces the need for more sophisticated distributed control techniques. In this paper, we present a method for distributed control using simple finite state automata. Each of the distributed entities is "controlled" by its associated automaton, in the sense that the entity examines the state of the automaton to determine its behavior. The result of the collective behavior of all of the entities is fed back to the automata, which change their state as a result of this feedback. We give a new method of analysis which derives the steady state behavior of this system as a whole, by decomposing it into two parts: describing and solving an imbedded auxiliary Markov chain, and analyzing the behavior of the system within each of the states of this auxiliary chain.

Key Words: *distributed algorithms, finite state automata, Markov chain, queueing theory, state aggregation*

1 Introduction

With the advent of powerful workstations, we have migrated from the centralized paradigm popular in the era of the large mainframe to a distributed paradigm that takes advantage of many cooperating processors available at a lower total cost. With this change, many new and exciting research problems have arisen in distributed systems. Typically, these problems, such as distributed communication and robot coordination, require the cooperation of several entities in performing a single task with little or no medium for control communication.

These problems have a common theme. In each, we wish a collection of entities to cooperate on a task which is most easily controlled centrally (that is, from "outside" the system). We would like the entities to perform this task without outside control, or in some cases, even without outside presence. We desire a self-contained control mechanism, capable of producing cooperation in the entities, with only a simple command from outside. In this paper, we develop such an efficient control scheme with the use of simple automata associated with each entity. These automata independently guide the entities, and take into account feedback that captures the composite effect of all the entities' actions.

Let us introduce this scheme with a simple game, called the Goore Game by Tsetlin, who describes it in [8]. Imagine that we have many players, none of whom are aware of the others, and a referee. Every hour, the referee asks each player to vote yes or no, then counts up the yes and no answers. A reward probability $r = r(f)$ is generated as a function of the fraction f of the players who voted yes. We assume that $0 \leq r(f) \leq 1$. A typical function is shown in Figure 1. Each player, regardless of how he voted, is

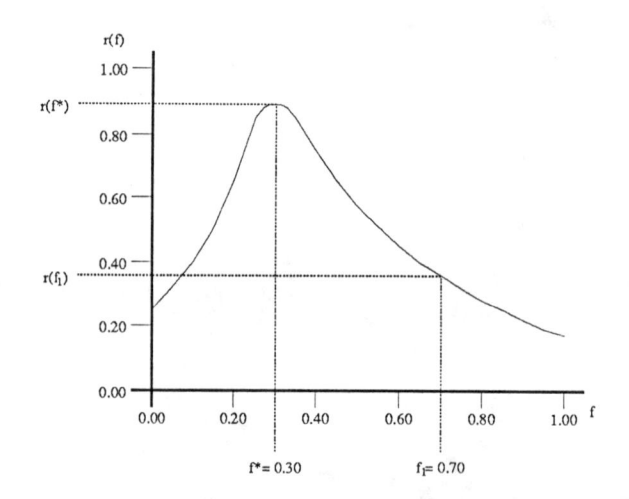

Figure 1: Typical Reward Function.

then independently rewarded (with probability r) or penalized (with probability $1-r$). For instance, let us suppose that at some point, the fraction of players voting yes was f_1. Then, the reward probability would be $r(f_1)$. Each player is then rewarded with probability $r(f_1)$. Note that the maximum of the example function occurs at $f^* = 0.3$. We can show the following: no matter how many players there are, we can construct automata such that exactly f^* of them (in this case, 0.3) vote yes—after enough trials—with a probability arbitrarily close to one. This property holds no matter what characteristics the function has—whether or not it is discontinuous, multimodal, etc. Note further that

---

*This work was supported by the Defense Advanced Research Projects Agency under grant MDA-972-91-J-1011, Advanced Networking and Distributed Systems.

the individual automata know neither the fraction f nor the reward function $r(f)$.

Moreover, each player plays solely in a greedy fashion, each time voting the way that seems to give that player the best payoff. This is somewhat unexpected. Greed affects outcomes in an unpredictable manner. An example of greed leading to significantly suboptimal outcomes is the famous prisoner's dilemma [3]. In this scenario, two entities (the prisoners) greedily optimize their own behavior, but together they produce (for them) a globally suboptimal result. This effect is common in greedy solutions. However, we will see that the method used here does not have this property, because the players do not attempt to predict the behavior of the other players. Instead, each player performs by trial and error, and simply preferentially repeats those actions which produce the best result for that player.

Most of the control and coordination tasks in distributed systems cannot be taken care of in a straightforward manner, because the distributed systems have no leader, or anything of the sort—in fact, that's what makes them distributed! Even if they did, it would be hard to get a list of assigned tasks to all the members efficiently. Consider, for instance, the problem of communication on an Ethernet. It would be convenient if some machine could be given the task of asking every other machine if they had anything to say, and then drawing up a list of machines to transmit in order. However, there is no such machine in a distributed system. One could be elected somehow, *then* the lists could be generated and distributed. Unfortunately, the medium to be used for electing a leader and distributing the transmission lists is the communication channel itself! The very resource being used to do the allocation is also the resource that is being allocated. It would be helpful if the machines could organize themselves without explicitly communicating the lists to each other. The method outlined here allows them to do that.

In this paper, we examine the principles involved in stochastically "guiding" *one* automaton. We give a method that allows us to approximate the performance of these automata as a whole, without going into the exhaustive detail about their individual behavior that would render an analysis intractable.

2 Single Automaton Behavior

The automaton design we considerrelies on the same paradigm described for the Goore Game; that is, automata perform by trial and error in an attempt to maximize some reward probability. This is usually most applicable in the instance of many automata, but we first examine the single automaton case. This will form the basis of our examination of the many automata case in the next section.

Consider a single finite state automaton which is capable of two actions (outputs) A_0 or A_1. Suppose that every second, the current output is examined by an external agent, and based on that action, a reward probability is determined. If the output is A_0, the reward probability is $r = r_0$, and if the output is A_1, the reward probability is $r = r_1$. With probability r, the automaton is then rewarded; with probability $1-r$, it is penalized. The automaton may then change its state as a result of its reward (or penalty). The cycle is continually repeated: the automaton chooses either A_0 or A_1, the corresponding reward probability is determined, and the automaton is rewarded or penalized, etc. The automaton only knows that it takes some action, which in some way affects whether it receives a reward or a penalty. What sort of design can be postulated for an automaton that performs better than one that chooses A_0 or A_1 randomly with probability 1/2 each time?

One possible design is as follows. (This automaton is called $\mathcal{L}_{2,2}$ in [8].) Let the automaton have two states, 1 and -1. If the current state is -1, the automaton chooses A_0; if it is 1, it chooses A_1. If a reward results, the automaton stays in the same state; if a penalty results, it moves to the other state. Suppose that r_0 and r_1 are 0.4 and 0.8, respectively. Below, we show that this automaton, over the long run, will choose A_1 three times as often as A_0, regardless of which state it starts in. Note that this results in an average reward probability of 0.7, which exceeds the random choice whose average reward probability would be 0.6.

The equilibrium behavior of the automaton can be modeled as a Markov chain, where the external reward is transformed into an internal transition probability. Define π_i ($i = -1, 1$) to be the steady state probability of finding the automaton in state i. Then, we get

$$\pi_1(1 - r_1) = \pi_{-1}(1 - r_0) \qquad (1)$$

which in this example yields

$$0.2\pi_1 = 0.6\pi_{-1}$$

Since these are the only two states, we can also write that

$$\pi_1 + \pi_{-1} = 1$$

which gives us $\pi_1 = 0.75$ and $\pi_{-1} = 1 - 0.75 = 0.25$.

If the automaton has more than two states, the limiting proportion of time that the automaton chooses A_1 (in this example) increases and approaches unity asymptotically (which would yield an average reward probability of 0.8). Suppose that we have $2n$ states, $\{i, -i \mid 1 \leq i \leq n\}$. If the current state is negative, the automaton chooses A_0; if it is positive, it chooses A_1. If a reward results, the automaton stays in states n or $-n$ if it is in either of those states; otherwise, it moves from state i to $i+1$ if i is positive, or from i to $i-1$ if i is negative. If a penalty results, the automaton moves from state 1 to -1 or *vice versa*, if it is in one of those states; otherwise, it moves from state i to $i-1$ if i is positive, or from i to $i+1$ if i is negative. In general, the automaton moves away from the center if it wins, and toward the center if it loses. This behavior is summarized in Figure 2.

The equilibrium behavior of this automaton can also be modeled as a Markov chain. The resulting balance equations give us the following.

$$\pi_i = \pi_1 \left(\frac{r_1}{1-r_1}\right)^{i-1} = \pi_1 \varphi_1^{i-1}, \quad i > 1$$

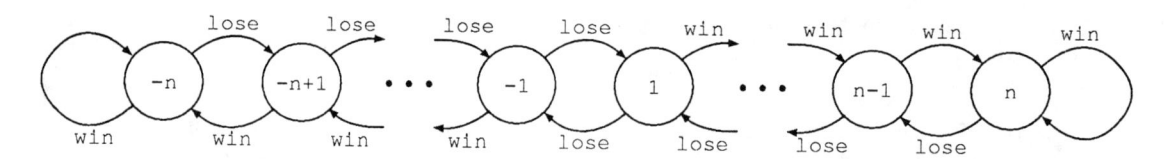

Figure 2: Automaton Design.

$$\pi_{-i} = \pi_{-1} \left(\frac{r_0}{1-r_0}\right)^{i-1} = \pi_{-1}\varphi_0^{i-1}, \quad i > 1$$

where $\varphi_0 = r_0/(1-r_0)$ and $\varphi_1 = r_1/(1-r_1)$. This in turn yields

$$\sum_{i=1}^{n} \pi_i = \pi_1 \cdot \frac{1-\varphi_1^n}{1-\varphi_1} \qquad (2)$$

$$\sum_{i=1}^{n} \pi_{-i} = \pi_{-1} \cdot \frac{1-\varphi_0^n}{1-\varphi_0} \qquad (3)$$

$$\pi_1(1-r_1) = \pi_{-1}(1-r_0) \qquad (4)$$

Knowing again that the probabilities sum to 1, we can write

$$\sum_{i=1}^{n} \pi_i + \sum_{i=1}^{n} \pi_{-i} = 1$$

$$\pi_1 \cdot \frac{1-\varphi_1^n}{1-\varphi_1} + \pi_{-1} \cdot \frac{1-\varphi_0^n}{1-\varphi_0} = 1$$

$$\pi_1 \left(\frac{1-\varphi_1^n}{1-\varphi_1} + \frac{1-r_1}{1-r_0} \cdot \frac{1-\varphi_0^n}{1-\varphi_0}\right) = 1$$

$$\pi_1 = \left(\frac{1-\varphi_1^n}{1-\varphi_1} + \frac{1-r_1}{1-r_0} \cdot \frac{1-\varphi_0^n}{1-\varphi_0}\right)^{-1} \qquad (5)$$

Substituting the values $r_1 = 0.8$ and $r_0 = 0.4$ in the above equations yields that the equilibrium probability of choosing A_1 is

$$\Pr(A_1) = \sum_{i=1}^{n} \pi_i = \frac{4^n - 1}{2 - 3(2/3)^n + 4^n} \qquad (6)$$

This probability goes to 1 as $n \to \infty$. In fact, for any r_0, r_1, such that $r_1 > r_0$, equations 2 and 5 together show that the probability of choosing A_1 goes to 1 as $n \to \infty$. Similarly, if $r_0 < r_1$, the probability of choosing A_1 goes to 0 as $n \to \infty$. Simply put, as the memory size gets larger, the automaton chooses the best option with increasing certainty.

In this example, there is only one automaton attempting to behave optimally. If, instead, the reward probability is a function of the *aggregate* behavior of many automata, is it possible to design the automata such that similarly expedient behavior results, even if none of the automata may communicate directly with each other? This is what we examine in the next section.

3 Multiple Automata Behavior

In this section, we consider what happens when we have many automata, interacting only through the reward function. Specifically, the automata are rewarded based on the *fraction* of automata performing a certain action, and not on the *particular* automata performing that action. We wish to find the proportion of time that k of N automata perform a certain action. Hopefully, if we design the automata properly, they will collectively behave in a way such that they spend a large fraction of time near the maximum reward point.

Consider a population of N automata, $\{\alpha_1, \alpha_2, \ldots, \alpha_N\}$, each capable of exactly one of two actions, A_0 or A_1, at discrete moments in time ($t = 0, 1, 2, \ldots$). We call this population a *system of automata*. For all m, $1 \leq m \leq N$, let the output of automaton α_m at time t be represented by $A_{u_m(t)}$. Also, let $a(t)$ represent the number of automata with output A_1 and $f(t)$ the fraction of automata with output A_1 at time t. That is,

$$a(t) = \sum_{m=1}^{N} u_m(t) \qquad (7)$$

and

$$f(t) = \frac{1}{N}a(t) \qquad (8)$$

For each moment t, we compute a reward probability $r = r(f)$ whose value depends solely on the fraction $f = f(t)$ ($f = 0, 1/N, 2/N, \ldots, 1$). Each automaton then independently receives a stimulus $x_m(t)$, which is a binary valued (reward) random variable. It is either a reward (with probability r), or a penalty (with probability $1-r$). We assume that the automata know nothing of the reward function r or even of the existence of other automata.

Clearly, there exists a k^* such that $r(k^*/N) \geq r(k/N)$ for all k. Assume that k^* is unique. Let us find the limiting proportion of time that $a(t) = k^*$. First, define $\Phi(k)$ to be the limiting proportion of time that k automata have output A_1; that is,

$$\Phi(k) = \lim_{T \to \infty} \frac{1}{T} \sum_{t=0}^{T-1} \zeta(a(t), k) \qquad (9)$$

where the indicator $\zeta(x, y)$ is defined by $\zeta(x, y) = 1$ if $x = y$, and 0 otherwise. We then ask: is it possible to design (finite state) automata in such a way that $\Phi(k^*)$ can be made arbitrarily close to 1? The answer is yes, although the behavior of the population is rather complex. The problem of the behavior in this context, essentially the Goore Game, has been examined by Tsetlin [8], but he only describes the construction and behavior of the automata, and does not develop a general method of analysis.

The automaton we use is the one defined in the previous section; the state diagram is displayed in Figure 2. The automaton is characterized by the memory size n—this size will be assumed to be the same for all automata in the population. For all m and t, let $s_m(t)$ be the state of automaton α_m at time t. We map states to outputs in a straightforward way. If $s_m(t) < 0$, then $u_m(t) = 0$; otherwise, $u_m(t) = 1$. The automaton is said to be *linear* [8]; that is, state transitions occur only between adjacent states, except for the self loops at the ends of the state space (n and $-n$). We use the mapping δ, where $\delta(s_m(t), x_m(t)) = s_m(t+1)$, to indicate that $s_m(t+1)$ is the state that results for automaton α_m when it is in state $s_m(t)$ and is subject to a stimulus (reward) $x_m(t)$.

We call this scheme the Goore Scheme. The motivation is to encourage behavior that produces a positive reward and to discourage behavior that produces a negative reward, that is, a penalty. We will show that for any population size N, it is always possible, with an appropriately large memory size n, to make $\Phi(k^*)$ arbitrarily close to 1.

Before we do so, however, let us consider the behavior of the system as the memory size of the automata and the number of automata increase without bound. Borovikov and Bryzgalov [1] show that when $n = 1$, that is, when the automata each have two states, the behavior is not optimal in the long run; in fact, with probability one, $f(t)$ approaches $1/2$ in the limit as $N, t \to \infty$. This is undesirable since it does not depend on the nature of the reward function; the reward function might even have a minimum at $f = 1/2$! Their demonstration of this result uses transforms, and like any such demonstration, their analysis cannot easily be related back to the original physical situation. Therefore, we show this result intuitively as follows.

Lemma 1 *Suppose that the memory size for each automaton is $n = 1$. Suppose further that there exists some number $\Delta r > 0$ such that $\Delta r \leq r(f) \leq 1 - \Delta r$ for all f. Let $f_0 = \lim_{t \to \infty} f(t)$. Then $\lim_{N \to \infty} f_0 = 1/2$.*

Sketch of Proof As N increases without bound, it suffices to describe the entire set of automata with a single fraction $f(t)$. Associated with this fraction is a reward probability $r(f(t))$. From this probability we can derive the fraction $f(t+1)$.

$$f(t+1) = r(f(t))f(t) + (1 - r(f(t)))(1 - f(t)) \quad (10)$$

Suppose that $f(t) > 1/2$. Using the law of large numbers, we may assume that as N goes to infinity, the fraction of automata rewarded goes to *exactly* $r(f(t))$. The fraction $f(t+1)$ consists of the portion of $f(t)$ that was rewarded and the portion of $1 - f(t)$

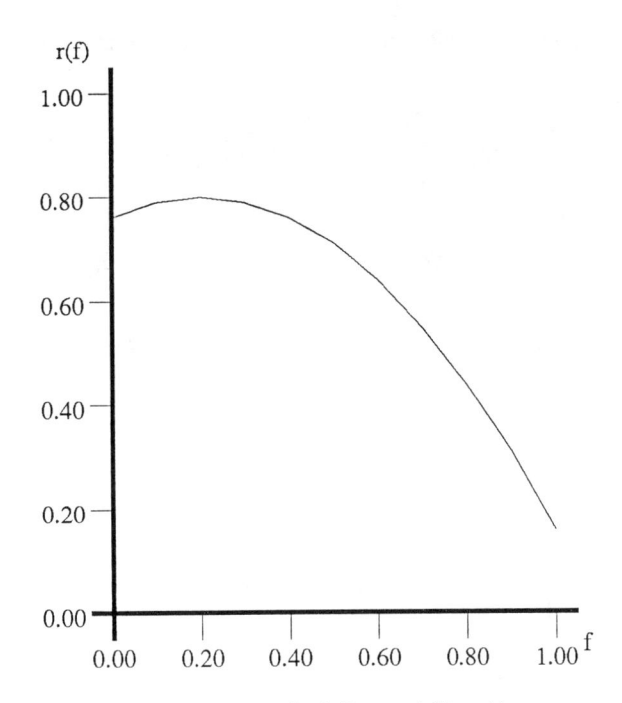

Figure 3: Example 1 Reward Function.

that was penalized. Since $f(t) > 1/2$, we know that $f(t) > 1 - f(t)$, and therefore,

$$\begin{aligned} f(t+1) &= r(f(t))f(t) + (1 - \Delta r)(1 - f(t)) \\ &\quad - (r(f(t)) - \Delta r)(1 - f(t)) \\ &\geq r(f(t))f(t) + (1 - \Delta r)(1 - f(t)) \\ &\quad - (r(f(t)) - \Delta r)f(t) \\ &= \Delta r f(t) + (1 - \Delta r)(1 - f(t)) \end{aligned}$$

or

$$f(t+1) \geq 1 - f(t) + (2\Delta r f(t) - \Delta r)$$

Again, since $1 - f(t) < f(t)$, we also get (by a similar argument)

$$f(t+1) \leq (1 - \Delta r)f(t) + \Delta r(1 - f(t))$$

or

$$f(t+1) \leq f(t) - (2\Delta r f(t) - \Delta r)$$

In summary, from the condition on $r(f)$, we see that

$$1 - f(t) + (2\Delta r f(t) - \Delta r) \leq f(t+1)$$
$$\leq f(t) - (2\Delta r f(t) - \Delta r)$$

Therefore, we can conclude

$$\frac{|f(t+1) - 1/2|}{|f(t) - 1/2|} \leq 1 - \frac{\Delta r(2f(t) - 1)}{(f(t) - 1/2)} = 1 - 2\Delta r \quad (11)$$

On the other hand, suppose that $f(t) < 1/2$. Then, by the condition on $r(f)$, we can say that

$$f(t) + (\Delta r - 2\Delta r f(t)) \leq f(t+1)$$
$$\leq 1 - f(t) - (\Delta r - 2\Delta r f(t))$$

by analogy to the above analysis. Again, we can conclude

$$\frac{|f(t+1) - 1/2|}{|f(t) - 1/2|} \leq 1 - \frac{\Delta r(2f(t) - 1)}{(f(t) - 1/2)} = 1 - 2\Delta r \quad (12)$$

Suppose finally that $f(t) = 1/2$. Then,

$$f(t+1) = (1/2)(r(1/2) + 1 - r(1/2)) = 1/2 \quad (13)$$

No matter what value $f(t)$ takes, $f(t+1)$ is closer to $1/2$ by at least a factor of $1 - 2\Delta r$. Therefore, $\lim_{N \to \infty} f_0 = 1/2$ (and the convergence factor is $2\Delta r$). □

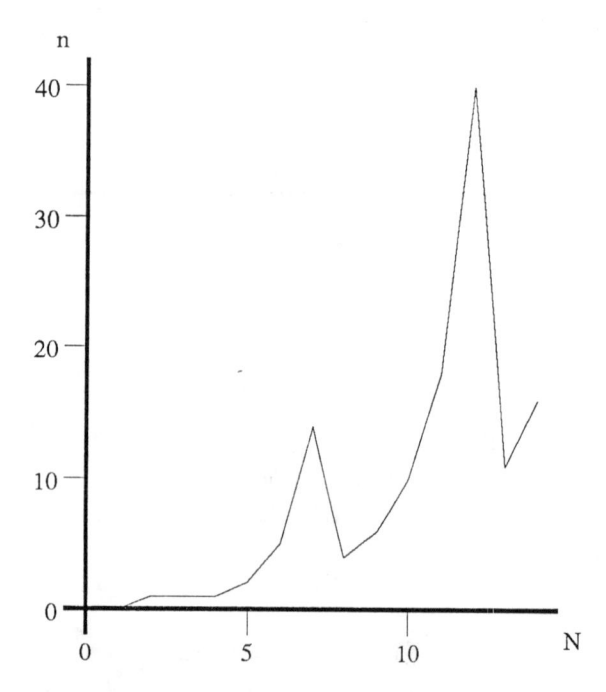

Figure 4: Increasing Memory Requirement To Maintain $\Phi(k^*) \geq 0.3$.

The corresponding exact analysis for $n > 1$ is extremely complex. However, based on simulations, and on the conclusions from the approximate analysis below in Section 3.1, we propose the following conjectures.

Conjecture 1 *For any value of N, there exists a value n_0 such that for all $n \geq n_0$,*

$$\lim_{t \to \infty} |f(t) - f^*| < \epsilon$$

This is to be distinguished from the similar

Conjecture 2 *For any value of n, there exists a value N_0 such that for all $N \geq N_0$,*

$$\lim_{t \to \infty} |f(t) - 1/2| < \epsilon$$

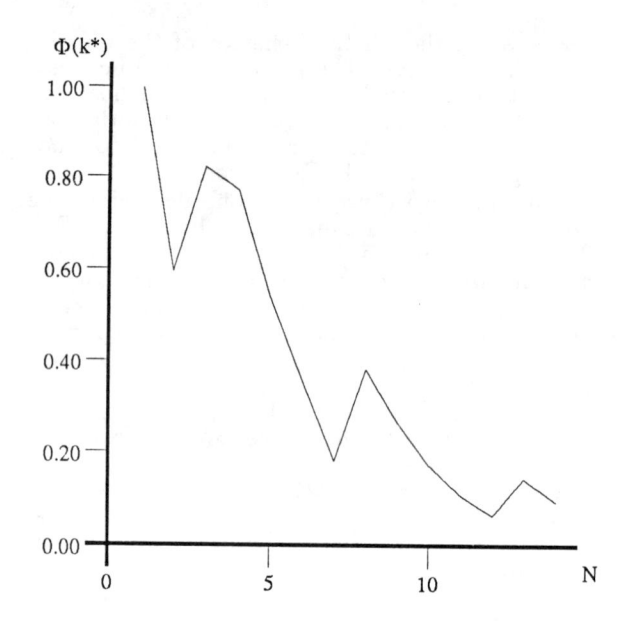

Figure 5: Decreasing Performance For Memory Size $n = 5$.

Conjecture 1 states that given any particular system with N automata, we can always set the memory size n high enough so that system operation is as close to optimal as desired. Conjecture 2 states conversely that given any memory size n for the automata, there is always some population size beyond which the system operates non-optimally; in fact, $f(t)$ again approaches $1/2$ asymptotically. Using the reward function $r(f) = -f^2 + 0.4f + 0.76$, shown in Figure 3, these two conjectures are illustrated through simulation in Figures 4 and 5. This function has a maximum at $f^* = 0.2$, so $k^* = 0.2N$, rounded off to the nearest integer. Suppose we would like $\Phi(k^*) \geq 0.3$. Figure 4 shows the increasing minimum memory size needed to maintain this level of performance. This illustrates Conjecture 1. Figure 5 shows $\Phi(k^*)$ decreasing as N increases, with memory size $n = 5$. This illustrates Conjecture 2. (The discontinuities in the graphs are due to the discrete jumps in the values of k^*; as noted above, k^* must be an integer. Thus, for instance, for N between 3 and 7, $k^* = 1$, but for N between 8 and 12, $k^* = 2$.)

3.1 State Aggregation

Our computer simulations illustrate these conjectures, but they do not explain why they seem to hold. Therefore, let us analyze this system as a Markov chain. The state space of the chain is an N-tuple whose m^{th} element, s_m, represents the state of α_m; the state is denoted by $\vec{s} = (s_1, s_2, \ldots, s_N)$. There are thus $(2n)^N$ states in the Markov chain. Let $\phi(\vec{s})$ for a Markov chain state $\vec{s}$ represent the number of positive elements in $\vec{s}$. We can then write the transition probabilities as follows.

$$q(\vec{s}, \vec{s'}) = \prod_{m=1}^{N} \Pr(x_m) \qquad (14)$$

where s'_m for all m is the result of the mapping $\delta(s, x)$ defined above; that is, $s'_m = \delta(s_m, x_m)$, where

$$\Pr(\text{reward}) = r(\phi(\vec{s})/N)$$

and

$$\Pr(\text{penalty}) = 1 - r(\phi(\vec{s})/N)$$

Define $P(\vec{s})$ to be the equilibrium state probability for the state $\vec{s}$. Then, we can write the detailed balance equations.

$$P(\vec{s}) = \sum_{\vec{s'}} P(\vec{s'}) q(\vec{s'}, \vec{s}) \qquad (15)$$

Knowing that the $P(\vec{s})$ sum to 1, we can solve for $P(\vec{s})$. Then,

$$\Pr(k \text{ automata are on}) = \sum_{\phi(\vec{s})=k} P(\vec{s}) \qquad (16)$$

Unfortunately, solving a Markov chain with $(2n)^N$ states is far from trivial, and the solution would only give us a set of probabilities, with no description of the dynamics of the system. Therefore, we choose to simplify (and thus approximate) the analysis by aggregating sets of states of the Markov chain. We implicitly assume that the behavior of the system is more or less the same in each of the states that make up any particular aggregate state.

Assume for the moment that $r(f) > 1/2$ for all f, so that at any time, most of the automata are in the extreme states, that is, near n or $-n$. This means that $f(t)$ is relatively stable; since the automata are at or near the end most of the time, state transitions between -1 and 1 (let us call these "trigger transitions," since they "trigger" changes in $a(t)$, and hence, $f(t)$) are relatively rare, and we can assume with little loss of precision that at most one trigger transition can take place at a time. For that reason, we call this the *well-behaved* case. (By contrast, we define *ill-behaved* systems to be those with $r(f) < 1/2$ for some f, and these are more difficult to analyze, so their treatment has been deferred. Qualitatively, however, the optimal behavior of these systems is still the same.) This characteristic will become important when we estimate the lengths of the intervals between trigger transitions. Suppose that out of the N automata, k are currently on the positive side of the state space. Note that with the exception of the sign of its current state, the dynamic behavior of an automaton is the same on either side of the state space. In other words, there is no way to distinguish between an automaton and its "mirror image." All other factors being equal, any one of the k automata on the positive side is just as likely to make the first trigger transition as any one of the $N - k$ on the negative side. Therefore, the probability that the next trigger transition goes from 1 to -1 (from positive to negative) is k/N, and the probability that it goes from -1 to 1 (from negative to positive) is $(N - k)/N$. The former corresponds to a decrease in $a(t)$ by one, and the latter to an increase in $a(t)$ by one. This suggests constructing the Markov chain in Figure 6, where the states represent the various values that $a(t)$ can take, rather than the various states of any particular automata. To avoid confusion, we call the former *system states*, and the latter *automaton states*.

This chain does not represent the sequence of system states at each discrete moment in time, but is rather an *imbedded Markov chain* which represents the sequence of system states at the instants just after trigger transitions. We can solve this chain for the equilibrium system state probabilities $\Pi(k)$, and in the following lemma, we show that it has the solution

$$\Pi(k) = 2^{-N} \binom{N}{k} \qquad (17)$$

Lemma 2 *Suppose that in any system state, any automaton is just as likely as any other to make a trigger transition. Then the above transition probabilities are valid, and*

$$\Pi(k) = 2^{-N} \binom{N}{k}$$

is the solution to the imbedded Markov chain.

Sketch of Proof Using the assumption in the statement of the lemma, we can write the following balance equation.

$$\Pi(k) = \Pi(k-1)\left(\frac{N-k+1}{N}\right) + \Pi(k+1)\left(\frac{k+1}{N}\right) \qquad (18)$$

In addition, we require that

$$\sum_{k=0}^{N} \Pi(k) = 1$$

It is then a simple matter of algebra to show that the solution to this system of equations is

$$\Pi(k) = 2^{-N} \binom{N}{k}$$

□

$\Pi(k)$ represents the visit ratios to the various system states, normalized to sum to unity. It has a maximum at $k = N/2$, so the system makes the most visits to that system state. $\Phi(k)$, however, depends not only on $\Pi(k)$, but also on the average time spent in that system state per visit. (For more on this general method, see Appendix B.) We now make an estimate of this average time.

Given any memory size n, we define the persistence time $\tau_n(k)$ to be the average time that the population

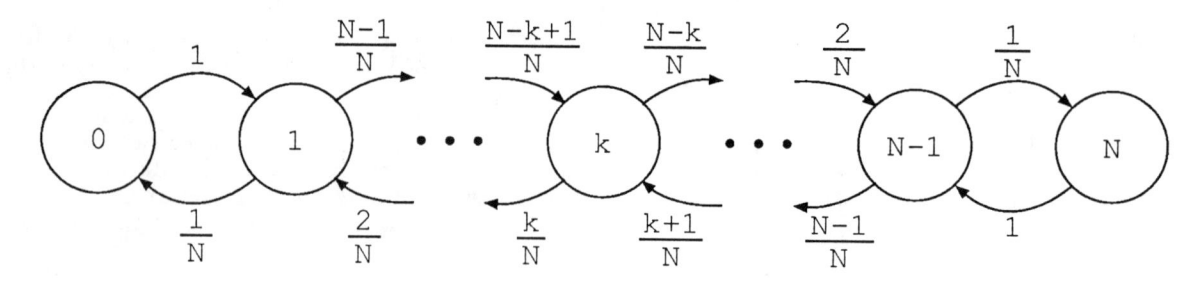

Figure 6: System State Diagram.

stays in system state k. The proportion of time that the population spends in system state k is then

$$\Phi(k) = \frac{\Pi(k)\tau_n(k)}{\sum_{k'=0}^{N} \Pi(k')\tau_n(k')} \quad (19)$$

Our object now is to estimate the persistence time $\tau_n(k)$.

Let $\bar{t}_{i,j}^n(r)$ be the average amount of time it takes for an automaton under reward probability r to move from automaton state i to automaton state j, with $1 \leq j < i \leq n$. (We can restrict our discussion to the positive side because the behavior on the negative end is identical, by symmetry, as discussed above.) When $i = n$, that is, at the end of the automaton state space,

$$\begin{aligned}\bar{t}_{n,n-1}^n(r) &= (1-r) + 2r(1-r) + 3r^2(1-r) + \cdots \\ &= 1 + r + r^2 + \cdots \\ &= \frac{1}{1-r} \quad (20)\end{aligned}$$

If, on the other hand, the automaton is currently at state i where $1 \leq i < n$, then we reason as follows. It will take the automaton at least one time unit to get to state $i - 1$. After the first time unit, either it has actually moved down to state $i - 1$ (with probability $1-r$), or it has moved up to state $i+1$ (with probability r), in which case it must first move back to state i before it can move to state $i - 1$. This gives us the recurrence equation

$$\bar{t}_{i,i-1}^n(r) = 1 + r(\bar{t}_{i+1,i}^n(r) + \bar{t}_{i,i-1}^n(r)), \quad 1 \leq i < n$$

which can be rewritten as

$$(1-r)\bar{t}_{i,i-1}^n(r) = 1 + r\bar{t}_{i+1,i}^n(r), \quad 1 \leq i < n \quad (21)$$

This recurrence equation can be solved by the usual z-transform techniques [4] (see Appendix A) to yield

$$\bar{t}_{i,i-1}^n(r) = \frac{1}{1-2r}\left(1 - \left(\frac{r}{1-r}\right)^{n-i+1}\right) \quad (22)$$

for $1 < i \leq n$, and

$$\bar{t}_{1,-1}^n(r) = \frac{1}{1-2r}\left(1 - \left(\frac{r}{1-r}\right)^n\right) \quad (23)$$

Immediately after a trigger transition, at least one of the automata—in particular, the one that made the trigger transition—must be in either state 1 or -1. Therefore, for sufficiently large n, the time this particular automaton takes to make a trigger transition *back* to the other side approximates the time before a trigger transition by *any* automaton. (When n is too small, the likelihood of multiple trigger transitions become high, and this invalidates the estimates of the persistence times.) This is true even though this automaton may not be the same as the one that made the last trigger transition. We can see this in two boundary cases for well-behaved systems. When r is close to $1/2$, there are many automata distributed evenly across the automaton state space, and any of these is as likely as any other to make a trigger transition. When r is close to 1, on the other hand, the likelihood is great that the automaton that last made a trigger transition will soon be in one of the end states, and again, any automaton is as likely as any other to make a trigger transition. We therefore claim that $\bar{t}_{1,-1}^n(r)$ is a good approximation to $\tau_n(k)$, and denote our estimate by

$$\bar{\tau}_n(k) = \bar{t}_{1,-1}^n(r(k/N)) \quad (24)$$

so the proportion of time spent in system state k is approximately

$$\Phi(k) \doteq \frac{\Pi(k)\bar{\tau}_n(k)}{\sum_{k'=0}^{N} \Pi(k')\bar{\tau}_n(k')} \quad (25)$$

We have now established the following approximation.

Approximation 1 *Assume that any automaton is just as likely as any other to make a trigger transition. Also assume that the persistence times are approximately proportional to the average travel time $\bar{\tau}_n(k)$. Then an approximation to the limiting probability that the system is in state k is*

$$\Phi(k) \doteq \frac{\binom{N}{k}\frac{1}{1-2r(k/N)}\left(1 - \left(\frac{r(k/N)}{1-r(k/N)}\right)^n\right)}{\sum_{k'=0}^{N}\binom{N}{k'}\frac{1}{1-2r(k'/N)}\left(1 - \left(\frac{r(k'/N)}{1-r(k'/N)}\right)^n\right)} \quad (26)$$

This approximation gives some insight into the Conjectures above. We see that the equilibrium system state probabilities are simply weighted binomial

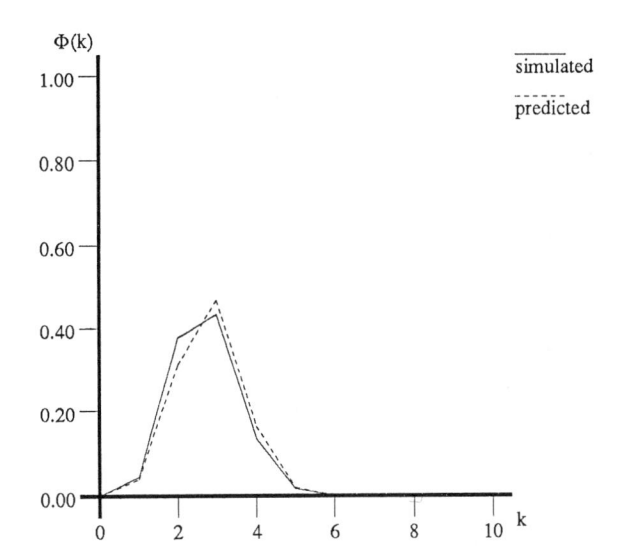

Figure 7: Steady State Probability Distribution for Example 1.

coefficients, where each weight is the persistence time associated with that system state. Suppose we have a reward function whose peak is at some f^* not equal to $1/2$. If we hold the population size N constant, and increase the memory size n, the persistence time for $k^* = f^*N$ will become larger and larger. Eventually, the system will spend most of its *time* at k^*, even though it makes more *visits* to the system state $k = N/2$, where the binomial coefficient is the greatest. This justifies Conjecture 1. If, instead, we hold the memory size n constant, and increase the population size N, the visit ratios to the system states in the vicinity of $k = N/2$ will grow larger and larger. Eventually, they will become so large that the greater persistence time for $k^* = f^*N$ is not enough to overcome the number of visits to $k = N/2$, and the system will spend most of its time around $k = N/2$. This justifies Conjecture 2.

We give two examples of systems of automata to show how well the approximation performs. In Example 1, there are $N = 10$ automata, each with a memory size of $n = 10$. The reward function is $r(f) = -f^2 + 0.4f + 0.76$, shown above in Figure 3. Recall that this function has a peak at $f^* = 0.2$, and that the optimal value of k^* is then 2. This example gives a flavor for the distribution of the fraction of time spent in various system states with a relatively small memory size, even when the reward function is relatively smooth. Figure 7 shows the estimated and simulated proportion of time spent in the various system states for these parameters. Note especially that even though some of the states have a reward probability less than $1/2$, the approximation is still accurate.

In Figure 8, we show the calculated steady state probabilities for Example 1 for various memory sizes n. Note that the system operates better and better as the memory size increases; in particular, the peak of the curve moves from $k = N/2$ for small values of n toward the optimal value $k = 2$ for large values of n.

In Example 2, there are $N = 10$ automata, each with a memory size of $n = 3$. The reward function is $r(f) = 0.9$ if $f = 1/N$ (0.1 in this case), and $r(f) = 0.6$ otherwise. Figure 9 shows the estimated and actual proportion of time spent in the various system states. Note that the probabilities are simply normalized binomial coefficients, except at $k = 1$ (that is, at $f = f^* = 0.1$), where it is much higher.

4 Other Considerations

So far we have only considered how much time, on average, the system spends in the optimal (or any other) system state. In any application, however, another parameter of interest is how long the system takes to *get* to the optimal condition. Since the system does not operate in equilibrium, we cannot speak of an exponential (or the like) convergence. Instead, we define the *walk period* ω^{-1} to be the average time between successive visits to the optimal system state, not counting the time actually spent in that optimal state. From the above discussion, it is clear that

$$\omega^{-1} = \frac{1}{\Pi(k^*)} \sum_{k \neq k^*} \Pi(k) \tau_n(r(k/N))$$

which we can write more concisely as

$$\omega^{-1} = \frac{1 - \Phi(k^*)}{\Phi(k^*)} \tau_n(r(k^*/N)) \qquad (27)$$

where $\Phi(k^*)$ is estimated from the above result. For a typical application, we usually want to maximize $\Phi(k^*)$ and to minimize ω^{-1}. Heuristics to do this can be found in [2] and [5].

Because of the possibly large walk periods, we might consider why we should use the Goore Game as a paradigm in these problems at all. If the reward function is known, why not use the value of f^* as a sort of probabilistic coin flip to determine the action of each automaton, since there is no walk period at all? The reason is that the Goore Scheme not only increases the likelihood that the percentage of automata performing a certain action is optimal when measured over a long period of time, it also increases that likelihood for each instant in time. For instance, suppose we were to take the above suggestion, and give each automaton a probability of f^* of performing action A_1. Then the probability that out of N automata, exactly k^* of them perform action A_1 is approximately

$$\Phi(k^*) = \binom{N}{k^*} f^{*k^*}(1-f^*)^{N-k^*}$$
$$= \binom{N}{k^*} f^{*Nf^*}(1-f^*)^{N(1-f^*)}$$

which can be shown to be less than or equal to $1/2$ for $N \geq 2$. But as we have seen above, with a large enough memory size n, the probability that exactly

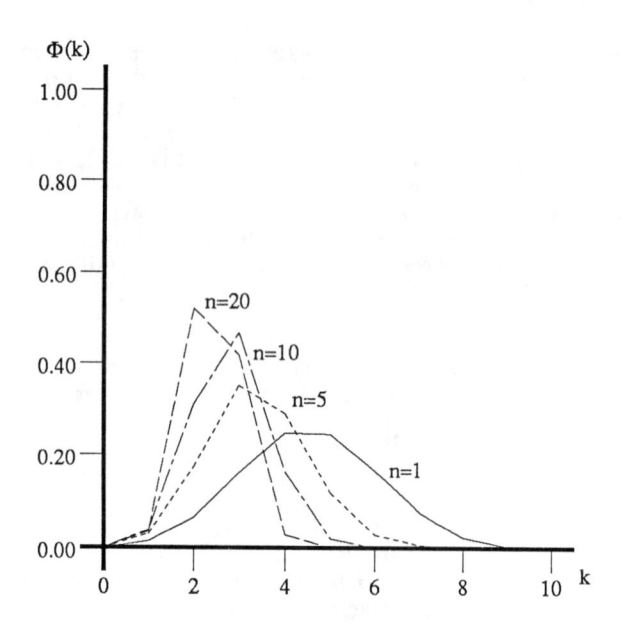

Figure 8: The Effect of Various Memory Sizes on Distribution.

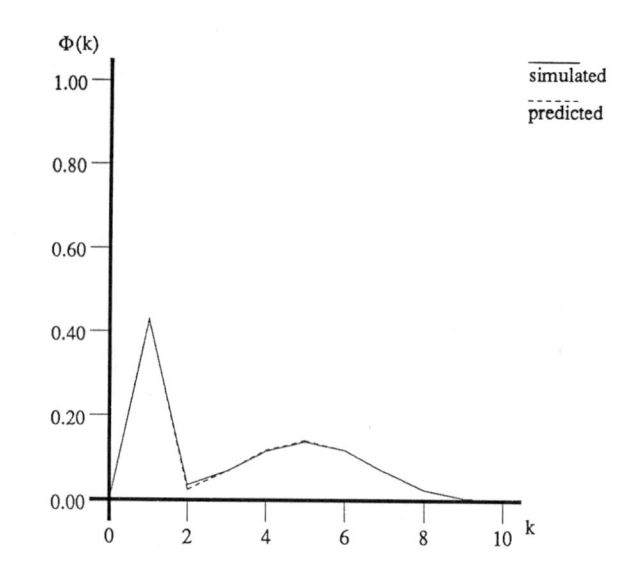

Figure 9: Steady State Probability Distribution for Example 2.

k^* automata perform action A_1 can be made as close to one as desired (given that one is willing to accept a correspondingly high premium on the walk period). Moreover, if the reward function changes, then the automata will adapt themselves automatically to adapt to the new function. This is not true when the automata are hard-wired to respond to a particular reward function. Most real life problems tend to create varying situations and this scheme allows the participants to react dynamically to these variations.

5 Summary

We have examined the problem of how to design automata so that they may work together cooperatively to achieve a common goal. We have taken a large class of systems, namely, the well-behaved systems, and derived a simple, quickly evaluated formula for the equilibrium system state probability distribution, which is approximate, but close enough for most purposes. We have described some other characteristics of these systems which also impact on the behavior of the systems, and given formulas for computing these parameters given the steady state probability distribution.

In future work, we plan to investigate the application of this scheme to the solution of real world problems. We intend to characterize the space of problems that are solvable by this method, and that are furthermore difficult to solve by other methods. We also propose to give specific solutions to various standard problems, and to detail necessary modifications to this scheme. We expect that there will be a wide range of tasks for which this technique is applicable.

A Solving for Persistence Time

In Section 3.1, we claimed that the solution to the recurrence equations 20 and 21 could be derived using z-transform techniques [4] to yield equations 22 and 23. In this appendix, we carry out this derivation. For any given n and r, we define

$$u_j = \bar{t}^n_{n-j,n-j-1}(r)$$

Then, from equations 20 and 21, we can write

$$u_0 = \frac{1}{1-r}$$

$$(1-r)u_{j+1} = 1 + ru_j$$

We define

$$U(z) = \sum_{j=0}^{\infty} u_j z^j$$

intending to discard any values of u_j for $j \geq n$. We multiply the recurrence equation above by z^j and sum from $j = 1 \to \infty$, and we get

$$\sum_{j=0}^{\infty}(1-r)u_{j+1}z^j = \sum_{j=0}^{\infty} z^j + ru_j z^j$$

$$\frac{1-r}{z}(U(z) - u_0) = \frac{1}{1-z} + rU(z)$$

$$\frac{1-r}{z}U(z) - \frac{1}{z} = \frac{1}{1-z} + rU(z)$$

$$\frac{1-r-rz}{z}U(z) = \frac{1}{z(1-z)}$$

$$U(z) = \frac{1}{(1-z)(1-r-rz)} = \frac{\frac{1}{1-2r}}{1-z} - \frac{\frac{r}{(1-r)(1-2r)}}{1-\frac{r}{1-r}z}$$

which we invert to get

$$u_j = \frac{1}{1-2r}\left(1 - \left(\frac{r}{1-r}\right)^{j+1}\right)$$

Using the substitution $j = n - i$, we get the equation claimed in the main text.

B System Decomposition

In the analysis presented in this paper, we decompose the system behavior into two parts: visit ratios and persistence time. Volkonskiy [9] makes use of this general method, but only for the simple case where the reward function is of the form $r(f) = r_0$ for $f \leq f_c$, $r(f) = r_1 < r_0$ for $f > f_c$, where $f_c < 1/2$ is some critical value. He also requires $r_1 > 1/2$. He then shows that for optimality, it is required that $\lim_{N\to\infty}(n/N) > \chi$, where

$$\chi = \frac{1 - H(f_c)}{\lg(\varphi_0/\varphi_1)}$$

and

$$H(f_c) = f_c \lg(1/f_c) + (1 - f_c)\lg(1/(1-f_c))$$

where $\varphi_i = r_i/(1-r_i)$. If $\lim_{N\to\infty}(n/N) < \chi$, then the automata spend most of their time in nonoptimal system states. Pittel [7] examines nearly the same problem. The only change is in the automata; he assumes that in a trigger transition, the automaton has an equal chance (that is, 1/2) of taking the other action, or staying with the same action. Using a different method of analysis, he comes to the same conclusion. He adds that "from the set of best decisions [which are not unique, since the reward function is piecewise constant], the automata choose one that allows them the most rapid detection of any disadvantages resulting from any deviations from that [choice]."

References

[1] V. A. Borovikov and V. I. Bryzgalov. A simple symmetric game between many automata. *Avtomat. Telemekh.*, Vol. 26(No. 4), 1965.

[2] A. Giessler, J. Hanle, A. Konig, and E. Pade. Free buffer allocation—an investigation by simulation. *Computer Networks*, Vol. 1(No. 3):191–204, July 1978.

[3] Douglas R. Hofstadter. Metamagical themas. *Scientific American*, May 1983.

[4] Leonard Kleinrock. *Queueing Systems, Volume 1: Theory*. John Wiley and Sons, 1975.

[5] Leonard Kleinrock. On flow control in computer networks. In *International Conference on Communications*, June 1978.

[6] Leonard Kleinrock. On distributed systems performance. In *ITC Specialist Seminar: Computer Networks and ISDN Systems*, pages 209–216, 1990.

[7] B. G. Pittel. The asymptotic properties of a version of the Goore game. *Probl. Peredachi Inform.*, Vol. 1(No. 3), 1965.

[8] M. L. Tsetlin. *Finite Automata and Modeling the Simplest Forms of Behavior*. PhD thesis, V. A. Steklov Mathematical Institute, 1964.

[9] V. A. Volkonskiy. Asymptotic properties of the behavior of simple automata in a game. *Probl. Peredachi Inform.*, Vol. 1(No. 2), 1965.

A Methodology for Evaluating Load Balancing Algorithms

Bharat S. Joshi   Seyed H. Hosseini   K. Vairavan

Department of Electrical Engineering and Computer Science
University of Wisconsin–Milwaukee
Milwaukee, WI–53201

Abstract

In general, a load balancing algorithm improves a system performance. Obviously, larger the difference between the task arrival rates at various processors, more the system is imbalanced and more improvement in the system performance is achieved using a load balancing algorithm.

The existing works which have used an experimental technique to show the improvement in the system performance under a load balancing algorithm have used an ad hoc procedure to select the task arrival rates for various processors. Thus, their experimental results necessarily may not provide a complete picture of the improvement in the system performance under their load balancing algorithms.

In this work, we present a systematic scheme for the selection of the task arrival rates at various processors such that experimental results reflect a complete picture of the improvement in the system performance under a load balancing algorithm. The idea has been motivated by the well-known Taguchi technique used in quality control.

1 Introduction

To improve the performance of a multiple processor system loads are balanced among the processors. A load is defined to be a task which can be an independent program or a partitioned module of a parallel task. Various load balancing algorithms have been proposed in the literature [1, 3-9, 11-15, 17].

A load balancing algorithm, in general, improves a system performance. However, the degree of the improvement in the system performance not only depends on the specific load balancing algorithm used, but also on the degree of uneven distribution of loads over the processors. Obviously, the more imbalanced the system is, the higher the degree of improvement in the system performance is achieved using a load balancing algorithm.

The existing experimental works have used ad hoc schemes to select the loads (i.e. task arrival rates) of the processors. Some works have assumed that the task arrival rates at all processors are the same. This is a very restrictive assumption to make and consequently it leads to a partial evaluation of a system performance under a given load balancing algorithm. Some other works have assumed that task arrival rates are different at various processors but have not selected the task arrival rates such that the entire range of values for the task arrival rates are considered. Thus, one still cannot have a complete picture of the system performance improvement under a given load balancing algorithm.

Of course, it is impractical to consider all the possible values for all the task arrival rates. A systematic scheme for the selection of values for the system parameters is the well-known Taguchi technique [16]. In that scheme, Taguchi has developed a set of tables which list combinations of the values for the system parameters such that the experimental results represent the entire range of values for the system parameters and consequently they provide a complete picture of a system behavior under study.

A shortcoming of the Taguchi technique is that the number of system parameters must be small. It is the purpose of this work to develop a methodology for the selection of the task arrival rates such that the experimental results truly represent the entire range of the values for the task arrival rates, especially for the systems with a large number of processors.

This paper is organized as follows.. In section 2, we propose our methodology for the selection of the task arrival rates. In section 3, we introduce a randomized load balancing algorithm. In section 4, we show the application of the proposed methodology in performance evaluation of the proposed load balancing algorithm. Finally, in section 5 we present the conclusion.

2 Description

Response time improvement under any load balancing algorithm depends on the system parameters such as arrival rates, service rates, and the number of processors in the system. To observe the improvement in the response time, it is not practical to consider all the possible values for all the system parameters. The alternative approach is to choose only a few values for each of the system parameters such that while the number of combinations is not too large and impractical, but it still covers the entire space of the system parameters ranges. In this section we introduce such a methodology.

2.1 A Methodology for Labeling a Processor

Depending on the load of a processor, in general, a processor is labeled as lightly, moderately, or heavily loaded. The existing works use one or more threshold levels to label a processor as above. An alternative and a more meaningful way to label a processor is based on the average response time at the processor. For example, consider a single processor system and assume that it is modeled as an $M/M/1$ queue. Thus, the average response time R is [10]

$$R = \frac{1}{\mu - \lambda}. \qquad (1)$$

Figure 1 plots R vs average arrival rate λ assuming that average service rate $\mu = 1$ task per unit time. As seen from this figure, the average response time is close to the service time, $1/\mu$ (minimal value) for small arrival rates. For large arrival rates (values close to μ) average response time becomes very large and unacceptable. Thus, according to this figure we may label a processor as follows:

- lightly loaded for $\lambda < 0.2\mu$, where average response time is almost the same as average service time.

- moderately loaded for $0.2\mu \leq \lambda \leq 0.8\mu$, where the average response time is larger than the average service time, but still an acceptable value.

- heavily loaded for $\lambda > 0.8\mu$, where the average response time is a lot more than the average service time, an unacceptable value.

2.2 A Methodology for Labeling a System

In multiple processor systems the arrival rates at the processors, in general, are different and it is not practical to consider all the possible combinations for all the system parameters including the arrival rates. We may try to consider only those combinations where load of every processor is selected to be any of the three values: low, moderate, or high as was discussed in the earlier section. But still considering all the possible combinations (i.e. 3^n where n is the number of processors) in a system with a large number of processors is not practical.

We propose an alternative practical scheme. This scheme depends on the fact that response time improvement by any load balancing algorithm depends on the degree of imbalance in the system, which in turn depends on the number of processors with low, medium, and high loads. The scheme labels a system as most imbalanced, moderately balanced, or balanced as follows:

- Most Imbalanced System

  A system is defined to be most imbalanced if only one of the processors receives all the tasks.

- Moderately Balanced System

  A system is defined to be moderately balanced if approximately half of the processors receive loads and the other half of the processors receive no load.

- Balanced System

  A system is defined to be balanced if all the processors receive the same number of loads.

An implementation of the above labeling scheme may be done as follows:

- Most Imbalanced System

  A system with one processor having an arrival rate of λ_I and the remaining processors having an arrival rate of zero.

- Moderately Balanced System

  A system with 50% of the processors having an arrival rate of λ_M and the remaining 50% of the processors having an arrival rate of zero.

- Balanced System

  A system with all the processors having an arrival rate of λ_B.

Assuming that the total arrival rate to the system is the same regardless of type of the system as labeled above, we find out the relationship between λ_I, λ_M, and λ_A as follows. Let the number of processors be n.

$$\begin{aligned} Total\ System\ Arrival\ Rate &= \lambda_I \\ &= \frac{50}{100} n \lambda_M \\ &= n \lambda_B \end{aligned} \qquad (2)$$

or $\qquad \lambda_M = \frac{2\lambda_I}{n} \quad$ and $\quad \lambda_B = \frac{\lambda_I}{n} \qquad (3)$

3 Application of the Methodology

A multiple processor system is considered to be balanced if the number of tasks at every processor is the same. Furthermore, by the Little's law [10], average response time, R, at a processor is

$$R = \frac{N}{\lambda} \qquad (4)$$

where λ and N are average arrival rate and average number of tasks at the processor, respectively. Thus, in a balanced multiple processor system the average response time at every processor must be the same. Considering that a load balancing algorithm balances a multiple processor system by making the number of tasks at every processor the same, by the Little's law, (4), the average task arrival rate at every processor must be the same in a balanced multiple processor system.

In general, arrival rates at processors are different. Let us assume that $\lambda_1, \lambda_2, \cdots, \lambda_n$ are the arrival rates at the processors $1, 2, \cdots, n$ respectively. In a system with the Poisson arrival rates and exponential service times, the average response time, R_i, at the processor i before balancing the loads is [10]

$$R_i = \frac{1}{\mu_i - \lambda_i} \qquad (5)$$

where λ_i and μ_i are the average arrival rate and the average service rate of processor i, respectively.

Hence, the average system response time, R_W, before balancing the loads among the processors is

$$R_W = \frac{1}{n^*}\sum_{i=1}^{n} R_i, \quad \text{where } n^* = \sum_{i=1,\lambda_i\neq 0}^{n} 1$$

In this work, first we consider only one type of task and a homogeneous system where all processors have the same speed. In section 3.3 we generalize it to the case where processors run various types of tasks. Thus, under the above assumption, $\mu = \mu_i$, for $i = 1, 2, \ldots, n$ and

$$R_W = \frac{1}{n^*}\sum_{i=1,\lambda_i\neq 0}^{n} \frac{1}{\mu - \lambda_i} \qquad (6)$$

Plugging the arrival rates from equation (3) into the equation (6) we get the average system response time before balancing the loads as follows:

(i) Most Imbalanced System

In this case, only one processor has arrival rate λ_I and the remaining $(n-1)$ processors have arrival rates of zero. Thus,

$$R_{WI} = \frac{1}{\mu - \lambda_I} \qquad (7)$$

(ii) Moderately Balanced System

In this case, 50% of the processors have the same arrival rate λ_M and the remaining 50% of the processors have arrival rates of zero. Thus,

$$R_{WM} = \frac{1}{\mu - \lambda_M} \quad \text{or} \qquad (8)$$

$$R_{WM} = \frac{1}{\mu - \frac{2\lambda_I}{n}}. \qquad (9)$$

(iii) Balanced System

In this case, all processors have the same arrival rate λ_B. Thus, as before,

$$R_B = \frac{1}{\mu - \lambda_B} \quad \text{or} \qquad (10)$$

$$R_B = \frac{1}{\mu - \frac{\lambda_I}{n}}. \qquad (11)$$

Another useful performance metric is the system distance.

Definition 1: The system distance at time t, Δ_t, is

$$\Delta_t = \sum_{i=1}^{n} |N_i^t - N_{ave}| \qquad (12)$$

where N_i^t is the number of tasks at processor i and $N_{ave} = 1/n \sum_{i=1}^{n} N_i^t$.

The system distance as defined above indicates how far the system is from being balanced. A better measure is the normalized system distance as defined below.

Definition 2: The normalized system distance at time t, Δ_t^N, is
$\Delta_t^N = \Delta_t/max\Delta$ where Δ_t is the maximum initial distance for a fixed total load. It will be shown that $max\Delta = 2(\lambda_I/(\mu - \lambda_I))(1 - 1/n)$ and it is the initial system distance for a load distribution where all the loads arrive at one node and zero load at other nodes.

(i) Most Imbalanced System

By Little's law $N_I = R_{WI} * \lambda_I$ where N_I is the average number of customers in the system, or

$$N_I = \frac{\lambda_I}{\mu - \lambda_I}$$

The system distance is:

$$max\Delta = (n-1)\frac{1}{n}\left(\frac{\lambda_I}{\mu - \lambda_I}\right)$$
$$+ \left(\frac{\lambda_I}{\mu - \lambda_I} - \frac{1}{n}\frac{\lambda_I}{\mu - \lambda_I}\right)$$
$$max\Delta = 2\left(\frac{\lambda_I}{\mu - \lambda_I}\right)\left(1 - \frac{1}{n}\right) \qquad (13)$$

The normalized system distance is 1.

(ii) Moderately Balanced System

By Little's law $N'_M = R_{WM} * \lambda_M$ where N'_M is the average number of customers per processor P_i for which $\lambda_i \neq 0$.

$$N_{ave} = \frac{1}{n}\left(\frac{n}{2}\right)\frac{\lambda_M}{\mu - \lambda_M}$$
$$N_{ave} = \frac{1}{2}\frac{\lambda_M}{\mu - \lambda_M}$$

The system distance is:

$$\Delta_t = \frac{n}{2}\left(\frac{1}{2}\frac{\lambda_M}{\mu - \lambda_M}\right) + \frac{n}{2}\left(\frac{\lambda_M}{\mu - \lambda_M} - \frac{1}{2}\frac{\lambda_M}{\mu - \lambda_M}\right)$$
$$= \frac{n}{2}\frac{\lambda_M}{\mu - \lambda_M}$$
$$\Delta_t = \frac{\lambda_I}{\mu - \frac{2\lambda_I}{n}} \qquad (14)$$

The normalized system distance is:

$$\Delta_t^N = \frac{\frac{\lambda_I}{\mu - \frac{2\lambda_I}{n}}}{2\left(\frac{\lambda_I}{\mu - \lambda_I}\right)\left(1 - \frac{1}{n}\right)}$$

$$\Delta_t^N = \frac{\mu - \lambda_I}{2\left(\mu - \frac{2\lambda_I}{n}\right)\left(1 - \frac{1}{n}\right)} \qquad (15)$$

It can be seen that the normalized distance $0 < \Delta_t^N < 1$.

(iii) Balanced System

The system distance is virtually zero.

3.1 A Load Balancing Algorithm

In a balanced multiple processor system, arrival rates at the processors are the same and equal to

$$\lambda = \frac{1}{n}\sum_{i=1}^{n}\lambda_i. \qquad (16)$$

In this section, we introduce a randomized distributed load balancing algorithm that balances a system by making the average task arrival rate at every processor equal to the average task arrival rate λ given by equation (16).

Algorithm

1. Every processor i upon the arrival of an external task will send it to every processor j including itself with equal probability of $1/n$ where n is the number of processors in the system.

2. Every processor j upon the reception of a job from another processor i will insert it in the job queue for execution.

The proposed load balancing algorithm indeed balances the loads among the processors as follows.

Theorem 1: Average arrival rate λ at every processor under the proposed load balancing algorithm is

$$\lambda = \frac{1}{n}\sum_{i=1}^{n}\lambda_i \qquad (17)$$

where λ_i is the average arrival rate at the processor i.

Proof: The arrival rate at the processor i from the processor j is $(1/n)\lambda_j$. Thus, the average arrival rate at every processor is

$$\lambda = \sum_{j=1}^{n}\lambda_j\frac{1}{n} \quad \text{or}$$

$$\lambda = \frac{1}{n}\sum_{j=1}^{n}\lambda_j \qquad \square$$

The following theorem gives the average response time at every processor.

Theorem 2: Average response time R_B at every processor is given as follows. Using the proposed load balancing algorithm and assuming Poisson arrivals from external world at the processors and exponential service times,

$$R_B = \frac{1}{\mu - \lambda} \qquad (18)$$

where λ is given in equation (16).

Proof: It has been shown [10] that the decomposition of a Poisson process into n sources with probabilities $p_1, p_2, \ldots, p_n$ generates Poisson processes at those sources. That is, sending an arriving task at a processor to any of the n processors with equal probabilities of $1/n$ generates a Poisson process (an arriving task) at every processor. Also, shown in [10] that superposition of n Poisson processes into one source remains a Poisson process. That is the arrivals of n Poisson processes, i.e. n tasks from n processors, generates a Poisson process (sum of the arrivals) at that processor. Thus, by the above properties of the Poisson process, the arrival of the tasks at each processor remains Poisson under the proposed load balancing algorithm, with the average arrival rate λ given in equation (16). As a result the average response time is governed by equation (18). $\square$

Thus, the average response time, R_B, of a balanced system is the same as the average response time of every processor and is equal to

$$R_B = \frac{1}{\mu - \lambda} \quad \text{or}$$

$$R_B = \frac{1}{\mu - \frac{1}{n}\sum_{i=1}^{n}\lambda_i} \qquad (19)$$

Replacing λ_i's with the arrival rates specified for each of the three types of load distributions given in section 2 gives the average response time R_B.

(i) Most Imbalanced System

In this case only one processor has non-zero arrival rate λ_i. Thus,

$$R_B = \frac{1}{\mu - \frac{1}{n}\sum_{i=1}^{n}\lambda_i}$$

$$R_B = \frac{1}{\mu - \frac{\lambda_I}{n}} \qquad (20)$$

(ii) Moderately Balanced System

Similarly, for the moderately balanced system, 50% of the processors have an arrival rate of λ_M and the remaining 50% of the processors have an arrival rate of zero. Thus,

$$R_B = \frac{1}{\mu - \lambda}$$

$$= \frac{1}{\mu - \frac{1}{n}\sum_{i=1}^{n}\lambda_i}$$

$$= \frac{1}{\mu - \frac{1}{n}\left(\frac{50}{100}n\lambda_M + \frac{50}{100}n(0)\right)}$$

$$R_B = \frac{1}{\mu - \frac{1}{2}\lambda_M}$$

Since by equation (3), $\lambda_M = 2\lambda_I/n$, we get

$$R_B = \frac{1}{\mu - \frac{1}{2}\frac{2\lambda_I}{n}}$$

$$= \frac{1}{\mu - \frac{\lambda_I}{n}} \qquad (21)$$

(iii) Balanced System

Finally, for the balanced system all the processors have the same arrival rate λ_B. Thus,

$$R_B = \frac{1}{\mu - \lambda}$$

$$R_B = \frac{1}{\mu - \frac{1}{n}\sum_{i=1}^{n}\lambda_i}$$

$$R_B = \frac{1}{\mu - \lambda_B}$$

Again by equation (3), $\lambda_B = \lambda_I/n$, or

$$R_B = \frac{1}{\mu - \frac{\lambda_I}{n}} \quad (22)$$

Note: The average steady state distance is zero under the proposed randomized load balancing algorithm.

3.2 The Effect of Communication Overhead on the Average System Response Time

To estimate the communication time overhead, an earlier model is used [2]. In this model when a task is transferred from a processor i to another processor j, the corresponding communication overhead T_c is

$$T_c = T_s + T_t \quad (23)$$

where T_s is the time it takes to set up a communication path between processors i and j and T_t is the time it takes to transfer the task from processor i to the processor j once a path has been established between them. In turn

$$T_s = d*t_s \quad \text{and} \quad T_t = \frac{sd}{v} \quad (24)$$

$$\text{or} \quad T_c = (t_s + \frac{s}{v})d \quad (25)$$

where d is the length of the path between processors i and j, t_s is the time it takes to set up a link between two neighboring processors, v is the speed of the link (in bits per unit time) between two neighboring processors and s is the size of the task in bits.

Thus, the average response time after balancing the loads among the processors with the proposed load balancing algorithm and when communication overhead is included is

$$\widetilde{R_B} = R_B + T_c \quad \text{or by equation (19)}$$
$$\widetilde{R_B} = \frac{1}{\mu - \frac{1}{n}\sum_{i=1}^{n}\lambda_i} + T_c \quad \text{or} \quad (26)$$
$$\widetilde{R_B} = \frac{1}{\mu - \frac{1}{n}\sum_{i=1}^{n}\lambda_i} + (t_s + \frac{s}{v})d_{ave} \quad (27)$$

where d_{ave} is the average diameter of the multiple processor system graph.

To find out the threshold level for the communication overhead T_c at which point the average system response time with and without the load balancing are the same, set

$$R_W = \widetilde{R_B} \quad (28)$$

or by equations (6) and (27)

$$\frac{1}{n*}\sum_{i=1,\lambda_i\neq 0}^{n}\frac{1}{\mu-\lambda_i} = \frac{1}{\mu-\frac{1}{n}\sum_{i=1}^{n}\lambda_i}$$
$$+(t_s+\frac{s}{v})d_{ave}. \quad (29)$$

Equation (29) gives the relationship between various system parameters at the threshold level.

3.3 Generalization

So far we have been considering that all the processors run the same type of task. Now, we generalize it to the case when processors run k different types of tasks. Let λ_{ij} denote the arrival rate of jth task type at processor i with probability P_{ij} for all $i = 1, 2, \ldots, n$ and $j = 1, 2, \ldots, k$. Thus, the total arrival rate λ_i at the processor i before load balancing is

$$\lambda_i = \sum_{j=1}^{k} P_{ij}\lambda_{ij}. \quad (30)$$

In this case, every processor can be modeled as a single queue with k servers of service rates $\mu_1, \mu_2, \ldots, \mu_k$ where μ_j is the service rate of the jth task type and $1/\mu_j$ is the service time of the jth task type [10], as shown in Figure 2. As before, considering Poisson arrivals and exponential service times for all different types of tasks, the average response time before balancing at the processor i is

$$R_i = \sum_{j=1}^{k} P_{ij}\frac{1}{\mu_j - \lambda_{ij}} \quad (31)$$

where $\sum_{j=1}^{k} P_{ij} = 1$.

As a result, the average system response time before balancing is

$$R_W^G = \frac{1}{n*}\sum_{i=1}^{n} R_i \quad \text{or}$$
$$R_W^G = \frac{1}{n*}\sum_{i=1}^{n}\sum_{j=1}^{k} P_{ij}\frac{1}{\mu_j - \lambda_{ij}}. \quad (32)$$

The total average arrival rate at every processor after balancing the loads among the processors with the proposed load balancing algorithm is

$$\lambda = \frac{1}{n}\sum_{i=1}^{n}\lambda_i \quad (33)$$

where λ_i is the average arrival rate of the external tasks at the processor i and given by the equation (30). Thus,

$$\lambda = \frac{1}{n}\sum_{i=1}^{n}\sum_{j=1}^{k} P_{ij}\lambda_{ij} \quad \text{or} \quad (34)$$

$$\lambda = \frac{1}{n}\sum_{i=1}^{n} P_{i1}\lambda_{i1} + \frac{1}{n}\sum_{i=1}^{n} P_{i2}\lambda_{i2} + \cdots$$

$$+ \frac{1}{n}\sum_{i=1}^{n} P_{ik}\lambda_{ik} \quad \text{or}$$

$$\lambda = \frac{1}{n}\gamma_1 + \frac{1}{n}\gamma_2 + \cdots + \frac{1}{n}\gamma_k \quad (35)$$

where γ_j is the total arrival rate of the jth task type at each processor after balancing the loads among the processors and with occurrence probability of $1/n$. or

$$\gamma_j = \sum_{i=1}^{n} P_{ij}\lambda_{ij}. \quad (36)$$

Thus, every processor can be modeled as a k-server single queue as shown in Figure 3.

Similar to the case of single type of task, using the decomposition and superposition properties of the Poisson process, the average system response time after balancing the loads is

$$R_B^G = \frac{1}{n}\sum_{j=1}^{k} \frac{1}{\mu_j - \gamma_j} \quad \text{or}$$

$$R_B^G = \frac{1}{n}\sum_{j=1}^{k} \frac{1}{\mu_j - \sum_{i=1}^{n} P_{ij}\lambda_{ij}}. \quad (37)$$

To include the communication overhead in the average system response time, we first estimate the average task size over all types of tasks with different arrival probabilities and sizes. The average task size at the processor i before balancing the loads and from the external arrivals is

$$S_i = \sum_{j=1}^{k} P_{ij} S_{ij} \quad (38)$$

where P_{ij} and S_{ij} are the probabilities of the jth task type and the average size of the jth type task at a processor i. Thus, the average task size at any processor after balancing the loads with the proposed load balancing algorithm is

$$S = \sum_{i=1}^{n} \frac{1}{n} S_i. \quad (39)$$

The average communication overhead per task is obtained from equation (25). Hence, the average system response time with the communication overhead included after balancing the loads among the processors by equation (37) is

$$\widetilde{R}_B^G = R_B^G + T_c \quad \text{or}$$

$$\widetilde{R}_B^G = \frac{1}{n}\sum_{j=1}^{k} \frac{1}{\mu_j - \sum_{j=1}^{n} P_{ij}\lambda_{ij}}$$

$$+ (t_s + \frac{S}{v})d_{ave} \quad (40)$$

where S is given by equation (39) and t_s, v, and d_{ave} are defined as before.

Note: A similar approach can be used to get the average system distances before and after balancing the tasks.

4 Experimental Results

Now, we present the performance results of the load balancing algorithm using the proposed load selection methodology.

Figure 4 shows the plots of the average response times R_{WI}, equation (7), R_{WM}, equation (9), and R_B, equations (20), (21), and (22) vs total system arrival rate for a 10-node system with the average service rate $\mu = 1$ (i.e. one task per unit time).

These are the observations from the plots in this figure.

- For a system where loads are not balanced among the processors, the more imbalanced the system state is, the faster the average system response time becomes unacceptable for the same total arrival rate to the system. For instance, response time becomes infinity at $\lambda = \mu$ for the system state of plot R_{WI} while it becomes infinity at $\lambda = (n/2)\mu$, and $\lambda = n\mu$ for the system states of plots R_{WM}, and R_B, respectively.

- For a system where loads are balanced among the processors, the more imbalanced the system state is, higher is the improvement in the average system response time, for the same total arrival rates to the system due to higher ratio of R_W/R_B. In general, we have

$$\frac{R_{WI}}{R_B} > \frac{R_{WM}}{R_B} > 1. \quad (41)$$

- As the system state becomes more balanced due to having either equal arrival rates at different processors or running a load balancing algorithm, the system average response time gets smaller and the threshold level for the total arrival rate to the system for acceptable average response time gets larger.

5 Conclusion

To observe the improvement in the performance of a system under any load balancing algorithm a new methodology for the selection of the task arrival rates at various processors has been proposed. The proposed methodology has the property that it selects the values for the arrival rates such that experimental results regarding the improvement in the system performance under a given load balancing algorithm represent the entire space for the arrival rates. As a result the experimental results represent a complete study of the system performance from completely balanced to moderately, and completely imbalanced states. The methodology may be used as a standard for measuring the performance of any load balancing algorithm or comparison between various load balancing algorithms.

The danger of not using a standard methodology such as the one introduced here is that the experimental results may partially but not completely represent the improvement in the system performance under a given load balancing algorithm.

The application of the methodology was shown on a proposed load balancing algorithm.

References

[1] I. Ahmad and A. Ghafoor. Semi-distributed load balancing on massively parallel multicomputer systems. *IEEE Transactions on Software Engineering*, SE-17, No. 10:987–1004, 1991.

[2] W.C. Athas and C. L. Seitz. Multicomputers: Message-passing concurrent computer. *IEEE Computer*, pages 9–23, 1988.

[3] George Cybenko. Dynamic load balancing for distributed memory multiprocessors. *Journal of Parallel and Distributed Computing*, 7, No. 2:279–301, 1989.

[4] Derek L. Eager, Edward D. Lazowska, and John Zahorjan. Adaptive load sharing in homogeneous distributed systems. *IEEE Transactions on Software Engineering*, SE-12, No. 5:662–675, 1986.

[5] A. Hac and T.J. Johnson. Sensitivity study of the load balancing in a distributed system. *Journal of Parallel and Distributed Computing*, pages 85–89, 1989.

[6] S. Hosseini, B. Joshi, B. Litow, M. Malkawi, and K. Vairavan. Graph coloring based distributed load balancing and its performance evaluation. *Proceedings Fourth Annual Parallel Processing Symposium*, pages 694–707, 1990.

[7] S. Hosseini, B. Litow, M. Malkawi, J. McPherson, and K. Vairavan. Analysis of a graph coloring based distributed load balancing algorithm. *Journal of Parallel and Distributed Computing*, Vol. 10, N0. 2:160–166, 1990.

[8] S. H. Hosseini, B. Litow, M. Malkawi, and K. Vairavan. Distributed algorithms for load balancing in very large homogeneous systems. *ACM-IEEE Computer Conference*, 29:397–404, 1987.

[9] S. H. Hosseini, B. Litow, M. Malkawi, and K. Vairavan. System modeling and performance analysis of a distributed load balancing algorithm. *Proceedings, IEEE 32nd Midwest Conference on Circuits and Systems*, 1989.

[10] H. Kobayashi. *Modeling and Analysis: An Introduction to System Performance Evaluation Methodology*. Addison-Wesley, 1978.

[11] Frank C. H. Lin and Robert M. Keller. The gradient model load balancing method. *IEEE Transactions on Software Engineering*, SE-13, No. 1:32–38, 1987.

[12] H.C. Lin and C.S. Raghavendra. A dynamic load-balancing policy with a central job dispatcher (lbc). *IEEE Transactions on Software Engineering*, SE-18, No. 2:148–158, 1992.

[13] S. Margaret, K. Efe, L. Delcambre, and L.N. Bhuyan. Load balancing with network cooperation. *IEEE Eleventh International Conference on Distributed Computing SYstems*, pages 328–335, 1991.

[14] L. Ni and K. Hwang. Optimal load balancing in a multiple processor system with many job classes. *IEEE Transactions on Software Engineering*, SE-11, No. 5:411–496, 1985.

[15] Lionel M. Ni, Xu Chong-Wei, and Thomas B. Gendreau. A distributed drafting algorithm for load balancing. *IEEE Transactions on Software Engineering*, SE-11, No. 10:1153–1161, 1985.

[16] M.S. Phadke. *Quality Engineering Using Robust Design*. Prentice Hall, 1989.

[17] John A. Stankovic. Simulations of three adaptive, decentralized controlled, job scheduling algorithms. *North-Holland Computer Networks*, 8:199–217, 1984.

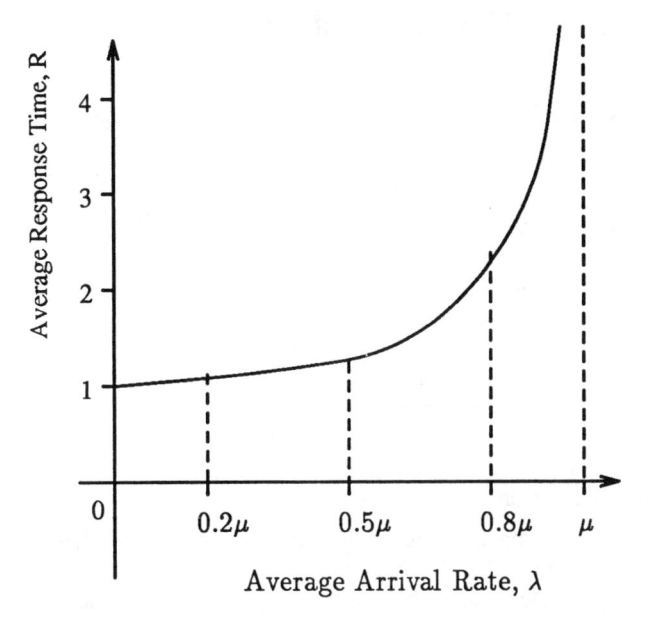

Figure 1: Average Response Time R vs Average Arrival Rate λ in a Single Processor System Modeled as an M/M/1 Queue

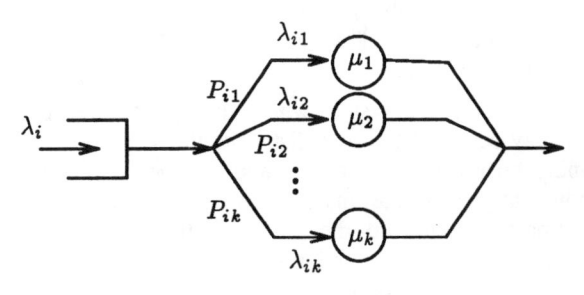

Figure 2: A Queueing Model for the Processor i Running k Different Types of Tasks Before Balancing the Loads Among the Processors

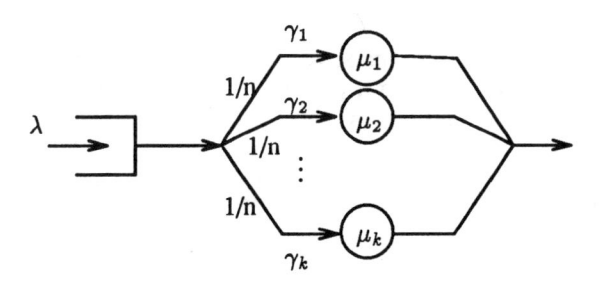

Figure 3: A Queueing Model for Every Processor Running k Different Types of Tasks After Balancing the Loads Among the Processors

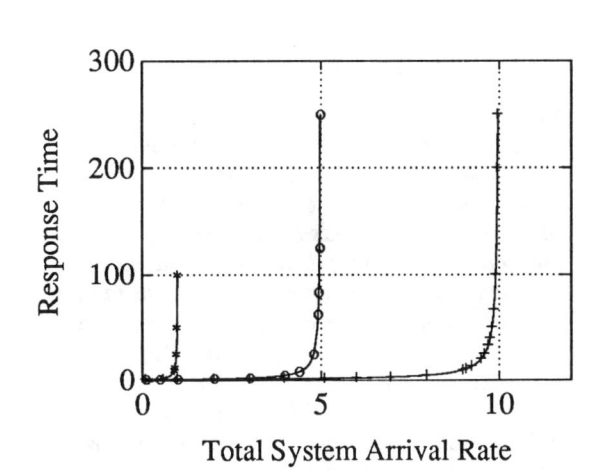

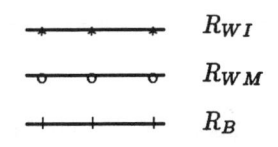

Figure 4: Average Response Time vs Total System Arrival Rate for Service Rate $\mu = 1$, n = 10

R_{WI}
R_{WM}
R_B

Distributed Computing Systems and Checkpointing*

Ken Wong and Mark Franklin

The Computer and Communications Research Center
Washington University, St. Louis, MO 63130

Abstract

This paper examines the performance of synchronous checkpointing in a distributed computing environment with and without load redistribution. Performance models are developed, and optimum checkpoint intervals are determined. The analysis extends earlier work by allowing for multiple nodes, state dependent checkpoint intervals, and a performance metric which is coupled with failure-free performance and the speedup functions associated with implementation of parallel algorithms. Expressions for the optimum checkpoint intervals for synchronous checkpointing with and without load redistribution are derived and the results are then used to determine when load redistribution is advantageous.

1. Introduction

The dual emerging technologies associated with gigabit networks [1] and high-speed processors (supercomputers), suggest the possibility of tackling very large, computationally intensive problems by coupling these technologies into a distributed computing environment. The large applications which make good candidates for this environment may produce results only after many hours even when multiple computers are employed. For example, several computing sites around the U.S. might be willing to cooperate (i.e., act as a distributed parallel processor) in tackling a difficult simulation problem. The computing sites may consist of computational resources from several vendors, and communcation between sites may require message transmission over long distances (thousands of miles) through several intermediate hops. Clearly, computing in this environment is much more precarious and we can expect higher resource failures rates than in a standard multiprocessor. Thus, a fundamental problem which must be addressed in this environment is that of providing effective computational progress in the face of resource failures.

---

* This research has been sponsored in part by funding from the NSF under Grant CCR-9021041.

In order to achieve maximum speed, the computational tasks must be assigned to the resources to exploit maximum parallelism. However, the possibility of a system failure (and therefore a complete restart) increases as larger numbers of processors are brought to bear on the application. Fault tolerant techniques must be used to insure finishing times which are comparable with fault-free performance.

One approach to providing higher reliability is to have each site periodically checkpoint by making a copy of the system state onto stable storage such as disk. When a failure occurs, each site can resume computing after it restores its system state by reading the latest checkpoint from its checkpoint storage. An important issue in such a system concerns the selection of checkpoint frequency. Checkpointing too frequently in a highly reliable system results in unnecessary overhead, while checkpointing too infrequently in a highly unreliable system results in the loss of large quantities of work — work which must be repeated after a failure.

Note also that in a system where the repair times are long, it may be beneficial to redistribute the load onto the remaining operational processors and resume computing (at a lower aggregate rate) instead of waiting for its repair. When repair is completed, the load could then be redistributed back onto the repaired processor. This approach allows for graceful performance degradation in the face of failures.

This paper examines the performance of synchronous checkpointing in a distributed computing environment with and without load redistribution. Performance models are developed, and optimum checkpoint intervals are determined. The analysis significantly extends earlier work by allowing for multiple nodes, state dependent checkpoint intervals, and a performance metric which is coupled with failure-free performance and the speedup functions associated with implementation of parallel algorithms. Expressions for the optimum checkpoint intervals for synchronous checkpointing with and without load redistribution are derived and the results are then used to determine when load redistribution is advantageous. Thus, the connected issues of checkpoint interval and load redistribution are considered and, for a given set of system and application parameters, an optimum checkpointing and load distribution scheme can be selected.

2. Optimum checkpointing

Optimum checkpointing for the single-node case has been studied extensively [2,3,4,5,6,7,8]. Optimum checkpoint intervals have been found by maximizing availability or minimizing response time. The objective function is typically convex, and analytic or numerical solutions can be found in many cases [8]. In most cases, a transaction-oriented environment is assumed where jobs or requests arrive from a Poisson source.

The optimum selection of checkpoint intervals for the multicomputer case has been sparsely studied. Gelenbe, et. al., developed a model which included the overhead of fault detection [9]. Gelenbe assumed that the nodes were homogeneous, the load at each node was identical, the nodes were tested periodically for faults, and there was an external source of jobs. In his development, requests sent to faulty nodes were routed to operational ones. Thus, the mean input rate to a node is a function of the job source rate, the number of faulty nodes, and the precision of fault detection. Based on these assumptions, expressions for the optimum checkpoint interval and optimum testing interval were obtained.

Our models consider a related situation but with the following differences:
1) Jobs are generated internally as the result of other jobs rather than coming from an external Poisson source.
2) Synchronous checkpointing is employed rather than an asynchronous checkpointing algorithm.
3) Fault detection is not explicitly modeled.

Our motivation is driven by a desire to model applications in a scientific computation environment rather than a transaction-oriented one. These differences lead to different models, solution techniques, and results.

We begin by considering the single-node case and then extend this to multiple nodes. A node can be viewed as being in one of three states: A) available, C) checkpointing, or R) recovering. For mathematical tractability and simplicity, we assume 1) Markovian state occupancy times, 2) failures form a Poisson process, and 3) failures only occur when a node is in the available state. This is reasonable when checkpoint and recovery times are small compared to the time that the node is available between such events.

The state transition-rate diagram for this Markov process is shown in Figure 1, and the parameters in the diagram are defined in Table I. After spending on average α^{-1} time units in the available state (A), the system will enter the checkpointing state (C). It spends on average β^{-1} time units saving the system state before it reenters the available state to resume computing. Occasionally, the system will fail. On average, the system will be available for ϕ^{-1} time units before this happens. When a failure occurs, the system will spend σ^{-1} time units recovering to the failure point before resuming the computation in the available state.

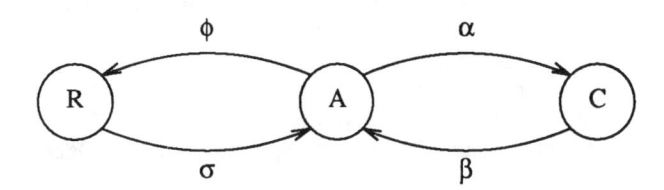

Figure 1. Single-Node State Transition Rate Diagram.

Parameter	Description
ϕ^{-1}	mean failure time
α^{-1}	mean time between checkpoints
β^{-1}	mean time to perform a checkpoint
σ^{-1}	mean recovery time

Table I. Model Parameters.

The availability (steady-state probability of being in the available state) π_A can be derived using standard CTMC (continuous-time Markov chain) techniques [10]:

$$\pi_A = \left[1 + \frac{\alpha}{\beta} + \frac{\phi}{\sigma}\right]^{-1} \quad (1)$$

Note that the mean recovery rate σ is a function of the mean checkpoint rate α since the amount of work to be repeated after a failure is related to the time between checkpoints. In order to determine how the availability π_A varies with the intercheckpoint frequency α, we must first express σ as a function of α.

The mean recovery time σ^{-1} consists of three time components: 1) a mean system repair time ρ^{-1}, 2) a mean state restoration time r, and 3) a mean recomputation time. The recomputation time is the time spent recomputing from the restored state to the failure point. If the system is never idle while in the available state, renewal theory says that the failure point will occur α^{-1} from the latest checkpoint since the failure and checkpointing processes are Poisson. If we assume that the system is never idle while in the available state, the mean recomputation time is

$$\sigma^{-1} = \rho^{-1} + r + \alpha^{-1} \quad (2)$$

The availability can now be written as:

$$\pi_A = \left[1 + \frac{\alpha}{\beta} + \phi\left[\rho^{-1} + r + \alpha^{-1}\right]\right]^{-1} \quad (3)$$

Setting the derivative of π_A with respect to α to 0 and solving for α leads us to the optimum checkpoint rate:

$$\alpha^{opt} = \sqrt{\phi \beta} \quad (4)$$

This corresponds to the result found in the literature [2,3]. The optimum checkpoint rate α^{opt} behaves as expected. That is, checkpoints should be taken more frequently (larger α) as failures occur more frequently (larger ϕ). Also, as checkpoints take less time (larger β), checkpoints can be taken more often (larger α) since there is less overhead associated with checkpointing.

At first, it may seem strange that the optimum checkpoint rate does not depend upon the repair and recovery parameters ρ and r. However, in the time interval between failures, the checkpoint frequency (α) controls only the overheads associated with checkpointing (through the number of checkpoints) and recomputation during recovery (through the intercheckpoint period). Changing the checkpointing frequency will not affect the repair and restore time components ρ^{-1} and r respectively.

The multi-node case offers us the opportunity to choose between several recovery methods. Consider two synchronous checkpoint recovery methods: one with load redistribution and one without load redistribution. Typically, if the down time after a failure is short, it is reasonable to wait for the failed node to recover before continuing the computation. However, if the failed node will be unavailable for a significant amount of time, it may make sense to redistribute the load among the remaining nodes, repeat the lost work, and then continue.

In addition to the three single-node model assumptions discussed earlier, we assume that 4) the fault-free speed-up curve is known, 5) the nodes are homogeneous, 6) the load is balanced across the processors, and 7) the processor utilization is approximately equal to the ratio of the speed-up to the number of processors. Assumption 4 is reasonable for many scientific computations. The fault-free speed-up is the ratio of the single-node and multinode finishing times in a fault-free system ($T(1)$ and $T(N)$) and is defined as:

$$S(N) = \frac{T(1)}{T(N)}, \qquad N \geq 1 \qquad (5)$$

Figure 2 shows two typical curves for $S(N)$. In the ideal situation, the speed-up with N processors would be N. Because of multiprocessor overheads, synchronization delays, and communication delays, however, the speed-up is generally less than N. The dashed curve indicates linear speed-up. The solid curve is approximately the same as the dashed curve for small numbers of processors, but then reaches an assymptote for larger numbers of processors. This deviation from linearity can be a result of a lack of sufficient parallelism, or heavy message traffic. We extend the speed-up measure to a faulty environment by defining the speed-up in a faulty environment $\bar{S}$ to be the ratio of the fault-free single-node finishing time $T(1)$ to the faulty multi-node finishing time $T^*(N)$; that is,

$$\bar{S}(N) = \frac{T(1)}{T^*(N)}, \qquad N \geq 1 \qquad (6)$$

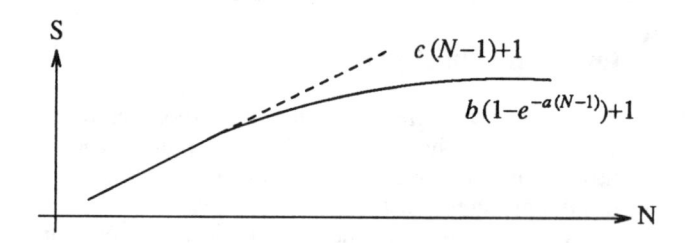

Figure 2. Speed-Up as a Function of Number of Nodes.

Assumptions 5 and 6 (homogeneous nodes and load balance) are made for illustrative purposes. Equivalently, the interfailure time, intercheckpoint time, and checkpoint duration at any node are stochastically identical to those on any other node. Although we make this last assumption for analytic tractability, the basic development would remain the same even without this last assumption, although the resulting equations would be more complex.

Assumption 7 is also made for analytic tractability. We assume that the fault-free utilization $U(N)$ is

$$U(N) = \frac{S(N)}{N} = \frac{T(1)}{T(N)} \frac{1}{N}, \qquad N \geq 1 \qquad (7)$$

Note that this is equivalent to assuming that the sum of the CPU time component of all processors is equal to the CPU time of a single processor system. This can be seen by noting that $U(N)T(N)$ is the CPU time of each processor. The sum of the CPU times of all N processors is $NU(N)T(N)$ which is equal to $T(1)$ when $U(N)$ is replaced by the righthand side of Equation 7.

3. Model I — synchronous checkpointing without load redistribution

Begin by considering the simplest case: synchronous checkpointing without load redistribution. The disadvantages of this approach for systems with many nodes are the high synchronization cost and low availability when repair times are slow. In this approach, all nodes checkpoint at approximately the same time. A two-phase commit protocol might be used to synchronize the start of a checkpointing phase. Once the checkpointing is done the system is available for normal computation. If any node fails, the whole system must go through a recovery phase. After recovery, the system is again operational with N nodes.

The system is equivalent to a single-node running N times as fast when operational, but also failing N times as often. Such a system can be in one of three states: A) all nodes are available, C) all nodes are checkpointing, or R) all nodes are recovering. The availability π_A of this system can be obtained from the single-node case by noting that the mean system failure rate is now $N\phi$ instead of ϕ. Furthermore, since the nodes can be idle during the intercheckpoint period, the mean recompute time is now given by $U(N)\alpha^{-1}$ where $U(N)$ is the fault-free utilization when there are N processors. Using equation 3, the availability is:

$$\pi_A = \left[1 + \frac{\alpha}{\beta} + N\phi\left(\rho^{-1} + r + U(N)\alpha^{-1}\right)\right]^{-1} \quad (8)$$

The objective is to maximize the availability of the system. Since the multi-node availability equation is identical to the single-node one except $N\phi$ replaced ϕ, and $U(N)\alpha^{-1}$ replaced α^{-1}, it is easy to see that the optimum checkpoint rate will be

$$\alpha^{opt} = \sqrt{N\phi\beta U(N)} \quad (9)$$

The speed-up using the optimum checkpoint frequency can now be derived. If $T(N)$ is the finishing time of the fault-free system with N processors, the finishing time of the faulty system is $T^*(N) = T(N)/\pi_A$ since π_A is the fraction of time that the faulty system is operational. From our definition of speed-up in a faulty environment,

$$\bar{S}(N) = \frac{T(1)}{T^*(N)} = \pi_A \frac{T(1)}{T(N)} = \pi_A S(N) \quad (10)$$

where $S(N)$ is the fault-free speed-up; that is, the speed-up in the faulty environment is reduced by a factor equal to the system availability. After substituting for α^{opt} (from 9) into the availability equation (8), equation 10 becomes:

$$\bar{S}(N) = \frac{S(N)}{1 + 2\sqrt{N\phi U(N)/\beta} + N\phi(\rho^{-1}+r)} \quad (11)$$

Figure 3 shows the speed-up curves for $N=4$ to $N=64$ processors for the parameters shown in Table II. Checkpoint and state restoration times are representative of times for writing and reading a few megabytes of data from moveable head disk and synchronizing the checkpoint and recovery activities. The mean failure time of 10^5 seconds is a typical value [11], while the mean repair times of 10^3 seconds and 10 seconds represent two short repair times. The dashed curve is the failure-free speed-up curve with exponential form (constants $b=128$ and $a=1/128$). The lower solid curve corresponds to the case when the mean repair time is $\rho^{-1}=10^3$ seconds. The other solid curve corresponds to the case when the mean repair time is smaller by two orders of magnitude.

Param.	Value	Description
β^{-1}	1 sec	Mean checkpoint time
a,b	1/128,128	Exponential fault-free speed-up params.
r	1 sec	Mean state restoration time
α	Optimum	Mean checkpoint rate
ϕ^{-1}	10^5 sec	Mean failure time
ρ^{-1}	$\{10^3, 10\}$ sec	Mean repair time

Table II. Model I Parameter Values.

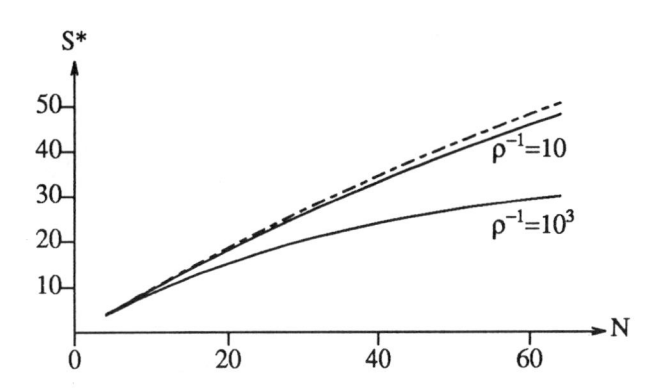

Figure 3. Speed-Up Versus Number of Processors (Model I).

4. Model II — synchronous checkpointing with load redistribution

In synchronous checkpointing without load redistribution, long recovery times due to permanent errors which can not be resolved by quick system resets forces the entire system to be idle for large time periods. In this situation, it would make more sense to work around the faulty node and redistribute the load onto operational nodes. But typically, the cost of load redistribution is significant. If the faulty node becomes operational immediately after the load is redistributed, it would have been better to wait for the faulty node to be repaired and not redistribute the load. Furthermore, in our analysis, the checkpoint interval is allowed to be dependent on the number of operational nodes. This section quantifies the overheads that justify a load redistribution and determines the optimum checkpoint intervals.

For homogeneous nodes, the system state can be defined in terms of the vector $S = (n_A, n_C, n_R, n_F)$ where the components correspond to the number of nodes in the states A, C, R, and F. These parameters are are shown in Table III. The state transition rate diagram is shown in Figure 4. In the available state $(N-k,0,0,k)$ (column 2, Figure 4), $N-k$ nodes are operational and k nodes are being repaired. When checkpointing is initiated from this state, the system enters the checkpointing state $(0,N-k,0,k)$ (column 4). After checkpointing, the system reenters the available state $(N-k,0,0,k)$. When a failure occurs, the system enters the state $(0,0,N-k-1,k+1)$ (column 1) where it downsizes (redistributes the load down to the $N-k-1$ operational nodes). After load redistribution, the system enters the available state $(N-k-1,0,0,k+1)$ (column 2) where it resumes computation with one less processor. Nodes are repaired (in parallel) while in state $(N-k,0,0,k)$. After a repair, the system is in state $(0,0,N-k+1,k-1)$ where the system takes a checkpoint and then upsizes (redistributes the load among the $N-k+1$ operational nodes).

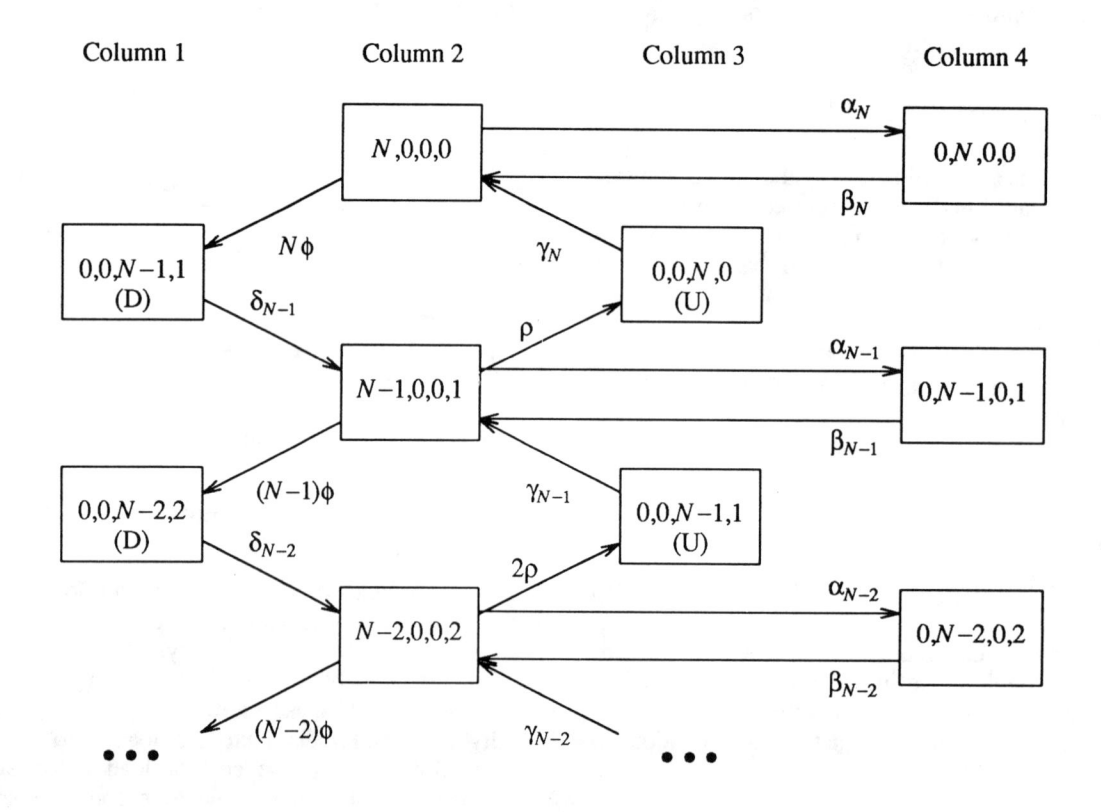

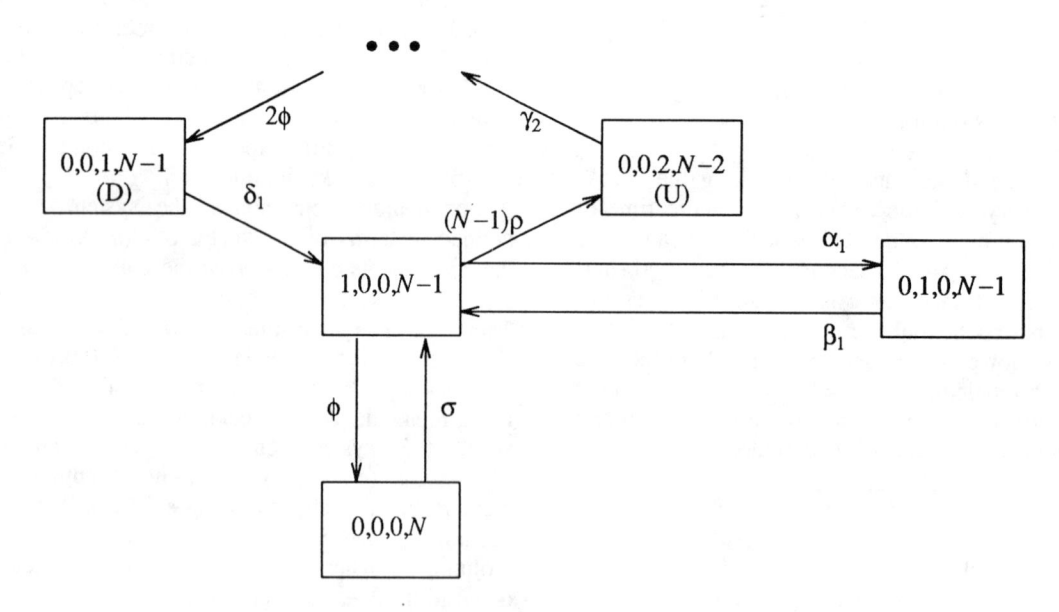

Figure 4. State Transition Rate Diagram (Synchronous Checkpointing With Load Redistribution).

Param.	Description
n_A	number of nodes in available state
n_C	number of nodes in checkpointing state
n_R	number of nodes in load redistribution state
n_F	number of failed nodes

Table III. Markov State Components.

In one case, the load is not redistributed after a failure. This occurs when there is only one operational node which then fails. In this case, the load can not be redistributed and the system must be repaired and lost work must be repeated.

The parameters in the state transition rate diagram are summarized in Table IV. The mean rates ϕ, and σ have the same interpretations as in the single-node case. In the multi-node model, the failure rate while in state $(N-k,0,0,k)$ is $(N-k)\phi$ since each of the $N-k$ operational nodes fail at a mean rate of ϕ. The mean rate α_k, $k=1,...,N$, is the multiprocessor equivalent to α and are the mean intercheckpoint rates when there are k operational nodes. The mean rate β_k, $k=1,...,N$, is the multiprocessor equivalent to β and are the mean checkpoint rates when there are k operational nodes. The two rates δ_k, $k=1,...,N-1$, and γ_k, $k=2,...,N$, are the recovery rates associated with downsizing (omitting a failed node) and upsizing (including a repaired node) respectively. During downsizing, the load must be redistributed, the state must be reloaded, and the work lost since the latest checkpoint must be repeated. The mean downsizing time is

$$\delta_k^{-1} = d_k + r_k + U(k+1)\alpha_{k+1}^{-1}, \qquad k=1,...,N-1 \quad (12)$$

where the first term is the mean load redistribution time, the second term is the mean state restoration time, and the third term is the mean recomputation time. During upsizing, a checkpoint is made and then the load is redistributed. The mean upsizing time is

$$\gamma_k^{-1} = \beta_k^{-1} + g_k + r_k, \qquad k=2,...,N \quad (13)$$

Param.	Description
N	Number of processors
k	Number of operational nodes
β_k^{-1}	Mean checkpoint time
$U(k)$	Fault-free utilization
r_k	Mean state restoration time
α_k	Optimum mean checkpoint rate
ϕ	Mean failure rate of a single node
ρ	Mean repair rate of a single node
d_k	Mean redistribution time (downsize)
g_k	Mean redistribution time (upsize)

Table IV. Model II Parameters.

Appendix I shows how the state probabilities can be computed using local balance equations and probability conservation.

Unlike the prior case, this system can continue to operate with failed nodes. However, when k nodes are under repair, the speed-up will be less than the N node case. Thus, our performance measure should account for variations in the speed-up due to node failures. We define the average speed-up to be

$$\bar{S}(N) = \sum_{k=1}^{N} S(k)\pi_{k,0,0,N-k} = \sum_{k=1}^{N} kU(k)\pi_{k,0,0,N-k} \quad (14)$$

where $U(k)$ is the fault-free utilization when k nodes are operational. Appendix I shows that the average speed-up can be derived as

$$\bar{S}(N) = \pi_{N,0,0,0}\left[\sum_{k=1}^{N} U(k)\binom{N}{N-k}\left(\frac{\phi}{\rho}\right)^{N-k}\right] \quad (15)$$

and the optimum checkpoint interval when there are k operational nodes is

$$\alpha_k^{opt} = \sqrt{k\phi\beta_k U(k)}, \qquad k=1,...,N \quad (16)$$

Thus the kth state-dependent checkpoint rate is identical to the optimum checkpoint rate of a system with k nodes using synchronous checkpointing without load redistribution.

Figure 5 shows the speed-up curves for $N=4$ to $N=64$ processors for the parameters shown in Table V. The parameters are the same as in Table II, but augmented by the load redistribution parameters d_k and g_k. For this example, we assumed that the mean checkpoint time ($\beta_k=\beta$), and the mean load redistribution times d_k and g_k are independent of the number of operational nodes. The dashed curve is the failure-free speed-up curve with exponential form (constants $b=128$ and $a=1/128$). The two solid curves are almost identical and indicate speed-ups which are not significantly worse than the one in a fault-free environment. This contrasts with the result in Model I where a longer mean repair time affected the performance substantially. Because Model II allows work to continue after redistributing the load, the affect of faulty nodes has a smaller impact on performance than in Model I.

Parameter	Value	Description
d_k	10 sec	Mean redistribution time (downsize)
g_k	10 sec	Mean redistribution time (upsize) ($g_k=d_k$)
Others		See Table II

Table V. Example Model II Parameters.

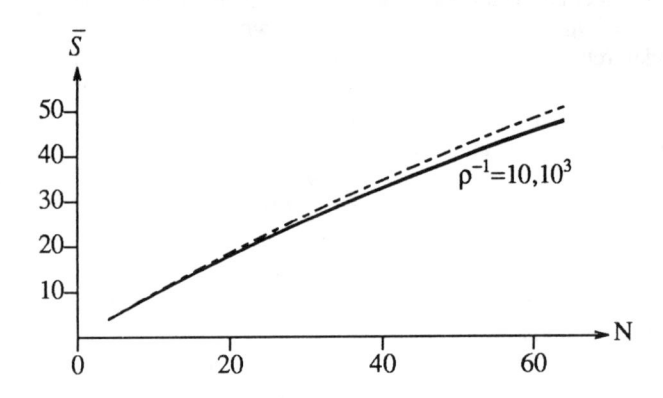

Figure 5. Speed-Up Versus Number of Processors (Model II).

5. An example

This section presents an example indicating how the expressions derived can be used to determine whether or not to employ load redistribution techniques. Table VI shows the parameter values which are used in this section's examples. In order to factor out the fault-free behavior from the examples, the fault-free utilization is assumed to be 1 ($U(k)=1$). Although $U(k)$ affects the absolute performance of the two algorithms, it will not affect their relative performance. Bracketed values in column two indicate that parameter values have been chosen from the interval indicated in brackets. The parameter values have been chosen as before to represent both typical and pedagogic cases. Both $N=8$ nodes and $N=64$ nodes have been evaluated to examine the effect of node population on performance.

Param.	Value	Description
N	[8,64]	Number of processors
β_k^{-1}	1 sec	Mean checkpoint time
$U(k)$	1.0	Fault-free utilization
r_k	1 sec	Mean state restoration time
α_k	Optimum	Mean checkpoint rate
ϕ	$[10^{-6}, 10^{-5}]$ sec^{-1}	Mean failure rate
ρ	$[10^{-4}, 10^{-1}]$ sec^{-1}	Mean repair rate
d_k	$[1, 10^{+2}]$ sec	Mean redistribution time (downsize)
g_k	$[1, 10^{+2}]$ sec	Mean redistribution time (upsize)

Table VI. Model II Parameter Values.

In order to focus on the fractional difference between the performance of the two algorithms, we use the ratio of the average speed-up $\bar{S}(N)$ to the ideal speed-up (N) as our performance measure and refer to this measure as the *efficiency* ε. In Model I (without load redistribution), the average speed-up is the speed-up given by Equation 11 since the system is only operational when all N processors are operational. However, in Model II (with load redistribution), the average speed-up is given by Equation 15.

$$\varepsilon = \frac{\bar{S}(N)}{N} \qquad (17)$$

Figures 6a and 6b show the effect of the mean repair rate ρ on the efficiency ε for different values of the mean load redistribution time $d_k=d$ and $N=8$ nodes. The solid (dashed) curves indicate the model II (I) efficiencies. Note that the horizontal axis is a log scale where ρ has been varied over four orders of magnitude.

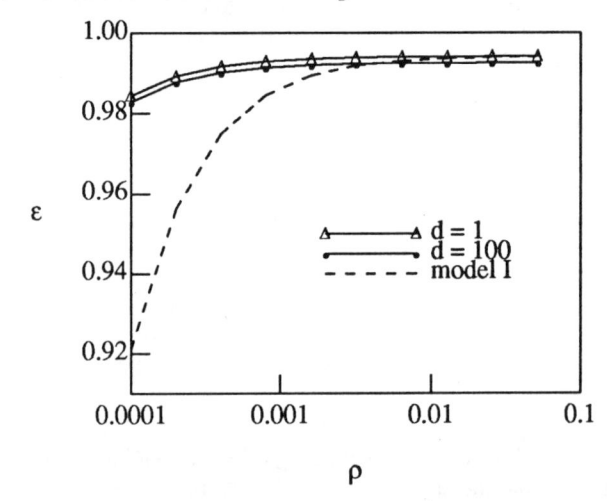

Figure 6(a). Efficiency (ε) Versus Repair Rate (ρ) (N=8 Processors, $\phi = 10^{-6}$ sec^{-1}).

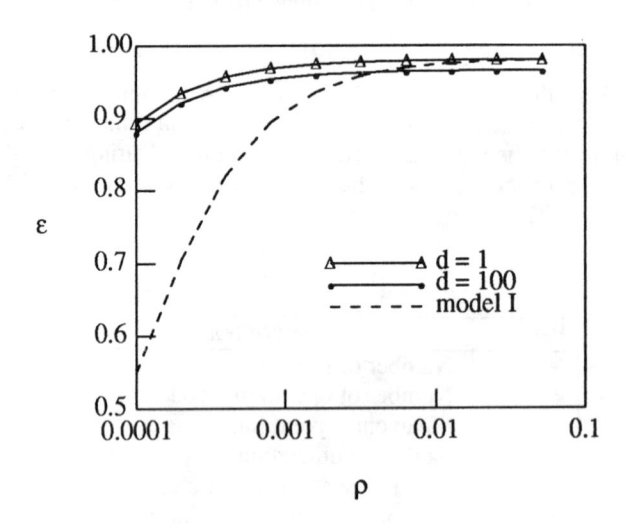

Figure 6(b). Efficiency (ε) Versus Repair Rate (ρ) (N=8 Processors, $\phi = 10^{-5}$ sec^{-1}).

Let ε_I and ε_{II} denote the efficiencies using models I and II respectively. The curves indicate that:
1) When the load redistribution cost is low (small d), the load should be redistributed for greater efficiency (i.e., $\varepsilon_{II} > \varepsilon_I$) since the system is more resilient to failures.
2) When the load redistribution cost is high (large d), the best strategy depends on the repair rate. The costs of

load redistribution must be offset by an increase in availability. Load redistribution is better ($\varepsilon_{II} > \varepsilon_I$) when repairs are slow (small ρ). Load redistribution is not better ($\varepsilon_{II} < \varepsilon_I$) when repairs are fast (large ρ).

3) The efficiency of model II is fairly insensitive to the repair rate ρ while the opposite is true of the efficiency of model I. Failures requiring a large repair time (small repair rate) are disastrous when the load can not be redistributed.

The curves also seem to suggest we should always redistribute the load since the efficiency of model I is never significantly better than that of model II. However, our next example shows that this is not always the case.

Figures 7a and 7b show the efficiency curves for the same parameter values used in the preceding example except that there are $N=64$ nodes instead of $N=8$ nodes.

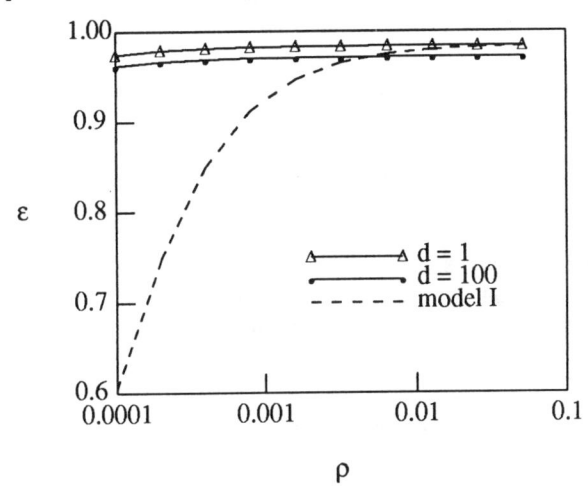

Figure 7(a). Efficiency (ε) Versus Repair Rate (ρ) (N=64 Processors, $\phi = 10^{-6}$ sec^{-1}).

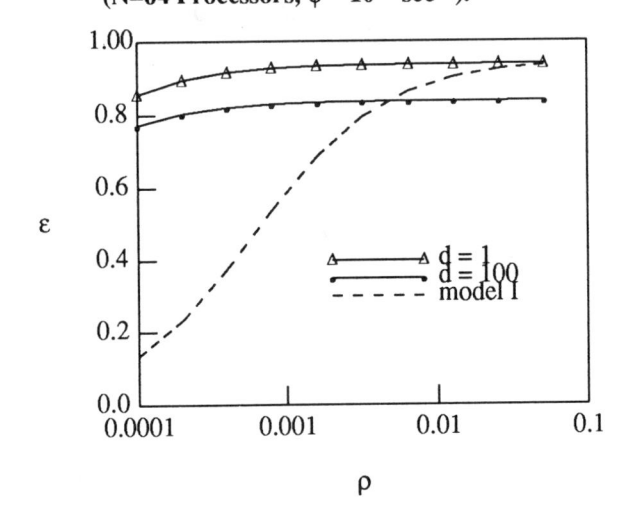

Figure 7(b). Efficiency (ε) Versus Repair Rate (ρ) (N=64 Processors, $\phi = 10^{-5}$ sec^{-1}).

The curves have the same general shapes as before but the details indicate additional features:

1) The efficiency in both models is less than before. This is due to the higher over-all system failure rate caused by a greater number of failure sources (nodes).
2) The repair rate has a more dramatic effect on the efficiency in model I than model II. For example, in order to have an efficiency in model I that is at least 0.80, the mean repair time can be no more than 250 sec (25 sec) when the failure rate is 10^{-6} sec^{-1} (10^{-5} sec^{-1}).
3) The efficiency in model II is less affected by the increased node population. It drops to only 0.80 even when the failure rate is high (10^{-5} sec^{-1}) and repair rate is low (10^{-4} sec^{-1}).
4) The load redistribution time d must be kept low in order to maintain high efficiency in model II, especially when failure rates are high. For example, when the failure rate is 10^{-5} sec^{-1}, there is a 10% difference between the efficiencies when $d=1$ sec and $d=100$ sec.

6. Conclusions and further research

The proper checkpointing strategy will be necessary to maintain high efficiency in long-running, massively parallel applications which are subject to failures. We have analyzed two checkpoint/recovery strategies for non-transaction-oriented systems: synchronous checkpointing with and without load redistribution. Optimum checkpoint rate(s) were determined analytically and have familiar forms. The models indicate operational regions where one is preferred over the other. In particular, synchronous checkpointing without load redistribution will have limited use in large node population applications because of its lack of resilience to failures. Synchronous checkpointing with load redistribution is more resilient to failures, but the load redistribution and checkpointing overheads must be kept small to maintain high efficiency. This becomes even more imperative with ever increasing node populations.

Although the material presented here assumes a symmetric system in which all nodes act identically (in the stochastic sense), it is a straightforward extension to handle the heterogeneous case or to add more state dependent considerations to the model (e.g., mean checkpoint time). Another related issue that can also be addressed in our framework is the distribution of tasks in a heterogeneous system.

Our models could easily be extended to include the possibility for handling transient and permanent failures differently. A transient failure is one in which the repair time is measured in seconds (e.g., software/hardware reset) whereas a permanent failure requires a much longer repair time which is measured in hours or even days. The response to a permanent failure might be to redistribute the load whereas the response to a transient failure might be to wait for recovery without load redistribution.

We are also in the process of modeling specific checkpointing strategies [12,13] and exploring alternative asynchronous strategies which take local snapshots and allow for partial operation during checkpoint periods.

The models presented in this paper characterize the system architecture explicitly and the task assignment indirectly through the fault-free speed-up curve. Another approach is to model the computational load by a task graph explicitly and the system architecture indirectly as affects on arc and/or node costs. We are also developing models using this alternative approach and trying to match the model parameters to real workloads (e.g., logic simulation) and use speed-up curves derived from experimental data. Our hope is that results from both approaches can be used iteratively to produce results which identify the fundamental parameters in determining task allocation in a faulty computation environment.

Appendix I
Optimum Synchronous Checkpointing With Load Redistribution

The Markov chain for Model II obeys local balance equations [14]. These equations can be written using four pairs of arcs for each row of states where row k corresponds to the states with k failed nodes:
1) the arcs coming into and going out of a downsizing recovery state (column 1);
2) the arc going out of an availabile state $(N-k,0,0,k)$ due to a failure and the arc going out of the available state $(N-k-1,0,0,k+1)$ due to a repair;
3) the arcs going into and out of an upsizing recovery state (column 3);
4) arcs going into and out of checkpoint states (column 4).

These arc pairs correspond to surfaces for states in columns 1, 2, 3, and 4 in the state transition diagram respectively. We equate the flows across these pairs of arcs. The solution to these local balance equations also satisfy the global balance equations in which the flow into each state is equal to the flow out of each state.

We first write the state probabilities for the active states (column 2) in terms of $\pi_{N,0,0,0}$. Then, all other state probabilities are written in terms of $\pi_{N,0,0,0}$. For the states in column 2 (excluding state $(0,0,0,N)$),

$$\pi_{N-k,0,0,k} = \pi_{N,0,0,0} \binom{N}{k} \left(\frac{\phi}{\rho}\right)^k, \quad k=1,\ldots,N-1 \quad (18)$$

For the state $(0,0,0,N)$, and then the states in columns 1, 3, and 4:

$$\pi_{0,0,0,N} = \pi_{N,0,0,0} \left(\frac{\phi}{\rho}\right)^N \frac{N\rho}{\sigma} \quad (19)$$

$$\pi_{0,0,N-k,k}^{(D)} = \pi_{N,0,0,0} \binom{N}{k} \left(\frac{\phi}{\rho}\right)^k \frac{k\rho}{\delta_{N-k}}, \quad k=1,\ldots,N-1 \quad (20)$$

$$\pi_{0,0,N-k,k}^{(U)} = \pi_{N,0,0,0} \binom{N}{k} \left(\frac{\phi}{\rho}\right)^k \frac{(N-k)\phi}{\gamma_{N-k}}, \quad k=0,\ldots,N-1 \quad (21)$$

$$\pi_{0,N-k,0,k} = \pi_{N,0,0,0} \binom{N}{k} \left(\frac{\phi}{\rho}\right)^k \frac{\alpha_{N-k}}{\beta_{N-k}}, \quad k=0,\ldots,N-1 \quad (22)$$

Using probability conservation, we can solve for $\pi_{N,0,0,0}$. The details can be found in [15]. Since all state probabilities have been written in terms of $\pi_{N,0,0,0}$ above, we have solved for all state probabilities.

The problem now is to find checkpoint rates α_k for $k=1,\ldots,N$ operational nodes which will optimize the average speed-up $\bar{S}(N)$.

$$\bar{S}(N) = \sum_{k=1}^{N} kU(k)\pi_{k,0,0,N-k}$$

$$= \pi_{N,0,0,0} \left[\sum_{k=1}^{N} kU(k) \binom{N}{N-k} \left(\frac{\phi}{\rho}\right)^{N-k} \right] \quad (23)$$

A necessary (but not sufficient) condition for optimality of the checkpoint rates is that the partial derivatives of $\bar{S}(N)$ with respect to the checkpoint rates be zero. But since $\pi_{N,0,0,0}$ is the only term in the $\bar{S}(N)$ expression that depends on the checkpoint rates α_k, the requirement for optimality is equivalent to finding the roots of the N equations:

$$\frac{d\,\pi_{N,0,0,0}}{d\,\alpha_k} = 0, \quad k=1,\ldots,N \quad (24)$$

Note that the recovery rates are state dependent. Recovery from the states in column 3 in which there were $N-k$ operational nodes ($k=2,\ldots,N$) involves checkpointing and then redistributing the load (including reloading the state); that is,

$$\gamma_k^{-1} = \begin{cases} 0, & k=1 \\ \beta_k^{-1} + g_k + r_k, & k=2,\ldots,N \end{cases} \quad (25)$$

The parameters g_k and r_k, $k=1,\ldots,N$, are the mean times for load redistribution and state restoration respectively. Recovery from state $(0,0,0,N)$ involves repairing the system, reloading the state, and then repeating work lost since the latest checkpoint.

$$\sigma^{-1} = \rho^{-1} + r_1 + U(1)\alpha_1^{-1} \quad (26)$$

Recovery from the states in column 1 in which there are $N-k$ operational nodes involves redistributing the load (including reloading the state) and then repeating the work lost since the latest checkpoint. The parameter d_k, $k=1,\ldots,N-1$, is the analog to g_k in the expression for γ_k and represents the load redistribution time.

$$\delta_k^{-1} = d_k + r_k + U(k+1)\alpha_{k+1}^{-1}, \quad k=1,\ldots,N-1 \quad (27)$$

After substituting the expressions for γ_k^{-1}, σ^{-1}, and δ_k^{-1} into the equations obtained from taking the N derivatives, the resulting derivatives can be shown to be quadratic in α_k with one non-negative root in each case. After some algebra, the optimum checkpoint rates can be shown to be

$$\alpha_k^{opt} = \sqrt{k \phi \beta_k U(k)}, \qquad k=1,...,N \qquad (28)$$

REFERENCES

1. J.S. Turner, "Design of a Broadcast Packet Switching Network," *IEEE Trans. on Comm.* **36**(6) pp. 734-743 (June 1988).
2. John W. Young, "A First Order Approximation to the Optimum Checkpoint Interval," *Communications of the ACM* **17**(9) pp. 530-531 (Sept. 1974).
3. K. Mani Chandy, James C. Browne, Charles W. Dissly, and Werner R. Uhrig, "Analytic Models for Rollback and Recovery Strategies in Data Base Systems," *IEEE Transactions on Software Engineering* **SE-1**(1) pp. 100-110 (March 1975).
4. E. Gelenbe and D. Derochette, "Performance of Rollback Recovery Systems under Intermittent Failures," *Comm. ACM* **21**(6) pp. 493-499 (June 1978).
5. Erol Gelenbe, "On the Optimum Checkpoint Interval," *Journal of the ACM* **26**(2) pp. 259-270 (Apr. 1979).
6. Asser N. Tantawi and Manfred Ruschitzka, "Performance Analysis of Checkpointing Strategies," *ACM Transactions on Computer System* **2**(2) pp. 123-144 (May 1984).
7. Kang G. Shin, Tein-Hsiang Lin, and Yann-Hang Lee, "Optimal Checkpointing of Real-Time Tasks," *IEEE Transactions on Computers* **C-36**(11) pp. 1328-1341 (Nov. 1987).
8. Victor F. Nicola and Johannes M. Van Spanje, "Comparative Analysis of Different Models of Checkpointing and Recovery," *IEEE Trans. Software Engineering* **16**(8) pp. 807-821 (Aug. 1990).
9. Erol Gelenbe, David Finkel, and Satish K. Tripathi, "Availability of a Distributed Computer System with Failures," *Acta Informatica* **23** pp. 643-655 (1986).
10. Kishor Shridharbhai Trivedi, *Probability and Statistics with Reliability, Queueing, and Computer Science Applications*, Prentice-Hall, Englewood Cliffs, New Jersey (1982).
11. X. Castillo, S. R. McConnel, and D. P. Siewiorek, "Derivation and Calibration of a Transient Error Reliability Model," *IEEE Trans. on Comm.* **C-31**(7) pp. 658-671 (July 1982).
12. Richard Koo and Sam Toueg, "Checkpointing and Rollback-Recovery for Distributed Systems," *IEEE Transactions on Software Engineering* **SE-13**(1) pp. 23-31 (January 1987).
13. Kai Li, Jeffrey F. Naughton, and James S. Plank, "An Efficient Checkpointing Method for Multicomputers with Wormhole Routing," *International Journal of Parallel Processing*, (June 1992).
14. K. Kant, *Introduction to Computer System Performance Evaluation*, McGraw Hill, New York (1992).
15. Ken Wong and Mark Franklin, "Distributed Computing Systems and Checkpointing," WUEE 92-115, Department of Electrical Engineering, Washington University (January 1992).

Formal Method for Scheduling, Routing and Communication Protocol

Lenore M. R. Mullin and Scott A. Thibault
Computer Science
U. of Missouri
Rolla, MO.

Daria R. Dooling and Erik A. Sandberg
Computer Science
U. of Vermont
Burlington, VT.

Abstract

The PRAM model has been shown to be an optimal design for emulating both loose and tightly coupled multiprocessors for unit time operations[10]. When virtual processors are required, multiplexing work to available processors is employed[8]. This introduces a form of latency incurred by operating system overhead. Further complications arise when bandwidth creates bottlenecking of work units. Blelloch showed[2] how to add parallel prefix operations(scans) to an extended PRAM model which uses unit step, not time operations. This paper shows how the Psi(ψ) Calculus[5, 6, 3] can be used to group work units, i.e. pipelining the work units, so that multiplexing is not required. We instead pipeline workunits to processors and show how the number of processors need not be equivalent to the number of data components. Partitioning array data structures and pipelining groups of partitions to processors can minimize latency and bottlenecking on distributed message passing multiprocessing architectures.

1 Introduction

Discovering what fundamental constructs apply over many classes of multiprocessing architectures is essential if parallel computation is to be fully realized. The PRAM model of computation is not just of theoretical interest for designs on tight or loosely coupled architectures, but as a potential basis for parallel programming paradigms and machines[11, 2]. This paper focuses on the parallel prefix operation, scan, a primitive PRAM operation, and its general use over a wide class of architectures using the ψ Calculus. The associative prefix operation, scan, matrix multiply, and outer product are basic building blocks to higher order matrix computation. In order to reason about and develop parallel and distributed algorithms for higher order functions, we first must focus on their underlying building blocks. The model developed for reduction and then extended to matrix multiply, is based on the PRAM model described in [2]. This model of computation is logarithmic step and used in our designs for matrix multiply. This paper describes the implementation of the formal model previously developed as applied to an interconnection network of processors.

Although Blelloch's PRAM initially required that the size of the argument did not exceed the number of processors[2], it quickly became apparent that problem sizes often exceeded the number of available processors. He determined that the scheduling, routing, and load balancing of multiple components within the local memories of available processors helped to reduce the processor-step complexity since local operations can be done sequentially.

Although some work has been done to extend the PRAM model, performance issues and I/O complexity have not been addressed[2, 8]. We extend the PRAM scan introduced by Blelloch[2] for SIMD computation to message passing distributed architectures, since the scan operation is a key component in many PRAM algorithms. We build on the HPRAM(Hierarchical PRAM) introduced by Heywood and Ranka [4] which allows *forking* to a specific set of processors and the XPRAM[11] which executes supersteps over p processors. In XPRAM, the time to execute each superstep incorporates not only the time to perform the local operations but the time it takes to send and receive messages from other processors. This model provides a form of synchronization at regular intervals so that packets can be transmitted between pairs of nodes. The XPRAM has been suggested in problems with massive parallelism due to its simplicity in managing high level communications. In the HPRAM model, the step size is the time it takes to compute a subsection of a scan e.g., plus the time it takes to *fork* and *join* over the available processors. We will show how the ψ Calculus can be used to partition array operations based on the memory hierarchy to pipeline operations to the available processors[8]. We will furthermore show how we can predict performance and aid in an ideal architectural configuration for scientific applications.

2 Goals

We describe a portable, scalable, uniform design for the prefix scan, matrix multiply and outer product that fits the parallel prefix PRAM model. There are 3 cases addressed herein, assuming each row or partial row of each matrix fits in each processor's local memory:

- one row per processor
- more than one row per processor

- a partial row per processor

To make the design portable and scalable as well as logarithmic step, we abstractly view the processors connected as a hypercube so that if the processors are **really** connected as a hypercube the performance curve looks logarithmic. If the number of rows or real processors is not a power of 2, we will still pretend it is by imagining that virtual processors contain the identity for the associative operation in use, such that the total number of real and virtual processors is a power of two.

We initially store the real processor addresses in a one-dimensional array or vector. From a one-dimensional array that holds the processors address, evolves a general mapping strategy. This paper presents a unified design for parallel prefix operations, matrix multiply and outerproduct that can perform over a wide range of architectures. Input to a compiler would be number of processors, addresses of each processors, local memory size, shared memory size, and structure or *shape*(if any) of the target architecture. For this paper we view the processors connected over a TCPIP network, i.e. there is no regular array topology.

3 Notation and Problem Description

Initially we view the processor addresses(e.g. socket addresses if our realization is in a Unix environment), as components of a vector that could be restructured(abstractly that is), into any arbitrary regular shape. We first present the reduction of a matrix A where the number of rows is equivalent to the number of processors in our interconnection network, and the number of components in each row exactly fits the local memory of each processor. One strategy assumes a master manages all activity, i.e. the master knows how many processors, p, are available. Let $\vec{p}_r$ represent the real processor vector of size p, i.e. the total number of components, $\tau\vec{p}_r$ is p where the components of $\vec{p}_r$ are real processor addresses. Let $\vec{p}$ denote the working processor vector that contains addresses of both real and virtual processors, i.e. the concatenation of $\vec{p}_r$ and $\vec{p}_v$ denoted by

$$\vec{p} \equiv \vec{p}_r \mathbin{+\!\!+} \vec{p}_v \qquad (1)$$

where $\vec{p}_v$ is defined whenever $\tau\vec{p}_v \equiv 2^{\lceil \log_2 p \rceil} - p$, and for $0 \leq j < \tau\vec{p}_v$

$$<j> \psi \vec{p}_v \equiv \vec{p}[j] \equiv id(\text{op}) \qquad (2)$$

Given that each row of the array we desire to reduce is placed in a processor, indexing any processor is defined whenever

$$\begin{aligned} \tau\vec{p} &\equiv (\tau\vec{p}_r) + (\tau\vec{p}_v) \\ &\equiv (\tau\vec{p}_r) + (2^{\lceil \log_2 p \rceil} - p) \end{aligned} \qquad (3)$$

and $\forall i$ s.t. $0 \leq i < (\tau\vec{p})$ with **op** a binary associative operation.

$$<i> \psi \vec{p} \equiv \vec{p}[i] \equiv \begin{cases} <i> \psi \vec{p}_r \equiv \vec{p}_r[i] & \text{if } 0 \leq i < p \\ id(\text{op}) & \text{otherwise} \end{cases}$$

Because we want to perfom a logarithmic number of steps, we need to view our processor vector abstractly as a hypercube configuration. We denote this by P^n with $n \equiv \lceil \log_2 p \rceil$ and define:

$$P^n \equiv < n \,\hat{\rho}\, 2 > \hat{\rho}\, \vec{p}$$

i.e. we restructure($\hat{\rho}$) the processor vector into a 2^n hypercube creating an n-dimensional array where the size of each of P's dimensions is 2, i.e.

$$\rho P^n \equiv < 2_0 \cdots 2_{n-1} > \equiv < n \,\hat{\rho}\, 2 > .$$

We first determine the number of iterations the reduction must perform based on the dimensionality, d, of the new hypercube configuration:

$$d \equiv \delta P^n \equiv \lceil \log_2 p \rceil \equiv n \qquad (4)$$

Sending the ith row of A, denoted by $\Leftarrow$, to it's correspondingly addressed processor is denoted by

$$<i> \psi \vec{p} \equiv \vec{p}[i] \Leftarrow <i> \psi A \equiv A[i;] \qquad (5)$$

but we want to describe how to send a group of rows to a group of processors, without using the cartesian coordinates of P^n, i.e. we want to use starts, stops and strides of addresses.

4 Logarithmic Step Reduction

With the processors viewed as a hypercube, P^n, the result of $_{\text{op}}\,\text{red}\,A$ is in the 0th indexed processor and defined by: (**Processor reduction**)

$$\begin{aligned} Pred : &\lambda P^n.\lambda(_{\text{op}}\,\text{red}).\text{if}\,[\delta P^n = 0\,, \\ &P^n\,,\,Pred\,((_{\text{op}}\,\text{red})P^n\,,\,_{\text{op}}\,\text{red})] \end{aligned}$$

where op is an associative binary operation. This logarithmic step expression reduces P^n s.t. with a row of A in each processor as shown in figure 1 for example, many operations are performed in parallel(abstractly that is, since we are performing the operations over a TCPIP communications network). To minimize latency, we envision a buffer attached to each processor equivalent to the size of the local memory. For the example **Pred** recurses three times. The first reduction is shown in figure 2 and the second in figure 3. **Pred** then terminates and the result is left in the first processor, i.e. $\vec{p}[0]$.

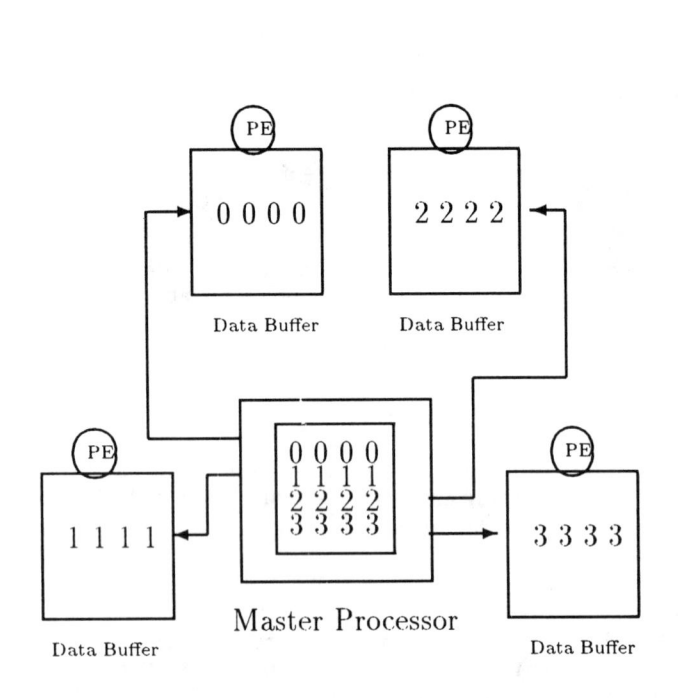

Figure 1: Example configuration of one row per processor.

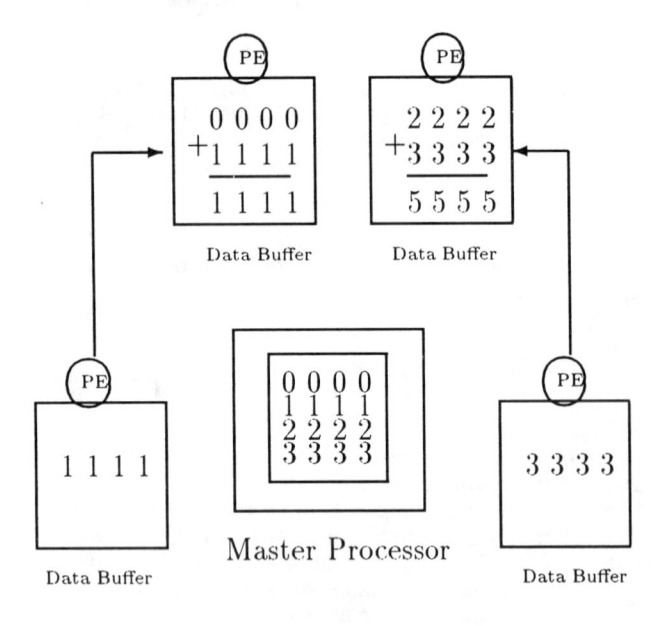

Figure 2: The first reduction in **Pred**'s execution.

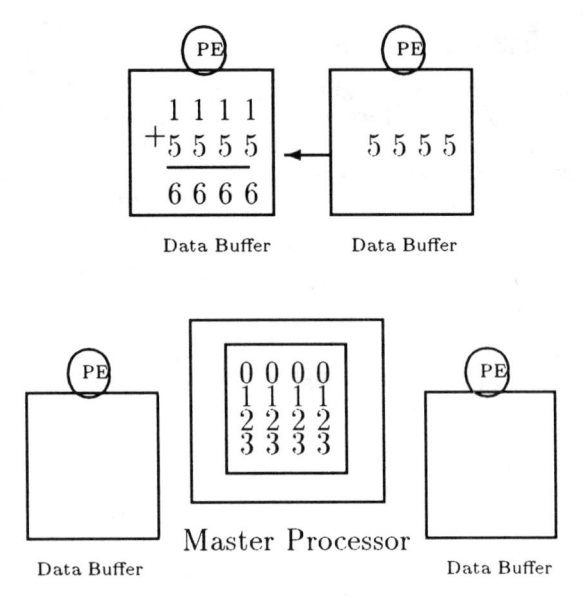

Figure 3: The last reduction of **Pred** with the result in the first processor.

4.1 Arrays that Don't Fit Exactly

What if the number of rows in A is greater than the number of processors? We want our design to still hold. Our original equation was:

$$<i>\psi\vec{p} \equiv \vec{p}[i] \Leftarrow <i>\psi A \equiv A[i;] \qquad (6)$$

If we restructure the data array A s.t. the extra rows get operated on sequentially, our original expression will still hold. Let A' [1] denote the restructured A s.t.

$$<i>\psi\vec{p} \equiv \vec{p}[i] \Leftarrow_{\text{op}} \text{red} \ (<i>\psi A') \equiv_{\text{op}} \text{red} \ A'[i;;] \qquad (7)$$

noting that in (7), each row of A is a plane in A' where the op **red** of the singleton plane sequentially reduces to a row, i.e.

$$<i>\psi A \equiv_{\text{op}} \text{red} <i>\psi A' \qquad (8)$$

Now a processor might contain more than one row to be reduced locally as shown in figure 4.

4.2 More Processors than Rows

Initially we assumed that the number of rows was a power of two then we developed the general case. We later extended the definition so that any number of rows could be reduced by partitioning the problem so that some operations were sequentially executed within each processor. We still have to address the issue of what to do if there are more processors than rows. For scientific problems that are 20000 by 20000 it is realistic to say that, if each component of the array is a floating point number, a row may not fit into a processor's local memory.

If we have more processors than rows we will need to partition the rows evenly to fully utilize the processors available to us, hence we need to view what

---
[1] See definition 12 in [7]

236

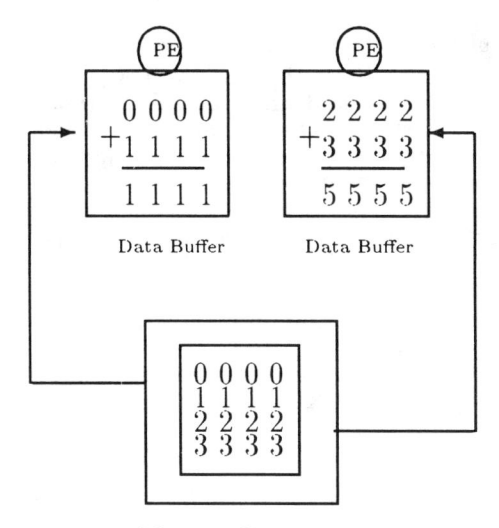

Figure 4: Example configuration of a reduction with more rows than processors.

Figure 5: Partitioning rows over more than one processor viewing $\vec{p_r}$ as a 2-dimensional array.

was previously called $\vec{p_r}$ as a 2-dimensional array of real processors where the first dimension represents the number of rows in the matrix to be reduced, and the second denotes the number of partitions of each row. For example, a matrix with two rows with four processors could be partitioned so that each row is partitioned over four processors as shown in figure 5. Restructuring the processor array, and denoting it by P we say

$$<i>\psi P \equiv P[i;] \Leftarrow_{\text{op}} \text{red}(<i>\psi A')$$
$$\equiv \text{op red } A'[i;;]$$

which means that each row of an array will now be broken up over many processors. We assume that the partitioning is broken up evenly, i.e. $(\rho A)[1] \mod \left\lfloor \frac{p}{(\rho A')[0]} \right\rfloor \equiv 0$. Letting c denote $\frac{(\rho A)[1]}{\left\lfloor \frac{p}{(\rho A')[0]} \right\rfloor}$ where $\forall j$, s.t. $0 \leq j < c$, thus the expression above means

$$<j>\psi<i>\psi P \equiv P[i;j] \Leftarrow_{\text{op}} \text{red}$$
$$A'[i;((j \times c) + 0) \cdots ((j \times c) + (c-1));]$$

It is the number of planes in A' that determines how many steps the reduction must make, noting again that each plane is sequentially reduced in each processor prior to invoking **Pred**. Therefore, given $m \equiv \lceil \log_2(\rho A')[0] \rceil$ we let the last dimension of P^n have a size equivalent to $\left\lfloor \frac{p}{(\rho A')[0]} \right\rfloor$ with the m leading dimensions equal to 2. We express this by saying

$$P^n \equiv < (m \, \hat{\rho} \, 2) \, ++ \, \left\lfloor \frac{p}{(\rho A')[0]} \right\rfloor > \hat{\rho} \, P$$

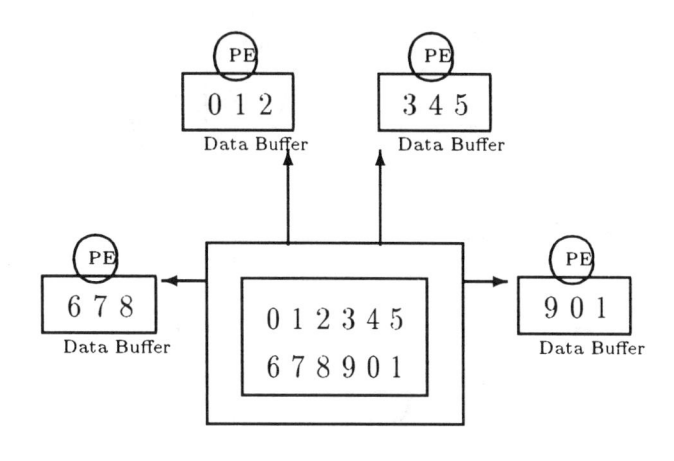

where

$$n \equiv \delta P^n \equiv m + 1$$

When **Pred** terminates, the result is in a vector of processors. We must therefore change the termination condition from 0 to 1 in our definition of **Pred** because we are putting 2-d not 1-d arrays into each processor. With all this we put the rows back together and say that the concatenation reduction(also a logarithmic step associative operation) of what is in the processors after applying **Pred** to P^n, is equivalent to the op red A' and as defined, sequential. For the example in figure 5, there is only one reduction and the result is in two processors and is concatenated together, as shown in figure 6. We express this as:

$$_{++}\text{red } Pred(P^n, \text{op red}) \equiv \text{op red } A' \quad (9)$$

and redefine **Pred** s.t.

$$Pred : \lambda P^n.\lambda(\text{op red}). \text{ if } [\delta P^n = 1,$$
$$P^n, Pred((\text{op red})P^n, \text{op red})]$$

4.2.1 Sequential Reductions in Local Memory

Pred used op red to describe the sequential reduction of each plane of A'. We now define **Sred** to encorporate the communications as well as sequential reductions. We will also extend the functionality of **Sred** to incorporate another operation and array so that the same design supports the inner and outer product, e.g. matrix multiply [7]. Note again, that the termination condition for **Pred** is $\delta P^n = 1$ due to our new formulation of P^n above. Initially, we'll assume that the size of each ith plane of A is less than or equal to the size of the local memory. Later, we'll relax this condition. From now on, we assume that when we say

$$<i>\psi P \equiv P[i;] \Leftarrow <i>\psi A' \equiv A'[i;;]$$

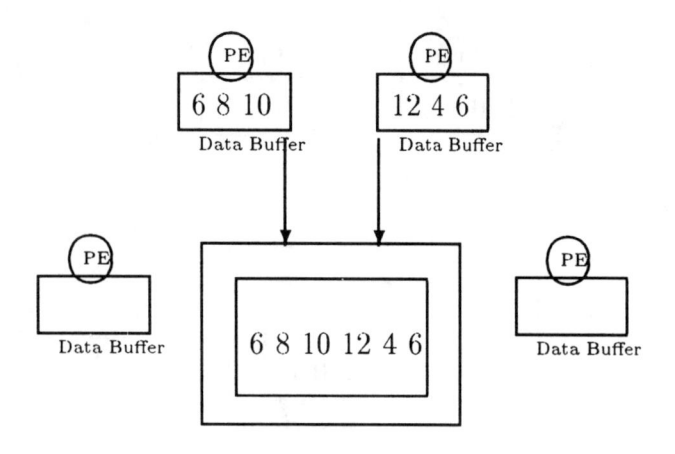

Master Processor

Figure 6: An example of the concatenation performed after invoking **Pred**.

that a row may be distributed over more than one processor.

Let **Sred**, for **S**equential **red**uction denote the lambda expression that defines how we will sequentially reduce $<i>\psi A'$ when A' has more than one row. From now on the sequential op **red** within each processor will be replaced by **Sred** and defined by the following, assuming that the row to be added is always ready in the buffer

op **red** : **Sred** : $\lambda A'.\lambda$op.
if $[(\rho A')[1] = 1$, $P_{\Leftarrow}\Omega_{<1\,2>} < 0 >_\psi \Omega_{<1\,2>} A'$,
  Sred $(1_{\triangledown}\Omega_{<0\,2>} A',$ op$)$ op $P_{\Leftarrow}\Omega_{<1\,2>} < 0 >_\psi \Omega_{<1\,2>} A']$

which means send in parallel each row of A's 2-dimensional planes to each row of P and sequentially reduce each row until all are reduced.

5 Parallel Prefix + Outer Product = Inner Product

So far, we have described how to perform a logarithmic step prefix scan/reduce operation for associative operations. We show in this section how we can use this design with outer product to perform matrix multiply. If we assume the parallel prefix is a primitive instruction, it is important to recognize how it may be incorporated with other parallel operations to produce useful computations. We have already implied in **Sred** that Ω describes parallelism. With this, we will show how the outer product, yet another primitive parallel operation, in conjunction with the parallel prefix describes an $O(\log n)$ addition step with n^2 parallel multiplies, given n processors, to produce the matrix multiplication of two conformably shaped matrices.

The matrix multiply is defined whenever B is an m by n matrix and A is an n by l. Let B^T denote the transpose of B. We then define the matrix multiply $B \odot A$ by

$$B \odot A \equiv_+ \text{red}\, B^T_{\otimes_\times} \Omega_{<1\,1>} A \qquad (10)$$

i.e. matrix multiply is the plus reduction of the outer product of each row of B^T with each row of A [7].

To accomplish this we need again to modify our design for **Sred** and **Pred** to perform another operation which will be a **no op** if we are just doing a reduction and a multiply if we are doing the matrix multiply, i.e. a plus reduction and an outer product. Similar to the way we restructured A we restructure B^T. We let B' denote the restructured B^T.

In the case of a simple reduction we would still perform the outer product but with the identity for the associative operation we chose. If we are not doing the matrix multiply, we still need to define a B' matrix that contains the identity for **op1**, i.e. $\forall \vec{i}$, $0 \leq^* \vec{i} <^* (\rho B')$

$$\vec{i}\psi B' \equiv id(op1)$$

letting **op0**$\equiv \otimes_{op1}$.

For the matrix multiply **op0**$\equiv \otimes_\times$ and **op1**$\equiv +$. Hence **Sred** and **Pred** are finally defined by:

op **red** : **Sred**: $\lambda A'.\lambda B'.\lambda$op0.$\lambda$op1.
  if $[(\rho A')[1] = 1$, $(P_{\Leftarrow}\Omega_{<1\,1>} < 0 >_\psi \Omega_{<1\,2>} B')$
    op0 $(P_{\Leftarrow}\Omega_{<1\,1>} < 0 >_\psi \Omega_{<1\,2>} A')$,
  Sred $(1_{\triangledown}\Omega_{<0\,2>} A', 1_{\triangledown}\Omega_{<0\,2>} B',$ op0, op1)
    op1 $(P_{\Leftarrow}\Omega_{<1\,1>} < 0 >_\psi \Omega_{<1\,2>} B')$
    op0 $(P_{\Leftarrow}\Omega_{<1\,1>} < 0 >_\psi \Omega_{<1\,2>} A')]$

Pred: $\lambda P^n.\lambda$op0.λ(op1 **red**).
  if $[\delta P^n = 1$, P^n , $Pred\,((\text{op red})P^n$, op **red**)$]$

where

$$B \odot A \equiv_+ \text{red}\, Pred(P^n , \otimes_\times , +\text{red})$$
$$\equiv_+ \text{red}\, B^T_{\otimes_\times} \Omega_{<1\,1>} A$$

An example should illustrate our design.

Example

Let
$$B \equiv \begin{bmatrix} 24 & 25 & 26 & 27 \\ 28 & 29 & 30 & 31 \\ 32 & 33 & 33 & 34 \end{bmatrix}$$

Let
$$A \equiv \begin{bmatrix} 0 & 1 & 2 & 3 & 4 & 5 \\ 6 & 7 & 8 & 9 & 10 & 11 \\ 12 & 13 & 14 & 15 & 16 & 17 \\ 18 & 19 & 20 & 21 & 22 & 23 \end{bmatrix}$$

The classical definition says:

$A \odot B \equiv$
$$\begin{bmatrix} (24 \times 0) + (25 \times 6) + (26 \times 12) + (27 \times 18) & \cdots \\ \vdots & \\ \cdots & (32 \times 5) + (33 \times 11) + (34 \times 17) + (35 \times 23) \end{bmatrix}$$

Our new definition says:

$+\text{red}\, B'_{\otimes_\times} \Omega_{<1\,1>} A' \equiv$
$$\begin{bmatrix} (<24\,28\,32> \otimes_\times <0\,1\,2\,3\,4\,5>) \\ + \\ (<25\,29\,33> \otimes_\times <6\,7\,8\,9\,10\,11>) \\ \vdots \\ +(<27\,31\,35> \otimes_\times <18\,19\,20\,21\,22\,23>) \end{bmatrix}$$

238

$$\equiv \left[\begin{array}{c} \left[\begin{array}{cccc} 24 \times 0 & 24 \times 1 & \cdots & 24 \times 5 \\ 28 \times 0 & 28 \times 1 & \vdots & 28 \times 5 \\ 32 \times 0 & 32 \times 1 & \vdots & 32 \times 5 \end{array} \right] \\ + \\ \left[\begin{array}{cccc} 25 \times 6 & 25 \times 7 & \cdots & 25 \times 11 \\ 29 \times 6 & 29 \times 7 & \vdots & 29 \times 11 \\ 33 \times 6 & 33 \times 7 & \vdots & 33 \times 11 \end{array} \right] \\ + \\ \vdots \\ + \\ \left[\begin{array}{cccc} 27 \times 18 & 27 \times 19 & \cdots & 27 \times 23 \\ 31 \times 18 & 31 \times 19 & \vdots & 31 \times 23 \\ 35 \times 18 & 35 \times 19 & \vdots & 35 \times 23 \end{array} \right] \end{array} \right]$$

Note that there are two ways to implement the new definition. As illustrated, each processor performs the outerproduct of two vectors resulting in a matrix. Upon completion of the outerproduct in each processor, **Pred** is invoked to perform the logarithmic step reduction of the matrices. If the outerproduct produced a matrix larger than the local memory size, it may have been advantageous to perform a scalar-vector outerproduct resulting in a vector. Using this method we would need to perform $B[0]$ invocations of **Pred** with $A[1]$ components versus one with $B[0] \times A[1]$ components.

6 Building the Design Model

The following are two different implementations of the distributed parallel prefix scan operation and matrix multiply. The first implementation uses one master processor to control all communication: the second distributes control. Experiments were run on a distributed system of RS6000s connected via an ethernet bus. In either implementation, the algorithm performs correctly regardless of the underlying communication and is thus scalable to any architecture.

6.1 Processors communicate with the master for future communications

To implement our model we reduce the formal lambda expressions given by **Sred** and eliminate the recursion. The **Sred** expression reduces to two looping constructs. The first, corresponds to the termination condition of the expression and sends the last row of each plane in A' to the proper processor. The second loop construct sends the remaining rows in each plane to the proper processor.

The expression for **Pred** is also reduced with the recursion removed. The outer loop is the number of reductions of the hypercube configuration that are performed. The inner loop sums the corresponding elements of the two components in the first dimension of P^n.

This implementation also includes the extension for matrix multiply. In this case a second operator is defined and the transposed B' matrix is sent with A' within the **Sred** expression.

The matrix multiply and reduction were tested on one to four RS6000's for varying sizes of square matrices. The results of the reduction are shown in figures 7 and 8. The speed up realized is not significant due to the reduction being fairly computationally inexpensive. However, it is still important to develop a good reduction algorithm, as it will be the fundamental basis for more computationally expensive operations (like the matrix multiply). The logarithmic performance is also not found in these results because only four processors are used. The matrix multiply, that has been built on the reduction, performs as desired. The results are shown in figures 9 and 10.

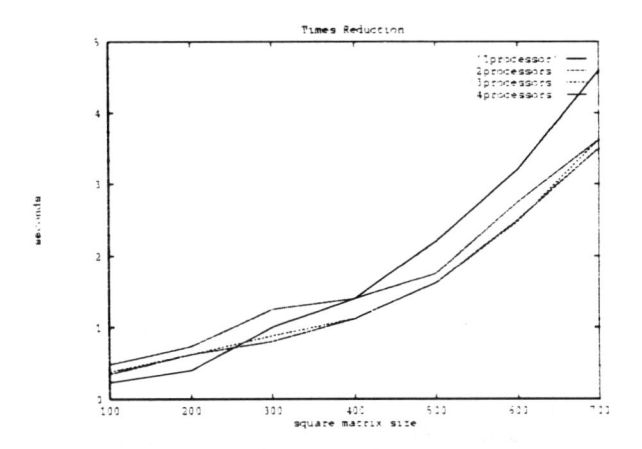

Figure 7: Timing results of the times reduction on one to four processors

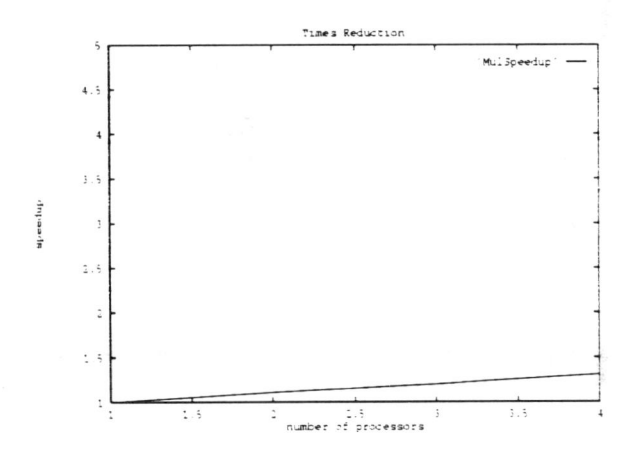

Figure 8: Relative speed up of the times reduction. The times used to calculate the speed up are with matrix sizes proportional to the number of processors.

This implementation could still be further optimized to balance the work done between the sequential operations and the time it takes to distribute partitions to each processor and return, to send the second partition to the first processor again. Future work would also include building the communication layer

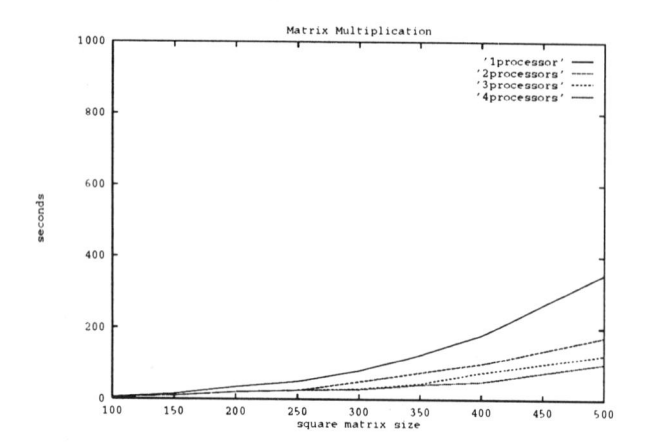

Figure 9: Timing results of the matrix multiply on one to four processors

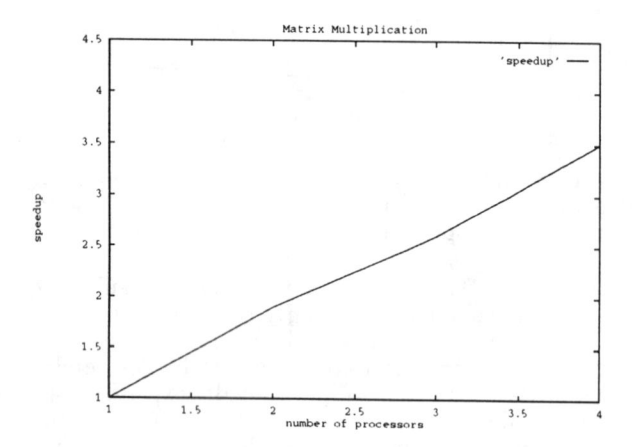

Figure 10: Relative speed up of the matrix multiply. The times used to calculate the speed up are with matrix sizes proportional to the number of processors.

for other architectures and examining some empirical results of using heterogeneous distributed systems.

6.2 Processors know all communications

This implementation differs from the implementation of section 6.1 in three ways. First, a tree structure of connections is used to communicate the problem and calculate solutions. Every node on the network has the same knowledge, therefore dispatching and control is propagated to parent nodes down the tree. Second, matrix multiply is implemented using the alternative method specified in section 5; it is described later in this section. Lastly, matrices reside on a Network File System, thus each processor performs disk I/O to obtain its partition of the input. Each communicates its piece of the answer up the tree to its parent.

A master processor collects the names of hosts which will be part of the network configuration and generates a communication table based on the processor vector $\vec{p}$ and the reshaped input matrix A'.

A processor accesses the communication table based on its position in the processor vector. Once a row is obtained, determining which processor to communicate with becomes a simple ψ function on that row. Which piece of the matrix a processor should access is also a simple ψ function based on the new shape of matrix A. **Sred** and **Pred** functions are similar at each node of this implementation as they are in the master of the first implementation.

In an effort to reduce local memory requirements and achieve a more fine grained parallelism, the matrix multiply algorithm implemented here performs a scalar-vector outerproduct for each element in a row of transposed B with the same row of A. The resultant vector is communicated upward at each step. This is why the major loop executed at each processor is executed $\rho B[0]$ times. For a reduce operation, the loop is executed only once. The first implementation does a vector-vector outerproduct with an entire row of transposed B and an entire row of A.

The same tests in section 6.1 were run on this implementation. We used one to five RS6000's and varied square matrix sizes. The results of the reduction operation are shown in figures 11 and 12. The speedup graph of the multiply reduce becomes linear after a matrix size of 400. Smaller sizes are not computationally intensive enough to realize linear performance.

The results of the matrix multiply operation are shown in figures 13 and 14.

For the parallel reduce operation, at each processor, we estimate $O(n)$ to be:

$$(n/p * n * k_{op}) + ((\log p * n * k_{op}) + (k_{send} * n) + (k_{recv} * n * \log p))$$

where n is the order of a square matrix, p is the number of processors, and k is a time constant. The first piece of this expression represents **Sred**; the second **Pred** and associated communication.

For a relatively large n, the second part of the equation is negligible, thus reducing $O(n)$ to:

$$n^2/p * k_{op}$$

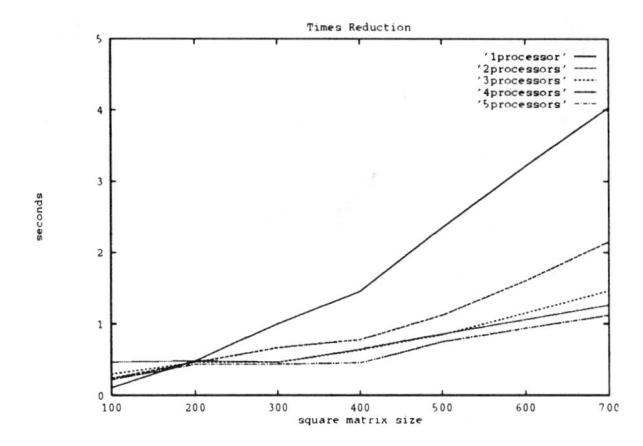

Figure 11: Timing results of the multiply reduction on one to five processors.

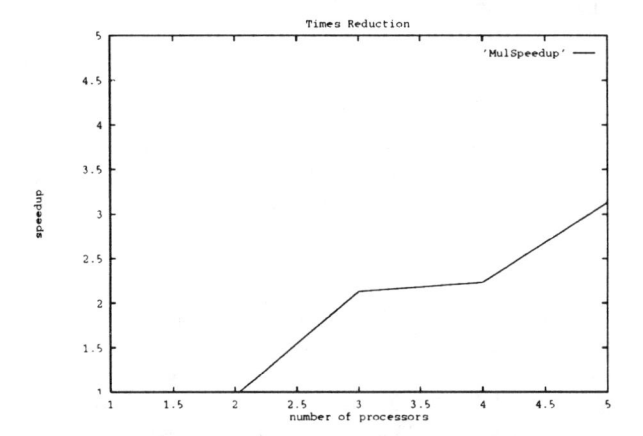

Figure 12: Relative speed up of the multiply reduction. Matrix sizes are proportional to the number of processors times 100. Speedup is the time for n processors/time for 1 processor.

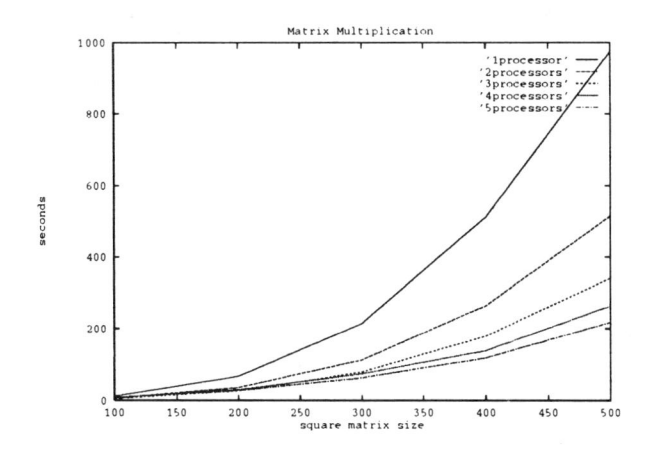

Figure 13: Timing results of the matrix multiply on one to five processors.

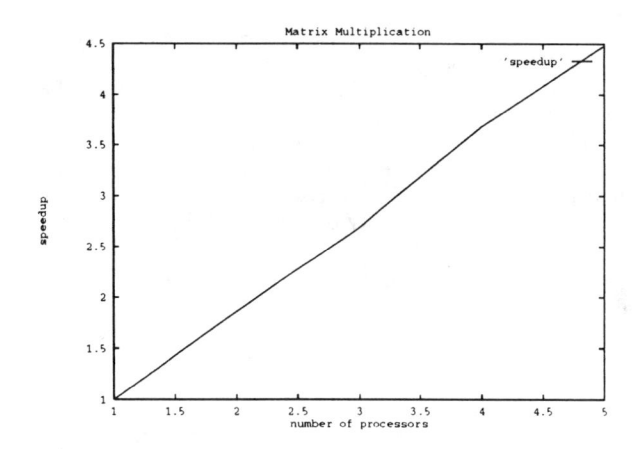

Figure 14: Relative speed up of the matrix multiply. Matrix sizes are proportional to the number of processors times 100. Speedup is the time for n processors/time for 1 processor.

At approximately $n/p = \log p$, the linear performance will no longer hold as the communication costs will outweigh the computational costs.

For matrix multiply, $O(n)$ is:

$$(k_{mult} * n/p * n) + (n/p * n * k_{op}) + (\log p * n * k_{op}) + (k_{send} * n) + (k_{recv} * n * \log p) + (k_{read} * n)$$

at each processor for n iterations. Simplifying the above, we have:

$$n^3/p * (k_{mult} + k_{op})$$

Some considerations to improve efficiency include putting matrix B in local memory and increasing pipelining during computation by having a larger communication buffer and adding more LANs.

7 Summary and Conclusions

Architecture independent designs are the key to portable scalable software. The PRAM model for the associative prefix operation performs on MIMD and SIMD multiprocessing architectures with both distributed and shared memory. Individual architectures may be insufficient when large scientific applications, which run for hours and perhaps days, are in question. We therefore need to address how architecture independent designs can be modified to include architectures connected by standard communications networks, such as TCPIP.

We showed in this paper how to extend the PRAM model over a TCPIP connected network of homogeneous workstations. We ran our experiments on 1-4 IBM RS6000's with one extra workstation working as a master. Our formal designs and code also run unmodified on SUN and IRIS workstations. The key difference between our designs and utilities such as PVM[9, 1] is that each step of our methodology is formal and can eventually be statically performed in a compiler. PVM requires some programmer intervention, hence errors can be introduced.

We also extended prefix operations to include the inner and outer product, e.g. matrix multiply. Although not discussed, we also extended the prefix scan to include certain non-associative operations as outlined in [7]. This and a detailed discussion of our new design for matrix multiply presented in [7], will be the topic of future reports.

For matrix reductions and matrix multiply(which uses the reduction) we performed timings using two methodologies (0) communication with the master for all future communications and termination and (1) a design which gives all processors knowledge of their subsequent communications. The design which carried all future communications was slightly faster but as the matrix size gets very large so does the communications packet which may become prohibitively large. The model that communicates with the master will always perform without constraints. We wonder what the threshold is in which performance degrades for (1) and increases for (0). With proper parameterizations as input, e.g. max packet size, matrix size, we could statically determine when to use one versus the other eventually mechanizing the process at compile time without programmer intervention. We plan to determine if our designs port to homogeneous multiprocessing MIMD and SIMD architectures. Eventually we would like to explore designs that include different speed cpus and hopefully heterogeneous architectures with a goal of load balancing statically. We plan to benchmark our designs with PVM.

We implemented matrix multiply two ways also. In one experiment we performed a vector to vector outer product with each processor versus a scalar to vector outerproduct. As expected, the former was faster because the cpu speed exceeded the communications speed, i.e. the later was, for a row with n components, n times slower due to communications overhead. What are the matrix sizes in which vector to vector outerproducts should be used versus scalar to vector outerproducts in the matrix multiply. What if a whole row does not fit? How can the outerproduct be partitioned? Can memory and communications network speed be factors in partitioning strategies? Can these methodologies be incorporated into an intelligent supercompiler for multiprocessing architectures and network configurations? We now we have a formal method to begin our investigations.

Acknowledgements

We thank the departments of Computer Science at the University of Missouri and the University of Vermont and the department of Electrical Engineering at Ecole Polytechnic at the University of Montreal for supporting this research. This work is also supported by NSERC.

References

[1] A. BEGUELIN, J. DONGARRA, A. GEIST, R. MANCHEK, AND V. SUNDERAM, *A Users Guide to PVM, Parallel Virtual Machine*, Oak Ridge National Laboratory. Report ORNL/TM-11826.

[2] G. E. BLELLOCH, *Scans as primitive parallel operations*, IEEE Transactions on Computers, 38 (1989), pp. 1526–1538.

[3] G. HAINS AND L. M. MULLIN, *An algebra of multidimensional arrays*, Tech. Report 782, Université de Montréal, 1991.

[4] T. HEYWOOD AND S. RANKA, *A practical hierarchical model of parallel computation: The model*, Tech. Report SU-CIS-91-06, School of Computer and Information Science, Syracuse University, Syracuse, New York 13244, 1991.

[5] L. M. R. MULLIN, *A Mathematics of Arrays*, Ph.D. dissertation, Syracuse University, December 1988.

[6] L. M. R. MULLIN, *Psi, the indexing function: A basis for ffp with arrays*, in Arrays, Functional Languages, and Parallel Systems, Kluwer Academic Publishers, 1991.

[7] L. M. R. MULLIN, D. R. DOOLING, E. A. SANDBERG, S. A. THIBAULT, *Formal Methods for the Scheduling, Routing and Communications Protocol of a Logarithmic Scan on a Message Passing Distributed Operating System: PRAM Algorithms Revisited*, Tech. Report CSEE/92/06-26, Department of Computer Science and Electrical Engineering, University of Vermont, Burlington, Vermont 05405, 1992.

[8] D. SKILLICORN, *Practical parallel computation i. models of computation*, Tech. Report 91-312, Department of Computing and Information Science, Queen's University, Kingston, Canada, 1991.

[9] V. SUNDERAM, *Pvm: A framework for parallel distributed computing*, Concurrency Practice and Experience, (1990).

[10] L. VALIANT, *A bridging model for parallel computation*, Communications of the ACM, (1990), pp. 103–111.

[11] L. G. VALIANT, *General purpose parallel architectures*, Tech. Report TR-07-89, Aiken Computational Laboratory, Harvard University, Cambridge, MA 02138, April 1989.

SESSION 7A:
File Systems and I/O

Nita Sharma, Chair

Accessing Remote Special Files in a Distributed Computing Environment

Joel Lilienkamp, Bruce J. Walker, Rich Silva

Locus Computing Corporation

ABSTRACT

This paper presents a general design for providing access to remote devices, pipes, and FIFOs, within a distributed computing environment. Though the design is presented in terms of SVR4 and Sun ONC, it is suffiently general to be built upon almost any underlying Unix system and distribution architecture. The design is applicable to all types of devices, and special attention is given to STREAMS oriented devices.

1. Introduction

Over the past decade or so significant advancements in the area of distributed computing have been made. The cost of hardware has been reduced substantially so that individual PCs and workstations are now commonplace. Local Area Networking technology is also more commonplace and is viewed as the principal mechanisms for providing sharing among these machines. System software is the key component necessary to provide this the appropriate level of sharing in this environment.

To date there are two significant software entries in the distributed computing arena. These are Sun's Open Network Computing system (ONC) and OSF's Distributed Computing Environment (DCE). Both of these systems provide a mechanism whereby files can be shared among systems in a reasonably transparent way. ONC provides this via the widely used Network File System (NFS), and DCE provides this using a variant of Transarc's AFS.

Both of these systems have their relative strengths and weaknesses. One significant deficiency they share is that neither of these environments provide transparent mechanisms for accessing remote special files. For the purposes of this paper special files are defined as devices and FIFOs. This paper presents a solution to this deficiency. It proposes a design which is applicable to both of these environments.

1.1 Motivations for Transparent Remote Access to Remote Special Files

While the existing standard distributed computing environments do not provide for remote access to special files, several distributed systems have provided such a feature [1,2,3,5,6,7,8,9,12]. None of these systems to date have provided this support in a manner which could easily be installed into any base system, thus making it a suitable candidate for adoption as a standard.

There are several motivations for providing transparent access to remote special files. These include the benefits of sharing resources in a distributed environment, the general desire of extending the distributed file system to all types of files, and providing a framework for transparent distributed processing for processes that have special files open.

A key advantage of providing transparent access to remote special files is a greater degree of resource sharing. Related to this is the cost savings that result from needing to buy less hardware. For example, printers and backup storage devices can be shared by users on a network. Fewer total backup devices can be used to backup data in such a system without needing to move the devices between machines.

The generally available distributed file systems export the entire file system name space to all of the participating systems. But the actual access that is exported is typically limited to files and directories; they do not export access to all special files. If all files in the namespace were exported then a greater percentage of programs written in for the single node would operate without errors in the distributed environment.

An additional motivation for providing transparent access to remote special files is to provide support for a distributed processing environment. In this context, distributed processing refers to the ability for processes to remotely exec or to migrate between nodes in a distributed system. Without support for transparent remote special file access, processes with them open could not remotely exec or migrate; they would effectively be pinned to the current execution node.

For a high performance multicomputer, it has been argued that a high performance transparent distributed computing environment is the answer for the system software [1,4,10,12,13]. Such an environment needs to have features beyond what standard distributed computing environments are offering today. The ability to provide transparent access to remote special files is a particularly important addition in this application.

The work for this paper was performed as part of a larger project termed "Transparent Network Computing", or TNC. The architectural scope of this project is described in [11].

1.2 Organization of the Paper

The second section of this paper discusses the overall goals of this design. The third section presents an overview of the total design. The fourth section describes how the basic I/O operations are implemented. The fifth section discusses special characteristics of STREAMS I/O. The final section discusses the future directions for this work.

2. Goals of Design

Several key goals for this design have been identified.

1. The solution should be as general as possible, so as to be as applicable as possible to any distributed computing environment. There is little value to be gained with a solution that is not appropriate for one or more standard distributed computing environments.

2. Once implemented on a particular base system, it should portable ported to other base systems with little or no rework necessary. To achieve this the software needs to be either replacement software or layered software that utilizes existing operating system hooks.

3. The design should implement special file access semantics that are consistent with existing standards for a single site system. Such standards include POSIX, X/Open, and SVID. In this way legacy software can operate in the distributed environment without modifications.

4. The performance of the resulting implementation should be good. It is probably not possible to provide strictly identical performance to the local case, since the bus speeds are typically much greater than LAN speeds and typically two I/Os are required at the client instead of one. But the design should still consider performance to be important.

3. Overview of the Design

The design described in this paper is presented in this paper in terms of System V Release 4. This is the platform on which the initial implementation was built. In general the design could be applied to other systems, but the terminology and details of the system interface would require minor changes.

The approach chosen for providing remote access to special files is to provide a new file system type, named *cspecfs*. This new file system interfaces to the system at the vnode operation switch. This interface was chosen because it is already provided in most UNIX implementations and hence will not require significant modifications to the base system in order to enable this new functionality.

The cspecfs file system uses a client/server model to provide distributed services. The client side is provided on all nodes. Users of remote special files access the device through the cspecfs client software, via the cspecfs vnode ops. First, these vnode ops determines the server node, which is the node where the special file is controlled and if it is a physical device, where it is physically attached. It then directs the operation request to that node. At the server node the request is received, and processed by the standard single-node vnode operations as if the request were generated locally. The pre-existing code need not be aware of local or remote issues and hence can work without any modifications. When the operation is completed, the result is returned to the client node.

Figure 1 shows the data structures used at the client and server nodes.

As described above, the cspecfs file system is layered above the existing special file support for the local

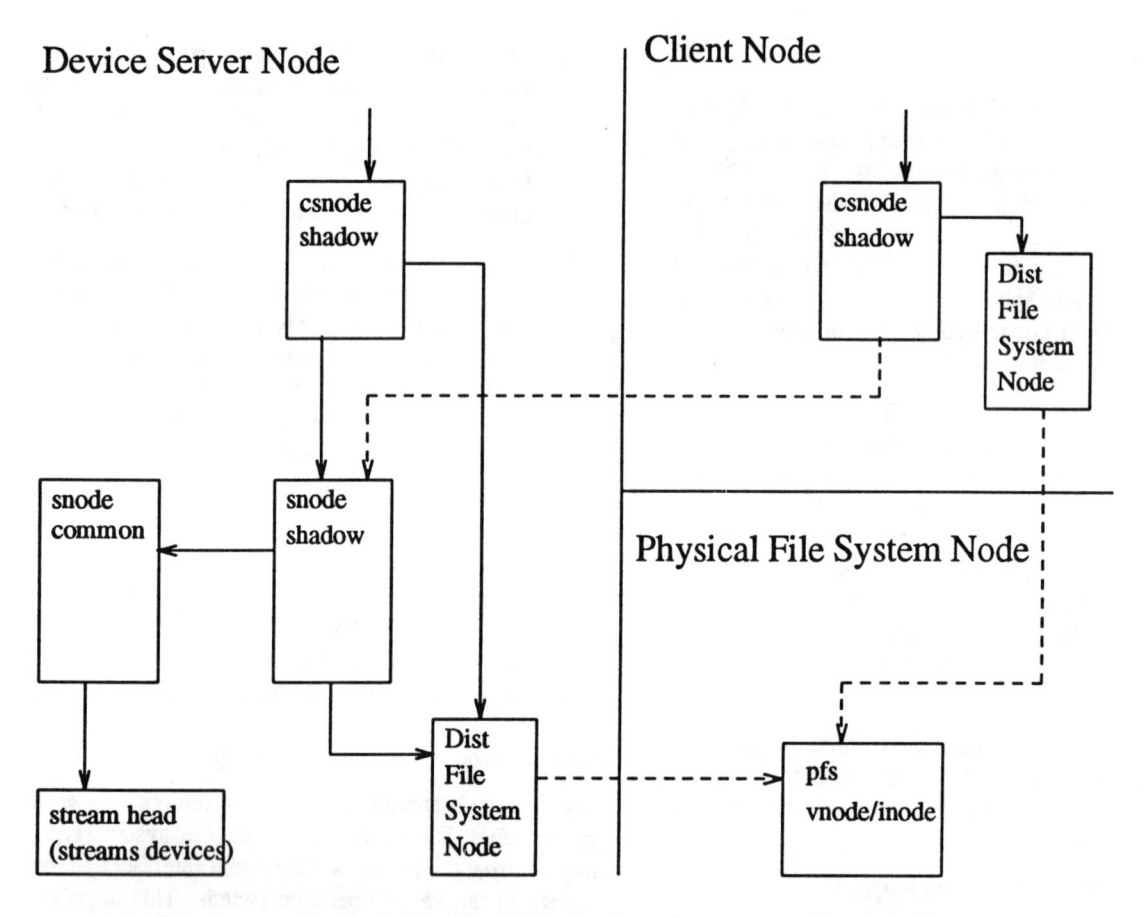

Figure 1. Distributed Device Data Structures at Client and Server

access case. This layering provides several advantages:

1. The design is modular: This makes development and testing more straightforward. The new code has a very specific function which is isolated from the existing code.

2. The lower level device code works without modification: Using a non-intrusive design, the implementation will be more palatable to system providers.

3. Supporting new devices is easy: Since the single node access software operates without modification, all that is required is the single-node drivers. The remote access code will not require modification to support the new device.

The cspecfs file system is layered above the underlying distributed file system. This too provides several benefits:

1. The device server node may be different from the node storing the file system. By separating these two concepts a more general solution is possible.

2. Any distributed file system can be used with this design. There is no consensus as to which distributed file system is the "best". There are strong advocates for both NFS and DCE, and other file systems have their followings too. By working with any of the file systems this design can appeal to all groups.

The design provides that clients communicate with the device server using a remote procedure call (RPC) mechanism. The protocols are general enough that any existing RPC facility can be used. For example, both ONC RPC and DCE RPC are suitable, though each has its own strengths and weaknesses. ONC RPC is widely available and its performance is fairly good, but is somewhat cumbersome to use. DCE RPC has a more general programming interface and has better capabilities for marshalling data, but it is not as widely available and its space and time performance characteristics are less than desirable. A message based system would also be feasible but was not explored.

On the device server node the recipient of the RPC will be a kernel thread acting as an agent for the client on the server. Typically, there will be a collection of these on each server node. These threads, called server threads, receive requests from the RPC mechanism, and assume the credentials of the client, so that permissions are properly enforced. When the action on behalf of the client is completed, any results are returned to the client, and the thread is for servicing other RPCs. The design assumes that it is acceptable for the server thread to sleep.

4. Basic I/O to Remote Devices

In this paper, six things are considered in the category of basic file I/O. Lookup is the operation when the special file is first looked up in the file system name space. Open and Close are operations which are used to set up structures to read and write files. Read and Write are the actual I/O operations. Ioctl is the operations to control special files. Attributes operations are typically file system operations regarding characteristics of the file from the file system perspective, including file ownership, permissions, and file times. Poll is a mechanism for event notification with respect to special files. These categories are discussed in the sections that follow.

4.1 Lookup

The special file lookup code is the same for all types of special files. During lookup the physical filesystem (e.g., UFS) call a routine specvp() to setup the appropriate vnodes. For the case of FIFOs, specvp() in turn calls fifovp(). For other special devices specvp() does the work itself.

If the underlying file system is a distributed file system, the specvp() and fifovp() routines will be called at the storage node of the file system. The first step in these routines is to determine the node where the special file will be controlled. For physical devices this node will be where the device is attached. There are several strategies for determining this. The simplest mechanism to do this is to add data to the device inode. Other strategies are to partition the device number space (e.g., major numbers map to particular nodes) or to keep additional data about the device elsewhere. FIFOs and pseudo-devices can be controlled anywhere. This design chose to implements them at the node where they are first opened after previously being unopened.

When the node has been identified it is returned to the client. If the client is also the server node or if the client is not the server node but is already a client, then the required structures exist already. Otherwise, the client node will create the underlying distributed file system vnode, and will then communicate with the server node. The server node determines the special file of interest, and returns a handle that uniquely identifies that special file on the server to the client. At the client this handle is stored so that future operations can communicate directly with the server.

4.2 Open and Close

The open and close operations are implemented in the cspec_open and cspec_close vnode operations. The steps to open a device in cspec_open are as follows:

— Determine which node node controls the stream. This information was determined during the lookup operation and stored in the csnode at that time.

— Increment the reference counts in the csnode.

— Send an open request to the server node. This request includes the process id, the session ID, the session device, and session flags (which are needed to ensure that a proper handling regarding controlling terminals is done).

— On the server node, call spec_open on the local shadow snode. If the open succeeds and returns back the same vnode (which means the device is not a clone device), return to the client node.

— If the spec_open fails return the error to the client.

— If the spec_open does not return the same vnode, the device was a clone device. As part of the clone operation the specfs shadow and common vnodes were dereferenced and new ones created. In this case return a handle for the new vnode to the caller.

— Back on the client node, it is necessary to detect if the device vnode has changed. If is has, it is necessary to create the new csnode.

The steps necessary to close a special file in cspec_close are considerably less complicated. A close message is sent to the server node. At the server, spec_close is called on the shadow snode. The per-node usage count is decremented at the server. The result is returned to the client, where the reference counts are similarly decremented.

4.3 Read and Write

Read and write operations are implemented in the cspec_read and cspec_write vnode operations. The cspec_read vnode op reads from the remote special file by sending a read message to the server. This message includes the necessary information regarding how much to read. If there is no data to be read and the read does not block, it returns immediately to the client. Otherwise it blocks at the server node until the data is ready. When data is read at the server, it is transferred back the client in the read response message. The client then transfers the data to the caller as if it were read locally. If an error occurs at the server, it is passed back to the client in the read response message where it is returned to the caller via an error code.

If multiple readers are waiting to read the device, the result is essentially the same as UNIX when all readers are local. Only one of the processes will get the data.

The cspec_write vnode op writes to the remote device. The data is copied from the caller and sent to the server in a write message. If the write blocks it will do so on the server node. When data is written control returns to the client node via the write response message. If an error occurs at the server, it is passed back to the client in the write response message where it is returned to the caller via an error code.

4.4 Ioctl

Ioctl operations are probably the most complicated to build in a distributed system, because ioctl takes an ioctl command argument which can require a somewhat arbitrary amount of data to be copied into or out from the user space. Furthermore, the ioctl commands are not all standardized. Individual drivers can define new ioctl commands.

One possible design would have the clients manage the copyin and copyout operations. The limitation with this approach is that the clients would have to know about all ioctls for all supported devices, so they could copy in or copy out the correct amount of data. Adding a new devices could require changing the client.

For these reasons this design chose to have to the server do the copyin and copyout operations directly. Since the user process may be remote, this requires that copyin and copyout be enhanced to work remotely.

The kernel thread on the server node assumes the credentials of the client. With a minor modification to standard copyin and copyout, if the user process is not running on the local node then a remote copyin or copyout routine is called. This routine sends a copyin or copyout message to the client hosts, with the data for copyout. Back at the client, the actual operation is performed. If it is a copyin, the result is returned in the response.

With this mechanism, the implementation of ioctl in the cspec_ioctl becomes straightforward. The client code sends the ioctl command and argument (which may be a pointer into user space on the client node) to the server node in an ioctl message. The agent on the server nodes sets its state so that the copyin and copyout operations will be directed back to the client, and then issues the ioctl command as if it were local. Any copyin and copyout will be detected and sent back to the client, but otherwise it is executed on the server. If the ioctl command blocks it will do so on the server. When completed, the server sends back an ioctl response message with any result or error return.

A few of the ioctl commands will be caught in the cspec_ioctl client and server routines to provide additional processing required for distributed STREAMS. These are all in the category of STREAMS control ioctls, and are described later.

4.5 Attributes

Special file attributes are managed either by the device manager or the file system. The operations cspec_getattr and cspecsetattr will be executed on the special file server node, although some of the attributes are passed to the distributed file system.

4.6 Poll

Poll operations require special handling because a client process can wait for several different events concurrently, and these events may be controlled on different nodes. Consequently the model used for the above operations of blocking at the device server is not practical.

The design for poll support thus requires a remote event notification feature. When a client issues a poll operation, any events on remotely controlled resources are registered on those nodes with a Poll Register message. This message supplies a handle to identify the client and identifies the resource and event being polled. On the server side the standard poll mechanisms are used. When all servers have been notified, the client sleeps. When an event occurs, callback is invoked, which sends a poll event message containing the client handle and the event status information from the server to the client. When this message is received at the client node, the sleeping the client is awakened. Processing continues on that node as if the event had occurred locally.

No complex mechanisms are required for cleanup. When the device is closed, any pending poll is canceled and the data structures are released. If a poll request comes in on a server where an event is already waiting, a second event watch need not be set up. In the event of client node failure the servers treat open devices as if a close occurred, and that close includes poll cleanup. Within the framework of the existing mechanisms all the necessary cleanup can be performed.

5. Special STREAMS I/O Characteristics

STREAMS I/O operates essentially in the same manner as other I/O. However, since STREAMS consist not of a single driver but also of module stacks and multiplexor links, there are some characteristics of STREAMS which require special consideration. These considerations are discussed in this section.

5.1 Single-node stack

To limit the complexity in the initial design, the choice was made to restrict STREAMS stacks to a single node. Hence all of the cspecfs functionality is built above the STREAMS layer. In this way, the existing STREAMS support including the module stacking mechanisms and inter-module communication works without modification. Likewise, all drivers and STREAMS modules will work without modification.

5.2 Multiplexing

STREAMS multiplexing is a feature by which multiple STREAMS can be connected to a single driver. Hence, a multiplexor driver is pseudo-driver one which has multiple Streams connected to it.

An upward multiplexor directs traffic up to one of several STREAMS, which are distinguished by different minor numbers associated with the same minor number, and hence a common driver. This structure works within the distribution framework described previously without additional mechanisms because all opens of devices that differs only in minor number will be directed to the same node, and so the stream stacks will all be built on that node.

A downward multiplexor directs traffic down to one of several STREAMS typically controlling different physical devices. These STREAMS are connected together by link operations. As long as all of these lower STREAMS exist on the same node no additional mechanisms are required. The next section discusses how to remove this restriction.

5.3 Cross-node Linkage

If a multiplexor driver needs to link to lower STREAMS stacks on remote nodes, additional mechanisms are required. This support needs to be done outside of the existing drivers and modules, and must impact the underlying STREAMS support as little as possible. The solution used is this design is build additional modules known as *aqueduct* modules. One of these modules is put on the node with the multiplexor driver. The other module is put on the node with the lower STREAMS stack to be linked. To the multiplexor driver and the lower STREAMS stack these aqueduct modules appear as ordinary STREAMS modules. In actuality they function as peers and provide the channel by which the multiplexor driver and the lower STREAMS stack can be connected together. Figure 2 illustrates the use of multiplexor modules.

The general algorithm to arrange this structure starts on the link node. The cspec_ioctl() routine traps the link ioctl request. This is necessary because the argument is a file descriptor which could not be easily interpreted on other nodes. This routine creates a handle for the open file and submits the request to the upper multiplexor driver.

The upper multiplexor driver first performs validity checks for the link request, and then sets up a "pseudo-stream head" for the remote stream stack. This pseudo-stream head includes data structures necessary for it to be linked to the multiplexor driver. The pseudo-stream head is connected to the client aqueduct module as if it were pushed. The multiplexor then sends an aqueduct link message to the node with the lower STREAMS stack. That node pushes the server aqueduct onto that STREAMS stack. When this is complete the node with the multiplexor driver simulates a link between the pseudo stream head and the multiplexor driver.

Aqueduct client and servers are logically a single pass-through module. The purpose is solely to transfer the message traffic between the upper multiplexor driver and the lower STREAMS stack, with the surrounding modules being unaware of the

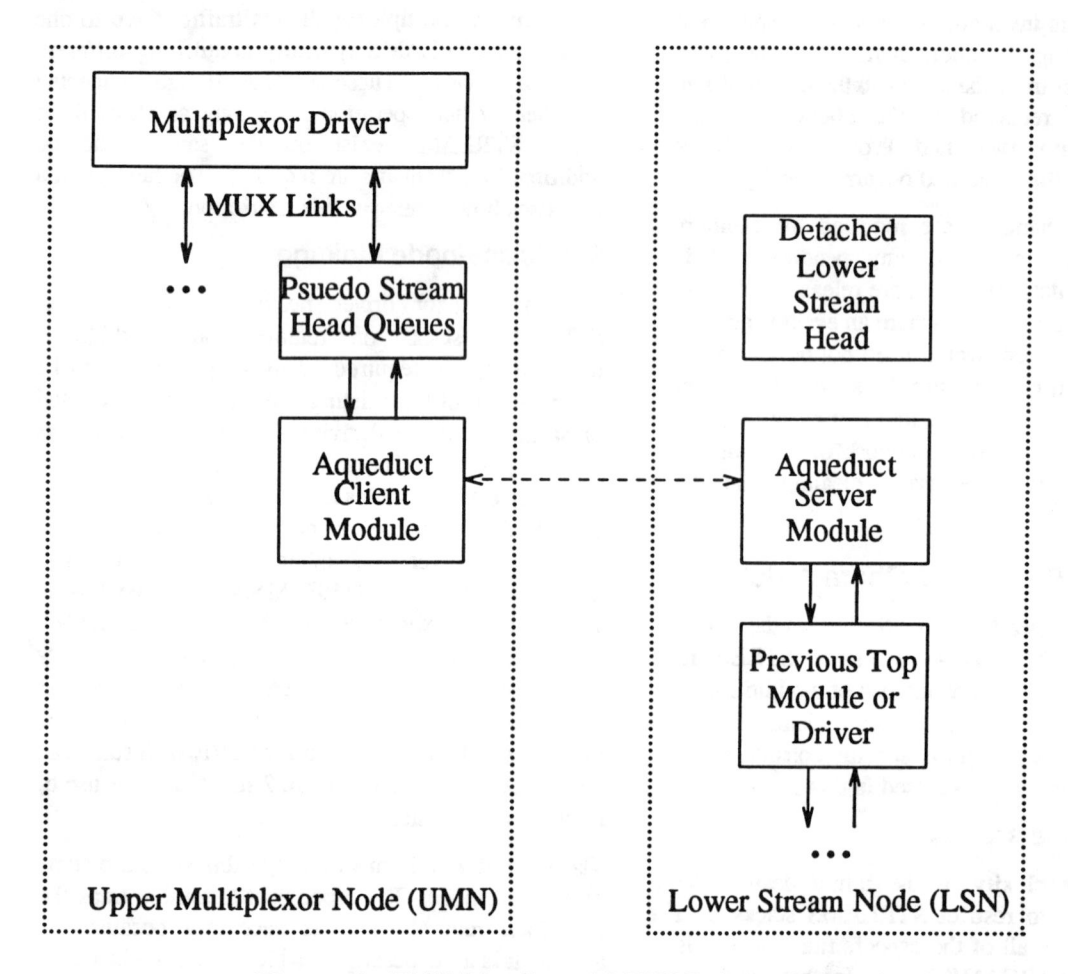

Figure 2. TNC Distributed MUX Drivers Using An Aqueduct

split. When the modules are set up, they contain a handle to the other's input queue so that the server routines can find the queue and transfer the data to the correct place.

6. Future Directions

While the design presented here is in some sense complete, there are a few areas of investigation for possible future improvements. These are discussed in this section.

6.1 Cache Coherency of Remote Block Devices

The design presented in his paper is suitable for both character and block devices. When block devices are read, however, the data is cached into the page cache (or buffer cache in some systems). No mechanisms are provided in this design to provide cache coherency. This is consistent with the design goal of being suitable for use with any distributed file system.

Some distributed file systems, NFS being the obvious example, do not provide mechanisms for absolute cache coherency, so providing cache coherency would be pointless. Other distributed file systems do provide for data cache coherency and it would be appropriate for this design to be able to take advantage of the mechanisms if they were provided.

The general strategy of using page-level tokens to ensure cache coherency is well understood. What needs to be researched is how to use the mechanisms available in a general way so that it can be applied to any of several coherent file systems. Also of interest is the mixing of strategies when both coherent and non-coherent distributed file systems are used together.

6.2 Distribution of Clone Device Management

The current design limits clone devices to the node controlling the clone. While this is a reasonable restriction for the first design, it would be appropriate that for clone pseudo-devices, that the control be done on the node that did the open. Doing so would help distribute the load among the nodes more effectively and possibly reduce subsequent network traffic.

6.3 Cross-node STREAMS Modules

The current design limits STREAMS stacks to a single node, except for the case of downward multiplexor links via aqueduct modules. In theory, it should be possible to put aqueduct modules between any pair of modules in a STREAMS stack, thus distributing the STREAMS processing between several nodes. In reality this is not easy because some STREAMS modules take advantage of the fact that the address space between modules is shared. Even were this not the case, there is still a question as to whether the parallel nature of the module processing outweighs the cost of copying data between nodes. There are probably some cases where it does. Hence it is an area of interest to understand when this is desirable and understanding better the mechanisms required to support it.

6.4 Memory-mapped Devices

The design presented in this paper does not address access to remote devices which are to be mapped into the virtual memory address space of the using process. Additional mechanisms to hook into the memory management support would be required. Since memory management implementations vary widely any solution would not be very portable. The performance of such an arrangement would probably be sufficiently poor as to make the value of such an effort dubious.

7. References

[1] Armand, F., Gien, M., Herrman, F., Rozier, M., Distributing UNIX Brings it Back to its Original Virtues", Proceedings of "Workshop on Experiences with Building Distributed (and Multiprocessor) Systems", Oct. 1989.

[2] Barak, A., Wheeler, R., "MOSIX: An Integrated Multiprocessor UNIX", USENIX - Winter 1989.

[3] Batlivala, N., et. al., "Experience with SVR4 Over Chorus", Proceeding of USENIX Workshop on Micro-Kernels and Other Architectures, April 1992.

[4] Bernhardt, M., "Intel and Locus Collaborate to Extend Paragon Supercomputer's Operating System Capabilities", Press Release, November 16, 1992.

[5] Briker, A., Gien, M., et. al., "Architectural Issues in Microkernel-based Operating Systems: the CHORUS Experience", Computer Communications, Butterword-Heinemann, Special Issue: Platforms for Distributed Applications, vol 14 #6, July/August 1991.

[6] Ousterhout, J. K., Cherenson, A. R., Douglis, F., Nelson, M. N., Welch, B., "The Sprite Network Operating System", Computer Magazine, February 1988.

[7] Popek, G., Walker, B., Chow, J., Edwards, D., Kline, C., Rudisin, G., Thiel, G., LOCUS: A Network Transparent, High Reliability Distributed System", Proceedings of the Eighth Symposium on Operating System Principles, Pacifig Grove, California, December 1981.

[8] Popek, G., Walker, B., *The LOCUS Distributed System Architecture*, MIT Press, 1985.

[9] Tanenbaum, A. S., Kaashoek, M. F., van Renesse, R., Bal, H. E., "The Amoeba Distributed Operating System -- A Status Report", Computer Communications, Butterword-Heinemann, Special Issue: Platforms for Distributed Applications, vol 14 #6, July/August 1991.

[10] Walker B., et. al., "Extending DCE to Transparent Processing Clusters", Winter Uniforum January 1992, San Francisco.

[11] Walker B., et. al., "Open Single System Image Software for the Multicomputer or MPP (Massively Parallel Processor)", Winter Uniforum March 1993, San Francisco.

[12] Welch, B.B., and Ousterhout, J. K., "Pseudo Devices" User-level Extensions to the Sprite File System", 1988 Summer Usenix Conference.

[13] Zajcew, R., et. al., "An OSF/1 Unix for Massively Parallel Multicomputers", 1993 Winter USENIX, January 1993, San Diego.

Performance Analysis of Distributed File Systems with Non-volatile Caches

Prabuddha Biswas
Digital Equipment Corp.
Nashua, NH.
biswas@xanadu.enet.dec.com

K.K. Ramakrishnan
Digital Equipment Corp.
Littleton, MA.
rama@erlang.enet.dec.com

Don Towsley
University of Massachusetts
Amherst, MA.
towsley@cs.umass.edu

C.M. Krishna
University of Massachusetts
Amherst, MA.
krishna@ecs.umass.edu

Abstract

In this paper we study the use of non-volatile memory for caching in distributed file systems. This provides an advantage over traditional distributed file systems in that the load is reduced at the server without making the data vulnerable to failures. We show that small non-volatile write caches at the clients and the server are quite effective. They reduce the write response time and the load on the file server dramatically, thus improving the scalability of the system. We show that a proposed threshold based writeback policy is more effective than a periodic writeback policy.

We use a synthetic workload developed from analysis of file I/O traces from commercial production systems. The study is based on a detailed simulation of the distributed environment. The service times for the resources of the system were derived from measurements performed on a typical workstation.

1 Introduction

Dramatic improvements in processor speeds has led to the I/O subsystem becoming the bottleneck in a computer system. Distributed file systems use caches at various points to remove the limitations due to this bottleneck [7,9,14]. The caches may be positioned at either the file server or at the client [12,16]. These traditionally have improved the performance of reads, both response times and throughput as seen by the user application. However, to provide a consistent view of the data seen by all of the clients of the distributed file system, and for reliability in the face of failures, write operations are often allowed to complete only after the data has been committed to stable storage, which has traditionally been the disk at the file server. Therefore, the dominant load on the file server is due to writes. It has been recognized that allowing writebacks from the clients can reduce this write-load on the server [7,12,18]. Further, the performance of writes can be improved by using a writeback policy for the server cache. This increases the number of clients that can be supported by a server and also reduces response times for user operations. However providing consistency and the ability to recover from failures remains a problem.

In the past, solutions have been proposed that allow for the data to be vulnerable to failures for a short period of time, while allowing clients to periodically writeback data to the server. This is often considered acceptable in operating systems such as Unix, wherein the user application is not given a guarantee that data is committed to the disk immediately, unless an explicit user-operation (fsynch) is used. Data loss and inconsistency cannot be tolerated in commercial applications and therefore non-volatile memory has to be used for writeback caches. Non-volatile Random access memory (NV-RAM) is becoming cheaper and is easy to incorporate into existing system designs without major changes to the file system. Products are commercially available which use NV storage to allow for the writeback of data at the server [11]. Several recent efforts have also quantitatively shown that the performance of the I/O subsystem improves with the use of NV write caches at the disk controller [4,10].

While the use of NV-RAM as a cache is becoming feasible, it is still sufficiently expensive [1,6] that a single large NV cache for the entire client cache or even the entire server cache cannot be used. In this chapter, we therefore consider the performance issues that arise when there is a separate read cache and a non-volatile write cache. In particular, we are interested in devising efficient management policies for the write cache at both the file server and the client's file subsystem. We consider two scenarios: one in which an NV write cache is placed only at the server and another in which NV caches are placed at both the clients and servers. We show that a small amount of NV-RAM at the clients and the server provides most of the performance achievable through a writeback scheme from a single large cache at the client and the server. When a writeback policy is used at the client in a distributed file system, policies are required to maintain consistency among the client caches [12,18]. We study the effect of the client NV write caches on the interactions generated by the consistency policies.

Previous studies of distributed file systems have either been based on measurement of prototype systems [2,7], analytic modeling techniques [9,14], or trace driven simulations [1,8,12,18]. We base our analysis on an extensive workload characterization based on file I/O traces collected on operational production systems [5,15]. We use these traces to parameterize a synthetic workload to drive a distributed file system simulation model.

In section 2 we present the traditional caching policies and also explain how an NV write cache can be used together with a volatile read cache. In the following section, we discuss the performance metrics used in this study. Section 4 includes a description of the traces and a discussion on how they are used for characterizing the workload. Section 5 presents the details of the simulation model and section 6 contains the results of the study. Finally, section 7 concludes with a summary of the major observations.

2 Caching Policies

In this study we model a distributed file system in which a number of client workstations access all files, including system executables, from a common file server system. The clients and the server have volatile file block caches. We study the effect of using non-volatile (NV) caches at the server and/or the clients to buffer writes coupled with different cache replacement algorithms. File blocks that are read are loaded into the volatile cache and the "least recently used" (LRU) replacement policy is used to replace blocks when the cache is full. When a single volatile file cache is used for both reads and writes, three alternative policies are traditionally used to handle write operations: write-through, writeback, and periodic writeback.

2.1 Cache Consistency Policies

With any form of writeback client cache management policy the problem of data consistency exists. When it is important to provide "strict" consistency (i.e. each client will always get the most up to date version of a file block it requests), a client cache consistency policy similar to that used in the Sprite distributed file system may be used. In this scheme all file open and close operations have to be performed at the file server and the file server keeps track of the last client that opened the file with the intent to update it. When a client opens a file that was updated and closed by another client then the server recalls the dirty blocks from the last writer. If the server detects that a file is concurrently opened by multiple clients and at least one client has the file open for writing, then it disables client caching for that file at all of the clients. To ensure that the client cache contains the most up to date information, the clients and the servers maintain a version number for each file. When a client opens a file and finds blocks from that file in its cache, it checks the version number of the file at the server to ensure that it is the latest version. If it is not the latest version, it removes the old file blocks from the cache. These policies are explained in greater detail in [12] and improvements to them have been investigated in [1,18].

2.2 Non-volatile Write Cache

File system measurement studies have shown that writes will be the primary load on the file server when large write through client file caches are used. Even when a periodic client cache writeback policy is used, most of the writes go through to the server to ensure data integrity and not as a consequence of cache size restrictions [2]. This has motivated the use of non-volatile caches to buffer writes so that a writeback policy can be used without the fear of losing modified file blocks. There are practical issues regarding how the NV cache of a crashed client can be accessed. These however, are outside the scope of this study and will not be considered.

We suggest a modified cache management policy to take advantage of the NV write cache. An updated file block is inserted into the NV write cache and the block is removed from the volatile read cache if it is present there. This avoids maintaining duplicate blocks in both caches. The volatile read cache is first searched when a file block is requested for read. If it is not found, then the write cache is searched. If the block is found in the write cache and it is found to be "clean" (i.e. an up to date version available at the server) then the block is removed from the write cache. A block in the write cache may become "clean" if one of the cache consistency or replacement algorithms causes it to be written back to the server. When the write cache is full, the LRU block is replaced and is written back to the server only if it is dirty. To avoid the scenario where an operation is stalled because the cache is full and a dirty block has to be committed to the server to make room, one can trigger the writing back of dirty blocks from the NV cache based on thresholds as demonstrated in [4] or use a periodic writeback policy.

Under a threshold based policy, the number of dirty blocks in the cache is tracked and the least recently used dirty blocks are purged from the NV cache as soon as the percentage of dirty blocks in the NV cache crosses a predetermined high-limit threshold. Purging of dirty blocks from the client NV caches to the server continues until the fraction of the dirty blocks in the cache drops below the low-limit threshold. We investigated such a policy in the disk cache context in [4] and recommended that write cache purging should be done when the disk is idle. In the DFS environment it is not possible for the client to know when the server is idle and therefore the client will purge its NV write cache when it deems necessary.

In the periodic writeback policy, each client checks its NV cache periodically (say every 5 seconds) and purges dirty blocks residing in the cache for a period longer than a certain interval (say, 30 seconds). A possible advantage of this method is that such a policy might be able to improve the file open time by reducing the cache consistency traffic resulting from the server having to check and flush the contents of the cache of the last writer of the file. The disadvantage of the periodic writeback policy is that file blocks may be prematurely written back to the server when it might be overwritten or deleted by the same client before it is ever accessed by any other client.

3 Performance Metrics

The metric that is of primary importance from the user/application perspective is the mean response time for read and write requests. When the request is satisfied in the client cache, then the read or write response time does not include a transaction with the server. When the request has to go to the server, the response time includes server execution and if there is a miss at the server cache, it includes access to the server disk subsystem. Since we are evaluating the impact of introducing NV storage to improve write response time, we focus on the effects of different NV storage management policies on the write response time. Since writeback caching policies at the clients can impact not only writes but also file open operations as a result of cache consistency policies, we also evaluate the effect of the policies on the mean file open response time when client caching is used. We look at the mean read response time to ensure that it is not adversely affected by the cache writeback policies.

We also look at the utilization of resources in the system to identify the bottleneck resource and to understand the capacity of the system to support a large number of clients. Since the server CPU is involved in the execution of different file system operations, including file opens, the resultant cache consistency mechanisms, handling network traffic and moving data, it has often been the bottleneck in the past [9,14]. With the increasing use of client caches and faster server CPUs, we anticipate the server disk subsystem to be the future bottleneck. We examine the utilization of the server CPU and disks while evaluating the different policies.

Finally, to understand the different caching policies and the reason for their effectiveness, we also look at the actual numbers of different operations going from the client to the server and at the server to its disks. For example, the mean response time of write operations is seriously impacted if they often find the NV write cache completely full with dirty blocks. The write cache has to "immediately" replace one dirty block to make room for the incoming block. Consequently, we present the number of these "immediate" write operations wherever applicable. In a distributed file system, the client-server interactions are not just dictated by the client/user workload, but are also caused by the mechanisms used to maintain consistency of data in the distributed environment. We therefore look at the contribution of the consistency mechanisms in detail by looking at the actual number of reads and writes at the server, the cache hit ratios at the server and client caches and the number of server disk operations with the different policies.

4 Workload and Parameterization

The characteristics of the workload we describe here are predominantly based on the analysis of file I/O activity observed at two operational, commercial sites. The traces were collected by instrumenting the I/O processing routines of the operating system. The instrumentation captured every I/O request and recorded detailed information about the system, storage device, file and process identification and disk block request information. A detailed description of the tracing mechanism, the traces and the characteristics of file I/O activity can be found in [5,15].

The functionality offered by a distributed file service is often identical to that offered at the local file system to allow applications to use it transparently. We extrapolate the results of the analysis of traces from two time sharing environments for use in the simulation of the distributed file system:

1. Scientific and Office (*Sci-Off*)
2. Office Applications and Decision Support (*Off-Day*).

The environment we consider here is of clients that access a file server for mass storage. Although it is common for clients to have local storage, particularly for maintaining the operating system executables, we assume here that the local disks are available for paging and swapping only. All access to data and operating system executables are done from the file server. This allows us to translate the file system trace data directly to the distributed environment.

4.1 File Access Characteristics

It is important to classify files according to their access and sharing properties. We show that the way a file is opened and the way the file is organized determines many of the important access characteristics.

Characteristics of files by the way they are opened has been presented in a previous paper [15]. We observe, across both traces, that the files opened for write-only (W-ONLY) are least likely to be shared. The files opened for both read and write (RW) are shared the most but are predominantly shared between two processes. The files opened for read-only (R-ONLY) have characteristics that lie somewhere between those of W-ONLY and RW files.

One can also classify the active files from the traces according to the way the blocks in the file are logically organized (accessed). The two categories are: sequential files and random access files.

We observe that the file access pattern, the file size distribution and access intensity depend on which of the above two categories a file belongs to. We see that 87-92% of the active files are sequentially accessed (Table 4.1), and the remaining are randomly accessed. But the random access files, are on an average, three times larger in size than the sequential files and account for a larger amount of file system activity.

	Sci-Off		Off-Day	
	Sequential	Random Access	Sequential	Random Access
Percent of Active Files	91.86%	8.14%	87.16%	13.18%
Mean File Size (Kbytes)	31.75	108.46	65.52	148.26
Mean Opens/File	9.71	32.25	6.37	10.01
Mean Reads/File	84.37	386.69	64.49	85.64
Mean Writes/File	21.10	57.02	22.63	34.53

Table 4.1: File Characteristics for Sequential and Random Access Files

4.2 Workload Parameters

A typical client interaction with the server involves a file open, several reads or writes and a file close. We break down the different workload components into the temporal characteristics of the file open-close information, the characteristics of the open operations and then estimate the read-write operations within an open-close session.

The number of active users (each of which is represented in our simulation as a distinct client) was obtained by identifying login sessions of distinct users. A ratio of the number of active users to the total number of users is found to be in the 1:5 to 1:6 range. This was calculated by taking the ratio of the average number of distinct users in a 1-hour interval to the total number of distinct users observed in a prime time period. The prime time period was 9 hours (8 a.m. to 5 p.m.) and 10 hours (7 a.m. to 5 p.m.) for the Sci-Off and Off-Day scenarios respectively.

Inter-Open Time

The time between two consecutive file open operations by a user, the inter-open time, is calculated from the the number of active users found in the trace, the total number of opens and the length of the trace interval. All of these measures were available from the file I/O trace data. We assume that the inter-open time is exponentially distributed, with mean given by:

$\# \text{ opens/sec. per user} =$
$\quad ((\text{total\# opens})/(\text{total trace time})) * (1/\# \text{ active users})$

mean inter-open time $= (1/\#\text{opens/sec. per user})$

Open-Close Time

The time between when a file is opened and closed is derived from the trace data. For example, for the Sci-Off trace we observe that about 90% of the open-close intervals are less than 5 seconds but that the remaining 10% of the open-close intervals are distributed over a wide range resulting in a large coefficient of variation. A 4-stage hyperexponential distribution was found to provide a good fit [3].

Open Characteristics

We observed that the organization and file open-mode is significant in determining the sharing and activity pattern of active files. Therefore, when a user opens a file we use the following three important characteristics to determine the amount and pattern of access to this file. These factors are:

1. The file open mode – i.e., is the file opened for reading or writing? This is given by the probabilities p_r and p_w shown in Figure 4.1 We observed that about 75% of all opens were done with the intent to read a file.

2. The "open-mode" category of the file being opened - whether the file is a R-ONLY, W-ONLY, or RW file (explained in section 4.1). Clearly an open for read cannot be directed at a file that belongs to the W-ONLY category and similarly a R-ONLY file cannot be opened for write. We therefore need to know the conditional probabilities p_{rr}, p_{rb}, p_{wb}, and p_{ww} as shown in Figure 4.1. For example, about 68-70% of open for reads are done on R-ONLY files whereas about 55-67% of the opens for write are directed to W-ONLY files.

3. The file organization – i.e., whether the file opened is a sequential or random access file. It was noted in Table 4.1 that about 87-92% of the active files are sequential files, but we observe this ratio does not hold across the open-mode file categories. For both traces that we use in this study, we find that the R-ONLY files predominantly tend to be sequential files while The RW files in the Sci-Off trace and the W-ONLY files in the Sci-Off trace contained a relatively larger fraction of random access files (Table 4.2).

			%Active Files	%Open Request	File Size (Kbytes)
Sci-Off	Read-Only	Sequential	31.76	50.58	17.5
		Random Access	0.55	0.87	86.9
	Write-Only	Sequential	32.49	4.43	66.8
		Random Access	2.27	13.59	60.5
	Read-Write	Sequential	27.61	22.26	6.9
		Random Access	5.32	8.27	131.1
Off-Day	Read-Only	Sequential	28.28	48.78	102.6
		Random Access	2.47	2.89	35.9
	Write-Only	Sequential	23.62	9.23	91.2
		Random Access	10.04	4.07	80.9
	Read-Write	Sequential	35.26	23.19	18.3
		Random Access	0.34	11.84	2991.5

Table 4.2: Percentage of Files, Opens and Average File Size for Six File Categories

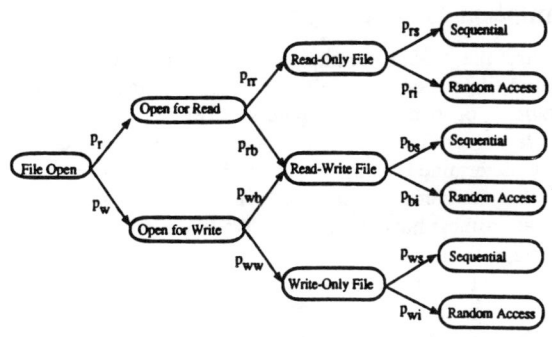

	p_r	p_{rr}	p_{ww}	p_{rs}	p_{bs}	p_{ws}
Sci-Off Trace	0.731	0.704	0.668	0.983	0.246	0.729
Off-Day Trace	0.758	0.682	0.549	0.944	0.694	0.662

Figure 4.1: File Open Characteristics
NOTE: Probabilities not shown in can be calculated..

Read-Write Characteristics

The way a file is read or written is depends on whether it is a sequential file or random access file. The total number of blocks accessed also depends on the file organization. The only exception we observed is that small files (< 48 KBytes in our case), irrespective of their file organization, are usually accessed in their entirety every time they are opened.

When a sequential file is opened, we assume that 80% of the time the entire file is accessed [2]. The rest of the time, we assume that on average 50% of the file is accessed. The fraction of the file accessed when the whole file is not accessed is drawn from a uniform distribution between 0 and 1. The starting point of access within the file is assumed to be randomly distributed, between the start of the file and a point such that the fraction accessed falls within the file.

When a random access file is opened for reading we assume that 40% of the file is accessed. Random access files are usually traversed using some form of an index structure and the file blocks containing the indices are more frequently read. Therefore we assume that 20% of the file is "hotter" than the rest of the file and that 80% of the file read operations are directed to it. Write operations to random access files occur significantly less frequently than writes to sequential files and do not display the skew in the access pattern. This is because the index blocks, which are read frequently, do not have to be updated as often. We match the amount of writes to a random access file within an open-close session to that observed in the trace data. Based on this, we use a mean value of 5% for the fraction of the random access file written in an average file activity session. The number of blocks written in a particular session is derived using a truncated exponential distribution and the blocks accessed are uniformly distributed across the file.

We model the reads and writes to files as requests from the client for 4K byte chunks. The number of read or write operations is determined by how much of the file is accessed.

Number of read/write operations =
$\quad$ (size of file * fraction of file accessed)/ 4K bytes.

5 Simulation Methodology

We use the CSIM simulation package [17] to model a distributed file system consisting of a number of active client workstations or personal computers accessing files from a single file server. The location of a file in the file system is typically determined using a global name service and we assume that the name server is collocated with the file server. The client systems have a rating of 24 SPECmarks [13]. They have a volatile in-memory file block cache. In addition, the clients may also have a non-volatile (NV) write cache. The server machine is also a 24 SPECmark system with 5 disk drives. The active files are assumed to be uniformly distributed over the five disks. A 5-disk configuration is chosen because it results in a well balanced system. The server also has a volatile file block cache and an optional NV write cache. The clients and servers are connected by an Ethernet.

5.1 Distributed Environment Model

The file server is modeled in detail including queues for the processing unit (CPU) and for each of the disks. In addition, the file system caches at the server are also modeled. At the client, only the CPU and file system caches are modeled. The CPU at both the server and the clients is modeled as a single server queue with a first-come-first-serve (FCFS) queueing discipline. The CPU service time includes the cost of file system operations like, open, close, read and write; processing cost for handling disk I/O and for performing network operations. These service times were derived from measurements on a RISC Ultrix workstation (Table 5.1). The CPU service time was assumed to be the same at both the client and the server. The service time for the disk was computed from the specifications of the device (Table 5.1). The service times for the file system cache replacement and consistency operations are also accounted for.

For this study the network was modeled as a single server queue with FCFS queuing discipline. We have assumed just two message size categories – small 64 byte messages for control operations and 4 KByte messages for the data movement operations between the clients and the server. All clients and the file server are assumed to be on a single 10 Mbits/sec. Ethernet segment. Studies have shown that this simple model may be acceptable if the network is not the bottleneck. The client and server CPU's are involved in processing the messages and we have accounted for the CPU service times for protocol processing and network I/O. The service time for the server representing the network is calculated based on the message size (Table 5.1).

Operation	CPU Service Time (msec)
File Open	3.0
File Close	1.0
File Read/Write	2.0
Disk Read I/O	1.0
Disk Write I/O	1.5
64 byte network I/O	0.4
4 Kbyte network I/O	1.5

Operation	Disk Service Time (msec)
Seek Time	16.0
Rotational Latency	8.0
Xfer time for 4 KByte	2.5

Message Size	Network Delay (msec)
64 bytes	0.05
4 KBytes	3.28

Table 5.1: Service Times used in Simulation

5.2 File System Setup

Prior to the simulation, the file system is initialized by the following procedure:

Step 1: The file characterization data derived from the traces gives us the information about the total number of active files for a fixed number of users. The simulation is run for a varying number of clients and we generate the number of active files according to the client population. If NCLIENTS denotes the size of the client population, then the number of active files is given by:

#*Active Files* =
 (#Active Files in Trace data / # Users in trace)*NCLIENTS

Step 2: We use the ratio of the number of sequential to random access files observed in the trace data (Table 4.1) to assign a file organization attribute to each active file.

Step 3: Files have specific access properties. Some are only accessed for reading (R_ONLY), others for writing only(W_ONLY) while the rest are both read and written (RW). It was found that the distribution of files in these three categories depends on the file organization (sequential or random access). The fraction of files in these three access categories was known for the two file organizations from the traces (Table 4.2) and was used to predetermine the access attribute for each file.

Step 4: Each file is then initialized to a certain size depending on its file open mode and organization. Table 4.2 shows the average file size for the different file categories observed in the file system traces. We use exponential distributions with the given means to derive the file sizes.

Step 5: The number of clients that access a file is determined by the appropriate file sharing distributions [3,15]. For a majority of the files the sharing characteristics (number of clients accessing file) is independent of the total number of clients. However, for a small set of files, the tail of the distribution, the number of clients accessing the file increases with client population size. This effect was captured in the empirical sharing distributions used. The specific clients that access a file are chosen by randomly selecting the number of clients determined by the sharing distribution. Once the identities of clients that access a file are determined, that file is put in the file list at that client.

This completes the initialization of the file system. Each file has a specific organization, a size and an open-mode category.

5.3 Client-Server Operations

A typical client interaction with the server involves a file open, several reads or writes and a close. We shall refer to all of the activity between the execution of an open and a close on a file as an "activity session". We cluster the read or write operations at the beginning of each activity session. The user at the client system is assumed to "think" for a certain amount of time before each file open request. It is also quite likely that a client may have multiple files open simultaneously. Therefore, we model each file open-close activity session at a client as an independent thread. The inter-open time between the start of each file open-close activity sessions, is fairly large, with a mean value of 17.5 seconds for the Sci-Off trace. In addition, the time between the last read/write activity and the closing of the file is also quite large, with a mean value of

42.5 seconds. In comparison, the total amount of time taken for the file open, all of the reads and writes and the close operation to complete, in an open-close activity session, averaged only about 1.8 seconds (which includes all the queueing time, network delay, etc.) for 700 clients in the baseline case. Therefore, an individual client presents a relatively light load to a server and we observe that a single server is able to support a large number of clients before a bottleneck resource in the server is saturated.

The client initiates activity by first opening a file. First, we determine whether the open request is for reading or writing the file based on the probabilities shown in Figure 4.1. A very simple file locality model is chosen. We have different probabilities of accessing the file categories. For example, if a file is to be read, we select a file from either the R-ONLY or RW pool for that client with probabilities (p_{rr} and p_{rb} respectively) specified in Figure 4.1. Files are chosen randomly from each pool. The client sends the open request to the file server that owns the file. We account for the service times on the client CPU for handling the open and for generating the network message. The CPU service time for the name lookup is accounted for. We also assume that 20% of the lookups result in a visit to the disk containing the name table information.

First we describe the operations at the server for a file that is not shared by any other clients. The server updates the file meta-data information of the file, records the client id and the mode (read or write) in which the file is opened. Again we assume that 20% of the opens result in a disk access to the meta-data information. The CPU cost for a file open is presented in Table 5.1.

Let us next consider the case where the file may be shared among multiple clients. If the clients use some form of cache writeback mechanism then the possibility of data inconsistency at the client caches arises. There are two different sharing cases to consider:

(a) Sequential Shared Files

Consider the case where another client had previously opened, updated and closed the file. The server always tracks the last writer to have closed the file. On encountering the next open, from the client of interest, the server sends a call back request to the last writer to flush all dirty blocks of this file. The open operation blocks until the last writer has flushed all dirty blocks and the operations have been handled at the server. The server then responds to the client with the current version number of the file. In the case where the version number received from the server is higher than the version number at the client, the client removes all of the blocks belonging to this file from its cache before signaling completion of the open request to the application. We account for the CPU, network and possibly disk overhead at the server, the last writer and the requesting client for these cache consistency operations.

(b) Simultaneously Shared Files

If one or more clients are found in the list of clients that already have the file open then the server checks if the current open is causing the file to become "write shared" i.e. a sharing mode in which one or more clients are updating the file. There are two ways in which an open causes the file to become "write shared"

1. The file is already opened by another client for write.
2. The file is being read by other clients while the current open is for write.

If the file becomes "write shared" as a result of an open, then cache consistency actions have to be taken. Clients which already have the file open are asked to flush their read and write caches and caching is disabled for the file. The open from the requesting client is complete at this point and all subsequent read and write requests are sent to the server. We assume UNIX-like semantics for write operations from these multiple clients.

After receiving the successful completion of the open from the server, the client reads or writes the file in the fashion described in the workload section. For a read request, first the read cache at the client is searched for the requested file block. If the read is not resolved there then the NV write cache is searched, if one is present. If the block is found in the write cache and it is found to be "clean" (i.e. it has been committed to the server) then it is removed from the write cache and inserted into the read cache. Blocks are maintained in the Least Recently Used (LRU) order in both the caches. If a requested block is not found in either of the client caches then the read request is forwarded to the file server.

A write request is handled in a slightly different fashion. When a file block is modified, it is inserted into the NV write cache at the client. An older version of the block, if present, is removed. If the written block was previously read into the read cache then it is removed from there at this time. This is done because the block is available for reads in the write cache. We assume that there are no difference in the access speed of the volatile and non-volatile caches. If the write cache is full, then the LRU block is replaced by the new block written. If the LRU block is dirty then it has to be written back to the server. The caches at the server operate exactly in the same way as the client caches. The only difference is that when a dirty block is removed from the server write cache, it is written to the appropriate disk.

In our simulation, we ensure that all shared data structures, for example the file meta-data at the server and all the caches at the server, have to be locked before they are updated. This is also true for accesses by the client to its local cache when a file is being flushed to the server. Therefore, we model the delays encountered by client operations as a result of lock conflicts. It must also be noted that we have not modeled file create and delete operations and have assumed that the clients have local paging devices.

6 Results

We look at the performance of alternative policies for managing the NV cache at the client and server and also quantify the actual performance improvement achieved by including NV caches. Further, we examine the sensitivity of system performance to variation in size of the NV cache. We base our results on a simulation of the environment described in Section 5, for different numbers of clients in the range 100 to 700. At 700 clients some of the server resources becoming heavily utilized. All of our studies are based on a single file server supporting a number of clients.

We define our baseline configuration to be a system in which each client has a volatile cache of 8 MBytes and the server has a 32 MByte volatile cache. The best case, without regard to vulnerability of the data in the cache, is to provide a writeback policy at all the caches. The writeback policy in the baseline case uses an LRU list for all the blocks in the cache. When a dirty block is replaced at the client, the block is written back to the server. When a dirty block is replaced at the server, that block is written to the disk. We shall refer to this as the "Writeback" policy. We compare the baseline "Writeback" policy with a "Periodic Writeback" policy where the caches are checked every 5 seconds, and any cache blocks that are dirty for more than 30 seconds are written back. This form of "Periodic Writeback" policy has been used in the Sprite distributed file system. The write response time is shown for varying number of clients in Figure 6.1, for a client population varying from 100 to 700 clients. We also compare, showing an upper bound, the "Write-thru" scheme where all writes are committed to the server's disk before an application's write is completed. Figure 6.1 shows that the "Write-thru" performance is not only poor even for low loads (since all writes suffer the overhead of going to the server's disk), but is also degrades dramatically at high loads due to saturation of the server's disk subsystem. The two writeback policies significantly reduce write response time and the server's I/O subsystem is not saturated even at 700 clients (Figure 6.1).

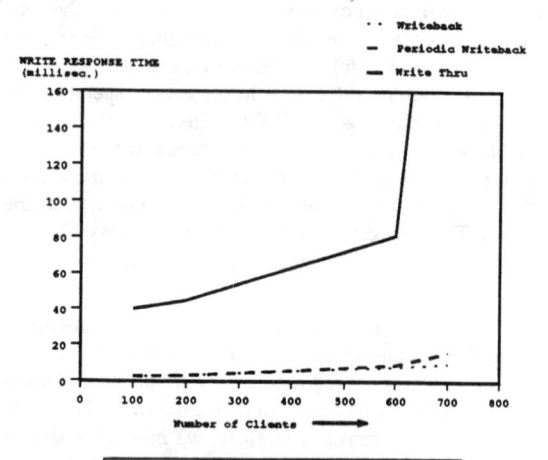

	Avg. Server System Disk Utilization(%)		
	100 clients	400 clients	700 clients
Writeback	7.9	20.2	56.4
Periodic Writeback	12.2	41.5	68.8
Writethru	12.3	43.8	79.2

Figure 6.1: Average Write Response Times and Server System Disk Utilization for different Cache Writing Policies. Client Cache = 8 MBytes, Server Cache = 32 MBytes.

While the performance of the writeback mechanisms are good, the problem of the vulnerability of the data in the volatile caches still remains. Therefore, when either a client, the network or the server fails, updates to the data may be lost, resulting in inconsistencies in the file system. We propose the addition of non-volatile (NV) write caches. Non-volatile memory is still quite expensive [1,6] and so we investigate algorithms to efficiently manage the write caches and also estimate the size of the write cache that will be required in the scientific and office environment that the synthetic workload represents.

6.1 Impact of the NV Write Cache at the Server

We begin with the introduction of an additional NV cache at the server alone, while maintaining the same amount of volatile cache at the client and server. We compare three different server NV write cache writeback policies:

1. "Periodic" writeback,
2. "Threshold" writeback, and
3. "LRU" writeback.

The volatile cache on the client uses a *Write-thru* policy, and the volatile cache on the server is used only for reads, with a simple LRU replacement policy. The server NV cache is assumed to have a capacity of 8 MBytes. Under the *Periodic* writeback policy, we use an aging time of 30 seconds for replacement. For the *Threshold* writeback policy, we use a Hi-Lim value of 90% and a Lo-Lim value of 50%. These threshold values are shown to be appropriate [3,4]. The interaction between the volatile read-cache and the NV write cache at the server was described in Section 2.2.

The variation in the mean write response time as a function of the number of clients for these three different policies is shown in Figure 6.2. The simple *LRU* writeback policy for the server NV cache performs relatively poorly at all loads compared to the other two policies because of a substantial number of "immediate" writes to the disk caused by the NV cache being full of dirty blocks. We observe two points of inflection for the simple *LRU* writeback policy, one at a load of 200 clients, the other at a load of 600 clients. In the 100 to 200 client range, the increase in the mean write response time is primarily due to an increase in the number of immediate writes from a full write cache. Between 200 and 600 clients, the mean write response time remains relatively flat. This is because there is substantial sharing which results in a higher number of over-writes ("write hits") on a dirty block in the NV cache). Beyond 600 clients, the server's CPU and disk becomes heavily utilized and this increases the write response time (Figure 6.2).

When we consider the *Periodic* writeback policy, the mean response time is substantially smaller at light loads compared to the *LRU* writeback policy. However, at 700 clients, the mean write response time with the *Periodic* writeback policy is only marginally better than the *LRU* writeback policy. This is because the server becomes heavily utilized due to the large number of disk writes generated by the *Periodic* writeback policy. In fact, across the entire loading range, the *Periodic* writeback policy produces a larger number of writes to the server disk than the *LRU* writeback. However, because a large number of these writes to the server disk are not synchronized with the user application's write operation, the write response time seen by the application is lower.

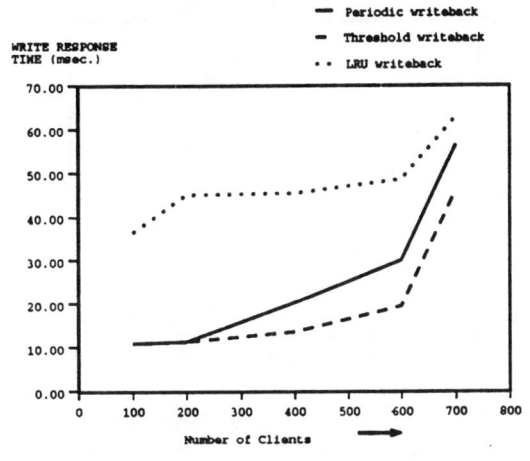

Figure 6.2: Average Write and Read Response Times. Server NV Cache = 8 MBytes.

	Avg. Read response (ms)		
	100 clients	400 clients	700 clients
Periodic	6.2	11.5	25.8
Threshold	6.2	11.2	25.5
LRU	6.2	11.5	23.9

Finally, when we look at the *Threshold* based writeback policy for the server NV cache, the write response time is even lower. Furthermore, we observe that the number of writes to the server disk is only marginally more than the *LRU* writeback policy. But, most writes to the server disk are not synchronous with the user application's writes, and therefore we see the substantial reduction in the write response time. In the case of 700 clients, the server CPU and disk are quite heavily used. This in combination with the limited size of the NV write cache, produces a relatively large number of immediate writes from a fully dirty NV write cache. As a result, the mean write response time increases substantially between 600 and 700 clients. The *Threshold* policy generates fewer writes to disk than the *Periodic* policy and the percentage of "immediate" writes is also lower for the *Threshold* policy than for the *Periodic* case.

An important consideration is that the application's read response time should not be affected by using a sophisticated policy for writeback from the server NV cache. This is because these policies may send several writes to the disk to clean the write cache (e.g., when the threshold is exceeded). Hence, the write traffic to the disk becomes bursty, and read operations that miss at the client may be queued at the server CPU or disk, behind a write to the server disk. We notice that at small loads, the mean read response time is not degraded at all, and is only impacted marginally even at very high loads when the server CPU and disk are heavily utilized(Table 6.1).

The policies for writeback from the server NV write cache include a number of parameters whose values affect performance. We studied the effect of these parameters on system performance. We found that a 30 second time-out age value is reasonable and use it in the rest of this study. As shown in [4], performance is insensitive to threshold values as long as Hi-Lim is not close to 100% and Lo-Lim value not too close to Hi-Lim. Therefore, a Hi-Lim of 90% and a Lo-Lim of 50% is chosen.

	Avg. Server CPU Utilization (%)			Avg. Server System Disk Utilization (%)		
	100 clients	400 clients	700 clients	100 clients	400 clients	700 clients
Periodic	11.6	46.7	75.9	12.1	40.8	69.4
Threshold	11.2	46.1	75.2	11.5	40.2	67.5
LRU	9.5	41.3	72.2	11.3	40.1	67.0

Table 6.1: File Server CPU and System Disk Utilizations with server NV cache

6.2 Server NV Write Cache Size Variation

In this subsection, we investigate the effect of varying the server NV write cache size for both the threshold based and periodic writeback policies. In Figures 6.3 and 6.4 we plot the average write response time for different server NV cache sizes at three different client load levels.

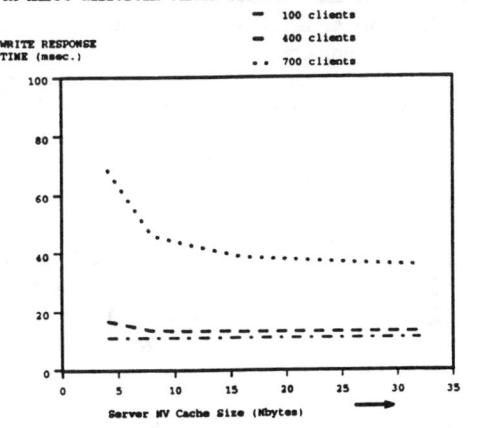

Figure 6.3: Server NV Cache Variation - Threshold Policy.

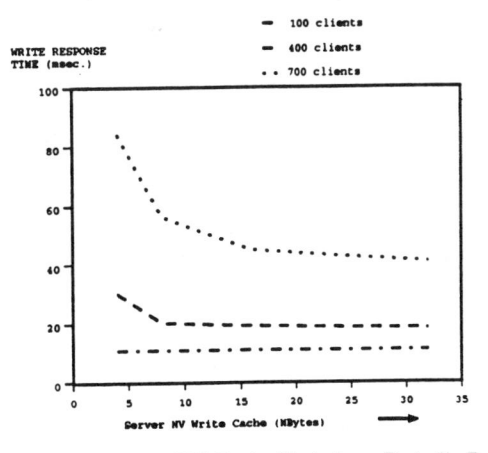

Figure 6.4: Server NV Cache Variation - Periodic Policy.

We observe that at 100 clients, 4 MBytes of server NV cache is more than adequate and the average write response time does not improve with larger caches. At 400 clients, there is a small improvement in the write response as the cache size is increased to 8 MBytes but thereafter there is no improvement in the response time. At 700 clients the write response time decreases dramatically (almost 33%) when the server NV write cache is increased from 4 MBytes to 8 MBytes but, thereafter, the write response time decreases but only slightly. We conclude that for this workload, an 8 MByte server NV write cache is adequate in the operational environment where the system resources are not heavily utilized.

6.3 Impact of NV Write Cache at the Clients

We now introduce a small NV write cache at the client in addition to the 8 MByte server NV write cache. The size of the NV write cache at the client is kept at only 0.5 MBytes. We compare the average write response time for this configuration with both the periodic and threshold-based writeback polices against one where there is no client NV write cache (Figure 6.5). We observe that the write response time with the client NV cache is substantially lower than when no client NV cache is used. The degradation of write response time with load is also more gradual when the client NV cache is used. We observe that the periodic writeback policy is better for small numbers of clients when the file server is lightly loaded (Table 6.2). But for large numbers of clients (600 and beyond) the threshold based policy is better. When a threshold based policy is used, dirty blocks are allowed to stay longer in the client caches and a large number of blocks are either overwritten or written back to the server by the cache consistency algorithms. This results in fewer writes to the server and consequently better performance.

When we use any form of writeback policy at the client it is necessary to introduce algorithms (as described in Section 2.2) to maintain data consistency at the clients and the server. Most of these cache consistency policies are invoked when a file is opened and therefore we need to ensure that the mean file open time is not seriously impacted by the introduction of the client NV write cache. We see from Figure 6.5 that the file open time for the periodic writeback policy is always greater than when no client write caching is used. However, for the threshold based writeback policy the mean file open time is higher only at very low loads (100 clients). At higher loads (400 and 700 clients), the mean file open time for the threshold case is, in fact, lower than the no-client cache case because the file server is not as heavily used as under the other two policies (Table 6.2). In Table 6.3 we look closely at the write traffic going from the clients to the server under the Threshold based and Periodic writeback policies. We look at the percentage of all the application writes that go to the server and further break down those writes going to the server into three categories – writes to maintain cache consistency, writes due to the invocation of the writeback policy (threshold or periodic), and immediate writes that are required when the client NV cache become completely full with dirty blocks and cannot accommodate an incoming dirty block.

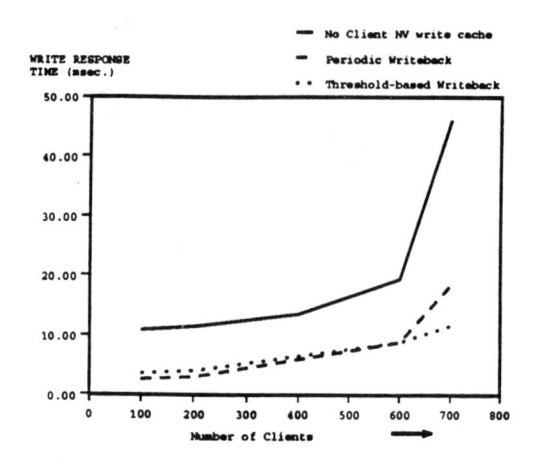

	Open response (ms)		
	100 clients	400 clients	700 clients
No client cache	51	67	119
Periodic	53	70	136
Threshold	54	67	97

Figure 6.5: Average Write and Open Response Times. Server NV Cache=8 MBytes, Client NV Cache=0.5 MBytes.

	Avg. Server CPU Utilization (%)			Avg. Server System Disk Utilization (%)		
	100 clients	400 clients	700 clients	100 clients	400 clients	700 clients
No client cache	11.2	46.1	75.2	11.5	40.2	67.5
Periodic	11.9	48.0	77.3	12.2	41.6	68.0
Threshold	8.9	40.1	71.6	10.1	36.0	61.4

Table 6.2: File Server CPU and System Disk Utilizations with client and server NV caches

	Threshold Policy			Periodic Policy		
	100 clients	400 clients	700 clients	100 clients	400 clients	700 clients
% Writes to Server	59.77	73.26	79.56	99.04	99.47	99.67
% Writes to Server - Consistency	41.14	69.24	82.44	9.43	40.31	55.85
% Writes to Server - Threshold/Periodic	42.30	21.20	11.37	90.53	59.60	44.13
% Writes to Server - Immediate	16.56	9.56	6.19	0.04	0.09	0.02

Table 6.3: Percentage of Writes from Clients to Server and Components of Write Traffic

The threshold-based policy performs fewer overall writes to the server and has a significantly higher fraction of writes due to consistency traffic than the periodic writeback policy. This indicates that the threshold policy adapts better to the dynamics of the workload and writes to the server only when it is required by the consistency mechanism. The number of writes to the server because the client cache is completely full with dirty blocks, however, is larger with the threshold-based writeback policy, compared to the periodic writeback policy. The periodic writeback policy is continually writing dirty blocks out, potentially keeping more of the client cache clean and, therefore, can handle bursts of writes at the client. So the write response time for the periodic writeback policy is better at low loads. But the significant reduction in the number of overall writes to the server with the threshold based writeback provides better performance at higher loads (Figure 6.5) so that the mean write response time is lower than under the periodic writeback at 700 clients.

6.4 Client NV Write Cache Size Variation

Next we look into the effect of varying the size of the client NV write caches while keeping the server NV cache constant at 8 MBytes. In Figure 6.6, we plot the variation of the average write response time as seen by the client application as the client NV write cache is varied from 0.25 MBytes to 2 MBytes.

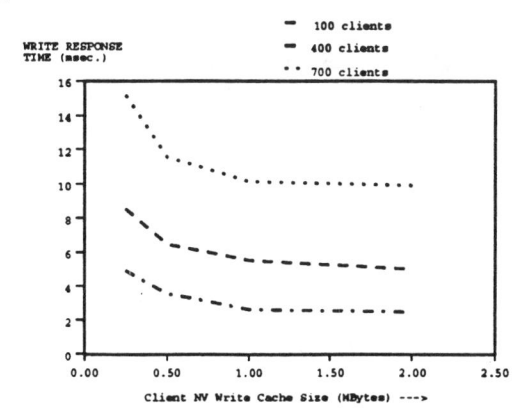

Figure 6.6: Impact of Client NV Cache Size on Average Write Response Times at Three Different Load Levels

We consider the system that uses the threshold based writeback policy at both the client and the server. We notice that at all load levels, the write response time decreases until the client NV write cache is increased to about 1.0 MByte. We reach a point of diminishing return for increased client NV write caches after that.

7 Conclusions

Distributed file systems use caches at various locations in order to alleviate the limitations due to the I/O bottleneck. Caches at both the file server as well as at the clients are commonly used. These traditionally have improved the performance of read operations as seen by the user application. However, in order to provide a consistent view of the data seen by all of the clients of the distributed file system, and for reliability in the face of failures, write operations are often allowed to complete only after the data has been committed to stable storage, which has traditionally been the disk at the file server. Therefore, the dominant load on the file server is writes. Allowing for writebacks from the clients reduces the load on the server but exposes the data to loss due to failures. Fortunately, non-volatile random access memory (NV-RAM) is becoming cheaper and we consider the performance issues when a non-volatile write cache is used together with a separate read cache.

The synthetic workload we use for this study is based on parameters derived from the analysis of I/O traces collected from operational commercial sites representing two interactive scientific and office environments. The important file access characteristics we model in the synthetic workload includes the file inter-open time, the file open-close time, the file sizes and most importantly, the characteristics of sharing. We also divide the active files into classes based on their file-open modes (e.g., Read-Only, Write-Only, Read-Write) and their organization (sequential, random access). We observe that the sharing characteristics are distinct among the different classes of files and that the access characteristics differ according to the file organization. Therefore, we divide the active files into six categories (sequential-read-only, random access-read-only, etc.) and look at the file size, file access pattern and sharing among these classes.

The study of the effectiveness of the NV write cache is based on a CSIM simulation model of a distributed environment of a large number of clients and a single file server. We parameterize the service times for the components at the client (CPU), the server (CPU, disk) and the network for the different file system operations (open, read, write, close) based on careful measurements of resource consumption on a representative workstation. We include the overhead for the cache consistency mechanisms and the system overheads for network I/O.

The primary observation we make from the study is that small NV write caches at the server and at clients is effective in reducing the write response time and the load on the file server dramatically, thus improving the scalability of the system. In fact, for this workload, we found that a NV write cache of 1 MByte at the client (with a volatile read cache of about 8 MBytes) and a NV write cache of 8 MBytes at the server (with a volatile read cache of about 32 MBytes) reduces the write response time by over 90% in comparison to having a simple write-through policy at the clients and the server even under light loads. We consider the mean write response time as the dominant metric in order to understand the effectiveness of the NV cache. We also study at the mean read response times, the mean response time of file opens and the resource utilizations at the server for each of the different cache writeback policies.

We studied the comparative benefits of two alternate writeback policies for the NV write caches. The first is a "periodic" writeback policy (checking every 5 sec. for dirty blocks older than 30 sec.) and the other is the proposed policy that we suggest here called the "threshold" based writeback policy. The threshold based writeback scheme uses a hysteresis policy for determining when to writeback dirty blocks from the NV write cache. At low loads, the policy for replacing blocks from the NV write cache is not critical as the system utilizations and the write response time is quite low. But at high loads, the "threshold" policy, which introduces a significantly lower load on the server than the "periodic" scheme, performs the best. In the "threshold" policy, dirty blocks tend to held longer in the write cache thereby increasing the probability of their being overwritten or being called back to the server only when it is required by another client. Another advantage of the "threshold" policy is that the performance of the policy is not sensitive to the exact choice of the threshold values.

We have shown that the use of NV write caches at the client and the file server with simple policies for managing these caches can result in substantial improvements in write response time and the ability to support a large number of clients.policies.

8 References

1. Baker, M.G., et al, "*No-Volatile Memory for Fast, Reliable File Systems,*" Proceedings of the 5th International Conference on Architectural Support for Programming Languages and Operating Systems (ASPLOS-V), October, 1992.

2. Baker, M.G., et al, "*Measurements of a Distributed File System,*" Proceedings of the 13th Symposium on Operating Systems Principles (SOSP), October, 1991.

3. Biswas, P., "*File Access Characterization and Analysis of Nonvolatile Write Caches,*" Ph.D. Thesis, University of Massachusetts, Amherst, May 1993.

4. Biswas, P., et al, "*Trace Driven Analysis of Write Caching Policies for Disks,*" Proceedings of the 1993 ACM Sigmetrics Conference on Measurement and Modeling of Computer Systems, May 1993.

5. Biswas, P., Ramakrishnan, K.K., "*File Access Characterization of VAX/VMS Environments,*" Proceedings of the 10th International Conference on Distributed Computing Systems, May 1990.

6. Copeland, G., et al, "*The Case For Safe RAM,*" Proceedings of the 15th International Conference on Very Large Data Bases, August 1989. .

7. Howard, J.H., et al, "*Scale and Performance in a Distributed File System,*" ACM Transactions on Computer Systems 6(1), February 1988.

8. Kure, O., "*Optimization of File Migration in Distributed Systems,*" Ph.D. thesis, Computer Science Division, University of California, Berkeley, CA, UCB-CSD-88-413, 1988.

9. Lazowska, E., Zahorjan, J., Cheriton, D., Zwaenepoel, W., "*File Access Performance of Diskless Workstations,*" ACM Transactions on Computer Systems 4(2), August 1986.

10. Menon, J., Hartung, M., "*The IBM 3990 Disk Cache,*" Proceedings of the IEEE Computer Society International COMPCON Conference, 1988. .

11. Moran, J., et al, "*Breaking Through the NFS Performance Barrier,*" Proceedings of the EUUG Spring 1990, Munich, Germany, April 1990. .

12. Nelson, M.N., et al, "*Caching in the Sprite Network File System,*" ACM Transactions on Computer Systems, February, 1988.

13. Nielsen, M.J.K., "*DECstation 5000 Model 200,*" Proceedings of the 36th IEEE Computer Society International Conference, COMPCON 1991, February 1991.

14. Ramakrishnan, K.K., Emer, J.S., "*Performance Analysis of Mass Storage Service Alternatives for Distributed Systems,*" IEEE Transactions on Software Engineering 15(2), February 1989. .

15. Ramakrishnan, K.K., et al, "*Analysis of File I/O Traces in Commercial Computing Environments,*" Proceedings of the 1992 ACM SIGMETRICS and PERFORMANCE '92 International Conference on Measurement and Modeling of Computer Systems, June 1992. .

16. Satyanarayanan, M., "*A Survey of Distributed File Systems,*" Technical Report CMU-CS-89-116, Department of Computer Science, Carnegie Mellon University, 1989.

17. Schwetman, H.D., "*CSIM Reference Manual,*" MCC Technical Report, ACA-ST-257-87 Rev 14, March 1990.

18. Thompson, J.G., "*Efficient Analysis of Caching Systems,*" Ph.D. thesis, Computer Science Division, University of California, Berkeley, CA, UCB-CSD-87-374, 1987.

Trading Disk Capacity for Performance

Robert Y. Hou, Yale N. Patt
Department of Electrical Engineering and Computer Science
University of Michigan, Ann Arbor 48109-2122

Abstract

Improvements in disk access time have lagged behind improvements in microprocessor and main memory speeds. This disparity has made the storage subsystem a major bottleneck for many applications. Disk arrays that can service multiple disk requests simultaneously are being used to satisfy increasing throughput requirements.

Higher throughput rates can be achieved by increasing the number of disks in an array. This increases the number of actuators that are available to service separate requests. It also spreads the data among more disk drives, reducing the seek time as the number of cylinders utilized on each disk drive decreases. The result is an increase in throughput that exceeds the increase in the number of disks. This suggests a tradeoff between the space utilization of disks in an array and the throughput of the array.

1 Introduction

Dramatic improvements in microprocessor and main memory speeds have far outpaced improvements in disk access times. This disparity has caused the storage subsystem, and the disk drive hardware in particular, to become a serious bottleneck for many applications. This also poses a problem for present applications as they are moved to faster machines and are no longer compute-bound.

For applications such as transaction processing, which are often characterized as consisting of numerous small requests uniformly distributed across the data space [Gray90, Holl92], disk caches may not be completely effective in reducing the number of disk accesses and improving disk access times. Therefore, disk arrays must provide high throughput to complete large numbers of transactions in a timely manner.

This paper considers the performance of three disk array architectures, non-redundant, RAID5 and mirrored, for workloads consisting of numerous small requests. It is shown that providing additional disks beyond those minimally required to store the data can increase throughput significantly. For example, doubling the number of disks in a mirrored array may provide up to 2.4 times the performance. The reason for the increase is two-fold. First, the number of disks available to handle requests increases. Second, the original data can be spread out among the additional disk drives, occupying a smaller fraction of the total cylinders on each individual disk, reducing the seek time for each request. For each of the three architectures, it is shown that the throughput improves linearly with the number of disks. That is, performance increases independent of the redundancy scheme used in the disk array. In addition, the increase in throughput is greater than the increase in the number of disks.

The remainder of this paper is organized as follows. Section 2 describes the basic tradeoffs of the three disk array architectures. Section 3 discusses the methodology, traces and simulator used in this paper. Section 4 examines the performance of non-redundant, mirrored and RAID5 disk arrays when eight disks are used. Section 5 compares these architectures when more than eight disks are used. Section 6 considers the impact of technology on our results. Section 7 provides some concluding remarks.

2 Disk Array Architectures

Many solutions have been proposed for increasing the throughput of a disk subsystem. A common solution is to increase the number of concurrently active disk drives in the subsystem. Disk striping [Sale86], or interleaving [Kim86], has been suggested for providing the high transfer rates required by some applications. Disk striping allows the data for a request to be accessed from multiple disks in parallel. Disk striping with a large stripe unit can also be used to form one logical disk capable of performing many concurrent accesses [Livn87]. We will refer to an array of disks with no redundancy as a non-redundant disk array and abbreviate it as NR.

Unfortunately, an increase in the number of disks also increases the probability of data loss due to disk failure. Several hardware redundancy schemes have been devised to improve reliability, including mirroring [Bitt88] and RAID5 [Patt88]. A mirrored array has double the number of disks and maintains two exact copies of the data. A RAID5 array has only one additional disk and maintains parity across all disks. Parity blocks may be striped across the entire array to remove the potential bottleneck of a single parity disk.

Mirroring the data in a disk subsystem doubles the number of disk drives in the array and duplicates the data to provide high reliability. These extra disks also improve performance by doubling the number of read requests that can be handled simultaneously. This can greatly increase the throughput provided by the disk array. Further, Bitton and Gray [Bitt88] have shown that selecting the disk which handles a read request based on the shorter seek distance can result in a 42% reduction in seek distance. Write requests, on the other hand, must be serviced by both disks containing copies of the old data. This reduces the improvement in throughput provided by mirrored disks. The two writes can also result in increased response times compared to non-redundant disks because the completion of both writes may be required before the request is considered complete.

RAID5 requires a much smaller increase in cost, specifically 1/N for a subsystem containing N disks. Each disk can handle a separate read request, so the additional disk augments the capacity for servicing read requests. RAID5 suffers in performance, however, when handling small writes. To keep the parity consistent, each write request requires that the parity which protects the written data be updated. The new parity value can be computed by combining the old data, the new data and the old parity. This requires four disk accesses, two to read the old data and parity and two to write the new data and parity. The four accesses required for each write request can significantly impact the throughput of a RAID5 disk array.

Clearly the performance of both redundancy schemes is highly dependent on the ratio of read to write requests. It has been shown that regardless of the read/write ratio, mirroring provides better performance per disk than RAID5 when the workload consists of numerous, small requests [Chen90]. This implies that when the throughput of the entire disk array is evaluated, the performance of mirrored disks greatly exceeds the performance of RAID5 arrays since mirrored disk arrays require more disks than RAID5 arrays. As will also be shown in this paper, even when the two arrays have an equal number of disks, mirrored disks outperform RAID5 arrays for all workloads except those consisting almost exclusively of read requests. The main reason for not using a mirrored disk array and obtaining higher throughput rates is the cost associated with the additional disks.

In many cases, obtaining high performance does merit the increased cost. Disk drives are often added to a disk subsystem to provide additional actuators and not necessarily for the additional storage [Gray90]. As will be shown, in addition to the extra actuators, the reduction in seek time contributes to increased performance. This indicates that the cost of a mirrored disk array may be acceptable for many systems.

3 The Experiments

3.1 Methodology

The amount of data accessed during our experiments is fixed throughout the paper at four full disks. A non-redundant disk array has no overhead, so any disks beyond four can be used to spread out the data to reduce the seek time. RAID5 requires an extra disk to store parity, and any disks beyond five can be used to spread out the data to reduce the seek time. A mirrored disk array requires four extra disks since it must maintain an extra copy of each data block. Therefore having more than eight disks reduces the seek time.

To clearly identify how many disks are being used in an array, we append the number of disks to the name of the architecture. Thus NR-8, Mirror-8 and RAID5-8 all contain eight disks.

3.2 Simulation

A trace-driven simulator was developed to analyze the performance of these architectures under different workloads and configurations. To start with, we use a standard disk which delivers modest performance. The disk drive parameters modeled by the simulator are for an IBM 0661 as shown in Table 1 [Holl92]. In section 6 we give results for a state-of-the-art disk and a future disk.

The disk drives are rotationally synchronized with respect to each other. Data is interleaved at the block level across all disks in each array. While recent studies indicate that larger striping units may be appropriate, we chose a single block since we are interested in transaction processing workloads which consist primarily of single block requests. The effect of the stripe unit on throughput requires further study.

The workload presented to the simulator is a stream of disk requests that is synthetically generated from a set of basic parameters. The starting positions of the requests are uniformly distributed among the data

bytes per block	4096
blocks per track	6
surfaces	14
cylinders	949
single track seek	2.5 ms
average seek time	12.7 ms
maximum seek time	25.5 ms
rotational speed	4318 RPM
seek time model	$2.0 + 0.01\ distance + 0.46\ \sqrt{distance}$

Table 1: Disk Drive Parameters

blocks [Gray90, Holl92]. The requests access one block of data. Each request is randomly chosen to be a read or write given the read/write ratio of the specific experiment. The interarrival rate is exponentially distributed.

The interarrival rate and read/write ratio are varied to create different workloads for each experiment. A lower interarrival rate means requests are issued at a faster rate, creating more work for the disk array. As the interarrival rate decreases, the array becomes saturated with requests and the response time increases. The read/write ratio also affects the response time for redundant arrays since write requests require extra disk accesses to complete. The average response time is used to compare the throughput of the different architectures under these workloads. As the response time is allowed to increase, the throughput of the system is also expected to increase until the system becomes fully saturated.

4 Comparing Base Architectures

We initially compare the three architectures for arrays of eight disk drives using workloads consisting of different ratios of read and write requests. We chose workloads containing 100%, 75%, 50% and 0% read requests. The results can be found in Figures 1 through 4, where throughput is shown as a function of the average response time.

Figure 1 shows the throughput of these architectures for workloads that consist of all read requests. NR-8, RAID5-8 and Mirror-8 each have eight disks. Since the amount of data is kept constant, NR-8 and RAID5-8 have unused disk space. NR-4 and RAID5-5 are shown for comparison purposes since NR-4, RAID5-5 and Mirror-8 each can store the same amount of data.

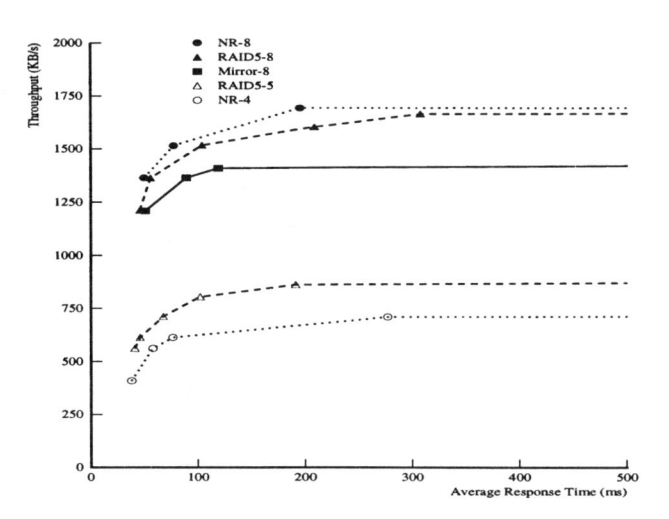

Figure 1: Read requests for eight disks

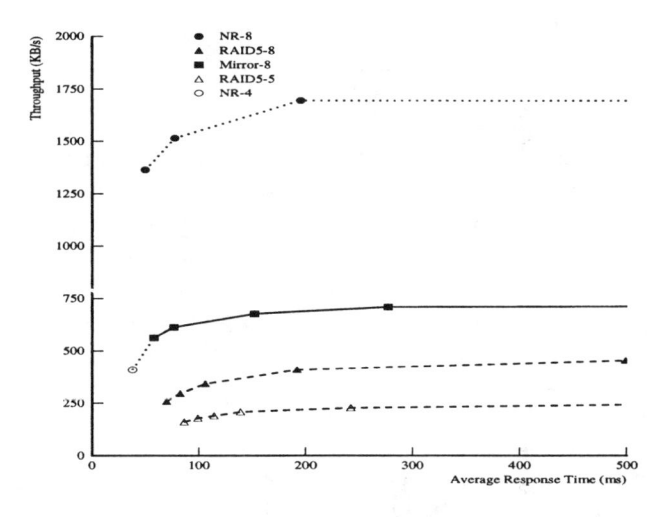

Figure 2: Write requests for eight disks

RAID5-8 and Mirror-8 obtain higher throughput than NR-4, but less than NR-8. NR-8 receives the maximum benefit of both additional actuators and seek time reduction, resulting in more than double the performance of NR-4. The RAID5 architecture requires additional allocation of storage for parity, increasing the space utilization of each disk. Thus, RAID5-8 provides lower throughput than NR-8 due to the increased seek time. Mirror-8 contains a duplicate set of data, using as many cylinders per disk as NR-4. As a result, seek time is not reduced except for light workloads, when a choice may be made to select the disk which can more quickly service a request. Note that for response times near 50 milliseconds, RAID5-8 and Mirror-8 perform similarly. Mirror-8 becomes saturated, however, as the response time increases past

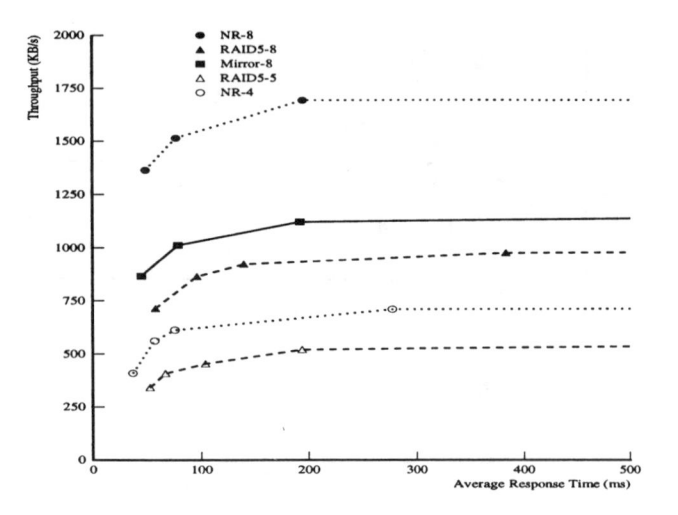

Figure 3: 75% read requests for eight disks

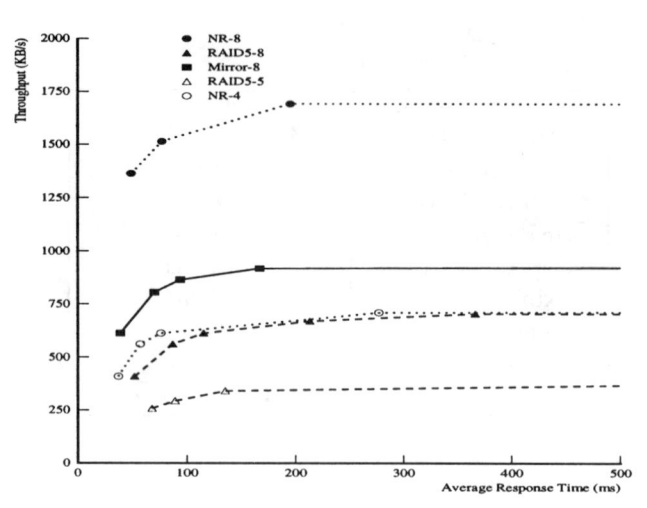

Figure 4: 50% read requests for eight disks

100 milliseconds while RAID5-8 does not saturate until close to 300 milliseconds.

Comparing the three architectures while keeping data capacity constant, Mirror-8 has the highest performance, followed by RAID5-5 and NR-4. The difference is completely accounted for by the additional actuators since there is no seek time reduction.

Figure 2 shows the throughput for workloads consisting of all write requests. As expected, Mirror-8 performance is identical to that of NR-4, since each pair of disks in Mirror-8 can match the corresponding single disk performance in NR-4 for a single write request. The RAID5 architecture does not perform well for these workloads because a write request for a single block requires a minimum of two disks to service it and the equivalent of four disk accesses to perform the read-modify-write operation.

Results for workloads containing a mixture of reads and writes are shown in figures 3 and 4. Mirror-8 consistently outperforms the other disk arrays except for NR-8. When the workload contains an equal number of reads and writes, RAID5-8 provides approximately the same performance as NR-4 by providing higher concurrency in servicing requests due to the extra disks, albeit at a higher average disk service time. For light workloads, however, NR-4 can service write requests more quickly and thus provide higher throughput than RAID5-8.

As can be seen from figures 1 through 4, RAID5-8 performs better than Mirror-8 for a stream of pure read requests, but its performance diminishes relative to Mirror-8 as writes are introduced into the request stream. For a workload of all writes, a RAID5 disk array requires the equivalent of four disk ac-

cesses to complete each request while a mirrored array only needs two accesses. One might therefore expect the performance of RAID5-8 to be almost half the performance of the mirrored array. This is not the case, however, due to the reduction in seek time for RAID5-8 accesses.

Mirror-8 easily out-performs RAID5-5 since both arrays contain the same storage per disk but Mirror-8 possesses additional actuators. For the workload of all read requests, this advantage, plus the ability to select between two sources for a specific request, allows Mirror-8 to attain nearly double the performance of RAID5-5. The comparison is not as straightforward for a workload of all write requests. With Mirror-8's eight disk drives, each write request accounts for one-fourth of the available disks. The same request serviced by RAID5-5, on the other hand, entails four disk accesses. With five disk drives, this accounts for four-fifths of its disks. Thus, RAID5-5 can service 25% / 80% = 31% of the write requests that Mirror-8 can in a given period of time.

As read and write requests entail the same activity for the non-redundant architecture, NR-8 maintains a constant performance in excess of twice that of NR-4, independent of the read/write ratio. The loss in throughput of mirrored and RAID5 disk arrays as compared to non-redundant arrays reflects the cost of implementing redundancy.

5 Increasing the Array Size

RAID5-8 gives a higher throughput than RAID5-5, which is not surprising since more actuators are avail-

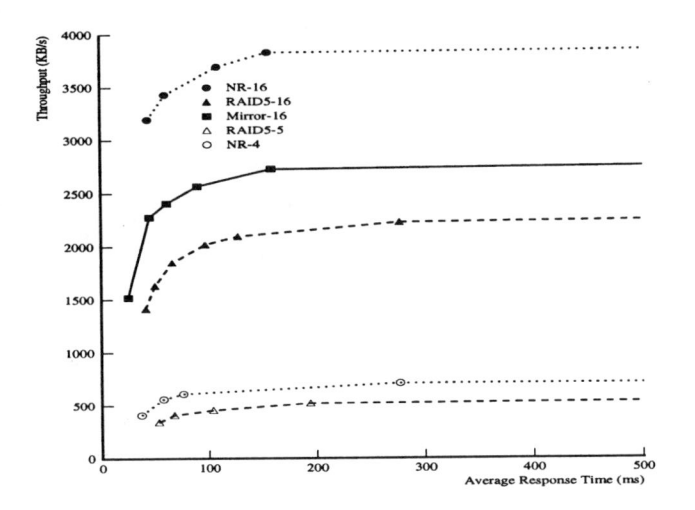

Figure 5: 75% read requests for sixteen disks

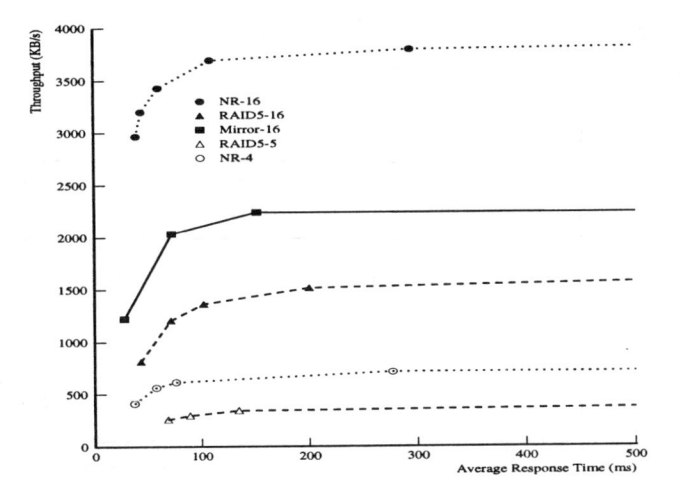

Figure 6: 50% read requests for sixteen disks

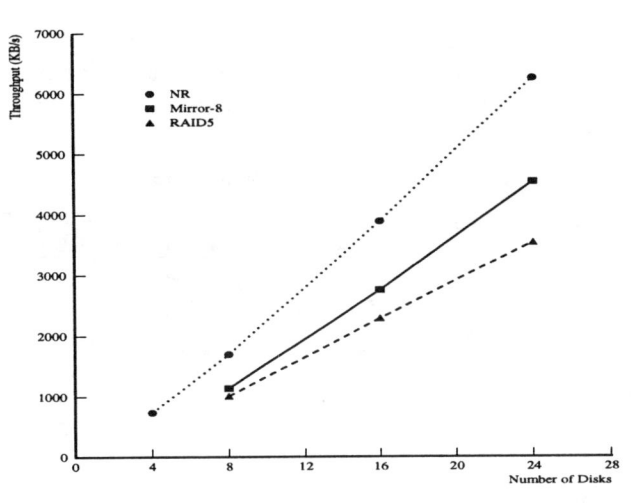

Figure 7: 75% read requests as function of disks

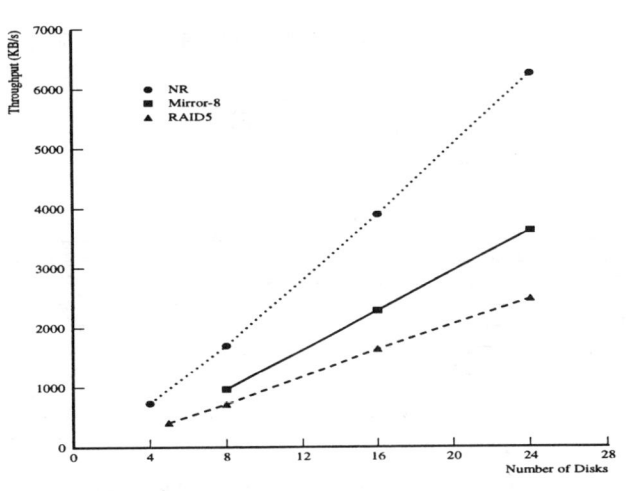

Figure 8: 50% read requests as function of disks

able to service the same workload. In addition, the seek time required for each disk request is reduced. Performance can be further increased if still more disks are added to the disk array. In this section, we examine the effect of adding more disks to the non-redundant, mirrored and RAID5 disk arrays. In particular, we will evaluate these architectures using sixteen disks. The results can be found in figures 5 and 6. Results for pure read and write workloads are similar to figures 1 and 2 and are not shown.

When the workload consists of both reads and writes, NR-16 performs the best, followed by Mirror-16 and RAID5-16. Comparing these results to figures 3 and 4, the extra actuators in RAID5-16 enable it to always provide higher throughput than NR-4. Mirrored disk throughput improves relative to RAID5 in both figures 5 and 6 since the seek time for mirrored disks is reduced more than it is for RAID5.

Figures 7 and 8 show the maximum throughput achieved when the number of disks in an array is varied. The increase in throughput is essentially linear. Pure read and write workloads exhibit similar behavior. The reason for this can be determined by examining the data in Tables 2 through 4.

Comparing the throughput per disk in each architecture as the array size increases, each disk in a larger disk array provides more throughput than each disk in a smaller disk array. Adding disk drives to a disk array provides two advantages. First, extra actuators are available to service independent disk requests. Second, the seek time is reduced since data is spread out among more disk drives. It appears that the advantage of adding disk drives does not diminish for a large number of disks. We are currently studying how far throughput scales with the number of disk drives.

Table 2: Effect of Multiple Disks (Mirrored)

Request	# of disks	avg seek time	throughput (KB/s)	throughput per disk (KB/s)
Read	8	12.7	1438	180
	16	8.9	3432	215
	24	7.4	5599	233
75% Read	8	12.7	1142	143
	16	8.9	2757	172
	24	7.4	4542	189
50% Read	8	12.7	954	119
	16	8.9	2308	144
	24	7.4	3625	151
Write	8	12.7	732	92
	16	8.9	1699	106
	24	7.4	2764	115

Table 3: Effect of Multiple Disks (RAID5)

Request	# of disks	avg seek time	throughput (KB/s)	throughput per disk (KB/s)
Read	5	12.7	911	182
	8	9.6	1666	211
	16	6.7	3807	238
	24	5.7	6026	251
75% Read	5	12.7	558	112
	8	9.6	1012	127
	16	6.7	2290	143
	24	5.7	3545	148
50% Read	5	12.7	408	82
	8	9.6	718	90
	16	6.7	1638	102
	24	5.7	2479	103
Write	5	12.7	264	53
	8	9.6	472	59
	16	6.7	1024	64
	24	5.7	1600	67

Table 4: Effect of Multiple Disks (Non-Redundant)

Request	# of disks	avg seek time	throughput (KB/s)	throughput per disk (KB/s)
Read/ Write	4	12.7	732	183
	8	8.9	1699	212
	16	6.6	3893	243
	24	5.6	6254	261

Matloff [Matl87] obtained similar results using an analytical model to evaluate the impact of additional disk drives on the maximum throughput attainable by a mirrored disk array, although his work can be generalized to a RAID5 disk array. Figure 9 compares his results, derived for a mirrored disk array, with ours for a workload containing 75% read requests. The results are similar for the other ratios of read and write requests.

Matloff assumed the seek time is a linear function of distance. This is not an accurate assumption since seek time is a non-linear function of distance when the distance is small. Thus his results are optimistic. For 24 disks, his results are 25% higher than ours.

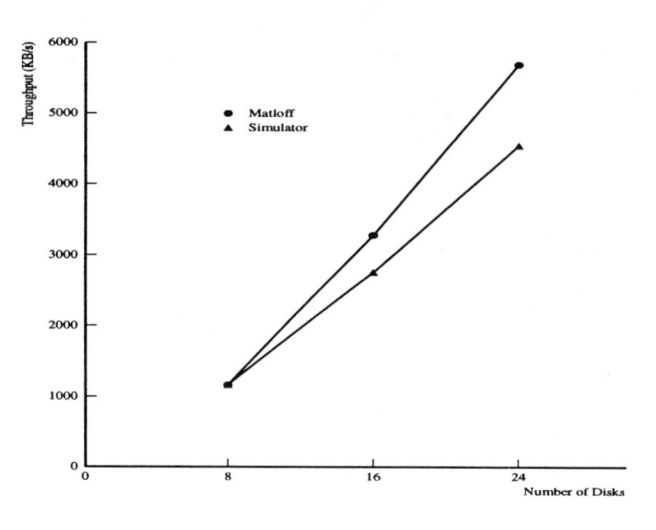

Figure 9: Comparison with Matloff

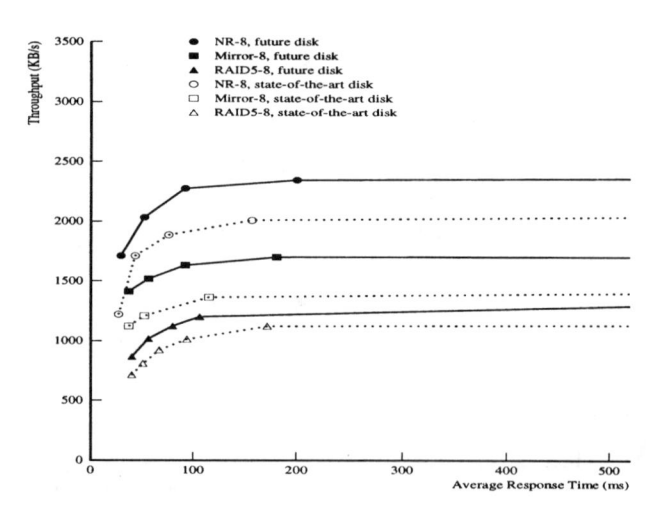

Figure 10: Reducing seek by 33% and 56% with no change in rotational speed

6 Impact of Technology

As stated in Section 3, the experiments presented thus far model a typical disk available today (see Table 1). Disk drive technology, however, is improving. It is important to understand how future technology will impact the results presented in this paper. In this section, we evaluate the effect of improvements in seek time and rotational latency on throughput. We use a workload containing 75% read requests since such a workload is more commonly encountered in practice than workloads containing only reads or writes.

We first consider the effect of reducing the seek time by 33% to represent a state-of-the-art disk drive and

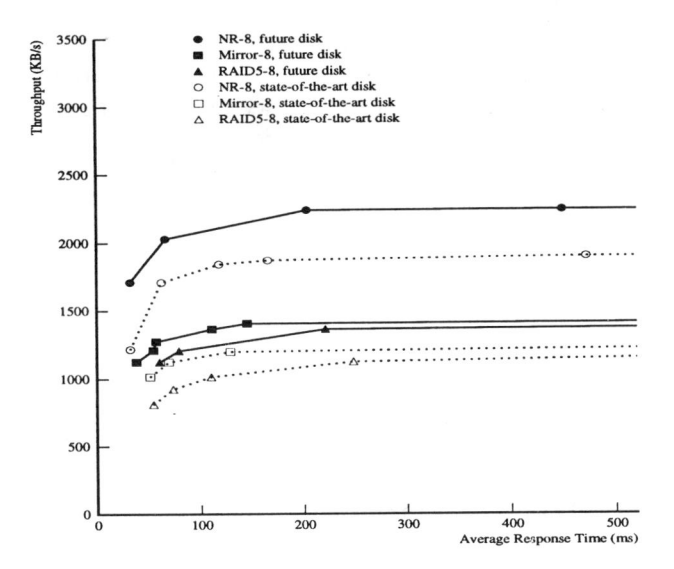

Figure 11: Increasing rotational speed to 5400 and 8000 RPM with no change in seek time

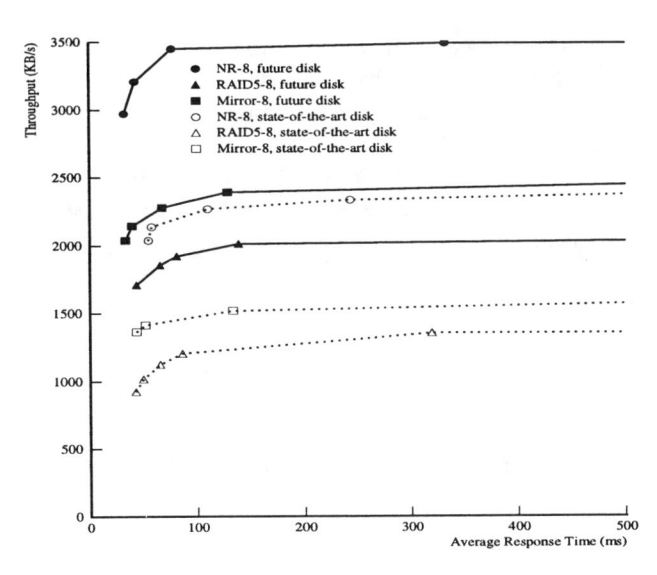

Figure 12: Reducing seek by 33% and 56% with rotational speed of 5400 and 8000 RPM.

56% to represent a future disk drive. The results can be seen in figure 10. Comparing figure 10 to figure 3, we observe that the performance of Mirror-8 improves relative to RAID5-8. The reason is the seek time is a much larger fraction of the total service time for Mirror-8 since RAID5-8 has already reduced its seek time by spreading data out among its disks. Thus reducing the seek time benefits Mirror-8 more than it benefits RAID5-8.

Next, we increase the rotational speed of the disk to 5400 RPM to model a state-of-the-art disk and 8000 RPM to model a future disk while using the original seek time model. This reduces the latency by 20% and 46%, respectively. Comparing figure 11 to figure 3, we observe that the performance of RAID5-8 improves relative to Mirror-8. An increase in the rotational speed aids the performance of RAID5-8 more since latency is a larger fraction of the service time. The latency is a larger fraction for read requests since the seek time has already been reduced. It is an even larger fraction for write requests since a write request incurs a full rotation penalty when performing the read-modify-write operation.

Finally, we change both the seek time and rotational speed in figure 12. Comparing figure 12 to figure 3, we see that the relative performances of the three architectures remain the same. This suggests that future technology will track the results derived in this paper.

7 Conclusion

We have studied the potential performance improvement obtained by trading disk drives and disk array capacity for throughput. Adding disk drives to a disk array without increasing the amount of data stored increases performance in two ways. First, extra actuators are available to service independent disk requests. Second, the seek time is reduced since data is spread out among more disk drives. These factors combine to increase throughput at a rate which exceeds the increase in the number of disks. For example, doubling the number of disks in a mirrored array improves throughput by as much as 140%.

We have also shown that the increase in throughput is independent of the redundancy scheme used in the disk array. This suggests that regardless of the disk array architecture used, throughput can be scaled to a desired value by increasing the number of disks.

These conclusions were also arrived at by Matloff [Matl87], although his results are greater than ours by up to 25%. In addition, there is one shortcoming with Matloff's work that we have addressed here. Matloff only evaluated the maximum throughput attainable by a mirrored array, independent of response time. As can be seen from our figures, this generally implies an average response time of 200 milliseconds or greater. This response time may be unacceptable for some transaction processing applications [TPC90]. Thus, it is important to understand how throughput increases for a range of response times.

Finally, we have compared the throughput and response times provided by three disk array architectures. As expected, the non-redundant disk array provided the best performance since it does not have any overhead. The redundant architectures, mirrored and RAID5, provide reduced performance due to the need to maintain redundancy. Mirrored disks always perform better than RAID5 disks in their basic configurations where the minimum number of disks is used for each architecture. Even when the two arrays have an equal number of disks, mirrored disks still outperform RAID5 arrays for all workloads except those consisting almost entirely of read requests. As disk drives become a commodity, we will see more computer systems use these redundant disk arrays to increase I/O performance.

The results given in this paper only consider workloads consisting of numerous small requests, as are typical of transaction processing applications. We believe our results also apply to workloads containing requests of variable sizes such as file system applications. This bears further study.

Many of the disk configurations evaluated in these experiments have unused disk space and we are investigating uses for this space. For example, it can be used to store infrequently used data or to replicate frequently accessed data. In addition, as disk capacities increase, users can afford to archive the latest versions of their data on disk in this unused area instead of on slow magnetic tape. Another example is a business that accesses customer data during the day and inventory data at night. The customer data can be placed on one half of the disk cylinders while the inventory data can be placed on the other half of the disk cylinders. In each case, the number of cylinders used by a set of data is less than the total number of cylinders. Therefore, the disk arm is restricted to a subset of the total cylinders, reducing the seek time. This implies it may be desirable to combine smaller disk arrays into a single large disk array.

Acknowledgements

This work is part of a larger research project in I/O being carried out at the University of Michigan, funded by NCR Corporation – E&M Columbia. We gratefully acknowledge NCR's support. We also wish to thank David Jaffe of MTI, Jai Menon of IBM, Richie Lary of DEC, and the members of our research group at Michigan, particularly Greg Ganger and Bruce Worthington, for all the technical discussions we have had on the various I/O issues.

Our research group is also fortunate to have the financial and technical support of several industrial partners. We are pleased to acknowledge them. They include NCR, Intel, Motorola, Scientific and Engineering Software, HaL, Hewlett-Packard, Micro Technology Incorporated and DEC.

References

[Bitt88] D. Bitton, J. Gray, "Disk Shadowing", *Proceedings of the Very Large Databases Conference*, September 1988, pp. 331-338.

[Chen90] P.M. Chen, G.A. Gibson, R.H. Katz, D.A. Patterson "An Evaluation of Redundant Arrays of Disks using an Amdahl 5890", *ACM Sigmetrics*, 1990, pp. 74-85.

[Gray90] J. Gray, B. Horst, M. Walker, "Parity Striping of Disk Arrays: Low-Cost Reliable Storage with Acceptable Throughput", *Proceedings of the 16th VLDB Conference*, August 1990, pp. 148-161.

[Holl92] M. Holland, G. Gibson, "Parity Declustering for Continuous Operation in Redundant Disk Arrays", *Architectural Support for Programming Languages and Operating Systems*, 1992, pp. 23-35.

[Kim86] M. Kim, "Synchronized Disk Interleaving", *IEEE Transactions on Computers*, November 1986, pp. 978-988.

[Livn87] M. Livny, S. Khoshafian, H. Boral, "Multi-Disk Management Algorithms", *SIGMETRICS*, 1987, pp. 69-77.

[Matl87] N. Matloff, "A Multiple-Disk System for Both Fault Tolerance and Improved Performance", *IEEE Transactions on Reliability*, June 1987, pp. 199-201.

[Patt88] D. Patterson, G. Gibson, R. Katz, "A Case for Redundant Arrays of Inexpensive Disks (RAID)", *ACM SIGMOD*, May 1988, pp. 109-116.

[Sale86] K. Salem, G. Garcia-Molina, "Disk Striping", *International Conference on Data Engineering*, 1986, pp. 336-342.

[TPC90] Transaction Processing Performance Council. "TPC Benchmark B - Standard Specification". Waterside Associates, Fremont, California. August 23, 1990.

SESSION 7B:
Protocols for Distributed Systems

J.J. Garcia-Luna, Chair

Partial Order Transport Service For Multimedia Applications: Reliable Service*

Paul D. Amer
Thomas Connolly
Computer and Information Science Dept
University of Delaware
Newark, DE 19716 USA

Christophe Chassot
Michel Diaz
LAAS du CNRS
7, avenue du Colonel Roche
31077 Toulouse France

Abstract

This paper introduces a Partial Order Connection (POC) protocol. Motivated in particular by multimedia applications, POC is an end-to-end connection that provides a partial order service, that is, a service that requires some, but not all objects to be received in the order transmitted. This paper discusses R-PO, a reliable version of POC which requires that all transmitted objects are eventually delivered. A metric based on the number of linear extensions of a partial order in the presence of no lost objects is proposed to quantify different partial orders. Means for its calculation is presented when P can be modeled as a combination of sequential and/or parallel compositions of Petri-nets. This metric allows one to compare and evaluate the complexity of different partial order services. [ACCD93] presents U-PO, an unreliable version which defines reliability classes for objects and permits the service to lose a defined number of each class of objects.

Key words: Estelle, FDT, multimedia, partial order, quality of service, transport protocol, transport service

1 Introduction and motivation

Current applications that need to communicate objects (i.e., packets, frames, protocol data units) usually choose between a fully ordered service such as that provided by TCP and one that does not guarantee any ordering such as that provided by UDP. What is more appropriate for some applications is a *partial order* service where a subset of objects being communicated must arrive in the order transmitted, yet some objects may arrive in a different order.

One motivation for a partial order service is the emerging area of multimedia communications. Multimedia traffic often is characterized either by periodic, synchronized parallel streams of information (e.g., combined audio-video), or by structured image streams (e.g., displays of multiple overlapping and nonoverlapping windows). Currently these applications must use and pay for a fully ordered service even though they do not need it.

A second motivation is based on the trend of increasing cpu power available in receiving workstations. With more intelligence at the destination to compensate for minor misorderings, it may pay to lower the demanded quality of service (QOS) of the communication from a total order to a partial order assuming that the latter service is more efficient and less costly.

This work considers quantifying, comparing and implementing various levels of partial order service. Two variations of a partial order service are defined. This paper investigates reliable partial order service (R-PO) which guarantees the eventual delivery of all transmitted objects according to a defined partial order; there can be neither loss nor duplication. Unreliable partial order service (U-PO) service classifies objects according to one of three reliability classes and is discussed in [ACCD93]. U-PO service makes a best effort to deliver all transmitted objects, but tolerates a well defined level of lost objects according to each reliability class.

Two hypotheses are made: (1) there exist applications that inherently need and could genuinely benefit from a partial order service, and (2) because of the additional flexibility in delivery to the user allowed in a partial order service, such a service would cost less in terms of memory and/or bandwidth and provide

---

*This work supported by CNET (Grant 92 1B 178) as part of a CNET-CNRS collaborative project on High Speed Multimedia Systems. Paul Amer supported, in part, by the US Army Communication Electronics Command (CECOM), Ft. Monmouth, and the Army Research Office (DAAL03-91-G-0086). Thomas Connolly supported by the Army Research Office (DAAL03-92-G-0070).

shorter expected delays than would a fully ordered one.

Given these hypotheses, several research questions become of interest. First, what metric(s) appropriately characterizes (i.e., quantifies) the work that must be performed to provide a particular R-PO service, and how is this metric computed? Such a formula would permit one to compare two or more R-POs and thereby, for example, provide a clearer means for charging for each service.

Second, what are the implementation difficulties in attaining the benefits of a R-PO service? How does a destination dynamically distinguish between acceptable and unacceptable orderings as objects arrive?

These questions and others will be considered as follows. Section 2 discusses and motivates a partial order service. Section 3 proposes a metric based on a partial order's set of linear extensions for quantifying and comparing the complexity of partial orders assuming R-PO service is desired. Formulae for calculating this metric are presented for the subset of partial orders that can be described by a limited composition of Petri-nets, a representation initially suggested in [LG90a] because of its natural association with multimedia applications. A Partial Order Connection (POC) protocol for providing R-PO service has been specified in Estelle. This specification and certain practical issues in its development are discussed in Section 4. Finally, Section 5 provides conclusions and directions of the authors' follow-up work.

2 Partial order service

A partial order service is needed and can be employed as soon as a complete ordering is not mandatory. When two objects can be delivered to a transport service user in either order, there is no need to use an ordered service that delays delivery of the second one transmitted until the first arrives.

An example application, used throughout this article, is an Anatomy and Physiology Instructor system described as "a simple multimedia application example based on the hypermedia paradigm and temporal relation specification" [LG90b]. Here a workstation displays multiple windows of video, audio, text, image, and animated image according to well defined synchronization and ordering requirements. The multimedia allows one to understand various parts of the human anatomy, say by combining an animated image and sound track of a heart pumping in one window while simultaneously providing general textual information (e.g., average heart rate) in another window. The consecutive images of the animation have an inherent order that is only partially dependent on the ordering of the textual information.

A second example application is that of refreshing structured information, say, a workstation screen/display containing multiple windows. In refreshing a workstation screen from a remote source, objects (icons, still or video images) that do not overlap have a "parallel" relationship (i.e., their order of arrival is independent) while overlapping screen objects have a "sequential" relationship and should be delivered in order. Why? Because objects that are even partially overlapped by others should arrive first for optimal redisplay efficiency.

Consider the four cases in Figure 1. In this case, a sender wishes to refresh a remote display that contains four active windows (objects) named {1 2 3 4}. Assuming the windows are transmitted in numerical order, an ordered service, also referred to as a FIFO channel, is shown in Figure 1.A. In this case, only one ordering is permitted at the destination. If window 2 is received before window 1, the transport service cannot deliver it or an incorrect image will be displayed.

An unordered service is desired in Figure 1.D. Here any of 4! = 24 delivery orderings would satisfy the application since the four windows can be refreshed in any order. As notation, 4 ordered objects are written 1;2;3;4 and unordered objects are written using a parallel operator: 1 || 2 || 3 || 4.

Figures 1.B and 1.C demonstrate two possible partial orders that permit 2 and 6 permitted orderings, respectively, at the destination. For N objects, there exist many possible partial orders. A question arises "how do these orders compare with respect to the work a protocol must perform to provide each one?"

Sending a set of objects in a partial order need not be a one time event as in a screen refresh example. In cases of periodic (i.e., cyclic) communication such as a multimedia presentation with synchronized video, sound and text streams, a partial order models each of a repeating pattern of objects. In this case, each repetition represents a single partial order snapshot in a stream of sequential periods of communication.

2.1 Related work

Other authors have considered theoretical consequences of channel ordering, or lack thereof, in the context of designing and verifying distributed algorithms [Lam78, NT87]. For example, Ahuja shows that some conclusions derived on the design of distributed algorithms need not have required FIFO ordering as a base assumption [Ahu90]. Ahuja, however, assumes a sending process dynamically builds the partial order and

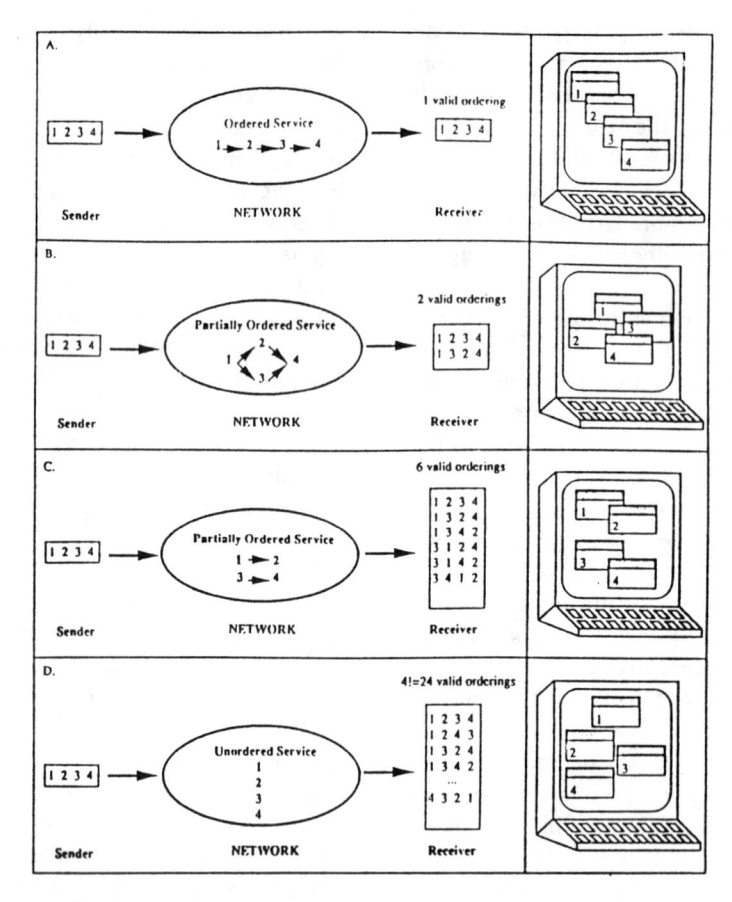

Figure 1: Ordered vs. Partial Ordered vs. Unordered Service

that no objects are ever lost [CKA93]. Our proposed work assumes a static partial order negotiated by the sender and receiver and U-PO service allows objects to be lost. Also, Ahuja's four data types do not permit all possible partial orders of objects as does our POC service.

[PBS89] defines a partial order on the messages communicated by a set of distributed processes and implements a protocol *Psync* that encodes the partial ordering within each message. The partial order is defined by the interleaved times that messages are sent and received in the shared message space of the multiple communicating processes and dynamically changes with each newly sent message. Our proposed work differs in its assumption of a *point to point* connection in which both sides agree *in advance* to a partial ordering of the data to be transferred.

Our proposed work does not consider the size or duration of objects being communicated; it focuses primarily on their delivery order. The temporal value of objects is taken into consideration when the service allows some level of permitted loss [ACCD93]. It is assumed that synchronization concerns in presenting the objects after delivery is a service provided on top of the proposed partial order service. Temporal ordering for synchronized playback is considered, for example,
in [AH91, HKN91].

3 Comparing partial order services

There are several known metrics that can be used for quantifying and/or comparing partial order transport services. For example, simple measures of a partial order's complexity are: its height, its width, and the number of relations. None of these simple measures however clearly correlates to the work a protocol would have to perform to provide a partial order service.

It is proposed here that the complexity of a partial order P be quantified by its set of linear extensions, denoted $L(P)$. Each linear extension in the set $L(P)$ is essentially one of the orderings of the objects that is permitted at the destination. The number of linear extensions of P, denoted $e(P)$, is thought as the best single number which measures the complexity of P [Sta86]. Clearly, $e($complete order on N objects$) = 1$, $e($no order$) = N!$ Shafer and Ahuja refer to this set as R_{send}, the reachable set of valid permutations at the destination [SA92].

It is argued here that $e(P)$ appropriately quantifies a desired partial order quality of service in communication networks. This is because the larger the number of permitted orderings allowed at the destination, the less overhead is required to provide acceptable object delivery. There will be, on the average, fewer out of order packets with a more flexible partial order.

3.1 Counting orderings

Given a particular partial order, just how many orderings are permitted at the destination? This question is important as it allows one to quantify a particular partial ordered service. The more reception orderings that a demanded partial order service allows, the less would be the relative cost for the service. Answering this question allows us to compare two or more partial order services.

Unfortunately no known formula exists for calculating $e(P)$ for any arbitrary partial order. Recently it has been shown that this problem is $\#P$-complete [BW91]. This means that a polynomial time algorithm (much less a simple formula) for computing $e(P)$ is unlikely to exist. There is an $O(N^5)$ algorithm for computing $e(P)$ for partial orders that are restricted to being in the form of a tree where N is the number of objects. Similarly, there is an $O(N^8)$ algorithm for computing $e(P)$ for any graph (and therefore for any partial order) where if the directions of the edges of P are not considered, any resulting cycles are disjoint[Riv89].

However if the partial orders under consideration are limited only to those that can be composed of sequential and parallel Petri-nets, calculation of $e(P)$ with this limitation is possible.

Little and Ghafoor suggest Petri-nets as a basis for modeling the synchronization and ordering of multimedia entities. They consider timed and augmented Petri-net models because of their desirable attributes of representation of concurrent and asynchronous events [LG90a, LG90b]. Their model is called Object Composition Petri Nets (OCPN), a model that has been extended to include the representation and specification of delays and jitters [DS92].

Using OCPNs, it is possible to represent arbitrarily complex synchronization. Of particular interest are those partial orders that can be represented by certain compositions of OCPNs. As suggested in Figure 2, consider those partial orders that can be represented by any number of *sequential* and/or *parallel* compositions of Petri-nets. Not all partial orders are representable.[1] since, in general, the total number of partial orders is much larger than the number of sequential-parallel partial orders [Sta74].

[1] For example, of the 15 and 63 partial orders of 4 and 5 objects, respectively, 1 and 15 partial orders cannot be composed.

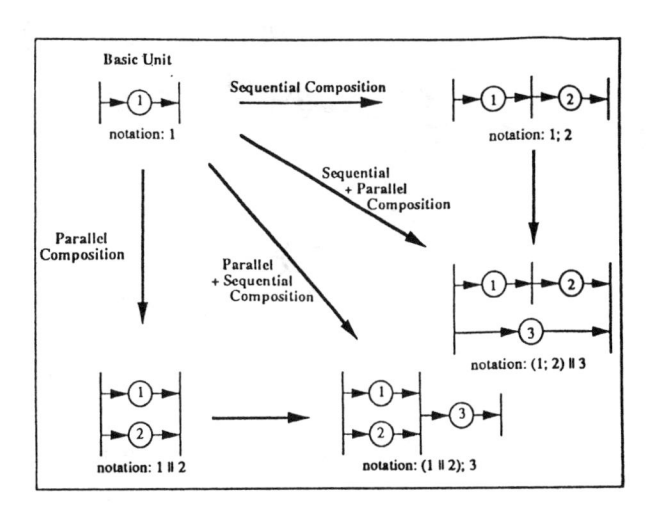

Figure 2: Basic Petri-net Compositions

A complex partial order example is shown in Figure 3. This Petri-net consisting of 19 objects represents the previously mentioned Anatomy and Physiology Instructor system [LG90b]. This example models a six parallel-window multimedia presentation of the heart's function and anatomy. It includes an animation sequence of two views of the heart (objects 1-12), two static text windows describing the heart's physical function (16;17), and a full motion video (14) with sound track (15).

Figure 3 can be composed using sequential and parallel composition as:

$((1 \parallel 2); (3 \parallel 4); (5 \parallel 6); (7 \parallel 8); (9 \parallel 10);$

$(11 \parallel 12)) \parallel (13; (14 \parallel 15)) \parallel 16 \parallel 17 \parallel 18 \parallel 19$

While every composition of Petri-nets can be represented as a partial order, not every partial order can be represented as a composition. These unspecifiable partial orders are precisely those that cannot be written using the operators ; and $\parallel$. Figure 2 also emphasizes that composing Petri-nets in sequence and then in parallel is not equivalent to composing them in parallel and then in sequence.

Let n denote the number of objects in the partial order defined by Petri-net X, and $e(X)$ denote the number of linear extensions defined by Petri-net X. If X has only $n = 1$ object in it, then $e(X) = 1$. If Petri-nets X_1 and X_2 with n_1 and n_2 objects, respectively, are combined sequentially (denoted $X_1; X_2$), then $X_1; X_2$ has $n_1 + n_2$ objects and

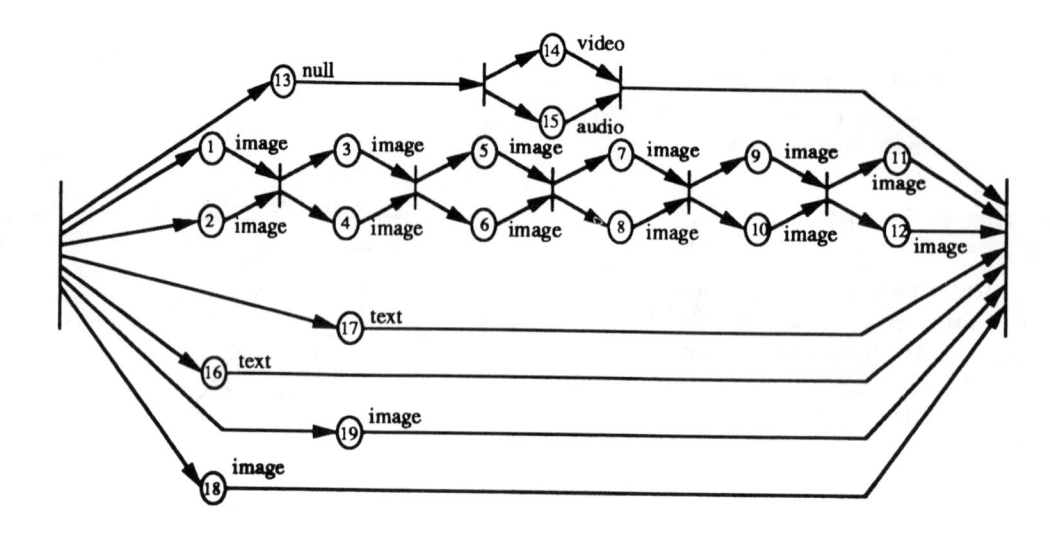

Figure 3: Complex Petri-net Composition Example [LG90b]

$$e(X_1; X_2) = e(X_2; X_1) = e(X_1) * e(X_2)$$

This formula indicates that for each linear extension of X_1, there exist $e(X_2)$ possible linear extensions that can follow.

If Petri-nets X_1 and X_2 are combined in parallel (denoted $X_1 \parallel X_2$), then $X_1 \parallel X_2$ has $n_1 + n_2$ objects and

$$e(X_1 \parallel X_2) = e(X_2 \parallel X_1) = \frac{(n_1 + n_2)!}{(n_1!) * (n_2!)} * e(X_1) * e(X_2)$$

Two extensions combined in parallel can be done so in all possible interleavings of all of the objects while still maintaining each one's relative order. The binomial function coefficient represents the interleavings between a single linear extension of X_1 and a single linear extension of X_2. This coefficient must then be multiplied by the number of possible linear extensions of X_1 and of X_2.

The order of multiple composition of Petri-nets does not affect the number of linear extensions of the final Petri-net. That is

$$e((X_1; X_2); X_3) = e(X_1; (X_2; X_3))$$

$$e((X_1 \parallel X_2) \parallel X_3) = e(X_1 \parallel (X_2 \parallel X_3))$$

For the second assertion above, it can be shown that both sides of the equality reduce to

$$\frac{(n_1 + n_2 + n_3)!}{(n_1!) * (n_2!) * (n_3!)} * e(X_1) * e(X_2) * e(X_3)$$

The first term is the multinomial function representing all of the interleavings of a single linear extension of X_1, a single one of X_2, and a single one of X_3. This term must then be multiplied by the number of possible linear extensions of each Petri-net X_1, X_2, and X_3.

In the mathematical theory of enumerative combinatorics, sequential and parallel Petri-net compositions are analogous to the "ordinal sum" and "disjoint union," respectively, of partial order sets. Those Petri-nets which can be composed of these two operations are analogous to what have been termed "series-parallel" partial order sets [Sta86]. That is, only 1 of the 16 possible partial orders of 4 objects is not analogous to a series-parallel partial order. From [Sta86, Example 3.5.4], the following formulae for our Petri-net compositions are known:

Given Petri-nets $X_1, X_2, \ldots, X_k$ with $n_1, n_2, \cdots, n_k$ objects, respectively, then $X_1; X_2; \cdots; X_k$ and $X_1 \parallel X_2 \parallel \cdots \parallel X_k$ have $N = \sum_{i=1}^{k} n_i$ objects, and

$$e(X_1; X_2; \cdots; X_k) = \prod_{j=1}^{k} e(X_j)$$

$$e(X_1 \parallel X_2 \parallel \cdots \parallel X_k) = \frac{N!}{\prod_{j=1}^{k}(n_j)!} * \prod_{j=1}^{k} e(X_j)$$

Recall that these formulae cannot be applied to every partial order; only those that can be represented by sequential-parallel compositions of Petri-nets.

3.2 Partial order metric

Using the Anatomy and Physiology Instructor example in Figure 3 and the formulae above, it can be shown that there are 5,417,717,760 valid orderings out of the total possible 19! (=121,645,100,408,832,000) orderings. While as a fraction of the total number, the number of valid orderings is relatively small (roughly $.4 * 10^{-6}$), this partial order service has significantly more flexibility than a total order which allows but one order. This significance or potential savings is best observed by considering the number of valid orderings on a normalized logarithmic scale.

We therefore propose a normalized partial order metric in the interval [0,1] where 0 represents ordered service, values from 0 to 1 represent increasingly more flexible partial order services, and 1 represents unordered service. The quantity that measures the flexibility of a partial order service modeled by Petri-net X containing n objects is denoted M and is calculated as:

$$M(X) = \frac{\log(e(X))}{\log(n!)}$$

The M value for the Petri-net in Figure 3 is therefore approximately .57, a value that provides a better intuition into Figure 3's flexibility. This metric M allows one to compare partial orders with respect to communication constraints.

[ACCD93] defines $e_i(X)$, the number of linear extensions in the presence of i losses. Then $e(X)$ becomes $e_0(X)$ and $M(X)$ becomes $M_0(X)$.

4 Implementation considerations

Given a particular partial order, what are the orderings that are permitted at the destination? While calculating $e(P)$ is valuable for evaluating and comparing partial orders, it remains a practical problem for a destination to determine as objects arrive if they are in one of the valid orders as defined by P. That is, is the arriving order a member of $L(P)$?

Enumerating $L(P)$ is equivalent to finding all possible topological sortings for a given partial order [Knu73]. Knuth provides an algorithm to find one arbitrary topological sort when given a partial order in the form of a set of ordered pairs that define ordering restrictions between pairs of objects. This algorithm is shown to have a linear complexity of $O(M + N)$ where M = number of ordered pairs used to describe the partial order, and N = number of objects in the partial order. Since just counting $e(P)$ is a difficult problem in general, certainly enumerating $L(P)$ is difficult.

Fortunately in practice, a destination need not enumerate $L(P)$ to decide if an arriving object can be delivered. The destination merely needs to see if the arriving object satisfies the defined partial order. Thus there are two problems: (1) how does a sender specify and communicate the partial order to destination? (2) and given the partial order, what algorithm does the destination use to evaluate an arriving object's validity with regards to order? These two questions are considered in the next two sections, respectively.

4.1 Establishing a connection

Initially a user must request a specific partial order service of interest. Then the partial order must be transmitted to the destination. It would be useful if the sender could encode a partial ordering in as few bits as possible since these bits must be transmitted every time the order changes. For the screen refresh example, this context will likely change before every refresh. For multimedia presentations that are more periodic in nature, it will suffice to transmit the partial order less frequently.

A partial order can be defined by a maximum sized set of ordered pairs $(i \prec j)$. Each pair indicates i must arrive before (i.e., precede) j. By maximum, it is implied that this set will include all pairs that can be derived via the transitive property of a partial order. That is, if $(i \prec j)$ and $(j \prec k)$ are included, then $(i \prec k)$ is also. For example, in Figure 1.B, the partial order is defined as the set $\{(1 \prec 2), (1 \prec 3), (1 \prec 4), (2 \prec 4), (3 \prec 4)\}$. Consider these pairs as 1's in an N by N matrix.

Proposition: If a partial order of N objects numbered 1 through N accepts (among possibly others) the linear extension 1,2,3,4,5,...,N, then the partial order can be represented by an upper triangular matrix where matrix location $(i, j) = 1$ iff $(i \prec j)$.

Proof: If a partial order accepts the sequence 1,2,3,4,5,...,N, then there can be no pair $(i \prec j)$ where $j < i$. Therefore there can be no 1 in the lower triangle of the matrix.

Since, without loss of generality, a sender can number objects such that the order 1,2,3,...,N is valid, one can encode any order uniquely by considering the 1's and 0's in the upper triangular matrix as a binary value. This value along with the number of objects in the partial order can be decoded by the destination to confirm the desired partial order. The number of bits to be sent is therefore $N(N-1)/2$. (Obviously, the diagonal is not needed.) Figure 4 contains the matrix for the example Petri-net in Figure 3.

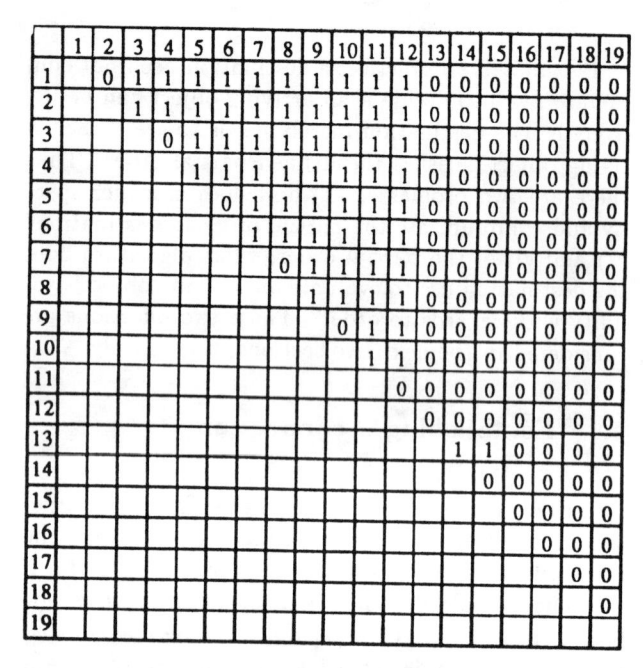

Figure 4: Maximal Partial Order Matrix for Little and Ghafoor Example

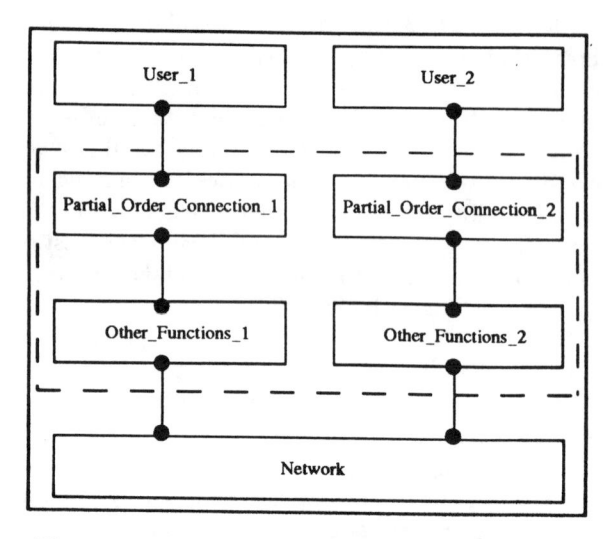

Figure 5: Architecture of Estelle Specification

4.2 Protocol specification

Once a destination knows the partial order, what algorithm should it use as objects arrive in determining which objects can be delivered immediately to the user, which must be buffered, and which must be discarded? A dynamic algorithm is needed which incrementally updates its information each time an object arrives.

[SA92] propose an algorithm using a channel grammar based on rewrite rules. This grammar is used for a hierarchical F-Channel, a model consisting of a set of channels, each of which is a partial ordered channel, and each of which contains objects that can overtake objects in channels higher in the hierarchy, but not lower in the hierarchy. However, the F-Channel model is used to derive qualitative results about distributed communication and does not permit the definition of all possible partial orders. Also, for our purposes, a matrix is more efficient.

Protocol POC[2] has been specified in Estelle, an ISO International Standard Formal Description Technique for specifying communication services/protocols and, more generally, distributed systems [ISO9074, BD87]. The specification defines a general architecture shown in Figure 5, and an extended finite state machine behavior for sending and receiving objects. The partial order service is placed inside a transport layer above other transport functions such as fragmentation/reassembly.

Without loss of generatlity, assume simplex communication where User_1 needs to transmit repeating periods of N objects to User_2. It is assumed that the partial order matrix has been transmitted accurately to User_2 and does not change during the association. Otherwise, it is necessary to first transmit and, if necessary, negotiate the partial order service. Changing the partial order during an association while some objects remain undelivered can result in unpredictable behavior if the new partial order is put into place too soon. Proper timing must be maintained. It needs to be studied just how quickly and often multimedia applications need to dynamically change contexts before adding this complexity into the protocol.

As with a classic reliable transport protocol such as TCP, User_1 gives objects to Partial_Order_Connection_1 (POC_1) which in turn then transmits the objects having up to S unacknowledged objects outstanding at any time (i.e., S is the sending window size). POC_1 buffers and retransmits objects until they are acknowledged. The underlying network service is assumed unreliable; it may lose, duplicate, and deliver objects to POC_2 in any order; not necessarily in the order transmitted.

POC_2 receives the objects and tries to deliver them to User_2. At any time, POC_2 can store up to R out of order objects (i.e., R is the receiving window.) Further out of order objects are discarded. Any time an object is delivered to User_2, POC_2 checks the buffers

---

[2] Available from the authors; not included here due to space limitations.

to see if as a result any stored objects have become deliverable. Because of repeating periods, POC_2 must distinguish identically numbered objects from different periods.

Protocol POC differs from a classic reliable one in several ways. (1) User_1 sends the objects according to the partial order, not necessarily in sequential order. This allows some extra degree of flexibility when, for example, User_1 is dynamically generating objects in real time where the order of generation is not deterministic. (2) Because of the partial order delivery service, at any point in time, there may be several objects that are deliverable to User_2, not merely a single object. Thus, on the average, it can be expected that fewer objects will be "out of order." (3) The windows S and R in fact are not windows in the classic closed interval sense. Rather they represent sets of objects whose numbers need not be consecutive. Thus deciding if an object is in a particular window and window update management are more complicated.

Finally, it is noted that *any* partial order can be represented as an upper triangular matrix, not only those that are series-parallel. Thus Protocol POC is applicable even in those cases where one cannot compute $M(X)$ exactly.

5 Conclusion

Motivated by multimedia applications, this work introduces a partial order transport service. In particular, a reliable version that must deliver all sent objects is considered. Consideration of an unreliable partial order service channel for applications that can tolerate loss is discussed in [ACCD93].

Different reliable partial order services can be quantified and compared based on $e(X)$, the number of linear extensions that they define. It is shown that $e(X)$ can be computed when the partial order can be expressed as sequential and parallel compositions of Petri-nets. By comparing $e(X)$ to the number of linear extensions permitted by an unordered service with the same number of objects, a metric over the interval [0,1] is proposed.

Multimedia applications frequently can tolerate well the loss of objects, particularly sound and video information streams. The authors are considering partial order service combined with varying degrees of reliability (i.e., permitted loss). One can view the tolerance of loss as an increase in the number of linear extensions permitted.

Using their Estelle specification, the authors are preparing a simulation model to investigate the relative performance of R-PO (and U-PO) service in comparison with an ordered service. The simulation will be used to determine the expected savings in retransmissions and buffer requirements at POC_2. As losses become more prominent, does a partial order service's savings grow exponentially, linearly or logarithmically? Exponential growth, for example, would underscore the value of a partial order service in an environment where one expects the underlying network quality of service to degrade.

This simulation will evaluate the expected memory/bandwidth performance improvements over an ordered service for various combinations of: (1) different partial orders and loss tolerances, (2) different distributions of disorder and loss supplied by the underlying service, and (3) different sender-receiver window set sizes. The goal is to better understand the potential performance gains when using a partial order service over increasingly less reliable networks and to better understand how well the metric $M(X)$ correlates to these gains. If the correlation is high, then can $M(X)$ can be used directly for charging purposes.

References

[ACCD93] P.D. Amer, C. Chassot, T. Connolly, and M. Diaz. Partial order transport service for multimedia applications: Part 2 - Unreliable service. Tech Report 93-033, LAAS du CNRS, Feb 1993.

[AH91] D. Anderson and G. Homsy. A continuous media I/O server and its synchronization mechanism. *IEEE Computer*, 24(10), 51–57, Oct 1991.

[Ahu90] M. Ahuja. FLUSH primitives for asynchronous dist'd systems. *Info Processing Letters*, 34(1), 5–12, Feb 1990.

[BD87] S. Budkowski and P. Dembinski. An intro to Estelle: A specification language for dist'd systems. *Computer Networks and ISDN Systems*, 14(1), 3–23, 1987.

[BW91] G. Brightwell and P. Winkler. Counting linear extensions is #P-complete. In *Proc 23rd ACM Symp on the Theory of Computing*, 175–181, 1991.

[CKA93] T. Camp, P. Kearns, and M. Ahuja. Proof rules for FLUSH channels. *IEEE Trans on Soft Eng*, to appear, 1993.

[DS92] M. Diaz and P. Senac. La synchronization d'objets multimedia. Tech Report 92-437, LAAS du CNRS, Nov 1992.

[HKN91] S.L. Hardt-Kornacki and L.A. Ness. Optimization model for the delivery of interactive multimedia documents. In *Proc Globecom 91*, 669–673, Phoenix, Dec 1991.

[ISO9074] Information Processing Systems - OSI. *ISO IS 9074: Estelle - A Formal Description Technique Based on an Extended State Transition Model.*

[Knu73] D. Knuth. *The Art of Computer Programming Vol 1: Fundamental Algorithms, 2nd ed.* Addison-Wesley, Reading, Mass., 1973.

[Lam78] L. Lamport. Time, clocks and the ordering of events in a dist'd system. *CACM*, 21(7), 558–565, Jul 1978.

[LG90a] T. Little and A. Ghafoor. Network considerations for dist'd multimedia object composition and communication. *IEEE Network Magazine*, 32–49, Nov 1990.

[LG90b] T. Little and A. Ghafoor. Synchronization and storage models for multimedia objects. *IEEE J on Selected Areas in Comm*, 8(3), 413–427, Apr 1990.

[NT87] G. Neiger and S. Toueg. Substituting for real time and common knowledge in asynchronous dist'd systems. In *Proc 4th Symp on Principles of Dist'd Computing*, 281–293, 1987.

[PBS89] L. Peterson, N. Buchholz, and R. Schlighting. Preserving and using context information in interprocess communication. *ACM Trans on Computer Systems*, 7(3), 217–246, Aug 1989.

[Riv89] I. Rival. *NATO Advanced Study Inst on Algorithms and Order.* Klumer Acadamic Publishers, 1989.

[SA92] K. Shafer and M. Ahuja. Process-channel(agent)-process model of asynchronous dist'd communication. In *Proc ICDCS 12*, 4–11, Yokohama, Japan, Jun 1992.

[Sta74] R. Stanley. Enumeration of posets generated by disjoint unions and ordinal sums. *Proc Amer Math Society*, 45(2), 295–299, Aug 1974.

[Sta86] R. Stanley. *Enumerative Combinatorics: Volume 1.* Wadsworth + Brooks/Cole Advanced Books & Software, Monterey, CA, 1986.

Starvation-Prevented Priority-Based Total Ordering Broadcast Protocol on High-Speed Single Channel Network

Akihito Nakamura and Makoto Takizawa

Dept. of Computers and Systems Engineering
Tokyo Denki University
Ishizaka, Hatoyama, Hiki-gun, Saitama 350-03, JAPAN
e-mail {naka, taki}@takilab.k.dendai.ac.jp

Abstract

In distributed applications like teleconferencing, various kinds of data like transactions, files, and voice have to be delivered to multiple destinations. Current high-speed networks like the FDDI provide high-reliable broadcast communication. However, since the processing speed of the communication entities is slower than the transmission speed of the network, the entities may fail to receive protocol data units (PDUs) transmitted through the network due to the buffer overrun. Some data units like control data have to be delivered to the destinations earlier than another PDUs. One approach to providing various kinds of communication by using a single-channel network is to give a priority to each PDU and to deliver higher-priority PDUs to the destinations earlier than lower-priority ones. In this paper, we discuss a distributed broadcast protocol which provides priority-based receipt ordering of PDUs for the application entities by using the high-speed single-channel network in the presence of the loss of PDUs. There is a starvation problem, i.e. lower-priority PDUs can be left waiting indefinitely in the receipt queue since higher-priority PDUs jump over lower-priority ones. In this paper, we present a method by which even lower-priority PDUs are delivered to the application entities in some pre-defined time by partitioning the receipt sequence of PDUs into runs, where each run is priority-based ordered.

1 Introduction

In distributed applications like teleconferencing in groupware [9], group communication among multiple communication entities is required in addition to conventional one-to-one communication [7, 12]. Current communication technologies like radio and optical fibers [2, 3] provide high-speed high-reliable data transmission among multiple entities. However, entities may fail to receive PDUs due to the buffer overruns [8] since the transmission speed of the network is faster than the processing speed of each entity. Hence, PDU loss is considered to be only failure in the high-speed network. In this paper, we would like to discuss how to provide atomic delivery of PDUs among multiple entities and some receipt ordering of them by using high-speed broadcast networks. Reliable broadcast communication systems have been discussed in [4, 5, 10, 11, 13, 17, 18, 19, 20, 22, 24, 25, 26, 27]. [22] presents a reliable broadcast protocol which uses one-to-one communication. [5, 10, 13] discuss centralized protocols which use Ethernet. [11] characterizes message ordering properties in a reliable broadcast protocol using the conventional one-to-one network. [24, 25, 19, 20, 21] present a *cluster* concept which is an extension of the conventional connection concept [12] to multiple service access points (SAPs) and shows how to establish the cluster by using the Ethernet MAC broadcast service. One important problem in designing protocols is which entity coordinates the cooperation of multiple entities. Most approaches [5, 10, 11, 22] adopt centralized control, where one master entity decides the correct receipt among multiple entities. In the centralized control, entities have to wait for the decision of the master entity. On the other hand, there is no master controller in the distributed control. The ISIS ABCAST protocol [4] adopts the distributed control where for each PDU p, there exists one entity which decides the correct atomic receipt of p. We discuss a cluster-oriented distributed broadcast protocol where every entity decides the correct atomic receipt of PDUs among all the entities in the cluster because we can take advantage of the underlying broadcast service. [24, 25, 26] present the TO (totally ordering) and OP (order-preserving) protocols on the broadcast networks. [19, 20] discuss an SPO (selectively partially order-preserving) protocol, where each entity rather sends each PDU p to a subset of the entities which are the destination of p than all the entities in the cluster, and each entity receives the PDUs destined to it from some entity in the same order as it sends.

In the distributed applications, various kinds of data like commands, texts, image, and voice are broadcast to multiple sites. For example, a control command has to be delivered to the destinations earlier than another data. One approach to delivering more-time-sensitive PDUs to the destinations earlier than less-time-sensitive ones is to give priority to each PDU. There are two kinds of priority-based transmission schemes for the broadcast communication, i.e. *controlled access* [14, 23] and *contention-based* [14, 16] ones. In this paper, we discuss contention-based priority schemes among multiple entities in a *cluster*. In the broadcast communication, it is important to consider in what order PDUs with priorities are received by each entity in the cluster. [21] presents a *priority-based total ordering* (PriTO) protocol, where every entity receives all the PDUs not only in the same order but also in the priority-based order. One problem is *starvation* (*indefinite blocking*), i.e. a lower-priority PDU p can be left waiting indefinitely in the receipt queue since higher-priority PDUs jump over p. In this paper, we present a PriTO protocol by which even lower-priority PDUs are delivered to the application entities in some pre-defined time by partitioning the receipt sequence of PDUs into *runs*, each of which is priority-based ordered and even higher-priority PDUs in one run R can not jump over ones in runs preceding R. Each entity receives the same sequence of the runs without starvation.

In section 2, we present a model of the broadcast communication. In section 3, we discuss the priority-based ordering of PDUs. In section 4, we discuss a protocol which provides the PriTO service by using high-speed one-channel. In section 5, we discuss how to resolve the starvation. Finally, we discuss the performance of the PriTO protocol in section 6.

2 Basic Concepts

2.1 Cluster

A communication system is composed of three layers, i.e. *application*, *system*, and *network* layers. Entities of the system layer provide reliable broadcast communication service for entities of the application layer by using high-speed broadcast communication service provided by the network layer. A *cluster* C [24, 25] is a set of *service access points* (SAPs) $S_1,...,S_n$ ($n \geq 2$). Each S_i is supported by a system entity E_i, and each application entity A_i takes reliable broadcast communication service through S_i ($i = 1,...,n$). Here, C is *supported* by $E_1,...,E_n$ (written as $C = \langle E_1,...,E_n \rangle$), and be *composed* of $A_1,...,A_n$. In this paper, we assume that C is established by multiple entities, e.g. by using a protocol presented in [24, 25].

2.2 Correct receipt among multiple entities

There are three levels of correct receipt among multiple entities in a cluster $C = \langle E_1,...,E_n \rangle$, i.e. *accepted*, *pre-acknowledged*, and *acknowledged* [24, 25].

(1) When a PDU p arrives at E_j, p is *accepted* by E_j.

(2) When E_j knows that every entity in C has accepted p, p is *pre-acknowledged* by E_j.

(3) When E_j knows that every entity in C has pre-acknowledged p, p is *acknowledged* by E_j.

At (2), although E_j knows that every entity in C has accepted p, some E_i still may not know that another entity has accepted p. For example, E_i has not received the acknowledgment of p from some E_h yet. (3) represents the highest correct level.

The service is modeled as a set of logs. A log L is a sequence of PDUs $< p_1 \ldots p_m \ ]$, where p_1 and p_m are the top and the last, denoted by $top(L)$ and $last(L)$, respectively. In L, p_i precedes p_j ($p_i \rightarrow_L p_j$) if $i < j$. Here, let L_1 be a log $< q_1 \ldots q_n \ ]$. $L||L_1$ denotes a concatenation of L and L_1, i.e. $< p_1 \ldots p_m \ q_1 \ldots q_n \ ]$. Here, let $L|_i^j$ ($i \leq j$) denote a subsequence $< p_i \ p_{i+1} \ldots p_{j-1} \ p_j \ ]$ of L. Each E_i has a sending log SL_i and a receipt log RL_i, which are sequences of PDUs sent and received by E_i, respectively. There are the following relations among the logs.

(1) RL_i is *order-preserved* iff for every E_j, $p \rightarrow_{RL_i} q$, if $p \rightarrow_{SL_j} q$. RL_i is *information-preserved* iff RL_i includes all the PDUs in $SL_1,...,SL_n$.

(2) RL_i and RL_j are *information-equivalent* iff RL_i and RL_j include the same PDUs. RL_i and RL_j are *order-equivalent* iff for every pair of PDUs p and q included in both RL_i and RL_j, $p \rightarrow_{RL_i} q$ iff $p \rightarrow_{RL_j} q$.

(3) RL_i is *preserved* iff RL_i is both order- and information-preserved. RL_i and RL_j are *equivalent* iff RL_i and RL_j are both order- and information-equivalent.

[**Definition**] A *one-channel* (1C) service is one where every receipt log is order-preserved and order-equivalent. □

The 1C service is abstraction of services provided by high-speed networks [2]. Although every entity receives PDUs in the same order, each entity may fail to receive PDUs due to the buffer overruns.

[**Definition**] *Order-preserved* (OP) service is one where every receipt log is preserved. *Total ordering* (TO) service is an OP service where every receipt log is order-equivalent with each other. □

In the TO service, every entity receives the same PDUs in the same order without any PDU loss.

3 Priority-Based Cluster Service

Let p and q denote PDUs. Each p has a unique sequence number $p.SEQ$ and a priority $p.PRI$. If p is broadcast after q, $p.SEQ > q.SEQ$. If p has higher priority than q, $p.PRI > q.PRI$. Let $p_{[r]}$ denote that p has priority r, i.e. $p.PRI = r$. In this paper, $r > 0$, and the system uses priority 0. Here, a notation p^i is used to explicitly denote that p is broadcast by E_i. $p.SRC$ shows an source entity of p.

[**Definition**] A log L is *priority-based ordered* iff for every p and q in L, (1) if $p.PRI > q.PRI$, then $p \rightarrow_L q$, and (2) if $p.PRI = q.PRI$, $p.SRC = q.SRC$, and $p.SEQ < q.SEQ$, then $p \rightarrow_L q$. □

[**Definition**] Two logs L_1 and L_2 are *priority-based-equivalent* iff L_1 and L_2 are information-equivalent

$$RL_1 = < c_{[3]}\ b_{[2]}\ y_{[2]}\ p_{[2]}\ a_{[1]}\ x_{[1]}\ q_{[1]}\ z_{[1]}\ ] \qquad SL_1 = < a_{[1]}\ b_{[2]}\ c_{[3]}\ ]$$
$$RL_2 = < c_{[3]}\ y_{[2]}\ b_{[2]}\ p_{[2]}\ x_{[1]}\ q_{[1]}\ z_{[1]}\ a_{[1]}\ ] \qquad SL_2 = < p_{[2]}\ q_{[1]}\ ]$$
$$RL_3 = < c_{[3]}\ p_{[2]}\ b_{[2]}\ y_{[2]}\ q_{[1]}\ x_{[1]}\ z_{[1]}\ a_{[1]}\ ] \qquad SL_3 = < x_{[1]}\ y_{[2]}\ z_{[1]}\ ]$$

Figure 1: Priority-based equivalent

$$L = < a_{[3]}\ b_{[2]}\ c_{[2]}\ d_{[1]}\ e_{[1]}\ f_{[2]}\ g_{[1]}\ h_{[1]}\ ]$$

$$R_1 = L|_1^3 = < a_{[3]}\ b_{[2]}\ c_{[2]}\ ] \qquad \sqsubseteq L$$
$$R_2 = L|_2^5 = < b_{[2]}\ c_{[2]}\ d_{[1]}\ e_{[1]}\ ] \qquad \sqsubseteq L$$
$$R_3 = L|_6^8 = < f_{[2]}\ g_{[1]}\ h_{[1]}\ ] \qquad \sqsubseteq L$$
$$R_4 = L|_5^8 = < e_{[1]}\ f_{[2]}\ g_{[1]}\ h_{[1]}\ ] \qquad \not\sqsubseteq L$$

Figure 2: Runs

$$L_1 = < \overbrace{a_{[3]}\ b_{[2]}\ c_{[2]}\ d_{[1]}\ e_{[1]}}^{R_{11}}\ \overbrace{f_{[2]}\ g_{[1]}\ h_{[1]}}^{R_{12}}\ ]$$
$$L_2 = < \underbrace{a_{[3]}\ c_{[2]}\ b_{[2]}\ e_{[1]}\ d_{[1]}}_{R_{21}}\ \underbrace{f_{[2]}\ h_{[1]}\ g_{[1]}}_{R_{22}}\ ]$$

Figure 3: Run-partition

$$RL_1: < \overbrace{b_{[3]}\ c_{[2]}\ e_{[2]}\ d_{[1]}}^{R_{11}}\ \overbrace{a_{[2]}\ f_{[2]}}^{R_{12}}\ ] \quad SL_1: < a_{[2]}\ b_{[3]}\ ]$$
$$RL_2: < \underbrace{b_{[3]}\ e_{[2]}\ c_{[2]}\ d_{[1]}}_{R_{21}}\ \underbrace{a_{[2]}\ f_{[2]}}_{R_{22}}\ ] \quad SL_2: < c_{[2]}\ d_{[1]}\ ]$$
$$RL_3: < \underbrace{b_{[3]}\ e_{[2]}\ c_{[2]}\ d_{[1]}}_{R_{31}}\ \underbrace{f_{[2]}\ a_{[2]}}_{R_{32}}\ ] \quad SL_3: < e_{[2]}\ f_{[2]}\ ]$$

(1) PriO service

$$RL_1: < \overbrace{b_{[3]}\ c_{[2]}\ e_{[2]}\ d_{[1]}}^{R_{11}}\ \overbrace{a_{[2]}\ f_{[2]}}^{R_{12}}\ ] \quad SL_1: < a_{[2]}\ b_{[3]}\ ]$$
$$RL_2: < \underbrace{b_{[3]}\ c_{[2]}\ e_{[2]}\ d_{[1]}}_{R_{21}}\ \underbrace{a_{[2]}\ f_{[2]}}_{R_{22}}\ ] \quad SL_2: < c_{[2]}\ d_{[1]}\ ]$$
$$RL_3: < \underbrace{b_{[3]}\ c_{[2]}\ e_{[2]}\ d_{[1]}}_{R_{31}}\ \underbrace{a_{[2]}\ f_{[2]}}_{R_{32}}\ ] \quad SL_3: < e_{[2]}\ f_{[2]}\ ]$$

(2) PriTO service

Figure 4: PriO and PriTO

and priority-based ordered. □

[Example] Suppose that E_1 broadcasts PDUs a, b, and c, E_2 broadcasts p and q, and E_3 broadcasts x, y, and z. The receipt logs RL_1, RL_2, and RL_3, and sending logs SL_1, SL_2, and SL_3 of E_1, E_2, and E_3 are shown in Figure 1. RL_1, RL_2, and RL_3 are priority-based equivalent because the receipt logs include the same PDUs which are priority-based ordered. It is noted that x and y are received in the sending order because they are broadcast by E_3 and have the same priority. □

[Definition] Let R be a subsequence of a log L, i.e. $L|_j^i$. R is a *run* in L (written as $R \sqsubseteq L$) if R is priority-based ordered. □

In Figure 2, R_1, R_2, and R_3 are runs of L. R_4 is not a run of L because $e.PRI\ (=1) < f.PRI\ (=2)$, i.e. R_4 is not priority-based ordered.

A log L is *run-partitioned* to runs $R_1,...,R_k$ if $L = (R_1 \parallel ... \parallel R_k)$. Figure 3 shows run-partitions of logs L_1 and L_2.

[Definition] Let $(R_{11} \parallel ... \parallel R_{1h})$ and $(R_{21} \parallel ... \parallel R_{2k})$ be run-partitions of logs L_1 and L_2, respectively. L_1 and L_2 are *run-equivalent* iff (1) $h = k (= m)$, and (2) R_{1i} and R_{2i} are priority-based equivalent for $i = 1,...,m$. □

In Figure 3, the run-partitions $(R_{11} \parallel R_{12})$ of L_1 and $(R_{21} \parallel R_{22})$ of L_2 are run-equivalent because R_{11} and R_{21}, and R_{12} and R_{22} are priority-based equivalent, respectively.

There are two kinds of broadcast communication service on the priority.

[Definition] The service of a cluster C is a *priority-based ordering* (PriO) service iff every receipt log in C is information-preserved and is run-equivalent with each other. The PriO service of C is a *priority-based total ordering* (PriTO) service iff all receipt logs in C are order-equivalent. □

[Example] Examples of PriO and PriTO services for a cluster $C = \langle E_1, E_2, E_3 \rangle$ are shown in (1) and (2) of Figure 4, respectively. Suppose that E_1 broadcasts PDUs a and b, E_2 broadcasts c and d, and E_3 broadcasts e and f. In (1) and (2), every entity receives all the PDUs broadcast in C. Hence, RL_1, RL_2, and RL_3 are information-preserved. R_{11}, R_{12}, and R_{13} are priority-equivalent, and so are R_{21}, R_{22}, and R_{23}. Hence, every receipt log is run-equivalent in (1) and (2). In the PriO service (1), same-priority PDUs may be received in any order, e.g. c and e, and a and f are received by the entities in different orders. On the other hand, all the entities receive the same PDUs in the same order in the PriTO service (2). □

4 Priority-Based Total Ordering (PriTO) Protocol

We would like to present a PriTO protocol for a cluster $C = \langle E_1,...,E_n \rangle$ by using the 1C service.

4.1 Transmission and receipt

Each E_i has the following variables to send and receive PDUs by using the 1C service ($j = 1,...,n$).

- SEQ = sequence number of PDU which E_i would transmit next.

- REQ_j = sequence number of PDU which E_i expects to receive next from E_j.
- AL_{jk} = sequence number of PDU which E_i knows that E_k expects to receive next from E_k ($k = 1,...,n$).
- $minAL_j$ = minimum of $AL_{j1},...,AL_{jn}$.
- PAL_{jk} = sequence number of PDU which E_i knows that E_k expects to pre-acknowledge next from E_j ($k = 1,...,n$).
- $minPAL_j$ = minimum of $PAL_{j1},...,PAL_{jn}$.
- PEQ_j = sequence number of PDU which E_j expects to pre-acknowledge next from E_j.

Each PDU p from E_i has the following control information.

- $p.SRC = E_i$, i.e. the entity which sends p.
- $p.SEQ$ = sequence number of p.
- $p.ACK_j$ = sequence number of a PDU which E_i expects to receive next from E_j ($j = 1,...,n$).
- $p.PRI$ = priority of p.

Here, $enqueue(L, p)$ denotes a procedure to put p in the tail of L. $broadcast(p)$ is a procedure to send a *service data unit* (SDU) of p at the 1C SAP. $delete(L, p)$ is a procedure which removes p in L. E_i broadcasts p according to the following *transmission* procedure.

[Transmission procedure] $p.SEQ := SEQ$; $SEQ := SEQ+1$; $p.ACK_j := REQ_j$ ($j = 1,...,n$); $enqueue(SL_i, p)$; $broadcast(p)$; □

When p is received, p jumps over lower-priority PDUs received in the receipt log. Here, an insertion operation ◁ named *priority-based insert* is introduced as follows.

[Priority-based insert] Let L be a priority-based ordered log $< p_1 ... p_m >$, and p be a PDU. A priority-based insert $L \triangleleft p$ is defined to be a priority-based ordered log $< p_1 ... p_{i-1}\ p\ p_i ... p_m >$ where $p_{i-1}.PRI \geq p.PRI > p_i.PRI$. □

For example, $< a_{[4]}\ b_{[3]}\ c_{[1]} > \triangleleft d_{[2]}$ is $< a_{[4]}\ b_{[3]}\ d_{[2]}\ c_{[1]} >$, and $< a_{[4]}\ b_{[3]}\ c_{[1]} > \triangleleft e_{[3]}$ is $< a_{[4]}\ b_{[3]}\ e_{[3]}\ c_{[1]} >$.

On receipt of p, E_i accepts p according to the following *accept* procedure. E_i creates a *pseudo-PDU* p^* which is the same as p except that p^* has no data. p^* is given a priority 0. E_i has two receipt logs RRL_i and PRL_i.

[Accept procedure]
if ($p^j.SEQ = REQ_j$) {
 $RRL_i \triangleleft p^{j*}_{[0]}$; $(PRL_i \parallel RRL_i) \triangleleft p^j$;
 $REQ_j := p^j.SEQ + 1$;
 $AL_{hj} := p^j.ACK_h$ ($h = 1,...,n$);
} □

p is priority-based inserted to a concatenation $PRL_i \parallel RRL_i$. Hence, PDUs in the receipt log $PRL_i \parallel RRL_i$ are ordered on the basis of the priority. On the other hand, the pseudo-PDU $p^*_{[0]}$ is inserted to the tail of RRL_i. This means that the pseudo-PDUs are ordered in the receipt order of the PDUs.

AL and $minAL$ are changed each time when a PDU is accepted. Here, PDUs in the receipt log are pre-acknowledged according to the following procedure.

[Pre-acknowledgment (PACK) procedure]
while (($p^j = top(RRL_i)$ is not a dummy) or
((p^j is a dummy) and ($p^j.SEQ < minAL_j$))) {
 $p^j := dequeue(RRL_i)$; $enqueue(PRL_i, p^j)$;
 if (p^j is a dummy) {
  $PEQ_j := p^j.SEQ + 1$;
  $PAL_{hj} := p^j.ACK_h$ ($h = 1,...,n$);
 }
} □

Each time when a PDU is pre-acknowledged, PAL and $minPAL$ are changed as presented in the PACK procedure. PDUs are forwarded to the application entity in the priority-based order by a log ARL_i according to the following procedure.

[Acknowledgment (ACK) procedure]
$NotEnd := \text{TRUE}$;
while ($NotEnd$) {
 if ($p^j = top(PRL_i)$ is not a dummy) {
  if ($p^j.SEQ < minPAL_j$) {
   $p^j := dequeue(PRL_i)$;
   $enqueue(ARL_i, p^j)$; $delete(PRL_i, p^{j*})$;
  }
  else $NotEnd := \text{FALSE}$;
 }
} □

[Example] Figure 5 shows an example of data transmission of an entity E_i in $C = \langle E_1,...,E_n \rangle$ by the PriTO protocol. Here, letters from a to j denote PDUs.

(1) First, E_i accepts a, b, and c which are priority-based ordered in the receipt log, i.e. PRL_i. The pseudo-PDUs a^*, b^*, and c^* of priority 0 are stored in RRL_i in the receipt order. Then, $d_{[2]}$ arrives at E_i.

(2) d is inserted in PRL_i and d^* in RRL_i by the priority-based insert as shown in (2). Here, suppose that a is pre-acknowledged. Hence, a^* is moved to PRL_i from RRL_i. Then, $e_{[2]}$ arrives.

(3) e and $e^*_{[0]}$ are priority-based inserted in $PRL_i \parallel RRL_i$. Suppose that b is pre-acknowledged. Then, $f_{[2]}$ arrives.

(4) f and $f^*_{[0]}$ are priority-based inserted in $PRL_i \parallel RRL_i$. Suppose that c is pre-acknowledged. Then, $g_{[1]}$ arrives.

(5) g and $g^*_{[0]}$ are priority-based inserted in $PRL_i \parallel RRL_i$. Suppose that d is pre-acknowledged. Since a is pre-acknowledged when d is accepted, a is acknowledged. a still stays in PRL_i because higher-priority PDUs are in PRL_i. Then, $h_{[4]}$ arrives.

(6) h and $h^*_{[0]}$ are priority-based inserted in $PRL_i \parallel RRL_i$. Suppose that e is pre-acknowledged. b is acknowledged. Then, $i_{[2]}$ arrives.

(7) i and $i^*_{[0]}$ are priority-based inserted in $PRL_i \parallel RRL_i$. Suppose that f is pre-acknowledged. c is pre-acknowledged when f is accepted. Hence, c is acknowledged. Since c is the top of PRL_i, c is moved from PRL_i to ARL_i. Although b is acknowledged, b is not passed to the application because h is not acknowledged. Then, $j_{[3]}$ arrives. □

4.2 Failure

In the 1C service, some entity E_i may fail to receive some PDU. E_i detects the PDU loss checking SEQ in PDUs. If E_i detects that it fails to receive a PDU from E_j, all the entities agree on which PDU they fail to receive by broadcasting the information on REQ. In [24, 26, 27], E_i rejects all the PDUs following the lost PDU in the receipt log, i.e. go-back-n scheme [28]. The PDUs rejected are broadcast again.

5 Starvation-Prevented PriTO Protocol

In the PriTO protocol, PDUs are forwarded to the application entities in the priority-based order, i.e. higher-priority PDUs are delivered prior to lower-priority ones. One problem is that lower-priority PDUs can be left waiting indefinitely in the receipt log even if they are acknowledged. A PDU p has to be left waiting in the receipt log until higher-priority PDUs which have jumped over p are acknowledged. In order to resolve the starvation problem, we adopt a method that PDUs left waiting in the receipt log for the prefixed time are forced to be delivered to the application entity. This means that a receipt sequence of PDUs is partitioned into runs.

[Example] Suppose that an entity E_i receives PDUs $a_{[1]}$, $b_{[3]}$, $c_{[4]}$, $d_{[2]}$, $e_{[2]}$, $f_{[2]}$, $g_{[1]}$, $h_{[4]}$, $i_{[2]}$ in this order. Suppose that a, b, and c are acknowledged on acceptance of g, h, and i, respectively. Here, E_i has a receipt log as shown in Figure 6 (1). a can be acknowledged after all the PDUs preceding a are acknowledged if every PDU to be received has priority less than or equal to a. However, if PDUs of priority greater than 1 are received successively, a is not passed to the application entity although a is acknowledged already. This is a starvation problem. One way to resolve the problem is that a is forced to be passed to the application entity if a is not passed in some prefixed time [Figure 6 (2)]. This means that one run $< c_{[4]}\ a_{[1]} >$ is created and passed to the application entity. In the cluster, every entity has to pass the application entity the PDUs in the same order as E_i. In order to do so, some protocol for synchronizing the run-partitions in the cluster is required. □

Each entity E_i in a cluster $C = \langle E_1,...,E_n \rangle$ has a new variable $TOSEQ_h$ ($h = 1,...,n$) which denotes a maximum sequence number of timed-out PDU from E_h. Initially, each $TOSEQ_h = NIL$. When each PDU p from E_h is acknowledged, a timer starts for p.

[Run synchronization (RSYNC)]

(1) The timer for p is expired in E_i. E_i stops the PACK and ACK procedures while E_i accepts PDUs. $TOSEQ_h := p.SEQ$. E_i broadcasts a Run-Sync PDU s where $s.TOSEQ_j = TOSEQ_j$ and $s.PEQ_j = PEQ_j$ ($j = 1,...,n$). s carries information on which PDUs are timed out and until which PDUs from each entity are pre-acknowledged in $s.TOSEQ_j$ and $s.PEQ_j$, respectively.

(2) Suppose that E_j receives the Run-Sync s from E_i. E_j stops the PACK and ACK procedures while PDUs are accepted. Then, $TOSEQ_h := s.TOSEQ_h$ if $TOSEQ_h = NIL$ or $TOSEQ_h < s.TOSEQ_h$ ($h = 1,...,n$). If E_j finds that the timer for q from E_k is expired and $TOSEQ_k < q.SEQ$, then $TOSEQ_k := q.SEQ$ ($k = 1,...,n$). E_j broadcasts a Run-Sync-PACK PDU sp where $sp.TOSEQ_h = TOSEQ_h$ and $sp.PEQ_h = PEQ_h$ ($h = 1,...,n$).

(3) If each E_k receives Run-Sync or Run-Sync-PACK PDUs from all the entities in C, E_k broadcasts a Run-Sync-ACK sa where $sa.TOSEQ_h = TOSEQ_h$ and $sa.PEQ_h = PEQ_h$ ($h = 1,...,n$).

(4) Suppose that every E_k receives the Run-Sync-ACKs from all the entities. Here, all the entities have the same $TOSEQ_j$ and PEQ_j ($j = 1,...,n$). First, the PACK procedure is executed and all the pseudo-PDUs pre-acknowledged are moved from RRL_i to PRL_i. Next, while $p^k.SEQ < minPAL_k$ for $p^k = top(PRL_i)$, p^k is acknowledged and p^* is removed. Then, the acknowledged PDUs which precede the PDU timed out lastly are forwarded to the application entities. Then, the PACK and ACK procedures are restarted. □

[Theorem] The PriTO protocol provides the PriTO service.

[Proof] Since the 1C service is used, every entity receives the PDUs in the same order. Suppose that some entity E_i fails to receive a PDU p ($p.SRC = E_j$). Since E_i does not send any PDU q such that $p.SEQ < q.ACK_j$, p and the PDUs following p are not pre-acknowledged. That is, only the PDUs preceding p can be moved to ARL_i in every E_i.

After the step (3) in the RSYNC procedure, every entity agrees on which PDUs are pre-acknowledged and are timed-out. Here, since each E_i stops the PACK and ACK procedures, AL is not changed even if E_i accepts PDUs during the RSYNC procedure. Further, at (4), all the entities agree on PDUs which are both acknowledged and timed-out, and move them to

$$
\begin{array}{rlll}
& ARL_i & PRL_i & RRL_i \\
(1) & <] & < c_{[4]}\, b_{[3]}\, a_{[1]}] & < a^*_{[0]}\, b^*_{[0]}\, c^*_{[0]}] \leftarrow d_{[2]} \\
(2) & <] & < c_{[4]}\, b_{[3]}\, d_{[2]}\, a_{[1]}\, a^*_{[0]}] & < b^*_{[0]}\, c^*_{[0]}\, d^*_{[0]}] \leftarrow e_{[2]} \\
(3) & <] & < c_{[4]}\, b_{[3]}\, d_{[2]}\, e_{[2]}\, a_{[1]}\, a^*_{[0]}\, b^*_{[0]}] & < c^*_{[0]}\, d^*_{[0]}\, e^*_{[0]}] \leftarrow f_{[2]} \\
(4) & <] & < c_{[4]}\, b_{[3]}\, d_{[2]}\, e_{[2]}\, f_{[2]}\, a_{[1]}\, a^*_{[0]}\, b^*_{[0]}\, c^*_{[0]}] & < d^*_{[0]}\, e^*_{[0]}\, f^*_{[0]}] \leftarrow g_{[1]} \\
(5) & <] & < c_{[4]}\, b_{[3]}\, d_{[2]}\, e_{[2]}\, f_{[2]}\, a_{[1]}\, g_{[1]}\, a^*_{[0]}\, b^*_{[0]}\, c^*_{[0]}\, d^*_{[0]}] & < e^*_{[0]}\, f^*_{[0]}\, g^*_{[0]}] \leftarrow h_{[4]} \\
(6) & <] & < c_{[4]}\, h_{[4]}\, b_{[3]}\, d_{[2]}\, e_{[2]}\, f_{[2]}\, a_{[1]}\, g_{[1]}\, a^*_{[0]}\, b^*_{[0]}\, c^*_{[0]}\, d^*_{[0]}\, e^*_{[0]}] & < f^*_{[0]}\, g^*_{[0]}\, h^*_{[0]}] \leftarrow i_{[2]} \\
(7) & < c_{[4]}] & < h_{[4]}\, b_{[3]}\, d_{[2]}\, e_{[2]}\, f_{[2]}\, i_{[2]}\, a_{[1]}\, g_{[1]}\, a^*_{[0]}\, b^*_{[0]}\, d^*_{[0]}\, e^*_{[0]}\, f^*_{[0]}] & < g^*_{[0]}\, h^*_{[0]}\, i^*_{[0]}] \leftarrow j_{[3]} \\
\end{array}
$$

Figure 5: Data transmission in the PriTO protocol

$$
\begin{array}{rlll}
& ARL_i & PRL_i & RRL_i \\
(1) & < c_{[4]}] & < h_{[4]}\, b_{[3]}\, d_{[2]}\, e_{[2]}\, f_{[2]}\, i_{[2]}\, a_{[1]}\, g_{[1]}\, a^*_{[0]}\, b^*_{[0]}\, d^*_{[0]}\, e^*_{[0]}\, f^*_{[0]}] & < g^*_{[0]}\, h^*_{[0]}\, i^*_{[0]}] \\
(2) & < c_{[4]}\, a_{[1]}] & < h_{[4]}\, b_{[3]}\, d_{[2]}\, e_{[2]}\, f_{[2]}\, i_{[2]}\, g_{[1]}\, b^*_{[0]}\, d^*_{[0]}\, e^*_{[0]}\, f^*_{[0]}] & < g^*_{[0]}\, h^*_{[0]}\, i^*_{[0]}] \\
\end{array}
$$

Figure 6: Run synchronization

the application in the priority-based order. Here, the same run is forwarded to every application. That is, every entity has the same receipt log which is run-equivalent with each other. Hence, the PriTO protocol provides the PriTO service. □

[**Example**] Figure 7 shows an example of the run synchronization. There are three entities E_1, E_2, and E_3.

(1) First, E_1, E_2, and E_3 receive the PDUs as shown in Figure 7 (1). For example, E_1 accepts PDUs a, b, c, d, e, f, g, h, ... in this order which is denoted by the sequence of the pseudo-PDUs, and a, b, c, d, e, f are already pre-acknowledged in E_1. a and d are forwarded to the application in E_2 and E_3, but not in E_1 yet. Suppose that the time-out (T.O.) occurs for a in E_1 and b in E_3. E_1 and E_3 broadcast Run-Sync PDUs.

(2) E_1, E_2, and E_3 broadcast Run-Sync-PACK and Run-Sync-ACK PDUs. Every entity agrees that b and PDUs preceding b are timed out by checking $TOSEQ$. PDUs preceding h are pre-acknowledged by checking PEQ, and all the PDUs preceding e are acknowledged. Suppose that a, d, and b are PDUs in the sequence of PDUs from the top to b.

(3) Then, a, d, and b are forwarded to the application entity in E_1. e and f are not forwarded because they are not acknowledged. c is not forwarded because it is not timed-out although it is acknowledged. Since a and d are passed already, only b is passed to the application entities in E_2 and E_3. E_1, E_2, and E_3 have the same priority-equivalent runs, i.e. $< a_{[5]}\, d_{[4]}\, b_{[1]}]$. □

6 Evaluation

The PriTO protocol is implemented in Sparc2 workstations interconnected by Ethernet. Each PriTO entity is running in one workstation. A cluster C is supported by n entities. In the evaluation, there are two levels of priority, i.e. 1 and 2. Each PDU is randomly assigned either priority 1 or 2 so that 10 % of PDUs have priority 2 and 90 % of PDUs have priority 1. Suppose that a PDU arrives at every entity every one time unit and every application entity takes a PDU every H time units. One time unit means how long it takes each entity to process one PDU. Since the high-speed network is used, application entities are slower than the network speed, i.e. $H \geq 1$. Suppose that every received PDU times-out when it takes T time units after the PDU is acknowledged.

Figure 8 and Figure 9 show for $n = 3,...,10$ the average delay time for PDUs of priority 1, 2, i.e. average time from when each PDU arrives at the PriTO entity until when the application entity takes the PDU. Figure 8 shows a case for $T = 10$ and $H = 20$. Figure 9 shows a case for $T = 50$ and $H = 20$. Compared with Figure 8, it is shown that lower-priority PDUs can be delivered earlier to the application entities if the time-out duration is decreased with the delay of the higher-priority PDUs varies small. The figures show that the delay time for PDUs of priority 1 is $O(n)$.

7 Concluding Remarks

In the high-speed network, entities may fail to receive PDUs due to the buffer overruns. One problem in using the priority concept is *starvation*, i.e. some lower-priority PDUs can be left waiting indefinitely in the receipt queue. In this paper, we have discussed a starvation-prevention broadcast protocol named a PriTO protocol which provides priority-based receipt ordering of PDUs by using the high-speed single-channel network. In the protocol, the receipt sequence of PDUs is partitioned into runs. PDUs in each run are ordered according to the priority. If there exists some PDU p which is acknowledged already but left waiting in the receipt log for a long time, p is forced to be forwarded to the application entities. Here, a run including p is created. Lower-priority PDUs in a run R can not jump over PDUs in runs preceding R. By this scheme, every entity receives the same sequence of runs while starvation is prevented. By the protocol, applications where various kinds of data are broadcast in a group of entities can be easily realized.

$$
\begin{array}{llll}
& ARL_i & PRL_i & RRL_i \\
& & \text{T.O.} \\
& & \downarrow \\
RL_1: & <\ldots] & < a_{[5]}\ d_{[4]}\ e_{[2]}\ f_{[2]}\ b_{[1]}\ c_{[1]} \ldots\ a^*_{[0]}\ b^*_{[0]}\ c^*_{[0]}\ d^*_{[0]}\ e^*_{[0]}\ f^*_{[0]}] & < g^*_{[0]}\ h^*_{[0]} \ldots] \\
RL_2: & <\ldots a_{[5]}\ d_{[4]}]\ < & e_{[2]}\ f_{[2]}\ b_{[1]}\ c_{[1]} \ldots\ \ b^*_{[0]}\ c^*_{[0]}\ e^*_{[0]}\ f^*_{[0]}\ g^*_{[0]}] & < h^*_{[0]} \ldots] \\
RL_3: & <\ldots a_{[5]}\ d_{[4]}]\ < & e_{[2]}\ f_{[2]}\ b_{[1]}\ c_{[1]} \ldots\ \ b^*_{[0]}\ \ \ \ c^*_{[0]}\ e^*_{[0]}\ f^*_{[0]}\ g^*_{[0]}] & < h^*_{[0]} \ldots] \\
& & \uparrow \\
& & \text{T.O.}
\end{array}
$$

(1) detection of timed-out PDUs

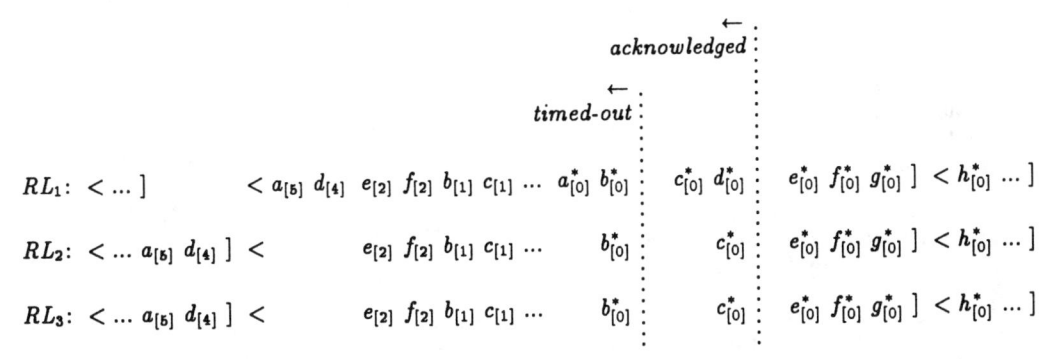

$\leftarrow$ acknowledged

$\leftarrow$ timed-out

$$
\begin{array}{ll}
RL_1: & <\ldots] \quad < a_{[5]}\ d_{[4]}\ e_{[2]}\ f_{[2]}\ b_{[1]}\ c_{[1]} \ldots\ a^*_{[0]}\ b^*_{[0]} : c^*_{[0]}\ d^*_{[0]} : e^*_{[0]}\ f^*_{[0]}\ g^*_{[0]}] < h^*_{[0]} \ldots] \\
RL_2: & <\ldots a_{[5]}\ d_{[4]}]\ < \quad e_{[2]}\ f_{[2]}\ b_{[1]}\ c_{[1]} \ldots\ b^*_{[0]} : c^*_{[0]} : e^*_{[0]}\ f^*_{[0]}\ g^*_{[0]}] < h^*_{[0]} \ldots] \\
RL_3: & <\ldots a_{[5]}\ d_{[4]}]\ < \quad e_{[2]}\ f_{[2]}\ b_{[1]}\ c_{[1]} \ldots\ b^*_{[0]} : c^*_{[0]} : e^*_{[0]}\ f^*_{[0]}\ g^*_{[0]}] < h^*_{[0]} \ldots]
\end{array}
$$

(2) agreement of pre-acknowledged and acknowledged PDUs and timed-out PDUs

$$
\begin{array}{ll}
RL_1: & <\ldots a_{[5]}\ d_{[4]}\ b_{[1]}] < e_{[2]}\ f_{[2]}\ c_{[1]} \ldots\ c^*_{[0]}\ e^*_{[0]}\ f^*_{[0]}\ g^*_{[0]}] < h^*_{[0]} \ldots] \\
RL_2: & <\ldots a_{[5]}\ d_{[4]}\ b_{[1]}] < e_{[2]}\ f_{[2]}\ c_{[1]} \ldots\ c^*_{[0]}\ e^*_{[0]}\ f^*_{[0]}\ g^*_{[0]}] < h^*_{[0]} \ldots] \\
RL_3: & <\ldots a_{[5]}\ d_{[4]}\ b_{[1]}] < e_{[2]}\ f_{[2]}\ c_{[1]} \ldots\ c^*_{[0]}\ e^*_{[0]}\ f^*_{[0]}\ g^*_{[0]}] < h^*_{[0]} \ldots]
\end{array}
$$

(3) termination of the RSYNC procedure

Figure 7: Example of run synchronization

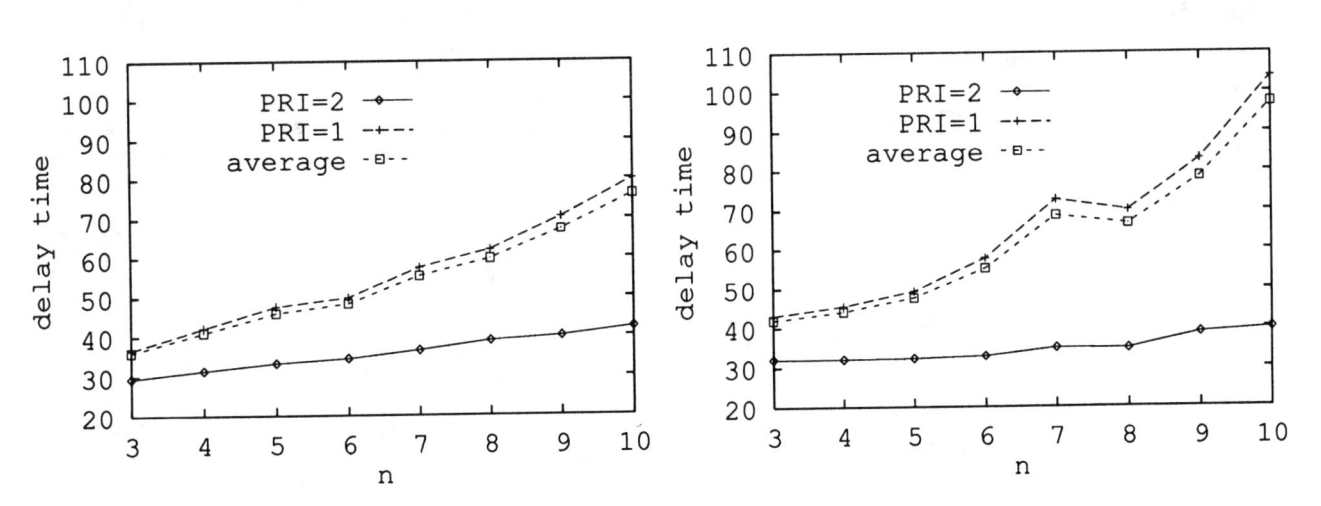

Figure 8: Delay time ($T = 10$)

Figure 9: Delay time ($T = 50$)

References

[1] Abramson, N., "The ALOHA System – Another Alternative for Computer Communications," *Proc. of the Fall Joint Computer Conference*, Vol.37, 1970, pp.281-285.

[2] American National Standards Institute, "FDDI Token Ring Physical Layer Protocol (PHY)," ANSI X3.148, 1988.

[3] American National Standards Institute, "Twisted Pair Physical Medium Dependent (TP-PMD)," ANSI X3 T9.5, 1990.

[4] Birman, K., Schiper, A., and Stephenson, P., "Lightweight Causal and Atomic Group Multicast," *ACM Trans. on Computer Systems*, Vol.9, No.3, 1991, pp.272-314.

[5] Chang, J. M. and Maxemchuk, N. F., "Reliable Broadcast Protocols," *ACM Trans. on Computer Systems*, Vol.2, No.3, 1984, pp.251-273.

[6] Chanson, S., Neufeld, G., and Liang, L., "A Bibliography on Multicast and Group Communications," *ACM SIGOPS Operating Systems Review*, Vol.23, No.4, Oct. 1989.

[7] Defense Communications Agency, "DDN Protocol Handbook," Vol.1–3, NIC 50004-50005, 1985.

[8] Doeringer, W. A., Dykeman, D., Kaiserswerth, M., Meister, B. W., Rudin, H., and Williamson, R., "A Survey of Light-Weight Transport Protocols for High-Speed Networks," *IEEE Trans. on Communications*, Vol.38, No.11, 1990, pp.2025-2039.

[9] Ellis, C. A., Gibbs, S. J., and Rein, G. L., "Groupware," *Comm. ACM*, Vol.34, No.1, 1991, pp.38-58.

[10] Garcia-Molina, H. and Kogan, B., "An Implementation of Reliable Broadcast Using an Unreliable Multicast Facility," *Proc. of the 7th IEEE Symp. on Reliable Distributed Systems*, 1988, pp.428-437.

[11] Garcia-Molina, H. and Spauster, A., "Message Ordering in a Multicast Environment," *Proc. of the 9th IEEE ICDCS*, 1989, pp.354-361.

[12] International Standards Organization, "OSI – Connection Oriented Transport Protocol Specification," ISO 8073, 1986.

[13] Kaashoek, M. F. and Tanenbaum, A. S., "Group Communication in the Amoeba Distributed Operating System," *Proc. of the 11th IEEE ICDCS*, 1991, pp.222-230.

[14] Kurose, J. S., Schwartz, M., and Yemini, Y., "Multiple-Access Protocols and Time-Constrained Communication," *ACM Computing Surveys*, Vol.16, No.1, 1984, pp.43-70.

[15] Lamport, R., "Time, Clocks, and the Ordering of Events in Distributed Systems," *Comm. ACM*, Vol.21, No.7, 1978, pp.558-565.

[16] Liu, M. and Papantoni-Kazakos, P., "A Random Access Algorithm for Data Networks Carrying High Priority Traffic," *Proc. of the 9th IEEE INFOCOM*, 1990, pp.1087-1094.

[17] Luan, S. W. and Gligor, V. D., "A Fault-Tolerant Protocol for Atomic Broadcast," *IEEE Trans. on Parallel and Distributed Systems*, Vol.1, No.3, 1990, pp.271-285.

[18] Melliar-Smith, P. M., Moser, L. E., and Agrawala, V., "Broadcast Protocols for Distributed Systems," *IEEE Trans. on Parallel and Distributed Systems*, Vol.1, No.1, 1990, pp.17-25.

[19] Nakamura, A. and Takizawa, M., "Reliable Broadcast Protocol for Selectively Ordering PDUs," *Proc. of the 11th IEEE ICDCS* 1991, pp.239-246.

[20] Nakamura, A. and Takizawa, M., "Design of Reliable Broadcast Communication Protocol for Selectively Partially Ordered PDUs," *Proc. of the IEEE COMPSAC'91*, 1991, pp.673-679.

[21] Nakamura, A. and Takizawa, M., "Priority-Based Total and Semi-Total Ordering Broadcast Protocols," *Proc. of the 12th IEEE ICDCS*, 1992, pp.178-185.

[22] Schneider, F. B., Gries, D., and Schlichting, R. D., "Fault-Tolerant Broadcasts," *Science of Computer Programming*, Vol.4, No.1, pp.1-15, 1984.

[23] Sharrock, S. M. and Du, D. H. C., "Efficient CSMA/CD-Based Protocols for Multiple Priority Classes," *IEEE Trans. on Computers*, Vol.38, No.7, 1989, pp.943-954.

[24] Takizawa, M., "Cluster Control Protocol for Highly Reliable Broadcast Communication," *Proc. of the IFIP Conf. on Distributed Processing*, 1987, pp.431-445.

[25] Takizawa, M., "Design of Highly Reliable Broadcast Communication Protocol," *Proc. of IEEE COMPSAC'87*, 1987, pp.731-740.

[26] Takizawa, M. and Nakamura, A., "Partially Ordering Broadcast (PO) Protocol," *Proc. of the 9th IEEE INFOCOM*, 1990, pp.357-364.

[27] Takizawa, M. and Nakamura, A., "Reliable Broadcast Communication," *Proc. of IPSJ Int'l. Conf. on Information Technology (InfoJapan)*, 1990, pp.325-332.

[28] Tanenbaum, A. S., "Computer Networks (2nd ed.)," *Englewood Cliffs, NJ: Prentice-Hall*, 1989.

Design and Analysis of a Hierarchical Scalable Photonic Architecture*

P.W. Dowd, K. Bogineni, K.A. Aly, J.A. Perreault
Department of Electrical and Computer Engineering
State University of New York at Buffalo
Buffalo, NY 14260
dowd@eng.buffalo.edu

Abstract - This paper introduces a hierarchical optical structure for processor interconnection and evaluates its performance. The architecture is based on *wavelength division multiplexing* (WDM) which enables multiple multi-access channels to be realized on a single optical fiber. The objective of the hierarchical architecture is to achieve scalability yet avoid the requirement of multiple wavelength tunable devices per node as with the WDM-based hypercube interconnection scheme introduced in [1]. Furthermore, single-hop communication is achieved: a packet remains in the optical form from source to destination and does not require cross dimensional intermediate routing. The wavelength multiplexed hierarchical structure features wavelength channel re-use at each level, allowing scalability to very large system sizes. It employs *acousto-optic* tunable filters in conjunction with passive couplers to partition the traffic between different levels of the hierarchy without electronic intervention. A significant advantage of the proposed structure is its ability to dynamically vary the bandwidth provided to different levels of the hierarchy. The architecture is compared to a wavelength-flat architecture in terms of physical and performance scalability.

1 INTRODUCTION

The *Fat-Tree* [2] was proposed as an interconnect strategy to support concurrent interprocessor communication through a hierarchy of limited-bandwidth spatial channels, whose number increases at levels closer to the root. The processors of a Fat-Tree are located at the leaves of a complete binary tree, and the internal nodes are space switches. The rate of bandwidth growth is influenced by the desired scalability and cost-performance ratio. A variation of the Fat-Tree network has been employed in Thinking Machine's CM-5 [3,4]. This paper introduces an optical-based approach, denoted as the *space-wavelength hierarchical architecture* (SWHA), that achieves the Fat-Tree objectives while also obtaining significant improvement in flexibility, performance and fault tolerance through *wavelength-division multiple access* (WDMA) photonic interconnection. Not only can the Fat-Tree strategy of providing increased bandwidth per link at levels closer to the root be obtained, but now *adaptable bandwidth allocation* can be achieved at each level: the bandwidth at each level does not need to remain fixed but can be *dynamically reallocated to adapt to changing communication requirements*. An advantage of this approach is that the system adapts to the users (programmers) instead of the users adapting to the system. Bandwidth reallocation is invisible to the users, and is initiated by the system to balance the per channel intensities described below. Furthermore, a highly scalable architecture is achieved, overcoming the fixed number of WDMA channels through *spatial re-use*. The hierarchy resembles a general m_i-ary tree, where an i-level node branches to one parent and m_i children. The *processors* (0-level nodes) are located at the leaves and the internal nodes are wavelength/spatial routing switches denoted as *FatNodes* due to its motivation from the Fat-Tree. The result is a system with a unity degree per processor yet unity diameter: any two processors can communicate without any intermediate routing. This is significant since the intermediate routing latencies may be much larger than the packet transmission time in an optical environment. One additional advantage of the proposed architecture is the independence of the number of channels in the WDMA network and the number of nodes interconnected by it.

In addition to a very large bandwidth, optical interconnects offer many desirable features such as a relaxed distance-bandwidth product, large fanout capability, low power requirement, reduced crosstalk and immunity to electro-magnetic interference. Computer architecture may employ optical interconnects at multiple system levels: chip-to-chip, module-to-module, board-to-board and node-to-node. However, little benefit is obtained by simply replacing metal interconnects with optical fiber in a one-to-one fashion since the result would be many expensive but under-utilized communication links. Furthermore, the true advantages of optical interconnections would not be harnessed due to the *speed mismatch* between the optical and electronic components. The low loss region of a single mode optical fiber has a bandwidth of about 30THz [5]: the optical media bit and packet throughput rates greatly exceed the capacity of the electronic interface components. *Wavelength-division multiplexing* (WDM) circumvents the speed mismatch by partitioning into many concurrent, *more manageable*, high speed channels. The WDM channels form a set that can be individually switched and routed. However, wavelength tunable transmitters and/or receivers are required. Section 2 contains a brief outline of their characteristics. Depending on the architecture, *optical self-routing* is achievable where a node only receives data destined to it and the system has the non-blocking connectivity characteristics of a crossbar [6]. Optical self-routing partitions the traffic, achieving a significant relaxation of the receiver subsystem design constraints since a node will not have to process all network traffic.

System scalability in this environment is limited by three main issues: *physical scalability* which bounds the maximum number of interconnected nodes through the OPB, *perfor-

---

*This work was supported by the National Science Foundation under Grant CCR-9010774 and ECS-9112435.

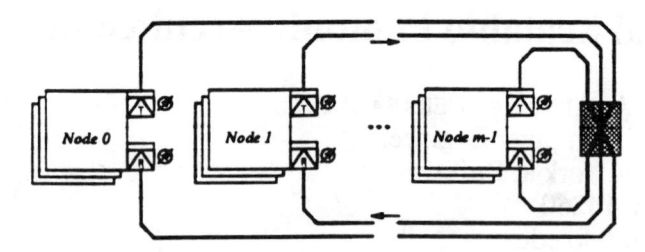

Figure 1: A star-coupled WDMA configuration shown with wavelength tunable transmitters and receivers.

mance scalability which is bound in the optical domain by the tunability of the optical devices (transmitters and receivers/filters) that limit the number of wavelength channels that are created, and scalability limitations when the cost or *complexity* grows faster than the performance. Physical scalability is examined by developing a framework to extend the system range beyond the OPB limit of a single star-coupled network shown in Fig. 1. Performance scalability is examined by using both spatial and wavelength multiplexing (multiple, but spatially separate, channels of the same wavelength) to extend the performance capacity beyond the limit of C channels imposed by the wavelength tunable device characteristics. Complexity scalability is supported through the hierarchical structures that retain a unity degree: a processor only requires a single transmitter and receiver regardless of system size. Our objective is to decouple the maximum system size and the number of wavelength channels, avoiding the situation where a system of M nodes requires M channels since this would create a situation where the scalability of the system is too dependent on the characteristics of the wavelength tunable devices.

A *wavelength-flat* but physically hierarchical structure, denoted as FHA, provides both physical and complexity scalability but is not performance scalable since the same wavelength space is shared by all processors. It achieves physical scalability by incorporating optical amplifiers within a hierarchical passive structure similar to the one considered for the SWHA. The resulting system is logically similar to a single star network of Fig. 1. The SWHA achieves (physical, performance and complexity) scalability through both spatial and wavelength multiplexing. The FHA and SWHA are both single hop architectures so the significant intermediate routing latencies of the WMCH, relative to the nominal packet transmission time, are eliminated. The SWHA is defined in Section 2. System scalability is analyzed in Section 3 in terms of power budget, complexity, and performance.

2 SWHA ARCHITECTURE

Both the physical limitations and performance requirements must be considered when developing scalable photonic architectures. The objective of this section is to provide a framework where system size can be varied within a desired range while maintaining a specified level of performance.

WDM networks require wavelength tunable transmitters and/or receivers to switch between the multiple channels created on the single optical fiber. A limited tuning range, transmitter linewidth and filter bandwidth constrain the maximum number of selectable wavelength channels. Wavelength tunable transmitters can be obtained through a number of techniques: fast tunable laser diodes [5], an array of non-tunable but different wavelength laser diodes, or LED *Spectral slicing* [7]. Wavelength selectivity can be achieved using electro-optic or acousto-optic filters with direct detection [8]. Acousto-optic devices have slower switching speeds (μs) but they offer the advantages of a broad tuning range, electronic control of tunability, and narrow filter bandwidth. Several implementations of an optical cross-connect based on an AOTF have been described in [5,8] where different wavelength channels can be routed independently to different output fibers. The selected wavelength is switched in an AOTF by varying the acoustic wave control frequency. This allows an individual wavelength to be switched or not switched. Multiple wavelengths may be switched with this device by the superposition of multiple acoustic control signals.

The SWHA interconnection network is based on a component called the *FatNode* which is a space/wavelength switch constructed from passive couplers and an acousto-optic tunable filter (AOTF). The AOTF is used as a wavelength-selective space-division switch to select a subset of wavelengths to switch. The architecture is defined in Section 2.1, the multi-level media access protocol is presented in Section 2.2, and the channel partition is discussed in Section 2.2.

2.1 Description

A mixed radix system is used to represent the node numbering. Let M (the total number of processors) be a decimal integer represented as a product of r factors:

$$M = \prod_{i=1}^{r} m_i \tag{1}$$

The processor identifier P, $1 \leq P \leq M$, can be represented as an r-tuple

$$P = (p_r, p_{r-1}, \ldots, p_1) \tag{2}$$

where $1 \leq p_i \leq m_i$ for all $1 \leq i \leq r$ and r denotes the number of hierarchical levels. The term *processor* is used to denote a node at the leaves of the tree (a 0-level node). An actual system might place m_0 processors at each 0-level node, perhaps interconnected through a shared metal bus as in [9], to amortize the cost of the communication subsystem over multiple processors depending on the cost, performance and typical communication requirements of the individual processors. Note that only the processors possess transmitters and receivers. All other i-level nodes, $1 \leq i \leq r$, are FatNodes that provide wavelength/spatial switching. The rest of this section describes the FatNode component, defines the SWHA topology, and the routing scheme.

FatNode: An i-level FatNode couples a total of $m_i + 1$ input fibers and $m_i + 1$ output fibers: one fiber to/from its parent node and m_i fibers to/from its children. Fig. 2 shows the architecture of the FatNode. The functionality of a FatNode can be described as a 2×2 switching element (the lower m_i links are passively coupled to a single fiber), as found in multistage interconnection networks, where each wavelength channel can be individually selected for a bar-connect or cross-connect configuration by the AOTF. This

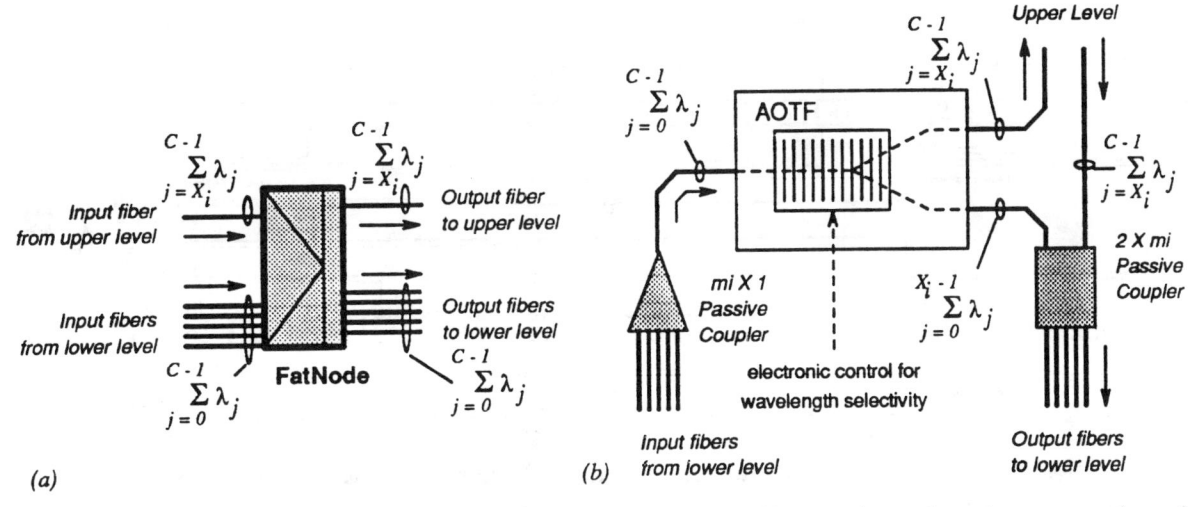

Figure 2: An i-level FatNode. (a) Graphical representation and (b) Possible implementation with two passive couplers and an acousto-optic wavelength tunable filter. The filter partitions the wavelength channels $\{\lambda_0, \lambda_1, \ldots, \lambda_{C-1}\}$ arriving from the lower level into two groups: $\{\lambda_0, \lambda_1, \ldots, \lambda_{X_i-1}\}$, which are retained locally; and $\{\lambda_{X_i}, \lambda_{X_i+1}, \ldots, \lambda_{C-1}\}$ which is the global traffic and passed to the upper level. Note that the link from the upper level contains no optical energy on channels $\{\lambda_0, \lambda_1, \ldots, \lambda_{X_i-1}\}$ so all traffic arrives along channels $\{\lambda_{X_i}, \lambda_{X_i+1}, \ldots, \lambda_{C-1}\}$ and is directly routed to the lower level.

is accomplished through the superposition characteristic of acousto-optic tunable filters. Although in principle an AOTF can cross-connect or bar-connect wavelength channels individually through the superposition of multiple acoustic control frequencies, a FatNode does not require this degree of sophistication to relax device design constraints and reduce device cost.

Spatial re-use of wavelength channels occurs at each of the r levels in this hierarchy. Limited by the characteristics of the optical devices, let C denote the total number of wavelength channels capable of being separated on a single fiber and $\mathbf{Z} = \{\lambda_0, \lambda_1, \ldots, \lambda_{i-1}, \lambda_i, \lambda_{i+1}, \ldots, \lambda_{C-1}\}$ denote the set of wavelength channels. An i-level FatNode is electronically configured to a *crossover channel* denoted as X_i, where $\lambda_{X_i} \in \mathbf{Z}$, such that bar-connections are established for channels channels $\{\lambda_0, \lambda_1, \ldots, \lambda_{X_i-1}\}$ and cross-connections are established for channels $\{\lambda_{X_i}, \lambda_{X_i+1}, \ldots, \lambda_{C-1}\}$. Essentially, this mapping is used to retain the local i-level traffic $\{\lambda_0, \lambda_1, \ldots, \lambda_{X_i-1}\}$, and forward the global traffic $\{\lambda_{X_i}, \lambda_{X_i+1}, \ldots, \lambda_{C-1}\}$ to the $(i+1)$-level FatNode. The dynamic reconfigurability characteristic is obtained by altering the wavelength channel partition at each level. Fig. 2(b) shows an implementation of a FatNode. Due to the traffic partitioning characteristics, traffic arriving from the upper level does not require partitioning and may avoid the AOTF and be coupled directly to the m_i nodes attached at the lower level. Only the lower level traffic must be partitioned.

Topology: Fig. 3 illustrates a 3-level structure where $M = 2 \times 3 \times 4$. An i-level FatNode, $1 \leq i \leq r$ partitions the traffic it receives according to its space-wavelength configuration. The partition points are defined as $\mathbf{X} = \{X_0, X_1, X_2, \ldots, X_r\}$ where $X_r = C$, $X_0 = 0$ and $0 < X_i < X_j < C$ if $i < j$ for all $0 < i < r-1$ and $1 < j < r$. Let $C_i = X_i - X_{i-1}$ denote the number of channels allocated for i-level communication, $1 \leq i \leq r$, such that $C = \sum_{i=1}^{r} C_i$. Channels $\{\lambda_{X_{i-1}}, \ldots, \lambda_{X_i-1}\}$ are used to support i-level communication.

The configuration remains fixed at the partition point and is not altered until the system is reconfigured to adapt to a change in the locality characteristics. The partition points $\mathbf{X}$ are shifted during reconfiguration which allows the system to adapt to a shift in traffic locality characteristics and dynamically reconfigure the amount of communication bandwidth provided at each level of the hierarchy. This relaxes the design constraints on the FatNode AOTF since fast tunability beyond the currently achievable microsecond switching speed is not required. Furthermore, narrow filter bandwidth is not required since individual channel selection is not needed.

Let M_j denote the number of j-level nodes in this hierarchy, given by $M_j = \prod_{i=j+1}^{r} m_i$, and $M = M_0$ as defined in Eqn. (1). Since there are a total of M_j j-level nodes, a total of $C_j M_j$ channels provide j-level communication. Therefore an r-level SWHA provides a total of

$$C = \sum_{j=1}^{r} C_j \prod_{k=j+1}^{r} m_k \qquad (3)$$

separate channels that may be concurrently accessed due to the combination of spatial and wavelength multiplexing. For example, consider the case of $M = 24$ in Fig. 3. If $C = 7$ and $\mathbf{X} = \{0, 4, 6, 7\}$, a total of $C = 29$ separate channels are effectively created.

Routing: Each processor is required to possess a receiver capable of receiving a total of r channels. A typical implementation of the receiver subsystem would be a single receiver and a (fixed or slow tunable) multi-channel filter such as an AOTF. Let $H_{Y,i}$ denote the i-level home channel of processor Y, $1 \leq i \leq r$. Node Y would have its multi-channel filter tuned to receive channels $\{H_{Y,1}, H_{Y,2}, \ldots, H_{Y,r}\}$ where $X_{i-1} \leq H_{Y,i} < X_i$. Routing is simple since the network has unity diameter and intermediate routing is not necessary. The

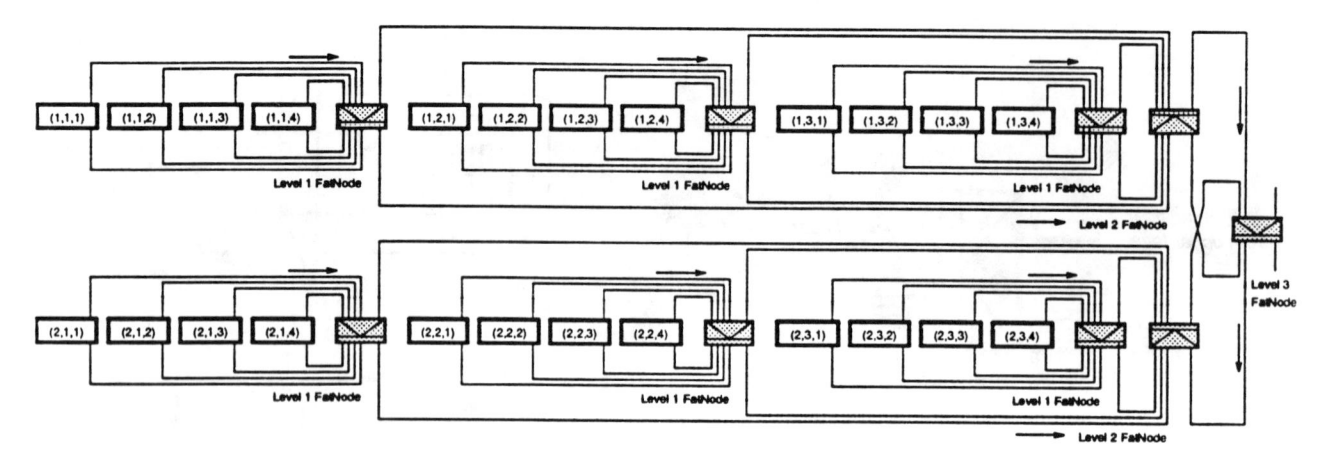

Figure 3: Spatial-wavelength hierarchical star-coupled architecture. A 3-level structure with $M = 2 \times 3 \times 4$ nodes.

routing algorithm must determine the appropriate level and channel based on the source and destination addresses, the channel partition $\mathbf{X}$, C, and M. Once the level and channel have been determined, the packet is transmitted according to the access protocol on the home channel of the destination.

In the example of Fig. 3, processor $A = (a_3, a_2, a_1)$ uses channels $\{\lambda_0, \lambda_1, \ldots, \lambda_{X_1-1}\}$ to communicate to processors with an address (d_3, d_2, d_1) if $d_3 = a_3$ and $d_2 = a_2$ but $d_1 \neq a_1$. Channels $\{\lambda_{X_1}, \lambda_{X_1+1}, \ldots, \lambda_{X_2-1}\}$ would be used if $d_3 = a_3$ and $d_2 \neq a_2$; and channels $\{\lambda_{X_2}, \lambda_{X_2+1}, \ldots, \lambda_{C-1}\}$ would be used if $d_3 \neq a_3$. Suppose source node $Z = (z_r, z_{r-1}, \ldots, z_1)$ wishes to transmit a packet to destination node $A = (a_r, a_{r-1}, \ldots, a_1)$. Determining the correct channel to transmit the packet is a two stage process:

1. Determine the minimum level of communication required to reach the destination through a digit-by-digit comparison of the source and destination address r-tuple: i-level communication is required if $z_i \neq a_i$ and $z_j = a_j$ for all $i < j \leq r$.

2. Determine the home channel of the destination processor A at that level. The i-level home channel of processor A is determined based on the allocation policy which in this case is interleaved and is given by

$$H_{A,i} = X_{i-1} + A \bmod [X_i - X_{i-1}] \quad (4)$$

Low-latency, high-throughput interprocessor communication is achieved with a unity diameter and a unity degree with SWHA. There are additional advantages with this approach:

▷ The bandwidth provided to each level of the hierarchy can be dynamically increased or decreased depending on the local/global communication characteristics. At least one channel must be allocated to each level to maintain complete connectivity.

▷ The design of the FatNode does not require AOTF tuning speeds greater than the microsecond speeds already achieved.

▷ The design constraints on the AOTF filter within a FatNode are further relaxed since individual channels do not need to be selected. Control is simplified since only a single acoustic frequency needs to be specified to identify the crossover point.

2.2 Multi-level Access Protocol

The SWHA architecture needs a multi-level media access protocol. Random access or static allocation protocols can be employed at the different levels of the hierarchy. The media access protocol considered in this paper for the SWHA is a multi-level generalization of the single level WDMA protocol described in [6]. Time is slotted on the channels at all levels of the hierarchy. The time-multiplexed protocol avoids collisions on all channels, eliminates the need to support media access level acknowledgments (coherence level acknowledgments are still required as in [9]), and is insensitive to propagation delay.

The time-wavelength diagram for a 3-level TDM-based media access protocol is shown in Fig. 4 where $M = 32 = 2 \times 2 \times 8$, $C = 6$, and $\mathbf{X} = \{0, 3, 5, 6\}$. The allocation map shows time slotted on all channels, and every node is assigned a slot on each channel per cycle. Slots on every channel are combined into groups of m_1. The 1-level clusters of the system are allocated slots in the group assigned to each of the M_1 clusters. Each processor does *not* maintain the table shown in Fig. 4: a processor determines its assigned slots in a decentralized fashion through the simple algorithm defined below based on $\mathbf{Z}$, $\mathbf{X}$, M, C and its own address. Execution of the slot assignment algorithm is needed only when reconfiguring to support the dynamic bandwidth reallocation.

Cycle Length: Let W_i denote the number of processors reachable by a processor through i-level communication ($W_0 = 1$):

$$W_i = \prod_{j=1}^{i} m_j \quad (5)$$

The cycle length depends on the number of nodes connected at that level: $\mathcal{L}_i = W_i$. Every node is assigned a slot on every channel at every level. In the example of Fig. 4, $\mathcal{L}_1 = 8$, $\mathcal{L}_2 = 16$, and $\mathcal{L}_3 = 32$.

Channel Partition: The SWHA allows the channel allocation to adapt to variations in reference locality on a process-by-process basis by shifting the partition configuration $\mathbf{X}$ through the retuning of the FatNodes. The i-level reference probability, denoted as p_i, represents the probability of targeting

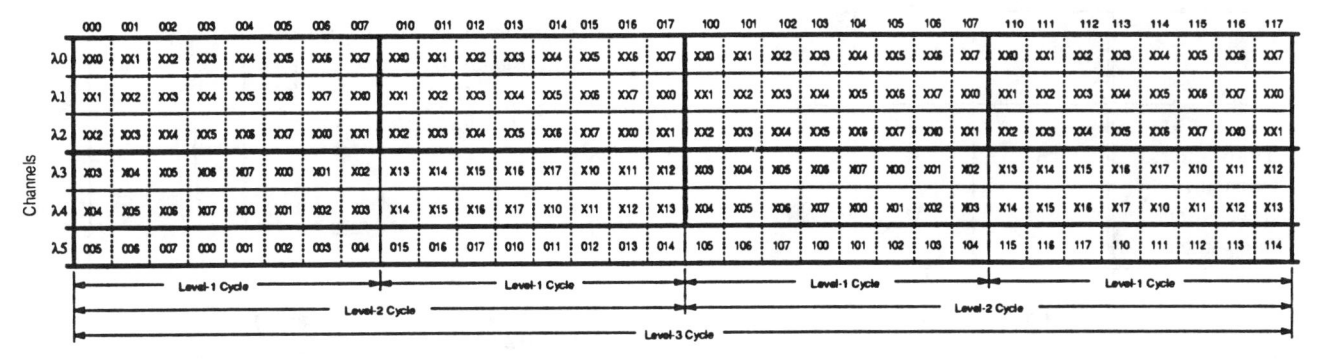

Figure 4: Assignment map for 3-level TDM-based protocol with $M = 2 \times 2 \times 8$ with $\mathbf{X} = \{0,3,5,6\}$. $\mathcal{L}_1 = 8$, $\mathcal{L}_2 = 16$ and $\mathcal{L}_3 = 32$.

a destination through i-level communication that can not be reached through $(i-1)$-level communication, $1 < i \leq r$. A fair number of channels need to be allocated to each level based on the relative traffic intensities with a minimum of one channel being assigned to each level to maintain complete connectivity. Let $\mathcal{C}_i = X_i - X_{i-1}$ denote the number of channels allocated to an i-level cluster:

$$\mathcal{C}_i = \left\lceil \frac{p_i \prod_{u=1}^{i} m_u}{\sum_{j=1}^{r} p_j \prod_{k=1}^{j} m_k} \right\rceil C \quad (6)$$

It can be inferred from Eqn. (6) that the channel partition is independent of m_1. It is shown in Section 3.2 that this partition achieves a uniform saturation load at each level.

3 SCALABILITY ANALYSIS

System scalability is primarily governed by three limitations: physical limitation due to optical power budget considerations, complexity limitations, and performance limitations due to the finite number of channels within the tuning range of optical sources and filters. Section 3.1 evaluates the physical scalability and Section 3.2 examines the delay-throughput performance via analytic models and discrete-event simulation.

3.1 Physical Scalability

Physical scalability is evaluated in terms of both power budget limitations and system complexity.

Power Budget: Physical scalability in both the FHA and SWHA architectures is achieved with optical amplifiers at the level hierarchical boundaries. For SWHA the incorporation of one amplifier within each FatNode is considered, being placed at the input to the AOTF. Let P_M represent the system power margin needed to guarantee a specified bit error rate according to the receiver sensitivity and $L_{FN}(n)$ represent the power losses within a FatNode component with n input and output ports. The required uniform amplifier gain at each level boundary is given by:

$$G = \max \left\{ \frac{1}{k} \left[\sum_{i=1}^{k} L_{FN}(m_i) - P_M \right] | k \in [1, r] \right\} \quad (7)$$

Fig. 5 compares the physical (power budget) scalability of

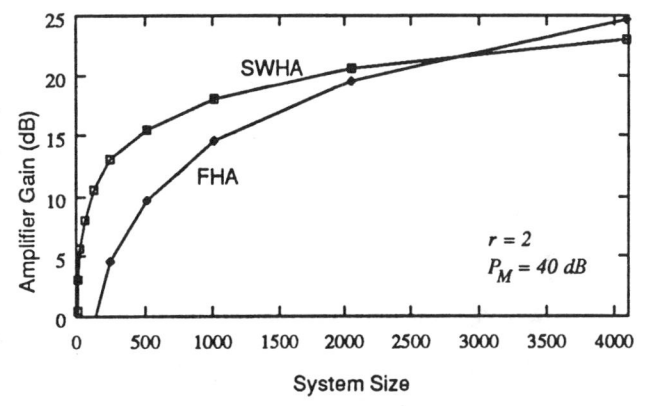

Figure 5: Required amplification (dB) at each level of the hierarchical architectures.

two-level SWHA and FHA using typical device losses and assuming a power margin $P_M = 40$ dB.

Complexity: The architectures employ tunable transmitters and fixed (slow-tunable) receivers. Both the FHA and the SWHA require only a single transmitter, while the WMCH requires r transmitters per node. A single receiver is sufficient for the FHA. An r-level SWHA may use a single receiver with an r-channel AOTF to monitor the incoming traffic from all r levels arriving on a single fiber. The WMCH needs one distinct receiver per dimension in each node as a result of its topological definition. Complexity expressions are summarized in Table 1, where the first two entries present the overall node complexity (transmitters and receivers) while the remaining entries present the interconnection network complexity (star couplers, AOTFs, amplifiers, and fiber links).

3.2 Performance

This section presents the SWHA delay-throughput performance evaluation via a queueing model validated by discrete-event simulation. The delay is defined as the time between the generation of a request and its delivery (and acknowledgment if necessary) to the destination. The total system throughput is defined as the total number of *concurrent* transfers per slot. D_i and Γ_i denote the delay and throughput of transfers that require i-level communication, for $1 \leq i \leq r$. Time is normalized to the channel slot length. The graphs contain

	WMCH	FHA	SWHA
Transmitters (tunable)	rM	M	M
Rcvr Filters (slow-tunable)	rM	M	M
Star couplers	$\sum_{i=1}^{r} \prod_{\substack{j=1,\\ j\neq i}}^{r} m_i$	$2\sum_{i=1}^{r} M_i$	$2\sum_{i=1}^{r} M_i$
AOTFs	None	None	$\sum_{i=2}^{r} M_i$
Amplifiers	None	$\sum_{i=2}^{r-1} M_i$	$\sum_{i=2}^{r} M_i$
Fiber links	rM	$2\sum_{i=1}^{r} M_i$	$2\sum_{i=1}^{r} M_i$

Table 1: Complexity expressions for WDM-based photonic architectures for processor interconnection.

plots of FHA performance also for comparison purposes.

Analytic Model: The hierarchy of the SWHA involves partitioning the channels among the system levels. The arrival process of new traffic generated at each processor has a geometric distribution with parameter g. The preallocation access protocol requires a separate buffer space for each channel to avoid head-of-line blocking [6]. Channel queues of all levels behave as Geom/D/1 queues when $m_1 \geq C$. The transmit queues are classified based on the number of nodes that use the corresponding channel as a home channel. There are $N_{ci} = W_i \bmod C_i$ queues for channels that are home channels for $\lceil W_i/C_i \rceil$ destination nodes (called *ceil*-queues), and $N_{fi} = C_i - (W_i \bmod C_i)$ queues belonging to channels that are home for $\lfloor W_i/C_i \rfloor$ destination nodes (*floor*-queues). Assuming infinite-capacity queues, the probability of an outgoing packet joining an i-level *ceil*-queue is $q_{ci} = \lceil W_i/C_i \rceil/W_i$ and that of joining a *floor*-queue is $q_{fi} = \lfloor W_i/C_i \rfloor/W_i$.

The average delay of i-level *ceil* and *floor*-queues is

$$\overline{D}_{ci} = 1 + \frac{W_i - 1}{2}\left[1 + \frac{gp_i q_{ci} W_i}{1 - gp_i q_{ci} W_i}\right] \quad (8)$$

$$\overline{D}_{fi} = 1 + \frac{W_i - 1}{2}\left[1 + \frac{gp_i q_{fi} W_i}{1 - gp_i q_{fi} W_i}\right] \quad (9)$$

and so the total average i-level delay is

$$\overline{D}_i = q_{ci}\overline{D}_{ci} + q_{fi}\overline{D}_{fi} \quad (10)$$

The overall average access delay for SWHA is expressed as the weighted sum $\overline{D} = \sum_{i=1}^{r} p_i \overline{D}_i$.

The i-level *ceil*- and *floor*-queues have slightly different saturation points of $g_{ci,sat} = 1/(p_i\lceil W_i/C_i \rceil)$ and $g_{fi,sat} =$

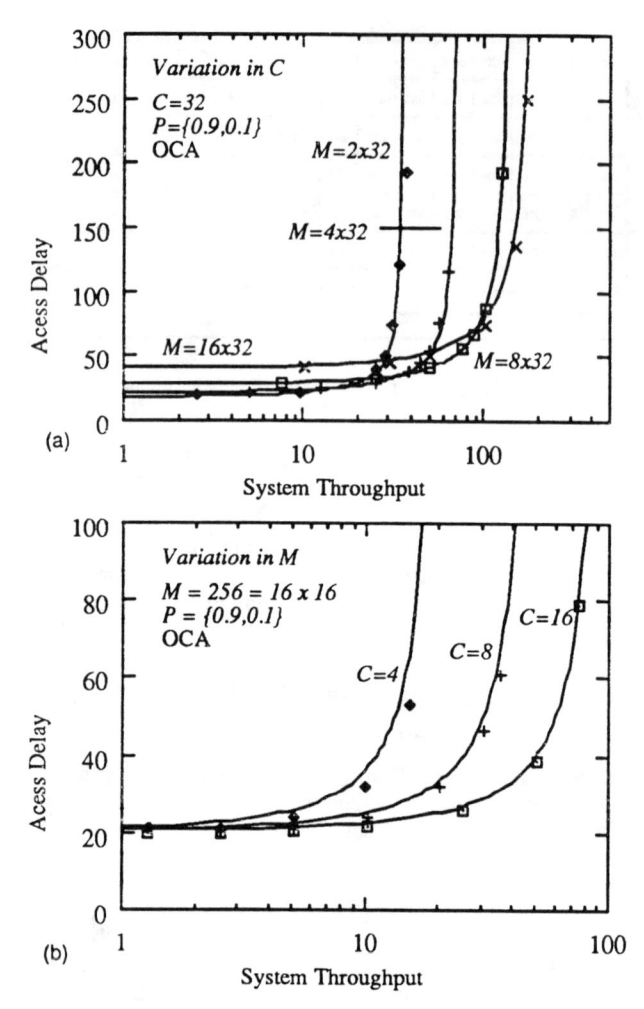

Figure 6: Validation of the SWHA analytic model.

$1/(p_i\lfloor W_i/C_i \rfloor)$, respectively. The system saturation load is determined by $g_{sat} = \min\{g_{ci,sat} \mid \forall i \in [1,r]\}$, since $g_{ci,sat} \leq g_{fi,sat}$. Due to the characteristics of the media access protocol, the throughput of an i-level *ceil* and *floor*-queue is

$$\Gamma_{ci} = \begin{cases} gp_i\lceil W_i/C_i \rceil & \text{if } 0 \leq g \leq g_{ci,sat} \\ 1 & \text{if } g > g_{ci,sat} \end{cases} \quad (11)$$

$$\Gamma_{fi} = \begin{cases} gp_i\lfloor W_i/C_i \rfloor & \text{if } 0 \leq g \leq g_{fi,sat} \\ 1 & \text{if } g > g_{fi,sat} \end{cases} \quad (12)$$

The total average i-level throughput can be determined taking into consideration the wavelength spatial re-use:

$$\Gamma_i = \begin{cases} [N_{ci}\Gamma_{ci} + N_{fi}\Gamma_{fi}] M_i & \text{if } 0 \leq g \leq g_{ci,sat} \\ [N_{ci} + N_{fi}\Gamma_{fi}] M_i & \text{if } g_{ci,sat} \leq g \leq g_{fi,sat} \\ C_i M_i & \text{if } g > g_{fi,sat} \end{cases} \quad (13)$$

and the overall system throughput is $\Gamma_{SWHA} = \sum_{i=1}^{r} \Gamma_i$. When the system has an optimal channel allocation, $g_{ci,sat} \approx g_{cj,sat}$

Figure 7: Impact of varying reference locality

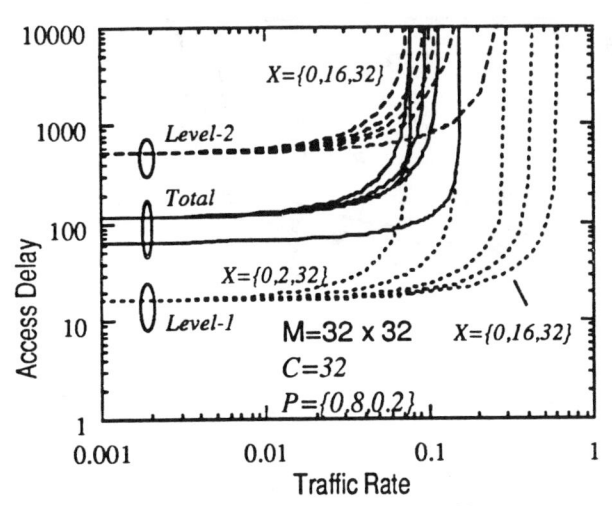

Figure 8: Impact of varying channel partition

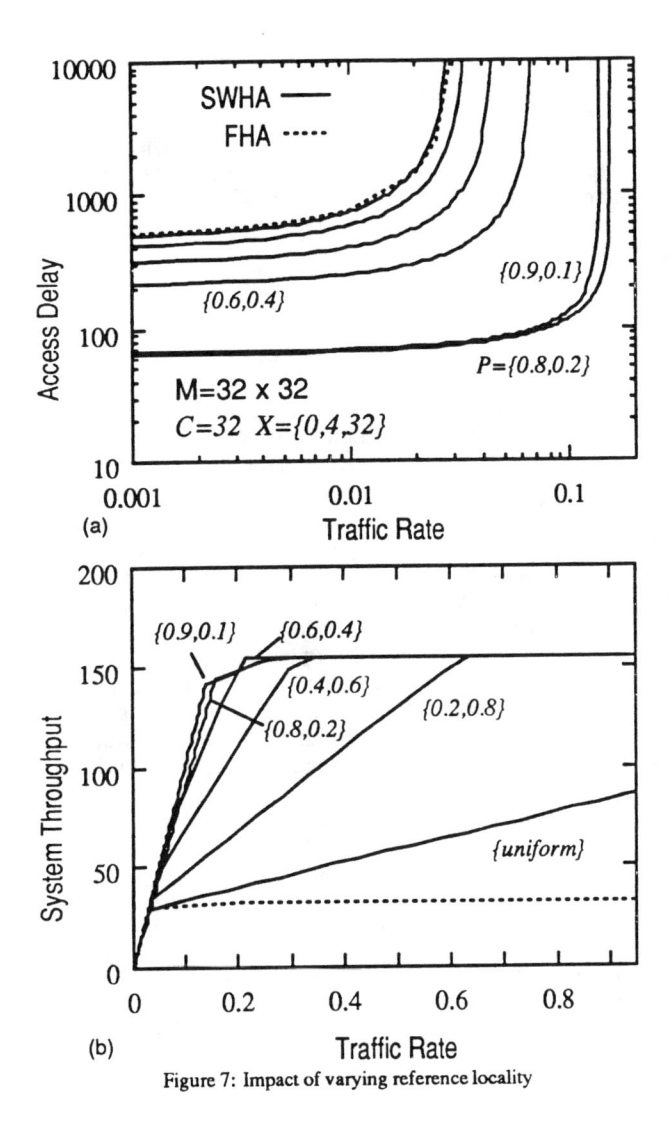

for $1 \leq i \leq r$ and $1 \leq j \leq r$, so the system saturates at all levels at the same traffic load. Stable behavior is still maintained when there is an imbalance which the model accurately illustrates in the graphs of Fig. 7.

Validation: A C-based discrete-event simulator is developed to validate the accuracy of the analytic model [10]. Steady state delay and throughput are measured and convergence is obtained through the replication/deletion method with a less than 2% variation from the mean. Fig. 6(a) plots the delay-throughput validation graphs for variations in number of channels as $C \in \{16, 8, 4\}$ with optimum channel partitioning, $M = 256 = 16 \times 16$ and locality $\{p_1, p_2\} = \{0.9, 0.1\}$. Fig. 6(b) plots the delay-throughput validation graphs for variations in system size. The system size is varied as $M \in \{64, 128, 256, 512\}$ with a configuration of $\{2 \times 32, 4 \times 32, 8 \times 32, 16 \times 32\}$, $C = 32$, and optimum channel partitioning for $\{p_1, p_2\} = \{0.9, 0.1\}$. The behavior of SWHA performance with varying different system parameters is next examined using a two-level system as a typical illustrative case.

Variation in communication locality: Fig. 7 examines the effect of varying the communication reference locality and compares it to the performance of FHA with the same system size and number of channels. Fig. 7(a) plots the average access time as a function of traffic rate. The delay characteristics of the SWHA with a uniform reference probability is same as that of FHA. As the reference probability is varied to increase the references to 1-level nodes while keeping the channel partition fixed, the average access delay decreases and capacity increases. The difference in cycle lengths at different levels together with the increased 1-level reference probability results in the decreased access delay. The given partition is optimum for reference probability $\{p_1, p_2\} = \{0.8, 0.2\}$, showing the highest system capacity in Fig. 7(a). Although the FHA and SWHA with uniform reference probability have the same delay characteristics, Fig. 7(b) shows that the SWHA achieves a significant increase in capacity even when there is no locality due to the spatial re-use of wavelength channels at each level of the hierarchy. The FHA cannot exploit locality due to its common wavelength space. The maximum throughput of $\Gamma_{max} = 156$ is obtained with the SWHA even with only a slight reference locality.

Variation in channel partition: Fig. 8 examines the impact of channel partition, showing the characteristics of the individual levels. Average access delay is plotted in Fig. 8. The 1-level cycle length is $\mathcal{L}_1 = 32$ since $W_1 = m_1 = 32$ and the 2-level cycle length is $\mathcal{L}_2 = W_2 = M = 1024$. When the traffic load is low, the average 1-level access delay is the average cycle synchronization time $\mathcal{L}_1/2 = 16$ slots and the average 2-level access delay is $\mathcal{L}_2/2 = 512$ slots as shown in Fig. 8(a). The low traffic delay is independent of channel partition. As the partition is varied to increase the channels allocated to 1-level communication, the 1-level delay decreases but the overall performance of the system may not improve. The optimum cases results in the minimum total delay and the maximum total system capacity. The system saturation point depends on the saturation points of the individual levels, $g_{sat} = \min\{g_{sat,1}, g_{sat,2}\}$, as shown in Fig. 8. This illustrates that maximum system performance can be maintained with varying reference locality through the dynamic re-allocation of bandwidth feature of the SWHA.

Variation in system size and number of channels: This

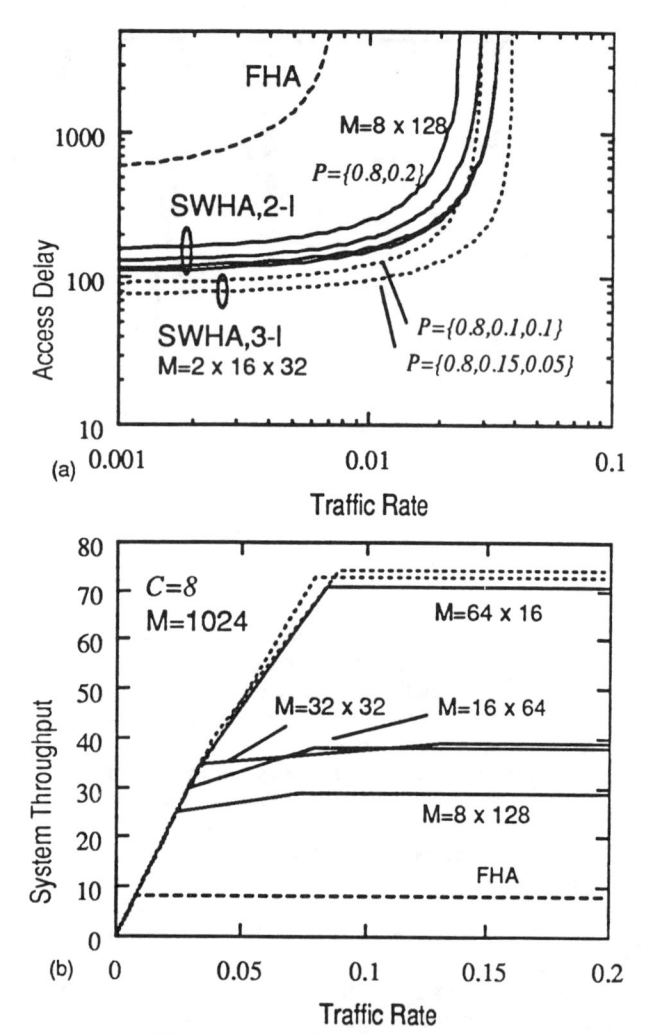

Figure 9: Impact of varying channel partition

section presents the impact of variations in M and C using Fig. 6. An optimum channel partition is used for each system configuration. Expansion results in increased average access delay if the reference probabilities remain fixed. Although C remains constant, the number of concurrently usable channels increases as the system size increases through channel re-use so a larger system has larger capacity (Fig. 6(b)). However, the marginal increase in capacity decreases as the system size increases for this example. For example, a 60% increase in maximum throughput occurs when the system is increased from $M = 2 \times 32$ to $M = 4 \times 32$ but the increase is reduced to 13% when the system is expanded from $M = 16 \times 32$ to $M = 32 \times 32$. Fig. 6(a) shows the delay-throughput characteristics as the number of channel increases using optimum channel allocation.

Variation in configuration: Fig. 9 plots the delay and throughput of 2-level and 3-level SWHA with a fixed system size of $M = 1024$. System expansion should take place, for both cost and performance reasons, by first expanding the lower levels size to the maximum as determined by OPB limitations. The improvement in throughput under this policy is due to the increase of spatial re-use of lower level channels (1-level in the figure). This policy results as well in lower system complexity, upon scaling up the system, as was noted by Table 1. The benefit of larger lower level sizes is maximized when communication locality is higher, since the contribution of the lower level throughput to the system throughput is higher.

4 CONCLUSIONS

This paper introduced a photonic-based single-hop structure for low-cost high-performance processor interconnection. The hierarchical approach preserved low cost while the combination of spatial and wavelength multiplexing, with a time multiplexed access technique, achieved excellent performance characteristics. In general, system scalability is hindered by the OPB, the number of channels realizable on a link, and the overall system complexity. The SWHA overcomes OPB and channel limitation by employing wavelength multiplexing and spatial re-use of channels at each level of the hierarchical architecture. An adaptable system results since the channels can be dynamically allocated to each level of the SWHA based on the reference locality. The performance of the architecture was examined through an analytical model and discrete-event simulation. The impact on the system performance was examined through variations in the communication locality, system size, configuration, number of channels, and channel partition.

REFERENCES

[1] P. W. Dowd, "Wavelength division multiple access channel hypercube processor interconnection," *IEEE Transactions on Computers*, vol. 41, pp. 1223–1241, Oct. 1992.

[2] C. E. Leiserson, "Fat-trees: Universal networks for hardware-efficient supercomputing," *IEEE Transactions on Computers*, vol. c-34, pp. 892–901, Oct. 1985.

[3] *"The Connection Machine CM-5 Technical Summary"*. Thinking Machines Corporation, October 1991.

[4] M. Lin, R. Tsang, D. Du, A. Klietz, and S. Saroff, "Performance evaluation of the CM-5 interconnection network," Tech. Rep. AHPCRC Preprint 92-111, University of Minnesota, Army High Performance Computing Research Center, Oct. 1992.

[5] C. A. Brackett, "Dense wavelength division multiplexing networks: Principles and applications," *IEEE Journal on Selected Areas of Communications*, vol. 8, pp. 948–964, Aug. 1990.

[6] K. Bogineni, K. M. Sivalingam, and P. W. Dowd, "Low complexity multiple access protocols for wavelength-division multiplexed photonic networks," *IEEE Journal on Selected Areas of Communications*, vol. 11, May 1993.

[7] M. M. Girard, C. R. Husbands, and R. Antoszewska, "Dynamically reconfigurable optical interconnect architecture for parallel multiprocessor systems," in *SPIE Proceedings (Optical Applied Science and Engineering)*, (San Diego, CA), July 1991.

[8] K. W. Cheung, "Acoustooptic tunable filters in narrowband WDM networks: System issues and network applications," *IEEE Journal on Selected Areas of Communications*, vol. 8, pp. 1015–1025, Aug. 1990.

[9] D. Lenoski, J. Laudon, K. Gharachorloo, A. Gupta, and J. Hennessy, "The directory-based cache coherence protocol for the DASH multiprocessor," in *Proc. 17th International Symposium Computer Architecture*, pp. 148–159, May 1990.

[10] P. W. Dowd, K. Bogineni, K. A. Aly, and J. Perreault, "Hierarchical scalable photonic architectures for high-performance processor interconnection," *IEEE Transactions on Computers*, (To Appear) 1993.

SESSION 8A:
Resource Management

Ray Bair, Chair

Reliable Management of Distributed Computations in Nexus [*]

Anand Tripathi Surya P. Koneru Clifton Nock Renu Tewari
Neeran M. Karnik Vijay Bandi Khaled Day Terence Noonan

Department of Computer Science
University of Minnesota, Minneapolis MN 55455

Abstract

This paper describes the approach taken for configuration management in the Nexus distributed operating system. Nexus uses kernel-level support for monitoring status of distributed components of an application. Periodic user-level messages are no longer required for status monitoring. Group and dependency relationships between such components can be defined by the programmer for the purpose of configuration monitoring and management. An object belonging to a distributed application can be monitored by its host kernel for some system-defined exception conditions. When any of these conditions arise, other objects are notified through signals or messages, as specified by the programmer.

1 Introduction

Workstation clusters connected by local-area networks offer great potential for high performance distributed computing by exploiting idle computing power for parallel processing. In this paper we discuss the facilities provided by the Nexus distributed operating system [15] for supporting configuration management of distributed computations. The objective of the Nexus design is to provide a set of simple, network-transparent abstractions to the programmer to utilize the distributed computing power and resources in such a cluster as a single monolithic computing facility. Nexus has been implemented on a cluster of Sun workstations. The Nexus approach centers around building distributed applications using object-based programming methods. The programming model is designed to be independent of any specific language.

Dealing with failure conditions is a major issue in distributed systems. Management of a distributed computation requires monitoring the status of its components and initiation of suitable recovery mechanisms and reconfiguration protocols under exception conditions. Most existing systems require periodic status messages (also referred to as *heartbeat* messages) to detect the failures of a distributed computation's components. This approach is highly sensitive to the frequency of such messages. Lower latency requirement implies higher message traffic and computation load to process such messages. Nexus exploits kernel-level mechanisms to monitor the objects of a distributed application. A network-wide service initiates programmer-defined actions when exception conditions are detected. This approach completely eliminates user-level heartbeat message traffic and latency problems.

The configuration management mechanisms described in this paper have been developed with the following objectives. The mechanisms should be compatible with the Nexus computation model and the UNIX [1] signal management. The primary reason here is to be able to exploit the object-based distributed programming capabilities of Nexus, which uses UNIX as its implementation base. There should be clear separation of mechanisms from any reconfiguration policies. A programmer should be able to implement any desired reconfiguration policies using these mechanisms. Using these mechanisms it should be possible to monitor an object for exception conditions or deliver a signal to it without requiring the knowledge of its location. Finally, these mechanisms should be usable by both the user-level applications as well as by the Nexus operating system components.

The next section presents a brief summary of other related work in the field. Section 3 describes the object-based computation model of Nexus. Section 4 presents the user-level view of configuration man-

---

[*] E-mail contact: tripathi@cs.umn.edu

[1] UNIX is a registered trademark of AT&T Bell Laboratories

agement primitives. Section 5 describes the system level protocols for configuration management.

2 Related Work

The various systems that have been developed in the past for supporting parallel and distributed computing in local area networks can be grouped into three general categories: parallel programming environments/tools, programming models/languages, and distributed operating systems. Programming environments are generally implemented as user-level software using the available operating system facilities. For this reason such systems are easily portable. Some of the examples of systems in this category are PVM [17], Express [5], and Isis [2]. In the second category we have distributed programming languages and models such as Argus [7], SR [1], and Conic [8]. In the third category we have distributed operating systems like Amoeba [14] Mach [10], Cronus [12], Clouds [11], and V system[4], which are kernel level implementations.

Parallel programming environments are implemented at the user-level using the standard protocols available for message passing. The foremost attractive feature of such systems is their portability to different computers because they do not require kernel modifications. Most such systems support programming in different languages and execution on heterogeneous platforms. The disadvantage of such systems is that they are not able to fully exploit the features of the underlying system for high performance. For example in an ethernet based environment, in many of such systems the broadcast communication is still performed using point-to-point messages. Stability of such systems can also become a problem when a long computation is spanned over a large number of computers.

Distributed systems often deal with groups of objects or entities. Instead of a single resource in conventional systems, a group of servers or resources are fundamental in distributed systems [6]. A process group in the V system is a set of processes identified by a single identifier, which can be distributed on various hosts in the network. The process group mechanism and multicast communication are used to implement distributed and replicated implementation of services. For reliable distributed computing Isis [2] provides process groups and group programming tools. Groups in Isis are viewed as a set of communication end points. Isis tools provide support for group communication, synchronization using locks, monitoring of group membership and site failures, and triggering of recovery. Express does not provide any general purpose support for defining groups. It is only recently that PVM has included support for process groups.

Reconfiguration for fault-tolerance requires mechanisms for two functions: monitoring of events and exception conditions, and specifications of the actions to be taken when such events occur. Most of the programming environments use periodic heartbeat messages for status monitoring. The group membership service in Isis supports facilities to monitor group membership and site failures and to trigger recoveries. Isis/Meta [9] uses rule-based specifications for configuration management. PVM and Express also support detection of process crashes, but do not support explicit mechanisms for reconfiguration. Both V system and Mach provide kernel-level support for exception handling. There are no mechanisms available to the programmer for conveniently specifying application-level global policies for status monitoring and configuration management. Such policies have to be implemented using kernel-level primitives in each component of the application. The approach adopted in Nexus eliminates user-level heartbeat messages by supporting remote signal monitoring/delivery, and allows application-level global specifications of actions to be taken when exception conditions arise. Similar to the Isis/Meta system, these specifications are rule-based.

Load balancing techniques are important in selecting the host machine for scheduling a process. As a part of the system-level configuration management functions, the operating system has to keep track of the current set of nodes in the system and their load status. In the V system, the least loaded machine is used for scheduling a process, thereby distributing the load among the machines in the cluster. PVM and Express adopt simple load balancing techniques in scheduling processes. Conic allows the programmer to control the mapping of a process on a specific host node; however, there is no support for load balancing. Mach provides an elaborate set of mechanisms for programmer-level control of scheduling policies for concurrent threads of a task; however, it does not include any user-transparent load-balancing mechanisms.

3 Nexus Computation Model

In Nexus, an object is an abstraction for some data or process. It is viewed as an instance of some abstract type, whose internal state can be accessed or modified only by invoking its interface procedures. Each abstract type is also an object in the Nexus system. We refer to such objects as *type-objects*. All type-objects are managed by a system-defined object called *NexusType*. By invoking operations on a type-object one can create or delete its instances; such operations are called *class operations*.

A 64-bit unique identifier (UID) is assigned to every object, which serves as a system-wide unique name for accessing it in the network. In accessing an object through its UID, the object's location is transparent to the client. The Nexus kernel supports request-reply based communication between objects. An object manager which is a UNIX process associated with each object implements the functional abstraction of the object. It receives the invocation messages sent to the object and executes the requested interface operations. This process is called *object manager*. Internal to the system is the concept of communication ports. Invocation messages sent to an object are delivered by the system to the port of its object manager process.

In Nexus, an *active object* represents a process; it encapsulates some data and the execution context of an activity. A *passive object* encapsulates data only. In case of active objects one object manager process is dedicated to each object whereas for passive objects, generally one manager process manages multiple instances. An object is *persistent* if its state continues to exist even after the process creating it has terminated.

The Nexus operating system's services are provided by a set of system-defined objects: *NexusType, Nexus Process Manager (NPM), NexusName Server, Nexus Configuration Manager (NCM)* which are always active on some hosts. Each Nexus host executes an instance of NPM whose primary function is to activate or deactivate object managers at its host, as requested by NexusType. Nexus Name Server supports mapping of programmer-assigned symbolic names for objects to their UIDs. There are two major functions of NexusType: (1) creation and management of type definitions in the system, and (2) maintenance of location and *active/inactive* status of the object managers of different types in the system. It also interacts with the Nexus Configuration Manager whose function is to monitor the status of some specified objects in the network.

To define a new object type the interface procedure *New* of NexusType is invoked; this procedure returns the UID for the newly created type-object. As a parameter to the New call the programmer specifies an executable file name which contains the code for the object manager. The programmer can also specify the *DOMAIN*, which is a set of preferred machines or architectures where the instances of the type are to be created. Tools such as the Nexus RPC compiler [16] and the Nexus Thread package are available to the programmer for building object managers. In defining a new type-object, the programmer has to specify how the class operations are to be implemented and how the instances are to be managed. There are two choices. One is to use the system-defined default implementation where each instance is an active object and the class operations are implemented by NexusType. To create a new instance, NexusType selects a node (based on the scheduling and load-balancing policies) and creates a UNIX process on that node to execute the object manager for the new instance. The second option allows type-objects and their instances to be managed by one or more UNIX processes that execute the code defined by the programmer.

4 Primitives for Configuration Management

To introduce the configuration management primitives of Nexus, we shall use a simple application example, the *existential worm* program described in [13], since it exhibits many of the requirements of a typical distributed application. This application has a *user interface* (or manager) process and some number of processes called *worm segments*, possibly running on different machines. The main function of the existential worm is to ensure that all segments are running at all times - if one segment dies a new one must be created in its place. In a practical application, each segment would perform some useful computation.

To implement the existential worm, facilities are needed for dynamically creating instances of the worm segment, monitoring the user interface process and the worm segments (possibly on remote machines), and for defining the actions to be taken when exceptions occur. It is also useful to be able to view all the segments as a group to simplify the specification of these actions as well as for multicast communication. These requirements are addressed by the primitives described below for supporting group management and dependency specifications.

4.1 Process Groups

In Nexus, a process-group is defined as a set of active objects which can be viewed as a single logical entity for communication and exception handling. The members of a process-group can be either active objects or process-groups themselves. Any object in the system can send a message to a group. Such a message is delivered to all currently active members of the group. The sender can also specify the number of replies expected from the group. The user sends a message to a group using the *invoke* call and waits for each reply serially. Members can communicate among each other using their logical indices or their *object-ids*.

A process group in Nexus can have objects of different types as its members, and the members of a group can be present at any set of nodes in the network. To keep the implementation simple, no special categories are defined for groups. In Nexus, the group is *indexed* such that the members can be addressed using their logical indices for the purpose of communication, status monitoring and exception handling. This is primarily for supporting parallel programming where the computation and communication performed by a process is based on its logical position in the group.

System functions are available to the programmer for creating and deleting process groups. A group is viewed as an object and is assigned a UID, which is called its *groupid*. A group object in Nexus is of a special system type called *GroupType* to distinguish it from other objects. The object that creates the group is the *owner* of the group. System functions are also available for adding or removing members of a group. A member can be deleted by specifying either its index in the group or its UID. It is also possible to replace a member with a specified index in the group, with another object. A set of system functions support queries about group configuration and membership information.

In the worm example, the user interface first defines a new type that represents a worm segment. This is done by calling the library function NexusTypeNew and specifying the file containing the binary code for the worm segment. The UID of this new type is stored in the variable *wormSegmentType*.

```
NexusTypeNew( wormSegmentCodeFile,
              &wormSegmentType);
```

It then spawns n worm segments in the network by creating instances of this newly created type. This is achieved by invoking the New operation on wormSegmentType using the *call* function of the Nexus RPC system. This invocation returns the UID of the newly created segment in the variable seg[i]. The user-interface process puts all these worm segments in one group. These steps are shown below:

```
CreateGroup(&seg_groupid);
for (i = 0; i < n ; i++) {
    call(wormSegmentType, "New", &seg[i]);
    AddMember(seg_groupid, seg[i]);
}
```

4.2 Exception Dependencies

A dependency is a cause-effect relationship between objects. In Nexus, a user defines a dependency so that, if some exception occurs on a particular active object (called the *trigger*) then a signal, and possibly a message is sent to another object, which is called the *target*. The target then takes appropriate action based on the context. The trigger-target dependency can be represented as:

$$\langle \text{trigger, exception} \rangle \implies \langle \text{target, action} \rangle$$

A dependency is registered with the NCM using the *AddDependency* call and removed using the *RemoveDependency* call. The exception defined for the trigger object can be (i) any UNIX signal, (ii) process termination, (iii) any user defined exception. The programmer can specify a UNIX signal, and any one of a set of pre-defined messages to be sent to the target when the exception occurs.

A set of *group exceptions* is also available to the programmer. It includes (i) group member addition/deletion, (ii) group member dependency changes, (iii) messages or signals addressed to the group. The trigger here is the UID of the group to be monitored. The target can be any active object or group object. In this way all group operations can be monitored as required.

In our example, the worm segments form a circular dependency, making every segment responsible for monitoring one other segment. The dependencies are set up such that, if the *ith* worm segment terminates, then the *(i+1)th* segment is notified, by sending the UNIX signal SIGUSR1. In addition all segments must be killed if the user interface is terminated. This can be done as follows:

```
for (i = 0; i < n ; i++) {
    AddDependency(seg[i], TERMINATION,
            seg[(i+1) % n], SIGUSR1);
}
AddDependency(user_interface, TERMINATION,
            seg_groupid, SIGKILL);
```

4.3 Setting Monitors

For each *trigger* object in a dependency, the Nexus kernel on the host machine of that object has to be informed. Only then will the kernel monitor the trigger for the specified exception and inform the NCM when it occurs. This monitoring can be activated using one of the following: (i) A *SetObjectMonitor* call to the NCM, specifying an active object to be monitored or (ii) a *SetProcessMonitor* call specifying a UNIX process to be monitored. An active object can make these calls to enable monitoring of itself for a particular exception, or some other object can make these calls on its behalf. Similarly there are two primitives to disable the monitoring by the kernel: (i) *ClearObjectMonitor* stops the monitoring of an active object by the Nexus kernel for the specified exception and (ii) *ClearProcessMonitor* does the same for a UNIX process.

In our example, user interface and each worm segment enable their own monitoring for the termination exception as follows:

```
SetProcessMonitor(SELF, TERMINATION);
```

4.4 Raising Exceptions

A provision is made to allow the user to simulate the occurrence of an exception on some trigger object of a dependency. The *RaiseException* call to the NCM gives the programmer the capability to force the target to perform some action based on an exception, even when the exception has not actually occurred. This is also useful when the exception which activates a dependency is not system-defined, and hence cannot be monitored by the kernel. The trigger, on reaching some condition, can raise the exception using this call and force the target to take appropriate action. For example if normal termination is to be distinguished from a *termination* exception, then a dependency can be defined based on *Normal Termination* and the process can make a *RaiseException* call for *Normal Termination* just before exiting. Similarly the user can request the NCM to send a signal (using *SendSignal*) to the target or trigger object of a dependency, thus simulating an exception and forcing the target into its signal handling routine.

The target object will usually specify the action to be taken on receipt of a signal using the UNIX *signal* system call. If a message is also sent to the target, it can receive and process the message in its signal handling routine. For example, each worm segment has a signal handler which is invoked when the process receives a SIGUSR1. This implies that its neighbor segment has terminated, and thus needs to be re-created. A new instance is created for the wormSegmentType and it is inserted in the group at the appropriate index. Using the Nexus primitives these steps can be implemented by the *ith* segment as shown below:

```
call (wormSegmentType, "New" &new_segid);
AddMemberAtIndex(seg_groupid,
        (i-1) % n, new_segid);
```

5 System Support for Configuration Management

This section describes the Nexus system architecture and its internal protocols in supporting configuration management, status monitoring, object location and dynamic binding.

5.1 System Components

5.1.1 Nexus kernel

The primary functions supported by the Nexus kernel are: request-reply based asynchronous inter-object communication, object location in the network, transportation of messages across the network, and support for status monitoring of objects at its node. It also participates in the status monitoring of some subset of nodes in the Nexus environment. The kernel executing at each node is also viewed as an object, with a UID assigned to it. One can communicate with a remote kernel using its UID.

To invoke an operation on an object, the client executes the *invoke* call. The important parameters to this call include the UID of the object and the invocation message. Another parameter can be used to indicate that no reply is expected from the callee object, and therefore the kernel need not maintain any information for this invocation.

The kernel caches the currently known port-ids for the objects that have been recently accessed. Entries in these caches are made whenever the kernel discovers the current port-id for an object from the request or reply message traffic. These caches are used in the object location protocol described in section 5.2.

The Nexus kernel also maintains a list of currently active object manager processes at its node. It maintains the association between the UNIX process-id, the Nexus UID, and the communication port-id. For each group, the kernel maintains the list of the local active objects belonging to the group. Any messages sent to a group are delivered by each kernel to its local members' ports.

The signal delivery system of UNIX has been modified to support signal monitoring in a distributed environment. For this purpose, the system call *SetProcessMonitor* directs the kernel to monitor the delivery of a specified signal to a given process on its node. Whenever the kernel delivers a signal to a process being monitored, it also sends a message to the NCM, informing it of this event.

5.1.2 Nexus Configuration Manager

The Nexus Configuration Manager is a system object that performs the function of maintaining the user-defined dependencies between objects. The NCM is replicated on a subset of the hosts.

When the user makes the *SetObjectMonitor* call the NCM queries NexusType for the process-id of the trigger object, and stores the pid-to-UID mapping in a local table. The NCM then requests the host kernel, using the *SetProcessMonitor* call, to monitor the process for the given exception.

When the Nexus kernel informs the NCM of the exception that occurred for a particular process, the NCM searches its tables for all occurrences of the corresponding object as a trigger in a dependency relationship. It then sends the appropriate signal (and message if any) to the corresponding targets. Since the NCM cannot directly signal an object on a remote machine it sends a message to the remote kernel requesting that the signal be delivered to that object.

Whenever any group operations are performed, the NCM searches the group dependency list to determine what action to take for such group exceptions. If the user defines a dependency in which trigger or target object is a group object, the dependency is expanded, at the time of its activation, for all existing members of the group. Whenever an object is added to a group, NCM informs the host kernel of that object, since group membership information is required by the kernel to support group communication.

The NCM also maintains a log of the context of the recently activated dependencies. The target can query the NCM for the cause of the signal. The context of the signal is the <trigger, exception> pair that activated the dependency. If the NCM detects that a node has crashed, it raises the termination exception for all the objects on that host.

5.2 Object Location Protocol

To send an invocation message to an object, the Nexus kernel needs the port id of the particular object manager that manages the requested instance. The kernel first looks up its local caches to see if it knows the location of the specified object. If the object has been accessed 'recently', then the corresponding port id will be available in the cache. If it isn't, the Nexus kernel is forced to query NexusType to find it. The kernel makes a *GetPort* call to NexusType, requesting it to return the list of port ids at which the specified object may be located. NexusType is the main service responsible for registering the locations of all Nexus objects, and therefore, the location of NexusType itself has to be known to the kernels on all machines. This problem is dealt with in section 5.3.2. NexusType searches its directories to locate the desired entry. If the required object manager is active, its port id is returned to the kernel.

If the object manager is inactive, NexusType activates the object manager on some workstation in the system. For this, NexusType makes a remote procedure call to the Nexus Process Manager (NPM) on the target machine, where the new object manager is to be executed. This target machine can be chosen using some load balancing algorithm, say, the least loaded machine in the system. Also, the user is allowed to specify a set of preferred machines or a set of machines to be excluded from consideration during this scheduling. The corresponding NPM then creates a UNIX process to execute the specified binary on its local host, assigns it a port-id, and returns this port-id to NexusType.

5.3 System Configuration Protocols

It is necessary for Nexus to keep track of the current configuration of nodes and system components, in order to provide a robust computing environment. This includes knowledge about which nodes are currently active, where NexusType instances are running, and some metric of the loads on the active machines.

5.3.1 Node Status Monitoring

Our approach to the problem of tracking the active nodes in the system is to organize the set of workstations in the system as a *logical ring*. Each kernel sends its status information to just two other nodes in the system, its neighbors in the ring. At boot-time, the kernel informs the NCM its intention to join the system. Since it has no means of knowing the location of NCM, it has to broadcast a message to the system-defined NCM group. NCM detects this message, inserts the new node into the ring, and broadcasts the new logical configuration of the system to all nodes. It also informs the newly booted kernel of the locations of the NexusType service. From then onwards, the kernel periodically receives the heartbeat messages from its neighboring machines. If any of its neighbors misses a heartbeat, the kernel reports this to NCM. If both neighbors of a node report that it is no longer sending status messages, NCM marks that node as *down*. It then rearranges the ring to exclude the failed node, and sends the new ring configuration to all kernels. Each kernel then restarts sending messages to its (potentially new) neighbors, and the new ring is established. When the failed node restarts, it again goes through the boot-time procedure and rejoins the system.

The advantage of our approach is that heartbeat messages are no longer broadcast, but only sent to two nodes. Similarly a node receives heartbeat messages from only two other nodes. Also, messages to a central entity (NCM) are necessary only in case of changes in the system configuration (addition or deletion of a node), which are relatively infrequent. So it does not create a bottleneck.

5.3.2 Location and Monitoring of System Components

Another problem in configuration management in Nexus is that all the kernels need to know the location of at least one instance of NexusType. The NexusType service is replicated on some subset of hosts, in order to provide better availability and load balancing. One possible solution is that each instance of NexusType could periodically broadcast heartbeat messages to all kernels, thus advertising its location. Instead, to avoid this broadcast traffic, we use our configuration management facilities, i.e. the NCM. All the instances of NexusType form a process group, which is monitored by the NCM. Whenever an instance of NexusType goes down, this event is detected by NCM. The other active instances of NexusType are informed about this, and they can recreate the failed instance on another node if necessary. Whenever NexusType comes back up, it contacts the NCM and asks to be added to its process group. This new instance of NexusType then uses a predefined protocol to join the other running instances and synchronizes its directories with those of the others. In either case, when the state of the NexusType process group changes, one of its members broadcasts the latest configuration to all the kernels. The kernels can then update their local caches to reflect the new status. Since this status update is idempotent, it is repeated a few times for greater reliability. Again, broadcast communication is needed only when the state changes, i.e. when an instance of NexusType goes down or comes up.

The NCM service is also replicated on some subset of hosts, so that a single point of failure is avoided. Further, the instances of NCM monitor one another, and in case one of them fails, it can be recreated on some available machine, in a worm-like fashion. This is achieved by putting all instances of the NCM into a group, and setting up dependencies so that, whenever any member of the group is terminated, the others are notified.

6 Discussion

The configuration management in the Nexus system using dependency specifications and group primitives provides the user a convenient environment for parallel programming on workstation clusters. The kernel level support for monitoring of exception conditions provides better latency in detecting remote status changes as compared to the use of periodic status messages. The overhead involved in supporting this scheme is in terms of some additional code that the kernel has to execute whenever it delivers a signal to any of its local processes. This code checks a table containing the list of local processes that are required to be monitored for some specified signals. When a trigger object incurs an exception, it takes 2 message-transmission delays and some processing time at NCM to deliver a signal to the target object.

The mechanism adopted in the Nexus system completely eliminates the need of user-level periodic status monitoring messages, thus reducing the message traffic. The configuration management mechanisms available to the application programmer are also used for managing the configuration of the Nexus operating system itself.

References

[1] Gregory Andrews, Ronald Olsson, Michael Coffin, Irving Elshoff, Kelvin Nilsen, Titus Purdin, and Gregg Townsend. An overview of the SR language and implementation. *ACM Transactions on Programming Languages and Systems*, 10(1):51–86, January 1988.

[2] Kenneth Birman. The Process Group Approach to Reliable Distributed Computing. Technical Report TR-91-1216, Cornell University, July 1991.

[3] Yih-Farn Chen, Atul Prakash, and C.V.Ramamoorthy. The Network Event Manager. *Proceedings of the Computer Networking symposium*, pages 169–178, 1986.

[4] David Cheriton. The V Distributed System. *Communications of the ACM*, March 1988.

[5] Parasoft Corporation. *Express 3.2 Introductory Guide*. Parasoft Corporation, 2500, E.Foothill Blvd, Pasadena, CA 91107, 1990.

[6] Luping Liang, Samuel Chanson, and Gerald Neufeld. Process Groups and Group Communications: Classification and Requirements. *IEEE-Computer*, February 1990.

[7] Barbara Liskov. Distributed Programming in Argus. *Communications of the ACM*, 31(3), March 1988.

[8] Jeff Magee, Jeff Kramer, and Morris Sloman. Constructing Distributed Systems in Conic. *IEEE Transactions on Software Engineering*, 15(6):663–675, June 1989.

[9] Keith Marzullo, Robert Cooper, Mark Wood, and Kenneth Birman. Tools for distributed application management. *IEEE Computer*, pages 42–51, August 1991.

[10] M.Young, A.Tevanian, R.Rashid, D.Golub, J.Eppinger, J.Chew, W.Bolosky, D.Black, and R.Baron. The Duality of Memory and Communication in the Implementation of a Multiprocessor Operating System. In *Proceedings of the 11th Symposium on Operating System Principles*, November 1987.

[11] P.Dasgupta, R.LeBlanc, M.Ahamad, and U.Ramachandran. The Clouds Distributed Operating System. *IEEE Computer*, pages 34–44, November 1991.

[12] Richard Schantz, Robert Thomas, and Girome Bono. The Architecture of the Cronus Distributed Operating System. In *Proc. of the 6th International Conference on Distributed Computing Systems*, pages 250–259, 1986.

[13] J.F. Schoch and J.A. Hupp. The Worm Programs - Early Experience with a Distributed Computation. *Communications of the ACM*, 25(3), March 1982.

[14] A. S. Tanenbaum, Robert van Renesse, Hans van Staveren, Gregory Sharp, Sape Mullender, Jack Jansen, and Guido van Rossum. Experiences with the Amoeba Distributed Operating System. *Communications of the ACM*, 33(12), December 1990.

[15] Anand Tripathi. An Overview of the Nexus Distributed Operating System Design. *IEEE Transactions on Software Engineering*, 15(6), June 1989.

[16] Anand Tripathi and Terence Noonan. Design of a Remote Procedure Call system for Object-Oriented Distributed Programming. Technical Report 92-20, University of Minnesota, Minneapolis, 1992.

[17] V.S.Sunderam. PVM: A Framework for Parallel Distributed Computing. *Concurrency: Practice & Experience*, 2(4), December 1990.

Management of Broadband Networks Using a 3D Virtual World

Laurence A. Crutcher, Aurel A. Lazar, Steven K. Feiner, and Michelle Zhou

Center for Telecommunications Research, Columbia University, New York, NY 10027-6699

Abstract

Just as broadband networks will enable user-to-user communications to extend from textual services to those employing multimedia, they will also enable a management environment that can take advantage of increased bandwidth and multimedia technology. The fundamental advances incorporated in such an environment can provide efficient solutions to the problem of information management. To establish this environment, we tackle the fundamental problems of observability and controllability of broadband networks. A virtual world provides a next-generation network management interface through which a user can observe and interact with the network directly in real time. The system we are developing uses a 3D virtual world as the user interface for managing a large gigabit ATM network. It provides the capability for experimentation in all aspects of network transport, control, and management.

1. Introduction

One of the most pressing issues to be tackled in the development and deployment of the next generation of communication systems is that of network control and management. In the past, this subject has been treated in an ad hoc fashion. However, the complexity of emerging broadband networks, in terms of both speed and size, require a more formal approach in which the control and management structures are an integral component of the overall network architecture. Such an approach will be mandatory in order to achieve the goal of pervasive high-speed communication among a large number of users and to support multimedia and distributed computation.

From a theoretical standpoint, the problem of network management and control can be viewed as one of controllability and observability of a large distributed system. A broadband network poses specific problems within this context as a result of its dynamics, size, and diversity of services. In this paper, we consider the properties of controllability and observability in terms of the degree of control and observation provided to a user operating as a network manager. We describe a system that we are building that provides advanced control, observation, and navigation capabilities to a network manager using the technology of virtual worlds. With this system, we aim to combine the power of high-performance computing and high-speed communication, using multimedia technology, to tackle the problems associated with managing and controlling a broadband network.

In the remainder of the paper, we explain the rationale for our approach, describe the structure of the system, and report on our prototype implementation. In the next section, we present the system architecture and show how the technology of virtual worlds can be used for network management and control. Section 3 reports on the state of our prototype, and in Section 4 we outline our current work on extending this prototype, and highlight the key research issues involved. We state our conclusions in Section 5.

2. System Architecture

We identify three major components in the proposed network management system:
- A management and control architecture that is structured and extensible. This architecture should assist in the realization of a system that is controllable and observable.
- Management services and protocols that can support a high level of interaction with the network in real time.
- The virtual world user interface through which the user can navigate, monitor, and manage the network.

The first two components are described in the next section. The user interface is discussed in Section 2.2.

2.1 Management and Control Structure

The management and control architecture is encapsulated in the Integrated Reference Model (IRM) [1]. This model has been developed by our group to provide a network-independent view of the structure and dynamics of the system to be managed, and of the services required for control and management on a range of time scales. The IRM is shown in Figure 1.

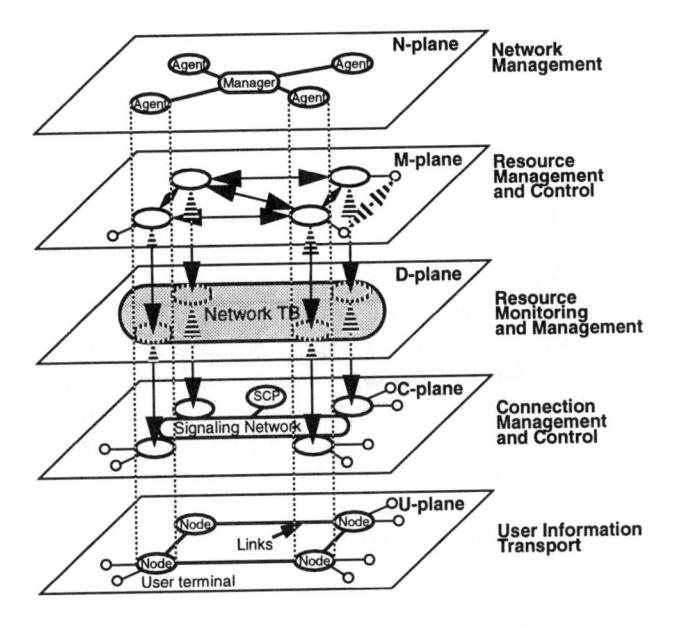

Figure 1: The Integrated Reference Model

The centerpiece of our model is the network telebase (D-plane). Here we represent all information regarding the network. This includes static, dynamic, and statistical information. In practice, the telebase comprises objects that are distributed throughout the network; conceptually the telebase represents a single information repository where network subsystems can read and write data for their own specific purposes, using D-plane data abstractions that suit their function. Two such subsystems are the Resource Control (M-plane) and Network Management (N-plane) planes. The M-plane embodies a set of distributed asynchronous algorithms that operate in real time to manage network resources. Routing algorithms are an example of a component of this plane. In contrast, the N-plane is perceived as operating on a longer time scale, with a centralized view of the network. Fault management and accounting are examples of components of this plane. The C- and U-planes represent the Connection Management and User Transport, respectively. Thus the C-plane embodies the algorithms and protocols associated with the signalling network, while the U-plane contains the protocols for user transport of services.

Further details of the IRM can be found in [1]. For the purpose of our discussion here, we note that the model allows us to systematically design and implement the network control and management system in a way in which the complexity of these systems is reduced and made manageable. The functional division according to time-scales and the unified representation of the network information are the key elements of the model in this respect. The inherent complexity of broadband networks means that attempting to build the management and control system without a structured approach such as that formulated in the IRM is analogous to providing a set of user protocols without a model such as the OSI Reference Model.

The Network Management plane provides the interface through which managers can communicate with all components of the network architecture. Actions in the virtual world are effected through the primitives provided by the services in this plane. The N-plane in our model shows a Manager/Agent structure of the type familiar from the OSI Management Architecture [2]. In terms of that architecture, everything in the IRM outside of the N-plane should be viewed as existing inside a Management Information Base (MIB). Access to other planes would occur via manager/agent interactions within the N-plane using a protocol such as CMIP (Common Management Information Protocol).

As detailed further in Section 3, our current prototype is built in an emulation environment in which we have bypassed the overhead of an OSI-style MIB. In parallel, we are implementing the OSI Management Architecture on TeraNet [3], a small scale gigabit ATM network that has been built at Columbia's Center for Telecommunications Research, and in this way plan to experiment with the management of an operational ATM network in a virtual world. However, the IRM is not constrained to fit the OSI Management Architecture, and there is some doubt over whether an implementation of that architecture can deliver the performance that we seek for our purposes, in terms of throughput of management information and response time to manager actions. Some specific areas of concern are the efficiency of the management protocol and the structure and organization offered by the MIB. While the OSI CMISE (Common Management Information Service Elements) provides the primitives required to get and set remote information, preliminary experience has shown that the protocols underlying these services are excessively complex and slow in execution even for the most basic operations. Similarly, the MIB provides an implementation-independent way in which to interface to managed objects, but does not lend itself to an efficient implementation. Furthermore, it does not address the issue of how the management database should be organized, as there is no overall logical relationship between management agents, and no communication between them. These issues are the subject of ongoing research by our group [4], [5], [6].

2.2 The User Environment

The most common type of network management tool in use today is the protocol analyzer. These analyzers are self-contained instruments that can be used to test specific aspects of the network, and perform limited diagnosis. A brief history of such machines can be found in [7]. More recently, the development of network management standards has led to the creation of more flexible tools. These tools are software-based and rely on advanced workstations to provide processing of management information together with 2D graphical display of information. We refer to this type of tool as a management workstation (MW). Although the functions of an MW may include protocol analysis, they generally have a much wider scope.

An MW provides remote access to the components of a network. Management protocols allow reading and writing of management information inside the network. The current generation of MWs is limited in three areas:
- *Monitoring Bandwidth.* The complexity of management protocols together with the low bandwidth of management connections result in low throughput of management information.
- *Semantic level of information.* Graphical displays provide a multifaceted representation of the state of the network. This is comprised of a mixture of abstractions including icons, graphs, tables, and textual reports. While this is a huge advance over a purely textual representation, it still presents a barrier between the behavior of the network and that perceived by an MW user.
- *Level of interaction.* The two limitations above combine to limit the degree of interaction with the network. Thus a user is typically an observer of the network rather than an actor in its operation.

The level of management provided by this type of MW can be summarized as *control and observation at a distance*. Despite the enormous advances in computer technology, 2D interfaces are still inadequate for visualizing and manipulating large datasets. In the case of a network crash, for example, the need to quickly understand and navigate through large datasets and spatial networking structures can only be satisfied by a significant increase in monitoring bandwidth.

In contrast, consider how we might use *virtual worlds,* which combine high-performance 3D graphics processors with 3D displays and interaction devices. We believe that a virtual world for network management could offer an answer to the navigation problem and, in conjunction with the bandwidth capabilities of gigabit networks, could provide the additional capability required for quick fault detection, isolation, and removal. Thus, advances in workstation and networking technologies mean that the obstacles described here can be removed. There are three consequences:
- The semantic level of the display (output) is raised so that objects and operations can be directly interpreted.
- Management information is organized hierarchically, but is available by random access, so that a user can obtain any information from any location at any time.
- The semantics of the user's input is explicit in terms of the objects to be manipulated and the operations to be performed.

We summarize the level of management provided by this type of MW as *direct control and observation*. Virtual worlds that are implemented using powerful workstations and graphics hardware give us the capability to fulfill some of these requirements. High-speed networks provide the raw bandwidth necessary to transmit management and control information at the rates necessary to interact with the network at the desired level. The need for efficient organization and access to this information, together with effective and efficient algorithms to process it, pose many interesting problems that are the basis of our ongoing research.

The contrast between the two types of management environment is illustrated in Figure 2. In this example, the user is observing the load on a set of Virtual Paths (VPs) inside the network, and as a result of these observations has decided to reroute some of the VPs. This is a typical scenario that may occur during fault or performance management in an ATM network. A conventional system is typified by the cycle of periodic snapshots of the state of the network being relayed to the manager, who is then required to interpret the state according to the events reported. In the example shown, the manager observes the average utilization on the links and relocates VPs by setting parameters in the routing tables. This mode of operation contrasts with that shown in the immersive environment. Here, the manager is able to navigate around the network and can observe the state of the system in real time, at a level of abstraction of his or her own choice. For the same scenario, the VPs inside a link are investigated by grabbing the link in question and observing the paths that are in place, abstractly presented as a set of cylinders inside the cylindrical link. The capacity of a VP is proportional to the diameter of its cylinder in this case, and its utilization is indicated by color coding. To relocate the VPs, the manager grabs the appropriate cylinders and moves them to the alternate link. A

Conventional System
Remote Action and Interpretation

Virtual World
Direct Visualization, Interaction, and Control

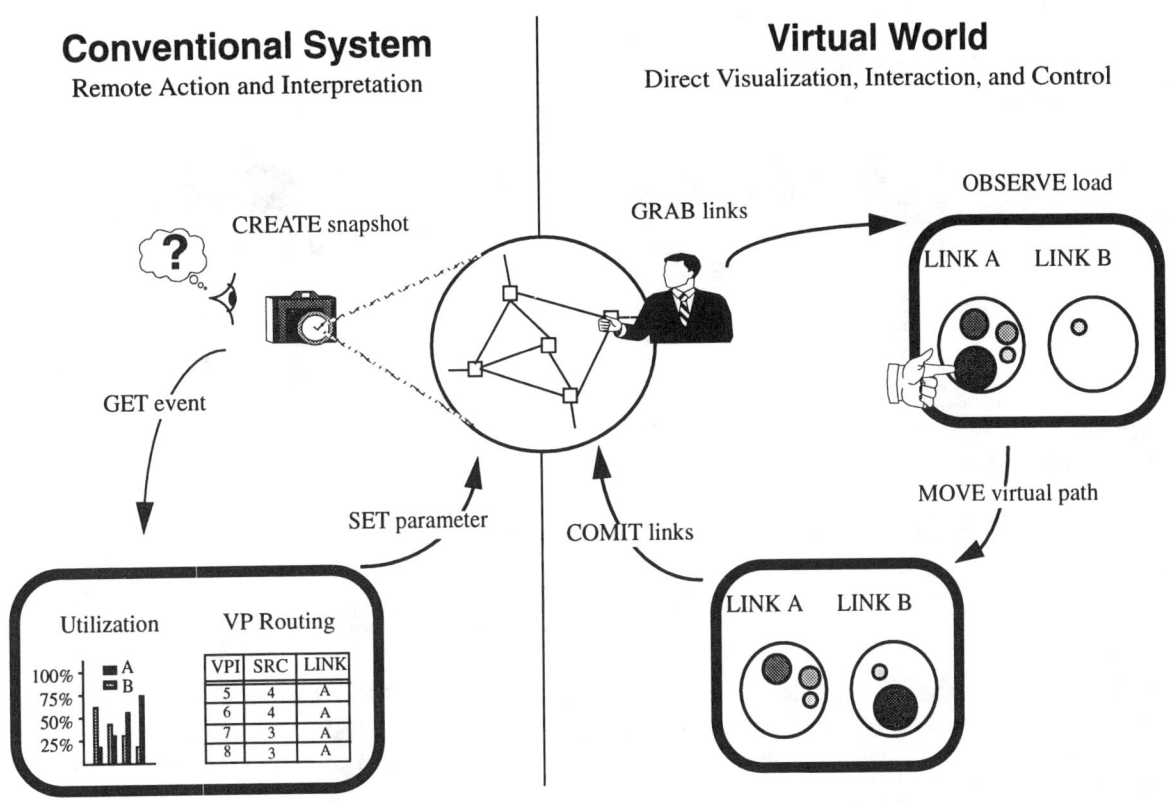

Figure 2: Conventional System vs. Virtual World

final commit operation, indicated by a hand gesture, translates the changes from the virtual world to the real network.

This example highlights some of the significant advantages of the virtual world over the conventional approach: high semantic level of interaction in real time, for both reading (observation) and writing (control and management) of the network state. Furthermore, users can operate at many levels of abstraction, under their own navigational control. In the example shown, the user has moved from an overall view of the network, where potential problems may be indicated by color coding, to a specific physical link and then to specific VPs. If it were desired, the user could navigate inside a VP to observe the cell-level behavior. Point failures could be detected in this way, as the user would see cell traffic flowing to the point of failure but not beyond it. The key idea here is that different levels of abstraction are useful in different situations, and the user is able to move between these levels with a minimum of effort. In terms of the IRM, all aspects of the network architecture are manageable in the virtual world, and the user has the capability to navigate horizontally within a plane, between nodes, and also vertically between planes to observe different facets of the network behavior. As an example of the latter case, the user should be able to move from the U-plane, to observe the state of the network in terms of the user information, to the C-plane where he or she can observe the state of the signalling network. Thus the multidimensional capabilities of the virtual world are reflected directly in the underlying management and control structure.

3. Prototype System

3.1 Design

To experiment with network management in a virtual world, we have built a test-bed comprising a *Visualization Engine* connected to a *Network Engine* via Ethernet. This test-bed is illustrated in Figure 3. The Visualization Engine comprises a high-performance graphics workstation with a liquid crystal stereo display system and an ultrasonic 3D mouse that tracks the user's 3D hand position and orientation.

The Network Engine executes a software emulation of a minimal subset of the IRM. The emulation is initialized with a user-specified configuration of physical (e.g., switches and links) and logical (e.g., VPs and calls) entities that are organized into a network database according to the principles of the D-plane in the IRM. The emulator con-

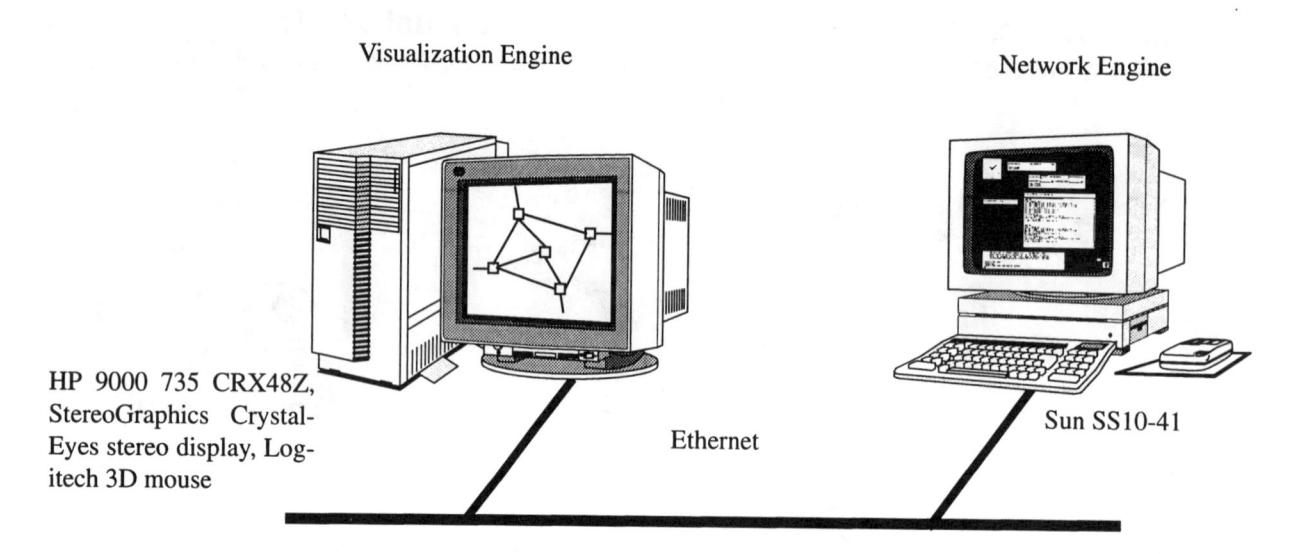

Figure 3: Experimental Test-Bed

tains a set of control and monitoring modules for the network, and a management interface through which a remote entity can observe and interact with the emulated network. The remote entity in this case is the Visualization Engine. Its user can observe the network in 3D and navigate among the physical and logical entities using the 3D mouse. The user may also invoke from a menu any of the management operations provided by the network emulator.

The structure of the software is shown in Figure 4. The lowest layer is the network itself, which for emulation purposes is initially specified by the configuration file. This file is written by the user in a high-level syntax that we have defined and is effectively compiled into a network telebase in the D-plane, during the emulation load phase. The remainder of the emulation component of the software is essentially an implementation of a subset of the IRM. The connection control is a minimal representation of the C-plane that allows connections to be set up between specified hosts with a specified quality-of-service, and deleted. C-plane services can be invoked either through a menu, so that connections are set up and closed individually, or via traffic generators, which are instantiated and generate connections on a continuous basis with a user-defined arrival and lifetime distribution. The resource control provides some M-plane functions to monitor the network and to change routing tables in the D-plane when appropriate.

The top layer in the network emulator is the Network Operations Service (NOS). This provides services to manage the network. We deliberately do not refer to it as the "management" layer since, although it encompasses typical management services that enable reading and writing of network data, the NOS layer also invokes higher-level actions on this data and, potentially, sets of such data. These may relate to any object in the network, from a particular element, such as a call, to the entire network itself, and can be either active or passive. Examples of active operations are "remove node" and "create virtual path", while passive operations include monitoring a specified call or path. This layer can be viewed as providing the language interface through which the network database is manipulated and monitored, and is similar in principle to that described in [8]. Thus the NOS layer directly provides the high-level functions that we feel are appropriate for effective network management. Working in emulation mode allows us to implement these functions without the overhead of lower-level management services such as those employed for CMISE.

In the Visualization Engine, the Network Operations are mapped into the virtual world through the VW Operations Service. This layer defines the relationship between data and actions in the virtual world and those in the network world. The functions in the NOS layer can be called directly since the interface between the two engines is implemented with remote procedure calls. Finally, the highest layer provides the interfaces to the components of the virtual world, through which the user can interact with the network.

3.2 Results

Our current prototype presents the user with several different views of the network being maintained by the emula-

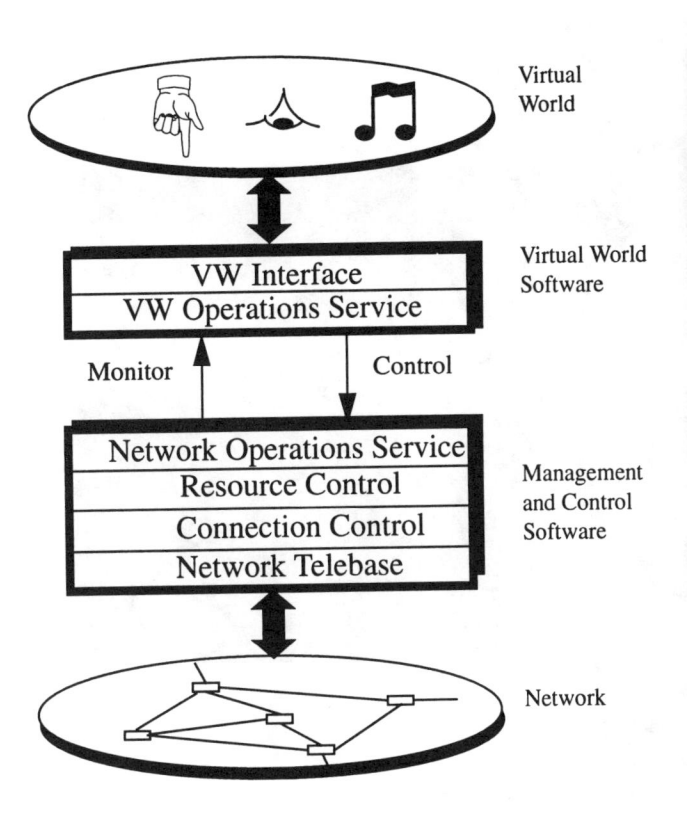

Figure 4: Software Architecture

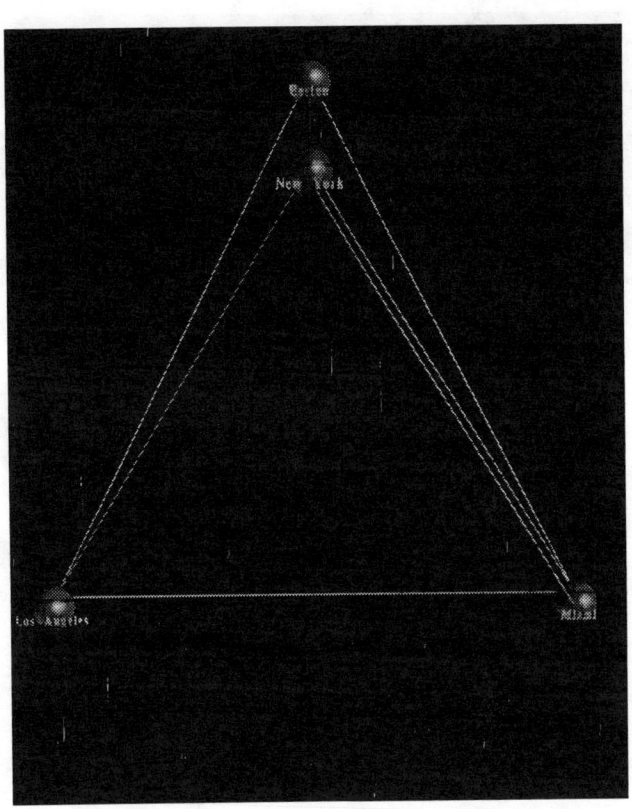

Figure 5: View of Physical Topology

tor. It relies on vendor-supplied software and hardware support for interactive 3D display and manipulation capabilities within a 2D Motif framework.

Figure 5 shows a view of the network's physical topology. Nodes are presented as spheres, links are presented as thin cylinders, and labels are presented as 3D text. The 3D mouse can be used to manipulate the network or camera to obtain a better view. The mouse's 3D position and orientation dynamically determine the position and orientation of the object being controlled. An additional button on the side of the mouse serves as a "clutch" that allows the user to momentarily disengage the 3D mouse from the object to which it is attached [9]. This makes it possible to translate and rotate objects relative to their previous position and orientation. We also provide a conventional Motif control panel to make precise adjustments.

The 3D mouse can be used to select a node or link to be examined in more detail. For example, the user may view the VPs inside a physical link, or may view a complete VP from source to destination.

To inspect the contents of a physical link, we display all VPs associated with a given physical link, as shown in Figure 6. The thin cylindrical link representation of the physi-

cal topology view is replaced with a thick cylindrical link that is sliced open to reveal the VPs inside it. The slicing is computed interactively so that the VPs are always exposed to the user no matter how the camera and network are positioned relative to each other. Each VP's diameter is proportional to its capacity. Several other windows, the contents of which are not shown here, present additional information. For example, a small overview of the entire network is included in a separate window to provide context.

In the complete virtual path display, shown in Figure 7, all nodes on the path are displayed. Additional information is displayed textually, which currently includes the precise virtual path capacity and the current load for each of the traffic classes supported by the network.

4. Research Thrusts

In this section, we briefly outline the way in which we are extending the virtual world user interface and the control and management capabilities, and indicate the areas in which we are conducting research.

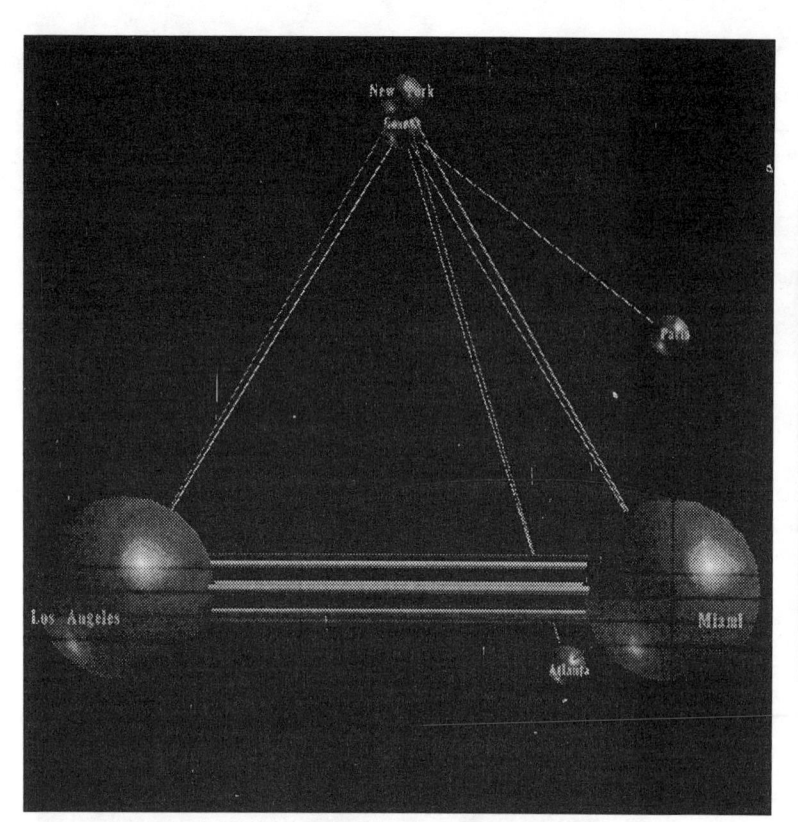

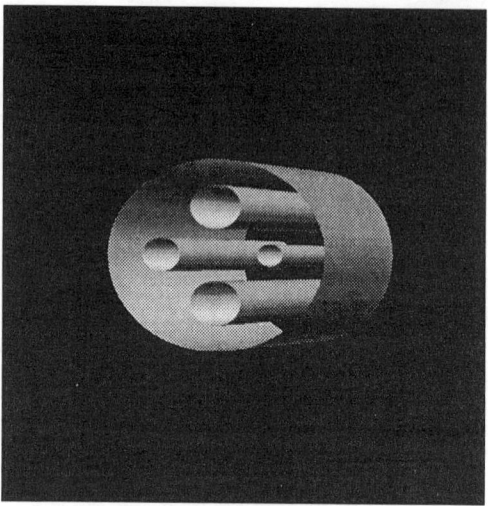

Figure 6: Inspection of Physical Links

Figure 7: View of Logical Topology

4.1 Control and Management

Our immediate plans are to extend the capabilities of the Network Engine so that we can investigate advanced management scenarios, such as rapid fault detection and repair, in the virtual world. As our main interest is to experiment with large systems, we will ultimately be limited by the performance of the emulation. We have already restricted the system to call-level emulation, as it is not possible to emulate cell-level behavior at Gbit/s speeds in the workstation environment we are currently using. Thus, to include cell-level dynamics and to investigate large systems of the type we imagine being deployed in the future, we plan to move the Network Engine into a parallel processing environment. Previously, we have built an emulator on a 32-node transputer machine [10], but even this does not provide the performance we require. We are currently working on an emulator that runs on a KSR supercomputer. The shared-memory architecture of the KSR is suited to an emulation of the IRM as it naturally reflects the logical model of the D-plane as a distributed database.

As previously noted, we are also exploring the implementation of the virtual world on top of the ISO Management Architecture (as in [11]) for the management and control of TeraNet, our gigabit ATM network. This network is limited to three nodes, but the experience of deploying the virtual world on an operational network is valuable in highlighting problems in real applications. This work will also enable us to investigate further the suitability of the OSI architecture and protocols for management of gigabit networks.

Our longer-term research concerns next-generation architectures and protocols for network management. The demands of the virtual world on the management system, in terms of throughput and response time for access to network information, focus this work. For example, we are currently working on the implementation of "grab" and "move" primitives in the management domain for the purpose of allowing a user to pick up a VP and move it from one physical route to another. This has significant implications for the underlying management operations, since a single VP may contain a very large number of calls which have to be re-routed with a minimum of disruption to users service. Thus, the operations provided in the virtual world provide very high-level primitives to the manager. In current management systems such as those using SNMP or CMIP, these would translate into a large number of simpler operations. It is clear that this would be so inefficient that it would be impractical to provide such services. Thus, our general observation is that high-level management operations require high-level primitives in the management service, which can equate directly with operations such as "grab" and "move". The realization of these services requires greater intelligence inside the network so that management agents can communicate on a peer level to carry out the actions required without overloading the management/agent interface. We will be reporting on this research in more detail at a later date.

4.2 Virtual World User Interface

There are two main research thrusts that we are addressing to design an effective virtual world for network management. The first is the development of a set of 3D interaction and visualization techniques that are appropriate for the domain of large networks. The second is the creation of a knowledge-based framework within which these techniques can be deployed. The goal is to customize automatically the information being presented and controlled, so that it meets the user's needs.

We are developing a set of 3D spatial metaphors for visualizing and manipulating different aspects of a network's structure and behavior, building on our previous work on developing virtual worlds for abstract data visualization [12]. Although a physical network has a physical representation, much of what we are interested in representing has a variety of abstract representations that can be mapped to spatial models. For example, the familiar 2D node and arc model of networks has been used in a number of research and commercial network monitoring systems [13]. Projects such as SemNet [14] have explored the utility of presenting semantic networks as 3D graphs through which the viewer can interactively navigate.

A key advantage of 3D graphics over 2D is that it offers an extra spatial dimension. This can be crucial in representing spatial data. For example, a nonplanar 2D graph can be represented in 3D without crossing arcs. Furthermore, the notion of direct manipulation [15], which is so important for 2D graphical interfaces, gains extra power in a virtual world that uses 3D stereo displays and interaction devices. User actions on virtual objects can then be modeled, when appropriate, on the familiar way that we interact with 3D physical objects.

Since we are interested in a network's behavior, rather than just its static topology, we are extending the basic directed-graph model to address behavior over time. One obvious approach is to represent temporal activity as data flows over the network, showing the individual packets. While this makes sense if time is slowed to speeds at which individual data can be viewed, if we run at full emulation speeds (let alone actual net speeds), individual data would not be discernible. In this case, we could instead model data flows as composite entities that represent traffic averaged over some finite temporal window. For example, flows might be visualized as the graphical attributes of the arcs through which they pass: a cylindrical arc's diameter may communicate density, while its color may indicate its data type.

Because of the massive amounts of data involved and the speed with which the simulation will proceed, facilities for viewing and reviewing emulated behavior will be extremely important. We will need the ability to journal significant stretches of network activity, and to run journaled activity at varying speeds, both forward and backward. Given the richness of even a single emulation run, one important issue will be developing ways to present summary visual representations to users that will allow them to get a high-level feel for what happened during a given period of time or in some selected part of the network. Here we anticipate exploring approaches such as "editable graphical histories," originally developed for static 2D user interfaces, which allow users to explore a graphical representation of previous activities [16].

We believe that sonic displays can be used in conjunction with graphical displays to help the user gain a better sense of network activity than can be achieved through purely visual virtual worlds. Information might be redundantly encoded in graphics and sound or different information may be presented in each medium [17]. We have recently acquired a sound processing system that allows sound sources to be positioned in 3D relative to the user [18] and will be incorporating this into our system. Such spatially localized sound could help direct the user's attention to relevant parts of the virtual world. For example, even if the network model surrounds the user, only that part directly within the user's field of view is visible at any point in time. If localized sound were used to encode selected aspects of network activity, the user could be quickly made aware of interesting phenomena that occur outside of their field of view. Visual and audio media could be used together to form a consistent spatial model of network activity.

Methods for eliding unneeded detail are vital for understanding the dynamic behavior of large networks. A variety of techniques may be applicable, including filtering the display to show only selected nodes, arcs, and data; and allowing the user to concentrate on a specific part of the network by selecting an appropriate 3D view. We will also be exploring the use of another approach, called "link suppression", first developed to present understandable maps of the network structure of complex hypermedia documents [19]. It uses hierarchy to group nodes and abstracts out high-level representations of their interconnections.

Finally, we will be building a knowledge-based presentation component, that will build on our ongoing work on the automated design of virtual worlds to explain abstract data [20] and concrete data [21]. Our approach will involve categorizing the visualization techniques that we are developing with regard to their applicability for expressing and controlling different kinds of network behavior. The idea is to build up a set of visualization policies that can be used by a rule-based system that will determine which interaction and visualization techniques to apply and when to apply them to best meet the needs of the user and situation.

5. Conclusions

The technology of virtual worlds is still in its infancy, and is not yet in a state where it could be considered practical and cost-effective for deployment in a real network management environment. However, progress is rapid, and we believe that for many applications 3D graphics environments will supersede the 2D systems that are now in common use. Interactive 3D environments are in many ways ideal for network management and control, as the network manager is faced with a complex system that is inherently multidimensional. Appropriate abstractions in the visualization world, together with advanced navigation capabilities, can assist the manager in coping with this complexity.

This use of virtual worlds is motivating our research into management and control architectures for the future. The complexity of broadband networks demands a more structured approach in this area than has been used in the past. The advanced real-time and multidimensional visualization and interaction capabilities provided by the virtual world place enormous demands on the underlying network structures, and there is a correspondence between the observation, control, and navigational requirements in the virtual world and the requirements of controllability and observability in the network architecture. If we can demonstrate controllability and observability of the network in the virtual world, then we have gone a long way to demonstrating the viability of our management and control structures.

Acknowledgments

Research on this project is supported in part by the Center for Telecommunications Research under NSF Grant ECD-88-11111, NSF Grant CDA-90-24735, and equipment grants from the Hewlett-Packard Company and Ascension Technology. We thank Ari Shamash and Sushil Da Silva for their work on the Logitech tracker process, Brad Paley of Digital Image Design for sharing his tracker support code, Cliff Beshers for his stereo display code, and Mun Choon Chan for his contribution to the network emulator software.

References

[1] A. A. Lazar, "A Real-Time Control, Management and Information Transport Architecture for Broadband Networks", *Proceedings of the 1992 International Zurich Seminar on Digital Communications,* March 1992.

[2] C. Sluman, "A tutorial on OSI management", *Computer Networks and ISDN Systems,* 17 (4&5), 270–278. 1989.

[3] R. Gidron, "TeraNet: a Multi-gigabits per second ATM Network", *Computer Communications,* 15 (3), April 1992.

[4] S. Mazumdar and A.A. Lazar, "Objective-Driven Monitoring", *IEEE Transactions on Data and Knowledge Engineering,* to appear.

[5] S. Mazumdar and A.A. Lazar, "Modeling the Environment and the Interface for Real-Time Monitoring and Control", *IEEE Transactions on Communications,* to appear.

[6] M. Tsuchida, A.A. Lazar, and N.G. Aneroussis, "Structural Representation of Management and Control Information in Broadband Networks", *Proceedings of the International Conference on Communications,* 1019–1024, 1992.

[7] J. Zinky and F. White, "Visualizing Packet Traces", *Computer Communications Review,* 22 (4), 1992.

[8] O. Wolfson, S. Sengupta, and Y. Yemini, "Managing Communication Networks by Monitoring Databases", *IEEE Transactions on Software Engineering,* 17 (9), 944–953, 1991.

[9] C. Ware and D. Jessome, "Using the Bat: A Six Dimensional Mouse for Object Placement", *Proc. Graphics Interface '88,* Edmonton, June, 1988, 119–124 (Palo Alto: Morgan Kaufmann, 1988).

[10] N.G. Aneroussis, A.A. Lazar, and M. Tsuchida, "A Multiprocessor Architecture for Real-Time Emulation of Management and Control of Broadband Networks", *Proceedings of the. IEEE 1992 Network Operations and Management Symposium,* Memphis, TN, April 6–9, 1992.

[11] A.A. Lazar, J. Biswas, K. Fairchild and H. Ng, "Exploiting Virtual Reality for Network Management", *Proceedings of the International Conference on Communications,* Singapore, November 16–20, 1992.

[12] S. Feiner and C. Beshers, "Worlds within worlds: Metaphors for Exploring n-dimensional Virtual Worlds". *Proceedings UIST '90 (ACM Symposium on User Interface Software and Technology),* Snowbird UT, 76–83, 1990.

[13] A. Dupuy, S. Sengupta, O. Wolfson, and Y. Yemini, "NETMATE: A Network Management Environment", *IEEE Network,* 5 (2), 1991.

[14] K. Fairchild, S. Poltrock, and G. Furnas, "SemNet: Three-Dimensional Graphic Representations of Large Knowledge Bases", in R. Guindon (ed.), Cognitive Science and its Applications for Human Computer Interaction, Hillsdale, NJ: Lawrence Erlbaum, 1988, 201–233.

[15] B. Shneiderman, "Direct Manipulation: A Step Beyond Programming Languages", *IEEE Computer,* 16 (8), 57-69, 1983.

[16] D. Kurlander and S. Feiner, "A Visual Language for Browsing, Undoing, and Redoing Graphical Interface Commands", in Chang, S. (ed.), Visual Languages and Visual Programming, Plenum Press, New York, 1990, 257–275.

[17] S. Smith, R. Bergeron, and G. Grinstein, "Stereophonic and Surface Sound Generation for Exploratory Data Analysis", *Proceedings of CHI '90,* Seattle WA, ACM Press, 1990, 125–132.

[18] E. Wenzel and S. Foster, "Real Time Digital Synthesis of Virtual Acoustic Environments", *Proceedings of the 1990 Symposium on Interactive 3D Graphics,* Snowbird UT, 1990, 139–140.

[19] S. Feiner, "Seeing the Forest for the Trees: Hierarchical Display of Hypertext Structure", *Proceedings of COIS '88 (ACM SIGOIS Conf. on Office Information Systems),* Palo Alto CA, 1988, 205–212.

[20] C. Beshers and S. Feiner, "Rule-Based Design of Virtual Worlds for Interactive Multivariate Visualization", *IEEE Computer Graphics and Applications,* 13 (4), July 1993.

[21] S. Feiner, B. MacIntyre, and D. Seligmann, "Knowledge-Based Augmented Reality", *Communications of the ACM,* 36 (7), July 1993.

Resource Management for Distributed Parallel Systems

B. Clifford Neuman   Santosh Rao

Information Sciences Institute
University of Southern California

Abstract

Multiprocessor systems should exist in the the larger context of distributed systems, allowing multiprocessor resources to be shared by those that need them. Unfortunately, typical multiprocessor resource management techniques do not scale to large networks. The Prospero Resource Manager (PRM) is a scalable resource allocation system that supports the allocation of processing resources in large networks and multiprocessor systems.

To manage resources in such distributed parallel systems, PRM employs three types of managers: system managers, job managers, and node managers. There exist multiple independent instances of each type of manager, reducing bottlenecks. The complexity of each manager is further reduced because each is designed to utilize information at an appropriate level of abstraction.

1 Introduction

Conventional techniques for managing resources in parallel systems perform poorly in large distributed systems. We believe that multiprocessor systems should exist in the broader context of distributed systems, allowing them to be shared by those that need them. To manage resources in distributed parallel systems, we have developed prototype resource management tools that manage resources at two levels: allocating system resources to jobs as needed (a job is a collection of tasks working together), and separately managing the resources assigned to each job.

This paper describes the model and implementation of these tools which were developed for use by the Prospero operating system, under development at the University of Southern California's Information Sciences Institute. The Prospero Resource Manager (PRM) presents a uniform and scalable model for scheduling tasks in parallel and distributed systems. PRM provides the mechanisms through which nodes on multiprocessors can be allocated to jobs running within an extremely large distributed system.

It is our belief that the common approach of using a single resource manager to manage all resources in a large system is not practical. As the system to be managed grows, a single resource manager becomes a bottleneck. Even within large local multiprocessor systems the number of resources to be managed can adversely affect performance. As a distributed system scales geographically and administratively, additional problems arise.

PRM addresses these problem by using multiple resource managers, each controlling a subset of the resources in the system, independent of other managers of the same type. The functions of resource management are distributed across three types of managers: system managers, job managers, and node managers. The complexity of these management roles is reduced because each is designed to utilize information at an appropriate level of abstraction.

While the development of PRM was motivated by the desire to support parallel computing across organizations in a distributed system, the same techniques can improve the scalability of scheduling mechanisms within independent tightly coupled multiprocessor systems. The abstractions provided also naturally suggest extensions that support fault-tolerant and real-time applications and debugging and performance tuning for parallel programs.

Throughout this paper we use the term *node* to denote a processing element in a multiprocessor system, or a workstation or other computer whose resources are made available for running jobs. A *job* consists of a set of communicating tasks, running on the nodes allocated to the job. A *task* consists of one or more threads of control through an application and the address space in which they run.

2 Contemporary approaches

Figure 1 shows the functions involved in the execution of a parallel application in a distributed environment. In the first step (1), the application is compiled and installed and information about resource require-

5	Program Execution	
4	Program Loading	Comm Libraries
3	Task to Processor Mapping	
2	**Processor Selection/Allocation**	
1	Initial Configuration	

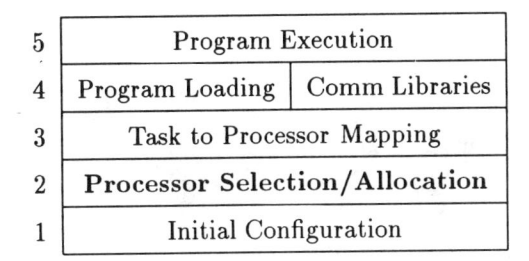

Figure 1: Support for distributed execution

ments and available resources are specified by the user or programmer. This information is used in (2) to select and allocate nodes on which the program will run. The tasks are mapped to the allocated nodes in (3) and the executable modules (the tasks) are loaded onto the appropriate nodes in (4). The execution of the program (5) depends on run-time communication libraries (also at 4) which in turn use information about the mapping of tasks to nodes (3).

Locus [10], NEST [1], Sprite [5] and V [13] support processor allocation, and remote program loading and execution (2,4,5) to harness the computing power of lightly loaded nodes. They primarily support sequential applications where task-to-task communication is not required. A critical issue for processor allocation in these systems is the maintenance of the database of available nodes. In Locus the target node for remote execution is selected from a list of nodes maintained in the environment of the initiating process. This approach is inflexible because the nodes available for remote execution do not change with changing load.

In NEST [1], idle machines advertise their availability, providing a dynamically changing set of available nodes; each user's workstation maintains the list of servers available for remote execution. Locus and NEST both require the application to maintain information about every possible target node, limiting the size of the pool from which nodes can be drawn. Additionally, resource allocation decisions in these systems are made locally by the application without the benefit of a high level view across jobs. This causes problems when applications run simultaneously.

Sprite [5] uses a shared file as a centralized database to track available nodes. Clients select idle nodes from this file, marking the entry to flag its use. While this approach appears simple, it requires a solution to problems related to shared writable files, including locking, synchronization and consistency. Fault-tolerance is also poor since failure of the file server on which the shared file resides disables the allocation mechanism completely. This approach does not scale beyond a few tens of nodes.

Theimer and Lantz experimented with two approaches for processor allocation in V [13]. In a centralized approach a central server selects the least loaded node from a pool of free nodes and allocates it. Nodes proclaim their availability based on the relationship of the local load to a cutoff broadcast periodically by the server. This approach has limited scalability and poor fault tolerance since the central server is a critical resource. In the distributed approach a client multicasts a query to a group of candidate machines selecting the responder with the lowest load. This approach suffers from excessive network traffic and was found to perform worse than the central server approach.

The UCLA Benevolent Bandit Laboratory (BBL) [6] provides an environment for running parallel applications on a network of personal computers. Like the other systems discussed, BBL provides processor allocation, and remote program loading and execution (2,3,4,5), incorporating the notion of a user-process manager separate from a systemwide resource manager. While this is an important step towards scalable resource management techniques, a single resource manager will be unable to handle all allocation requests for a large systems.

Parallel Virtual Machine (PVM) [12] and NetExpress [9] allow users to run parallel applications on a collection of workstations. In the initial configuration phase, users specify a list of nodes on which they have started daemon processes. Based on this configuration, PVM and NetExpress map a job's tasks to nodes, load and execute the tasks, and support communication between tasks (3,4,5). There is no support for high-level resource allocation functions (2) that assign nodes to jobs with the goal of efficient system utilization. All nodes specified by the user are available to the job whether or not they are already in use by other jobs.

Efficient management of a pool of processors becomes very important when the system scales to large numbers of nodes, spanning multiple sites. The emphasis of the Prospero Resource Manager is the allocation of nodes across and within jobs (2). The job manager eliminates the need for users to enumerate all hosts on which their applications might run, while the system manager efficiently manages the system's resources. While PRM also supports task mapping, program loading, and execution (3,4,5), it is the allocation function (2) that distinguishes it from PVM and NetExpress. We encourage the integration of the PRM allocation methods with both packages.

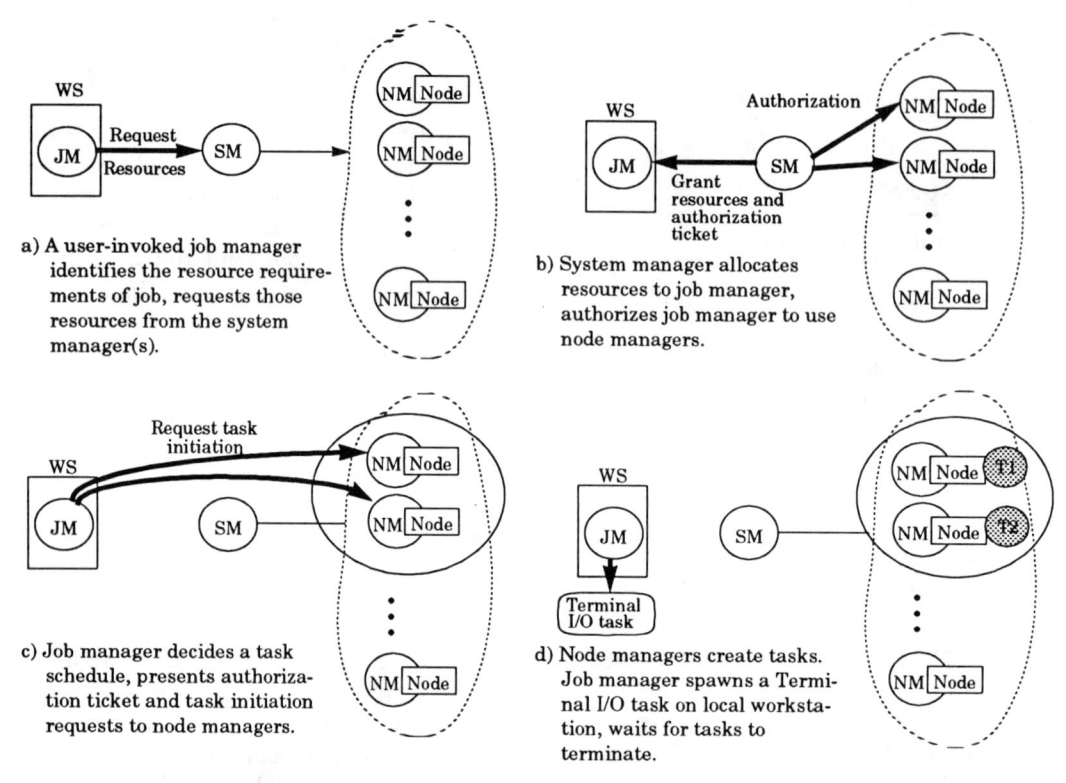

Figure 2: Running a job with PRM

3 Scalable resource management

Users have difficulty dealing with extremely large systems because, although only a small subset of the available resources are needed, it is difficult to identify the resources that are of interest among the clutter of those that are not. Today's users are able to cope because only a tiny portion of the world's resources are available to them. Managing the world's resources is a daunting task, but the problem is simplified when it is reduced to managing only a subset of the resources.

We believe it should be possible to organize *virtual systems* in which resources of interest are readily accessible, and those of less interest are hidden from view. The organization of such systems should be based on the conceptual relationship between resources and the mapping to physical locations should be hidden from the user. These concepts form the basis of the Virtual System Model, a new model for organizing large distributed systems [8].

To apply the concepts of the Virtual System Model to the allocation of resources in large systems, we have chosen to divide the functions of resource management across three types of managers: the system manager, the job manager, and the node manager. The system manager controls a collection of physical resources, allocating them to jobs when requested. The job manager is responsible for requesting the resources needed by a job, and once allocated, assigning them to the individual tasks in the job. The node manager runs on each processor in the system, loading and executing tasks when authorized by the system manager and requested by the job manager. Each manager makes scheduling decisions at a different level of abstraction, some concerned with the high level performance of the system, and others concentrating on particular jobs.

3.1 The system manager

The full set of resources that exist in a system will be managed by a set of system managers. For example, one or more system managers might manage the nodes in a parallel computer, or the resources local to a particular site. System managers allocate their resources across jobs as needed. We do not believe that it is possible to build a single system manager to manage all resources in a large system. As the system to be managed grows, a single system manager would become a bottleneck. To avoid this problem, our system supports multiple system managers, each responsible for a collection of resources. For example, one system manager can be responsible for the processors on a multiprocessor system and when necessary for performance or other reasons, multiple system managers may exist, each controlling a disjoint subset of the processors on the multiprocessor. An independent system manager might manage the resources available on one or more workstations.

The system manager is a hierarchical concept. Several sets of resources may be managed by different system managers, with a higher level system manager responsible for the entire collection. The control of resources could then be transferred from one system manager to another as directed by a higher level manager.

The system manager keeps track of the resources for which it is responsible, maintaining information about the characteristics of each resource, whether it is currently available, and if assigned, the job to which it is assigned. The system manager responds to status updates from node managers and resource requests from job managers. Status updates provide information needed to make allocation decisions including availability and load information. Resource requests identify the resources required by a job, their characteristics, as well as connectivity constraints, but only in well defined ways. It is possible to extend the system manager to accept messages from higher level managers (or other entities) adding or removing resources from its control.

When a resource request is received from a job manager, the system manager determines whether suitable resources are available as defined by the characteristics specified in the request. If so, the system manager assigns them to the job, notifies the node managers responsible for each resource that the resource has been assigned to a specific job manager, and informs the job manager of the resources that have been assigned. If the requested resources are not available the system manager can, at the job managers option (and subject to the scheduling policy of the system manager), assign a subset of the requested resources and/or reserve the resources for assignment when they become available.

3.2 The job manager

Although multiple system managers are necessary for scalability, the application needs a single point of contact for requesting resources. In our system, this point of contact is the job manager. The job manager acts as an agent for the tasks in a job, providing a single entity from which the tasks will request resources. In this capacity the job manager provides the abstraction of a virtual system to a job, managing the resources that have been allocated to a job by the system managers responsible for each resource. Although it is possible for a job to have more than one job manager, in most cases only one exists.

The job manager is part of a job and is aware of the specific requirements and communication patterns of the tasks it manages. As such, the job manager is better able than the system manager to allocate resources to the individual tasks within a job. This is the same argument used in favor of user-level thread management on shared-memory multiprocessors [2]. In fact, we allow the job manager to be written by the application programmer if specific functionality is required, though we do not expect this to be a common practice.

We plan to eventually provide alternative job managers to support fault-tolerant and real-time applications. Such job managers would add additional requirements to the resources requested from system managers, and might assign individual tasks to multiple nodes. Similarly, a job manager is planned that will collect information needed for debugging and performance tuning. The programmer would then be able to select job managers tailored to the needs of the application or the phase of program development; when an application is ready for production use, a different job manager could be substituted.

At the time a job is initiated, the job manager identifies the job's resource requirements. Using the Prospero Directory Service [7], if available, or a configuration file otherwise, it locates system managers with jurisdiction over suitable resources and sends allocation requests. If the system managers respond affirmatively, the job manager allocates the resources to the tasks in the job, contacting the node manager for each resource to initiate the loading of programs onto the appropriate processors. If the system manager refuses the allocation request, the job manager will try to identify alternate resources from other system managers. If necessary, the job manager will additionally create tasks to handle I/O to the terminal or to files on the local system.

Once the job has been initiated on the assigned nodes, the job manager monitors the execution of the program. During program execution the job manager responds to requests from the job's tasks for additional resources, reallocating them from other tasks or requesting additional resources from suitable system managers. In this phase the job manager also maintains information about the mapping of logical task identifiers to node identifiers, for use by the communication library.

3.3 The node manager

The third component of our resource management suite is the node manager. A node manager runs on each processor in the system, eventually as part of the kernel but in the current implementation as a user-level process. The node manager accepts messages from the system manager identifying the job managers that will load and execute programs. When requested by an authorized job manager, the node manager loads and executes a program. The node manager notifies the job manager about events such as the termination and failure of tasks. The node manager also keeps the system manager informed about the availability of the node for assignment. The node manager caches information needed to direct messages for other tasks to the node on which the task runs.

3.4 Application invocation

Each program that executes under PRM has associated with it information about the virtual system on which it will run. This information is stored either in a configuration file or as attributes of the program in the Prospero Directory Service [7]. When a program is invoked, a new job manager is created and the job manager finds a suitable processor or set of processors by contacting system managers identified by the virtual system associated with the program.

Figure 2 shows the steps involved in running an application using PRM. Our goal is for users to invoke programs as if they were local to a workstation. When the program is invoked, a job manager is automatically started on the workstation[1]. The job manager determines the resource requirements of the job and sends requests to one or more system managers. If the requested resources are available the system manager informs the node manager responsible for each resource that the resource has been assigned to a particular job manager and it returns a list of the assigned resources to the job manager. The job manager further allocates the assigned resources to the job's tasks then contacts the node manager for each resource to invoke the application. Upon receipt of a request from the authorized job manager, each node manager loads the application task.

During job execution, the job manager responds to requests from the job's tasks for additional resources (additional processors for example) and to preemption and migration requests from the system managers responsible for the resources in use and, if necessary, attempts to obtain additional resources from other system managers. The job manager acts as an agent for

[1] Though in some cases, it might migrate to another node.

a) User invokes application program on his workstation.

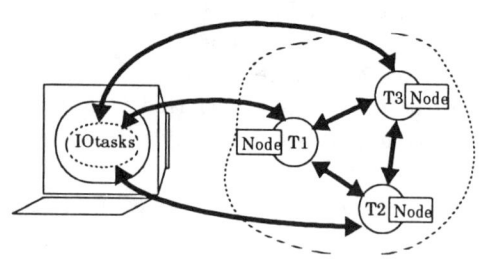

b) A set of tasks are created. Tasks execute the program, communicate with each other and perform terminal I/O.

Figure 3: Input/Output using PRM

the user, hiding the details of parallel execution; the user's environment and shell are maintained on the workstation and the job manager decides where each command is to execute, hiding the details from the user for whom local sequential execution and parallel execution appear identical.

3.5 Discussion

By separating the job and system manager, the system manager becomes much simpler. The system manager is concerned only with the allocation of resources between jobs, eliminating application specific functionality. The job manager is part of a job, and has more information about the requirements and communication patterns for the tasks it manages. Thus, the job manager is in a better position to allocate resources to tasks once resources have been allocated to the job. Because the job manager is part of the job, it can be customized or even rewritten if application specific functionality is required.

4 Implementation and performance

The current implementation of the Prospero Resource Manager runs on a collection of Sun3, Sparc, and HP9000/700 workstations, connected by a local or wide-area network. Even though PRM's emphasis is on resource allocation, we provide an application programming interface (in the form of macros and libraries) that provide the user with a programming and execution environment similar to that on a multicomputer. Heterogeneous execution environments are supported; the tasks in a job may execute on different processor types, and the set of nodes executing a job need not share a common filesystem. In the latter case PRM handles program loading and I/O to shared files. This is shown in figure 3.

Msg len (bytes)	4	64	1024	4096	8192
Latency (msec)	4.4	4.6	5.9	15.7	28.5

Table 1: Effect of message length on latency

Application programs are based on message-passing and are coded in C. A library is provided with PRM for sending and receiving tagged messages, broadcasting, and global synchronization. In designing this library, a layered approach has been used to facilitate easy integration with low-level communication protocols. In the present implementation, these library functions use an Asynchronous Reliable Delivery Protocol (ARDP) that transmits and receives sequenced packets over the Internet using UDP. We are currently implementing a version of the communication library layered on top of the Mach *port* mechanism [4]. The global synchronization and reduction primitives rely on centrally maintained state information. To the extent possible, we plan to develop distributed implementations of these primitives, perhaps building on the primitives provided by ISIS [3].

PRM's transparent message routing mechanism frees the programmer from having to explicitly keep track of task to node mappings. At the application level, messages are addressed using *task-identifiers* (*tids*), which are translated to an internet-address/port pair by the communication library. The node manager assists tasks in this translation using a mapping table furnished by the job manager. Such translations are then cached in the local address space of the task to reduce address translation overhead for subsequent communication with the same task.

4.1 Running jobs under PRM

Multiple users may share a common PRM environment. Once setup, system and node managers run as server processes. The system manager maintains the *availability status* for each node, and allocates available nodes to jobs when requests are received. Depending on options specified at setup, a node manager may make its processor unconditionally available for running jobs, or available only within specified time windows, or when no user is logged onto the workstation (or a combination of the latter two options). Node managers notify their system manager of any changes in node availability.

A user initiates a job by invoking a job manager process on the workstation, specifying a configuration file from which resource requirements of the job are to be read. Typically, this file contains the number of nodes required to run the job, the number and lo-

Number	Message Length				
of tasks	4	64	1024	4096	8192
4	33.3	34.6	37.8	181.8	342.9
8	68.4	70.0	83.7	347.3	560.6

Table 2: Latencies for broadcast operation (msec)

cation of I/O tasks, the path names for executable files and the host names of one or more system managers that can potentially satisfy the resource requirements. The current implementation requires the user to write a configuration file for the job. In a future release, static resource requirements will be generated by a compiler (possibly with some help from the programmer) and stored as file attributes. At run time, the user may override static specifications and specify runtime requirements as command line arguments to the job manager.

Terminal and file I/O are handled by two special tasks created with every job. The job manager schedules these I/O tasks on nodes with local I/O devices. For example, an I/O task may run on a file-server, performing file-I/O on behalf of the tasks. The terminal I/O task supports interactive execution. It is analogous to the host task in the host-node model of execution. Users can customize this task for job initialization functions, such as prompting the user for interactive input and distributing this input to the appropriate tasks.

4.2 Performance

Table 1 shows the measured average latencies for synchronous *send* operations as a function of message size. Experiments were conducted with a pair of tasks running on two Sun 4/60 workstations. After an initial message to obtain the internet-address and port of the destination from the node manager, the sender executed a loop, repeatedly sending messages to the receiver, which sent back an acknowledgment. On the sender, the total time spent in the loop was measured using the `gettimeofday()` system call. The increase in latency for messages up to 1K bytes is due primarily to variations in the overhead imposed by the ARDP library and Unix system calls. Longer messages are split into 1 K byte chunks and require the processing of additional packets. We are improving our code to reduce the overhead imposed by the ARDP library.

Table 2 shows latencies for broadcast operations as a function of message length and number of tasks. Broadcast is implemented in two phases. Data is first transmitted sequentially but asynchronously to all recipients using *send* operations. A second series of sends provides synchronization, assuring recipients that all other recipients have received the data. Broadcast latencies are of the order of $2n$ times the latency of a *send* operation were n is the number of recipients.

We are also testing our system using real scientific applications. The *Ocean* program from the SPLASH benchmark suite from Stanford University [11] studies the role of eddies and boundary currents in influencing large-scale ocean movements by solving a set of partial-differential equations. We started with a message-passing version of Ocean available for the Connection Machine (CM-5). To port this program to the PRM platform, we wrote a set of macros and routines to implement the CMMD library functions [14] using equivalent calls from our own library. The host program from the CM-5 version was incorporated into the terminal I/O task and handles interactive input. We are also using PRM to develop a simulator for large networks of neurons.

5 Future directions

The current implementation demonstrates only a few of the benefits of our resource management model. The greatest benefit of the model is its flexibility. The prototype provides a framework within which we can try experimental solutions to interesting problems, and upon which interesting tools may be built.

Among our planned experiments are the use of interchangeable scheduling policies by the system manager. Because our model supports multiple system managers, multiple scheduling policies can be applied simultaneously to disjoint sets of resources. We also plan to explore options for hierarchical configuration and dynamic reconfiguration of the nodes for which a system manager is responsible.

We plan to extend the job manager to make use of information such as task memory and I/O requirements, and intertask communication graphs to find an optimal assignment of tasks to nodes. We also plan to add support for preemptive scheduling across tasks when insufficient processing resources are available for the job. As discussed in section 3, we plan to develop special job managers to support fault-tolerant and real-time applications, debugging, and performance tuning.

We must also extend the node manager to support suspension of tasks and to allow the job manager to initiate non-interfering operations on the resources of the suspended tasks that it manages. In particular this will allow the migration of a task to an alternate node. The role of the node manager in translating task identifiers to host addresses would then include invalidation of stale translations cached by the tasks.

Our communications primitives are still quite rough. We intend to fine tune the current mechanisms, and where communication between nodes is possible using high-performance mechanisms specific to the host system (*e.g.*, within a single multiprocessor) we will use those mechanisms. We will also support execution of user programs originally developed for other platforms by linking them with the appropriate set of communication libraries. The macros for CMMD library calls in the Ocean program already represent a step in this direction.

I/O to files is still a limiting factor for many applications. This is especially troublesome when the processors on which an application runs are separated geographically from the disk on which a file is stored. The file I/O task plays an important role, supporting read and write operations to files on computers that do not export their file system. We are extending this protocol to support file caching.

Finally, with the ability to run applications on multiprocessor systems across wide-area networks, security will become a critical problem. It is unlikely that sites would make their resources available to others if there are no methods for protection. Security mechanisms are needed to control access to remote nodes, to allow remote tasks to securely retrieve data that might be stored across a wide-area network, and to account for the use of processing resources. We plan to incorporate further security mechanisms into the software we develop, concentrating initially on authentication and authorization mechanisms to be applied when a request is received by the system and node managers.

6 Conclusions

The growth of a distributed system brings with it increased complexity for the management of available resources. While it is possible to manage resources in different parts of the system separately, such an approach makes life difficult for the users and programmers who must interact with more than one entity to obtain the resources needed by an application. Unfortunately, centralized management techniques for parallel systems are not suitable for large distributed systems either.

The Prospero Resource Manager provides a solution between the two extremes. An individual manager controls a subset of the resources in the system independent of other managers of the same type. The system manager controls resources that are physically or administratively related. The job manager controls resources that are logically related, *i.e.* those resources needed by a particular job. When resources are needed, an application requests resources from its job manager which in turn requests the resources from one or more suitable system managers. The resources obtained are then reallocated across the tasks in the job. In this capacity the job manager acts as an agent for the user, presenting the abstraction of a virtual system.

The current prototype demonstrates the usefulness of the model and provides a framework within which we can experiment with different approaches and upon which interesting tools may be built. Section 5 highlighted the flexibility of the model. The true test of the model will be the extent to which it is employed in future systems.

Acknowledgments

Ed Lazowska, John Zahorjan, and Hank Levy contributed to discussions about the Virtual System Model. The initial idea of separate job and system managers for scheduling tasks on a multiprocessor system was proposed by Stockton Gaines and Dennis Hollingworth. Rafael Saavedra provided code for the CM-5 version of Ocean and also guided the implementation of the communication library. Bradford Clark, Ali Erdem and Ronald Wood implemented some of the functions in the communication library as part of a class project at USC. Celeste Anderson, Steven Augart, Gennady Medvinsky, Rafael Saavedra, and Stuart Stubblebine commented on drafts of this paper.

References

[1] R. Agrawal and A. K. Ezzat. Processor sharing in NEST: A network of computer workstations. In *Proceedings of the first International Conference on Computer Workstations*, pages 198–208. November 1985.

[2] Thomas E. Anderson, Brian N. Bershad, Edward D. Lazowska, and Henry M. Levy. Scheduler activations: Effective kernel support for the user-level management of parallelism. *ACM Transactions on Computer Systems*, 10(1):53–79, February 1992.

[3] Kenneth P. Birman and Thomas A. Joseph. Exploiting virtual synchrony in distributed systems. In *Proceedings of the 11th ACM Symposium on Operating Systems Principles*, pages 123–138, November 1987.

[4] David L. Black, David B. Golub, Daniel P. Julin, Richard F. Rashid, Richard P. Draves, Randall W. Dean, Alessandro Forin, Joseph Barrera, Hideyuki Tokuda, Gerald Malan, and David Bohman. Microkernel operating system architecture and Mach. In *Proceedings of the USENIX Workshop on Microkernels and Other Kernel Architectures*, pages 11–30, April 1992.

[5] F. Douglis and J. Ousterhout. Transparent process migration for personal workstations. Technical Report UCB/CSD 89/540, Computer Science Division, University of California, Berkeley CA 94720, November 1989.

[6] R. E. Felderman, E. M. Schooler, and L. Kleinrock. The Benevolent Bandit Laboratory: A testbed for distributed algorithms. *IEEE Journal on Selected Areas in Communications*, 7(2):303–311, February 1989.

[7] B. Clifford Neuman. The Prospero File System: A global file system based on the Virtual System Model. *Computing Systems*, 5(4), Fall 1992.

[8] B. Clifford Neuman. *The Virtual System Model: A Scalable Approach to Organizing Large Systems*. PhD thesis, University of Washington, June 1992.

[9] ParaSoft Corporation, Pasadena, CA 91107. *NetExpress 3.2 Introductory Guide*, 1992.

[10] G. Popek and B. Walker, editors. *The Locus Distributed System Architecture*. M.I.T. Press, Cambridge, Massachusetts, 1985.

[11] J. P. Singh and J. L. Hennessey. Finding and exploiting parallelism in an ocean simulation program. *Journal of Parallel and Distributed Computing*, 15(1), May 1992.

[12] V. S. Sunderam. PVM: A framework for parallel distributed computing. Technical Report TM-11375, Oak Ridge National Laboratory, 1991.

[13] M. A. Theimer and K. A. Lantz. Finding idle machines in a workstation-based distributed system. *IEEE Trans. Software Engineering*, 15(11):1444–1458, November 1989.

[14] Thinking Machines Corporation, Cambridge, MA. *CMMD Reference Manual*, Oct. 1991.

This research was supported in part by the Advanced Research Projects Agency under NASA Cooperative Agreement NCC-2-539. The views and conclusions contained in this paper are those of the authors and should not be interpreted as representing the official policies, either expressed or implied, of ARPA or NASA. To obtain the software described in this paper, send mail to info-prospero@isi.edu asking for information about the Prospero Resource Manager. The authors may be reached at USC/ISI, 4676 Admiralty Way, Marina del Rey, CA 90292-6695, USA. Telephone +1 (310) 822-1511, email bcn@isi.edu, srao@isi.edu.

SESSION 8B:
Performance Evaluation

Arun Somani, Chair

Analytical Performance Evaluation of Data Replication Based Shared Memory Model

Siniša Srbljić and Leo Budin

University of Zagreb, Faculty of Electrical Engineering
Avenija Vukovar 39, 41000 Zagreb, Croatia

Abstract

The proposed distributed shared memory model is based on a data replication scheme that provides an environment for a collection of processes that interact to solve a parallel programming problem. In the implementation of the scheme we suppose that the replicas of the shared data are present at each node and that an appropriate coherence protocol for maintaining the consistency among the replicas is applied. The performance of the distributed computation is very sensitive to the data-access behavior of the application and to the applied coherence protocol. Communication cost is regarded as an appropriate performance measure. Therefore, we first introduce a model characterizing the computation behavior with five workload parameters. Second, we formally describe the coherence protocols as cooperating state machines in order to evaluate their communication costs as functions of workload parameters.

1: Introduction

In a distributed shared memory environment the inherently present message passing mechanism together with underlying hardware and software is hidden from the application [1], [2], but they heavily influence the performance of the distributed computation. Therefore, to improve the performance of such systems, appropriate models for the performance analysis and prediction are needed. The models have to take into consideration enough subtle details, in order to accomplish eventual fine tuning of the computation behavior.

In this paper we describe a methodology for performance evaluation of distributed shared memory system based on data replication. In this scheme data are replicated at every node of the distributed system and suitable coherence protocols for maintaining the consistency among replica are applied. A substantial number of data replication coherence protocols have been designed and analyzed [3]-[5]. We analyze eight protocols obtained by modification of seven well-known decentralized cache coherence protocols designed for the bus-based multiprocessors (Write-Once, Write-Through, Synapse, Illinois, Berkeley, Dragon, and Firefly [6], [7]). The Write-Through protocol is modified into two distributed versions. Message passing is the only used mechanism in these modified protocols. For the sake of simplicity, in this paper we analyze in details the Write-Through protocol. The detailed description of all the protocols is given in [8], [9].

In Section 2 we describe the structure of the distributed system. In order to simplify the presentation we concentrate only on the features needed for the application of the Write-Through coherence protocol. The formal model of a coherence protocol based on the Mealy state-machine is given in Section 3. In section 4 we first define the workload parameters and develop an analytic method for performance evaluation. Performance is expressed as steady-state average communication cost per *read* and *write* operation. Finally, in Section 5, the eight modified coherence protocols are mutually compared and some simulation results are discussed.

2: The distributed system model

In this section, we present the essential features of the distributed system under consideration. We describe the distributed system structure, the structure of nodes in the model, and the mechanism of the shared memory operation execution. The description is restricted to the Write-Through protocol to simplify the discussion, but can be easily modified for other coherence protocols.

In the system there is a set of $N+1$ nodes. Each node has a local memory and a processing element. We assume fault free communication between nodes and the implementation of the message passing mechanism through channels that behave like first-in/first-out queues. Thus, every message sent is delivered and not corrupted. We suppose that in each node only one *application process* accesses the memory.

The global address space is decomposed into M disjoint shared data blocks that can be identified by unique index j ($j=1,...,M$). A data block is collection of data that does not necessarily have to be stored consecutively in memory. For the sake of simplicity, we deal with the full-replication scheme, i.e., we assume that the shared data blocks are replicated at each node. Every copy of a data block at each node is controlled by its *protocol process*. The *application process* at one of the nodes can access an arbitrary data block j issuing a *read* or *write* request to the corresponding local *protocol process*. Further on, we concentrate our analysis on only one data block, say jth, and only on the *protocol processes* associated with the copies of that particular data block.

The *protocol processes* are implemented as *Mealy state machines*, as described in Section 3, that produce sequences of atomic *actions* for the fulfillment of a particular request. Some requests are executed locally and produce only one action. Others have to be executed network wide producing sequences of actions in more then one node. In such *distributed operations*, *protocol processes* communicate by message passing hidden to the *application processes*.

The *protocol processes* associated with the copies of the same data block in all nodes, except one of them which we distinguish by index $N+1$, are identical. These *protocol processes* have two input queues: a *local queue*, where the requests from a local *application process* are enqueued, and a *distributed queue* for enqueuing the messages from other *protocol processes*. The *protocol process* at node $N+1$ has only a *distributed queue*, where both the requests from its local *application process* and messages sent from other nodes are enqueued. The Mealy machine at this node is also slightly different from the Mealy machines in other nodes with indices $i=1,...,N$.

Protocol process at node $N+1$ is responsible for global sequential filtering of concurrent distributed operations and is therefore named a *sequencer*. The other *protocol processes* are later on referred to as *clients* [1]. Since we are analyzing the *protocol processes* associated with the copies of only one data block, the node whose *protocol process* is the *sequencer* may also be called the *sequencer*. Analogously, those nodes whose *protocol processes* are *clients* may also be referred to as *clients*. It will be clear from the context whether we are talking about the *sequencer* and the *clients* as *protocol processes* or as nodes. The brief description of interactions between *clients* and the *sequencer* is as follows:

- The *sequencer* can communicate with all the *clients*, but *clients* communicate only with the *sequencer*, and not among themselves.
- The *application process* in the *sequencer* starts the execution of the *read* or *write* operation by sending a request message into its *distributed queue*. The *application process* in one of the *clients* initiates the execution of the operations by putting the request message into the *local queue* of its *protocol process*. This message starts the execution of the first action of the operation. If the operation is executed locally, then this action is the only one that is executed.
- If one of the *clients* initiates the execution of a distributed operation, then the first action of the *protocol process* in the *client* sends a permission-asking message into the *distributed queue* of the *sequencer*. The *sequencer's distributed queue* sequences the *clients' distributed* operations together with its own operations. The actions initiated from the *sequencer's distributed queue* may send invalidation or grant messages into the *distributed queues* of the *clients*. In that case, the executions of the distributed operations terminate in the *clients* by the execution of the actions initiated from their *distributed queues*.
- When the execution of the *client's* distributed operation requires a response from the *sequencer*, the pending requests in the *local queue* are temporarily disabled until the response from the *sequencer* is obtained. Therefore, the first action of a distributed operation initiated from the *local queue* disables further requests from the same queue, whereas an action initiated by the response message from *client's distributed queue* enables further requests.

To keep the copies of the same shared data block consistent, we globally sequence the actions of the different operations. Three assumed features which preserve the sequence order of the operations started from one of the nodes, and insure the same sequence of the action executions of the different operations at all nodes are: first in/first out communication channels, first in/first out queues and disable/enable mechanisms associated with *local queues*.

3: The formal model of a data replication coherence protocol

To enable detailed analysis of different coherence protocols, we introduce the formal model described by Mealy machines. First, we introduce the formalized notation and describe the general outlook of the machine and later on we use them for modeling the distributed Write-Through coherence protocol. This model serves as a modeling paradigm for other coherence protocols [8], [9].

A particular operation is initiated by the first message taken out of the *local queue* of the *client* or by dequeuing a message from the *distributed queue* of the *sequencer*.

A *message* consists of two parts: a message token and additional parameters. A message token is represented by a five-tuple (***type, operation_initiator, object_name, queue, parameter_presence***), where:

- ***type*** is the type of the message (in the Write-Through protocol there are six message types: R_REQ and W_REQ for read and write request messages, R_PER and W_PER for permission-asking messages, R_GNT for the grant message and W_INV for the invalidation message);
- ***operation_initiator*** is the index of the node which starts the execution of the operation ($i=1,...,N+1$);
- ***object_name*** selects one of the shared memory blocks that is later on named as *shared object* ($j=1,...,M$);
- ***queue*** points to the queue from which the message came (l - for *local queue*, d - for *distributed queue*);
- ***parameter_presence*** marks the presence of additional parameters in the queue beside the message token (0 - additional parameters are not present, r - *read* operation parameters are present, w - *write* operation parameters are present, ui - complete new user information part of a copy is present).

For every replica of the shared object in each node one Mealy machine is introduced. In each of the *clients*, the Mealy machines are the same.

A Mealy machine is a finite automaton with output defined as a six-tuple $MM=(Q, \Sigma, \Omega, \delta, \lambda, q_0)$. The finite *set of states* Q is equal to the set of states of a shared object copy (for the protocol in consideration the set consists of the VALID and the INVALID state for the *client's* machine, and contains only the VALID state for the *sequencer's* machine). The finite *input alphabet* Σ consists of all message tokens. The *transition function* δ maps $Q \times \Sigma$ to Q. The *output alphabet* Ω is determined by a set of *output routines*. The *output function* λ maps $Q \times \Sigma$ to Ω (this function determines which of the output routines will be executed on a particular input and the present state). The *starting state* q_0 is INVALID in the *client's* machine and VALID in the *sequencer's* machine.

Table 1: Mealy machine transition table for a copy of jth ($j=1,...,M$) shared object at ith client ($i=1,...,N$) for Write-Through protocol

1 - a message token as input symbol
2 - a state of a copy of shared object as a state of Mealy machine, the first row is labeled with the starting state
3 - a new state defined by function δ
4 - an output routine as output symbol defined by function λ
5 - error (errors are not analyzed by the given protocol)
6 - $k \neq i$, $k = 1,...,N+1$

client i a copy of shared object j	read operation		write operation	
	(R_REQ, i, j, l, r)	(R_GNT, i, j, d, ui)	(W_REQ, i, j, l, w)	(W_INV, k^6, $\bar{j}$, d, 0)
INVALID[2]	INVALID[3] 2[4]	VALID 3	INVALID 4	INVALID
VALID	VALID 1	error[5]	INVALID 4	INVALID

Table 2: Set of Mealy machine output routines for a copy of jth ($j=1,...,M$) shared object at ith client ($i=1,...,N$) for Write-Through protocol

1	pop (parameters_r(j)); return (parameters_r(j)), user_information(j))
2	pop (parameters_r(j)); push (N+1, (R_PER, i, j, d, 0)); disable(l)
3	pop (user_information(j)); return (parameters_r(j)), user_information(j)); enable(l)
4	pop (parameters_w(j)); push (N+1, (W_PER, i, j, d, w), parameters_w(j));

The output routines are described as concatenation of *simple functions*. The implementation of the considered model requires the following seven simple functions:

- Function **pop(*variable*)** updates the contents of a specified variable. The content of ***variable*** is popped from a queue from which the message token came. There are three variables in this model. The user information part of a copy of the jth shared object is defined by the content of the variable ***user_information(j)***. Variables ***parameters_r(j)*** and ***parameters_w(j)*** temporarily store additional parameters of *read* and *write* operations. respectively. The structure of the last two variables depends on the organization of the user information part of a copy.
- Function **push(*destination, message_token, additional_parameters*)** sends the ***message_token*** and ***additional_parameters*** to the destination nodes. The message is sent to a queue specified by the parameter ***queue*** in the ***message_token***.
- Function **except(*address_list*)** determines that the message has to be sent to all nodes excluding those listed in ***address_list***.
- Function **change(*parameters_w(j), user_information(j)*)** updates the content of the variable ***user_information(j)*** according to the *write* operation parameters defined in the ***parameters_w(j)*** variable.
- Function **return(*parameters_r(j), user_information(j)*)** returns the data to the *application process* according to the

Table 3: Mealy machine transition table for a copy of jth ($j=1,...,M$) shared object at the sequencer for Write-Through protocol

1 - $k=1,...,N$

sequencer $N+1$ a copy of shared object j	read operation of sequencer	write operation of sequencer	read operation of client	write operation of client
	(R_REQ, N+1, j, d, r)	(W_REQ, N+1, j, d, w)	(R_PER, k^1, $\bar{j}$, d, 0)	(W_PER, k^1, $\bar{j}$, d, w)
VALID	VALID 101	VALID 102	VALID 103	VALID 104

Table 4: Set of Mealy machine output routines for a copy of jth ($j=1,...,M$) shared object at the sequencer for Write-Through protocol

101	pop (parameters_r(j)); return(parameters_r(j), user_information(j))
102	pop (parameters_w(j)); change (parameters_w(j), user_information(j)); push (except (N+1), (W_INV, N+1, j, d, 0))
103	push (k, (R_GNT, k, j, d, ui), user_information(j))
104	pop (parameters_w(j)); change (parameters_w(j), user_information(j)); push (except (k, N+1), (W_INV, k, j, d, 0))

read operation parameters specified by the content of ***parameters_r(j)***.

- Functions **disable(*l*)** and **enable(*l*)** control the dequeuing from the *local queue l*.

For the Write-Through coherence protocol, a copy of the shared object at the *sequencer* is always valid. All the changes of the shared object are always passed to the *sequencer*. Therefore, the Mealy machine for a copy in the *sequencer* has only the VALID state. The copy of the shared object at the *client* can be in one of two states: VALID (i.e., consistent with the copy at the *sequencer*) and INVALID (i.e., not consistent with the copy at the *sequencer*). Transitions between these two states of the *client's* machine are shown in Fig. 1. The whole transition function and output routines of the *client's* machine are presented by Table 1 and Table 2, respectively. Tables 3 and 4 describe the *sequencer's* machine.

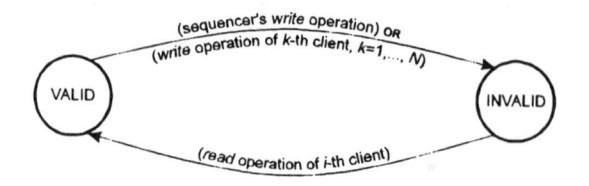

Figure 1: The state of the copy at ith client for Write-Through protocol.

The described formal model for the Write-Through protocol serves as a paradigm for the formal description of different protocols. In Appendix A, we only illustrate the transition state diagrams for other seven well-known cache coherence protocols which we have modified for use in a distributed environment. Detailed descriptions of the adapted protocols can be found in [8] and [9].

4: Performance evaluation

In this section we use the formal model for performance analysis of a distributed shared memory system. We assume that the cost of accessing locally available data is negligible and that the communication cost due to message exchanges between *clients* and the *sequencer* can be considered as a performance measure. Therefore, we first estimate the communication costs associated with different modes of operation executions and second, we introduce a model for the data access behavior of the application. We characterize the workload as a specific deviation from an ideal one that consists of *application processes* accessing disjoint data objects. We introduce some deviation parameters and compare the performance of different coherence protocols for some of their typical values.

4.1: Traces of actions and their communication costs

Every access to the shared memory is initiated by one of the *application processes* of the distributed computation. *Application processes* put the read or write requests into the appropriate queues of their *protocol process*. These messages initiate sequences of actions that we call traces of actions, or shortly *traces*.

It can be shown that for a given coherence protocol the set of all traces TR is finite [8] and that every operation execution results in exactly one trace from the set TR. The set of traces has to be determined by a thorough analysis of the applied coherence protocol [8], [9]. Every trace $tr_h \in TR$ depends on: the type of operation, the state of the copies of the shared object, and on the interaction of operations that are executed concurrently on the same object.

With each trace tr_h we associate the corresponding trace communication cost cc_h which is established by summing up the communication costs of all actions in the trace. We distinguish four different action communication costs:
- the communication cost is zero if the action is executed inside a node;
- the unit communication cost is associated to the action sending an inter-node message that contains only the message token (i.e., with *parameter_presence* = 0);
- the communication cost of $S+1$ units is associated to the action sending an inter-node message (with *parameter_presence* = ui) that contains the message token and the updating user information;
- the communication cost of $P+1$ units is associated to the action sending an inter-node message (with *parameter_presence* = w) that contains the message token and the *write* operation parameters.

The set of traces for the Write-Through protocol, that we use in this paper to demonstrate the proposed methodology, consists of six traces. We describe each trace and its communication cost for one of the shared objects, say jth.

The *client's read* operation of the copy in VALID state generates trace tr_1 with only an action executed locally with the communication cost $cc_1 =0$. If the copy is in INVALID state, trace tr_2 is generated with communication cost $cc_2=S+2$. First, the read permission-asking message token is sent to the *sequencer* which responds with a read grant message token joined with user information (Fig. 2.).

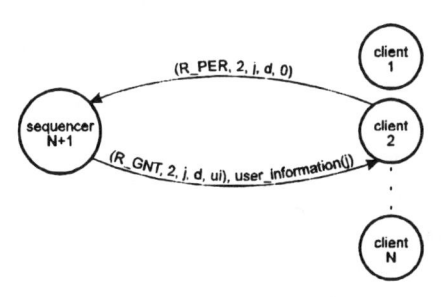

Figure 2: The messages in trace tr_2

Traces tr_3 and tr_4 are initiated by the *client's write* operation to the shared object in VALID and INVALID states, respectively. The messages emerging in traces are illustrated in Fig. 3. Both traces have the same communication cost $cc_3=cc_4=P+N$. Namely, the write permission-asking message token together with write parameters are passed from the *client* to the *sequencer* with cost $P+1$, and after that the *sequencer* sends invalidation message tokens to the remaining N-1 *clients*.

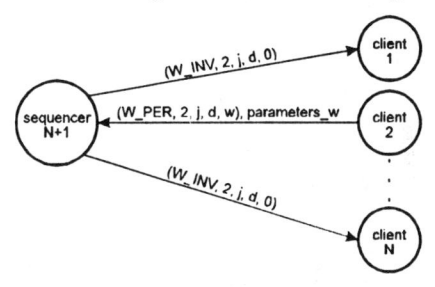

Figure 3: The messages in traces tr_3 and tr_4

Traces tr_5 and tr_6 are generated by *sequencer's* operations. A *read* operation executes locally on the copy that is always VALID with the zero cost, i.e., $cc_5 =0$, whereas the *write* operation initiates trace tr_6 sending N invalidation message tokens to all *clients* with communication cost $cc_6 =N$. (Fig. 4)

The defined trace communication costs will be used to evaluate the cost of the distributed computation.

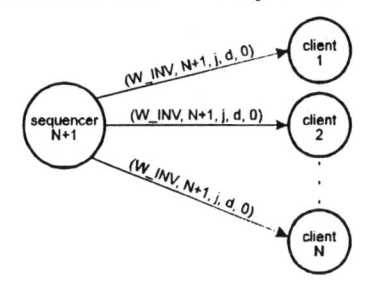

Figure 4: The messages in trace tr_6

4.2: Workload characterization

The performance of the distributed shared memory system is very sensitive to data-access behavior of the distributed computation. Therefore, a generalized characterization of workload is useful so that different coherence schemes can be compared with respect to only few workload parameters.

We assume that the workload consists of a collection of processes that behave in a stochastic steady-state manner.

Concerning the communication cost, we denote as an *ideal workload* the computation in which every object is accessed in one and only one node. That is, an ideal workload is a computation without shared data.

If, in an ideal workload, node i issues the *read* and *write* requests to object j, we call node i the *activity center* for object j. Further on, we concentrate our analysis only on *clients* associated with the copies of one object. The activity center *read* operation (Ar) and *write* operation (Aw) may be considered as the only two random events of the sample space that are mutually exclusively exhaustive. Also, their occurrences are statistically independent in time. Therefore, the sum of the probabilities of the *read* operation $p(Ar)$ and the *write* operation $p(Aw)$ is equal to one. If we introduce the parameter $\rho = p(Aw)$ for the *write* operation in the activity center, then the probability of the *read* operation is $p(Ar)=1-\rho$.

We analyze three *deviations from an ideal workload* and call them: *read disturbance*, *write disturbance* and *multiple activity centers disturbance*. For each deviation we determine the event sample space and introduce the corresponding parameters, as follows:

- In the workload with *read disturbance* only activity center i can start a *read* operation (Ar) and a *write* operation (Aw), whereas some number α ($\alpha<N$) of other *clients* can start only a *read* operation ($Or_k, k \neq i$). The sample space consists of $\alpha+2$ events: Ar, Aw, and α events Or_k. If the probabilities are expressed as $p(Aw)=\rho$ and $p(Or_k)=\sigma_k$, the probability for an activity center *read* operation $p(Ar)$ can be determined. To simplify the presentation of performance evaluation we assume the homogeneous case where $p(Or_k)$ are all equal, i.e., $p(Or_k)=\sigma_k=\sigma$. In that case, $p(Ar)=1-p(Aw+\sum_{k=1,...,\alpha}Or_k)=1-\rho-\alpha\sigma$.

- In the workload with *write disturbance* only activity center i can start a *read* operation (Ar) and a *write* operation (Aw), whereas some number α ($\alpha<N$) of other *clients* can start only *write* operation ($Ow_k, k \neq i$). The sample space consists of $\alpha+2$ events: Ar, Aw, and α events Ow_k. If the probabilities are expressed as $p(Aw)=\rho$ and $p(Ow_k)=\xi_k$, the probability for an activity center *read* operation $p(Ar)$ can be determined. To simplify the presentation of performance evaluation we again assume the homogeneous case where $p(Ow_k)$ are all equal, i.e., $p(Ow_k)=\xi_k=\xi$. In that case, $p(Ar)=1-p(Aw+\sum_{k=1,...,\alpha}Ow_k)=1-\rho-\alpha\xi$.

- In the workload with *multiple activity centers disturbance* more than one *client* can behave as activity center. If there are β *clients* declared as activity centers then the sample space consists of 2β events. To simplify the analytic performance comparison we consider only the homogeneous case with equal read and write probabilities at all activity centers. In that case, if the total write probability is ρ, the probabilities of *write* and *read* operations at a particular node k are $p(Aw_k)=\rho/\beta$ and $p(Ar_k)=(1-\rho)/\beta$, respectively.

The five parameters ρ, σ, ξ, α and β describe an assumed synthetic workload, although they may be obtained by estimating the relative frequencies of events in some real distributed computation. Parameters and the communication costs per trace are input to the performance comparison model. All model parameters are summarized in Table 5.

Table 5: Parameters of the model

N	- number of *clients* (Section 2)
α	- number of *clients* that start *read* or *write* operations (Section 4.2)
β	- number of *clients* declared as activity centers (Section 4.2)
ρ	steady-state probability of the activity center *write* operation (Section 4.2)
σ	- steady-state probability of *read* operation of one of α *clients* (Section 4.2)
ξ	- steady-state probability of *write* operation of one of α *clients* (Section 4.2)
S	- communication cost of user information part of copy transmission (Section 4.1)
P	- communication cost of *write* operation parameters transmission (Section 4.1)
acc	- steady-state average communication cost per operation and per shared object (Equation 1)

4.3: Steady-state average communication cost as a performance measure

We define as a performance measure the average communication cost, denoted by acc, of an operation accessing a shared object in the stochastic steady-state computation. The average communication cost can be expressed as:

$$acc = \sum_{tr_h \in TR} \pi_h \, cc_h, \quad (1)$$

where cc_h is the communication cost for trace tr_h, π_h is the steady-state probability that operation execution will result in trace tr_h, and TR is the set of all traces for a given coherence protocol ($\sum_{tr_h \in TR} \pi_h = 1$).

The probabilities π_h are functions of the parameters ρ, σ, ξ, α and β. These functions can be determined for the steady-state behavior of the interacting Mealy machines for a particular coherence protocol.

We analyze in detail the derivation of the expression for the average communication cost of the workload with read disturbance deviation for the Write-Trough protocol, and give only the final formulae for the other two deviations. The same methodology can be used to express the average communication costs for other coherence protocols [8], [9].

We recall from Section 4.2 that the *read* and *write* operations are treated as random events from sample space and that they are mutually exhaustive and their occurrences are statistically independent in time. Therefore, a specific sequence of operations can be treated as a sequence of repeated independent trials. We denote the events by symbols Ar, Aw and Or_k for activity center *read* operation, activity center *write* operation and other *client's read* operation, respectively. The probability of a specific sequence of operations is equal to the product of probabilities of the individual items. To obtain the probability of a specific outcome, the probabilities of all sequences giving this outcome have to be summed up. We symbolize the sequence of trials by a string of event symbols, e.g., $ArOr_kOr_kOr_kArAw$, with an exponent denoting the multiple consecutive appearance of the same symbol, e.g., $Ar(Or_k)^3ArAw$.

In *read disturbance deviation* from ideal workload at an activity center *read* and *write* operations are allowed, whereas in α other *clients* only *read* operations can be executed. Therefore, in an activity center four traces can emerge: tr_1 or tr_2 for *read* operation, and tr_3 or tr_4 for *write* operation. The other α *clients* produce only traces tr_1 and tr_2.

In the activity center, the execution of the *read* operation will result in trace tr_1 if at least one *read* operation of the activity center has been executed previously. The *read* operations of the other α *clients* do not change the state of the activity center copy. Therefore, an arbitrary number of Or (Or=$\sum_{k=1,...,\alpha} Or_k$) events from other *clients* can be interpolated between two consecutive Ar events giving as the outcome trace tr_1. So, the probability of trace tr_1 is $\pi'_1 = p(tr_1) = p(\sum_{x=0,...,\infty} Ar(Or)^x Ar) = (1-\rho-\alpha\sigma)^2/(1-\alpha\sigma)$. With π' are denoted the steady-state probabilities of the activity center traces, whereas with π'' are denoted the probabilities of the traces of the one of other α *clients*. The probability of trace tr_2 is the probability that the *read* operation event Ar follows the *write* operation event Aw. Again, between these two events an arbitrary number of Or events can emerge, and we have: $\pi'_2 = p(tr_2) = p(\sum_{x=0,...,\infty} Aw(Or)^x Ar) = \rho(1-\rho-\alpha\sigma)/(1-\alpha\sigma)$.

A *write* operation execution of activity center can result in one of two traces: tr_3 or tr_4. The execution will result in trace tr_3 if at least one *read* operation of the activity center has been executed previously, and in trace tr_4 if at least one *write* operation of the activity center has been executed previously. With the same reasoning as before, we have the probability for trace tr_3: $\pi'_3 = p(tr_3) = p(\sum_{x=0,...,\infty} Ar(Or)^x Aw) = \rho(1-\rho-\alpha\sigma)/(1-\alpha\sigma)$ and probability for trace tr_4: $\pi'_4 = p(tr_4) = p(\sum_{x=0,...,\infty} Aw(Or)^x Aw) = \rho^2/(1-\alpha\sigma)$.

A *read* operation execution of one of the α *clients* can result in one of two traces: tr_1 or tr_2. The execution will result in tr_1 if at least one *read* operation of the same *client* has been executed previously. The other *read* operations have no influence on the state of that copy. Let Z_i be a random event denoting a *read* operation which is executed outside that *client*. The steady-state probability of that event is $p(Z_i) = 1-p(Aw+Or_i) = 1-\rho-\sigma$. Now, the steady-state probability of trace tr_1 can be expressed as: $\pi''_1 = p(tr_1) = p(\sum_{x=0,...,\infty} Or_i(Z_i)^x Or_i) = \sigma^2/(\rho+\sigma)$. The execution will result in trace tr_2 if at least one *write* operation of activity center has been executed previously giving: $\pi''_2 = p(tr_2) = p(\sum_{x=0,...,\infty} Aw(Z_i)^x Or_i) = \sigma\rho/(\rho+\sigma)$.

The total steady-state probabilities for the traces of the same type tr_h can be calculated by expression $\pi_h = \pi'_h + \alpha\pi''_h$. They are:

$$\pi_1 = (1-\rho-\alpha\sigma)^2/(1-\alpha\sigma) + \alpha\sigma^2/(\rho+\sigma),$$
$$\pi_2 = \rho(1-\rho-\alpha\sigma)/(1-\alpha\sigma) + \alpha\sigma\rho/(\rho+\sigma),$$
$$\pi_3 = \rho(1-\rho-\alpha\sigma)/(1-\alpha\sigma),$$
$$\pi_4 = \rho^2/(1-\alpha\sigma).$$

Using (1) with appropriate communication costs cc_h for traces, introduced in Section 4.1, the communication cost per operation can be expressed as:

$$acc = \pi_1(0) + \pi_2(S+2) + \pi_3(P+N) + \pi_4(P+N). \quad (2)$$

Putting the derived probabilities in (2), we obtain the following average communication costs per operation and per shared object for read disturbance deviation:

$$acc_{RD} = (\rho(1-\rho-\alpha\sigma)/(1-\alpha\sigma) + \alpha\sigma\rho/(\rho+\sigma))(S+2) + \rho(P+N). \quad (3)$$

Putting $\sigma=0$ or $\alpha=0$ into eqn. (3), the communication cost for ideal workload acc_{ID} can be obtained:

$$acc_{ID} = \rho((1-\rho)(S+2) + P+N),$$

and if, additionally, there are no *write* operations at the activity center, i.e., if $\rho=0$, the communication cost is equal to zero.

Similar reasoning for *write disturbance deviation* gives the following total steady-state trace probabilities:

$$\pi_1 = \pi'_1 = p(ArAr) = (1-\rho-\alpha\xi)^2,$$
$$\pi_2 = \pi'_2 = p((Aw+Ow)Ar) = (\rho+\alpha\xi)(1-\rho-\alpha\xi),$$
$$\pi_3 = \pi'_3 = p(ArAw) = \rho(1-\rho-\alpha\xi),$$
$$\pi_4 = \pi'_4 + \alpha\pi''_4 = p((Aw+Ow)Aw) + \alpha p(Ow_i) = \rho(\rho+\alpha\xi) + \alpha\xi,$$

where $Ow = \sum_{k=1,...,\alpha} Ow_k$. Putting these probabilities into (2), the average communication cost per operation is:

$$acc_{WD} = (\rho+\alpha\xi)(1-\rho-\alpha\xi)(S+2) + (\rho+\alpha\xi)(P+N). \quad (4)$$

Finally, for *multiple activity centers deviation* the total steady-state trace probabilities are:

$$\pi_1 = \beta p(\sum_{x=0,...,\infty} Ar_i(X_i)^x Ar_i) = (1-\rho)^2/(1+(\beta-1)\rho),$$
$$\pi_2 = \beta p(\sum_{x=0,...,\infty} Aw(X_i)^x Ar_i) = \beta(1-\rho)\rho/(1+(\beta-1)\rho),$$
$$\pi_3 = \beta p(\sum_{x=0,...,\infty} Ar_i(X_i)^x Aw_i) = \rho(1-\rho)/(1+(\beta-1)\rho),$$
$$\pi_4 = \beta p(\sum_{x=0,...,\infty} Aw(X_i)^x Aw_i) = \beta\rho^2/(1+(\beta-1)\rho),$$

where $X_i = \sum_{k \neq i, k=1,...,\beta} Ar_k$, and $Aw = \sum_{k=1,...,\beta} Aw_k$. Using (2), the average communication cost per operation can be expressed as:

$$acc_{MAC} = (\beta(1-\rho)\rho/(1+(\beta-1)\rho))(S+2) + \rho(P+N). \quad (5)$$

5: Analytical performance comparison of coherence protocols with respect to read disturbance

We used the proposed methodology to analyze the performance of distributed computation in the distributed shared memory system implemented by eight coherence protocols. Here, we compare the performances only for read disturbance deviation from ideal workload. The obtained analytical results are compared with the results of simulation.

5.1: Analytical performance comparison of coherence protocols

The steady-state average communication costs per operation and per shared object for read disturbance deviation from ideal workload for eight coherence protocols [8] are given in Table 6. These expressions were obtained by a thorough analysis of the protocols. To give an impression of the outlook of the protocols, we have added in Appendix A the state transition diagrams for these protocols. It should be pointed out that in these diagrams emerge some states not mentioned in the description of the Write-Through protocol.

Table 6: The steady-state average communication cost per operation and per shared object for read disturbance deviation from ideal workload

Protocol	Average communication cost per operation acc
Write-Through	$acc_{WT}=\rho(P+N+2)+(\alpha\sigma\rho/(\rho+\sigma))(S+2)$
Write-Through-V	$acc_{WV}=\rho(P+N)+(\rho(1-\rho-\alpha\sigma)/(1-\alpha\sigma)+\alpha\sigma\rho/(\rho+\sigma))(S+2)$
Write-Once	$acc_{WO}=(\alpha\sigma\rho/(\rho+\sigma))(S+N+1)+((\alpha\sigma\rho^2/(\rho+\alpha\sigma)^2)(S+4)+(\alpha\sigma\rho/(\rho+\alpha\sigma))(P+N+2)$
Synapse	$acc_{SY}=(\alpha\sigma\rho/(\rho+\alpha\sigma))(S+2N+2)+(\alpha\sigma\rho/(\rho+\sigma))(S+2)$
Berkeley	$acc_{B}=(\alpha\sigma\rho/(\rho+\alpha\sigma))(N)+(\alpha\sigma\rho/(\rho+\sigma))(S+2)$
Illinois	$acc_{I}=(\alpha\sigma\rho/(\rho+\alpha\sigma))(S+N+4)+(\alpha\sigma\rho/(\rho+\sigma))(S+2)$
Firefly	$acc_{F}=\rho(N(P+1)+1)$
Dragon	$acc_{D}=\rho(N(P+1))$

(a) Write-Once, Synapse, Illinois, Berkeley ($S=5000$)

(b) Write-Through-V ($S=100$)

(c) Dragon, Firefly ($S=5000$)

(d) Dragon vs. Berkeley ($S=5000$)

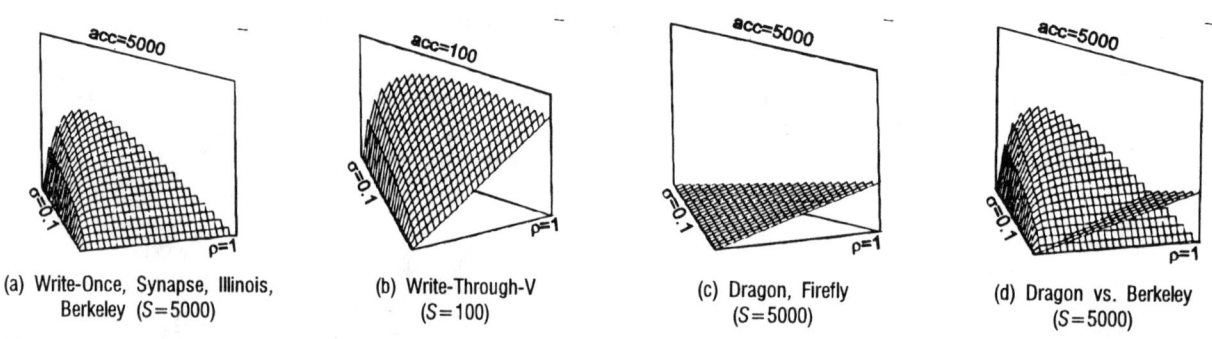

Figure 5: The characteristic surfaces of the steady-state average communication cost per operation and per shared object for read disturbance deviation from ideal workload ($N=50$, $\alpha=10$, $P=30$)

(a) Write-Once, Synapse, Illinois, Berkeley ($S=5000$)

(b) Write-Through-V ($S=100$)

(c) Dragon, Firefly ($S=5000$)

(d) Dragon vs. Write-Through ($S=5000$)

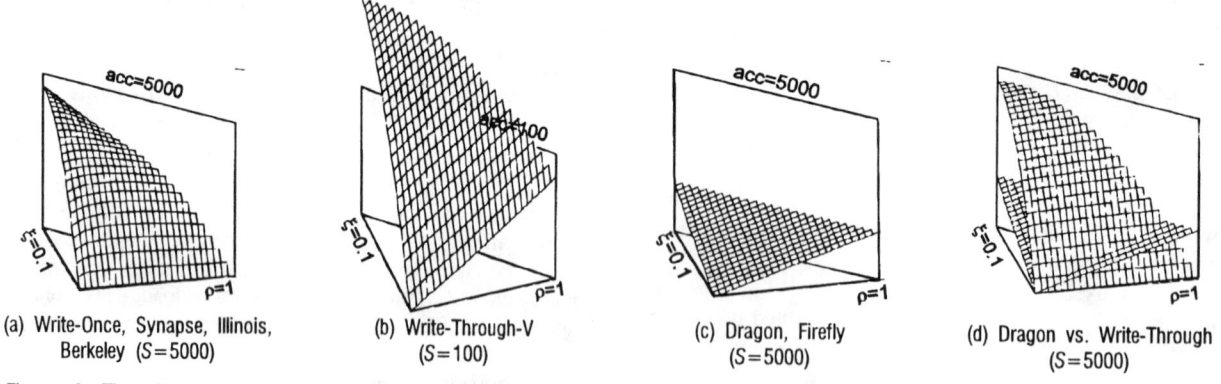

Figure 6: The characteristic surfaces of the steady-state average communication cost per operation and per shared object for write disturbance deviation from ideal workload ($N=50$, $\alpha=10$, $P=30$)

We use the equations from Table 6 to compute the communication costs for some particular values of the workload parameters for different coherence protocols. Computed results are represented in Fig. 5 for read disturbance deviation, while the characteristic surfaces for write disturbance deviation are given in Fig. 6. By inspecting the diagrams in this figure, and by additional observation of the equations, interesting general conclusions come into mind for read disturbance deviation:

- For $\rho=0$ all coherence protocols incur $acc=0$, because all nodes in the steady-state have a valid copy and *read* operations are executed locally.

- For an ideal workload ($\sigma=0$) Synapse, Write-Once, Illinois and Berkeley incur $acc=0$, because these protocols have the ability of locally executing the *write* operations. Write-Through and Write-Through-V protocols incur $acc_{WT}=\rho(P+N+2)$ and $acc_{WV}=\rho(P+N)+\rho(1-\rho)(S+2)$ respectively, because user information changes are always passed to the *sequencer*. Dragon and Firefly protocols incur $acc_D=\rho N(P+1)$ and $acc_F=\rho(N(P+1)+1)$ respectively, because user information changes are always passed to all nodes.

Table 7: A comparison of analytical and simulation results for Write-Once and Write-Through-V protocol
$N=3$, $\alpha=2$, $P=30$, $S=100$

	Write-Once Protocol		
σ	Analytical Results acc_a	Simulation Results acc_s	$100 \times (acc_a - acc_s)/acc_a$ (%)
0.5	0	0	0
0.4	0 36.661	0 36.153	0 1.38
0.3	0 34.110 54.041	0 33.290 52.202	0 2.40 3.40
0.2	0 30.088 45.133 54.576	0 30.371 42.710 53.690	0 -0.93 5.36 1.62
0.1	0 22.566 30.551 34.778 37.400	0 22.115 28.730 32.910 38.129	0 2.00 5.96 5.37 -1.94
0.0	0 0 0 0 0 0	0 0 0 0 0 0	0 0 0 0 0 0

	Write-Through-V Protocol		
0.5	0	0	0
0.4	0 34.200	0 35.840	0 -4.79
0.3	0 31.480 48.971	0 29.792 48.017	0 5.36 1.94
0.2	0 27.400 41.200 51.600	0 25.274 41.879 50.377	0 7.75 -1.64 2.37
0.1	0 20.600 30.320 38.485 46.133	0 20.509 29.167 37.188 45.306	0 0.44 3.80 3.37 1.79
0.0	0 7.000 14.000 21.000 28.000 35.000	0 7.256 13.510 20.580 27.566 35.023	0 -3.60 3.50 2.00 1.55 -0.06
	0.0 0.2 0.4 0.6 0.8 1.0	0.0 0.2 0.4 0.6 0.8 1.0	0.0 0.2 0.4 0.6 0.8 1.0 ρ

- Protocol Berkeley incurs the minimum communication cost in comparison with Write-Through, Write-Through-V, Write-Once, Illinois and Synapse, because in the steady-state, an activity center becomes the *sequencer*.
- Protocol Illinois incurs *acc* lower than the Synapse scheme, because Illinois dynamically updates the address of the *client* which has the only valid copy.
- The Synapse incurs *acc* lower then Write-Through-V if $P>S+N$. If $P<S+N$, a line $\rho=\alpha\sigma(S+N-P)/(P+N+2)$ separates two regions where Synapse or Write-Through-V protocol incur minimum *acc*.
- A line $\rho= -\alpha\sigma(S/(S+2))+S/(S+2)$ separates two regions where Write-Through-V or Write-Through protocol incur minimum *acc*.
- In Fig. 5d Dragon vs. Berkeley are compared. The performance comparison of Dragon and Berkeley protocols shows that for $NP>S+2$ the Berkeley protocol incurs *acc* lower then the Dragon protocol. For $NP<S+2$ and $\alpha=1$, the line $\rho=\sigma(S+2-NP)/(P+N+2)$ separates two regions where the Dragon or the Berkeley protocol incur minimum *acc*.

Additionally, the numerical performance comparison between the Write-Once and the Write-Through-V protocols is presented in Table 7. The values are double-bordered if the communication costs are lower, single-bordered if the costs are higher for the corresponding protocol, and thick-bordered if the costs are equal. In the same table the simulation results, discussed in the next section, are also given.

5.2: Comparison between analytical and simulation results

We simulated the behavior of coherence protocols by executing the protocols implemented in a multitasking Ada environment [10]. The implementation allows the simulation with real or synthetic workloads. For synthetic workloads, the *application processes* at each node randomly generate the *read* or *write* operations in concordance to specified stochastic steady-state workload parameters.

The comparison between the simulation and analytical results is given in Table 7 for the Write-Once and the Write-Through-V protocol. In this example, there are $N=3$ *clients*. One of them is the activity center, whereas two other nodes ($\alpha=2$) start only the *read* operations. The data structure is decomposed into $M=20$ shared objects. The probabilities of the accesses to all of the shared objects are the same. If only one shared object is considered, then the probability of the *write* operation at the activity center, the probability of the *read* operation at the activity center and the probability of the *read* operations at one of the other *clients* for that object are ρ, $1-\rho-2\sigma$ and σ, respectively. These probabilities are assumed to be the same for all shared objects.

To eliminate the influence of the transient period, the first 500 operations are neglected. Approximately 1500 operations from the steady-state period are taken into consideration for each pair of parameters ρ and σ. From the data given in Table 7 it is visible that the maximum discrepancy between analysis and simulation is less than ±8%.

6: Conclusion

In this paper, we have described the methodology for the performance evaluation of data replication based distributed shared memory systems implemented with various coherence protocols. We used the proposed methodology to compare different coherence protocols. For comparison purposes, we applied a synthetic workload characterized by five parameters which can be also used to estimate the behavior of real distributed computation. The obtained results indicate that the choice of a coherence protocol is a significant design decision problem since the performance differences for a given workload can be quite large. We applied our analytical comparison model for a class of coherence protocols that we have constructed by the modification of well-known cache coherence protocols, but the methodology is convenient for general use. We feel that the model can be applied to implement a classifier for the development of adaptive data replication coherence protocols with self-tuning capability based on run-time information. The model is also a sound basis for further research. We consider its modifications in order to include other types of operations (eject operation, synchronization operation) and the influence of some distributed system parameters, such as the size of the free memory pool.

Appendix A: State transition diagrams for coherence protocols

Transitions between different states of the *client's* and *sequencer's* copies for Synapse, Illinois, Write-Once, Firefly, Dragon and Berkeley protocols are illustrated. Only the operations that change the states of the copies are presented.

Synapse:

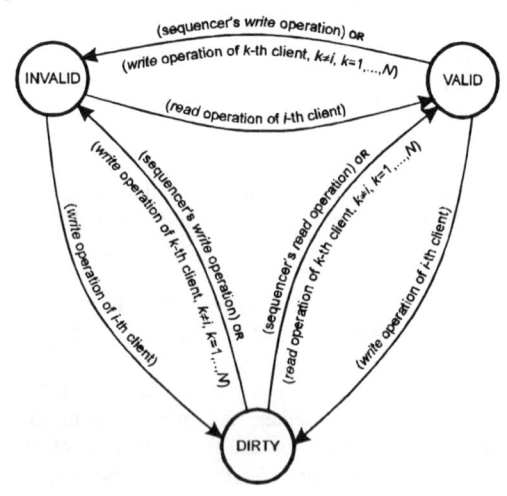

Figure 7: States of a copy at *i*th client ($i=1,..., N$) for Synapse protocol

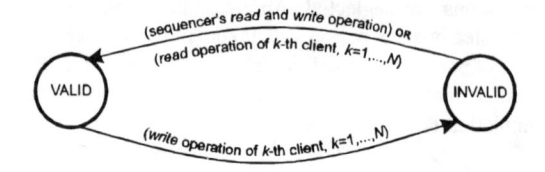

Figure 8: States of *sequencer's* copy for Synapse protocol

Illinois: The state transition diagrams for the Illinois protocol is the same as for the Synapse protocol The difference between these two protocols is that the *sequencer* in the Illinois protocol updates all the time the address of the *client* which has the copy in DIRTY state.

Write-Through-V: The *client's write* operation at the Write-Through-V protocol updates the copy at the *sequencer* and its own copy. The *sequencer's* copy has only one state: VALID.

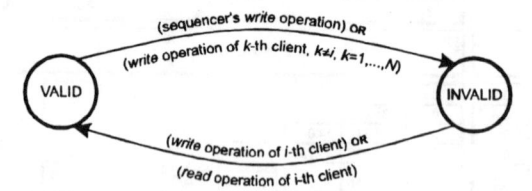

Figure 9: States of a copy at *i*th client ($i=1,...,N$) for Write-Through-V protocol

Write-Once: The *sequencer's* state transition diagram for the Write-Once protocol is the same as for the Synapse protocol. The *write* operation of *k*th *client* changes the state of the *sequencer's* copy from VALID to INVALID only if *k*th *client's* copy is in RESERVED or INVALID state.

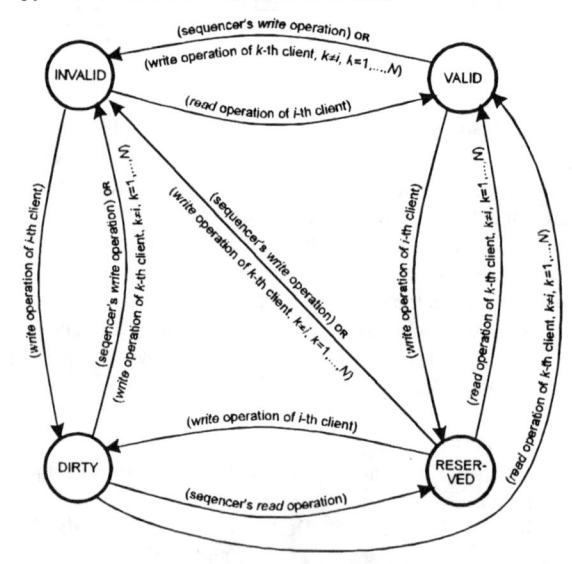

Figure 10: States of a copy at *i*th client ($i=1,..., N$) for Write-Once protocol

Dragon: The role of the *sequencer* can be taken by different nodes during protocol execution. The *sequencer* broadcasts the write operation parameters to all *clients*. The copy at the *sequencer* has only one state: SHARED-DIRTY. The copy at the *client* has also only one state: SHARED-CLEAN.

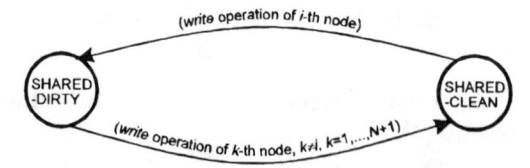

Figure 11: States of a copy at *i*th node ($i=1,..., N+1$) for Dragon protocol

Firefly: The copy at the *sequencer* has only one state: VALID. The copy at the *client* has also only one state: SHARED. The *client* always passes the *write* operation parameters to the *sequencer*. The *sequencer* broadcasts the *write* operation parameters to all *clients*.

Berkeley: The role of the *sequencer* can be taken by different nodes during protocol execution. The copy at the *sequencer* can be in one of two states: DIRTY or SHARED-DIRTY. The copy at the *client* can be in one of two states: VALID or INVALID.

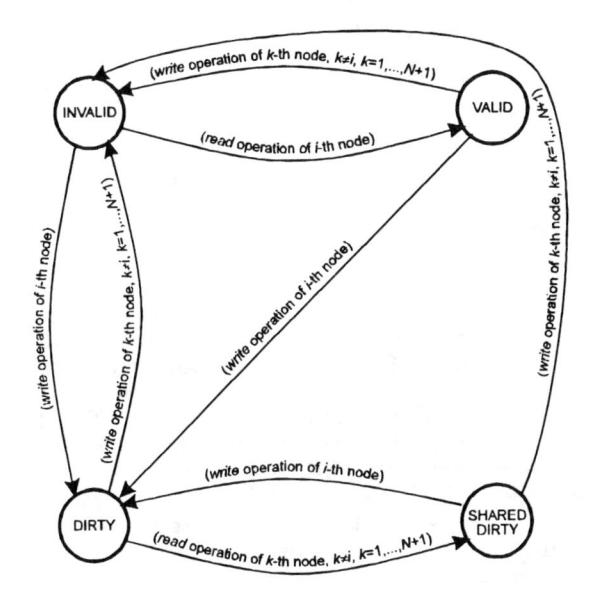

Figure 12: States of a copy at *i*th node ($i=1,..., N+1$) for Berkeley protocol

Acknowledgments

This research has advanced through valuable discussions with Dalibor Vrsalović (Ready Systems Corporation, California) and Zvonko Vranešić (University of Toronto). The authors are grateful to Vlado Sruk (University of Zagreb, Faculty of Electrical Engineering) who implemented the coherence protocols into the multitasking Ada simulator and prepared the results of the simulation. The authors also thank Neven Elezović, Hrvoje Bunjevac, Andrea Budin, Tomislav Grčanac, Joško Radej, Goran Omrčen-Čeko (University of Zagreb, Faculty of Electrical Engineering) and Zoran Ivković (University of Delaware) for many fruitful discussions and suggestions.

References

[1] M. Stumm and S. Zhou, "Algorithms Implementing Distributed Shared Memory", *IEEE Computer*, Vol. 23, No. 5, May 1990, pp. 54-64.

[2] P. Stenstrom, D. Vrsalovic, and Z. Segall, "Shared Data Structures in a Distributed System - Performance Evaluation and Practical Considerations", in. *Proc. Int. Seminar on Performance of Distributed and Parallel Systems*, Kyoto, Japan, December 1988.

[3] B. Ciciani, D.M. Dias, and P.S. Yu, "Analysis of Replication in Distributed Database Systems", *IEEE Transactions on Knowledge and Data Engineering*, Vol. 2, No. 2, June 1990, pp. 247-261.

[4] M. Thapar and B. Delagi, "Cache Coherence for Large Scale Shared Memory Multiprocessors", *ACM Computer Architecture News*, Vol. 19, No. 1, March 1991, pp. 114-119.

[5] D. Chaiken, J. Kubiatowicz, and A. Agarwal, "LimitLESS Directories: A Scalable Cache Coherence Scheme", *ASPLOS-IV Proceedings, Santa Clara*, California, April 8-11, 1991, pp. 224-234.

[6] Q. Yang, L.N. Bhuyan, and B.-C. Liu, "Analysis and Comparison of Cache Coherence Protocols for a Packet-Switched Multiprocessor", *IEEE Transaction on Computers*, Vol. 38, No. 8, August 1989, pp. 1143-1153.

[7] J. Archibald and J.-L. Baer, "Cache Coherence Protocols: Evaluation Using a Multiprocessor Simulation Model", *ACM Transactions on Computer System*, Vol. 4, No. 4, November 1986, pp. 273-298.

[8] S. Srbljić, "Model of Distributed Processing in Flexible Manufacturing Systems", Ph.D. dissertation, Institute for Electronics, Faculty of Electrical Engineering, University of Zagreb, Croatia, November 1990. (Work published in Croatian, original title: "Model distribuirane obrade u prilagodljivim proizvodnim sustavima")

[9] S.Srbljić and L.Budin, "A Formal Model of Data Replication Coherence Protocols", Technical Report, Institute for Electronics, Faculty of Electrical Engineering, University of Zagreb, Croatia, November 1991.

[10] V.Sruk and S.Srbljić, "Comparison of Data Replication Coherence Protocols for Distributed Systems", Technical Report, Institute for Electronics, Faculty of Electrical Engineering, University of Zagreb, Croatia, January 1993.

Hierarchical Distributed System Network Design with Cost-Performance Tradeoffs*

Nita Sharma
nCUBE Corp.
919 East Hillsdale Blvd
Foster City, CA 94404
nita@ncube.com

Dharma P. Agrawal
Department of Elec. and Comp. Eng., Box 7911
North Carolina State University
Raleigh, NC 27695-7911
dpa@ncsu.edu

Abstract

Design of a large distributed system (DS) is becoming increasingly important and with its added popularity, it is crucial to define its topology based on some objective function. This paper introduces a reliability-based systematic approach for defining the topology of a DS network in a hierarchical form, given the traffic requirements, a set of cluster topologies and the cost constraints. Our scheme first identifies a group of permissible inter-cluster links which yields the maximum network reliability to cost ratio and then selects the gateways within each cluster for balancing the traffic through the inter-cluster links and the node degrees within each cluster. The usefulness of our method lies in a simultaneous consideration of the cost and the network reliability. Some examples are included to illustrate our design procedure.

1 Introduction

There has been an increasing use of networks both for private memory parallel systems and distributed systems (DSs). This has led to a spur of activities in defining topologies of new networks. For multicomputers, one of the major problems faced with is how to design a network with a low connectivity and a reasonable diameter. In designing any DS network, it is desirable to maximize the network reliability for a given cost. Network reliability, a commonly used measure of connectivity, is defined as the probability that all processors in a network can communicate successfully with each other.

Many algorithms have been developed to design networks with required specifications [1] [2] [4] [6] [10] [12] [15]. However, very little work has been reported on the design of hierarchical network, with the reliability in mind. Catuneanu et al [3] describe a compute-intensive algorithm which leads to a topology with the maximum overall reliability network, for a given permissible network topology and cost.

In summary, all previous design algorithms are based on the assumption that removal of a link from the network reduces the cost of the network. This assumption is not valid in any realistic system, wherein there exist given average traffic requirements between processors. The removal of a link from a network results in diversion of that link traffic to the remaining links. This may force an increase in their capacity requirements, so as to avoid performance degradation, and hence, there may be an overall increase in the cost. The problem of designing a network is complex because the cost constraint has to be met, while maximizing the network reliability. Each link of a DS network contributes to the network reliability as well as to the cost of the network. Furthermore, each additional link is associated with a port addition cost for each of the two processors that the link connects. In addition to the aforementioned issues, decisions on the choice of gateways needs to be made for each cluster. Gateways are defined as those nodes of the cluster which are used to interconnect various clusters together. The choice of gateways affects the traffic balance in the network and the node degree balance within each cluster, as is discussed in a later section. This implies that the design problem is far more complex in a hierarchical network.

Our work introduces an algorithm which chooses a subset of the permissible inter-cluster topology that maximizes the network reliability to cost ratio by considering traffic requirements between the processors in the network. We also introduce an algorithm to optimally select gateway nodes for each cluster, given the cluster topologies, as defined by the characteristics of each physical location.

2 Modeling of a Hierarchical Network

A computer network can be modeled as a graph $G = (V,E)$, where the set of vertices/nodes V of the graph correspond to the processors of the network and the set of edges E of the graph correspond to the communication links between processors in the network.

To make the description of the design process simpler, we restrict ourselves to a 2-level hierarchical network, wherein level one nodes are grouped as a cluster and level 2 serves to interconnect clusters of level one nodes to constitute the network.

2.1 Network Modeling

Corresponding to the 2-level hierarchical network, [14], we create two levels of models. The first level,

---

[0]*This work was done when Ms. Sharma was at NCSU and has been supported in part by the Army Research Office under grant no. DAAL03-91-G-0031 and SRC.

called the Network Graph Model, NGM(c,e) consists of modeling each cluster as a macro-node in the graph and the inter-cluster links as edges in the graph. The second level of model, the Cluster Graph Model, CGM(p,e), is the set of models for the individual clusters (CMs). The inter-cluster traffic between any two clusters is the sum of the traffic flowing between all node pairs in the two clusters.

2.2 Notations
NGM : Network graph model
CM : Cluster model
CGM: Cluster Graph Model (set of CMs)
cl_i : Cluster i
R : Network reliability
ΔR : Change in network reliability by link removal
R_{new} : Network reliability of the subnetwork
K: Cost of the network
ΔK : Change in network cost by link removal
p_{x_i} : probability that link x_i is working
q_{x_i} : $(1 - p_{x_i})$ = probability that link x_i is faulty
C_i: Capacity of link i
λ_i : Average message rate on link i
γ_{jk} : Average message rate between Nodes j and k
μ_{jk} : Average message length from Node j to Node k
$\frac{1}{\mu_i}$: Average message length on link i
n: maximum number of inter-cluster links to replace a link i of the network graph model (user-specified)
l_{max} : maximum number of inter-cluster links to replace a link i of the NGM (computed)
g_{ik}^j : gateway i from Cluster k to Cluster j
g : Maximum number of allowable gateways for a cluster
m_j : Mean node degree of Cluster j
d_{j-min} : Minimum node degree of Cluster j
$norm_j$: Normalized degree of Cluster j = (m_j - d_{j-min})
$T_{i,jmax}$: Maximum traffic from any node of Cluster j through inter-cluster link i
f_i : Fraction of traffic flow through gateway i
k_{1i} : Traffic balance factor of Cluster i
k_{2i} : Node Degree balance factor of Cluster i
w_1 : Weight assigned to the traffic balance factor
w_2 : Weight assigned to the degree balance factor
O_j : Objective function for Cluster j

2.3 Input Parameters
The following parameters are given as the specifications of the network:

1. The average traffic between all node pairs is known.
2. The permissible NGM topology is known.
3. The maximum number of links permissible between any two clusters is known.
4. Cluster topologies are specified.
5. Permissible gateways in each cluster are specified.
6. The cost per unit distance of installing a link of a given capacity is known.
7. The distance between all pairs of clusters is known.
8. The maximum allowable time delay on each link is specified.

2.4 Assumptions
The following assumptions are made:

1. Distance between any two clusters is independent of the two specific nodes that the link joins. This assumption is valid since distances between clusters are much larger than distances between the nodes of a cluster.
2. At the NGM level, all links in parallel between any two clusters can be grouped together as a single link for the purpose of cost computation. This assumption is valid, considering that the distance between two clusters of a hierarchical system is substantially large as compared to the distance between nodes of a cluster.
3. Each link is full-duplex in operation.
4. Every link can operate only in two states. This assumption states that every link is either in the working (ON) or failed (OFF) state.
5. Reliability of every link is known.

3 Design Algorithm
The design algorithm can be best described as follows:

begin
    Create the NGM.
    Create the CGM.
    Design the network at the NGM level.
    Choose gateways for each CM and number of inter-cluster links.
end.

3.1 Design at the NGM level
Step 1:
In this step, we start with the permissible topology at the NGM level and determine the capacity needed for each of the links.

For simplicity, the traffic flowing through each link has been assumed symmetric. We shall focus on one-way message flow rate, since in the case of asymmetric traffic, we can determine the direction of maximum traffic flow for each link and then use that factor to decide the capacity of each link.

It is also reasonable to assume that the routing of messages between macro-nodes of the NGM takes the shortest route in terms of the distance traveled. Since the traffic between all cluster pairs is known, the average one-way message rate in each of the links can be found. It is assumed that the message arrival rate is Poisson, with λ_i messages on an average on link i and exponentially distributed messages results in an average of $1/\mu_i$ bits per message on link i.

Let γ_{jk} messages/sec represent the rate of traffic between macro-nodes j and k (one-way traffic). For link i, the average one-way message rate is $\lambda_i = \Sigma_{j,k} \gamma_{jk}$ where the link i is included in the shortest path from macro-node j to macro-node k.

Let μ_{jk} be the average length of a message from macro-node j to macro-node k. The average message length passing through link i can be given by [13]:

$$\frac{1}{\mu_i} = \Sigma_{link i} \frac{\gamma_{jk}\mu_{jk}}{\Sigma_{link i}\gamma_{jk}}$$

Thus, the capacity of link i,
$C_i = \frac{\lambda_i}{\mu_i} + \frac{1}{\mu_i T_i}$
where T_i is the maximum allowable time delay through link i.

Step 2:
Obtain the network reliability expression, R, for the permissible topology of the NGM [7] [9]. Compute the cost, K, of the topology using the distance between the clusters (length of the links), the capacity calculated in Step 1, and the cost per unit distance for the assigned capacity of each link. As explained in [8], MTFF can be easily derived from a network reliability expression.

Step 3:
Continue Step 4 and choose the subset of the permissible topology, which has the maximum reliability to cost ratio, until at least one of the following conditions occur:

1. A preset number of networks N_{max} (specified by the user) have been tried.

2. The network reliability has reached the minimum allowable reliability value (specified by the user).

3. All possible networks have been examined.

Step 4:
For each link in the network, compute the reduction in network reliability by removing the link. This is done by substituting $p_{x_i} = 0$ in the reliability expression obtained in Step 2, where p_{x_i} is the probability that link x_i is working.

Let R_{new} be the network reliability obtained by dropping the link and R be the network reliability with all links in the network.

Then, $\Delta R = R - R_{new}$.

For each link dropped, find the increase in capacities of other links, since the traffic is routed differently. Thus, compute the change in cost, ΔK. If the cost of the new network is greater than the original network, ignore the new network. Consider only those links whose removal reduces the overall cost. For all links considered, compute the new ratio R_{new}/K_{new} and operate only on all those networks.

3.2 Design at the CGM

Once the NGM topology has been decided, gateways have to be selected for each CM. The choice of the gateways dictates the traffic through the inter-cluster links and the number of such gateways governs the network reliability and the cost.

Routing within the cluster always uses the shortest path. If several gateways are at the same distance from a node, the gateway which has the lesser traffic flow is selected. It is obvious that, as the number of inter-cluster links increases, the network reliability increases as well. However, the cost of adding ports for the gateways also increases. Hence, it is necessary to trade-off costs and reliability.

Our heuristic algorithm is based on minimizing an objective function described as :

Objective Function

The overall objective function is computed as
$O_j = w_1 k_{j1} + w_2 k_{j2}$
where the weights w_1 and w_2 can be assigned by the user, depending on which cost is more dominant in a particular application/system.

k_{j1} : Traffic Balance Factor
k_{j2} : Degree Balance factor

The algorithm for design at the CGM level can be summarized as follows:

begin
order the inter-cluster links by their significance in the reliability at the NGM level.
   For each link in the ordered list do
   begin
   for each of the two clusters that the link connects do
   begin
     Compute the maximum number of links
     to substitute the link, l_{max}.
     For each choice of number of gateways,
     compute the objective function.
     Select the set of gateways and number of links
     which minimizes the objective function.
   end.
   end.
end.

It is necessary to select some ordering of links to fix the gateways. The contribution of each link in the network reliability can be found after the computation of the network reliability, as done in the NGM design (Step 2 - Section 3.1). By choosing reliability as a primary criterion, we select the link with the maximum contribution in the network reliability as a starting point and work with links in the order of decreasing contributions. The contribution of a link in the network reliability expression is computed as a ratio of the sum of all terms containing the working probability of that link to the total network reliability.

For each link in the NGM, a choice needs to be made about the number of links to replace the chosen link. The total capacity of the new links is equal to the capacity of the substituted link, as computed earlier in the design at the NGM. For each cluster, the choice of gateways is crucial in deciding the traffic balance through each gateway and the number of additional links governs the increase in number of ports at the gateways, while increasing the network reliability.

Maximum allowable inter-cluster links

The link capacity C_i, of link i, is decided during the design at the NGM stage. In an ideal case, if n links replace link i, each should have a capacity of

$\frac{C}{n}$. If $T_{i,jmax}$ is the maximum traffic flowing from any node in the Cluster j through the inter-cluster link i, every link replacing link i should have capacity at least $T_{i,jmax}$, so that there is no split of the traffic from any cluster node, between the links replacing link i. Thus, the maximum allowable number of links to replace link i is $\lfloor \frac{C_i}{T_{i,jmax}} \rfloor$.

Let l_{max} = maximum allowable links to replace link i.

Then $l_{max} = \min(\lfloor \frac{C_i}{T_{i,jmax}} \rfloor, n)$

where n is specified by the user as the maximum number of allowable links to substitute link i in the NGM, each of capacity $\frac{C_i}{n}$.

Traffic Balance factor

As explained earlier, to keep the link usage balanced, it is necessary to establish a penalty for relatively heavily used links. For each possible choice of gateways, compute the traffic balance factor.

For example, consider a network with three clusters cl_1, cl_2, cl_3. Let $g_{11}^2, g_{21}^2, \ldots g_{k1}^2$ be the gateways linking cl_1 and cl_2 and $g_{11}^3, g_{21}^3, \ldots g_{m1}^3$ be the gateways for links between cl_1 and cl_3. Say, in the NGM, the shortest path from cl_2 to cl_3 is through cl_1 (refer to Fig. 2). Assume that we start with selecting $g_{11}^3, \ldots, g_{m1}^3$.

It is not possible to estimate the relative traffic proportions through gateways $g_{11}^2, \ldots g_{k1}^2$, since the gateways of cl_2 have not been fixed. Hence, it is not possible to estimate the relative proportions of the traffic through gateways $g_{11}^3, \ldots g_{m1}^3$, of the traffic from cl_2 to cl_3. We consider only traffic flowing from nodes of cl_1 to nodes of cl_3 to estimate the relative proportions of traffic on the links. Similarly, in any other network, only traffic from nodes within the cluster is used to decide the cost of imbalanced usage of inter-cluster links.

Let the equation for this traffic balance factor in a Cluster j for a choice of r (r can vary from 2 to g) gateways be:
$k_{1j} = (\Sigma_{i=1}^r \Delta t_i)$

where $\Delta t_i = \Delta f t_i$; if $\Delta f t_i > 0$
= 0; otherwise.

f_i = fraction of the traffic flow through gateway i.
$\Delta f t_i = f_i - \frac{1}{r}$
g = maximum number of allowable gateways

Thus, $\Delta f t_i > 0$, if the fraction of traffic through gateway i is greater than the balanced state of having an equal fraction of $(1/r)$ through each gateway.

Degree Balance Factor

Choosing a node as a gateway increases the node degree and hence the number of ports. We assume a non-linear increase in the cost to ensure that a node degree within each cluster is not excessively larger than any other node.

For example, we assume that increasing the degree of a node from 2 to 4 costs more than increasing the degree from 2 to 3 each for two nodes.

If m_j = mean degree of the Cluster j, and
and d_{j-min} = minimum degree of the Cluster j,

define a normalized degree for Cluster j as
$norm_j = (m_j - d_{j-min})$;

To accommodate the non-linearity of port increase, and to allow low degree node to permit more ports, we introduce an equation,
degree balance factor $k_{j2} = \frac{(\Sigma_{i=1}^r (\Delta d_i)^2)(norm_j + (d_i - m_j) + 1)}{\Sigma_{i=1}^r (\Delta d_i)}$,
where Δd_i = increase in degree of the Node i.
and d_i = initial degree of Node i before the link addition.

for $\Sigma_{i=1}^r \Delta d_i \leq l_{max}$

The normalized degree when added to $(d_i - m_j + 1)$ has the minimum value of 1 and increases as d_i increases. This factor ensures that the degree balance factor of a low degree node is less than that of a high degree node, when equal number of ports are added to both.

For each set of gateways, compute the traffic balance factor and then compute the degree factor by considering the increase in degrees of the gateways in proportion to the traffic flowing through each gateway.

3.3 An alternative approach for gateway selection

In section 3.2, the design is based on the assumption of replacing a given inter-cluster link by a set of links, k, of equal capacity. The number of links, k, is decided by the minimization of the objective function. An alternative approach to the design issue may be based on a user-specified number of links, u, to replace any inter-cluster link. However, each of these links may have a different capacity. The problem of design at the CGM lies in determining the capacities of each of the u links and the set of gateways, corresponding to these links, so as to minimize the objective function. For example, i gateways can be chosen from g gateways in $\binom{g}{i}$ ways, with i varying from 1 to g. For each of these choices of i, compute the traffic balance factor. The ratio of the traffic through the i gateways decides the capacity requirements of the links at those gateways. If C_{ri} is the capacity requirement at gateway r for a choice of i gateways, then the number of inter-cluster links from gateway r can vary from 1 to $\lfloor \frac{C_{ri}}{C_{min}} \rfloor$, where C_{min} is the user-specified minimum capacity of a link. For each of these choices, compute the degree balance factor. For all i gateways, these possibilities will be $\Pi_{r=1}^i \lfloor \frac{C_{ri}}{C_{min}} \rfloor$. For the choice of i gateways, choose the set of links which minimizes the degree balance factor. Then compute the objective function over all possible choices of i. Choose the value of i which minimizes the objective function. This decides the gateways and inter-cluster links.

Figure 1 gives the flowchart for each of the links in the NGM, using this algorithm.

4 Analysis of the Algorithm
4.1 Correctness

Observation 1 Our design algorithm at the NGM level is based on cost and reliability considerations.

Observation 2 Our algorithm at the NGM, produces the optimal solution, with an assumption of fixed link costs.

Observation 3 The number of gateway and inter-cluster link choices is $O(g^{nl})$ where g is the number of permissible gateways for each cluster, n is the number of links to replace any inter-cluster link and l is the number of links in the NGM.

Observation 4 The choice of gateways at the cluster level optimizes the traffic and degree balance.

4.2 Complexity Analysis

To perform the time complexity analysis of our algorithm, an assumption regarding regularity of the network is made and the worst case analysis is done. Assume that the network has c clusters, each with m nodes. There are l links in the NGM. Each link of the NGM can be replaced by at most n parallel links in the final topology and each cluster has at most g gateways.

Network Modeling : To compute the NGM, $O(m.c)$ steps are needed to find the inter-cluster communication.

Network Reliability : Computing the network reliability of the NGM is a non-polynomial time algorithm [5] of $O(2^{2c})$, in case of a fully connected network. However, since the number of clusters and inter-cluster links is small, this can be computed in a reasonable time.

Inter-cluster routing : Finding the shortest path between all possible pairs of clusters is of $O(c^3)$.

Cost Computation : In the NGM with l links, cost computation will take $O(l)$ time.

Steps 3 and 4 at the NGM level : To keep the NGM connected, a minimum of (c-1) links are required. Hence, in the worst case, Step 4 has to be executed (l-c+1) times. In the worst case, for each iteration of Step 4, all paths may have to be recomputed which is $O(c^3)$ steps. The new reliability computation is a simple substitution in a fixed expression and hence may be ignored.

Thus, Steps 3 and 4 have a complexity of $O(c^3(l-c+1)) = O(lc^3 - c^4)$.

Sorting the inter-cluster links : In the first step of design at the CGM level, all inter-cluster links are sorted. This requires $O(l.logl)$ steps.

CGM Design : This step takes a $O(m^3. l. 2^g)$ steps.

As seen from the above discussions, the dominant factor in the computation time required by our algorithm is the CGM design process and the network reliability computation for the NGM.

5 Example

Consider the NGM in Figure 3 (a). Figure 3 (b) shows CM 0. In this example, we consider the CGM level design for Cluster 0 inter-cluster link 0. The traffic from Cluster 0 to Cluster 1 is shown in Table 1. Assume that n = 8; and C_0 is 50 units and that the possible gateway choices are Nodes 0, 1 and 2 (user-specified).

Assume that w_1 and w_2 are each equal to 1. From Table 1, $T_{0-max} = 6.5$, and hence $C_0/T_{0-max} = 7.6$; Hence, $l_{max} = \min(\lfloor 7.6 \rfloor, 8) = 7$.
$m_0 = 2.4$ and $norm_0 = (2.4 - 2) + 1 = 1.4$;

Since r > 2 (refer to the Traffic Balance Factor), the possible choices of two gateways are 0 and 1; 0 and 2; or 1 and 2.

Two gateways :
Choice 1: Nodes 0 and 1.
Traffic through Node 0 is from Nodes 0 and 4 and equals 9 bits/sec.
Traffic through Node 1 is from Nodes 1, 2 and 3 and equals 12 bits/sec.
$f_0 = 9/21$ and $f_1 = 12/21$.
$\Delta ft_0 = -1/14$; and $\Delta ft_1 = 1/14$;
$\Delta t_0 = 0$, and $\Delta t_1 = 1/14$;
The traffic balance factor, $k_{10} = 1/14$;
$f_0 : f_1$ as 3:4 and hence with node degrees of 3 and 4 for Nodes 0 and 1, we get a degree balance factor of (25/7). No other possible choices of node degrees are possible since the next choice of degrees for Nodes 0 and 1 is 6 and 8 and (6+8) exceeds l_{max}.

The objective function for this choice of gateways is $1/14 + 25/7 = 51/14$

Choice 2: Nodes 0 and 2
Traffic through Node 0 is from Nodes 0 and 4 and equals 9 bits/sec.
Traffic through Node 2 is from Nodes 1, 2 and 3 and equals 12 bits/sec.
The traffic balance factor, $k_{10} = 1/14$;
Choosing node degrees of 3 and 4 for Nodes 0 and 2, we get a degree balance factor,
$k_{20} = 41/7$. No further choices of node degrees are possible.

The objective function for this choice of gateways is $1/14 + 41/7 = 83/14$

Choice 3 : Nodes 1 and 2
Traffic through Node 1 is from Nodes 0 and 1 and equals 7.5 bits/sec.
Traffic through Node 2 is from Nodes 2, 3 and 4 and equals 13.5 bits/sec.
The traffic balance factor, $k_{10} = 1/7$;
The traffic proportions are in the ratio of 15:27. The choice of minimum node degrees for Nodes 1 and 2 is 15 and 27. However, this is not permissible since (15+27) exceeds the l_{max}. Hence, this choice is neglected.

Three gateways :
The only possible choice of three gateways is 0, 1 and 2.
Traffic through Node 0 is from Nodes 0 and 4 and equals 9 bits/sec.
Traffic through Node 1 is from Node 1 and equals 2.5 bits/sec.

Traffic through Node 2 is from Nodes 2 and 3 and equals 9.5 bits/sec.

Since no possible choices of node degrees are possible, we reject this choice. The choice of the minimum objective function is gateways 0 and 1 and with 7 links to replace inter-cluster link 0.

Note: The choice of a single gateway is eliminated unless no other possible choice is allowed by the degree balance factor. For example, in the above case, if choices of nodes 0 and 1; and nodes 0 and 2 had not been permitted by the l_{max} restriction, Nodes 0, 1 and 2 would have been considered individually. Since, in the case of single gateways, the traffic balance factor always equals one, one need to compare only the degree balance factors.

6 Results

The algorithm at the NGM level has been tested for two sample NGMs with three cases of random traffic and link distances generated. The average message lengths are between 150 to 500 bits/message and the average message rates are between 0.5 and 2.0 messages/second. The link lengths are randomly distributed between 5 and 50 units. Non-linear capacity costs are chosen so as to represent a practical system.

It is assumed that:

$p_{x_i} = 0.9$ for all i and

$q_{x_i} = 0.1$

No restrictions are imposed on the maximum number of subnetworks to be considered or the minimum allowable network reliability (refer to Step 3 -NGM level design).

Two different algorithms are compared:

1. The 'best' solution is generated by considering all possible subnetworks of the permissible topology. A subnetwork is generated from its 'parent' topology by removing a link. Subnetworks which disconnected the NGM are discarded. The subnetwork with the maximum reliability to cost ratio is the 'best' solution.

2. In our algorithm, subnetworks are also generated by removing a link from the 'parent' network. But they were discarded based on two conditions:

    (a) The subnetwork which disconnects the graph.

    (b) The subnetwork which has a cost greater than that of its 'parent' topology.

I. NGM -1 (network 1)
(refer to Figure 4)
a. Random Pattern I
The permissible topology has a network reliability of 0.976 and a cost of 1027.81.
(refer to Figure 5 a and Table 2)
b. Random Pattern II
The permissible topology has a network reliability of 0.976 and a cost of 1654.87.
(refer to Figure 5 b and Table 3)
c. Random Pattern III
The permissible topology has a network reliability of 0.976 and a cost of 1207.632.
(refer to Figure 5 c and Table 4)
II. NGM -2 (network 2)
(refer to Figure 3)
a. Random Pattern I
The permissible topology has a network reliability of 0.916 and a cost of 1089.31.
(refer to Figure 6 a and Table 5)
b. Random Pattern II
The permissible topology has a network reliability of 0.916 and a cost of 1822.97.
(refer to Figure 6 b and Table 6)
c. Random Pattern III
The permissible topology has a network reliability of 0.916 and a cost of 2339.43.
(refer to Figure 5 c and Table 7)

It is observed that in the aforementioned examples, the 'best' solution and our algorithm generated the same solution. Though no generalization can be made on the basis of this result, it is obvious from observing the number of subnetworks considered by the two algorithms that the removal of a link increases the cost in some cases and decreases the cost in some other. This further strengthens our assumption that the cost of each link is not fixed and that the cost of the network cannot be predicted, merely by the number of links in the network.

7 Conclusion

The algorithm described in this paper considers traffic requirements and generates a subset which has a higher network reliability to cost ratio than the permissible topology, at the network graph model level. At the cluster level, it chooses a set of gateways that balance the traffic and node degrees within the cluster. The algorithm can be easily modified to design task-based systems, and to a r-level hierarchy.

References

[1] K. K. Aggarwal, Y. C. Chopra, and J. S. Bajwa, *Topological Layout of Links for Optimizing the Overall Reliability in a Computer Communication System*, Microelectronics and Reliability, Vol. 22, No. 3, March 1982, pp. 347-351.

[2] F. Beichett, and A. Stark, *Optimum Topological Layout of Communication Networks*, Microelectronics and Reliability, Vol. 29, No. 3, 1989, pp. 387-391.

[3] V. M. Cacatuneanu, Fl. Popentru, G. Albeanu, D. Vlasceanu, and A. Vatasescu, *Optimal Topological Design of Large Telephone Networks*, Microelectronics and Reliability, Vol. 30, No. 4, 1990, pp. 705-711.

[4] Y. C. Chopra, B. S. Sohi, R. K. Tiwari, and K. K. Aggarwal, *Network Topology for maximizing the terminal reliability in a Computer Communication Network*, Microelectronics and Reliability, Vol. 24, No. 5, 1984, pp. 911-913.

[5] S. Hariri, and C. S. Raghavendra, *SYREL: A Symbolic Reliability Algorithm based on Path and Cut-set methods*, IEEE Trans. Computers, Vol. C-36, No.10, Oct. 1987, pp. 1224-1232.

Table 1: Traffic from Cluster 0 through Inter-cluster link 0

Node	Traffic in bits/sec
0	5.0
1	2.5
2	3.0
3	6.5
4	4.0

[6] S. P. Jain, and K. Gopal, *An Improved Method of selecting Network Topology for Optimal Terminal Reliability*, Microelectronics and Reliability, Vol. 26, No. 2, 1986, pp. 255-259.

[7] A. Kumar, *On Evaluation of Reliability and Integrated Performance-Reliability Parameters For Distributed Systems*, Ph.D Thesis, 1989, N.C. State University, 137 pages.

[8] S. V. Makam, and C. S. Raghavendra, *Dynamic Reliability Modeling and Analysis of Computer Networks*, Proc. 1983 Int. Conf. Parallel Processing, pp. 496 - 502.

[9] D. Mandaltsis, and J. M. Kontoleon, *Overall Reliability Determination of Computer Networks with Hierarchical Routing Strategies*, Microelectronics and Reliability, Vol. 27, No. 1, 1987, pp. 129-143.

[10] K. T. Newport, *Incorporating Survivability Considerations directly into the Network Design Process*, Proc. 1990 IEEE Infocom, pp. 215-220.

[11] S. Rai, and D. P. Agrawal, *Distributed Computing Network Reliability*, Tutorial Textbook, IEEE Computer Society Press, 1990, 347 pages.

[12] M. A. Schroeder, and K. T. Newport, *Augmenting Tactical Communication Networks to enhance Survivability*, MILCOM '88: 21st Century Military Communication- What's possible ?, Proc. 1988 IEEE 21st Military Communication Conference, pp. 507-513.

[13] M. Schwartz, *Computer-Communication Network Design and Analysis*, Englewood Cliffs, NJ, Prentice Hall, Inc. 1977.

[14] N. Sharma, and D. P. Agrawal, *Hierarchical Reliability of Large Networks*, Proc. Third IEEE Symposium on Parallel and Distributed Processing, Dec. 1991, pp. 444 - 451.

[15] U. Sharma, K. B. Misra, and A. K. Bhattacharya, *Optimization of CCNs: Exact and Heuristic Approaches*, Microelectronics and Reliability, Vol. 30. No. 1, 1990, pp. 43-50.

Table 2: Random Pattern I- network 1

	Processing Time	No. of subnetworks examined
'Best'	0.5s	47
'Our algorithm'	0.2s	20

Table 3: Random Pattern II- network 1

	Processing Time	No. of subnetworks examined
'Best'	0.6s	47
'Our algorithm'	0.3s	27

Table 4: Random Pattern III- network 1

	Processing Time	No. of subnetworks examined
'Best'	0.6s	47
'Our algorithm'	0.3s	28

Table 5: Random Pattern I- network 2

	Processing Time	No. of subnetworks examined
'Best'	1.1s	63
'Our algorithm'	0.5s	27

Table 6: Random Pattern II- network 2

	Processing Time	No. of subnetworks examined
'Best'	1.1s	63
'Our algorithm'	0.7s	33

Table 7: Random Pattern III- network 2

	Processing Time	No. of subnetworks examined
'Best'	1.1s	63
'Our algorithm'	1.1s	63

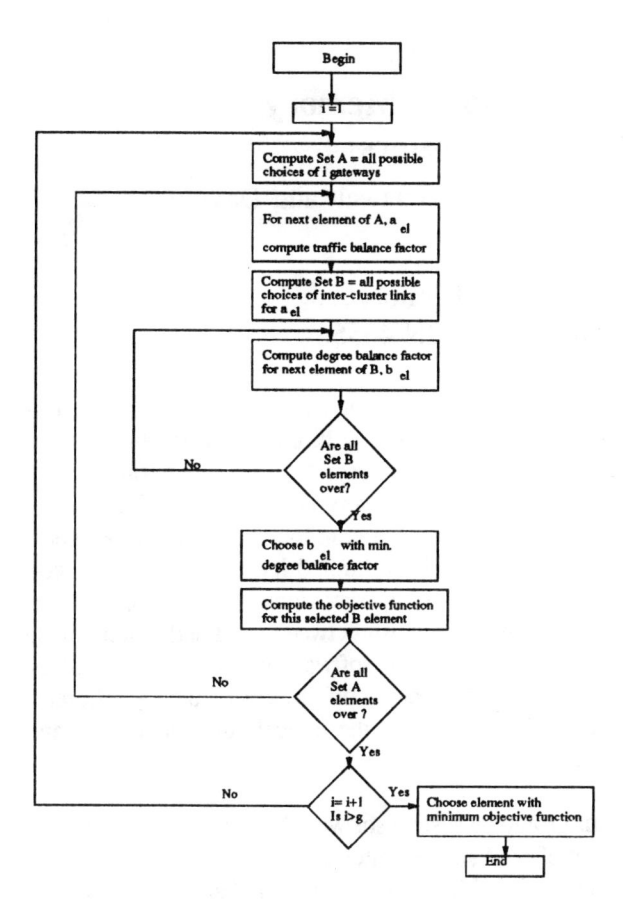

Figure 1: Flowchart of the alternative approach

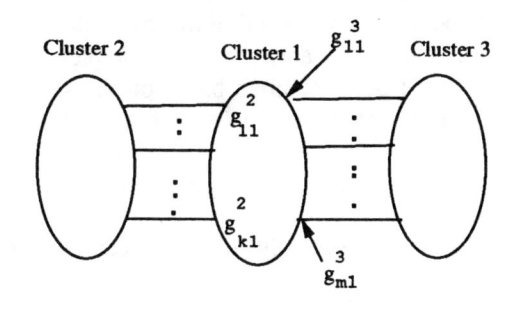

Figure 2: Traffic Balance

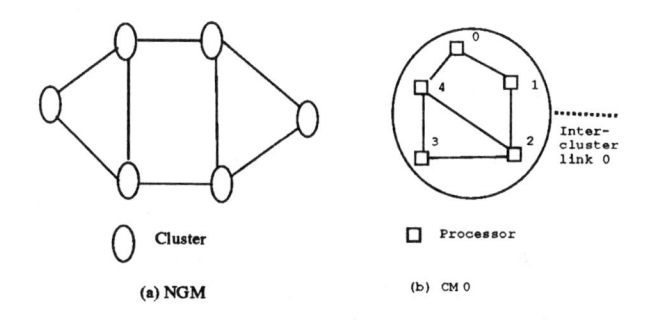

Figure 3: Example
(a) NGM
(b) CM 0

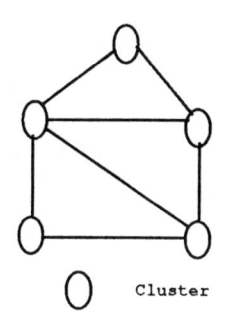

Figure 4: NGM 1

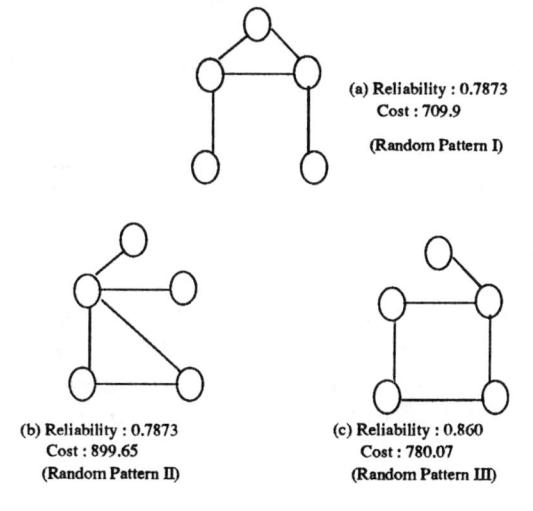

Figure 5: Solutions to NGM 1
(a) Reliability : 0.7873
    Cost : 709.9
    (Random Pattern I)
(b) Reliability : 0.7873
    Cost : 899.65
    (Random Pattern II)
(c) Reliability : 0.860
    Cost : 780.07
    (Random Pattern III)

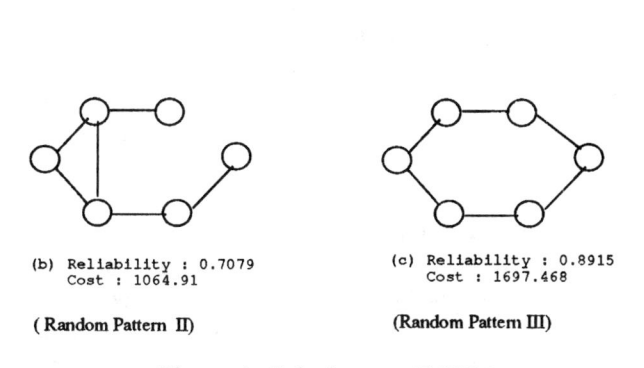

Figure 6: Solutions to NGM 2
(a) Reliability : 0.7742
    Cost : 752.4
    (Random Pattern I)
(b) Reliability : 0.7079
    Cost : 1064.91
    (Random Pattern II)
(c) Reliability : 0.8915
    Cost : 1697.468
    (Random Pattern III)

High-Performance Distributed Shared Memory Substrate for Workstation Clusters

Arindam Banerji, Dinesh Kulkarni, John Tracey, Paul Greenawalt and David Cohn

Distributed Computing Research Laboratory
University of Notre Dame, Notre Dame, IN 46556

Abstract

In order to exploit the latest advances in hardware technology, application developers need high-performance, easy-to-use cooperation tools that span interconnections of standard hardware. Distributed shared memory has been proposed as such a cooperation tool, but performance problems have limited its usefulness. This paper argues that a new approach to distributed shared memory implementation can make it a effective tool in its own right and a foundation for other tools. It describes a prototype implementation that allows sharing of memory resources in a workstation cluster. The prototype is based on an innovative, low-overhead messaging protocol which utilizes the high bandwidth of the underlying hardware, while adding very little latency overhead. Finally, the interface exported by this software is designed to function effectively as a substrate for a variety of cooperation tools.

1: Introduction

Clustered workstations offer the same potential peak processing power as a modern multiprocessor, but this power is difficult. Gigabit fibers provide bandwidth comparable to that of multiprocessor backplanes, and latency within at least an order of magnitude. Thus, the hardware is available, and this paper presents a new system software approach designed to exploit it. It proposes coupling a distributed shared memory implementation with efficient communication to form a canonical substrate that can serve as the foundation for a variety of cooperation tools. Early experimental results from a prototype implementation are reported.

The use of shared memory as a foundation for cooperation tools has its origins in the design of multiprocessors [Li86]. Some multiprocessors use physically shares memory while others provide shared memory emulation. Applications use this (emulated) shared memory either directly or through system software tools built on top of it. The physical interconnection bus in a shared memory multi-processor (SMMP) hides the distinction between remote and local memory; locality effects only latency, not access method. Users generally have found shared memory a good cooperation tool for SMMPs, but performance problems have limited its usefulness in clustered systems. Clustered workstations do not have a bus and normally do distinguish between local and remote memory. However, system software that emulates an SMMP bus also reduces locality differences to latency differences and makes the cluster the logical equivalent of a multiprocessor.

Our prototype system software has been designed to make a set of workstations interconnected with high-bandwidth optical fiber channels look like a shared-memory multiprocessor. An extension to the operating system, called the *pager*, allows a portion of each machine's address space to be logically shared throughout the cluster. Classic distributed shared memory implementation techniques have been modified based on the speed and reliability of the optical links to offer high-performance. This efficiency is based upon three factors:

- The characteristics of a new generation of communication hardware
- A thin and extremely efficient communication protocol
- An implementation with minimal overhead compared to message passing

In addition, the software architecture of the pager provides extendibility and an easy to use programming interface.

This paper begins with a brief overview of the pager design followed by a description of the hardware resources used for the construction and evaluation of this prototype. The performance of the pager and its various components are described in Section 4. This is followed by a discussion of the prototype pager implementation and an analysis of the performance results. Section 6 details the pager software architecture and its use as an operating substrate. The paper ends with a discussion of the advantages of this approach and describes some of the future work already under way.

2: Pager Overview

The pager substrate provides location independent access to the memory resources of all machines within a cluster. Pager instances communicate with each other through a special-purpose *message protocol* that is a client of the *device driver* for an optical fiber communication link. Figure 1 illustrates the relationship between the pager, the

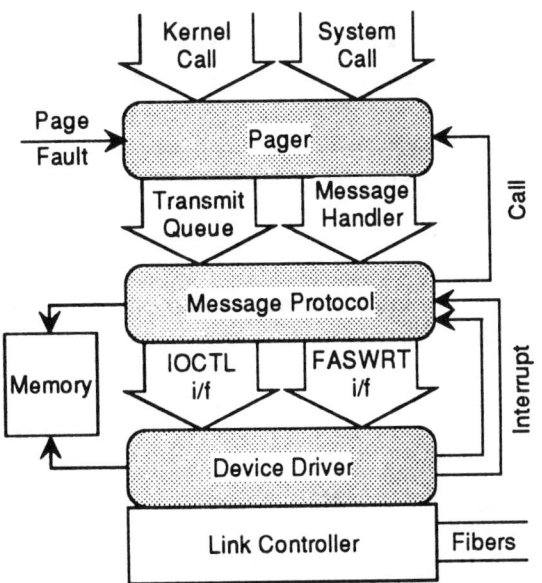

Figure 1 - Implementation Relationships

message protocol and the device driver. This section summarizes the pager services and semantics; a more detailed discussion is presented later.

The pager substrate is implemented as a distributed virtual file system. This allows the pager to install its own page fault handler for each *virtual memory segment* that it uses. It defines a name space that spans all of the machines in a cluster. Each vnode in this file system corresponds to a uniquely named DSM virtual memory segment, or *memory object*. The pager augments the traditional vnode interface with a system call interface for manipulating these segments. Clients of the pager use the name of the memory segment as a memory object handle. They map a DSM segment into their address space by *allocating* an object with a given name. Sharing is achieved when multiple clients allocate an object with the same name. Once the segment has been allocated, clients may allocate its pages by using a page allocation interface that closely resembles the malloc interface. Once a page has been allocated by any client of an object, all other clients have access to the page. Page sharing between DSM objects is driven by page faults, generated by client-access of the pages. In addition, system calls are provided to allow explicit movement of pages between objects.

In order to provide complete DSM functionality, the pager provides two synchronization mechanisms. Clients that need guaranteed continuous access to a set of pages may choose to *pin* those pages to the local machine. This acts much like the locking protocols supported by other DSM implementations [Li86] [Ra89] [Co92]. In addition, support is provided for event notification. Thus, a receiving client can be notified whenever a sending client moves pages into the segment. Notification is based on installable callback routines which are normally defined during segment allocation. These routines are then activated on the occurrence of specified events.

A specialized message protocol handles all cooperation traffic between instances of the pager. This is a thin layer that implements an end-to-end protocol on top of a standard optical link device driver. It relies on the controller hardware to detect errors and failures and provides interrupt service routines to handle these conditions. It allows clients, such as the pager, to define other interrupt service routines which handle normal messages. When a message is received, the device driver transfers it from the hardware to memory and notifies the communication subsystem. The subsystem then checks the message type and activates the appropriate service routine. To transmit, a client calls a routine that places the message on a transmit queue and then activates the subsystem.

3: The Interconnection

The pager prototype was implemented on a three-machine cluster of IBM Risc System/6000 machines. The 500-series of RS/6000 support interconnection via high-bandwidth fiber optic channels. They feature an expansion slot on their CPU planar board which accommodates a serial optical channel converter (SOCC). The SOCC supports two fiber optic channels; each channel provides full-duplex point-to-point communication at approximately 220 Mbits per second with a maximum packet size of 60 KBytes. The resulting communications channel supports data transfer between workstations with bandwidth comparable to that for processor-to-memory transfers.

4: Pager Performance

The performance of the pager subsystem is influenced by three primary factors:
- The capabilities of the serial optical link hardware
- The behavior of the message protocol
- The pager's software overhead

This section explains how each of these factors was measured.

A number of experiments were conducted to measure the communication performance of the pager software. These generally involved sending data from one machine to another and then sending the same amount of data back. The resulting transfer times were then plotted against message size and the following three parameters were computed:
- Latency - The time it takes for the first bit of a short message to arrive.
- Incremental Bandwidth - The fastest rate at which data can be transferred, essentially the incremental slope of the time vs message size curve.
- Asymptotic Bandwidth - The average data transfer rate including "end of packet effects" which tend to slow things down.

4.1: SOL Hardware Capabilities

Our first experiment was designed to determine the actual data carrying capacity of the serial optical link (SOL) hardware. We measured the round trip transfer time between two RS/6000 model 530s running AIX Version 3.2. Messages of various sizes were sent. The smallest consisted of a just a 44-byte header; larger ones were in increments of 4 KBytes up to 56 KBytes (just less than the 60 KByte maximum packet size). For each size, transfer times were averaged over 60 to 100 trials.

The Y intercept in Figure 2 shows that for very small

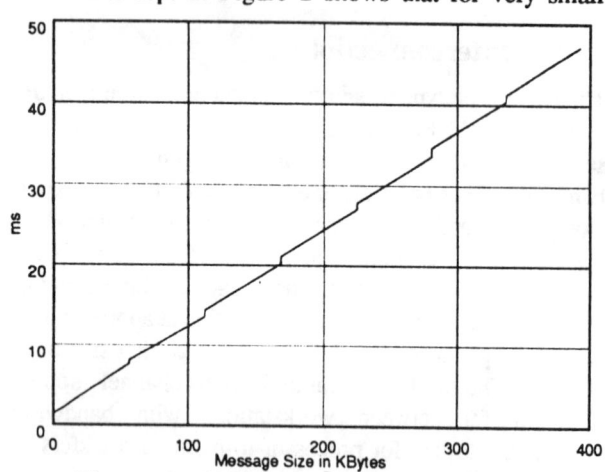

Figure 2 - Hardware Round Trip Times

packets, the round trip time is approximately 1.4 msec. Thus, the latency of the SOL device driver and hardware is half of this, or 0.7 msec. This is the minimal start-up cost for each transaction across the SOL. The small discontinuities or jumps in the graph are due to the optical link's maximum packet size of 60 KBytes. Sending more than the maximum packet size requires multiple invocations of the SOL device driver. The associated packet overhead averages 0.8 msec, although the first two invocations took only 0.4 msec. The slope of the straight portions of the graph implies an incremental bandwidth of 150 Mbits/sec in each direction; discounting the initial latency, the average slope gives an asymptotic bandwidth of 130 Mbits/sec. The graph is essentially linear over a wide range of transmission sizes (we ran as high as 560 KBytes), indicating that the hardware can sustain high throughput rate.

4.2: Message Protocol Behavior

The next experiment assessed the performance of the message protocol performance. Again, a series of round-trip data transfers was used. This time, communication was between two user processes, not between kernel extensions. Thus, we will incur a penalty each time we cross the boundary between the user space and the kernel space. The message protocol was designed to accept requests from user processes so that its performance could be easily evaluated.

For comparison, we ran a set of four tests. In addition to evaluating the message protocol over the serial optical link, we evaluated UDP over an ethernet, UDP over the serial optical link and PVM [Su90] over an ethernet. UDP provides services similar to the message protocol and PVM offers some additional features. The transfer times for different sized messages are shown in Figure 3.

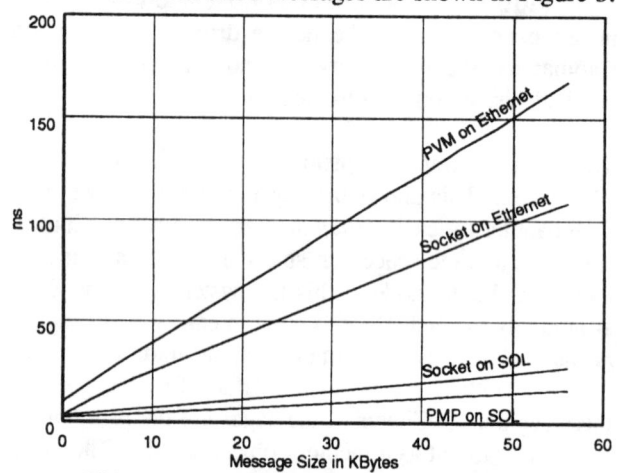

Figure 3 - Protocol Round Trip Times

The three communication parameters: latency, incremental bandwidth and asymptotic bandwidth were calculated and are listed in Table I. It is clear from the table that the user space to kernel space transition is costly, particularly in terms of bandwidth. However, it is also clear that the special purpose message protocol has significantly better performance than UDP, which is a light-weight, general purpose member of the TCP/IP communication suite. UDP over the serial optical link is better than over the ethernet, but by as much as the raw bandwidth would imply. Finally, the increasingly popular PVM system is further limited by its daemon-based implementation.

4.3: Pager Shared Memory Performance

The main purpose of the pager is to implement distributed shared memory using the well-known page fault mechanism [Fl89]. Pages are moved between machines in response to page faults. Since the pager is implemented as a virtual file system kernel extension, it can efficiently handle page faults. It communicates directly with the device driver and is notified of page faults by the AIX kernel. The this software veneer that provides the paging services adds minimal overhead.

A good measure of DSM performance is page load time. This is the time between the generation of a page request and the availability of the required page. For a remote page, this has two important components: communication time and paging software overhead. The communication involves a request indicating which page is required and the response containing the required page; paging software overhead involves locating the page, managing housekeeping information and providing other checks and services.

Table I - User-Level Latency & Bandwidth

Experiment	Latency	Incremental	Asymptotic
SOL Hardware	0.68 ms	159 Mbs	131 Mbs
Message Protocol	1.09 ms	64.9 Mbs	63.9 Mbs
UDP on SOL	1.59 ms	38.0 Mbs	37.7 Mbs
UDP on Ethernet	1.56 ms	8.69 Mbs	8.52 Mbs
PVM on Ethernet	5.00 ms	**	5.80 Mbs

Repeated measurements showed that for the 4 KByte pages of AIX 3.2, the page load time is approximately 1.90 msec. Previous experiments showed that the message protocol requires 1.57 msec to send a short message followed by a 4 KByte message, we conclude that the paging software overhead is 0.33 msec, or only 17% of the total page load time.

5: Pager Implementation

The pager prototype is implemented as an AIX distributed virtual file system, with a pager instance appearing on each machine in the cluster. The instances cooperate through a specialized message protocol to create a single common substrate view. This protocol is a separate component and exists independently of the pager. The pager virtual file system uses the vnode interface and the AIX memory management interface. It maintains and manipulates all information pertaining to the DSM segments and the pages contained therein.

5.1: Message Protocol

The interface exported by the message protocol allows clients, such as the pager, to transmit packets over the link and to install handlers for the receipt of specific message types. The protocol's interface is available to user-level clients and is the basis for the performance tests described in Section 4.2. However, it has been designed for trusted clients. Prior to discussing the protocol implementation, it is necessary to look at the link controller and serial link device driver interfaces.

The serial optical link controller [Ir90] contains buffers, a sequencing engine, an optical receiver and control registers. The controller transmits messages as a sequence of 256-byte frames with an appended 16-bit cyclic redundancy check. When message transmission or reception completes or an unexpected event happens, the controller fires an interrupt to inform the device driver.

The device driver exports three kinds of interfaces:
- The IOCTL interface allows clients to perform controller-specific actions such as obtaining information about the processor, transmitting a message, etc.
- The FASWRT interface provides kernel-level clients a fast-path data transmission facility that goes directly to the controller.
- Interrupt Handlers installed by device driver clients are used to notify the clients of hardware failure, data reception, status changes, etc.

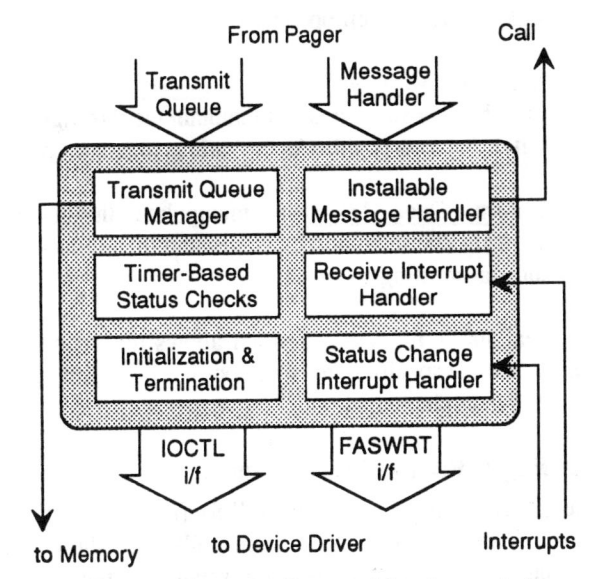

Figure 4 - Message Protocol Implementation

The message protocol seen in Figure 4 provides two interfaces. One allows clients to install message handlers for various message types. A client defines a message type by using this interface to notify the message protocol of the callback routine to be associated with this type. When such a message arrives, the protocol realization activates this routine, with a pointer to the message as a parameter. The other interface allows clients to place messages on the protocol's transmit queue. These interfaces are designed for minimum overhead by giving the clients responsibility for any advanced services.

The major components of the protocol implementation are:

- Receive Interrupt handler - called by the device driver on the arrival of any message that uses this protocol. This component does some initial checks and then calls the appropriate message handler for the received message type.

- Status Change Interrupt Handler - called by the device driver whenever any hardware errors occur or a change in the hardware status is detected.

- Timer Based Status Checks - from time-to-time ensure that the status of the link is appropriate and that the all neighbors can still be reached. It is also responsible for responding when a neighboring machine becomes reachable.

- Initialization and Termination Components - open the link, perform initial sanity checks, set up the reachability matrix, bring down the link methodically and perform all cleanup operations.

- Installable Message Handler Component - manipulates the data structures that maintain the information pertaining to the callbacks for various message types.

- Transmit Queue Manager - manipulates the queue, allowing clients to add messages and then removing and transmitting them.

An installable error handler which allows the clients to deal with some specific error situations has been designed, but not yet implemented.

5.2: Pager Virtual File System

The pager virtual file system (VFS) [IB90] shown in Figure 5 exports a set of system calls that allow the manipulation of shared memory segments, the pages contained in the segments, movement of pages, synchronization and event-notification. These may be used by

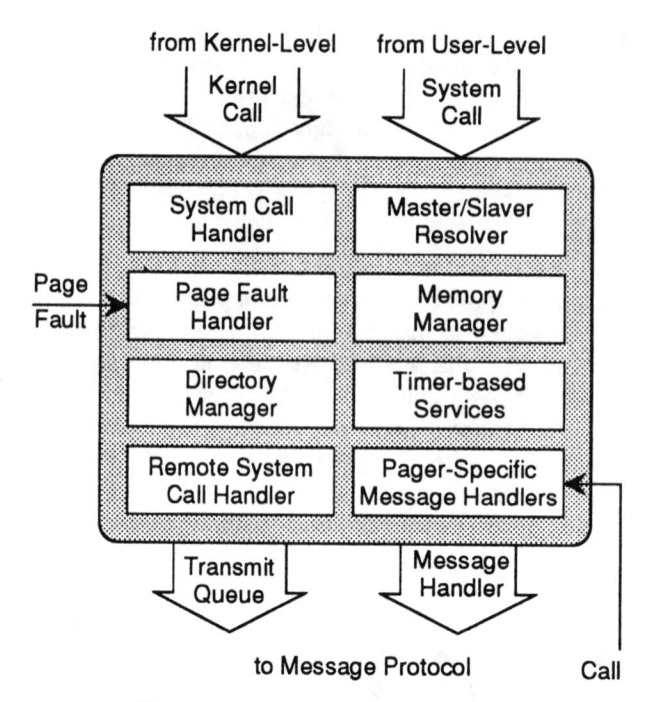

Figure 5 - Pager Implementation

either kernel-level or user-level clients, with only marginally different semantics. This section describes the functionality of the major components of the pager VFS.

The *directory manager* maintains per-page information for all the segments that are handled by the VFS. This includes hints about current location, if the page is not local; hints about previous location, if it is local, and page-control bit status, such as whether the page is pinned. In essence, the directory manager maintains a complete map for all the pages that it handles.

The *memory manager* manipulates the allocation and deallocation of pages within each DSM segment. Free pages are maintained in a heap and allocated ones in a sparse hash table. After allocation and deallocation, this component also ensures that fragmentation is minimized. It uses a best fit algorithm to allocate pages within a segment.

The *page fault handler* forms the core of the pager VFS. All page faults generated on segments managed by this VFS are passed to this handler by the AIX kernel. If the page is not available locally, the handler finds its location from the directory manager and makes a PAGE-FAULT request. When the page is returned by the remote machine, the handler pins it locally for a short period, and then completes the page fault process. The pinning avoids unnecessary thrashing [Fl89] [Ni91].

The *master/slave resolver* manages and controls the name space of the segments within the cluster. Whenever a memory object is allocated, this protocol ensures that only one object with that name exists in the cluster. It uses a two-phase commit protocol to ensures name uniqueness. Thus, only one machine within the cluster holds the actual memory object pertaining to the DSM segment; the other machines maintain a proxy for this object.

The *system call handler* implements all the calls exported by the pager VFS. It determines whether a call should be forwarded to a remote machine or whether it should be resolved locally. It calls the appropriate routine within the memory manager, the directory manager or the master/slave resolver to handle the system call. It checks return codes and takes appropriate actions.

The *remote system call handler* implements all system calls that originated on foreign machines. It essentially performs the same function as the system call handler, except that error recovery and completion are done differently.

The *pager-specific message handler* implements and installs all message handlers specific to this VFS with the message protocol realization. On receipt of a message from the message protocol layer, this component retrieves the appropriate information from the message and invokes the target component that handles the message.

The *timer-based services* handle the reliability features of the pager VFS. They ensure that system calls do not hang, that messages are resent, etc. In addition, they are used for housekeeping and cleaning up data structures.

6: An Operating System Substrate

The pager uses an object-based definition of shared memory. Clients allocate a memory object consisting of multiple pages and can then allocate individual pages within that object. These pages can be moved between machines, forming the basis for other cooperation mechanisms. This section describes the memory object services and the kind of cooperation mechanisms that can be built on top of them.

6.1: DSM Substrate - Architecture

The pager represents regions of memory as memory objects with several associated resources. The pager guarantees that the name of each memory object is unique within the cluster. Each object has a set of pages whose maximum number is set at allocation. Finally, each has one or more associated callback routines to handle event notifications.

The pager interface exports five kinds of location-independent, re-entrant operations:

- Object allocation and deallocation - An allocation call specifies object name and maximum size. It returns a handle to either an existing object or a newly created object. ("Allocations" of existing object return handles to those objects.) The initial allocation call causes pager to globally define a memory segment of maximum size and initializing a descriptor; all calls cause it to map the segment into the client's address space and return a valid segment descriptor. Thus, multiply allocated objects become shared in the sense of classic DSM.

- Page allocation and deallocation - When a client adds pages to a memory object, a pointer to the initial offset within the new pages is returned. The pager ensures that all page allocation calls to the same object are serialized. If a client refers to a location someone else has allocated, a page-fault causes the page to be mapped into the client's address space. If the page had never been allocated, an exception is generated. This limited protection is acceptable since the pager is a substrate for trusted services.

- Page movement between objects - A client can name source and destination objects and ask that a set of pages be copied or moved. This is useful, for example, in implementing 4.3 BSD sockets. Sending a packet between two processes involves just moving a set of pages between the source pager object and the destination pager object.

- Callback routine installation and manipulation - Events, such as the arrival of a page, may require that a memory object notify a client. For example, a process may be waiting on the socket mentioned above and must be awakened when the pages arrive.

- Control flag manipulation - Sometimes the normal, or default, behavior of a memory object may not allow a client to use it successfully. For example, the page-fault mechanism for moving pages can lead to thrashing and starvation. Therefore, a client can control the behavior of a memory object through control flags.

As we have noted, the pager is a flexible distributed shared memory substrate on which a number of cooperation tools can be built.

6.2: Cooperation Tools

A significant community of parallel application developers favor the UNIX socket interface, others feel comfortable with the Linda tuple space, while still others prefer to use PVM messaging. The pager's software architecture allows it to easily support each of these cooperation tools, as well as shared memory. The pager's low-overhead ensures good performance of these higher-level tools. On the other hand, using the pager as a building block makes tool implementation considerably simpler, significantly reducing development and maintenance costs. The range of tools which can be implemented on the pager includes:

- BSD Sockets - Sockets are a classic communication mechanism which provide a reliable byte-stream between unrelated processes. A socket implementation based on the messaging protocol of Section 5.1 can provide good performance to clients.

- Linda - Linda [Ah88] is a language-level view of a shared data space. This data space, also known as the tuple space maps directly to a memory object. Additional metadata is maintained on a per tuple basis to hold name and type information. Tuples are put into or removed from the space by allocating and deallocating the required pages.

- File Systems - Many UNIX-based file-systems optimize performance by mapping active files into virtual memory. Extending this by mapping the files into a memory object automatically provides cluster-wide sharing of open files. This suggests that it may also be possible to share devices throughout the cluster. If devices, such as disks, are mapped to the substrate, they will be globally visible.

6.3: Ease of Use

As discussed in previous sections, the pager is designed as a very thin and efficient software veneer to achieve good performance with implementations in existing operating systems.

Since the pager was designed both for direct use and as a substrate for operating system services, one might assume that it would have a complex interface. However, special care has been taken to ensure that the interface is easy to use. Its few calls have well-defined semantics as illustrated in the following small code segment:

```
// A code fragment illustrating use of pager
// Allocate obj, get obj & callback ids
// Callback optional, allows greater page
//    movement control

ret_code = pager_object_alloc (size, object-
    _name, &address, &object_id, flags, &call-
    back, &callback_routine_id);
..
// Allocate a few pages
ret_code = pager_alloc_page (object_name,
    object_id, num_pages,
    &offset_within_object);
..
// Use pages, then de-allocate them
ret_code = pager_free_page (object_id, object-
    _name, offset);
// Deallocate object and then we are done
ret_code = pager_object_dealloc (object_name,
    object_id, address,
    callback_routine_id);
```

These calls are further simplified by the standard `malloc` interface.

7: Discussion

At this point, the pager is still in the prototype stage. Our early experiments indicate that it is capable of providing the connectivity needed to join workstations into a valuable distributed computing structure. The pager design is also a valuable tool for assessing operating systems and cooperation structures.

7.1: The Value of Distributed Shared Memory

Distributed shared memory has long been recognized as a convenient cooperation tool. However, performance considerations have limited its usefulness. Our prototype pager has shown that it is possible to reduce page load times by a factor of five from previous work [An90]. By reducing software overhead to only 17% of communication time, we have shown that DSM can be almost as efficient as raw message passing.

Future experiments will investigate ways to further reduce this overhead. We will exploit locality of reference and transfer multiple pages whenever we encounter a page fault. Also, we will evaluate pre-paging when the communication channel is idle.

We are in the process of evaluating the impact of DSM on large, compute intensive applications. Early results are promising, particularly for asynchronous algorithms and those which exploit the pagers facility to pin pages.

7.2: The Substrate Structure

Perhaps the most important contribution of the pager work is the substrate approach to building cooperation mechanisms in clustered environments. Hardware advances, especially in communication links, are exploited through the high-performance message protocol, which has been designed especially for the pager prototype. Also, the architecture of the pager itself allows interesting opportunities to dynamically extend the very nature of the substrate.

DSM implementations have traditionally been geared towards application-level clients. By contrast, the pager's clients are operating system services. This critically affects the design, implementation and performance of the prototype. With system-level clients, the pager need not maintain any per-process information or perform general and extensive error checking. This makes the implementation small and reduces the DSM overhead to a minimum. Clients maintain their own per-process information and perform specific error-checking to ensure security. This allow the prototype to be built far closer to low-level kernel interfaces, such as that of the device-driver, and avoids expensive context change operations such as those encountered by daemon-based implementations of cooperation protocols.

Since optical communication links have far greater bandwidth and much better performance robustness with increasing traffic than LANs, a page transfer operation is relatively inexpensive. In addition, their error rates are remarkably low and recovery can be left to pager's clients. Thus, the message protocol achieves high performance by offering basic services and letting higher-level entities provide guarantees of more specialized services.

The initial pager prototype has only been tested on a small workstation cluster. By limiting the number of machines, we have limited communication latencies. With our experiments, all machines are within one hop of each other. If a message packet has to be routed through switches, latency will increase, and if intermediary hosts are used, the latencies become disastrous. Future work will consider a hierarchical structure, or a cluster of clusters, to mitigate the latency problem.

References

[Ah88] Ahuja, S., et. al., Linda and Friends, *IEEE Computer*, Vol. 19, No. 8, August, 1986, pp. 26-34.

[An92] Ananthanarayanan, R., et. al. Application Specific Coherence Control for High Performance Distributed Shared Memory, in *Proceedings Symposium on Experiences with Distributed and Multiprocessor Systems*, 1992.

[An90] Ananthanarayanan, R., et. al. *On the Integration of Distributed Shared Memory with Virtual Memory Management*, Technical Report, Georgia Institute of Technology, GIT-CC-90/40, 1990.

[Ba89] Bal, H., *The Shared Data-Object Model as a Paradigm for Programming Distributed Systems*, Ph.D. Dissertation, Vrije Universiteit, 1989.

[Bl92] Blount, M., *DSVM6K: Distributed Shared Virtual Memory on the Risc System/6000*, IBM Research Draft, 1992.

[Ca91] Carter, J. et al Implementation and Performance of Munin, *Proc 13th ACM Symp on Operating System Principles*, ACM, pp. 152-164.

[Co92] D. Cohn et. al. A Universal Distributed Programming Paradigm for Multiple Operating Systems, *Proc Symp on Experiences with Distributed and Multiprocessor Systems*, USENIX.

[Fl89] Fleisch, B. and Popek, G., Mirage: A Coherent Distributed Shared Memory Design, *Proceedings of the 12th ACM Symposium on Operating Systems Principles,* December, 1989, pp. 211-223.

[Fo88] Forin, A., Barrera, J., Young, M. and Rashid, R., *Design, Implementation, and Performance Evaluation of a Distributed Shared Memory Server for Mach*, Technical Report CMU-CS-88-165, Carnegie-Mellon University, August, 1988.

[IB90] *AIX Kernel Extensions and Device Support Programming Concepts for IBM RISC System/6000*, IBM, Part No. SC23-2207-00, 1990.

[Ir90] Irwin, J. and Mathis, J., "Serial I/O Architecture and Implementation", *RISC System/6000 Technology*, IBM, Part No. SA23-2619-00, 1990.

[Li86] Li, K., *Shared Virtual Memory on Loosely Coupled Multiprocessors*, Ph.D. Dissertation, Yale University, YALEU/DCS/RR-492, September, 1986.

[Ni91] Nitzberg, B. and Lo, V., Distributed Shared Memory: A Survey of Issues and Algorithms, *IEEE Computer*, Vol. 24, No. 8, August 1991, pp. 52-60.

[Ra89] Ramachandran, U., Ahamad, M. and Khalidi, M., Coherence of Distributed Shared Memory: Unifying Synchronization and Data Transfer, *Proceedings of the 1989 International Conference on Parallel Processing*, Volume II, August, 1989, pp. 160-169.

[Sc92] Scott, M. and Garrett, W., "Shared Memory Ought to be Commonplace", *The Third Workshop on Workstation Operating Systems (WWOS-III)*, IEEE, 1992.

[Su90] Sunderam, V. "PVM: A Framework for Parallel Distributed Computing", *Concurrency: Practice and Experience*, Vol. 2, No. 4, 1990.

Author Index

Agrawal, D.P.	336
Agrawal, P.	114
Agrawal, V.D.	114
Aly, K.A.	289
Ambrosiano, J.J.	102
Amer, P.D.	272
Bal, H.E.	5
Bandi, V.	298
Banerji, A.	344
Biswas, P.	252
Bogineni, K.	289
Braun, T.	76
Brown, J.C.	102
Bryant, R.	144
Buczkowska, T.	68
Budin, L.	326
Butler, R.M.	50
Chassot, C.	272
Chen, T.	160
Coddington, P.D.	179
Cohn, D.	344
Colombet, L.	121
Connolly, T.	272
Crandall, P.E.	42
Crutcher, L.A.	306
Dannevik, W.P.	102
Day, K.	298
Desbat, L.	121
Diaz, M.	272
Dobosiewicz, W.	92
Dooling, D.R.	234
Dowd, P.W.	289
Eltgroth, P.G.	102
Evans, J.B.	136
Farrara, J.D.	102
Feeney, J.	160
Feiner, S.K.	306
Fletcher, J.	174
Fox, G.C.	84, 160
Franklin, M.	224
Frieder, G.	160
Frost, V.S.	136
Fry, M.	68
Gburzynski, P.	92
Ginige, T.	68
Greenawalt, P.	344
Grimshaw, A.S.	34
Hariri, S.	84
Homer, P.T.	187
Hosseini, S.H.	216
Hou, R.Y.	263
Joshi, B.S.	216
Judd, M.	34
Kaashoek, M.F.	5
Karnik, N.M.	298
Karpovich, J.F.	34
Kleinrock, L.	1, 206
Koneru, S.P.	298
Krishna, C.M.	252
Kulkarni, D.	344
Kung, H.T.	4
Lazar, A.A.	306
Lee, T.-Y.	129
Leveton, A.L.	50
Lilienkamp, J.	244
Lusk, E.L.	50
Ma, C.C.	102
Ma, J.	152
Manke, J.	21
Mechoso, C.R.	102
Ménard, F.	121
Messina, P.	100
Minden, G.J.	136
Mirin, A.A.	102
Mukherjee, B.	59
Mullin, L.M.R.	234
Nakamura, A.	281
Neuman, B.C.	316
Neves, K.	21
Nicholas, J.B.	129
Nock, C.	298
Noonan, T.	298
Obradovic, Z.	174
Parashar, M.	84
Park, J.	84
Patt, Y.N.	263
Perreault, J.A.	289
Petr, D.W.	136
Pramanick, I.	196
Quinn, M.J.	42
Raghavendra, C.S.	129
Rahko, K.	152
Ramakrishnan, K.K.	252
Ranka, S.	160
Rao, S.	316
Richards, A.	68
Sahai, V.	144
Sandberg, E.A.	234
Schlichting, R.D.	187
Schmidt, C.	76

Schwan, K.	59	Towsley, D.	252
Seneviratne, A.	68	Tracey, J.	344
Sharma, N.	336	Tripathi, A.	298
Siegel, H.J.	30	Tung, B.	206
Silva, R.	244	Vairavan, K.	216
Skjellum, A.	13	Varma, A.	144
Spahr, J.A.	102	Villoldo, J.	114
Srbljic, S.	326	Walker, B.J.	244
Strayer, W.T.	34	Wehner, M.F.	102
Sunderam, V.	170	Wicks, T.	21
Takizawa, M.	281	Wilhelm, B.	160
Tanenbaum, A.S.	5	Wong, K.	224
Tewari, R.	298	Yu, F.-K.	84, 160
Thibault, S.A.	234	Zhou, M.	306

IEEE Computer Society Press

Press Activities Board

Vice President: Ronald G. Hoelzeman, University of Pittsburgh
James H. Aylor, University of Virginia
Mario R. Barbacci, Carnegie Mellon University
Bill D. Carroll, University of Texas
James Farrell III, VLSI Technology Inc.
Barry W. Johnson, University of Virginia
Duncan H. Lawrie, University of Illinois
Murali Varanasi, University of South Florida
Ben Wah, University of Illinois
Marshall Yovits, Indiana University — Purdue University
Staff Representative: True Seaborn, Publisher

Editorial Board

Editor-in-Chief: Jon T. Butler, US Naval Postgraduate School
Assoc. Editor-in-Chief: Pradip K. Srimani, Colorado State University
Oscar N. Garcia, The George Washington University
Joydeep Ghosh, University of Texas, Austin
Uma G. Gupta, University of Central Florida
A.R. Hurson, Pennsylvania State University
Ez Nahouraii, IBM
Frederick E. Petry, Tulane University
Dhiraj K. Pradhan, University of Massachusetts
Charles Richter, MCC
David Rine, George Mason University
A.R.K. Sastry, Rockwell International Science Center
Ajit Singh, Siemens Corporate Research
Murali R. Varanasi, University of South Florida
Staff Representative: Henry Ayling, Editorial Director

Press Staff

T. Michael Elliott, Executive Director
True Seaborn, Publisher

Henry Ayling, Editorial Director
Mary E. Kavanaugh, Production Editor
Lisa O'Conner, Production Editor
Regina Spencer Sipple, Production Editor
Penny Storms, Production Editor
Edna Straub, Production Editor
Robert Werner, Production Editor
Perri Cline, Electronic Publishing Manager
Frieda Koester, Marketing/Sales Manager
Thomas Fink, Advertising/Promotions Manager

Offices of the IEEE Computer Society

Headquarters Office
1730 Massachusetts Avenue, N.W.
Washington, DC 20036-1903
Phone: (202) 371-0101 — Fax: (202) 728-9614

Publications Office
P.O. Box 3014
10662 Los Vaqueros Circle
Los Alamitos, CA 90720-1264
Membership and General Information: (714) 821-8380
Publication Orders: (800) 272-6657 — Fax: (714) 821-4010

European Office
13, avenue de l'Aquilon
B-1200 Brussels, BELGIUM
Phone: 32-2-770-21-98 — Fax: 32-3-770-85-05

Asian Office
Ooshima Building
2-19-1 Minami-Aoyama, Minato-ku
Tokyo 107, JAPAN
Phone: 81-3-408-3118 — Fax: 81-3-408-3553

IEEE Computer Society

IEEE Computer Society Press Publications

Monographs: A monograph is an authored book consisting of 100-percent original material.

Tutorials: A tutorial is a collection of original materials prepared by the editors, and reprints of the best articles published in a subject area. Tutorials must contain at least five percent of original material (although we recommend 15 to 20 percent of original material).

Reprint collections: A reprint collection contains reprints (divided into sections) with a preface, table of contents, and section introductions discussing the reprints and why they were selected. Collections contain less than five percent of original material.

Technology series: Each technology series is a brief reprint collection — approximately 126-136 pages and containing 12 to 13 papers, each paper focusing on a subset of a specific discipline, such as networks, architecture, software, or robotics.

Submission of proposals: For guidelines on preparing CS Press books, write the Editorial Director, IEEE Computer Society Press, PO Box 3014, 10662 Los Vaqueros Circle, Los Alamitos, CA 90720-1264, or telephone (714) 821-8380.

Purpose

The IEEE Computer Society advances the theory and practice of computer science and engineering, promotes the exchange of technical information among 100,000 members worldwide, and provides a wide range of services to members and nonmembers.

Membership

All members receive the acclaimed monthly magazine *Computer*, discounts, and opportunities to serve (all activities are led by volunteer members). Membership is open to all IEEE members, affiliate society members, and others seriously interested in the computer field.

Publications and Activities

Computer **magazine:** An authoritative, easy-to-read magazine containing tutorials and in-depth articles on topics across the computer field, plus news, conference reports, book reviews, calendars, calls for papers, interviews, and new products.

Periodicals: The society publishes six magazines and five research transactions. For more details, refer to our membership application or request information as noted above.

Conference proceedings, tutorial texts, and standards documents: The IEEE Computer Society Press publishes more than 100 titles every year.

Standards working groups: Over 100 of these groups produce IEEE standards used throughout the industrial world.

Technical committees: Over 30 TCs publish newsletters, provide interaction with peers in specialty areas, and directly influence standards, conferences, and education.

Conferences/Education: The society holds about 100 conferences each year and sponsors many educational activities, including computing science accreditation.

Chapters: Regular and student chapters worldwide provide the opportunity to interact with colleagues, hear technical experts, and serve the local professional community.